THE STRUGGLE FOR CIVIL LIBERTIES

THE STRUGGLE FOR CIVIL LIBERTIES

Political Freedom and the Rule of Law in Britain 1914–1945

K. D. EWING

and

C. A. GEARTY

OXFORD
UNIVERSITY PRESS

OXFORD

UNIVERSITY PRESS

Great Clarendon Street, Oxford OX2 6DP

Oxford University Press is a department of the University of Oxford.
It furthers the University's objective of excellence in research, scholarship,
and education by publishing worldwide in

Oxford New York

Athens Auckland Bangkok Bogotá Buenos Aires Calcutta
Cape Town Chennai Dar es Salaam Delhi Florence Hong Kong Istanbul
Karachi Kuala Lumpur Madrid Melbourne Mexico City Mumbai
Nairobi Paris São Paulo Singapore Taipei Tokyo Toronto Warsaw

and associated companies in Berlin Ibadan

Oxford is a registered trade mark of Oxford University Press
in the UK and in certain other countries

Published in the United States
by Oxford University Press Inc., New York

British Library Cataloguing in Publication Data

Data available

Library of Congress Cataloging in Publication Data
Ewing, K. D. (Keith D.)
The struggle for civil liberties: political freedom and the rule of law in Britain,
1914–1945/K.D. Ewing and C. Gearty.
p. cm.
Includes bibliographical references and index.
1. Great Britain—Politics and government—1901–1936. 2. Great Britain—Politics and
government—1936–1945. 3. Civil rights—Great Britain—History—20th century.
4. Law—Great Britain—History—20th century.
I. Gearty, C. A. II. Title.
DA576.E95 1999 941.083—dc21 99–047701
ISBN 0–19–825665–5

1 3 5 7 9 10 8 6 4 2

Typeset in Baskerville
by Hope Services (Abingdon) Ltd.
Printed in Great Britain
on acid-free paper by
Bookcraft Ltd.,
Midsomer Norton, Somerset

Preface

What are civil liberties? How are they protected in Britain? What is the role of the judges as defenders of civil liberties? These are the three central questions which form the focus of this book, with the analysis concentrating on the period from 1914 to 1945. But although rooted in the first half of the twentieth century, we hope nevertheless that the study will have a strong contemporary resonance, and will be of interest to those engaged in current debates about the protection of civil liberties. Like so many other areas of the law, civil liberties as a discipline can only fully be understood by examining the historical, political, and ideological forces which have helped to shape it: all modern legal disciplines bear the legacy of their past.

In this case the legacy has been one of struggle against restraint, as suggested by an examination of some of the great events of the first half of the twentieth century. These include the First World War; the Bolshevik Revolution and the formation of the Communist Party of Great Britain; the General Strike and the miners' lock out of 1926; economic depression, unemployment and the hunger marches in the 1920s and 1930s; and the rise of fascism in the 1930s. We also examine in some detail developments in Ireland and subsequently Northern Ireland throughout the period, and consider the implications for civil liberties of the Easter Rising in 1916, the campaign for Irish independence, and the Unionist government established in Northern Ireland in 1921.

Many of these incidents and events are of course well known. But in writing this book it became painfully clear to us that the civil liberties dimension to them has been either lost or neglected. As a result some scholars have unwittingly fed successive generations an account of civil liberties in the United Kingdom which is at best complacent, and at worst wholly out of touch with reality. In addressing some of these issues in detail for the first time in the legal literature, we hope to show that much of the traditional learning and teaching in this country is founded upon myth: there is a clear disconnection of principle from practice, of fact from fiction. One aim of this book is to question many of the current assumptions which exist about freedom in Britain.

Our account takes us back to the first half of the twentieth century, seen sometimes as the golden age of liberty in Britain, a time when it is thought by some that the common law was steadfast in its defence of political freedom. But the reality was very different: during all of this period either the whole or parts of the jurisdictions considered were governed by emergency legislation of one kind or another, in which civil liberties were explicitly subordinated to other concerns. And throughout this period the common law proved to be impotent, with the judges developing and applying common law rules in a manner which showed extraordinary deference to the executive. The consistency of such obsequiousness at least invites a re-examination of the political role of the courts.

This book began life some time ago, and has metamorphosed into something rather different from what was originally intended. Inevitably we have incurred substantial debts to a number of people, particularly for their patience as the focus of this work radically changed. We should in particular like to thank Richard Hart who commissioned this work, and our earlier work *Freedom under Thatcher*, on which this volume builds. We should also like to thank OUP for their support over what now seems like many years, and in particular John Louth and Mick Belson. Finally a word of thanks to the staff of the various libraries on the holdings of which we have drawn extensively, and to our colleagues at King's College, London for contributing to what is an extremely congenial and supportive place in which to work.

KDE
CAG
17 October 1999

Contents

Table of Cases

Table of Legislation

1

Introduction

A remarkable feature of civil liberties scholarship in Britain is the lack of certainty about the boundaries of the discipline. In his path-breaking work first published in 1963, Harry Street set out to review each of the 'fundamental liberties' without, however, explaining why they were 'fundamental' or why they were selected for consideration.[1] The author of the sixth edition is slightly more explicit, announcing that the book examines 'the state of English law as it relates to the liberties that are recognised as most fundamental to the fulfilment of human aspirations'.[2] But which 'liberties' are fundamental to human aspirations and why? And which liberties are more 'fundamental' than others to the fulfilment of these aspirations, and why? The uncertainty about the boundaries of the discipline is highlighted when it is revealed that there is some variation in the subjects covered in the original and most recent editions of this pioneering study. It is true that there is a substantial hard core of material which remains constant across the editions, including police powers, public protest, freedom of expression, freedom of movement and freedom from discrimination. But a number of important topics which appeared in the first edition were excluded from the sixth and seventh, including in particular 'freedom to work', which initially appeared with the observation that 'Britain lags behind in its industrial charter',[3] an observation which appears no less relevant some thirty-six years later. There is no account of the exclusion of this item from the sixth edition, though its importance (together with so-called 'second generation' rights) is recognised in the seventh.[4]

Street's book held the field for some considerable time. It was later to be accompanied by two weighty casebooks of considerable scholarship.[5]

---

[1] H Street, *Freedom, the Individual and the Law* (1963), p 11.

[2] G Robertson, *Freedom, the Individual and the Law* (6th edn, 1989), p 17.

[3] Street, n 1 above, p 231.

[4] G Robertson, *Freedom, the Individual and the Law* (7th edn, 1993), p xi. Their exclusion is justified on the surely contestable ground that 'their acceptance as social goals is in this country rather more secure (government cuts and thrusts notwithstanding) than the civil freedoms which [the] book is concerned to explain and enhance' (p xii).

[5] S H Bailey, D J Harris, and B L Jones, *Civil Liberties: Cases and Materials* (1980), and P O'Higgins, *Cases and Materials on Civil Liberties* (1980). Paul O'Higgins is a particularly important and influential figure in the study of civil liberties law and practice.

Both were important and each advanced the subject considerably in a number of ways, and by their example help us in our quest to mark out the territory of the discipline. The collection by Bailey, Harris and Jones, *Civil Liberties: Cases and Materials*, first published in 1980 and now in its fourth edition, announces that it concentrates on *'civil* liberties (rights)' with 'only occasional and incidental coverage of economic and social rights'.[6] But no attempt is made to define civil liberties or to explain how something might be said to fall within its ambit, save only that prisoners' rights are included 'as an example of an area in which the law of civil liberties is in the process of change',[7] suggesting perhaps not only the fluid content of the subject but also the fluid nature of its boundaries.[8] As a result we are left to deduce theoretical insights from the contents where we find that civil liberties is about police powers, public order, emergency powers and the response to terrorism, freedom of expression (including censorship and obscenity, contempt of court, governmental secrecy and national security), the right to privacy, freedom of religion, freedom from racial discrimination, freedom of movement (with particular reference to immigration control), and prisoners' rights.

These books of cases and materials have now been joined by a number of textbooks on the subject, the most voluminous of which is David Feldman's *Civil Liberties and Human Rights in England and Wales*, published in 1993. Running to 927 pages here was an opportunity to provide a definitive account of what the subject is about in what has rightly come to be regarded as one of the leading studies. Although the author somewhat disarmingly informs us that any 'selection of liberties which might be examined is bound to reflect the personal interests of the author', and expresses the hope that his choice of material is 'not entirely unrepresentative of more general concerns',[9] Feldman nevertheless also advances the cause of our inquiry some way. There is implicit in the title of the book a distinction between civil liberties and human rights, and while it is true that the distinction is not fully developed in the text itself it is nevertheless one which is clearly worth exploring. There is also a valuable account in Chapter 1 of why it is desirable to protect individual freedom and of the different theories and approaches to protection, as well as an account of different types of 'rights' and the different purposes which they serve. The author appears, however, to favour a justification

---

[6] 1st edn, p v. Emphasis in original.   [7] Ibid.
[8] A suggestion reinforced by the exclusion of the topic from the fourth edition for reasons of space.
[9] At p vii.

based on the moral autonomy of the individual, and to determine the boundaries of the discipline by what is necessary to promote and protect personal freedom in the widest sense. So in a comprehensive survey Feldman leads us at one extreme from life, liberty and physical integrity, through privacy and expression, to equality and social and economic rights at the other extreme. But like many of those who have gone before him, Feldman does not address the question of where human rights end and civil liberties begin: the reader is left to reflect that the terms are used as synonyms rather than antonyms.

Civil Liberties and Political Participation: The Legacy of Marx

So we return to the question as yet unanswered by the literature: what do we mean by civil liberties? How do we clarify the boundaries of our inquiry? The starting point is to consider with Feldman whether there is a difference between what are sometimes referred to as human rights and what we refer to as civil liberties, and if so to develop that difference and consider its implications. Such a distinction is in fact well established, having been made by the young Marx in his famous essay *On the Jewish Question* as long ago as 1843, in which he identifies *droits de l'homme* on the one hand and *droits du citoyen* on the other. As expressed in the eighteenth century French and American constitutional texts to which he refers, the former include such things as freedom of conscience and religion, but also in the 'most radical constitution', the French Constitution of 1793, liberty, security and property. Of these Marx writes that:

not one of the so-called rights of man goes beyond egoistic man, man as a member of civil society, namely an individual withdrawn into himself, his private interest and his private desires and separated from the community. In the rights of man . . . society appears as a framework extraneous to individuals, as a limitation of their original independence. The only bond which holds them together is natural necessity, need and private interest, the conservation of private property and their egoistic persons.[10]

In other words, *droits de l'homme* are about protecting the *autonomy* of the *individual*: his or her private life, his or her freedom of conscience, and his or her freedom of artistic expression, to say nothing of his or her freedom of private property. (They were, however, at least perceived as human rights, and had not at that time been embraced by the corporate form—that most remarkable instrument of humanity.[11]) *Droits du citoyen*, in contrast, are 'partly *political* rights, rights which are only exercised in

---

[10] K Marx, 'On the Jewish Question', in K Marx, *Early Writings* (1975), p 230.
[11] See now *Groppera Radio AG v Switzerland* (1990) 12 EHRR 321.

community with others'.[12] What defines their content, Marx maintains, are those measures which facilitate '*participation* in the *community*, in the *political* community or *state*. They come under the category of *political free-dom* or *civil rights*'.[13] Marx does not give much indication of what would fall within this category, though he does refer to freedom of the press, and by extension would presumably include matters such as the right to vote or universal suffrage, and political freedoms such as freedom of asso-ciation, freedom of assembly and freedom of expression—at least to the extent that these facilitate participation in the political life of the com-munity. Yet although there may thus be a difference between *droits de l'homme* and *droits du citoyen*, there are also important overlaps which sug-gest that we cannot reject all manifestations of the former. It would, for example, be a rather fragile right to freedom of assembly which operated in a culture in which the police had an unconstrained power of arrest, or an unconstrained power of search and seizure. So, with one caveat, here we have two quite different disciplines with two quite different pur-poses.

The distinction drawn and developed by the young Marx provides a valuable starting point for our quest to discover the purpose of civil lib-erties, and the boundaries within which they operate. We are therefore concerned not with all of the matters which appear in the US Bill of Rights (on which Marx did not dwell) or the European Convention on Human Rights (on which he could not dwell), but only with those liber-ties which are designed to promote a sense of political engagement. It is true that these texts contain provisions of this latter kind (more true of the ECHR and its protocols than the US Bill of Rights), provisions which might properly be considered as *droits du citoyen*, even if the right to vote—the most central of all *droits du citoyen*—appears in the ECHR only as something of an afterthought. But they also contain much more, and indeed to the extent that these texts include what might be referred to as *droits du citoyen*, they are largely overshadowed by *droits de l'homme*—the right to privacy, the right to freedom of religion and conscience, and the right to private property. This is not, however, to diminish the impor-tance of human rights, or indeed to deny the importance of human rights as instruments in a democratic society. Nor is it to deny that one of the purposes of a democratic society is to sustain those human rights which contribute to the dignity and security of the individual without which there can be no effective right of political participation. But in this sense

---

[12] Marx, n 10 above, p 227. Emphasis in original.   [13] Ibid. Emphasis in original.

the boundaries of human rights are even more opaque than the boundaries of civil liberties, with a greater rhetorical than substantive content.

We are, however, moving into much more highly contestable territory, contestable for a number of reasons. Implicit in the observations of Marx to which we have referred is more than a distinction of purpose between *droits du citoyen* and *droits de l'homme*. There is also a suggestion that the two are contradictory rather than complementary, serving what may sometimes be conflicting goals: one is designed to fuel the engine of democracy, and the other to act as its brake. Certainly the priority accorded the individual by the language of human rights can undermine the effective operation of civil liberties as guarantors of democracy. This point was drawn out more clearly when Marx referred to article 2 of the French Declaration of the Rights of Man of 1791, which provided that the 'goal of all political association is the conservation of the natural and imprescriptible rights of man'. He also referred to the similarly worded French Declaration of the Rights of Man of 1793 which by article 1 provided that government is 'instituted in order to guarantee man the enjoyment of his natural and imprescriptible rights'. As might be predicted, both texts are strongly criticised by Marx, who was particularly scornful that 'a people which is just beginning to free itself'—as was the case of the French people in the late eighteenth century—should presume to reduce 'the political community' to a mere *means* for the conservation of these so-called rights of man'.[14] The great mystery for Marx was why the political emancipators had set matters on their head in this way, 'so that the end appears as the means and the means as the end'.[15] So here we have a claim not only that civil liberties are different from human rights, and that the two are contradictory disciplines, but moreover that in the instruments with which Marx was concerned, the former are subordinated to the latter.

This begs many questions, some of which will form an important focus of our study. First and most obviously, to what extent is it still accurate to say that *droits de citoyen* are subordinated to *droits de l'homme*? Even if the argument can be sustained in the case of eighteenth and nineteenth century France, can the same judgement be made about more modern and contemporary civil and political societies? Can a judgement made in the nineteenth century about the eighteenth really be credible in the century of democracy? Secondly, to which human rights or *droits de l'homme* are the rights of political citizenship or *droits de citoyen* subordinated? And if

---

[14] Ibid, p 231. Emphasis in original.   [15] Ibid, p 232.

rights of political citizenship are subordinated to the so-called rights of man, to what other interests or values may these rights of political citizenship be subordinated? Thirdly, if it is the case that this process of subordination is constrained neither by history nor geography but is a phenomenon of wider or even universal application, are there any particular institutional devices by which it is secured or consolidated? Marx had in his sights two particular texts in which the controversial claims were made (the 1791 and 1793 French Declarations of the Rights of Man), and we have referred to several others, including the European Convention on Human Rights. But how far can this theory be sustained in a constitution which on the one hand secures *droits du citoyen*, but does not—formally at least—recognise the so-called *droits de l'homme*, though they may be recognised in other branches of the law? The last question is of course particularly pertinent for an inquiry about the place of civil liberties in Britain in the first half of the twentieth century.

Civil Liberties and the Rule of Law: The Legacy of Dicey

It is against this background that we can turn our attention to consider how civil liberties are protected in British law. Do they have a subordinated status or are they ends in themselves? And if they do have a subordinated status, how is this subordination achieved? In order to consider these issues we must begin with the principles upon which the British constitution is built. Unlike many other countries the civil liberties of British citizens are not protected in any formal way by a constitutional text interpreted by the courts. Indeed the civil liberties of the people of this country appear to be particularly vulnerable by virtue of the constitutional principle of parliamentary sovereignty whereby Parliament is free to make or unmake any law whatsoever. This is not to suggest the inevitable effectiveness of a written code of entrenched rights, since it does not follow from the formal protection of rights in this way that they cannot be subordinated by the courts to other political ends, as is arguably the case in the USA.[16] Nor indeed is this to suggest that the existence of a formal guarantee of rights in a written code is the only way by which civil liberties can be protected; in fact the absence of such a

---

[16] See *Schenck v United States* 249 US 47 (1918); *Debs v United States* 249 US 211 (1918); *Gitlow v New York* 268 US 652 (1924), and *Whitney v California* 274 US 357 (1926). See the extraordinarily prescient comments of James Connolly, 'Ballots, Bullets, Or—?', in P Berresford Ellis (ed), *James Connolly: Selected Writings* (1973), p 202. The cases are considered in their historical context by S Walker, *In Defence of American Liberties* (1990). See also C Gearty, 'Citizenship and Freedom of Expression', in R Blackburn (ed), *Rights of Citizenship* (1993), ch 14.

framework of protection was celebrated as a distinguishing virtue of the British constitution by its greatest exponent, A V Dicey in his celebrated and still influential *Introduction to the Study of the Law of the Constitution*, which conveniently for the purposes of this study was first published in 1885.

Dicey argued that civil liberties in this country are protected not by a single constitutional document but by the common law, and specifically by the Rule of Law which was said to have three component parts or 'conceptions'.[17] The first of these is that 'no man is punishable or can be lawfully made to suffer in body or goods except for a distinct breach of the law established in the ordinary legal manner before the ordinary courts of the land'. 'In this sense', he continues, 'the rule of law is contrasted with every system of government based on the exercise by persons in authority of wide, arbitrary, or discretionary powers of constraint'. Dicey's second conception is what might be referred to as the principle of equality by which he meant 'not only that with us no man is above the law', but that 'here every man, whatever be his rank or condition, is subject to the ordinary law of the realm and amenable to the jurisdiction of the ordinary courts'. According to Lord Chief Justice Hewart this means that 'Everyone, whatever his position, Minister of State or Government official, soldier or policeman, is governed by the ordinary law of the land and personally liable for anything done by him contrary to that law'; and also that everyone is 'subject to the ordinary Courts of Justice, civil and criminal'.[18] Dicey's third principle involved invoking the Rule of Law in 'a different sense', on this occasion as 'a special attribute of English institutions'. What this meant was that the 'constitution is pervaded by the rule of law on the ground that the general principles of the constitution (as for example the right to personal liberty, or the right of public meeting) are with us the result of judicial decisions determining the rights of private persons in particular cases brought before the courts; whereas under many foreign constitutions the security (such as it is) given to the rights of individuals results, or appears to result, from the general principles of the constitution'.[19]

Much ink has been spilled criticising Dicey and in particular his contention that civil liberties are protected by the common law, a point to which we return. For the moment, however, it is necessary to address the concern that Dicey's theory was simply a metaphor for a more general

---

[17] A V Dicey, *Introduction to the Study of the Law of the Constitution* (10th edn by E C S Wade, 1959), p 188.

[18] Lord Hewart, *The New Despotism* (1929), p 26.

[19] Dicey, *Introduction to the Study of the Law of the Constitution*, n 17 above, p 195.

political theory, no more and no less than an embodiment of the values of
liberal individualism which was to used to attack the emerging collectivist
State and its institutions.[20] As conceived by Dicey the Rule of Law was
thus an ideological stick with which to beat progressive political forces.
This is a point which was made forcefully by Jennings in a blistering attack
on Dicey,[21] in the course of a critique of the report of the Committee on
Ministers' Powers in 1932.[22] Jennings points out that the antithesis
between 'regular law' and 'arbitrary power' is false, in the sense that regular law may confer arbitrary power, citing as examples the Defence of
the Realm Consolidation Act 1914 and the Emergency Powers Act 1920,
both of which conferred wide powers on ministers to deal with war-time
and peace-time emergencies. These are considered fully in Chapters 2 and
4 below. Everybody agreed, said Jennings, that if the Rule of Law meant
that 'no act ought to be done by anybody without legal authority', then
the rule of law ought to be obeyed: this, however, was a characteristic of
all constitutions and was not peculiar to the British constitution. But insofar as Dicey employed the Rule of Law to mean that public authorities
ought not to have large powers, that is an opinion of 'a conservative
Liberal-Unionist of the Victorian era' and that as such it was 'not a legal
doctrine at all'.[23] But if it were not a legal doctrine, in what sense was it a
political doctrine, and how did it connect with political ideology?

The starting point in the search for an answer to that question lies in
Dicey's contempt for collectivism ('the school of opinion often termed
socialism')[24] which is abundantly clear in his companion volume *Law and
Public Opinion in England,* first published in 1905. In the Introduction to the
second edition which appeared nine years later, Dicey traced the emergence of collectivist influence to the extension of the franchise, and the
perception on the part of the poor that 'political authority can easily be
used for the immediate advantage, not of the country but of a class'.[25]
The danger of democracy was thus that while it prevented the enactment
of legislation which 'the people are unwilling to accept', it gives 'inadequate security for the passing of laws which are wise and good', and in
particular gives inadequate protection from the influence of the socialist
for those who believe that nothing 'can benefit the people as much as does
the maintenance of political freedom'. Indeed Dicey was to argue that
democracy and socialism were incompatible, with the latter encouraging

---

[20] See especially M Loughlin, *Public Law and Political Theory* (1992), ch 7.
[21] W I Jennings, 'The Report on Ministers' Powers' (1932) 10 *Public Administration* 333.
[22] Cmd 4060 (1932).   [23] Jennings, n 21 above, p 342.
[24] A V Dicey, *Law and Public Opinion in England* (2nd edn, 1914), p 64.   [25] Ibid, p lxv.

its enthusiasts 'to think lightly of individual freedom, and to suggest the very dubious idea that in a democracy the wish of the people may often be overruled for the good of the people'.[26] Dicey appears to embrace a vision of democracy which reserves a key role for certain individual rights, including the right to own private property, condemned by the socialist who 'wishes to substitute for it the passion for common ownership by the State', thereby further demonstrating that 'the democratic ideal as understood by Englishmen is inconsistent with the ideals of socialism'.[27] But what has Dicey's antipathy to collectivism to do with the Rule of Law? The answer lies in the fact that he lamented not only the emergence of socialist thought, but also what he saw as its emerging influence on the development of public policy and on legislation.

Dicey was concerned in particular with recent legislation which had 'given judicial or quasi-judicial authority to officials who stand more or less in connection with, and therefore may be influenced by, the government of the day, and hence have in some cases excluded, and in others indirectly diminished, the authority of the law Courts'.[28] And for good measure Dicey had earlier been heard to complain that these public authorities or administrative tribunals, whose members did not have security of tenure, were 'always more or less connected with the Government of the day' and their decisions 'apt to be influenced by political considerations'.[29] This tendency 'to diminish the sphere of rule of law' was shown, for example, by the 'judicial powers conferred upon the Education Commissioners by the Education Act 1902, on various officials by the National Insurance Acts 1911 and 1913, and on the Commissioners of Inland Revenue and other officials by the Finance Act 1910'.[30] So far as the National Insurance Act 1911 is concerned this was condemned both for its aims and administrative methods, in the case of the latter the resolution of disputes about the scope of the Act by administrative tribunals rather than the ordinary courts being 'enough to prove' that there now existed in England a system 'bearing a marked resemblance to the administrative law of France',[31] a regime which he attacked on the ground that public officials are thereby 'exempted from the ordinary law of the land, protected from the jurisdiction of the ordinary tribunals, and subject in certain respects only to official law administered

---

[26] Dicey, *Law and Public Opinion in England*, n. 24 above, pp lxxii–iii.   [27] Ibid, p lxxvi.

[28] A V Dicey, *Introduction to the Study of the Law of the Constitution* (8th edn, 1915), p xxxviii.

[29] Dicey, *Law and Public Opinion in England*, n 24 above, p xliii.

[30] Dicey, *Introduction to the Study of the Law of the Constitution*, n 28 above, p xxxviii.

[31] Dicey, *Law and Public Opinion in England*, n 24 above, p xliii.

by official bodies'.[32] Socialist legislation it seems was inconsistent with the Rule of Law, proper respect for which would prevent the introduction of collectivist measures.

Civil Liberties and the Principle of Legality

As articulated by Dicey the principle of the Rule of Law is not particularly helpful: it serves to confirm the suspicions of several commentators that as a principle, the Rule of Law is simply a synonym which reflects certain values of a liberal legal system which in turn reflects certain political values. But it does not follow that the principle of the Rule of Law is necessarily empty of substance, or that we should go the whole hog with Jennings who claimed that 'the antithesis between "regular law" and "arbitrary power" is false'.[33] It does follow, however, that if the Rule of Law is to be a meaningful principle of universal application, we must start again, perhaps from a much less ambitious and certainly much less value-loaded base, recognising that 'the rule of law is just one of the virtues which a legal system may possess and by which it is to be judged', thereby rejecting any attempt to confuse the principle with 'democracy, justice, equality (before the law or otherwise), human rights of any kind or respect for persons or for the dignity of man'.[34] To do otherwise is simply to appropriate an invaluable principle as a metaphor for a political theory, which in one extreme version encompasses nothing less than 'ideas about the requirements of justice and fairness between government and governed'.[35] To do otherwise is also to misunderstand the Rule of Law both as a principle and in terms of what it can be expected to yield, for it does not follow that the role of the Rule of Law as properly understood is peculiar to any particular political philosophy, while its use as a label by those who adhere to an inarticulate theory adds nothing but an empty slogan to the course of debate. Thus if the practice of government or public officials is unjust or unfair why not say so and explain why? How is the argument strengthened by the parallel claim that the action in question is also, and for this reason alone, contrary to the Rule of Law? Is not the Rule of Law in this sense a tautology, a largely redundant concept robbed of any integrity or value?

---

[32] Dicey, *Law and Public Opinion in England*, n 24 above, pp 190–1.

[33] Jennings, n 21 above, p 342.

[34] J Raz, 'The Rule of Law and its Virtue' (1977) 93 LQR 195, at p 196. Also P P Craig, 'Formal and Substantive Conceptions of the Rule of Law' (1995) 1 *Diritto Pubblico* 35.

[35] T R S Allan, *Law, Liberty, and Justice* (1993), p 21.

There are those who would argue that the Rule of Law is incapable of rehabilitation in this way. In his famous study on the origin of the Black Act, E P Thompson sought to vindicate the value of the Rule of Law, arguing that some modern radicals have overlooked the 'difference between arbitrary power and the rule of law'. Although there were 'shams and inequities which may be concealed beneath this law', the Rule of Law itself by 'the imposing of effective inhibitions upon power and the defence of the citizen from power's all-intrusive claims' was 'an unqualified human good'.[36] This immediately drew a number of criticisms, notably from the American legal historian, Morton Horowitz who was unable to 'see how a Man of the Left can describe the Rule of Law as an "unqualified human good" '. For although the Rule of Law 'undoubtedly restrains power', it also 'prevents power's benevolent exercise', by creating 'formal equality' (a 'not inconsiderable virtue') and at the same time '*promotes* substantive inequality by creating a consciousness that radically separates law from politics, means from ends, processes from outcomes'. Indeed 'by promoting procedural justice it enables the shrewd, the calculating, and the wealthy to manipulate its forms to their own advantage'.[37] Other critics have argued in a similar vein, with Bob Fine contending that 'the rule of law was directly connected with the emergence of absolute private property right' and that one cannot be dissociated from the other.[38] In other words far from being 'an unqualified human good' the Rule of Law is an instrument for sustaining the power of private property and consequently the domination of one class (the bourgeousie who own the means of production, distribution and exchange) over another (the working class who own nothing but their labour power). This is certainly a view of the Rule of Law to which our analysis of Dicey discussed above, adds credence.

The controversy generated by E P Thompson's observations thus draws us immediately into the traditional socialist suspicion about the virtue of liberal legal concepts, of which the Rule of Law is perhaps the pre-eminent. It is not just that the Rule of Law is a synonym for liberalism generally; there is also the claim that behind its apparently neutral facade lurks a structure of class domination. The law is a reflection of the power of the ruling class, one of the instruments by which it maintains that control: 'According to Marx, the state is an organ of class *rule*, an

---

[36] E P Thompson, *Whigs and Hunters* (1975), p 266.
[37] M Horowitz, 'The Rule of Law: An Unqualified Human Good?' (1977) 86 *Yale LJ* 561. Emphasis in original.
[38] B Fine, *Democracy and the Rule of Law* (1984), p 188.

organ for the *oppression* of one class by another; it is the creation of "order", which legalises and perpetuates this oppression by moderating the conflict between the classes'.[39] The Rule of Law is thus the rule of class by law and to the extent that it provides equality under the law it does so to protect certain interests above all others between unequal individuals.[40] Although as a matter of form '[t]he law protects everybody equally', it is a society based on private property, with the main purpose of the law being to protect 'the property rights of every merchant, industrialist and manufacturer'.[41] How thus can the law offer equal protection to those whose interests it fails to recognise, and how can those who have nothing invoke the protection of the law? How then can it seriously be contended that the Rule of Law is an 'unqualified human good', particularly when there is 'not a single state, however democratic, which has no loopholes or reservations in its constitution guaranteeing the bourgeoisie the possibility of dispatching troops against the workers, of proclaiming martial law, and so forth, in case of a "violation of public order" '?[42] In other words, the Rule of Law also provides the means for the protection of a particular political structure. Not only that: by providing a cloak of legality for repressive measures, it provides a cloak of legitimacy.

So can anything be rescued from the Rule of Law as a legal principle? It seems reasonably clear that if it is to be recognised as a principle with any substance or meaning of universal application, it can only be on different terms, on the basis of the Rule of Law as expressing a principle of legality.[43] By this we mean the principle that those who exercise power over others must have legal authority for their actions. No more and no less: it does not imply any moral or substantive content of the law beyond the obligation that government should be conducted in accordance with the law. As such the principle of legality is nevertheless crucially important as a precondition of liberty and a precondition of the right to political participation (though this is not to deny that the content of the law may continue to be based on liberty of property or that it may continue to operate to protect property relations).[44] This is not to say, however,

---

[39] V I Lenin, 'The State and Revolution' (1918), in V I Lenin, *Selected Works 2* (1971), p 291.
[40] See Thompson, n 36 above, p 259.
[41] V I Lenin, 'The State' (1919), in V I Lenin, *Selected Works 3* (1971), pp 269–70.
[42] V I Lenin, 'The Proletarian Revolution and the Renegade Kautsky' (1918), in Lenin, ibid, p 82.
[43] Cf J Jowell, 'The Rule of Law Today', in J Jowell and D Oliver (eds), *The Changing Constitution*, (3rd edn, 1994), ch 3.
[44] Cf H Collins, *Marxism and Law* (1982) who writes at p 144 of the danger of a celebration of legality sliding into 'a wholesale acceptance of the Rule of Law'.

that the principle of legality will have no bearing on substantive questions, for although the principle does not on its own directly provide a legal framework for the protection of civil liberties, it may do so indirectly. In an advanced liberal democracy grounded in legality, many of the rights of political participation will have a clear statutory base, as for example in the case of the right to vote in Britain. Having been created by law, these rights may be removed or qualified only by law, and although this is always possible, the principle of legality at least clothes these rights with the protection of a legal process which must be complied with before any removal or qualification can be effective. In other words, the principle of legality offers an important measure of procedural protection to substantive rights secured by political struggle, even if does not guarantee the substance of the rights themselves or indeed prescribe a process which must be followed before revocation or qualification.

In the British system it is of course the case that not all rights of political participation had a statutory base in this way. Indeed as we shall see in the British system there were very few rights of political participation formally guaranteed by law, this being true for example of vast areas relating to the freedom of association, assembly and expression. But it does not follow that because political freedom in these areas is constructed on a much less secure base, the principle of legality is any the less important as a check on arbitrary government. So although the principle of legality does not guarantee the right to freedom of expression, there can be no freedom of expression or any other kind of freedom if the police are free with impunity to intimidate and violate the privacy of anyone who dares to criticise the government. Similarly, although the principle of legality does not guarantee the right to freedom of assembly, there can be no freedom of assembly if the police are free to disrupt marches and processions with impunity. In the absence of legal authority the principle of legality means that such action (at least in principle) can be restrained and a remedy sought in the courts. It is true of course that legislation might well expressly provide the police with such arbitrary power, in which case it might well be argued that this is precisely the principle of legality in action: legislation has given to the police the power to do whatever they want, and to determine the scope of their own powers. But in the absence of such an eventuality or similar eventualities (in which case arguments from principles of legality would be as futile as they would be quixotic) the principle of legality permits us to retrieve the Rule of Law as a doctrine of utility and value. This is a matter to which we return, but as we shall see full compliance even with formal legality

is itself a challenge which not all governments in twentieth-century
Britain have been able to meet.

Civil Liberties and the Principles of Legality

The first requirement of the principle of legality may seem self evident,
and perhaps it ought to be. Simply, it requires government to have legal
authority for whatever it does on behalf of those whom it represents. This
is similar to the first limb of Dicey's first principle which he appeared to
presume was easily reflected by the demands of the common law. This
was, however, most surprising, for this is not a principle which has been
fully recognised by English law, as can be demonstrated in a number of
ways. Above all it is demonstrated by the fact that legality is met not by
the requirement that the government must have legal authority for its
conduct, but by the requirement that what the government does must
not be unlawful.[45] The two are not the same, with the result that the government was and is free to violate the freedoms of citizens even though
it has no formal legal authority to do so, provided that it does not violate any established personal or property rights of the individual in the
process. Often arbitrary conduct of the government will cross the line of
legality as occurred in *Entick v Carrington*[46] where it was held that the
Secretary of State had no authority to issue a warrant to search the home
of John Entick for seditious papers even where this was claimed to be in
the interests of State necessity. In that case what was under attack by the
courts was not the exercise of arbitrary power but the coincidence that
there had been a trespass, that is to say a violation of established property rights. As later cases relating in particular to the surveillance activities of the Special Branch and the secret service were to demonstrate,[47]
it did not always follow that the unrestrained exercise of public power
would coincide with the violation of any common law right of the individual.

Apart from this requirement for legal authority what else may the principle of legality be said to require? It may be maintained that legal
authority is not enough per se, but that a second set of requirements
demand that the government must have legal authority which is (i) clear,
for otherwise people would be unable to determine the scope of their
obligations; (ii) published in advance, for otherwise people would not
know of their obligations when they violated them; and (iii) prospective,

---

[45] *Malone v Metropolitan Police Commissioner* [1979] Ch 344.
[46] (1765) 19 St Tr 1030.   [47] See especially Chapter 3 below.

for otherwise people would be penalised for doing something which was lawful at the time it was done. It also means that there should be no indemnities for government officials, for otherwise they would be excused the consequences of failing to comply with the principle of legality. We may refer to these as the secondary principles of legality, to which we might add another, namely the requirement that the law should not be used to confer unduly wide discretionary powers. As we have seen this is a matter of some difficulty. On the one hand it is not discretion which is necessarily the enemy of legality, as Dicey would have us believe; much depends on the nature of the discretion and on the extent to which the manner of its exercise is subject to scrutiny. But on the other hand it would be difficult to justify as being consistent with the Rule of Law a statutory provision authorising a minister to do whatever he or she likes. It is true that the power in question would be authorised by law and so would meet the first requirement of the condition of legality. But it can hardly be argued that a power to do whatever one likes is consistent with the secondary principles of legality which we have identified and which follow inexorably even from the most elementary conception of law.

In practice, however, discretionary power does not take this form, but may for example enable a minister to take certain measures if statutory preconditions are met, as in the case of the Emergency Powers Act 1920. This authorises the proclamation of a state of emergency 'at any time' where 'it appears to His Majesty that there have occurred, or are about to occur, events of such a nature as to be calculated, by interfering with the supply and distribution of food, water, fuel, or light, or with the means of locomotion, to deprive the community, or any substantial portion of the community, of the essentials of life'. Once made, a proclamation authorises His Majesty to make such regulations as he 'deems necessary' for a wide range of purposes for securing the essentials of life of the community. It is open to question whether legislation of this kind gives adequate guidance or adequately constrains the circumstances in which the power may be used or the steps which may be taken in its purported exercise: such powers may be thought to come close to the type of discretion which confers authority on the minister to do whatever he or she likes, and so to sail close to the wind of, if not to cross, the principle of legality. The case for the control of discretionary powers is not the province of any particular political philosophy; as Sypnowich points out writing from a perspective clearly on the Left, '[u]nfettered discretion can doubtless lead to arbitrariness' and that as a result 'a just legal system will seek, not to eliminate discretion, but to regulate and control it, within the framework of the rule of law'.[48] One way by which this can be done is for the courts to ensure that any discretionary powers are not exercised improperly in the sense that they are not used for a purpose or in a manner which was clearly not intended by Parliament: in intervening in this way the courts are upholding rather than undermining the principle of legality by 'acting as guardians of Parliament's purpose'.[49]

The third requirement of the principle of legality brings us to the boundaries of the principle, and reminds us of the concern that even in a more rational form any conception of the Rule of Law may be elusive. The third requirement is for an autonomous and accountable legal process: the government must be answerable to an independent judiciary for the way in which its powers are exercised, to ensure that there is no excess or abuse. By autonomy what we have in mind is an aspect of the notion of judicial independence, a requirement of singular importance. It would be hardly consistent with the principle of legality if those who made the rules were also empowered to determine what they were to mean in any particular case. It would be tantamount to conferring upon the government official the ability to determine the limits of his or her own power, unconstrained by the boundaries erected by the law. But on the other hand there are very real concerns about whether there can be any such thing as an independent judiciary: we are reminded of the condemnation by Marx in *The Civil War in France* of the 'sham independence' of the 'judicial functionaries' which had 'but served to mask their abject subserviency to all succeeding governments'.[50] This can take a number of forms, including 'the high degree of *ideological congruence*'[51] that exists between ministers, legislators and judges who are for 'the most part agreed on the fundamental features of the social order'.[52] This is partly 'to do with who judges are', being drawn mostly from 'the same narrow segment of the population from which is also recruited the majority of people who exercise [political] power'.[53] As such it is said that they 'not uncommonly see themselves as the guardians of the social order against anyone, including ministers, who seeks to change it in ways they find unacceptable'.[54]

---

[48] C Sypnowich, *The Socialist Concept of Law* (1990), p 72.
[49] Jowell, n 43 above, p 73. See *Padfield v Minister of Agriculture, Fisheries and Food* [1968] AC 997.
[50] K Marx, 'The Civil War in France', in K Marx and F Engels, *Selected Works* (1968), pp 291–2.
[51] R Miliband, *Socialism for a Sceptical Age* (1994), p 76. Emphasis in original.
[52] Ibid.
[53] R Miliband, *Capitalist Democracy in Britain* (1982), p 116.
[54] Ibid.

This tends to suggest that the best we can settle for is functional rather than genuine independence in the deepest sense of that term. This has two virtues, neither of which should be underestimated: the first is a separation of personnel in the sense that members of the the judicial branch are not also members of the executive or legislative branches of government; and the second is a separation of function in the sense that members of the executive do not exercise judicial functions and that members of the judiciary are not compromised by assuming executive functions. But even in this weak sense the capacity and potential for an autonomous legal process has been undermined historically by a system of patronage which has seen appointments being made on political grounds, and which has also witnessed ministers of the crown being elevated to the Bench to adjudicate on disputes about legislation which they may have had a hand in creating. As Robert Stevens has demonstrated, for much of the period under consideration in this book the most senior court in the country was 'highly politicalized', this being true of both judicial decisions 'as well as in political activities'.[55] In the pages which follow we shall see that this politicalization was a feature of at least some of the judges in the lower courts as well, with the position of the Lord Chief Justice in particular raising important questions about independence even in this weak sense of the term.[56] But so far as the House of Lords is concerned, Stevens has argued that political judges (appointed in recognition of their political affiliation) were 'an integral part of the appellate scene until the 1930s',[57] referring to Lords Atkinson and Shaw who were appointed by Balfour and Asquith respectively 'because they were party men and party men were needed to ensure that the appellate functions of the House were handled from the appropriate political viewpoint'.[58]

Civil Liberties, Political Participation and the Role of Parliament

The Rule of Law as political ideology was not the only charge levelled against Dicey: Jennings was also to challenge the claim that 'it is the courts that have invented the modern Constitution', arguing that the 'greater part of the law of the Constitution is to be found in the special

---

[55] R Stevens, 'Judges, Politics, Politicians and the Confusing Role of the Judiciary', in K Hawkins (ed), *The Human Face of the Law* (1997), p 250.

[56] See especially Chapter 2 below. On lower levels still see D N Pritt, *Law, Class and Society. Book 2: The Apparatus of the Law* (1971), pp 61–74.

[57] R Stevens, *Law and Politics. The House of Lords as a Judicial Body, 1800–1976* (1979), p 217.

[58] At p 246.

statutes which regulate the powers and duties of public authorities, legislative and administrative'.[59] This would be true of much of the law and
practice of civil liberties, and in particular the rights of political participation. Indeed it is now quite clear that the common law was a serious
obstacle to the development of such rights, and that the common law
barriers had to be removed by legislation. This was not true in the case
of all such rights, though in order more fully to understand the processes
at work it is necessary to distinguish between two different types of civil
liberties or rights of political participation: we refer to these as primary
and secondary rights respectively. The former are in many respects the
most fundamental yet also the most badly neglected: they deal with the
right of the individual to participate directly in the process of government, whether as an elector, a candidate for election, or as an elected
representative. The latter are in many respects well covered by the literature and fully understood: they deal with the right of the individual to
influence the government but as such they do not require (though they
are a precondition of) a fully democratic form of government and a
'healthy public life',[60] while the existence of such forms of government
through the extension of primary rights will go a long way to enhance
the value and impact of the secondary rights. These latter include freedom of assembly and expression. It is in respect of primary rights in particular that the intervention of Parliament has been critical to remove the
roadblocks placed by the common law and to lay the foundations of liberal political society.

On this as on other points Dicey seriously misrepresents reality. In so
doing he also reinforced the view that his version of the Rule of Law was
a deeply ideological weapon. What did the common law have to say
about the franchise and about the role of the elected representative?
Unsurprisingly, in relation to both it reflected the values which the common law had been developed to embrace, with historians teaching us that
the common law developed to meet 'the needs of a commercial society',
to permit 'the development of a world in which men of property could
do what they would with their own'.[61] So far as the franchise is concerned, it was itself considered as a property right, the exercise of which
was contingent on the ownership of property until well into the twentieth century, reinforcing the view that its purpose was to protect prop-

---

[59] Jennings, n 21 above, pp 341–2.
[60] See R Luxemburg, 'The Russian Revolution', in M-A Waters (ed), *Rosa Luxemburg Speaks* (1970),
p 365, at p 389. See further, P Frölich, *Rosa Luxemburg* (1940), pp 276–8.
[61] C Hill, *Intellectual Origins of the English Revolution* (1972), p 256.

erty.[62] But so far as the common law was concerned, the franchise was not only economically exclusive, it was also enjoyed exclusively by men: 'it was a principle of the unwritten constitutional law of this country that men only were entitled to take part in the election of representatives to Parliament',[63] a perfectly rational principle in a society which had denied married women the right to own property in their own name until 1882.[64] At this point the cases are not simply reinforcing our evidence in relation to the deeper ideology of the Rule of Law, but they are also thrusting a fatal blow into the heart of the principle of equality before the law, which self-evidently did not exist, not even as a matter of form, quite apart from any questions of substantive equality which might otherwise have arisen at the time.

Related problems were to arise in the context of the role of the elected representative, with the rule of the common law threatening to stunt the growth of the Labour Party and to frustrate the development of its collectivist programme. In *Amalgamated Society of Railway Servants v Osborne*[65] the House of Lords held that trade unions could not impose a compulsory levy on their members to promote parliamentary representation generally and the Labour Party in particular.[66] This heavy blow to freedom of association was justified mainly on the ground that the promotion of parliamentary representation was not an object of trade unionism which was referred to in any of the legislation conferring a legal status on trade unions. But Lord Shaw of Dunfermline (joined by Lord James of Hereford on this point) decided the case on the quite different ground that the payments were 'unconstitutional and illegal' because they required any trade union sponsored candidate to accept the Labour Party whip and vote accordingly, thereby creating a financial inducement which 'destroys or imperils that function of freedom of advice which is fundamental in the very constitution of Parliament'.[67] In a full frontal attack on a disciplined system of party government, Lord Shaw's speech reveals quite clearly the concern about the threat to established

[62] See Blackstone, *Commentaries on the Laws of England* (7th edn, 1775), i, p 158: 'The commons consists of all such men of property in the kingdom, as have not seats in the house of lords; every one of which has a voice in parliament, either personally or by his representatives'. He continues by observing 'The counties are therefore represented by knights, elected by the proprietors of lands: the cities and boroughs are represented by citizens and burgesses, chosen by the mercantile part or supposed trading interest of the nation' (ibid, p 159).

[63] *Nairn v The University Court of St Andrews*, 1907, 15 SLT 471, at p 473. See subsequently *Nairn v St Andrews University* [1909] AC 147, esp at p 163.

[64] Married Women's Property Act 1882.   [65] [1910] AC 87.

[66] For a full account, see S and B Webb, *The History of Trade Unionism 1666–1920* (1920), pp 608–31, and K D Ewing, *Trade Unions, the Labour Party and the Law* (1982), ch 2.

[67] [1910] AC 87, at p 115.

authority of universal suffrage and working class representation in Parliament through working class parties.[68] Quoting Locke he said that 'the people having reserved to themselves the choice of their representatives, *as the fence to their properties*, could do it for no other end but that they might always be freely chosen, and so chosen freely act and advise, as the necessity of the commonwealth and the public good should upon examination and mature debate be judged to require'.[69]

So it was Parliament rather than the common law which in fact created the rights of political participation, the primary rights to which we have referred. This was done in direct conflict with the principles which the common law reflected, which were property-based principles of liberty rather than politically-based principles of equality. It is paradoxical perhaps that these achievements should be secured and that steps in the direction of equality should be taken by elected representatives who were themselves under a legal duty to preserve the privileges of those by whom they were elected. But none of these triumphs was secured without political struggle to reshape the pillars on which the Diceyesque Rule of Law was built. This was true of much of the political pressure that produced the electoral reform legislation of 1832 and 1867, and it was also the case with the suffragettes, particularly in the period between 1903 and 1914.[70] Their campaigning for the right to vote took a number of different forms of public protest both peaceful and violent,[71] and led to hunger strikes and force-feeding of imprisoned suffragettes.[72] The immediate statutory consequence of the campaign was the Public Meeting Act 1908, which was passed in order to prevent disruption at political meetings,[73] though it proved to be something of a dead letter. In fact it was not until after the end of the First World War that the first step in the direction of women's suffrage was taken, with the Representation of the People Act 1918 providing that women over the age of 30 could vote.[74] The same Act also removed the property qualification (as a householder or lodger on the one hand, or occupier of property over

---

[68] It was not, however, an attack on the idea of working class representation in Parliament nor indeed the idea of State allowances for MPs (introduced in 1911), Lord Shaw acknowledging that such payments may be 'a tribute to character, or a recognition of talent, coupled with a desire that these should be secured for the service of the State' (at p 114).

[69] J Locke, *Two Treatises of Government* (1963 edn), p 461. Emphasis added.

[70] See R T B Fulford, *Votes for Women* (1957).

[71] See *R v Hewitt* (1912) 28 TLR 378; *R v Joachim* (1912) 28 TLR 380; and *R v Beckett* (1913) 29 TLR 332.

[72] See *Leigh v Gladstone* (1909) 26 TLR 139.

[73] See Parl Debs, 19 December 1908, cols 2328–42.

[74] For consideration of this issue by Dicey, see Dicey, *Introduction to the Study of the Law of the Constitution*, n 28 above, pp lxii–xvi.

a prescribed value on the other) before men could be entered on the register of electors. Thus in 1918 men were entitled to be registered on the basis of residency alone,[75] though it was not until 1928 that the franchise was extended to women on the same terms.[76]

But it was not only in relation to the franchise that Parliament proved to be the source of rights of political participation: the same was true also of the right to be an elected representative. In *Osborne* it was held in effect that the working class could have representation in Parliament provided that they adapted to the values of the existing constitution in which the role of Parliament was to advise and deliberate in the 'national interest', rather than to act in a concerted and predetermined way to promote the sectional interests of a particular class. It is well known, however, that this decision was unsustainable and the political pressure for its reversal irresistible: the right of trade unions to promote political objects, including support for the Labour Party and the election of parliamentary candidates, was restored by the Trade Union Act 1913. The freedom was not, however, unlimited, with the Act providing that a trade union had first to conduct a ballot of its members and establish a separate political fund which in turn had to be financed by a separate levy of the members. More significantly, in an important gesture of recognition of the civil liberties of trade union members who may not support the Labour Party, any member of a union with political objects had the right to claim exemption from the obligation to pay the levy and a right not to be subjected to any disability or disadvantage for doing so. It is true, however, that this concession did not halt the forward march of Labour and indeed if anything proved to be helpful to the cause of parliamentary representation, by providing a supply of money which could be used only for political purposes. And although the Act did not expressly address the point raised by Lord Shaw, it gave clear legal authority to trade union political activity, and little was heard in the courts thereafter of the Lockean objections which he had raised.

Civil Liberties and the Paradox of Parliamentary Sovereignty

We have seen that Parliament played a critically important role in creating the framework in which political participation was possible in Britain at the start of the twentieth century, for example by developing

---

[75] Representation of the People Act 1918, s 1.
[76] Representation of the People (Equal Franchise) Act 1928, s 1.

the principle of universal suffrage. Paradoxically, however, Parliament could also be a source of restraint on civil liberties, with C B Macpherson demonstrating that having unleashed the power of universal franchise, an immediate and constant preoccupation has been to tame and diminish its liberating potential.[77] Parliament was supreme and indeed for Dicey the legal sovereignty of Parliament was 'the dominant characteristic of our political institutions' and meant 'neither more nor less' than the right of Parliament 'to make or unmake any law whatever'.[78] In a passage quoted by Dicey with approval, Blackstone had written even more powerfully that Parliament 'hath sovereign and uncontrollable authority in the making, confirming, enlarging, restraining, abrogating, repealing, reviving, and expounding of laws, concerning matters of all possible denominations, ecclesiastical, or temporal, civil, military, maritime, or criminal: this being the place where that absolute despotic power, which must in all governments reside somewhere, is entrusted by the constitution of these kingdoms'.[79] For Dicey this supremacy of Parliament complemented the Rule of Law on the ground that 'the sovereignty of Parliament, as contrasted with other forms of sovereign power, favours the supremacy of the law, whilst the predominance of rigid legality throughout our institutions evokes the exercise, and thus increases the authority, of Parliamentary sovereignty'.[80] One obvious problem with Dicey's observations is that they appear to relate only to the first of his three conceptions of the Rule of Law, that is to say the principle of legality: the principle of parliamentary sovereignty may contribute to the 'supremacy of the law', but this tells us nothing about the content of the law.

Parliament was thus the instrument through which political power was won by the people (the instrument through which they secured their political sovereignty),[81] but it was also the instrument through which that political power was exercised (the instrument by which they asserted their political sovereignty). Yet it did not follow that a sovereign legislature was required only to legislate or that questions would not arise relating to the democratic content of that legislation. For as Bernstein and others have pointed out on the Left, democracy must mean more than majority rule: it must also include 'an idea of justice, that is, equality of rights for all

---

[77] C B Macpherson, *The Life and Times of Liberal Democracy* (1977).
[78] Dicey, *Introduction to the Study of the Law of the Constitution*, n 17 above, pp 39–40.
[79] Blackstone, *Commentaries*, n 62 above, i, p. 160.
[80] Dicey, *Introduction to the Study of the Law of the Constitution*, n 17 above, p 406.
[81] By winning the franchise even though it may have been 'grudgingly conceded': Miliband, *Socialism for a Sceptical Age*, n 51 above, pp 24–5.

members of the community, and this sets limits to the rule of the majority'.[82] We are thus immediately faced with the dilemma of democracy which is that only a sovereign Parliament can satisfy the requirement that the political and legal sovereign be representative and accountable, but in a representative and accountable democracy only a sovereign Parliament can impose controls on the exercise of that sovereign power. The dilemma is in fact that a sovereign Parliament in the democratic age is asked to perform two quite different and contradictory functions; the first being to ensure that the wishes of the electorate are carried out with speed and efficiency, and the second being to ensure that in carrying out these wishes legislation is not passed to erode civil liberties or to confer wide and unrestrained powers on the part of the government, thereby diminishing the very process for which the government for the time being is merely a trustee.

At the start of the democratic age, the trick was to hold this difficult balance between the legislative and scrutiny functions of the legislature, which in turn suggested the need for effective institutional arrangements if the latter function in particular was to be fulfilled when the independence of Parliament was already being eroded by the demands of the party system. Yet it is clear that this second function was even at this early stage vulnerable and subject to serious limitations. This is not to condemn the principle of parliamentary sovereignty or indeed strong party government, but to question whether the sovereignty of Parliament was effectively maintained in both of its aspects. The problem did not appear unduly to trouble Dicey, who addressed the matter in the most complacent terms. What were the safeguards to ensure that the despotic potential of Parliament was not transformed into a despotic reality? Returning to Dicey, the first it seems was the requirement that 'the commands of Parliament' could be 'uttered only through the combined action of its three constituent parts' (Queen, the House of Lords and the House of Commons);[83] the second appears to be the wise restraint of Parliament itself in the sense that 'Parliament has looked with favour and jealousy on all exemptions of officials from the ordinary liabilities of citizens or from the jurisdiction of the ordinary courts';[84] and the third was the fact that when the need for 'discretionary powers brings about the recourse to exceptional legislation', the powers so conferred 'must always be exercised "under the supervision of the courts" '. Thus 'however

---

[82] E Bernstein, *The Preconditions of Socialism* (1993), p 141.
[83] Dicey, *Introduction to the Study of the Law of the Constitution*, n 17 above, p 407.
[84] Ibid, p 409.

extraordinary', powers which are conferred or sanctioned by statute are 'never really unlimited' for they are 'confined by the words of the Act itself, and, what is more, by the interpretation put upon the statute by the judges', who are 'influenced by the feelings of magistrates no less than by the general spirit of the common law'.[85]

Whether these constraints on the sovereignty of Parliament were even in theory ever a sufficient safeguard of liberty is of course open to question. Part of the problem in the real world of Britain at the turn of the century was that with the gradual extension of the franchise the function of Parliament was transformed from that of an independent source of restraint in a nineteenth-century nightwatchman State into the instrument through which the executive governed in the twentieth century, armed increasingly with a democratic mandate and a programme of social and economic reform. The emerging democratic impulse had two implications, one institutional and the other consequential. So far as the institutional impact is concerned, this was expressed most clearly in the enactment of the Parliament Act 1911 which as Dicey acknowledged in the eighth edition published in 1915, 'greatly increased the share of sovereignty possessed by the House of Commons and has greatly diminished the share thereof belonging to the House of Lords'.[86] The significance of this of course was to reduce the capacity of Parliament to scrutinise the work of the government, though paradoxically it is difficult to lament the reduction of the power of the unelected chamber as the country was moving inexorably in the direction of universal franchise. The consequential impact of the democratic impulse was the exercise of great powers on the part of the government in the social field—in areas such as housing, education and national insurance—designed to address the expectations of the electorate. In the process great powers were conferred upon ministers and on government departments, and although there is of course cause to welcome this development, one problem with the willingness of Parliament to defer to the executive on matters of social and economic policy was that this risked creating a habit of quiescence, which might spread to questions of personal and political freedom.

There were in truth few constraints on the power of the executive ('a committee for managing the common affairs of the whole bourgeousie'?)[87] governing through Parliament (elected members of 'the ruling class' to

---

[85] Dicey, *Introduction to the Study of the Law of the Constitution*, n 17 above, p 413.

[86] Dicey, *Introduction to the Study of the Law of the Constitution*, n 28 above, p xxiv.

[87] K Marx and F Engels, 'The Communist Manifesto', in Marx and Engels, *Selected Works*, n 50 above, p 31, at p 37.

'misrepresent the people'?).[88] For as the franchise was about to be extended further, and at the same time that working class representation in Parliament was becoming a reality, so legislation was being passed by Parliament authorising the making by the executive of regulations of the most far-reaching kind. Admittedly the legislation (the Defence of the Realm Acts 1914–15) was passed in war-time and the powers in question were conferred for the duration of the war only. But the fact is that this legislation was passed, that wide powers were taken to suppress political opposition to the war, and more significantly, if we may anticipate the reader's likely retort, that many of these powers were retained after the war as permanent laws. Thus many of the restrictive provisions of the Defence of the Realm Regulations were given permanent effect in the Official Secrets Act 1920 while a standing power to re-introduce them in peace-time was conferred upon the government by the Emergency Powers Act 1920, these being subsequently used with some venom to crush the General Strike in 1926.[89] Equally significant are measures such as the Incitement to Disaffection Act 1934 and the Public Order Act 1936 both of which can trace their origins to war-time powers.[90] But although these measures clearly make the point, there is a danger that they do so too forcefully. For as we shall see, the second paradox of parliamentary sovereignty is that in the period under discussion in the area under discussion it was in fact Parliament which offered the most effective resistance to the illiberal tendencies of government, though there were clearly some spectacular failures, not the least of which was the Official Secrets Act 1911, passed on the eve of our era.[91]

Civil Liberties, Parliamentary Sovereignty and the Courts

If Parliament was to prove to have a patchy record in controlling the executive, what about the judiciary? The principle of parliamentary sovereignty clearly had important implications for the constitutional role of the courts. As Dicey pointed out the three traits of parliamentary sovereignty were 'first, the power of the legislature to alter any law, fundamental or otherwise, as freely and in the same manner as other laws; secondly, the absence of any legal distinction between constitutional and other laws; thirdly, the non-existence of any judicial or other authority

---

[88] Marx, 'The Civil War in France', n 50 above, at p 292.
[89] See Chapter 4 below.   [90] See Chapters 5 and 6 below.
[91] For details of the content of this measure and the circumstances of its passage, see Chapter 2 below.

having the right to nullify an Act of Parliament, or to treat it as void or unconstitutional'.[92] This contrasted with a subordinate law-making body characterised first by 'the existence of laws affecting its constitution which such a body must obey and cannot change; hence, secondly, the formation of a marked distinction between ordinary laws and fundamental laws; and lastly, the existence of some person or persons, judicial or otherwise, having authority to pronounce upon the validity or constitutionality of laws passed by such law-making body'.[93] Examples of such subordinate law-making bodies included the legislatures of France, Belgium and the USA, the judges in the case of the last mentioned being the 'guardians of the constitution' and the 'only adequate safeguard which has hitherto been invented against unconstitutional legislation'.[94] This is not to say that Dicey approved of such a regime, and we may readily endorse his suggestion that it is somewhat 'anomalous' that 'the legislative assembly of an independent nation may not be a sovereign assembly'.[95] For in contrast to a constitution based on popular sovereignty and parliamentary supremacy, a system in which judges are the guardians of the constitution is also a system in which the judicial branch is effectively sovereign.

Yet it is unclear why, apart from the natural superiority of the middle class Englishman and the natural superiority of English ways, Dicey was dismissive of this kind of arrangement and such an apparently warm supporter of parliamentary sovereignty, particularly in view of its democratic and emancipatory potential which appear to have caused him such alarm.[96] It did not follow, however, that the courts in England had no role to play in moderating the impact of legislation: we have seen Dicey's view that 'however extraordinary' powers which are conferred or sanctioned by statute are 'never really unlimited' for they are 'confined by the words of the Act itself, and, what is more, by the interpretation put upon the statute by the judges', who are 'influenced by the feelings of magistrates no less than by the general spirit of the common law'.[97] The point is made forcefully by Lord Justice Vaughan Williams in *R v Local Government Board, ex parte Arlidge* where he said that:

[92] Dicey, *Introduction to the Study of the Law of the Constitution*, n 17 above, p 91.
[93] Ibid, at p 92.
[94] Ibid, at p 137.   [95] Ibid, p 121.
[96] Dicey *Introduction to the Study of the Law of the Constitution*, n 28 above, pp lxii. Note also the contextually misplaced Diceyesque lament of Lord Justice Farwell in *Conway v Wade* [1908] 2 KB 844, at p. 856.
[97] Dicey, *Introduction to the Study of the Law of the Constitution*, n 17 above, p 413.

an Act of Parliament may be so worded as expressly to authorise a procedure inconsistent with the principles of justice recognised by the common law of England. Parliament is omnipotent. Rules, however, made under statutory authority, although express, may, in my opinion, be inoperative because they are ultra vires, or inconsistent with the principles on which English law is based. At all events, when rules are silent, such a rule, inconsistent with the principles on which the common law is based, cannot be implied.[98]

In this way, 'majority decisions were filtered through the common law doctrine of the sovereignty of Parliament and . . . the legislative output of Parliament was in turn filtered through the judgment of judges wedded to the common law conceptions of individual rights and the rule of law'.[99] But just like the Parliaments which conferred the powers in the first place there was a suspicion that the courts too were going soft on the Rule of Law.

This suspicion applied both in terms of failing adequately to constrain the exercise of discretion on the one hand, and in terms on the other of failing to ensure the application of full procedural safeguards in the determination of people's rights and duties by the officers of state who had been established to deal with such matters. The latter point is illustrated most clearly by the landmark decision in *Local Government Board v Arlidge*[100] where in reversing the Court of Appeal the House of Lords cannot be accused of being driven by the 'general spirit of the common law', at least in all of its aspects. In that case, all the more extraordinary for the fact that it involved a statutory encroachment on property rights, the respondent had been served with a closing order by the Hampstead Borough Council on the ground that a house which he leased was not fit for human habitation. An inspector was appointed under the Act to hold a public inquiry, attended by the respondent who gave evidence and who was accompanied by his solicitor. The inspector submitted his report together with the shorthand notes of the proceedings to the Local Government Board which confirmed the refusal of the council to withdraw the closing order. The respondent then challenged the decision of the Board on the ground that he should have been given a copy of the inspector's report and an opportunity to make representations to the Board before it reached its decision. But the House of Lords rejected these claims, holding that the Board in this case had discharged its duty to act in good faith and to listen fairly to both sides. That being so, 'the

---

[98] [1914] 1 KB 160, at pp 175–6.
[99] D N MacCormick, 'Jurisprudence and the Constitution' [1983] 36 CLP 13, at p 18.
[100] [1915] AC 120.

only authority that can review what has been done is the Parliament to which the Minister in charge is responsible'.[101]

There is not much evidence here of the right to have one's liberties determined 'in the ordinary legal manner before the ordinary courts of the land', indeed not much evidence of the right to have one's liberties determined in accordance with an ordinary legal procedure. In determining the procedures to be followed by the Board, it did not follow that these had to be based on the procedures which would be adopted by a court of law, for when Parliament entrusts bodies such as the Local Government Board to enforce 'obligations on the individual which are imposed in the interests of the community',[102] it must be taken 'to have intended' the Board 'to follow the procedure which is its own, and is necessary if it is to be capable of doing its work efficiently'.[103] Indeed 'that the judiciary should presume to impose its own methods on administrative or executive officers is a usurpation. And the assumption that the methods of natural justice are *ex necessitate* those of Courts of justice is wholly unfounded'.[104] So where 'the question of the propriety of procedure is raised in a hearing before some tribunal other than a Court of law there is no obligation to adopt the regular forms of legal procedure. It is sufficient that the case has been heard in a judicial spirit and in accordance with the principles of substantial justice'.[105] For present purposes it is important to note that there is not much evidence here of the ordinary courts being alert to protect what were considered at the time to be fundamental liberties, in this case the peaceful enjoyment of one's property. For in reaching this decision the House of Lords was prepared to bend with the political winds (in this case those blowing in the direction of social liberalism),[106] clearly mindful of the fact that the question before the court was clearly 'one affecting property and the liberty of a man to do what he chooses with what is his own'.[107]

Yet although few are likely to lament this decision, or the willingness of some of the judges to move with the times, paradoxically it does present problems: if the courts were prepared to defer so readily on matters relating to property, what price personal and political liberties? For the style of deference appropriate in a case involving the regulation of private property was not necessarily appropriate for violations of personal or political liberty, the winds of change requiring the emergence of a new

---

[101] [1915] AC 120, at p 134 (Viscount Haldane LC).　　　　[102] Ibid, at p 132.

[103] Ibid.　　　　　　　　　　　　　　[104] Ibid, at p 138 (Lord Shaw of Dunfermline).

[105] Ibid, at p 140 (Lord Parmoor).　　　[106] See L T Hobhouse, *Liberalism* (1911).

[107] [1915] AC 120, at p 130 (Viscount Haldane LC).

and more sophisticated judicial approach to reflect the emerging new political structures and principles. Whereas in the past restrictions on property rights might have been scrutinised with extreme care, now it was time to do the same with restrictions on personal and political liberties: if the common law is not flexible it is nothing. Yet as we shall see the judges proved unable to make that distinction, and indeed *Arlidge* may well have been an aberration,[108] the happy coincidence of the presence of so many Liberal Law Lords on a point of such deep political sensitivity:[109] the deference to restrictions on property rights was not matched by a rigorous examination of restrictions on personal or political liberties,[110] and indeed the deference to attacks on property rights was not sustained for long. Normal service was resumed during the war when, remarkably, war-time measures regulating property proved more vulnerable to judicial scrutiny than those regulating personal and political liberty.[111] Indeed there is not a single case of significance in the Law Reports of legislation passed between 1914 and 1945 to restrict personal and political liberties being restrained in its scope by the judicial power of interpretation.[112] The common law and the principles on which it was based proved to be remarkably robust: there was no space reserved in the common law for association, assembly or expression, and none was created.[113]

Civil Liberties, the Courts and the Common Law

The last sentence appears in some ways directly to contradict Dicey and indeed much of the learning which British public lawyers have absorbed since their first days at law school. The traditional view has always been that civil liberties in Britain were protected by the common law and that their violation has been the fault of Parliament. But as we have seen this is self-evidently not true in the case of what we refer to as primary rights of political participation, which were won by Parliament challenging

---

[108] For similar sentiments but in a different context see *Board of Education v Rice* [1911] AC 179.

[109] See Stevens, 'Judges, Politics, Politicians and the Confusing Role of the Judiciary', in Hawkins (ed), *The Human Face of Law*, n 55 above, p 250. The Liberals on the court were Haldane LC and Lords Parmoor and Shaw of Dunfermline.

[110] *Despard v Wilcox* (1910) 26 TLR 118 is a good illustration of this point.

[111] See Chapter 2 below.

[112] On the contrary in perhaps the most famous case of the period, *Liversidge v Anderson* [1942] AC 206 (dealing with powers of internment without trial) the House of Lords distorted the language of the legislation to authorise a detention for which there would otherwise have been no authority. See Chapter 8 below.

[113] Cf Lord Browne-Wilkinson, 'The Infiltration of a Bill of Rights' [1992] PL 397.

established common law principles. So far as what we refer to as secondary rights of political participation are concerned, it is true only indirectly, with the result that in those areas where Parliament did not intervene, there continued to be cause for concern about the capacity of the common law and the ability of the courts to provide a vigorous protection for civil liberties. Given its purpose to promote and protect rights of private property, it seems most likely that the common law would be at its best in the safeguarding of property rights, and in some difficulty when being called upon to defend conduct which was unconnected with the right to property or which presented a direct challenge to property rights. Indeed the most famous of all English civil liberties cases is incapable of being separated from its roots in property law. This is the decision in *Entick v Carrington*[114] in which as we have seen it was held that the King's Secretary had no authority to issue a warrant to search the home of John Entick for seditious papers. In reaching this decision the court was not moved by the need to preserve freedom of expression or accountability on the part of government. The concern was rather different, and was expressed as anger at a violation of the 'great end, for which men entered into society', namely 'to secure their property', a 'right which is preserved sacred and incommunicable in all instances, where it has not been taken away or abridged by some public law for the good of the whole'.[115]

So in *Entick v Carrington* personal liberty was protected because of the happy coincidence of personal interests and property rights. But it would be misleading to suggest that this is the only basis for the protection of liberty by the common law: the other is revealed by the famous decision in *Beatty v Gillbanks*[116] of which Dicey thought that 'No better instance can be found of the way in which in England the constitution is built up upon individual rights than our rules as to public assemblies'.[117] It was in that case that the Queen's Bench Division upheld appeals by members of the Salvation Army who had been bound over to keep the peace for refusing to obey a magistrate's instruction not to march through the streets of Weston-super-Mare for fear of provoking violence by a rival group masquerading under the name of the Skeleton Army. In a powerful judgment Field J accepted the magistrates would have been entitled to act as they did if the disturbances had in fact been either intended by

---

[114] (1765) 19 St Tr 1030.
[115] Per Lord Camden LCJ, at p 1066. Emphasis added.
[116] (1882) 9 QBD 308, followed in *R v Londonderry Magistrates* (1891) 28 LR Ir 440.
[117] Dicey, *Introduction to the Study of the Law of the Constitution*, n 17 above, p 271.

the Salvation Army or had been a natural and necessary consequence of their acts. But in fact the disturbance was caused by the unlawful resistance of the Skeleton Army and not the conduct of the Salvationists who were guilty of no offence in passing through the streets: the former was an 'unlawful organisation' which had 'no possible right to interfere with or in any way obstruct the Salvation Army in their lawful and peaceable processions'. In upholding the rights of the latter to assemble freely, Field J concluded by repudiating the proposition that 'a man may be convicted for doing a lawful act if he knows that his doing it may cause another to do an unlawful act'.[118]

What does *Beatty* tell us about the status of political liberty in English law? It tells us that where the individual is not standing on a property right, his or her liberty may not be interfered with if the conduct is not unlawful. But as in *Entick v Carrington*, the common law again is not here protecting the right of political liberty: there is still no right to freedom of assembly or freedom of expression recognised by the common law. Rather it is protecting the right of the individual not to be restrained unless he or she has done something unlawful, which may or may not protect political freedom, but then only incidentally and collaterally. This is a very insecure base on which to build a theory of political liberty, particularly as there is no fixed definition of what constitutes unlawful action, so that the general principle can readily be swallowed in the shifting sands of its exception. In other words, the right to do that which is unlawful is exposed to the danger of new heads of liability being introduced by a sovereign Parliament, or just as likely by the common law itself which proved to be as efficient in controlling and regulating political freedom as it did in protecting it. For all the efforts to place *Beatty v Gillbanks* on a pedestal (not only by Dicey), it was in truth an exceptional decision, an aberration. There was until very recently little evidence before or since *Beatty v Gillbanks* of the common law recognising the right to freedom of assembly, with the traffic of judicial decisions being all the other way.[119] As defendants in subsequent proceedings were to find out, political action in practice will invariably be unlawful for any one of a number of reasons.

An indication of the true position is provided by *O'Kelly v Harvey*,[120] all the more significant for testing the courts on a matter of political controversy rather than the ephemera which was *Beatty v Gillbanks*. The case followed a proposed meeting to be held by the Land League, an organisation formed in Ireland in 1879 with the aim of reducing rents and

---

[118] (1882) 9 QBD 308, at p 314.
[119] See now *DPP v Jones* [1999] 2 All ER 257.   [120] (1883) 15 Cox CC 435.

eventually achieving tenant ownership. On this occasion a meeting was arranged to persuade tenant farmers not to pay their rent. Advertised as a 'Great Land Demonstration' to be addressed by Charles Stewart Parnell, it was met by counter-advertising calling on the 'Orangemen of Fermanagh' to assemble in their thousands to 'put a stop to all treasonable proceedings in our loyal county'. Fearing that there would be a breach of the peace, Harvey, a magistrate, ordered the Land League meeting to disperse and in the course of doing so 'laid his hand on the plaintiff, in order to separate and disperse the plaintiff' and the persons who had assembled. The subsequent action for damages for assault and battery was unsuccessful on the ground that the defendant was under a duty to take whatever steps were necessary to preserve the peace and that the decision to disperse the meeting was consistent with said duty, even though this meant denying the right of peaceful assembly and even though 'the danger to the public peace arose altogether from the threatened attack of another body on the plaintiff and his friends'.[121] *O'Kelly v Harvey*[122] thus demonstrates clearly the paradox that political freedom depended not upon the law, but upon the benevolent exercise of discretion by a public official, contrary to everything which Dicey preached. Yet as we shall see in the pages which follow, it is this decision and not *Beatty v Gillbanks*[123] which best captures the spirit of the common law.

There is always the temptation to dismiss *O'Kelly v Harvey* as dealing with the special problems raised by the Irish Question. But that would be a mistake, for the suffragettes were also to find that *Beatty v Gillbanks* was more froth than ale. In *Despard v Wilcox*[124] the appellants were members of the Women's Freedom League who had assembled in Downing Street to present a petition to the Prime Minister, several of their number having previously been convicted for trying to present a petition to him at Westminster.[125] The Prime Minister was not present when they arrived so they waited for several hours, during which time a crowd of onlookers also assembled. When he did eventually arrive the Prime Minister refused to speak to the defendants, and two hours later the police arrested two of their number who said they were pickets of the League, and then cleared Downing Street, in the process arresting

---

[121] At p 445, per Law LC who 'frankly own[ed]' that he could not understand the decision in *Beatty v Gillbanks*, particularly having regard to its facts. In his view 'any needless assemblage of persons in such number and manner and in such circumstances as are likely to provoke a breach of the peace, was itself unlawful'.

[122] (1883) 15 Cox CC 435.   [123] (1882) 9 QBD 308.   [124] (1910) 26 TLR 118.

[125] *Pankhurst v Jarvis* (1909) 26 TLR 118.

the other defendants who had refused to leave. They were convicted by the magistrates on grounds which are unclear, but in upholding the convictions the Divisional Court rejected an argument based on *Beatty v Gillbanks* that the appellants were using the highway lawfully, and 'the fact that people assembled to watch them did not make their use unlawful'. In the view of the Lord Chief Justice (Alverstone) the women were liable for the 'natural consequences of their action', namely that their conduct over several hours 'led to obstruction' by 'crowds of idle people, and perhaps worse' who were 'rejoicing in the prospect of seeing these unfortunate women being taken away to prison'. Although there were other grounds on which the convictions were upheld, there is nevertheless enough here to indicate that *Beatty v Gillbanks* had been turned on its head, providing further evidence of a rather spineless principle: if the reasoning in *Despard* had been applied in *Beatty*, the appeal by the Salvationists would have failed.

Conclusion

It is appropriate here to draw together some of the threads which have been woven through this chapter. Our first concern has been to highlight the lack of any coherence about the way in which some scholars define what they mean by civil liberties. The tendency to conflate civil liberties with human rights is in our view deeply and profoundly mistaken: the two are different disciplines serving different and sometimes contradictory goals. We have also argued that the main purpose of civil liberties is to promote political participation and that as such it is a discipline which encourages the development of an active political culture: it is about freedom *to* rather than freedom *from*. Seen in these terms the discipline is designed to promote and reinforce popular participation in political life and as such to underpin the power of the franchise and the capacity for reform of a wide and varied kind. As a result it presents a serious dilemma for liberal democracy and its exponents, a point which we have already noted as having been nicely identified by C B Macpherson and others. Writing in the radical tradition, Macpherson argues for the need to 'pay attention to the relation between democratic institutions and the underlying structure of society', and emphasises not only that 'liberal democracy has typically been designed to fit a scheme of democratic government onto a *class-divided* society', but that the concept of liberal democracy 'became possible only when theorists—first a few and then most liberal theorists—found reasons for believing that "one man, one vote" would not be dangerous to property, or to the continuance of class-divided societies'.[126]

We have also argued that the traditional foundation of civil liberties in English law—Dicey's conception of the Rule of Law—is very unstable: as others have shown it is no more than a rhetorical statement which embraces a number of political principles fundamental to the values of a particular conception of liberal democracy, designed to protect these values and principles from the dangers of collectivism. To the extent that the Rule of Law as understood by Dicey purports to offer a coherent vision for the protection of civil liberties through the medium of the common law, it fails quite fundamentally to do so. In order to explain the failure it is necessary to acknowledge that civil liberties take two forms, which we describe as primary and secondary. The former include rights of direct political participation, such as the right to vote. These have depended upon Parliament for their introduction, and in this sense it is Parliament which has been the principal guarantor of political liberty in Britain. The latter include rights of political influence which may exist with or without the franchise. Although there have been few statutory provisions guaranteeing these measures, it is also the case that they are not formally recognised by the common law, and will be protected by the common law only collaterally as incidents of other principles which the common law does protect.[127] To the extent that there was any substance in Dicey's Rule of Law (which we doubt), this had all but evaporated even within his own lifetime, which he comes close to acknowledging himself in a note on the *Arlidge* case in 1915.[128] Parliament was in the process of metamorphosis, adapting to the demands of the democratic age as the engine of executive-driven change while even the courts were (quite properly) beginning to reveal a deference to the authority of democratic institutions,[129] albeit one that was to be short-lived.

This is not to deny that there is substance in the Rule of Law which as a principle of legality remains a constitutional principle of great importance, without which there can be no political freedom. Yet in the pages which follow we advance the claim that civil liberties in Britain in the first half of the twentieth century have not been effectively underpinned

---

[126] Macpherson, *The Life and Times of Liberal Democracy*, n 77 above, pp 9–10. Emphasis in original.

[127] Cf now *DPP* v *Jones*, n 119 above.

[128] See A V Dicey, 'The Development of Administrative Law in England' (1915) 31 LQR 148.

[129] In addition to *Arlidge* above, see also *Kruse v Johnson* [1898] 2 QB 91. But compare *Roberts v Hopwood* [1925] AC 578, though contrast the decision of the Court of Appeal ([1924] 1 KB 514).

by legality, particularly if the principle is expanded to the limited extent that we suggest. The period under review is one in which political liberty was violated in some cases without legal authority, and in others by legal authority which conferred a virtually unlimited, unconstrained and largely unaccountable discretion on the executive. Partly this is a failure of Parliament, never certain of its role as the defender as well as the source of much of the political freedom in this country, lacking effective institutional mechanisms of governmental scrutiny. Indeed by the time the male franchise was fully extended in 1918, the process of government control of Parliament was complete and irreversible, a process which paradoxically was required by the emergence of popular sovereignty mediated through the framework of party government. But partly this erosion of political liberty was also a failure of the courts, wedded to common law principles created in the eighteenth century and robustly defended ever since, in the manner explained in the foregoing paragraph and at earlier points of this chapter. As we shall see, in this respect the common law was a metaphor for civil liberties and political freedom generally, in the sense that these existed to serve and were permitted only to the extent that they did not seriously challenge or frustrate an established political and social order. The boundaries of political freedom were to prove both narrow and constrained: it was a case of freedom for all except those who dissent.

2

The First World War

The First World War was one of the twentieth century's great cata-
clysmic events. So far as Great Britain is concerned, it had long-term
social, economic and political consequences, quickening the pace of
reform on all fronts. So far as the present enquiry is concerned, the war
is equally significant even though its domestic legal and civil liberties
implications have not been fully examined by modern scholars. Perhaps
it is difficult to be seen to complain too loudly about selected restraints
on individual liberty at home when 2.5 million British servicemen and
women were being killed or wounded on the fields of Flanders and elsewhere.[1] Yet it remains true that the period leading up to the war, and
the war-time period itself, saw major institutional innovations affecting
political freedom on the one hand, as well as enduring restrictions on the
civil liberties of the people of this country on the other. As we shall see
some of these restrictions were introduced as temporary measures under
the Defence of the Realm Act. But as we shall also see, many of the
restrictions either survived the reason for their original introduction or
were revived in a different form at a later date. The First World War
offers a fascinating study of a state in crisis and of the ease with which
liberal values may be surrendered in times of emergency. It also offers a
valuable insight into the role of the different institutions of government,
tending to reveal a largely unaccountable executive restrained only by a
sometimes quiescent legislature and a compliant judiciary. As such the
experience of war tends to confound the complacency of Dicey, writing
only thirty or so years earlier, that liberty in Britain was effectively protected by the common law and an independent Parliament.

The First World War saw many restrictions imposed on the personal and
political liberties of the people of Britain in the interests of victory over
'the common enemy'. Among these were the measures which prolonged
the life of Parliament for the duration of the war,[2] thereby suspending

---

[1] On war-time casualties, see J M Winter, *The Great War and the British People* (1986). See also
H C Debs, 4 May 1921, cols 1033–4. Casualties in the legal profession are considered by T E
Scrutton, 'The War and the Law' (1918) 34 LQR 116. Obituaries were carried by the *Solicitors'
Journal*.

[2] Parliament and Registration Act 1916, s 1 (amending Parliament Act 1911, s 7), amended in
turn by Parliament and Local Elections Act 1917, s 1, Parliament and Local Elections (No 2) Act
1917, s 1, and Parliament and Local Elections Act 1918, s 1.

elections, and thereby denying the people an opportunity directly to express a view on how the war was being waged. Thus although the life of Parliaments had been reduced from a maximum of seven to a maximum of five years by the Parliament Act 1911, the Parliament which was elected in 1910 was not dissolved until 1918. Secondly, major restrictions of civil and political liberties were authorised by the Defence of the Realm Acts 1914–1915, emergency legislation which was rushed through at the beginning of the war to give to the government wide-ranging powers to make regulations without reference to Parliament, to take steps necessary to secure the defence of the realm. As we shall see these powers were used to introduce far-reaching restrictions on freedom of association, freedom of assembly, and freedom of expression, and as we shall also see these and other powers were used by the government to attack the activities of the war-time peace movement and those engaged in anti-war activities in major industrial centres such as Clydeside. Although the Defence of the Realm Acts and the regulations made thereunder form the main focus of this chapter, it is not to be overlooked that personal and political liberties were undermined thirdly in a number of other ways by a *pot pourri* of restrictive legislation passed without much hesitation by Parliament at a time of acute stress. The Aliens Restriction Act 1914 authorised regulations to be made imposing restrictions on the immigration and free movement of aliens;[3] the National Registration Act 1915 set up a compulsory national register of all persons between the ages of fifteen and sixty-five; and the Military Service Act 1916 introduced military conscription with only limited and controversial rights of conscientious objection.[4]

Preparing for War

'By 1903', writes French, 'the construction of the German navy had locked Britain and Germany in a state of mutual fear. The British feared that the Germans intended to invade them, and the Germans were afraid that the Royal Navy would launch a surprise attack to sink their new

---

[3] These were in addition to the powers which could be exercised in respect of aliens under the Defence of the Realm Regulations, and in addition to prerogative powers in respect of aliens, on which see *R v Commandant of Knockaloe Camp, ex parte Forman* (1917) 34 TLR 4 (prerogative power to detain enemy aliens registered under the Aliens Order).

[4] See J M Rae, *Conscience and Politics. The British Government and the Conscientious Objector to Military Service, 1916–1919* (1970). See also B Stewart, *Breaking the Fetters* (1967), chs 8–12, and more recently L Bibbings, 'State Reaction to Conscientious Objection', in I Loveland (ed), *Frontiers of Criminality* (1995), ch 3.

ships while they lay peacefully at anchor'.[5] Although both countries were wrong, 'by 1908–9 public fears of an invasion' (whipped up by the popular press and 'patriotic writers' of fiction such as William Le Queux who wrote tirelessly of a country swarming with German spies) 'had reached fever pitch with the news that the Germans might be about to accelerate their shipbuilding programme'.[6] Responding to public alarm, a subcommittee of the Committee of Imperial Defence was appointed in March 1909 to examine the situation: chaired by R B Haldane, the Secretary of State for War, the subcommittee also included the Home Secretary, the Postmaster General, the Metropolitan Police Commissioner, the Director of Military Operations, and the Director of Military Training. They agreed that 'an extensive system of German espionage exists in this country' and made a number of recommendations to deal with the threats of espionage and subversion, including the establishment of a secret service on the one hand and a new statutory framework for dealing with espionage on the other.[7] The implementation of both these recommendations was not, however, an example of the constitution at its best, whether in terms of the Rule of Law being vindicated or in terms of the excessive zeal of the executive being tempered by Parliament.

Considering first the establishment of a secret service, a small committee of the sub-committee had met and reported that 'a great need' existed for the establishment of a secret service bureau and recommended that it should be separate from any government department, but in close touch with the Admiralty, the War Office and the Home Office. In terms of funding it was said that no accurate estimate could be made, but on the basis of a staff of four (!) plus a subsidy to a private detective firm it was proposed should be enlisted, the cost would be somewhere in the region of £2,160 per annum.[8] This report was read to the subcommittee at its third and final meeting, but it was 'of so secret a nature that it is thought desirable that [the recommendations] should not be printed or circulated'.[9] A single typed copy was made, the affairs of the Bureau thus being 'shrouded in secrecy from the start'.[10] The

[5] D French, 'Spy Fever in Britain, 1900–1915' (1978) 21 *Historical Journal* 355.

[6] Ibid, p 358.

[7] See PRO, CAB 16/8, Report of the Sub-Committee, 24 July 1909. Reform was also to be strongly advocated by the secret service itself (PRO, KV 1/1, KV 1/2, and KV 1/35). See below.

[8] See PRO, CAB 16/232, Conclusions of the Sub-Committee requested to consider how a secret service bureau could be established in Great Britain. The number of staff employed by the secret service had risen to 844 by the Armistice. See PRO, KV 1/49.

[9] See PRO, CAB 16/8, 24 July 1909.

[10] French, n 5 above, p 362. For a full account of the origins of the secret service see C Andrew, *Secret Service* (1986). For the document, see PRO, CAB 16/232, n 8 above.

sub-committee accepted these conclusions and made recommendations as to the functions of the new organisation, based on the report of its committee. At that stage it was anticipated that the new organisation would have responsibility for gathering information about the intentions of foreign governments by employing agents overseas, while also addressing the question of foreign spies in this country. To the latter end the proposed Bureau would 'keep in touch through the Home Office, who would nominate an officer for the purpose, with the county and borough police, and, if necessary . . . send agents to various parts of Great Britain with a view to ascertaining the nature and scope of the espionage that is being carried out by foreign agents'.[11]

The first appointments were made in October that same year (1909), though such was the extent of the secrecy about the initiative that no announcement even of the existence of the service was made to Parliament for five years.[12] But apart from announcing that 'on the advice of the Committee of Imperial Defence, there was established at the War Office an Intelligence Department', the Prime Minister did not even then give much away: he did not reveal how the service went about its business, to whom it was accountable, under what restrictions or guidelines it operated, how many people were employed by it and in what capacity, or what was the size of its budget.[13] In the meantime, however, the new Department or Bureau had immediately set about the 'construction of [the] legal and administrative machinery' necessary to enable it to perform its duties.[14] The first priority was to ensure the enactment of a new Official Secrets Act to replace the Act of 1889,[15] said to be 'cumbrous and unpractical', neglecting to confer a power to 'complete one's evidence by preliminary search on suspicion', while failing also to prohibit photography or sketching in the vicinity of a military or naval establishment. 'Such a state of the Law', wrote a representative of the Bureau 'seemed more appropriate to some Gilbertian Utopia than to modern England'.[16] Although claiming to have 'initiated' the 1911

[11] See PRO, CAB 16/8, 24 July 1909. See also Public Record Office, *MI5: The First Ten Years, 1909–1919* (1997), pp 3–4.

[12] H C Debs, 18 November 1914, col 412.

[13] The existence of the Bureau was also acknowledged in the Lords a week later by Viscount Haldane in a debate on 'The Spy Peril'. He was slightly more forthcoming than the Prime Minister, but not on the critical issues. See H L Debs, 25 November 1914, col 145.

[14] PRO, KV 1/35.

[15] Although not passed with German espionage in mind, the Official Secrets Act 1889 had been used effectively in two cases involving German spies. See *The Times*, 16 October 1910 (the Helm case), and *The Times*, 29 August 1911 (the Schultz case).

[16] PRO, KV 1/35. It was generally felt by the security boffs pre-1911 that 'no action, in the present state of the law, can be taken to prevent German investigations' (PRO, KV 1/2).

Act,[17] it is clear that the need for legislation of a wide-ranging kind was well understood before the Bureau was created, and indeed that the formation of the Service and the amendment of the 1889 Act were seen by some as two sides of the same coin.[18] Nevertheless 'the Bureau's protests against the impossible situation were soon crowned with success' when in a 'short and masterly speech' the Secretary of State for War (Viscount Haldane) introduced the Official Secrets Bill in the Lords on 25 July 1911,[19] deliberately to strengthen the hand of the Bureau with 'much more drastic remedies'.[20]

Claimed by the Intelligence Department to be 'an excellent instrument that served [its] needs until the exigencies of war produced the still more effective Defence of the Realm Act and Regulations',[21] the Bill passed through the Lords without incident. It was then introduced by a nervous government into the Commons on 18 August 1911, 'a Friday afternoon when only 117 MPs were present to vote on the only division it faced'.[22] Completing all its stages on that day, the Bill took less than an hour in the process, the entire proceedings occupying no more than ten columns of Hansard.[23] Some of those present were inevitably critical of the indecency of the government's haste, with one backbencher claiming that it was 'a very unusual and very extraordinary thing to pass such a Bill without an opportunity of discussing it'. But these and other concerns were met with the rather bland assurances from the Under Secretary of State for War (Colonel Seely) that 'in no case would the powers be used to infringe any of the liberties of His Majesty's subjects'; and from the Attorney General (Sir Rufus Isaacs) that 'there would be no danger to anyone engaged in something perfectly innocent'. By the time the Bill reached its Third Reading one backbencher was moved to complain that undertakings to amend the Bill made during the Second Reading had not been honoured while another was so 'distressed' that he insisted that the House was 'entitled to hear an appeal that in the interest of the public service this Bill be allowed to pass so quickly'. An appeal was duly made by the Under Secretary of State for War who at the same time

[17] PRO, KV 1/35.

[18] See PRO, CAB 16/8, Report of the Sub-Committee, 24 July 1909.

[19] Ibid. The Sub-Committee had concluded that the Bill should be introduced by the War Secretary rather than the Home Secretary in order to 'excite less opposition', believing that 'the plea of its being a measure of precaution of great importance to national defence' would help assuage critics (PRO, CAB 16/8, Report of the Sub-Committee, 24 July 1909).

[20] H L Debs, 25 November 1914, col 145.   [21] Ibid.

[22] French, n 5 above, p 361.

[23] H C Debs, 18 August 1911, cols 2251–60. For the House of Lords, see H L Debs, 25 July 1911, cols 641–7. For further details, see D G T Williams, *Not in the Public Interest* (1965), ch 1.

reassured the House that 'the actual change in the law is slight' and that 'none of His Majesty's loyal subjects run the least risk whatever of having their liberties infringed in any degree or particular whatever'. These are extraordinary remarks in the light not only of the content but also the subsequent use of the 1911 Act.

Section 1(1) provides that it is an offence for any person ('for any purpose prejudicial to the safety or interests of the State') to approach, be in the neighbourhood of, or enter a 'prohibited place'.[24] It is also an offence to make any sketch, plan, model, article, or note 'which is calculated to be or might be or is intended to be directly or indirectly useful to an enemy', as well as to obtain or communicate to any other person information intended or likely to be of benefit to an enemy.[25] More controversial are the provisions of section 1(2) which provide that it is unnecessary to show that an accused person 'was guilty of any particular act tending to show a purpose prejudicial to the safety or interests of the State'. It is enough in the absence of any such act being proved against the accused that 'if, from the circumstances of the case, or his conduct, or his known character as proved, it appears that his purpose was a purpose prejudicial to the safety or interests of the State'. But while this last measure rightly occupied much of the time in the cursory parliamentary debates, there were other equally important measures in the 1911 Act which were entirely overlooked, not the least of these being the notorious section 2 which complemented the more serious offence in section 1.[26] As is well known, the new section 2 (the marginal note of which refers to the 'wrongful communication of information') was a provision of extraordinary breadth, applying not only to information about a 'prohibited place' or confidential information, but also to any information which has been obtained by the accused 'owing to his position as a person who holds or has held office under His Majesty, or as a person who holds or has held a contract made on behalf of His Majesty, or as a person who is or has been employed under a person who holds or has held

[24] The term 'prohibited place' is defined in s 3. See p 42 below

[25] See *R v Parrott* (1913) 8 Cr App Reps 186 (Germany an enemy even though not at war). This was the only one of the five pre-war prosecutions to be reported and the only one to involve an Englishman.

[26] In 1909 when the Bill was proposed by the Sub-Committee on Imperial Defence, it was proposed to amend the 1889 Act only to deal with espionage, and that care should be taken not to trespass on press freedom. It was also agreed that for this purpose there should be new powers of search. It is true that there were proposals also to punish those who knowingly published secret information, following the recent publication in a daily newspaper of secret information relating to the construction of a battleship. But this was to be the subject of a separate Bill, to be introduced only after consulting the press. See PRO, CAB 16/8, Report of the Sub-Committee, 24 July 1909.

such an office or contract'. It was an offence for any person to communicate this information, 'other than to a person to whom he is authorised to communicate it, or a person to whom it is in the interest of the State his duty to communicate it'.

Although sections 1 and 2 are the most significant of the measures in the 1911 Act, a number of others merit consideration. The first is section 3 which defines the term 'prohibited place', a crucial phrase used in both of the two preceding sections. It is true that not all the offences in sections 1 and 2 applied only in respect of prohibited places, but some did, notably the offence of entering a prohibited place in section 1. Under the 1889 Act the term 'prohibited place' was not used, but it was an offence to enter what were in effect government-owned military establishments 'for the purpose of wrongfully obtaining information'. The 'places which were barred from public access were [thus] but few', a limitation thought by Haldane to be too narrow in view of the 'many other places which have grown up in importance in the last twenty years'. Section 3 in defining the term 'prohibited place' thus extends the locations from which the public may be excluded to cover not only government defence installations but also other places where it may be 'just as important that strangers should not go', such as 'a private dockyard where a Government warship is being built'.[27] It also gave a rather open-ended and largely unreviewable power to the government ('a power which will only be exercised in time of emergency')[28] by defining a 'prohibited place' to include any place belonging to His Majesty which is 'for the time being declared by a Secretary of State to be a prohibited place . . . on the ground that information with respect thereto, or damage thereto, would be useful to an enemy'. Although sections 1 to 3 thus contained the substance of the principal new offences created by the Act, their scope and application were extended by sections 4 and 5. The former provided expressly that the Act should apply to attempts and incitement, while the latter provided that anyone charged with a felony under the Act (section 1) could be convicted of a misdemeanor (section 2) if the circumstances so warranted.

These then were the main provisions of the 1911 Act, designed to deal with the German spy and also those who supplied information to the spy. Other measures dealt with the harbouring of spies and with the powers of the police to enforce the Act. So far as the former is concerned, sec-

---

[27] H L Debs, 25 July 1911, col 643 (Viscount Haldane).   [28] Ibid.

tion 7 made it an offence not only knowingly to harbour any person who has committed or who is about to commit an offence under the Act, but also to allow any such person to meet or assemble in any premises owned or controlled by the accused. Moreover, if someone harboured another contrary to the Act or permitted another to use premises for a meeting or assembly contrary to the Act, it was an offence wilfully to refuse to disclose to the police 'any information which it is in his power to give in relation to any such person'. So far as police powers are concerned three important initiatives were taken. The first was the power in section 6 for police officers to arrest without a warrant anyone committing or suspected of having committed an offence under the Act, a power which surprisingly was not included in the 1889 Act. Secondly, section 8 provided that although the consent of the Attorney General was required for a prosecution under the Act, it was not necessary to have this consent before an individual was charged or a warrant issued for his or her arrest. This change clarified an uncertainty which had arisen under the 1889 Act where the requirement of the Attorney General's consent to prosecution had been 'construed to mean that you could not arrest without the fiat of the Attorney General', with the result being that 'many of these persons with whom we wished to interfere were a long way off before any warrant could be obtained for their arrest'.[29] Thirdly, new and very extensive powers of entry and search were given to the police in section 9, these becoming a precedent for other restrictive legislation later in the century, and the basis for very controversial police action as late as 1985.

Civil Liberties in Wartime: Defence of the Realm Acts 1914–1915

War was declared on 4 August 1914. The government moved immediately to take emergency powers, the first measure being the Aliens Restriction Act 1914 passed the next day, to give 'the Home Secretary untrammelled power to exclude and expel aliens, without any rights of appeal or even the right to make representations, and without any protection for refugees'.[30] It was followed by the Defence of the Realm Act 1914, which was passed through the House of Commons on 7 August 1914 'with lightning speed, without a word of protest, in that spirit of decision and confidence which has marked the war measures of this

---

[29] H L Debs, 25 July 1911, col 643 (Viscount Haldane).
[30] G Robertson, *Freedom, the Individual and the Law* (6th edn, 1989), p 316. See *R v Chiswick Police Station Superintendent, ex parte Sacksteder* [1918] 1 KB 578.

Parliament'.[31] In an awkwardly drafted manner the Act empowered the government ('His Majesty in Council') to issue regulations 'as to the powers and duties of the Admiralty and Army Council . . . for securing the public safety and the defence of the realm'. It also authorised the trial by court-martial of persons contravening regulations designed to (a) prevent persons communicating with the enemy or obtaining information for purposes calculated to jeopardise the success of military operations; or (b) secure the safety of any means of communication, or of railways, docks or harbours. Anyone charged with a breach of any of these regulations was to be tried 'in like manner as if such persons were subject to military law and had on active service committed an offence under section five of the Army Act'.[32] In seeking leave to introduce the Bill (which was presented as a measure for the 'Trial of Spies by Court Martial'), the Home Secretary explained simply that it was 'extremely desirable in cases of tapping wires or attempts to blow up bridges that there should be an immediate court to consider the offence of the offenders'.[33] After responding to a single backbench intervention seeking reassurance that any regulations made under the Act would not apply retrospectively (an assurance duly given), the Home Secretary (Reginald McKenna) was given leave to introduce the Bill which was read the first time, and ordered to be printed. It was then immediately read a second time, whereupon the House resolved itself into Committee and the Bill 'reported without Amendment, read the third time, and passed', the entire procedure consuming no more than two columns of Hansard.

Several weeks later the Defence of the Realm (No 2) Act 1914 authorised also the trial by court-martial of anyone contravening on the one hand regulations 'to prevent the spread of reports likely to cause disaffection or alarm', and on the other those regulations designed to secure the safety of any area proclaimed by the Admiralty or Army Council to be an area 'which it is necessary to safeguard in the interests of the training or concentration' of the forces. The amending legislation also authorised the making of regulations to suspend legal restrictions on the acquisition or use of land, contained in measures such as the Defence Acts 1842–1875. Like the first Defence of the Realm Act which preceded it, the amending measure passed through all its stages in the Commons in a single session, and was passed without a division. There was, how-

---

[31] H M Bowman, 'Martial Law and the English Constitution' (1916) 15 *Michigan Law Review* 93.
[32] For an account of the Defence of the Realm Acts, see C Townshend, *Making the Peace: Public Order and Public Security in Modern Britain* (1993), ch 4.
[33] H C Debs, 7 August 1914, cols 2191–3.

ever, some unease expressed at Second Reading in the course of the only discussion to take place, the exchange between the Home Secretary who introduced the Bill and Charles Trevelyan, an active member of the Union for Democratic Control, which as we shall see was the leading organisation of the war-time peace movement. Trevelyan was particularly concerned that the additional power to try by court-martial for the breach of regulations made to prevent the spreading of false reports would be 'interpreted by the military authorities to prevent the expression of speech or in writing of any political opinions on the actions of the Government'.[34] Giving an assurance that the measure would not be used in this way, the Home Secretary pointed out, however, that the power was necessary to deal with a recent case in which an unnamed man had stated that 'the Black Watch had been cut up and the wounded brought home to this country'. In his view it was 'most desirable that the spreading of false reports of that kind, which may cause disaffection and do cause alarm, should be punished, and it is obvious that it is only false reports of that kind which it is here proposed to make punishable'. Moreover, 'the actual language' of the proposed provision was 'extremely reasonable', though the government did indicate that it would be willing to adopt a more appropriate form of words, but none was suggested.[35]

Although even these laws were said to be 'unprecedented in character',[36] it was perhaps inevitable that yet further extensions of government power would be taken, and this was duly done in the Defence of the Realm Consolidation Act 1914, the third Defence of the Realm statute to be passed within the space of four months. Despite being ostensibly a consolidating measure, this third Act also included a number of fresh provisions which had been requested by the Admiralty and the War Office, thereby 'placing larger powers in the hands of the authorities'.[37] As such it formed the basis of the government's legal powers to make regulations for the remainder of the war, though these powers were added to by amending legislation on a number of occasions. The Consolidation Act in fact restructured the powers of the government in a number of ways, some of which were quite subtle yet nevertheless very important. In the first place, a much wider power was created to make regulations, though this appears to have passed over the heads of parliamentarians (though not the courts)[38] in the course of the debates (considerably

---

[34] H C Debs, 26 August 1914, col 88.   [35] Ibid, col 89.
[36] T Baty and J H Morgan, *War, Its Conduct and Legal Results* (1915), p 73.
[37] H L Debs, 27 November 1914, col 204 (Haldane LC).
[38] See especially *R v Halliday* [1917] AC 260, per Lords Atkinson and Wrenbury. See also Baty and Morgan, n 36 above, p 80. See below.

lengthier than on the two earlier occasions), and was not referred to by the Home Secretary who again introduced the Bill. Thus whereas regulations could previously be made 'as to' the powers and duties of the military authorities for securing the public safety and the defence of the realm, now there was a wider power to issue regulations for securing the public safety and defence of the realm simpliciter, an important change which appeared to address suggestions that the first two Acts were not adequately drafted to bear the weight of the regulations that had been made thereunder.[39] The Consolidation Act, however, retained the distinction to be found in the previous measure between the power to make regulations on the one hand, and the power to authorise the trial by court-martial of anyone who acted in breach of the regulations on the other. But unlike the earlier measure which permitted trial by court-martial only in the case of regulations for prescribed purposes, the Consolidation Act permitted regulations to be made authorising the trial by courts-martial (or in the case of minor offences courts of summary jurisdiction) of persons 'committing offences against the regulations', the intention being that this should be any of the regulations and not simply those dealing with issues such as those designed to prevent persons communicating with the enemy or the spreading of false reports, or those made in respect of a defended harbour or proclaimed area.

This change would overcome the surprising difficulty which had arisen under the first Defence of the Realm Act, namely that it was 'not possible to impose any penalty for many offences committed outside defended harbours and proclaimed areas' with the result that many breaches of the regulations could therefore be committed with 'impunity'.[40] This appears to be based on a construction of the 1914 Act that although there was a wide power to make regulations, any offences could only be tried before a court-martial and not otherwise, yet courts-martial had authority only to deal with alleged breaches of a narrowly defined category of regulations. But although the Consolidation Act extended the jurisdiction of courts-martial to cover all but minor offences (for which express provision was made for summary trial by the civil

---

[39] See Baty and Morgan, n 36 above, pp 73 et seq. And see G R Rubin, *Private Property, Government Requisition and the Constitution* (1994), pp 25–6. As Lord Atkinson pointed out in *Halliday* (n 41 above, at p 275), 'the second statute, though it covers the same ground as the first, goes much beyond the first in its scope, and differs from the first in the methods it authorizes for securing the public safety and defence of the realm, inasmuch as it provides that the regulations to be issued may not only deal with the powers and duties of the Admiralty, and so forth, and with the punishment of offenders against certain of its provisions, but it empowers His Majesty, during the war to issue regulations for securing directly the public safety and the defence of the realm. These are wide words'.

[40] H L Debs, 27 November 1914, col 205. See also Baty and Morgan, n. 36 above, p 77.

courts), curiously the Act also provided that the general power to try offenders by court-martial applied 'in particular' to any measures made for one of a number of now expanded prescribed purposes. In addition to the matters contained in the previous Act specific provision was made for the trial by court-martial of anyone alleged to have violated any regulations designed to secure the safety of His Majesty's forces and ships, or to secure the navigation of vessels in accordance with directions given by or under the authority of the Admiralty. Quite why it was thought to be necessary to specify particular powers in this way is far from clear, and it became even less clear when in Committee the Home Secretary resisted an amendment which would have added to the list of prescribed items on the ground that the subject matter of the amendment (to prevent attempts by nationalists in Ireland to disrupt the 'free' enlistment of soldiers) was adequately covered by the general powers.[41] But whatever the explanation the key point is that the breach of any regulations could now be tried by court-martial (save in the case of minor offences which were to be dealt with by the summary courts). Also important is the fact that the powers of the courts-martial were extended so that someone convicted of an offence 'committed with the intention of assisting the enemy' was 'liable to suffer death'. This is a provision which proved to be extremely controversial and is a matter to which we return below.

By the time of this third measure, parliamentary patience was beginning to wear thin. Two issues in particular were raised in connection with the Consolidation Bill, the first of which related to the proposed power to make regulations authorising the trial by court-martial of anyone offending against regulations designed to prevent the spread of reports likely to cause disaffection or alarm. The point was pursued on this occasion by Lord Robert Cecil who complained that the power would 'enable the Government to suppress any reports of any kind of which they disapprove', even though they may be true.[42] He was concerned also by the proposed application to reports which might cause disaffection, which as he pointed out 'is not disaffection to His Majesty or disaffection to the Crown; it is simply "disaffection" '. Did it mean disaffection to the government with the result that the government could punish someone for 'reports which were not in any way damaging to the interests of the country, but were damaging to the interests of the Government?'[43] The concern was by no means academic, for a few members of the House clearly had in mind a recent incident involving the *Globe* newspaper which had

---

[41] H C Debs, 25 November 1914, col 1271. [42] H C Debs, 23 November 1914, col 910.
[43] Ibid. For discussion of similar issues under the Emergency Regulations 1926, see Chapter 4 below.

reported that there were 250,000 armed Germans living in London. This led to an intervention on behalf of the government, the editor being sent a letter in 'peremptory' terms warning against any further reporting of such 'false' statements and indicating in menacing terms that it had the power to make the 'desire for suppression effective'. Despite being stoutly defended by the Home Secretary, 'having regard to the great wickedness of alarming the London public', it is clear that he was embarrassed by the affair and stung by the criticism that the power could be used for 'the suppression of news merely for the purpose of saving the skin of the Government'. Although the government nevertheless thought it necessary to continue to ask the House to give it powers of this kind, the Home Secretary indicated that he was prepared to accept an amendment in Committee.[44] The Act was thus amended to apply only to preventing the spread of 'false reports' or reports likely 'to cause disaffection to His Majesty'.[45] A third amendment deleted the power to try by court-martial anyone breaching regulations designed to prevent the spread of reports likely to cause 'alarm', another bone of contention that had been gnawed effectively by Lord Cecil.[46]

This, however, was not the only issue of controversy to emerge during the passage of the Consolidation Bill. A rather different point (which was not picked up in the Commons) erupted in the House of Lords in connection with the extension of the military jurisdiction in the trial of offenders, in the sense that all cases involving a breach of the regulations could now be tried by courts-martial which as we have seen were to have new powers to sentence convicted British subjects to death. These proposals attracted the strongest condemnation, from Earl Loreburn, the Earl of Halsbury, and Lord Parmoor. Their complaint was that the Bill 'places at the option of the Executive the power to deny any British subject when they think fit the right which he now has to have the trial for his life before an ordinary [civil court]'.[47] Earl Loreburn 'very much . . . regretted' this proposal 'to place the life of the British subject at the mercy of a military Court-Martial, even though the Court of Assize may be sitting within fifty yards'.[48] For his part the Earl of Halsbury accepted that 'there are rights which should not necessarily be insisted upon in time of war', but he nevertheless complained that 'this wholesale sweep-

---

[44] H C Debs, 23 November 1914, cols 915–16. On the *Globe* incident and press censorship generally, see H L Debs, 8 November 1915, col 181, and in particular the criticism of the government by Earl Loreburn and Lord Parmoor (the latter in particular giving a robust defence of free speech).

[45] See H C Debs, 25 November 1914, cols 1265–8.   [46] Ibid, col 1268.

[47] H L Debs, 27 November 1914, col 207 (Earl Loreburn).   [48] Ibid, col 207.

ing away of them is greatly to be deprecated' and expressed reluctance 'to surrender all the liberties and protections which been built up . . . for many generations, just because at this particular time there are some things that you may wish to do more quickly than at any other time'.[49] Stronger still was Lord Parmoor who claimed that 'at periods of panic and in war times there is an amount of prejudice and bias which makes it all the more necessary that every British civil subject should have the rights and protection which not only the Common Law but also the Statute Law of this country have given him over a long series of years'. He continued by doubting whether 'there is any precedent for taking away the rights of a British subject as regards ordinary trial by a jury directed by a skilled Judge', and claiming that 'Courts-Martial have neither the procedure nor the experience that our ordinary Courts have. They have not, in fact, the safeguards that we have built up in the civil Courts in order to protect an innocent man who may be wrongly charged'.[50]

The strength of opposition to this particular proposal clearly surprised the government which promised to bring forward a fresh Bill which would restore the right of British subjects to trial by jury in the civil courts for breach of the regulations. The subsequent Bill was the subject of lengthy debate in both Houses and it was now accepted by the government, in a rather belated celebration of constitutional principle, that the controversial provisions of the Consolidation Act contained 'an extremely novel proposal, and created a very unique situation'[51] which violated 'the traditions of our Constitution' that citizens of this country are 'amenable to civil tribunals, and courts-martial are for the purposes of the discipline of those who serve in the Army and Navy'.[52] As eventually enacted the Defence of the Realm (Amendment) Act 1915 permitted offences under the regulations to be tried by a civil court with a jury instead of by court-martial (s 1(1)). The right to trial by jury in a civil court was restricted to British subjects not subject to military law (civilians), who had asserted their right to be tried in this way 'within six clear days from the time when the general nature of the charge is communicated to [them] (s 1(2))'.[53] So that the arrested persons might make a properly informed decision, the Act also provided that 'as soon as practicable after arrest', the general nature of the

---

[49] Ibid, col 208.   [50] Ibid, col 210.   [51] H C Debs, 24 February 1915, col 288.
[52] Ibid, col 289–90.
[53] For a criticism that these measures did not go far enough in restoring constitutional principle, see (1915) 59 *Sol Jo* 295, and 343 where tribute is paid to Lord Parmoor for his attempt to retain the ordinary criminal courts both for British subjects and aliens.

charge was to be communicated to the suspected person in writing, it
being provided further that the suspect was to be given written notice of
his or her right to claim to be tried by a civil court with a jury (s 1(2)). It
was also provided that a civil court was empowered to sit in camera where
the interests of national safety so required.[54] The right to elect trial by
jury in a civil court was not, however, unqualified, the Act permitting its
suspension by Proclamation in 'the event of invasion or other special military emergency arising out of the present war' (s 1(7)). This was seen by
the government to be an important provision which preserved the right
to use the machinery of military justice, when it was decided necessary to
do so, though the Attorney General (Sir John Simon) undertook on behalf
of the government not to use the power 'wantonly or without real and
extreme necessity'.[55] In fact the power was invoked in respect of Ireland
in 1916,[56] when a Proclamation was issued at the time of the Easter
Rising, and when 'a German invasion of Ireland was feared'.[57]

Yet although these were important concessions won by parliamentary
pressure, they ought not to be exaggerated. Notwithstanding the triumphs on freedom of expression and trial by jury, the war-time experience is generally one of parliamentary neglect and ineffectiveness, not
only in terms of the delegation of so much power to the executive in the
first place, but also in terms of a failure adequately to ensure that regulations were given proper consideration before they were promulgated.
It is true that the delegation of law-making powers to ministers was by
no means unknown even in 1914, before the more recent growth of the
bureaucratic state. There were, however, also precedents in some cases
for the possibility of at least some parliamentary scrutiny of the exercise
of powers of delegated legislation which even in 1914 might take one of
a number of forms. This is not to suggest that such basic requirements
of constitutional government are an adequate safeguard against abuse by
the executive, but they are at least an elementary requirement which was
significantly lacking in these war-time powers. Perhaps more than any
other experience this century it is the unsupervised authority claimed by
the executive in 1914 and 1915 which best deserves Lord Hewart's
famous sobriquet, even though Hewart himself played a full part in conferring these powers on the administration as Member of Parliament for
Leicester and as Solicitor General from December 1916.[58] These were

[54] See s 1(3). See n 136 below.   [55] H C Debs, 24 February 1915, col 291.
[56] S R & O 1916 No 256. See Chapter 7 below.
[57] *R v Governor Wormwood Scrubbs Prison, ex parte Foy* [1920] 2 KB 305. See Chapter 7 below.
[58] He became Attorney General in 1919 and Lord Chief Justice in 1922. See Chapter 3 below.

admittedly difficult times, affording 'a signal opportunity for departmental legislation'.[59] But as we have seen at least Lord Parmoor was alive to the dangers of authoritarian government in war time.[60] Surely he was not the only parliamentarian with the insight to recognise that it was precisely in times of panic and crisis that the need for vigilance was at its greatest.

The Defence of the Realm Regulations

The Defence of the Realm Regulations were first promulgated on 12 August 1914 and were amended at frequent intervals thereafter.[61] Although they were very detailed, consolidated regulations were issued at monthly intervals by the Stationery Office, so that people were at least aware of their content even if they lacked a certain democratic legitimacy. The Regulations began by providing somewhat optimistically that 'The ordinary avocations of life and the enjoyment of property will be interfered with as little as may be required by the exigencies of the measures required to be taken for securing the public safety and the defence of the Realm' (reg 1). This was followed by a stirring and reassuring rendition of the Rule of Law, it being provided that 'ordinary civil offences will be dealt with by the civil tribunals in the ordinary course of law' (reg 1). In practice, however, the avocations of life were extensively disturbed and although civil offences continued to be dealt with in the civil courts, the scale and breadth of restriction imposed by the regulations contrived to ensure that the nation was regulated well beyond the 'ordinary course of law'.[62] The Regulations in fact gave the authorities an extensive range of powers and consequently imposed restrictions on personal and civil liberties of a quite extraordinary scope, so much so that it is impossible to cover them all here or indeed even to give a full account of their range. Some were predictable and clearly necessary for a war-time emergency (such as those regulating the entry and approach to places of national

---

[59] Lord Hewart, *The New Despotism* (1929), p 96.

[60] Lord Parmoor was opposed to Britain's participation in the War and was 'a principal champion of the conscientious objector'. He also took a great interest in the League of Nations after the war was over. He served in the first Labour government as Lord President of the Council and shared with Lord Haldane responsibility for speaking on behalf of the government in the Lords. A Liberal politician (and MP) before the War, he was raised to a peerage in 1914 on Asquith's recommendation. See *Dictionary of National Biography 1941–1950*, pp 186–7. See also Lord Parmoor, *A Retrospect* (1936).

[61] S R & O 1914 No 1231. The following account is based on the Defence of the Realm Consolidation Regulations, S R & O 1914 No 1699, as subsequently amended.

[62] For a critique, see Baty and Morgan, n 36 above, p 113.

and military importance), others involved the erosion of civil and political freedom (such as those authorising the police to impose restrictions on freedom of movement, freedom of assembly and freedom of expression), while others were positively bizarre (such as the shortlived regulation 40D which made it an offence for a woman with venereal disease to have sexual intercourse with a soldier).[63] We concentrate on some of the more important measures and those which are more relevant to our inquiry, though in the course of doing so we do not confine our treatment at this stage to those provisions which deal only with the erosion of civil liberties as we have defined that term in Chapter 1.

As might be expected in war time, the military authorities were given extensive powers in relation to *private property*. These included the taking of any land and constructing military works thereon; the taking of any buildings or other property (including gas, electricity and water installations); and causing any buildings, structures or property to be destroyed.[67] They were also permitted to 'do any other act involving interference with private rights of property which is necessary' for the aforementioned purposes (reg 2). Although these measures were wide enough to authorise the taking of property to accommodate the clerical staff of the Ministry of Munitions,[65] provisions were also introduced to facilitate the taking of unoccupied property to house workmen employed in the production, storage or transport of war material.[66] Indeed in certain circumstances a landlord was prohibited from initiating legal proceedings to recover the property without first obtaining the consent of the Ministry of Munitions.[67] The wide provisions relating to property were also complemented by special powers relating to the 'production, manufacture, treatment, use, consumption, transport, storage, distribution, supply, sale or purchase' of any article where it was 'necessary or expedient' to maintain the food supply.[68] In relation to food, there was also a power of requisition 'as may be directed' by the Food Controller 'on such terms as he may direct', with compensation payable with a 'reasonable profit' though not necessarily the 'market price'.[69] Apart from the authority thus to take private property, the Regulations also provided

---

[63] S R & O 1918 No 367, Regulation 4; revoked S R & O 1918 No 1550.

[64] See generally Rubin, n 39 above. On the question of compensation, see *In re a Petition of Right* [1915] 3 KB 649. But see also *Attorney General v De Keyser's Royal Hotel* [1920] AC 508.

[65] *Sheffield Conservative and Unionist Club (Ltd) v Brighton* (1916) 32 TLR 598.

[66] S R & O 1915 No 235, Regulation 1 (inserting a new Regulation 2(e)).

[67] S R & O 1917 No 1008, Regulation 1, adding to Regulation 2A.

[68] S R & O 1917 No 5, Regulation 1, inserting a new Regulation 2F.

[69] Ibid. The office of the Food Controller (the title of the Minister of Food) was established by the New Ministries and Secretaries Act 1916, s 3.

that the military had 'a right of access to any land or buildings or other property whatsoever' (reg 3). Power was also granted for the use of land for military training (reg 4), the closing of roads (reg 5), the removal of vehicles (reg 6), the requisition of the output of factories (reg 7), and taking possession of factories (reg 8). Additional powers were granted to the military authorities to regulate or restrict the carrying on of any work in a factory or workshop, and to require the work to be done in accordance with military instructions in order to make the factory or workshop 'as useful as possible for the production of war material' (reg 8A).[70]

Apart from these wide provisions in respect of private property, a second group of regulations dealt with *the 'clearance of areas' and the control of meetings, recreations and fairs.* Under the former (the 'clearance of areas'), the authorities were empowered to clear areas of inhabitants (reg 9), to require the closure of pubs and other licensed premises (reg 10), and to 'require every person within any area . . . to remain in doors between such hours as may be specified' (reg 13). More controversially, under the latter (the 'control of meetings') a new regulation 9A was issued in 1916 which 'for the first time' empowered the Home Secretary, or a chief officer of police, a mayor, or magistrate if authorised by the Home Secretary, to issue an order prohibiting the holding of a meeting or procession.[71] This power, 'a startling inroad on the right of public speech'[72] which anticipated important and controversial developments in the common law some twenty years later,[73] was strongly criticised as 'a retrograde step of great importance, since it has hitherto been an axiom of British Constitutional Law that a meeting, otherwise lawful, could not be legally prohibited on the ground that it would provoke other persons to a breach of the law'. No less an authority than Dicey was cited in aid of the established proposition that 'neither the government nor the magistrates, can . . . solely on the ground that a public meeting may provoke wrongdoers to a breach of the peace, prevent loyal citizens from meeting together peaceably and for lawful purposes'.[74] But this was to change under the new regulation which could be exercised 'where there appears to be reason to apprehend' that the holding of any meeting 'will give rise to grave disorder . . . or that the holding of any procession will conduce to a breach of the peace or will promote disaffection'. The occasion for

---

[70] Inserted by S R & O 1915 No 235.   [71] S R & O 1916 No 702, Regulation 3.
[72] (1916) 60 *Sol Jo* 442. See also (1917) 61 *Sol Jo* 659.
[73] *Thomas v Sawkins* [1935] 2 KB 249. See Chapter 6 below.
[74] 'North Briton', *British Freedom 1914–1917* (1917), p 31. The passage from Dicey is in A V Dicey, *Introduction to the Study of the Law of the Constitution* (8th edn, 1915), p 283.

the introduction of this measure was a pacifist demonstration proposed to be held in Trafalgar Square on Easter Sunday 1916 which it was believed 'would undoubtedly have given rise to a very serious riot in London', though in practice it is not known how widely the power was used.[75] It was claimed in Parliament by Herbert Samuel, Home Secretary at the time the regulation was made, that the Trafalgar Square meeting was the only one that was suppressed while he was Home Secretary,[76] but there were others, and there is some evidence of meetings being banned without the authorisation of the minister.[77]

A third executive power related to *the freedom of movement of the civilian population* and dealt with matters such as the deportation and internment of individuals, extraordinary powers relating to personal liberty and freedom of movement. As originally introduced in 1914, regulation 14 allowed for the deportation of individuals from one part of the country to another. There was no need for the deportee to have committed an offence; it was enough that he or she was 'suspected of acting, or of having acted, or of being about to act in a manner prejudicial to the public safety or the defence of the Realm'. The only other condition was that it appeared 'to the competent naval or military authority that it is desirable that [the person in question] should be prohibited from residing in or entering any locality'. These conditions being met, there was no provision for the formality of a hearing or anything of the kind; the respon-

[75] In practice it seems that other steps were taken to prevent or disrupt anti-war meetings. According to D Hopkin, 'Domestic Censorship in the First World War' (1970) 5(4) *Journal of Contemporary History* 151, the government's 'best ally was the pro war public', with meetings being 'wrecked by mobs composed very often of uniformed soldiers'. It is said that the authorities simply 'stood aside' and 'let the tide of public opinion do the work they could not easily do themselves' (p 165). For complaints about the disruption of meetings of the Society of Friends, see (1916) 60 *Sol Jo* 296. Several other examples are to be found in 'North Briton', n 74 above, pp 28–31. See also R Challinor, *The Origins of British Bolshevism* (1977), p 127. There is also evidence of police intimidation of organisers, with the threat of prosecution on account of what was likely to be said at a meeting. See H C Debs, 29 June 1916, col 1167.

[76] H C Debs, 12 December 1917, cols 1287–9. Samuel in fact made a very interesting speech in the course of which he said that there was no right in the executive to prohibit a public meeting, except under the powers of the Defence of the Realm Act. Otherwise, he continued, 'the duty lies on the executive of protecting meetings in the interests of the right of free speech' (col 1288). Admittedly it 'is in war-time a most distasteful duty, because the natural sympathies of the police, of the Government, and of the military will probably be very little with the persons whom it will be their duty to protect. Nevertheless, that duty has to be performed', and in his view 'as a rule it is performed' (ibid). Samuel was in fact applauded for his restraint by 'North Briton', n 74 above, pp 32–3, and in particular for his refusal to exercise the power to suppress in respect of two peace meetings in South Wales in 1916.

[77] For examples of the use of Regulation 9A with the clear authority of ministers, see I McLean, *The Legend of Red Clydeside* (1973), pp 93–4. For examples of meetings being banned by the police, see H C Debs, 10 December 1917, col 859. It is not clear whether this was done under the purported authority of Regulation 9A or whether the Home Secretary was required specifically to authorise each exercise of the power conferred by the regulation.

dent was simply required to leave the area 'within such time as may be specified in the order'.[78] Additional powers (said to be 'milder as well as more effectual' than the suspension of habeas corpus)[79] were added by Sir John Simon[80] in 1915 under regulation 14B, authorising the Home Secretary to impose restrictions on the personal liberty of individuals where it appeared 'expedient in view of the hostile origin or associations of any person' for 'securing the public safety or the defence of the Realm'.[81] Under the regulation, which not unsurprisingly gave rise to considerable unease in Parliament and elsewhere,[82] the minister could issue an order requiring an individual 'either to remain in, or to proceed to and reside in, such place as may be specified in the order, and to comply with such directions as to reporting to the police, restriction of movement, and otherwise as may be specified in the order, or be interned in such place as may be specified in the order'.[83] In the case of anyone detained who was not 'a subject of a state at war with His Majesty', provision was made in the vaguest of terms 'for the due consideration' of 'any representations he may make against the order' by an advisory committee 'appointed for the purpose of advising the Secretary of State with respect to the internment and deportation of aliens', each

---

[78] See also the proviso inserted by S R & O 1915 No 235, Regulation 5. 612 people were removed or excluded from certain areas under Regulation 14 between 4 August 1914 and 30 June 1918: PRO, KV 1/51.

[79] *R v Halliday* [1917] AC 260, per Lord Finlay LC, at p 270.

[80] During his brief tenure as Home Secretary for the first time. See H C Debs, 17 June 1915, col 840.

[81] S R & O 1915 No 551, Regulation 3. Needless to say this measure caused civil libertarian hackles to rise and was the subject of comment in Parliament on a number of occasions. In raising the matter on 2 March 1916, the Unionist Mr W W Ashley complained about the erosion of constitutional safeguards and likened the powers in Regulation 14B to 'the system of the Bastille, of *lettres de cachet*, and of the Star Chamber' (col 1238). Unsurprisingly the Home Secretary (by now Herbert Samuel) rejected these charges drawing attention to the right of review by the Advisory Committee, which included two judges, Sankey J and Younger J), and to the fact that the Home Office always acted on the advice of the Committee. Although the Committee did not 'hear counsel or anyone employed for the purpose of advocacy', it frequently heard solicitors and people were always able to get legal advice. And although respondents were not given details of the case against them which was only revealed at the hearing in the course of examination, steps were taken to ensure that a written statement would be given in general terms of the charge. But people might be interned before a hearing of the Committee, there being no question of bail. It was also revealed that internment was used in some cases because there was not enough evidence to bring criminal charges against persons suspected of an offence. See H C Debs, 2 March 1916, col 1236. See also H C Debs, 23 March 1916, col 427 et seq. See further, A W B Simpson, *In the Highest Degree Odious: Detention without Trial in Wartime Britain* (1992).

[82] See H C Debs, 23 March 1916, col 427 (*Howsin* case). (See also *Ex parte Howsin* (1917) 33 TLR 527.) The *Solicitors' Journal* was immediately concerned that such regulations were ultra vires. See (1915) 59 *Sol Jo* 557.

[83] 216 people were interned under these powers and another 40 had their movements restricted: PRO, KV 1/51.

committee to be presided over by a person 'who holds or has held high judicial office'.[84]

Limitations on the *unauthorised collection and communication of information* in the Regulations took two principal forms. One related to the protection of military information (reg 18), and the other to the publication of false statements or reports (reg 27). So far as the former is concerned, there had grown up since 1912 an arrangement whereby newspaper proprietors co-operated with the Admiralty and War Office in regulating the conduct of the press. These measures had been introduced as an alternative to censorship to prevent the leakage of valuable information to a potential enemy. Although the arrangements worked 'surprisingly well'[85] they were superseded in 1914 by an official Press Bureau (with the Solicitor General at its head)[86] in which the press played no formal role.[87] The functions of the Bureau were to control the supply of information to the newspapers and to examine telegrams and cables sent and received by each newspaper.[88] Regulation 18 gave the system of executive censorship the support of legal compulsion by providing that it was offence 'without lawful authority' to 'collect, record, publish or communicate' any 'information with respect to the movement, numbers, description, condition, or disposition of any of the forces, ships or war materials of His Majesty or any of His Majesty's allies'.[89] It was also an offence to collect, publish or communicate information which was 'calculated to be or might be directly or indirectly useful to the enemy'. So far as criticism and dissent in newspapers and elsewhere is concerned, regulation 27 (as

[84] The grounds for the challenge of an internment order were not specified, nor was the procedure to be adopted by the committee. See Lord Shaw of Dunfermline in *Halliday*, n 79 above. On the unwillingness of the courts to review the exercise of this power (which they had earlier refused to invalidate on grounds of ultra vires) see *Ex parte Howsin* (1917) 33 TLR 527.

[85] Hopkin, 'Domestic Censorship in the First World War', n 75 above, p 153.

[86] The first head was Sir Stanley Buckmaster, later Lord Buckmaster. For a critique of his perception of his role, see (1914) 59 *Sol Jo* 68.

[87] For an account of the various methods of censorship employed during the war see H L Debs, 4 May 1915, col 910.

[88] For details of the work of the Bureau, see Hopkin, n 75 above, pp 153–6. For a powerful criticism of its activities, see H C Debs, 31 August 1914, col 453. Although not a statutory body, its existence is acknowledged in S R & O 1918 No 765, introducing a new Regulation 18C. It is unclear what executive authority it purported to exercise, but there is at least one report that the publication of the *Jewish Times* was 'prohibited by the authorities for a short period' as a result of 'a breach of the regulations of the Press Bureau with regard to the publication of information which might indicate the ground or route covered by hostile aircraft': (1915) 79 JP 283.

[89] See H L Debs, 4 May 1915, col 916 under the heading 'Military Prosecution of Journalist' where it was revealed that it was not the intention of the War Office to take such action in the future except 'in regard to information concerning matters which have to be treated with the greatest secrecy'. The government defended the prosecution as being neither 'too arbitrary' nor 'too severe'. See also *Fox v Spicer* (1917) 116 LT 86. See further S R & O 1916 No 561 extending Regulation 18 to information relating to the passage of ships.

expanded in 1916)[90] prohibited any person from spreading false reports; spreading reports or making statements intended or likely to cause disaffection to His Majesty; or spreading reports or making statements intended or likely to prejudice the recruiting, training, discipline, or administration of any of His Majesty's forces (later extended to include the police and the fire service).[91] The restriction applied in respect of anything said by word of mouth, or in writing, or published in a newspaper, book or circular. It applied also in respect of plays, exhibitions and films. Mere possession of an offending document was an offence unless the accused could prove that he or she had no intention of distributing it to other persons.[92]

Further restrictions on freedom of speech were to be found in those regulations which appeared under the general heading of measures dealing with *interference with military duties and war supplies*. The most significant of these was clearly regulation 42 by which it was an offence for any person to attempt to cause mutiny, sedition, or disaffection among any of His Majesty's forces or among the civilian population, a measure used most notably in 1916 as one weapon for suppressing the political and industrial unrest on Clydeside. A particular victim of its terms was the socialist leader John MacLean who was jailed in 1916, and again in 1917 for passionate anti-war speeches. An amendment in 1915 also made it an offence to impede, delay, or restrict the production, repair or transport of war material or any other work necessary for the successful prosecution of the war.[93] The purpose of this measure was to deal with the incitement to take part in strikes. It is true that it was already an offence in some circumstances under the Munitions of War Act 1915 to engage in strikes, but this applied only to the participants and not also the organisers. The weakness of this measure was revealed in July 1915 on the occasion of a miners' strike in South Wales when it was 'borne in upon the Government' that 'it was impossible . . . to fine 200,000 strikers', leaving the organisers of the action (the union officials) untouched.[94] The government proposed initially to close this 'loophole' in the Munitions of

---

[90] S R & O 1916 No 317, Regulation 2. For a critique of the scope of these powers see (1916) 60 *Sol Jo* 506. See also Regulation 27A inserted by S R & O 1916 No 253, prohibiting press reporting of parliamentary proceedings held in secret session.

[91] S R & O 1918 No 267, Regulation 4.

[92] On the application of Regulation 27, see *Kaye v Cole* (1917) 86 LT 1084. For evidence of the oppressive use of the power, see H C Debs, 23 March 1916, cols 423–4.

[93] S R & O 1915 No 1134, Regulation 4. Note also S R & O 1916 No 614, Regulation 4 (new Regulation 42A making it an offence to attempt to induce a member of the forces to act in breach of duty).

[94] R Page Arnot, *The Miners: Years of Struggle* (1953), p 169.

War (Amendment) Bill 1916, but it was thought that 'this would cause such widespread opposition that the Bill as a whole would be held up for it', with the result that 'the desired regulation was slipped in as an amendment to Defence of the Realm Regulation 42'.[95] Further restrictions were imposed on the right to strike long after hostilities had ceased, with regulation 43C (made in 1919) extending to workers in the electricity supply industry the statutory restrictions on industrial action (to the extent that it involved the wilful and malicious breach of contract) by gas and water workers contained in the Conspiracy and Protection of Property Act 1875.[96]

As might be expected the Regulations conferred sweeping powers on the police. Under regulation 51 the competent naval or military authority was empowered to *enter and search private premises*, if need be by force, 'at any time of the day or night', if the authority had reason to suspect that an offence against the Regulations was being or had been committed thereon or that the premises were being used for a purpose prejudicial to the public safety or the defence of the realm. The authority could seize and destroy 'anything found therein' which the authority believed was being used in breach of the Regulations or for a purpose prejudicial to the public safety or the defence of the realm. Where a report or statement in breach of regulation 27 appeared in a newspaper the authority could seize and destroy 'any type or other plant used or capable of being used for the printing or production of the newspaper', thereby in effect suppressing the newspaper in question.[97] Regulation 51 was amended in 1915 to enable police constables to exercise the powers of entry, search and seizure on the same basis as the military authorities.[98] Unlike regulation 51, regulation 51A authorised entry only with a warrant,[99] which could be issued where a justice of the peace was satisfied that a document was about to be produced from the premises in question containing information in breach of regulations 18 or 27.[100] Regulation 51A was

---

[95] I McLean *The Legend of Red Clydeside*, n 77 above, p 47. See also S R & O 1918 No 1033, Regulation 3 (new Regulation 34B) for additional restrictions on strikes.

[96] S R & O 1919 No 132. See Chapter 4 below.

[97] For a contention that these powers were ultra vires see (1915) 60 *Sol Jo* 915.

[98] S R & O 1915 No 551, Regulation 6.   [99] S R & O 1915 No 715, Regulation 6.

[100] A problem arose about the actions of the police under Regulations 51 and 51A, it being officially acknowledged that the powers were exercised in relation to pamphlets not included in any Home Office circulars 'and which did not, in fact, in any way contravene Regulation 27'. In order to secure 'proper and uniform action in this matter', a Home Office circular was issued in June 1916 instructing the police not to proceed in relation to any matter not on the Home Office circular without referring to the competent military authorities. Given that the police were thus acting unlawfully under Regulation 51A even though a warrant was required, what does this tell us about the magistracy? See H C Debs, 29 June 1916, col 1153.

thus largely preventive. But neither regulations 51 nor 51A empowered the authorities to enter private premises for the purpose of attendance at meetings, an omission addressed by regulation 51B which provided that:

Where a competent naval or military authority, or any superior officer of police, is of opinion that a meeting or assembly is being or about to be held of such a character that an offence against these regulations may be committed thereat, he may authorise in writing a police constable or other person to attend the meeting or assembly, and any police constable or person so authorised may enter the place at which the meeting or assembly is held and remain there during its continuance.[101]

Regulation 51B did not confer a power 'to stop or disband a meeting',[102] though this was already provided for in regulation 9. The new measure simply authorised police surveillance and as such anticipated a lively debate which was to erupt in the 1930s about whether the police had a common law right to enter meetings against the wishes of the organisers.[103]

Apart from these extensive powers of entry, search and seizure of property, the regulations also introduced three wide-ranging *police powers of stop and search, and arrest of individuals*. Regulation 52 conferred on any police officer or any soldier or sailor engaged on sentry patrol, or other similar duty, a power to stop vehicles travelling along the public highway, and a power to search and seize the vehicle (and search anything found therein) on suspicion that the vehicle was 'being used for any purpose or in any way prejudicial to the public safety or the defence of the Realm'. Regulation 53 in turn conferred on a police officer and any soldier or sailor engaged on sentry patrol, or other similar duty, a power to stop (though not search) and question individuals, an apparently random power (at least so far as the police were concerned) which did not require suspicion that the person detained should have committed an offence against the Regulations or otherwise. Nevertheless individuals were under a 'duty' to 'stop and answer to the best of [their] ability and knowledge any questions reasonably addressed to them', failure to do so being

---

[101] S R & O 1917 No 127, Regulation 6.

[102] H C Debs, 28 February 1917, col 2030 (Sir George Cave).

[103] *Thomas v Sawkins* [1935] 2 KB 249, on which see Chapter 6 below. The regulation was wonderfully ambiguous on the point, stating expressly that the powers conferred 'shall be in addition to and not in derogation of any other powers' of the law enforcement bodies. When the matter was raised in the House the Home Secretary simply explained that 'The Regulation relates only to meetings of such a character that offences against the Regulations made for securing the public safety and the defence of the realm may be committed thereat. It does not, therefore, contemplate interference with trade unions or other lawful organisations. No power to stop or disband a meeting is created by the Regulation' (ibid). And that was it!

an offence.[104] This was in addition to the principal power of arrest which was contained in regulation 55 enabling the military or the police to arrest without a warrant not only any person suspected of having committed an offence against the Regulations, but also anyone whose behaviour was of such a nature as to give reasonable grounds for suspecting that he or she had acted, was acting, or was about to act in a manner prejudicial to the public safety or the defence of the Realm. It was thus not necessary for the purposes of an arrest that the person concerned was suspected of having committed an offence. Once arrested, however, the citizen could be both photographed and fingerprinted, an offence being committed by anyone who refused to allow prints or photographs to be taken. The only safeguard in the case of someone who neither had been nor was subsequently convicted of an offence against the Regulations, in which case (but only in such a case) both the prints and the photographs were to be destroyed 'as soon as they are no longer required' and in any case immediately after the end of the war.[105]

The final group of provisions which may be noted here relate to *the trial of offenders*. These were to be found in regulations 56 to 58, extensively amended following the enactment of the Defence of the Realm (Amendment) Act 1915. As we have seen this had been passed following concern in the House of Lords during the passage of the Defence of the Realm Consolidation Act 1914 about the proposed extension of the jurisdiction of courts-martial to try breaches of the Regulations by civilians.[106] Although the purpose of the 1915 amendments was to enable breaches of the Regulations to be tried by civil courts and civilians to elect to be tried by a civil court, the amended Regulations nevertheless gave the military authorities a considerable presence in the administration of criminal justice. Under regulation 56(3) where a person was 'alleged to be guilty of an offence other than an offence declared by these Regulations to be a summary offence, the case shall be referred to the competent naval or military authority who shall forthwith investigate the case and determine whether or not the case is to be proceeded with'. If

---

[104] See (1918) 82 JP 92.

[105] S R & O 1916 No 231, Regulation 5. It is unclear what safeguards there were to prevent abuse in the exercise of these powers apart from that recognised in *Kruse v Johnson* [1898] 2 QB 91, namely that if the police officer 'acts capriciously or vexatiously, he can be checked by his immediate superiors, or he can be taught a lesson by the magistrates should he prefer vexatious charges' (at 101). But it takes a great deal of faith to accept these as being adequate. Although the magistrates would deal only with summary cases under the Regulations, it has been said that the magistrates were 'bitter partisans': H C Debs, 6 April 1916, col 1101.

[106] On the amendments see S R & O 1915 No 235.

it was decided that the case should be proceeded with the alleged offender could claim the right to be tried by a civil court with a jury, at which point the case would be 'handed over, for the purposes of trial, to the civil authority' (reg 56(6)(a)). If on the other hand the alleged offender made no such claim the case could be tried by way of court-martial unless there were 'general or special instructions given by the Admiralty or Army Council' directing that the case should not be tried by court-martial (reg 56(6)(b)).[107] In order to ensure that suspects could make an informed choice about the form of their trial, regulation 56(8) gave effect to the obligation to this effect in the 1915 Act by providing that an alleged offender was to be given as soon as practicable after his or her arrest 'written notice in a prescribed statutory form of the general nature of the charge and of his [or her] right [where appropriate] to claim to be tried by a civil court with a jury instead of being tried by court-martial'.[108] The only exception from this regime, which also reversed the burden of proof in the case of some offences,[109] was made for so called 'press offences' which were referred in the first instance to the Director of Public Prosecutions (or the Lord Advocate in Scotland) rather then the military authorities.[110]

Although it has not been possible to give a detailed account of the Defence of the Realm Regulations in all their glory, the foregoing may be enough to indicate that such an account is unnecessary. For it should be clear that the Regulations gave to the military and civilian authorities the power to restrict the civil liberties and personal freedoms of individual citizens and others resident in this country. On some occasions the power was direct—such as the power to restrict freedom of association and assembly, either by banning meetings or by authorising a police presence at meetings. Also into this category fell the power to restrict freedom of expression in general and freedom of the press in particular by regulating the content of what may be said or published, and effectively authorising the suppression of newspapers, though admittedly only after minimum standards of due process had first been met. On other occasions the power was indirect in the sense that wide discretionary powers

---

[107] See the point made in *Kaye v Cole*, n 92 above.

[108] Note Regulation 58, on which see *R v Pearce, ex parte Raynes* (1918) WN 291.

[109] S R & O 1915 No 551, Regulation 8, inserting a new Regulation 58B.

[110] Regulation 56(13), inserted by S R & O 1915 No 532, Regulation 3 (later amended by S R & O 1918 No 1121, Regulation 5, on which see (1918) 62 *Sol Jo* 780). For the significance of this see (1915) 59 *Sol Jo* 540–1 (decisions on press offences had previously been taken by the military authorities). For an unusually sensitive application of this provision see *Fox v Spicer* (1917) 116 LT 86, for comment on which see (1917) 81 JP 137.

conferred on the authorities had the potential to be used in a discriminatory way and in a manner hostile to those who promoted dissent and opposition to the war. It takes a great deal of faith in the fairness and integrity
of the military authorities to be unconcerned by the despotic potential of
the power to order the deportation or internment of individuals, in the former case on account of no more than their having behaved 'in a manner
prejudicial to the public safety or the defence of the Realm' and in the latter on no more than their suspected 'hostile origin or association'. And it
takes just as much faith in the fairness and integrity of the police and military authorities to be unconcerned by the wide powers given to stop and
search, to question and interrogate, and to arrest, photograph and finger-
print individuals, not because they were suspected of having committed an
offence, but simply because there were reasonable grounds for believing
that they too were acting in 'a manner prejudicial to the public safety or
the defence of the Realm'. We turn now to consider how these powers were
used, first in relation to the war-time peace movement, and secondly in
relation to the activities of the socialists on Clydeside.

The Peace Movement

The government faced very little opposition at the beginning of the war.
The country was swept along by a profound sense of jingoism, and by
an expectation that the conflict would soon be over.[111] The mood in
some quarters began to change, however, when the full horrors of war
became more widely known and when it was realised that the campaign
would be a long one. The most important of the so-called pacifist groups
operating at the time was the Union of Democratic Control,[112] in relation to which it is tempting to draw parallels with the later Campaign for
Nuclear Disarmament.[113] The UDC aimed to persuade the government
to seek a negotiated end to the war, believing that 'the best way to secure
a lasting peace was to terminate the conflict by a compromise settlement
rather than military victory'.[114] It was led by a number of 'influential

[111] See Challinor, n 75 above, p 123.
[112] For a full account of the UDC see M Swartz, *The Union of Democratic Control in British Politics
during the First World War* (1971).
[113] A Special Branch report prepared in 1917 by Sir Basil Thomson identified two different anti-
war organisations operating in Britain at the time. These he described as pacifist and revolutionary
respectively. The UDC was one of the former and has been described as 'an important organ of
opposition to governmental policy in Britain during the First World War' (Swartz, n 112 above, p
1). The revolutionary groups included the Shop Stewards and Amalgamation Committee (Rank and
File Movement), the Industrial Workers of the World, Workmen's and Soldiers' Councils, and the
Herald League.
[114] Swartz, n 112 above, p 66.

intellectuals, publicists and politicians, such as Bertrand Russell, Norman Angell, and James Ramsay MacDonald',[115] and attracted support not only from Radical Liberals but also from within the Labour Party as the war progressed. Indeed no fewer than nine members of the first Labour Cabinet in 1924 had been members of the UDC.[116] By the end of 1915 the UDC had a membership of over 300,000 in 107 affiliated organisations, this rising to 650,000 in 300 organisations by the end of 1917. Apart from its high profile opposition to the war, it has been suggested that the UDC had a much more lasting impact on the political landscape, contributing to the disintegration of the Liberal Party and the movement of many of its members to Labour when individual membership became possible in 1918.[117]

So far as the war is concerned, the UDC issued a manifesto in September 1914, shortly after its foundation. This stated 'four cardinal points for a lasting peace settlement'.[118] These were as follows:

(1)   No Province shall be transferred from one Government to another without the consent by plebiscite or otherwise of the population of such Province.

(2)   No Treaty, Arrangement, or Undertaking shall be entered upon in the name of Great Britain without the sanction of Parliament. Adequate machinery for ensuring democratic control of foreign policy shall be created.

(3)   The Foreign Policy of Great Britain shall not be aimed at creating alliances for the purpose of maintaining the 'Balance of Power', but shall be directed to concerted action between the Powers, and the setting up of an International Council, whose deliberations and decisions shall be public, with such machinery for securing international agreement as shall be the guarantee of an abiding peace.

(4)   Great Britain shall propose, as part of the Peace Settlement, a plan for the drastic reduction, by consent, of the armaments of all the belligerent Powers, and to facilitate that policy shall attempt to secure the general nationalisation of the manufacture of armaments and the control of the export of armaments by one country to another.[119]

The campaign to promote these goals was carried out in a number of ways. They included the distribution of pamphlets, the holding of public

---

[115] Ibid, p 1.

[116] For the influence of the UDC on Labour Party foreign policy, see S White, *Britain and the Bolshevik Revolution; A Study in the Politics of Diplomacy 1920–1924* (1979), pp 216–24.

[117] See Swartz, n 112 above, p 222.   [118] Ibid, p 41.

meetings, and the publication of a journal, *The UDC*, through which the leadership 'expressed their dissent regularly and forcefully'.[120]

As might be expected this activity attracted a great deal of attention, with the UDC having to endure personal attacks on its senior officers (both inside and outside Parliament),[121] and the inevitable calls for its suppression.[122] The government responded in a number of different ways but was never able finally to remove a significant irritant which on the contrary grew in strength as the war continued. Thus the UDC and its members were the subject of various forms of surveillance and harassment. These included police visits to the homes of activists (on one occasion in Exeter the police allegedly entering without a warrant and demanding to be provided with a list of local UDC subscribers);[123] police attendance at meetings (on one occasion in Southampton allegedly hiding under the table);[124] and the prosecution of its leading official and speaker, E D Morel, whose book *Truth and War* was both important and influential.[125] Only three days after a Cabinet discussion on 20 August 1917 laid stress on 'the importance of taking more active steps to combat peace propaganda' the competent military authority at Whitehall issued a warrant to search Morel's house in London. He was then 'arrested, tried, convicted and imprisoned' for six months, 'within a fortnight' for breach of an obscure regulation: contrary to regulation 24, Morel had 'solicited a correspondent to transmit (otherwise than by post) two of his publications to Romain Rolland [a French intellectual and novelist], who was living in Switzerland'.[126] It ought perhaps to be noted that in 1915 Morel had been granted permission by the government to send literature to neutral states. This was qualified in 1916, however, first in respect of *The UDC*, and later in respect of his *Truth and War*. Later that year the War Office announced that it was prohibiting the distribution of all UDC literature abroad, on the ground that it 'contained material the enemy might use for propaganda purposes'.[127]

[119] See Swartz, n 115 above, p 42.   [120] Ibid, p 65.

[121] See H C Debs, 5 April 1916, col 1186.

[122] See H C Debs, 10 May 1916, col 629. For the government the Home Secretary replied that they had no such powers of suppression.

[123] H C Debs, 15 November 1916, col 774.

[124] H C Debs, 19 November 1917, col 861. The problem of disruption of UDC meetings is covered by 'North Briton', n 74 above, pp 29–30.

[125] On the influence of this work, see White, *Britain and the Bolshevik Revolution*, n 116 above, p 220.

[126] Swartz, n 113 above, p 178.

[127] Ibid, p 123. There were no fewer than 54 publications which were banned from leaving the country by 26 April 1917. Apart from all publications of the UDC, they included *Forward*, *Labour Leader*, and other socialist material, as well as the *Cambridge Magazine* and the *Meteorological Journal*: PRO, KV 1/46, Annexure 2.

The main problem for the authorities, however, was not the sending of material to French intellectuals, but in knowing how best to deal with the literature of the peace movement designed for domestic consumption. The first incident of significance was the raid on the premises of the National Labour Press which published both the *Labour Leader* (the official organ of the Independent Labour Party) and UDC pamphlets. This was done under the authority of regulation 51A which, as we have seen, authorised a justice of the peace to issue a warrant to a police officer to enter and search premises from which it was believed there was about to be issued publications the contents of which would be an offence against either regulation 18 or 27. It appears that the raid had been authorized after the work of the UDC had been raised in Parliament on 19 July 1915 by the Tory, Herbert Nield, who complained that the UDC and kindred organisations, including the Independent Labour Party, 'are holding over 200 meetings weekly', and also 'issuing quantities of literature in which the attitude of the late and present Governments, as also the true facts relating to the origin of the War, are misrepresented in order to mislead and dupe the public'.[128] The Attorney General (Sir Edward Carson) was asked 'whether he will cause prompt and effective measures to be taken to put an end to this agitation and to prosecute those who take part in it'. Allegations were also made that the UDC was funded by Germany, a claim hotly denied by Arthur Ponsonby, a prominent member of the UDC who claimed that 'the Union of Democratic Control have repeatedly denied that they have received any money from German sources', and offered to allow the government to inspect its accounts.

Responding to the parliamentary pressure of 19 July 1915 (when in the course of an exchange Ponsonby also welcomed police attendance at UDC meetings),[129] the Attorney General (Sir Edward Carson) instructed the Director of Public Prosecutions (Sir Charles Mathews) to authorise a police raid of the Manchester and London premises of the National Labour Press which duly took place on 18 August 1915 (while Parliament was in recess).[130] According to *The Times*, the issue of the *Labour Leader* scheduled for publication on the following day 'was already on the machines and some copies had been printed'. These were confiscated, and before the paper was allowed to go on printing, the page proofs had to be submitted to the authorities. As a result some material was censored, including a letter from a correspondent on 'Trade Unions and

[128] See H C Debs, 19 July 1915, cols 1161–3.   [129] Ibid, col 1163.
[130] For an account, see Hopkin, n 75 above, p 159.

Conscription'. The space occupied by the letter—two-thirds of a column—was left blank save for a notice explaining the circumstances of the police raid.[131] Apart from seizing and censoring copies of the *Labour Leader*, the police also seized UDC literature. According to Swartz, 'The London police seized seven or eight hundred of its pamphlets (as well as those of other organisations) and eighty copies of E D Morel's *Ten Years of Secret Diplomacy*; the Manchester police seized only samples of the UDC pamphlets stocked by the National Labour Press, because they doubted whether a magistrate would have ordered many of them destroyed'. This caution appeared well placed for when the material was brought before the Salford magistrates by the police seeking its destruction, they were 'not convinced of the illegality of the seized material', though admittedly their London colleagues did not entertain the same doubts and duly ordered the destruction of peace movement literature.[132]

The proceedings in London in fact led to an attempt to challenge the validity of regulation 51A, by the authority of which the raid took place.[133] Under the regulation any material which had been seized by the police had to be brought before a court of summary jurisdiction. The owner could then be summonsed to show cause as to why it should not be destroyed, and these proceedings could be held in camera if the public interest so required.[134] As already suggested the London magistrate (Alderman Sir John Knill) was satisfied that the publications contained statements likely to prejudice relations with foreign powers and likely to prejudice recruitment. The owners were duly summonsed and after various in camera hearings the magistrate ordered that the material be destroyed. In an application for certiorari it was argued on behalf of the applicants that the procedure was irregular because of the invalidity of the regulation to the extent that it authorised proceedings to be held in camera, contrary to the practice of open justice which had

---

[131] *The Times*, 19 August 1915. *The Times* had itself been the subject of a prosecution under Regulation 27, despite its well known 'devotion to patriotism'. See (1915) 79 JP 280.

[132] Nevertheless the incident caused some embarrassment, not only because of the result but also because it had been sanctioned without the knowledge of the Home Secretary in breach of the current practice that he should be 'consulted regarding . . . legal proceedings which had any political object', claiming also that 'the final decision in questions of policy rested with him' (Swartz, n 112 above, p 118). The Salford offices were raided again and pamphlets seized and destroyed on the authority of the Home Secretary who appears to have proceeded on the basis that the pamphlets in question could be suppressed because their destruction had been authorised by the magistrate in London a year or so earlier. See H C Debs, 6 April 1916, col 1351. For a strong attack on the operation of these powers, see H C Debs, 23 March 1916, cols 414–59.

[133] *Ex parte Norman* (1916) 114 LT 232. See above, p 58.

[134] S R & O 1915 No 551, Regulation 8, amending principal Regulation 8. For strong criticism of the use of the power in this case see (1915) 59 *Sol Jo* 740.

been asserted as recently as 1913 by the House of Lords in *Scott v Scott*,[135] an important and well-known case. The argument was based on the provision in the Defence of the Realm Consolidation Act 1914 authorising the trial of minor offences in courts of summary jurisdiction.[136] Following the decision in *Scott*, it was submitted that 'use of the expression "trial" excludes the notion of any proceedings being held in camera'. But perfectly predictably, Avory J rejected the argument on the ground that the proceedings under regulation 51A did not constitute a trial, though just as predictably perhaps he did not express a view as to the nature of the proceedings if they were not a 'trial'! In holding the regulation intra vires the judge was strongly influenced by the 'obvious' insight that 'when the whole object of these proceedings is to suppress the publication of certain documents, the hearing in public of a matter of this description would bring about the very mischief which the proceedings were intended to prevent'.[137]

The successful defence of regulation 51A barely disguises the fact that the National Labour Press raid was an embarrassment for the government,[138] leading not only to unwanted pressure in the House but

---

[135] [1913] AC 417.

[136] It was also submitted by counsel in argument that 'section 1(3) of the Defence of the Realm (Amendment) Act 1915 expressly confers on the court the power to exclude the public in the case of a felony; no such power was conferred in the case of minor offences. The only inference, therefore, that could be drawn in the absence of such an express enactment was that no such power existed'. But the point does not appear to have been addressed by the court. In fact powers to hear cases in camera (other than the matters in Regulation 51A) were conferred by Regulation 58 (S R & O 1915 No 551, Regulation 8) to be exercised where necessary in the 'public interest' in addition to any existing powers to this effect. The use of the power to hear cases in camera was very controversial and led to the Home Secretary issuing a circular to magistrates urging them to exercise 'great care' in the use of the 'limited power' ((1915) 79 JP 596). This did not fully address concerns, the matter being raised at some length in both the Commons and the Lords. See H C Debs, 23 March 1916, col 414 and H L Debs, 7 March 1917, cols 408–9 where Lord Sheffield complained about the 'unreasonable use' of the power and that magistrates were 'very indifferent' to the 'pious hopes' of the Home Secretary on which the circular was based.

[137] (1916) 114 LT 232, at p 234. For the sequel to this case see *Norman v Mathews* (1916) 32 TLR 303 (DC) (1916); 32 TLR 369 (CA) where in Westminster County Court in an action against the DPP and the Police Commissioner for detinue of documents seized during the raid the court heard the case in camera and struck it out. In the course of a review of that decision an attempt was made unsuccessfully to argue that Regulation 27 was ultra vires on the ground that it was being used not only to prevent the publication of 'untrue' statements, but also 'to prevent the expression of political opinions'. The case also established the right of the county court to sit in camera, though on the basis of *Scott v Scott*, above, rather than Regulation 58.

[138] There appear nevertheless to have been many such raids. Indeed according to 'North Briton', n 74 above, p 37, the scale of the raids was 'unprecedented in English history', and that 'cases are so numerous that little will be gained by referring to specific instances'. For examples of raids on the ILP branches and the No Conscription Fellowship as well as other organisations, see H C Debs, 29 June 1916, cols 1171–2. It was incidents such as this which led to the attack on the magistracy by Philip Snowden as being 'partisans' who 'cease to be judicial bodies and simply become the tools of the Executive Government or of the military authorities' (H C Debs, 29 June 1916, col

also a realisation that the Defence of the Realm Regulations were not up to the job of countering the propaganda of the UDC and the peace movement generally, despite the accommodating stance of the courts.[139] Growing concern about the literature of the peace movement led the Home Secretary (Sir George Cave) in November 1917 to seek two important amendments to the Regulations. One would make it an offence 'to spread reports or make statements intended or likely "directly or indirectly to impede or interfere with the successful prosecution of the war" '. The Home Secretary is said to have told the War Cabinet that a measure of this kind 'would enable us to stop certain pamphlets and newspapers which are not now directly hit by the Regulations'.[140] The other proposed amendment would require pamphlets and leaflets to be approved by the Press Bureau, the official but non-statutory body which we have already encountered.[141] The first of these proposals was rejected, the Cabinet being unwilling to 'delegate any such arbitrary power to the Home Secretary', but the second was accepted, and became regulation 27C.[142] It was subsequently explained by the Home Secretary that the purpose of the amendment was 'to prevent the circulation of a leaflet which infringes Regulation 27 or 42 before the authorities have knowledge of it, and so to give an opportunity to take proceedings in time'. But on this occasion, as on so many others, the measure backfired. The UDC submitted its pamphlets to the Press Bureau as required (though not all peace groups did, their members thus risking imprisonment) and then distributed them with the note 'Passed by the Censor' on the front cover. According to Swartz, 'the dissenters were amused at the irony of having the government's imprimatur inscribed on their literature'.[143] Needless to say, the government was not equally amused and regulation 27C was thus amended within a month of its promulgation.

1171). Members of the Fellowship had previously been prosecuted under Regulation 27 in connection with leaflets urging the repeal of the Military Service Act 1916 ((1916) 80 JP 236).

[139] See also *Kaye v Cole* (1917) 86 LT 1084 (undermining the right to a speedy trial).

[140] Swartz, n 112 above, p 192.

[141] For full details, see Hopkin, 'Domestic Censorship in the First World War', n 75 above.

[142] S R & O 1917 No 1190, Regulation 5. For strong criticism on civil libertarian grounds see (1917) 62 *Sol Jo* 81, and 170 where it is said that its opinion on the matter 'coincided with that very generally held'. Cf (1918) 82 JP 187. For an earlier rejection by the government of this form of censorship in relation to the Press as being 'entirely contrary to our institutions', see H L Debs, 8 November 1915, col 205.

[143] Swartz, *The Union of Democratic Control*, n 112 above, p 191. But not all peace groups were willing to have their publications censored in this way. 'The Society of Friends felt that this regulation was opposed to the principles of Christian liberty', and a number of its members were prosecuted for failing to comply with its terms. See Lord Parmoor, n 66 above, pp 122–4.

As a result it became necessary only to submit literature to the Bureau at least 72 hours before its publication or distribution.[144]

Announcing the amendment to the House of Commons the Home Secretary explained that every leaflet would be examined by the 'Censor', and if it contravened the Regulations, steps could be taken at once to prevent its issue, though the 'ultimate decision would rest with the courts'. He drew attention to the particular advantage of the amendment which was that it would no longer be the duty of the Press Bureau 'to give its sanction to pamphlets, which, although not illegal, may nevertheless be of an undesirable nature'. In fact no attempt was made to challenge any UDC literature in the courts and in that sense regulation 27C appeared to make little difference in practice. The government it seems was constrained by the requirement of having to prove that any objectionable statements in peace propaganda were 'false'—perhaps living to regret its willingness to accept Lord Robert Cecil's amendment to the Defence of the Realm Consolidation Act 1914. Although much of the peace literature was thought by the government to be misleading and alarming, and although there was a strong desire to prosecute, the fact is that 'the Home Office adhered to the argument that the UDC's challenge to the makers of British foreign policy had to be taken up in the first instance by the Foreign Office. The latter could do so only by making an explicit statement of war aims which, even if capable of precise formulation, might have lent substance to some of the Union's accusations'. The government, which had considered 'the problem of dealing with the literature of the Union of Democratic Control' at the highest level, was thus impaled on the horns of a dilemma: prosecute under regulation 27 in the knowledge that 'the only demonstrably false statements contained in [the literature] deal with subjects we could not permit to be publicly discussed in a court of law'; or accept and tolerate the fact that its activities would be the subject of damaging, misleading, but influential attacks.

These changes to the Regulations, largely ineffective though they were, accompanied a parallel attempt to counteract the activities of the UDC. Unable to control the propaganda of the movement, the government responded, without statutory authority it may be said, by making public money available to fund a body called the National War Aims Committee which it had set up in June 1917 with the specific aim of countering the propaganda work of the peace movement.[145] Selected details of the work of this body were given to the House of Commons on

---

[144] S R & O 1917 No 1190, Regulation 5. And see H C Debs, 10 December 1917, cols 856–7.
[145] A full account is to be found in Swartz, n 112 above, pp 188–91.

13 November 1917 by the Joint Parliamentary Secretary to the Treasury (Captain F Guest).[146] He explained that the Committee had been set up in the summer of 1917, 'when there were indications of considerable pacifist propaganda being fermented in certain industrial centres in England', or in the words of Sir Edward Carson, 'subterranean' influence of a 'pernicious and pestilential character'. The purpose of the Committee, said to be 'of an educative and of a satisfying character', was to 'steady' and 'stiffen' the morale of workers at home. Accordingly its terms of reference included assisting 'the country during the ensuing months of strain to resist insidious influences of an unpatriotic character'. It is clear that leading political figures played a prominent part in the activities of the Committee. The enterprise was established by the government; Guest, from the Treasury bench, was the chairman; and the Prime Minister and members of the Cabinet were among the Presidents. The government was not, however, prepared to give 'details either of expenditure or of personal employment in connection with this work'. It is difficult to resist the charges of some parliamentarians that the government's refusal to supply more information about the Committee was 'deplorable', that it was the improper use of 'public money for political purposes', and that it involved the 'corrupt expenditure of public funds'.

The main activity of the Committee, it seems, was to arrange for speakers for meetings throughout the country in the 300 or so constituencies in which it was claimed that local committees were to be set up. The Committee also arranged with the Home Office that it would be provided with intelligence about pacifist meetings so that rival meetings could be organised as a 'counter-blast'. Yet despite 'governmental co-operation and financing' the Committee failed in its 'attempts to counteract the Union of Democratic Control and other dissenting groups'. According to Swartz, it was 'ineffective, if not incompetent'. An investigation of its work by the Select Committee on National Expenditure in 1918[147] revealed that after the War Cabinet had decided in October 1917 that the expenditure of the Committee should be a charge on public funds, 'the money found by the voluntary subscribers, amounting to about £9,000, was refunded to them by the Government'. The Select Committee reported that the estimated expenditure of the National War Aims Committee for the six months ending 31 March 1918 was £118,858, but that the actual expenditure was much less,

---

[146] H C Debs, 13 November 1917, cols 286 et seq.
[147] Report from the Select Committee on National Expenditure, 3rd Report, HC 59 (1918), paras 103–12.

amounting to only £28,058 during the eight months from August 1917 to 31 March 1918. This was still considerably more than the UDC spent during the entire war.[148] The Director and Editor-in-Chief each received an annual salary of £1,500, and eight other officials were paid between £1,000 and £300 per annum. A subsistence allowance of £1 per day when away from home, railway fares and a fee for each meeting were paid to each speaker, with campaigns in each constituency lasting about four weeks. The Select Committee was critical of the payment of the £9,000 (for which there should at least have been parliamentary approval) and also of the high salaries of the chief officials 'having regard to the nature of the work to be done'.[149] Otherwise the report was remarkably restrained, though it did draw attention also to larger scale expenditure on propaganda by the Department of Information.[150] Set up in 1917 under the supervision of Lord Carson with a staff of 485, the Department absorbed the work of a number of different agencies including the War Propaganda Bureau and 'a Bureau managed . . . through the Home Office out of an Emergency Vote, which we were informed was drawn from the Secret Service Vote'.[151]

'Red Clydeside'

Apart from the peace movement, the Defence of the Realm Regulations were deployed to deal with other forms of unrest on the home front. An area of some difficulty in this respect was Clydeside, particularly in 1915 and early 1916, with strong political opposition to the war helping effectively to ignite the simmering grievances of the munitions workers, on whom a successful outcome obviously depended in some measure.[152] It

---

[148] Swartz, n 112 above, pp 191–2.

[149] At para 111. 'The majority of these gentlemen were connected with the Press, and the salaries seem to have been fixed upon the basis of what they would have received if they had continued in that connection' (ibid).

[150] This is more fully explored in Report from the Select Committee on National Expenditure, 6th Report, HC 97 (1918).

[151] It was also reported that the Treasury 'appear to have no cognisance of the expenditure of these Departments beyond that of the War Propaganda Bureau' (HC 97 (1918), para 1). For the Government response, see Cd 9201 (1918), where its was said to be 'neither customary or desirable' for the Treasury to have cognisance of secret service money. The project had been funded from three sources: a vote of credit through the National Health Insurance Commission, a confidential head in the vote of credit, and secret service funds; the Treasury knew about the first two.

[152] Although this was perhaps the best known source of socialist opposition to the war, it was not the only one. See generally, Challinor, n 75 above, ch 6. In addition to the illustrations of many of the forms of harassment referred to throughout this chapter, Challinor refers also to well-documented complaints of the use of agent provocateurs and government spies within anti-war organisations.

is perhaps important to identify two quite separate, though intimately connected, strands of dissent when considering the anti war activity on Clydeside.[153] So far as the political wing of the Labour Movement is concerned, it is true that at least initially, the Labour Party in Parliament supported the war effort. But it was opposed from the start by both the Independent Labour Party (which was affiliated to the Labour Party as a socialist society) and by the British Socialist Party which had been formed in 1911 as an offshoot of the Social Democratic Party. Although the total membership of both was fairly small, it seems reasonably clear that their influence in Glasgow was disproportionately high: it was there that the BSP had grown to such an extent that it was able to recruit a paid organiser for Scotland. The BSP also produced in John MacLean perhaps the only truly revolutionary figure in Britain this century.[154] Although there are now those who would question the effectiveness of his vigorous and unremitting campaign against the war, MacLean nevertheless appears as a man of great vision, courage and influence. Dismissed from his job as a school teacher for his socialist activities, MacLean ('so intelligent and highly educated') conducted an indefatigable crusade. He has been described by David Kirkwood, one of his contemporaries 'as sincere as sunlight and as passionate as a typhoon',[155] and by another as an 'indomitable and irrepressible revolutionary figure'.[156]

So far as the industrial wing of the Labour Movement is concerned, here too the official trade union organisations largely supported the war, or at least were not prepared to be seen to frustrate its progress. But on Clydeside, a centre of the munitions industry, there was growing concern about working conditions particularly after the introduction of the Munitions of War Act 1915. As Hinton points out, the Act was 'designed to reinforce employers' control of labour against the pressures of wartime full employment and to facilitate the introduction of diluted labour'. 'To this end', he continues, 'strikes were made illegal, restrictive practices suspended and the free movement of labour restricted by the device of the "leaving certificate" ' whereby workers were required to seek the permission of their employer before they could terminate their employment.[157] It was against this background of greatly enhanced employer power that the influential Clyde Workers' Committee (CWC), consisting mainly of shop stewards and other workplace representatives, emerged to

[153] For background, see W Kendall, *The Revolutionary Movement in Britain 1900–1921* (1969), p 105.
[154] See N Milton, *John MacLean* (1973).   [155] D Kirkwood, *My Life of Revolt* (1935), p 114.
[156] W Gallacher, *Revolt on the Clyde* (1936), p 20.
[157] J Hinton, 'The Clyde Workers' Committee and the Dilution Struggle' in A Briggs and J Saville (eds), *Essays in Labour History 1886–1923*, vol 2 (1971), p 152, at p 161.

safeguard workers' interests. Revisionist history tends to the view that the role and influence of the CWC is exaggerated and that the 'Clyde shop steward leaders were by no means uniformly opposed to the conduct of the war'.[158] It has been claimed, for example, that the activities of the Committee were 'more dominated by simple industrial motives than has hitherto been realised and scarcely rose above immediate, syndicalist, industrial union activities'.[159] Still, 'most of the leaders of the CWC were revolutionaries, conscious of belonging to a political vanguard'[160] and indeed their numbers included influential figures, not the least of whom was the chairman, William Gallacher, later to be a founder member of the Communist Party of Great Britain and subsequently Communist Member of Parliament for West Fife. It is also the case that the CWC was held primarily responsible for the wave of industrial unrest which gripped Clydeside for about twelve months from February 1915 over a wide range of issues, though dilution (the use of unskilled workers to do the work of craftsmen) appears to have been a major bone of contention.

Hinton claims that the suppression of the CWC 'was the result of a well planned offensive directed by the Labour Department of the Ministry of Munitions',[161] though this is a judgement that has since been contested.[162] The result of the 'offensive', if there was such an offensive, was the imprisonment and deportation of the political and industrial leadership, which effectively broke the Committee by the middle of April 1916. But before this climax was reached, a number of other incidents indicate the growing impatience of the authorities with political and industrial developments in Glasgow in late 1915 and early 1916. These included the suppression of *Forward*, then 'the principal socialist journal in the West of Scotland',[163] following its publication of the account of a meeting between Lloyd George (the Minister of Munitions) and Clydeside munitions workers in St Andrew's Hall, Glasgow on Christmas Day 1915. An official report of the meeting, which had been arranged to encourage the Glasgow workers to accept dilution, was issued by the Press Bureau which had 'particularly requested that no account of [the] meeting should be published other than a general statement that the meeting was held', explaining that 'at the meeting many things may have been said the publication of which is not desirable in the national interest'. Only the authorised version of the Minister's speech was to be published and no reference was to be made to any disturbance that might

[158] Kendall, n 153 above, pp 105–6.
[159] Ibid, p 106.
[160] Hinton, 'The Clyde Workers' Committee', n 157 above, p 165.
[161] Ibid, p 153.
[162] McLean, n 77 above, p 74.
[163] Ibid, p 11.

have taken place.[164] This, however, was not received by *Forward* which proceeded to report a blow by blow account of the meeting which appears to have been dominated by several hundred noisy supporters of the CWC and which ended in the humiliation of the Minister who was barely able to make himself heard amid the din of protest. According to one leading study Lloyd George's speech 'was in part drowned altogether by the commotion', and contrary to the official report of the Press Bureau ('the meeting was on the whole good humoured'), the meeting 'broke up in disorder'.[165]

Predictably the retribution was swift. A decision to suppress *Forward* was taken on 31 December 1915, several days after the publication of the offending article. Similar measures were taken against John MacLean's paper, *Vanguard*, which had also published details of the meeting including the oft-quoted lines, 'Seldom has a prominent politician been treated with so little respect by a meeting of the workers. It is evident that the feeling of servility towards their masters no longer holds first place in the minds of the Clyde workers'. The action was taken under regulation 51 which as we have seen enabled the authorities, without a warrant, to enter and search premises where there was reason to suspect that they were being used for any purpose prejudicial to the public safety or the defence of the Realm, or that an offence against the regulations was being or had been committed thereon. Regulation 51 then authorised the seizure of offending material, and in the case of newspaper offices where a report had appeared in breach of regulation 27, the seizure of any plant necessary for its printing or publication. Armed with this authority, the police not only visited the offices of the newspapers, but also seized copies from newsagents and visited the homes of subscribers,[166] missing only the copy deposited under the Copyright Act in the National Library of Scotland.[167] When the matter was raised in the House of Commons for the first time it was explained by Lloyd George that the action had been taken because the paper had been 'deliberately inciting the workers . . . not to carry out an Act of Parliament which has been passed by this House in order to promote the output of munitions'.[168] Subsequently rejecting claims that the suppression of *Forward*

---

[164] McLean, *The Legend of Red Clydeside*, n 77 above, pp 53–4.

[165] Ibid, pp 52–3, based on an account which appeared in the surviving copy of the banned newspaper.

[166] *The Times*, 4 January 1916.

[167] McLean, n 77 above, p 253.

[168] H C Debs, 4 January 1916, col 803. It had earlier been explained by the Under Secretary of State at the War Office (H J Tennant) that the action had been taken under Regulation 27 (col 802).

was a direct result of the embarrassment of the Minister, the action was justified also on the basis of regulation 42, with Lloyd George citing articles stretching back to the summer of 1915 and indicating that the suppression of *Forward* had been under review since the previous November.[169] But it seems that few were persuaded.[170]

The suppression of *Forward*, and later *Vanguard*, lasted for about a month.[171] This, however, was only the prelude to much more drastic action. On 2 February 1916, the police raided the Socialist Labour Press, broke the machinery and suppressed the forthcoming issue of the *Worker*, the newspaper of the CWC, for the publication of an article entitled 'Should the Workers' Arm?' which had appeared in the fourth issue on 29 January.[172] This was followed by the arrest on 6 February of John MacLean and on the following day, 7 February, of leading CWC officials, namely William Gallacher (chairman) and John Muir (editor of the *Worker*), together with Walter Bell, the paper's printer. This was not the first time that MacLean had been in trouble with the authorities. He had, as already suggested, carried a tireless campaign against the war, running a regular Sunday meeting in Bath Street, 'where the transport offices had been turned into an army recruiting centre',[173] which became 'the largest of its kind in the city and quite a local institution'. In this, writes Kendall, Glasgow, and perhaps MacLean, were unique, 'as in most other cities anti-war orators were in danger of being pulled off their platform, brutally beaten and chased off the streets'.[174] MacLean had previously been imprisoned for five days in 1915 for making statements likely to prejudice recruiting contrary to regulation 27(c). He had stated at a Bath Street meeting that 'I have been enlisted in the Socialist Army for fifteen years. God damn all other armies!', and at another meeting that any soldier who shot another soldier in the war was a murderer.[175] The arrest in February related to speeches MacLean had made at six different meetings thereafter, mainly in opposition to military conscription and dilution.

---

[169] H C Debs, 10 January 1916, cols 1402–15.

[170] For a full and exhaustive account of this incident, see McLean, n 77 above, pp 55–62.

[171] For examples of other difficulties encountered by the socialist press on Clydeside, see Challinor, n 75 above, p 127.

[172] According to *The Times*, 4 February 1916, 'The Glasgow police, acting on military instructions, raided the printing and publishing offices of the Socialist Labour Party and seized all available copies of the the *Worker*, the organ of the Clyde Workers' Committee, the fifth issue of which was in preparation. Later the police raided the printer's and seized all the type portion belonging to another newspaper'.

[173] H McShane, *No Mean Fighter* (1978), p 66.   [174] Kendall, n 153 above, p 112.

[175] See Milton, n 154 above, pp 99–100.

Before the trials of MacLean, Gallacher, Bell and Muir at the High Court in Edinburgh in April, a strike was called at the factory of Sir William Beardmore on 17 March following the revocation two weeks earlier of David Kirkwood's rights as convenor of shop stewards. Kirkwood was also a key figure in the CWC and it has been suggested that the employer's conduct was designed deliberately to provoke a strike as a pretext to break the Committee. When the dispute spread to other works the decision was taken, on 23 March, to arrest and deport three shop stewards as well as two other CWC leaders, one of whom (McManus) was engaged at a location which had not joined the strike, thereby giving some credence to the view that the aim was to break the Committee while also breaking the strike. The decisions to deport were taken under the authority of regulation 14 which as we have seen allowed for the deportation of individuals from one part of the country to another. There was no need for the deportee to have committed an offence; it was enough that he or she was 'suspected of acting, or of having acted, or of being about to act in a manner prejudicial to the public safety or the defence of the Realm'. The only other condition was that 'it appeared' to the competent naval or military authority that 'it is desirable that [the person in question] should be prohibited from residing in or entering any locality'. These conditions being met, there was no provision for the formality of a hearing or anything of the kind; the respondent was simply required to leave the area 'within such time as may be specified in the order'. On this occasion the Parliamentary Secretary in the Munitions Department (Dr Addison) announced that the 'method of deporting these men was resorted to in the first instance because a criminal trial would require an interval of six weeks or two months before it could be held, and it was felt that immediate action was necessary'.[176] In other words, it was done expressly to avoid the formalities of the law.

In his autobiography, David Kirkwood tells how he was arrested by four armed detectives at 3 o'clock on the morning of 25 March 1916:

I was sleeping the sleep of the just. I was awakened by a violent rat-tat-tat at the door.
My wife said: 'That's them for ye noo'.
The same thought flashed through my mind. I went to the door and asked who was there. A voice answered: 'The police. Open the door'.
'I will do nothing of the kind', I answered.

---

[176] H C Debs, 28 March 1916, col 567.

'You'd be better to open it. We have a warrant under the Defence of the Realm Act to take you to the Central Police Office. If you do not open the door, we shall batter it in.'

I opened the door. There were four detectives with revolvers at their sides.[177]

On his arrival at the Central Police Station Kirkwood claims that he had been court-martialed the day before (in his absence) and sentenced to deportation. Later that same day he was taken to Queen Street Railway Station, 'handed a single ticket for Edinburgh and a ten shilling note, and put inside the barrier'. He and his colleagues were thus 'cast adrift' for an indefinite period without even the opportunity to challenge the decision before a judicial authority. Leaving behind his wife and five children, Kirkwood was 'suddenly transferred to a strange city', arriving in a blinding snowstorm with inadequate funds and nowhere to stay.[178] For the government the end justified the means. It is true that the deportations did not bring an immediate end to the strike, and on the contrary provoked its extension to other factories. But this in turn led to the further deportation of another five shop stewards, and the prosecution and conviction of individual strikers for breach of the Munitions of War Act 1915, which by section 2 provided that it was an offence to take part in a strike unless 21 days' notice had been given to the Board of Trade.[179]

Yet despite these last death throes, the 'deportations broke the Committee',[180] and the strike was over by the end of March, followed within a few weeks by the trials of MacLean on the one hand, and Gallacher, Bell and Muir on the other. MacLean was charged under regulation 27 for statements likely to prejudice recruiting, training and discipline; and under regulation 42 for attempting to cause mutiny, sedition and disaffection among the civilian population, and for attempting to impede and delay the production of war material. He was alleged to have made a number of inflammatory statements against conscription and dilution, to have encouraged the Clyde workers to strike and to have urged those who had guns to use them. 'Workers were being made slaves to suit the bloody English capitalists, which was pure Kaiserism and

---

[177] Kirkwood, n 155 above, p 129.

[178] For a full account see Kirkwood, ibid, pp 129–33.

[179] For an account of the prosecutions of the strikers see G R Rubin, *War, Law, and Labour* (1987), pp 95–104. An attempt to justify the government's conduct of the strike was made in a parliamentary statement by the Parliamentary Secretary to the Ministry of Munitions. See H C Debs, 28 March 1916, cols 564–7. This statement gave rise to the most extraordinary outburst from Sir Edward Carson who rose to ask whether 'it has been considered whether these men are not guilty of assisting the King's enemies, and thereby are guilty of high treason?' (col 566).

[180] Hinton, n 157 above, p 183.

Prussianism.' At another meeting 'he did not advise his hearers to strike, but they should sell or pledge their alarm clock and sleep in the morning and not go to their work'. In a trial which attracted 'considerable interest',[181] the only witnesses against MacLean were police officers, twenty-three in total, 'who attended the various meetings as part of their duty, and for the most part made written reports of the speeches from memory afterwards. One detective said he wrote two lines of shorthand on the back of a label'. The trial lasted only two days, with MacLean being found guilty on four of the six counts against him, the jury taking only sixty-five minutes to reach its verdict. Passing sentence the Lord Justice General observed that this was not the first time that MacLean had been convicted for contravening the Defence of the Realm Regulations. Determined not to follow the example of the earlier 'very light sentence', he sentenced the accused to three years' penal servitude. On being taken from the dock MacLean waved his hat to the crowd in the gallery where a verse of 'The Red Flag' was sung. Four members of the choir were arrested by the police and brought before the court on the following day for contempt, for singing while the judge was still on the bench. Following 'most humble apologies' the accused, all working men, were each ordered to pay a fine of £2 or go to prison for two weeks.[182]

Like MacLean, the trials of Gallacher, Bell and Muir took place in Edinburgh. They were charged under regulation 42, it being alleged that the article in the *Worker* of 29 January contained statements likely to cause sedition and impede the production and transport of munitions. It was maintained by counsel that the offending article 'Should the Workers Arm' 'meant exactly the opposite of the meaning extracted from it by the Crown'. 'It was', he said, 'intended to prevent strikes and discourage violence, although couched in rhetorical and lurid language'.[183] Nevertheless all three were found guilty, and after a strong plea in mitigation in which counsel for the accused stated that they 'disavowed the meaning attached to the article, and humbly apologised for its publication', Gallacher and Muir were each sentenced to twelve months' and Bell, the printer, to three months' imprisonment. In passing sentence the Lord Justice General 'commented on the extreme gravity of [the offence] but said that, having regard to the apology the accused had tendered,

---

[181] *The Scotsman*, 12 April 1916.

[182] These details are drawn from *The Times*, 12–14 April 1916. The case is also reported in *The Scotsman*, 12–14 April 1916.

[183] According to McLean, n 177 above, p 73 the 'most cursory reading of the article shows that the answer the writer implied to his own question was "No"'.

and to their unimpeachable characters, he would not inflict as he would otherwise have done, a sentence of penal servitude'.[184] Both the political and industrial leadership of the anti-war forces were thus removed, either by deportation or imprisonment, amateurs in class warfare pitched against the ruthless efficiency of the ministry and its powerful allies in the local business community. The crisis over, Gallacher and Muir were released in February 1917; the deportees returned several months later, shortly before the release of MacLean on 30 June, having served only fourteen months of his sentence.[185] It seems that political expediency operated here too, just as it did in having him removed to prison in the first place. Gallacher has suggested that MacLean's early release coincided less with the calm which had returned to the workplaces of the Clyde, than to the fact that Lloyd George was to be made a freeman of the city of Glasgow.

But whatever the reason for his release, MacLean's freedom was short-lived for his revolutionary and anti-war activities soon brought him into conflict with the authorities yet again.[186] He was arrested on 15 April 1918—less than a year after his second release from prison and only several months after his appointment as Soviet Consul in Scotland—and charged with sedition.[187] At the trial on 9 May, it took 'fully ten minutes' to read the indictment in the course of which he was accused of having 'addressed meetings in Glasgow, Lanarkshire and Fife between the dates of 20 January and 4 April 1918, and there making statements likely to prejudice recruiting and cause mutiny and sedition among the people'. There were eleven charges, 'but in essence his main crime was his call to the workers to follow the example of their Russian comrades, go forward, and strike the first blow for the revolution on 1 May'.[188] At one of the meetings MacLean was accused of having advised the workers to 'break all laws' and 'to take control of Glasgow City Chambers, the Post Office, and the banks, and urged that the House of Commons should be superseded by a Soviet, saying that he did not care whether they met at

[184] *The Times*, 14–15 April 1916. The more lenient treatment of the three in the *Worker* prosecution than of MacLean was a matter of some embarrassment for Gallacher who was later to write that 'If MacLean held high the banner of revolutionary struggle, we dragged it, or allowed it to be dragged, in the mire': Gallacher, n 156 above, p 119.

[185] A good account of prison conditions, and in particular the hardship suffered by MacLean, is provided in Gallacher, ibid, p 122.

[186] On MacLean's activities after his release from prison, see Gallacher, ibid, p 171.

[187] MacLean was 'more than any other individual regarded by the Russians as the authentic voice of the British Revolution' (Kendall, n 153 above, p 284). He was also appointed to the Honorary Praesidium of the First All Russian Congress of Soviets. But he refused to join the Communist Party of Great Britain following its foundation under Lenin's direction in 1920.

[188] Milton, n 154 above, p 167.

the usual place or at Buckingham Palace'.[189] Addressing the jury the Lord Advocate said that there was nothing in the law as currently framed to prevent people talking about socialism 'however inappropriate it might be, but there came a time when such discussion of social questions became seditious'. They all had a duty, he continued, to protect themselves from men like MacLean 'unless they wanted to be overtaken by the same catastrophe as befell Russia'.[190] For his part, MacLean refused to plead, refused to enter the witness box and conducted his own defence. The jury found him guilty without troubling to retire, but only after he had delivered a famous speech lasting some seventy-five minutes in which he stood not as the accused but as the accuser of capitalism ('the most infamous, bloody, and evil system which mankind had ever witnessed') which was 'dripping with blood from head to foot'.[191] He was sentenced to five years' penal servitude, but released on 3 November 1918, and was imprisoned again before his death in 1923.

The Role of the Courts

We have seen that the government was given great powers by the Defence of the Realm Consolidation Act 1914 to make regulations to deal with the emergency. We have seen also that wide powers were in fact taken, restricting personal liberties and political freedom in a number of ways. And we have seen further how these powers were used in an attempt to crush political and industrial opposition at home. The question which now arises is simply this: how did the courts respond to these war-time measures and to their application in particular cases? Should the courts stand back and allow a one-dimensional approach to government? Should civil libertarian concerns play a part in supervising the exercise of war-time powers? If so, should an attempt be made to reconcile the needs of government with the liberties of the individual? We have encountered the very powerful performances of at least some of the Law Lords during the debates surrounding the Defence of the Realm Consolidation Act 1914 when it was proposed to extend the powers of the courts-martial. A strong restatement of civil libertarian concerns by some unlikely and improbable champions led to the introduction of the Defence of the Realm (Amendment) Act 1915 preserving the right to trial by jury in civil courts. But we have also encountered a number of cases,

---

[189] *The Times*, 10 May 1918.   [190] Milton, *John MacLean*, n 154 above, p 170.
[191] John MacLean, 'Condemned From the Dock. His Famous Speech Against War and Capitalism' [n d].

including *Ex parte Norman*,[192] in which the courts seemed particularly sensitive to the needs of the government during the emergency. How typical were these decisions?

Before turning to the cases, and the principles which the courts applied, it is useful to consider just how extensive, or otherwise, were the powers of the courts in war-time. It is true that they could not challenge the primary legislation, such as the Defence of the Realm Acts which delegated so much authority to the executive (though as we have seen, as legislators some of the Law Lords had played an important part in shaping the content of some of that legislation). On the other hand, the courts were charged with the duty of ensuring that the extensive measures taken under primary legislation came within the scope of the enabling power. In view of the fact that so much power was taken in the form of delegated legislation under the Defence of the Realm Act with little or no parliamentary scrutiny, this placed the courts in a crucially important and perhaps an unprecedentedly responsible position. Yet the role of the courts lay not only in determining whether regulations were ultra vires or not. Even those regulations which were clearly valid had to be interpreted, and here again the courts had an important role in determining how executive power was to be shaped and used in any particular situation. But these were not the only challenges which the courts faced. Apart from the validity and interpretation of statutory material, questions were also to arise about the scope and content of the common law with its capacity both on the one hand to reinforce through the Royal Prerogative the emergency powers of government, and on the other allegedly to protect the individual from the arbitrary exercise of executive authority. Again, how was this balance to be struck?

Cases would typically start life in the King's Bench Divisional Court, presided over by the Lord Chief Justice. Most of them were disposed of at this stage, though a few did proceed to the Court of Appeal, but only two of what might be described as having civil liberties implications went all the way to the House of Lords, and of these one was not heard until 1920 by which time of course the Armistice had been signed.[193] The key court was thus the Divisional Court which had been presided over by Lord Reading since 1913. Described by one biographer as 'a liberal imperialist',[194] Rufus Isaacs had been elected to Parliament in 1904 and

---

[192] (1916) 114 LT 232.
[193] See respectively *R v Halliday* [1917] AC 260 and *Attorney General v De Keyser's Royal Hotel Ltd* [1920] AC 508.
[194] *Dictionary of National Biography 1931–1940*, at p 463.

from 1911–13 had been Attorney General in the Liberal government (and unusually as such was a member of the Cabinet).[195] His position as Lord Chief Justice during the war was extraordinary in the sense that 'his statesmanlike qualities were throughout the war increasingly employed on special duties of the highest order imposed upon him by the successive governments of Great Britain'.[196] At the outbreak of war his help was called for to assist the Treasury in framing financial and legislative plans for the domestic emergency,[197] and in September 1915 he led an Anglo-French mission to the USA seeking American credit for supplies urgently needed for carrying on the war, achieving a 'brilliant' success by securing a loan of 500 million dollars (to be spent in the USA).[198] On his return to judicial duties, 'the government continued to take constant advantage of his advice',[199] and he was advanced to a viscountcy in the birthday honours of 1916, adding this to his appointment as GCB in 1915. His 'appetite whetted for wider responsibilities', Reading was appointed in September 1917 as High Commissioner of the King in the USA, Ambassador Extraordinary and Minister Plenipotentiary to deal with 'complicated strands of Anglo-American finance',[200] and was kept engrossed in financial matters even after his return to London in November, 'where the British War Cabinet required his assistance'.[201] An Earldom was conferred upon him later that month.[202]

Yet despite all his work for and with the government, and despite its showering of honours and awards upon his shoulders, Isaacs continued to sit as Lord Chief Justice, albeit intermittently. In his absence Reading's place was taken by Darling J (once famously described as 'an impudent little man in horsehair'),[203] as the senior puisne judge in the King's Bench

---

[195] For comment see (1915) 60 *Sol Jo* 1 which condemned the inclusion of Simon and Carson (Reading's successors) in the Cabinet.

[196] *DNB*, n 194 above, at p 465.

[197] On which see the tribute paid to the Lord Chief Justice by the Prime Minister at the Lord Mayor's banquet in (1915) 59 *Sol Jo* 63, a report which also carries details of the speech of Lord Reading in response.

[198] On his return he also addressed the Lord Mayor's banquet. See (1915) 60 *Sol Jo* 63.

[199] *DNB*, n 194 above.

[200] For comment on this appointment see (1918) 62 *Sol Jo* 205. Although there was no reason to grudge Lord Reading his chance of adding to his great services to the State, it was noted that other great judges had been content with their position in the courts. The unique event was said to be the subject of an impressive scene when the Solicitor General on behalf of the Bar expressed to Lord Reading 'their deep sense of the devotion to duty and of public spirit which led him to accept a great and exacting office' ((1918)) 62 *Sol Jo* 215). For details of the speech of the Solicitor General and of Lord Reading's reply, see ibid, p 238.

[201] *DNB*, n 194 above.

[202] For full details, see S Jackson, *Rufus Isaacs. First Marquess of Reading* (1936).

[203] See S H Bailey, D J Harris and B L Jones, *Civil Liberties: Cases and Materials* (4th edn, 1995), p 422.

Division. Darling, a Conservative, had been appointed a High Court judge in 1897, after having served eight years as a Member of Parliament without distinction ('a competent party man rather than a . . . politician with any original contributions to make').[204] The appointment was not without controversy, with *The Times* devoting a leader to rumours that the Lord Chancellor (Halsbury) was contemplating Darling's elevation to the Bench. Without mentioning him by name, it was said that the subject of the rumour was a man of 'acute intellect and considerable literary power', but that he had given no sign of legal eminence and that his appointment, were the rumours to be true, would be 'on political grounds'.[205] Darling's appointment to the Queen's Bench Division was announced two days later, whereupon '*The Times* returned to the charge; Asquith gave expression to his doubts; [and] much indignation was expressed in the Temple'.[206] Although there is no record of Darling having the same symbiotic relationship with the executive during the war as his senior colleague, his war-time service was not without reward in the sense that his work was recognised by the distinction, 'unusual in the case of a serving judge', of being made a Privy Councillor in 1917.[207] Darling's strong support for the war extended to the publishing of letters and poems in the press, usually anonymously, in response to issues of controversy. These included a remarkable letter to *The Times* in which he noted the difficulty of convicting of 'any crime, such as piracy or murder on the high seas, the crews of German submarines now in English custody'. Given that they were in 'all probability mere murderers, as several members of the Cabinet have called them', he proposed that they should be left to perish at sea: there was no 'legal obligation to rescue them from the drowning deserved'.[208]

Reading and Darling thus help to explode the myth of an independent judiciary standing as a bulwark between the executive and the citizen. Yet together they sat in most of the cases dealing with crucial regulations affecting personal and political liberty, and they decided them all in favour of the government. The issues dealt with were many and varied, and included on the one hand attempts to challenge deportations under regulation 14 and on the other the extent of police powers under regulation 55. In one regulation 14 case, *Ronnfeldt v Phillips*,[209] an order that

---

[204] *DNB*, n 194 above, p 211.
[205] *The Times*, 26 October 1897.   [206] *DNB*, n 204 above, p 211.
[207] Ibid, at p 212. See also (1917) 62 *Sol Jo* 146.
[208] See D Walker-Smith, *The Life of Lord Darling* (1938), p 183.
[209] (1918) 34 TLR 556, aff'd [1918] WN 328 (Bankes, Warrington and Scrutton LJJ).

a Welsh coal exporter should leave the Cardiff area within four days was upheld, the order having been made on the basis of rumours that the plaintiff (whose father had come to Britain in 1859) had said that the Kaiser's head would soon be on the coinage of this country. Although there was 'very, very little ground for suspecting' that the plaintiff was about to act in a manner prejudicial to the public safety, Darling J nevertheless refused to declare the deportation order ultra vires, being satisfied that the military authorities had acted honestly, even if they 'may have suspected without much reason'.[210] A similarly indulgent view of the powers of the public authorities was taken in *Michaels v Block*[211] where the plaintiff was arrested by order of the military authorities on the basis of information supplied by the Chief Constable of Portsmouth. In an action for damages for his alleged false imprisonment in a prisoner of war camp, the plaintiff argued that he had been wrongfully arrested under regulation 55 which empowered the authorities to arrest any person whose behaviour is of such a nature as to give reasonable grounds for suspecting that he has acted, is acting or is about to act contrary to the public safety. It was argued that this 'highly penal statute . . . must be strictly construed' and that someone could be arrested on account of such behaviour, only if the behaviour in question had been witnessed by the arresting officer. But this was rejected by Darling J who held that '"behaviour" must include all such acts as the competent naval or military authority may be credibly informed of'.[212] Regulation 55 was 'part of legislation passed hurriedly while the country [was] at war', and should be construed according to the maxim *salus populi suprema lex*.[213]

These and other cases provide important insights into the judicial approach to the interpretation of the Regulations by the military and civil authorities. Perhaps more important were those cases such as *R v Halliday*,[214] to which reference has already been made, and which concerned attempts not to test the application of a regulation in any particular case, but to challenge its very validity. This case concerned one Arthur Zadig who had been born in Germany in 1871 and had become a naturalised British subject in 1905. He was interned in October 1915

---

[210] (1918) 34 TLR 556, at p 557. This test for the exercise of the power was laid down (by Lord Reading CJ, Scrutton and Avory JJ agreeing) in *R v Denison, ex parte Nagale* (1916) 85 LJ KB 1744 (the case of the Boston (Lincs) dealer in human hair). *Ronnfeldt* is interesting also because the plaintiff was unable to obtain a copy of the police report on which the decision was based, this being protected by Crown privilege.

[211] (1918) 34 TLR 438.   [212] Ibid.   [213] Ibid.

[214] [1916] 1 KB 738 (King's Bench Division and Court of Appeal); [1917] AC 260 (House of Lords).

under regulation 14B which as we have already seen permitted the internment without trial of 'any person of hostile origin or associations' where
it appeared to the minister expedient for securing the public safety or the
defence of the realm. Detained in an internment centre in Islington, north
London, Zadig issued a writ of habeas corpus addressed to Halliday, the
commandant of the detention centre, arguing that his detention was
unlawful because regulation 14B was ultra vires. Unusually (no doubt
because the case was particularly important), the Lord Chief Justice
presided over a court of five judges.[215] But predictably all five rejected the
application with little ceremony or explanation, despite the significance of
the issue, both in terms of what was being attempted by the applicant (to
invalidate the regulation), and in terms of what was at stake (the liberty
of the individual). The five judgments run to less than three pages of the
Law Reports, the longest being that of the Lord Chief Justice who did at
least manage to turn the page. In doing so he rejected the argument that
the regulation was ultra vires, asserting that 'In the ordinary course in
times of peace, if it had been intended to impose obligations or restrictions upon the subject they would have been submitted to Parliament in
a Bill. But by reason of the emergency arising out of the war and the
necessity of providing for the national safety without delay Parliament
thought that the making of the necessary provisions for that purpose
might be entrusted to His Majesty in Council'.[216] Suffice to say that these
rather vacuous remarks failed to address the rather important points of
principle and substance that had been put by counsel for Zadig.

Although Reading and Darling were thus key figures, they did not sit
in all of the relevant cases and it is also true that in principle their decisions were the subject of appeal. But only two of what we would call the
civil liberties cases were appealed to the Court of Appeal, and in neither
of these was the Divisional Court reversed. The Court of Appeal (members of which also assisted the government during the war)[217] equally

---

[215] Lord Reading CJ, Lawrence, Rowlatt, Atkin and Low JJ. In view of his famous dissent in
Liversidge v Anderson [1942] AC 206 it is not irrelevant to note here that Atkin J thought the regulation 'well within' the powers given by the parent Act and could see 'no reason for invoking any limitations upon it'. In his view 'this is a mere question of prevention' (at p 743). For *Liversidge v Anderson*,
see Chapter 8 below.

[216] [1916] 1 KB 738, at p 741.

[217] For example Pickford J (who became Master of the Rolls as Lord Sterndale) was appointed
to an inquiry into the origin and conduct of operations in the Dardenelles. See Special Commissions
(Dardanelles and Mesopotamia) Act 1916, s 1 where he is expressly named; other members included
Field-Marshal Lord Nicholson and Admiral of the Fleet Sir William May. Pickford also presided
over a conscientious objectors' tribunal, and is said to have done so 'as some in a similar position
did not, judicially'. See *Dictionary of National Biography 1922–1930*, p 679, at p 681. For concern about
the extrajudicial work of the judges see (1918) 62 *Sol Jo* 513.

disposed of Zadig in three pages, with only Swinfen Eady LJ troubling to write.[218] 'Parliament', he wrote, had 'expressed its intention with irresistible clearness'.[219] Counsel for Zadig had argued that the general words of the statute ought not to be construed so as to take away the rights of the subject, but to this Swinfen Eady LJ replied simply by noting that 'in the present case the language of the statute is free from ambiguity'.[220] The point was returned to in the House of Lords,[221] where it was not denied that the literal wording of the enabling Act was wide enough to authorise a measure such as regulation 14B. But 'it was strongly contended that some limitation must be put upon these words, as an unrestricted interpretation might involve extreme consequences', including 'the infliction of the punishment of death without trial'. It was argued further that 'general words in a statute could not take away the vested rights of the subject or alter the fundamental law of the Constitution' and that a construction of the statute 'said to be repugnant to the constitutional traditions of this country could not be adopted'. The drift of the argument would appear to be that in order to make regulations depriving the individual of his or her liberty, express powers would be required, that there was no such power 'for imprisonment without trial', and that the lack of an intention to create such a power was strengthened by the fact that the 1915 Act made specific provision for 'the trial of British subjects by a civil Court with a jury'.[222] But although there was some considerable force in these arguments they were comprehensively rejected by the majority, the only note of equivocation coming in a blistering attack by Lord Shaw of Dunfermline in a dissenting speech,[223] perhaps unprecedented and certainly unequalled, eclipsing by

---

[218] Swinfen Eady LJ was to succeed to the position of Master of the Rolls in 1918 amid concern that the position might be offered to Sir George Cave the Home Secretary, a suggestion that drew the response that high judicial office 'ought not to be made the sport of political circumstances' ((1918) 62 *Sol Jo* 302).

[219] At p 745.   [220] Ibid.

[221] [1917] AC 260, in which remarkably the Lord Chancellor (Finlay) presided, and the Attorney General (F E Smith) and Solicitor General (Sir Gordon Hewart) appeared for the government. The other members of the court were Lord Atkinson (the first Irish barrister to go direct from the Irish Bar to the House of Lords); Lord Wrenbury (famous as H B Buckley in the field of Chancery law generally and company law in particular); Lord Dunedin (a Scottish judge of some distinction who had served in the Conservative Cabinet as Secretary for Scotland between 1903 and 1905); and Lord Shaw of Dunfermline, whom we have already encountered.

[222] At p 268.

[223] Lord Shaw poured scorn on the judgments of the courts below as constituting no less than 'a suspension and a breach of those fundamental constitutional rights which are protective of British liberty' (at p 276). In his view the Defence of the Realm Act did not authorise a power to intern people without trial, tracing the parliamentary history of the legislation and highlighting the care which Parliament had taken particularly in 1915 to provide safeguards for those charged with a breach of the Regulations. With impeccable logic, Lord Shaw thought it improbable that Parliament

far the better known contribution of Lord Atkin twenty-five years later.[224]

In dismissing the appeal (with costs!) the Lord Chancellor thought it 'a sufficient answer' that 'it may be necessary in a time of great public danger to entrust great powers to His Majesty in Council, and that Parliament may do so feeling certain that such powers will be reasonably exercised'.[225] Lord Dunedin thought 'the fault, if fault there be, lies in the fact that the British Constitution has entrusted to the two Houses of Parliament, subject to the assent of the King, an absolute power untrammelled by any written instrument obedience to which may be compelled by some judicial body'.[226] But he did not go so far as to concede the myth of Diceyism, for he went on to say that 'the danger of abuse' was only 'theoretically present' and 'practically, as things exist . . . absent'.[227] Thus were 'a regulation to be framed . . . to intern the Catholics of south Ireland or the Jews of London the result would, I think, be the speedy repeal of the Act which authorises the regulation'.[228] A similarly complacent note was struck by Lord Atkinson who commented that however 'precious the personal liberty of the subject may be, there is something for which it may well be, to some extent, sacrificed by legal enactment, namely, national success in the war, or escape from national plunder or enslavement'.[229] Such deference to the executive in war time is perhaps understandable and perhaps even appropriate, but it was to lead the judges down an unfortunate path which not only made a mockery of Dicey's faith in the self-correcting mechanisms of the British constitution but also led to a total abdication by them of their role.[230] Thus Lord Atkinson confessed that he 'never could appreciate the contention that

had intended that the government could freely avoid protections so scrupulously introduced by the simple expedient of internment to none of which the protections would apply. More generally, he was concerned that the government was effectively claiming unlimited and unreviewable powers of arbitrary government for the duration of the war, becoming in the process a Committee of Public Safety (but with powers 'far more arbitrary than those of the most famous Committee of Public Safety known to history' (at p 291). Pursuing this point he asked whether the powers claimed by the government under the Act would embrace 'a power not only over liberty alone but also over life'. 'If there is a power to lock up a person of hostile origin and associations because the Government judges that course to be for public safety and defence, why, on the same principle and in exercise of the same power', inquired Lord Shaw, 'may he not be shot out of hand?' (at pp 290–1). The Attorney General was left to reply that the 'graver result seemed to be perfectly logical' (at p 291), a reply more extraordinary for the fact that it appeared to leave the majority unmoved.

[224] *Liversidge v Anderson* [1942] AC 206. See Chapter 8 below.
[225] At 268–9. See also his defence of the government against charges that civil liberties had been too readily sacrificed to the war in H L Debs, 7 March 1917, cols 419–22.
[226] At pp 270–1.   [227] At p 271.   [228] Ibid.   [229] At p 271.
[230] For critical assessments of the decision, see (1917) 61 *Sol Jo* 438 and 454; (1917) 33 LQR 206. On the Divisional Court in particular see (1916) 80 JP 61. For a defence see T E Scrutton, 'The War and the Law' (1918) 34 LQR 116, at p 130.

statutes invading the liberty of the subject should be construed after one manner, and statutes not invading it after another',[231] while even more remarkably the Lord Chancellor dismissed the claim that internment should be sanctioned only after judicial inquiry on the ground that no tribunal for investigating the question 'can be imagined less appropriate than a Court of law'.[232]

It was in fact not until the war was over that any change could be detected in the judicial attitude, the judges no longer 'fighting by their sons'.[233] A decision of some significance is *Chester v Bateson*[234] in which the plaintiff challenged the validity of regulation 2A(2) which required landlords to obtain the approval of the Minister of Munitions before instituting proceedings to evict munitions' workers from their homes.[235] In holding a Defence of the Realm Regulation ultra vires for the first time, Darling J asked himself whether 'it is a necessary, or even reasonable, way to aid the securing of public safety and the defence of the realm to give power to a Minister to forbid any person to institute any proceedings to recover possession of a house so long as a war worker is living in it'.[236] In answering his own question in the negative, Darling J replied that an 'extreme disability' of this kind 'can be inflicted only by direct enactment of the Legislature itself, and that so grave an invasion of the rights of all subjects was not intended by the Legislature to be accomplished by a departmental order such as this one of the Minister of Munitions'.[237] In a concurring judgment, Avory J (also to be accorded the honour in 1932 of being made a Privy Councillor while a serving judge) commented that the purpose behind the regulation was 'without doubt' reasonable, namely to prevent the disturbance of munitions workers in their homes.[238] The regulation was, however, objectionable to the extent that it deprived 'the King's subjects of their right of access to the Courts of justice and renders them liable to punishment if they have the temerity to ask for justice in any of the King's Courts'.[239] In his view, nothing less than 'express words in the statute' would authorise or justify a measure of this kind.[240] In the same vein Sankey J wrote that he would be 'slow to hold that Parliament ever conferred such a power unless it expressed it in the clearest possible language, and should never hold that it was given indirectly by ambiguous regulations made in pursuance of any Act'.[241]

[231] At p 274.   [232] At p 269.   [233] Scrutton, n 230 above, at p 117.
[234] [1920] 1 KB 829.   [235] See S R & O 1917 No 1008.
[236] [1920] 1 KB 829, at p 833.   [237] Ibid.
[238] At p 835.   [239] At p 836.   [240] [1920] 1 KB 829, at p 836.   [241] Ibid, at p 838.

Chester v Bateson represents a softening of judicial attitudes which was reflected in the same year in a decision of Salter J quashing an order of the military authorities for the requisitioning under regulation 2B of 239 puncheons of rum.[242] The standard of review had suddenly changed, with Darling J now requiring the government to show that regulations were necessary or at least reasonable for the promotion of statutory objectives rather than merely being (at its highest in war-time) 'reasonably capable of being a regulation for securing the public safety and defence of the realm',[243] a standard so low that it permitted regulations authorising the requisition of a crop of raspberries.[244] The established canons of construction were suddenly restored, with the Divisional Court now requiring personal liberty to be compromised only by express powers whereas in *Halliday* these had been surrendered to the needs of war. *Chester v Bateson* is in fact a very awkward case, serving to illuminate the extent to which in a time of national stress, when the need for judicial vigilance was greatest, the courts fell into line behind the administration, in the same way as an army might fall into line behind its generals. (It was thus not only in the munitions industry that there was a clear dilution of standards!) Also unfortunate is the fact that *Chester v Bateson* was about asserting claims in respect of private property (which were seen to attract a sympathetic judicial response) whereas cases like *Halliday*, *Ronnfeldt* and *Michaels* were about rather more serious questions relating to personal liberty (which were seen to attract judicial indifference), thereby inviting some obvious political conclusions to be drawn. A vigorous application of the standard of review and the canons of construction adopted in *Chester v Bateson* would have yielded a much different outcome in *Halliday* (and in other cases as well) and would have gone some way to protect the easy erosion of civil liberties during the war. It

---

[242] *Newcastle Breweries Ltd v R* (1920) 36 TLR 276 (on the ground that it denied those whose goods had been requisitioned of their right to a fair market value and to a judicial determination of the amount). See G R Rubin, *Private Property*, n 39 above, ch 8. See also *Attorney General v Wilts United Dairies Ltd* (1921) 37 TLR 884 (CA), reversing (1921) 37 TLR 296 (Bailhache J). See too *Attorney General v De Keyser's Royal Hotel Ltd* [1920] AC 508 which was perhaps an even more pronounced illustration of a sea change in judicial attitudes after the war. According to Lord MacMillan in an obituary of Lord Dunedin who delivered the leading judgment it was a vindication of 'the right of the owner of property requisitioned by the Crown for the defence of the realm to receive compensation' (*Dictionary of National Biography 1941–1950*, p 608, at p 610).

[243] *Lipton Ltd v Ford* [1917] 2 KB 647, at p 654 (Atkin J). Cf *R v Halliday*, n 214 above, esp per Lord Atkinson where he raised the possibility that the courts might intervene to declare ultra vires and void a regulation which 'enjoined or required something to be done which could not in any reasonable way aid in securing the public safety and the defence of the realm' (at p 272). But see also Lord Wrenbury at p 307 who suggested that it was enough that the power was exercised 'honestly'.

[244] See *Lipton Ltd v Ford*, n 243 above. But the shift was not universal. Compare the Lord Chief Justice in *R v Inspector of Leman Street Police Station, ex parte Venicoff* [1920] 3 KB 72.

was not only Darling J who was prepared to surrender the rule of law to
the maxim *salus populi suprema lex*.[245]

Conclusion

The First World War was the most serious crisis which the emerging
democratic State had yet to face. It was also the most significant period
this century in terms of its impact and the legacy it bequeathed to the
law and practice of civil liberties. For it is not an exaggeration to say that
the way in which the crisis was met has had an enduring impact on the
power of the State on the one hand, and the political and personal freedoms of the individual on the other. Thus it serves to consolidate several
of the themes identified in Chapter 1, such as the idealism rather than
the accuracy of Dicey's Rule of Law. The Defence of the Realm Acts
1914–1915 were hardly a triumph of the ordinary law: 'never in our history has the Executive assumed such arbitrary power over the life, liberty and property of British subjects'.[246] Nor could the response of the
courts to these powers be in any way described as a triumph of the 'general principles of the constitution', at least to the extent that these were
defined to include 'the right to personal liberty'. The way in which the
crisis was met also exposes as ill-founded the attempt by Dicey to suggest
that his principle of the Rule of Law and the principle of parliamentary
sovereignty were somehow inevitably complementary. Although the latter is an essential pre-condition of democracy, the idea that Parliament
would protect the people from oppression appeared rather less sustainable in 1918 than it did in 1914, while the idea that the judges would
moderate the impact of legislation (which was 'never really unlimited')
did not seem to mean so much after the *Halliday* case. Zadig's continued
detention is surely not what Dicey had in mind when he wrote of legislation being interpreted in accordance with the 'general spirit of the common law'.

In terms of the other themes underlying this book, it is clear that the
war-time experience raised important questions of constitutional principle
and constitutional practice. So far as questions of *constitutional principle* are
concerned, the most important lesson relates to the effect of the war on
the principle of legality. Although not an example of the primacy of ordinary law, it can hardly be a matter for criticism or condemnation that
the government operated during war-time under emergency powers. But

---

[245] *Ronnfeldt v Phillips* (1918) 34 TLR 438, at p 438.
[246] Baty and Morgan, n 36 above, p 112.

there is nevertheless a balance to be struck between having the powers necessary to conduct the war on the one hand, and upholding the constitutional principles in whose name conflict is often justified on the other. So far as the principle of legality is concerned, it was sacrificed initially in the Defence of the Realm Act 1914, a statute which was thought inadequate to bear the load of the extensive powers taken in its name: there had never been 'any statutory regulations which appeared to outrun so breathlessly the statutory powers actually conferred'.[247] And it was sacrificed subsequently by the amending Defence of the Realm Consolidation Act 1914 which admittedly gave power to the government to issue regulations 'for securing the public safety and the defence of the realm', but in doing so conferred so wide a discretion as effectively to give an unlimited power to enable the executive to do as it wished. The granting by Parliament to the executive of so much discretion was matched only by its failure to ensure even a modest level of scrutiny and accountability: there was no requirement that the regulations should be approved by Parliament. It was for the government and the government alone to decide what was to be done to secure the public safety and the defence of the realm.[248]

But apart from the assumption of such power by the government, for all practical purposes a power without limits, constitutional principle was undermined also by the extraordinarily close relationship between the executive and the judiciary. Here was a government acting under the authority of legal rules which it had a free hand in drafting without any effective parliamentary accountability, supervised by courts many of whose judges were actively engaged in a non-judicial capacity in assisting the very government it was their constitutional duty to control. It is straining credulity in these circumstances to contemplate a vital concept of legality, certainly to the extent suggested in Chapter 1 above. Even in war-time there is an expectation that a measure of constitutional government will survive, an essential precondition of which is the independence of the judiciary. But as with Parliament, some of the judges exposed themselves as being badly compromised not only by serving the

---

[247] Ibid, p 80.

[248] The point ought perhaps not to be exaggerated, for there were a few brave souls, in both the Commons and the Lords, who were prepared to question the administration and who as a result won a number of concessions, which were to benefit the peace movement in particular. Civil liberties issues were also raised from time to time in the course of debates. See for example H L Debs, 7 March 1917, col 402, with a notable intervention by Lord Parmoor who attacked the threat to civil liberties, particularly by internment without trial, the restrictions on free discussion, and the holding of trials in camera.

interests of government while simultaneously continuing to hear cases, but also by throwing their weight so uncompromisingly behind the government and '*salus populi*' in the cases which came before the courts for adjudication. It is true that the judges could not challenge the primary legislation which gave the government so much power in the first place.[249] They were, nevertheless, obliged to ensure that government powers were not over-reached, a responsibility which was at least recognised by Bailhache J when he wrote in one case that the courts were specially charged to safeguard the liberty of the subject 'as one of their most sacred duties'.[250] But apart from the lone voice of Lord Shaw of Dunfermline in the Zadig case there is little evidence of this rhetoric being translated into reality, the House of Lords and the other courts being content to leave the matter to the good sense of Parliament.

So far as *constitutional practice* is concerned, the problems here flow inexorably from the defects of constitutional principle which we have identified. The war effectively saw the formal suspension of civil liberties, with elections postponed indefinitely and the freedom to oppose existing only to the extent that it was tolerated by the authorities. The government responded ruthlessly, by using its control of the law-making machinery (in this case by the making of regulations) not only to take powers to control dissent, but also to use these powers to intimidate and suppress its critics. We have seen the introduction of wide-ranging measures for the internal exile and internment without trial of people resident in this country (including British subjects), and the restriction of freedom of expression by measures designed on the one hand to protect military information and on the other to control dissent and opposition by prohibiting the publication of false or seditious information. In certain prescribed circumstances the authorities could seize and destroy 'any type or other plant used or capable of being used for the printing or production of the newspaper', thereby in effect suppressing the newspaper in question. We have also encountered examples of these powers being used, including the raid on the premises of the *Labour Leader*, the pacifist ILP newspaper, and more remarkably the temporary suppression of *Forward*, the Scottish socialist newspaper which had published an account of Lloyd George's humiliation at the hands of the Clydeside shop stewards. The imprisonment of Morel of the UDC, and John MacLean, the Glasgow revolutionary, serve only to reinforce the point that dissent

---

[249] Though for disappointment at the performance of the American judges who could, see F Pollock, 'Abrams v United States' (1920) 36 LQR 334.

[250] *R v Vine Street Police Station Superintendent, ex parte Liebmann* [1916] 1 KB 268, at p 275.

would not be tolerated, as do the imprisonment and deportation of the shop stewards who were concerned as much with the erosion of living standards as they were with opposition to the war.

Yet although these developments were clearly of great importance, the practical effects of the war and the war-time measures extended long beyond the victory of 1918. As an editorial note in the Statutory Rules and Orders for 1920 points out, 'Certain provisions of the Defence of the Realm Regulations and certain orders made thereunder have to varying extents been incorporated in the Statute Book by Act of Parliament',[251] including the Firearms Act 1920, the Dangerous Drugs Act 1920, and the Shops (Early Closing) Act 1920.[252] But perhaps more significantly they also included the Official Secrets Act 1920 which was introduced in order to strengthen (rather than repeal) the Official Secrets Act 1911, which had been passed during the phoney war and which continued to be invoked during the war itself.[253] It is true of course that not all of the Defence of the Realm Regulations were absorbed into the legislation passed immediately after the war and that most of the regulations were in fact simply revoked.[254] On the other hand, however, it is equally true that the process of absorption did continue in the sense that the restrictive general legislation of the 1930s—such as the Incitement to Disaffection Act 1934 and the Public Order Act 1936—can trace its ancestry back to at least some of the war-time Orders in Council. Here again what began life as emergency powers to deal with the defence of the realm gradually became part of the general law and as such part of the peace-time powers of the public authorities for dealing with dissent and opposition. It was also the case that the government's attraction to emergency powers authorising wide-ranging legislation led to the enactment of the Emergency Powers Act 1920,[255] a measure which it was said 'rivets for all time the provisions of [the] Defence of the Realm Act Regulations on the country'.[256] The 1920 Act forms part of the story of the next two chapters.

[251] Statutory Rules and Orders 1920, vol 1, p 468.
[252] See also the Aliens Restriction (Amendment) Act 1919 which extended the 1914 Act in the sense that for a year after its enactment, the powers contained in the latter could be exercised at any time, and not just when a state of war existed or when there was some other imminent national danger or great emergency, as the 1914 Act required. The 1919 Act also introduced further restrictions on aliens generally, and on former enemy aliens in particular.
[253] See (1916) 70 JP 148; (1918) 72 JP 276.
[254] Though this did not happen immediately with the end of the war (see Termination of the Present War (Definition) Act 1918 and War Emergency Laws (Continuance) Act 1920), with Defence of the Realm Regulations being prolonged and deployed in a manner for which they could hardly have been intended. See *Inkpin v Roll* (1922) 86 JP 61, and Chapter 3 below.
[255] See G S Morris, 'The Emergency Powers Act 1920' [1979] PL 317.
[256] H C Debs, 25 October 1920, col 1420.

3

The Communist Party of Great Britain

Having dealt with the threat to civil liberties during the First World War, we turn our attention now to the emergence of the Communist Party of Great Britain (CPGB) and the steps taken by the public authorities to suppress it. The reaction to the rise of communism at times bordered on the hysterical and the full panoply of State power was used—unsuccessfully—to crush it. We begin this chapter by outlining the formation and objects of the Party in order to place the reaction of the public authorities in proper perspective. We then consider the response of the authorities, which as well as prosecutions under emergency regulations, included various forms of surveillance, and restrictions on freedom of expression and freedom of assembly. These different forms of State harassment culminated in the sedition trial of 1925 which led to the imprisonment of leading CPGB officers for periods of between twelve and eighteen months. Despite the contemporary notoriety and importance of this case, it has largely washed over generations of law students who will find no reference to it in any of the standard textbooks on civil liberties which are currently in use.[1] The suppression of communism did not, however, end with the 1925 trial. Restrictions on free speech and public assembly introduced during the General Strike of 1926 appeared to apply disproportionately against communists, a matter which we address in Chapter 4.

The remarkable feature of the State response to communism was its relative informality so far as the student of law is concerned. The crusade against communism in the 1920s did not produce more than a single case considered worthy of reporting in the Law Reports.[2] The big political trials which did take place leave few traces and are available mainly in newspaper reports. They are, however, worth retrieving and this we have attempted to do. By the same token the crusade against communism was conducted without the need to enact special legislation. Admittedly the Emergency Powers Act 1920 permitted emergency regulations to be made to deal with the consequences of large-scale industrial

---

[1] There is, however, a brief account in D G T Williams, *Keeping the Peace* (1967), pp 185–6.
[2] *Inkpin v Roll* (1922) 86 JP 61. The next major case was *Elias v Pasmore* [1934] 2 KB 164.

unrest,[3] which would include the campaign work of the communists and their sympathisers. But the only direct statutory initiative was the Incitement to Disaffection Act 1934—a response to communist attempts to subvert members of the armed forces. Yet this was rather belated— even if MI5 had campaigned for something along these lines ever since 1921—and its absence did not in any way inhibit the prosecutions of 1925. All of which is to state the obvious, namely that the threat to political freedom and civil liberties can arise in a variety of forms and from the State in all of its guises—executive, legislative and judicial. In this chapter we seek to show how these different branches of government were deployed against the Communist Party of Great Britain and in the process we endeavour to retrieve a story which so far has fallen outside the boundaries of traditional legal education.

Formation, Principles and Tactics

The Russian Revolution took place in October 1917, giving rise to consequences (such as the nationalisation of the banks) which were 'not an agreeable task for a British Court of Justice to consider'.[4] In January 1919, writes Pelling, 'the Russian Bolsheviks announced the formation of a Communist International (Comintern)' conference in Moscow later that year.[5] But because of hostility to the Revolution and the blockading of Russia, it was difficult for British representatives to attend. However, the Marxist parties which already existed in Britain—including the British Socialist Party and the Socialist Labour Party—'realised the significance of the occasion and began to consider how they could consolidate themselves into a Communist Party, so as to become a component of the new International'.[6] Encouraged by the Communist International to 'drop their differences and form a united party',[7] the Communist Party of Great Britain, founded 'on the basis of the Soviet system, the dictatorship of the proletariat and affiliation to the Third International',[8] was established at a Unity Convention held in London in July 1920.[9] Apart from the British Socialist Party and the Socialist Labour Party,

---

[3] The Act could in principle be used where the emergency was caused by other factors, though it never has been.

[4] *Russian Commercial and Industrial Bank v Comptoir D'Escompte de Mulhouse* [1925] AC 112, at p 123, per Cave LC.

[5] H Pelling, *The British Communist Party: A Historical Profile* (1958), p 5.

[6] Ibid.   [7] Ibid, p 6.

[8] L J MacFarlane, *The British Communist Party: Its Origin and Development until 1929* (1966), p 56. See CPGB, *Constitution and Rules* (1921).

[9] See *Official Report of the Communist Unity Conference* (1920).

those represented included the Workers' Socialist Federation, the South Wales Socialist Society and the National Shop Stewards' and Workers' Committee Movement. These different organisations were not always unanimous in their support for the venture, and it appears that the 159 delegates represented anything from between 4,000 and 5,125 people. Several hundred others were brought into the Party shortly afterwards by the absorption of a number of other groups, including the Communist Labour Party (based in Scotland) and Sylvia Pankhurst's Workers' Socialist Federation (which had changed its name to the Communist Party (British Section of the Third International)).[10]

The new party was the British section of the Communist International,[11] the statutes of which stated in the preamble that its aim was 'to fight by all available means, including armed struggle, for the overthrow of the international bourgeoisie and for the creation of an international Soviet republic as a transitional stage to the complete abolition of the State'.[12] The dictatorship of the proletariat was said to be the only possible way to liberate mankind from the horrors of capitalism. The supreme authority of the Communist International was the World Congress of all the national parties, which was to meet annually to discuss and 'decide the most important questions of programme and tactics'. Congress was also charged with the responsibility of electing the Executive Committee of the Communist International which had authority under the statutes to issue instructions which were binding on all parties and organisations belonging to the International. The executive also had the power to demand that parties expel groups or persons who offended against international discipline, and the right to expel from the International those parties which violated decisions of the World Congress. According to MacFarlane, the major influence with the Executive Committee was the Russian Party. 'It alone had successfully made a revolution', he wrote, 'and its leaders, especially Lenin and Trotsky, were accepted as the masters of revolutionary strategy'. The domination of the Russian Party was increased by the fact that Moscow became the permanent home of the International as a result of the failure of the Revolution to spread. The statutes appeared, at least in form,

[10] See MacFarlane, n 8 above, pp 56–72. See also on the formation of the party, J Klugmann, 'The Foundation of the Communist Party of Great Britain' (1960) 4 *Marxism Today* 1; J Klugmann, *History of the Communist Party of Great Britain*, vol 1 (1968), ch 1.

[11] 'The Party is affiliated to, and adheres to the Statutes and Theses of the Communist International': CPGB, *Constitution and Rules* (1921).

[12] The Theses and Statutes of the Third International are reproduced in J Degras (ed), *The Communist International 1919–1943, Documents, Vol.1 1919–1922* (1956).

to anticipate the possibility of the seat of both the World Congress and the Executive Committee being movable annually.

Two days after the adoption of the statutes of the Communist International, the second Congress approved Conditions of Admission to the International.[13] The aim here was to exclude social democratic or reformist elements and to eliminate the danger of 'dilution by unstable and irresolute groups'. Some of the twenty-one conditions appeared to go beyond this and are of particular interest in the light of subsequent responses by the public authorities in Britain. Thus condition 3 stated that communists 'are obliged everywhere to create a parallel illegal organisation which at the decisive moment will help the party to do its duty to the revolution'. Also important was condition 4 which imposed a duty 'to carry on systematic and energetic propaganda in the army'. Where such agitation was prevented by emergency laws, 'it must be carried on illegally'. A similar obligation was imposed by condition 9 in respect of trade unions, in the sense that every party wishing to join the International 'must carry on systematic and persistent communist activity inside the trade unions, the workers' councils and factory committees, the co-operatives, and other mass workers' organisations'. Communist cells which 'must be completely subordinate to the party as a whole' were to be established in these organisations which would be won for the communist cause by 'persistent and unflagging' work. Finally for present purposes, we may note condition 14 which provided that every party wishing to join the International was obliged to give unconditional support to any Soviet republic in its struggle against counter-revolutionary forces. They were also to carry on 'unambiguous propaganda' to prevent the dispatch of munitions to the enemies of the Soviet republics.

The close connection with Moscow no doubt explains the hostility and suspicion displayed by the public authorities in London. 'Like the Roman Catholic minority of the Elizabethan age', writes Pelling, 'the Communists were feared not only for their own revolutionary potential but also because they seemed to be the agents of a hostile foreign power'.[14] But the connections were not only ideological: it was well-known in government circles that from its earliest days the Party was funded by the Third International which provided 'considerable financial aid'.[15] According to a Home Office report in 1922, up until March

---

[13] This document is also reproduced in Degras, ibid. See also MacFarlane, n 8 above, pp 62–3.
[14] Pelling, n 5 above, pp 27–8.
[15] PRO CAB 24/166, CP 273 (24), Cabinet Committee on Industrial Unrest, 30 April 1924, Appendix, p 4.

1922 roughly £60,000 was received, and during that year a further £80,000 was allotted. The Third International was also known to subsidise the expenses of party candidates at general elections (with £2,500 being made available in 1924) and to pay for the salaries of full-time party officials such as William Gallacher. Yet despite this financial support, the Party was 'constantly in great financial difficulties which appear[ed] to be due to the comparatively heavy expenditure which [was] incurred on literary propaganda'. The Party not only received money from abroad, but also was given instructions as to how it should be spent, it being reported for example that in December 1923 the Executive Committee of the Third International (IKKI) instructed the British Party 'to endeavour to raise the circulation of Communist press (sic) and utilize not less than 30 per cent of the income of the Party including the subsidy of the IKKI in combating the Government . . . and the bourgeousie by means of printed matter'.[16]

Yet despite support from overseas, and despite being 'extremely active',[17] Party membership remained very small for the first decade of its life, and did not reach 5,000 until June 1925, climbing steadily from 2,000 in 1921. It is true that membership doubled to over 10,000 between June 1925 and October 1926, during the historic miners' lockout of that year. But thereafter it began to slide again, falling to 3,200 in December 1929 and 2,555 in November 1930.[18] Circulation of the Party's newspapers was rather higher, though *The Communist* (1921–1923) never exceeded 60,000 and the *Workers' Weekly* (1923–1927) peaked at 80,000. By the end of the decade the *Workers' Life* (1927–1929)) had fallen back to 24,000.[19] Yet despite its relatively small membership, the Party operated on a number of fronts. With Lenin's encouragement,[20] it was committed to both parliamentary action and to seeking affiliation to the Labour Party, which was immediately refused.[21] It was, however,

[16] This paragraph draws on PRO, CAB 24/166, CP 273 (24), ibid. See also pp 149–50 below.

[17] Ibid, para 3.

[18] The figures relating to Party membership are not uncontroversial. These are drawn from MacFarlane, n 8 above, App D, as are the circulation figures for the Party's newspapers. For an account of the Party press, see Klugmann, *History*, n 10 above, pp 213–21.

[19] *The Communist* folded after it had libelled J H Thomas. The *Workers' Weekly* suffered a similar fate. See *The Times*, 25 November 1926, and the *Workers' Weekly*, 21 January 1927. The proprietor and editor of the newspaper were also sentenced to four months' imprisonment in a separate incident for criminal libel. See *The Times*, 5 March 1927. Libel proceedings were also instituted against *The Sunday Worker* in 1927. See *The Times*, 3 May 1927. See further, p 203 below, n 257.

[20] On which see his letter to the Unity Conference: *Official Report of the Communist Unity Conference* (1920), p 64.

[21] The saga is rehearsed in the CPGB pamphlet, *The Communist Party and the Labour Party. All the Facts and All the Correspondence* [n d].

possible for members of the CPGB also to be members of the Labour Party and to stand as Labour Party candidates at local and parliamentary elections.[22] Indeed, at the general election in 1922, two communist candidates were elected, one of whom 'stood as an official Labour candidate and the other as a Communist but without Labour opposition'.[23] It was not until 1924 that Labour ruled Communists ineligible to stand as Labour Party candidates,[24] and it was not until 1925 that it ruled that members of the CPGB were ineligible to be individual members of the Party,[25] although they could still attend party conference as trade union delegates.[26]

So far as trade union work is concerned, the Red International of Labour Unions (known as Profintern) had been formed in Moscow in 1920 to promote the political and industrial tactics of the International. As MacFarlane points out, the CPGB was as a result 'the first party in Britain to attempt to draw all its members into trade union activity'.[27] Under the direction of Profintern, however, the tactic of organising independent revolutionary unions was rejected in the case of Britain in favour of revolutionary work within the existing trade unions. The aim was 'to carry the policy of the party into the trade unions by organising its members at branch, district and executive level. In this way it was hoped to ensure that the attitude taken up by party members on an issue which arose in any area would be determined by the needs of the class struggle and not by the purely local or sectional interests of those directly involved'.[28] The engine for this work was to be a body born in 1924 under the name of the National Minority Movement. According to MacFarlane:

The militant trade unionists in the Minority Movement would act through Minority Movement groups to influence the policy of their union branches along lines determined by the Communist leaders of the Movement. In time it was hoped that the Minority Movement would become the majority movement in the trade unions. This would open the way to transforming them from bodies

[22] For background. see R McKibbin, *The Evolution of the Labour Party 1910–1924* (1974), pp 191–205.

[23] Pelling, n 5 above, p 25. On parliamentary activity, see Klugmann, *History*, n 10 above, pp 181–94.

[24] See *Labour Party Report 1924*, pp 38–40 for a justification of this decision by the National Executive Committee.

[25] Ibid, p 131. According to Ernest Bevin, 'the Communists could not conscientiously reconcile the Communist basis with the basis of evolutionary democracy that the Labour Party represented: *Labour Party Report 1925*, p 183. For a full account, see Klugmann, *History*, n 10 above, pp 309–24.

[26] This, however, was discouraged in 1925, and affiliated organisations were asked to take steps to avoid it. See *Labour Party Report 1925*, p 38.

[27] MacFarlane, n 8 above.   [28] Ibid.

concerned with trying to improve the conditions of the workers under capitalism to a movement dedicated to the overthrow of capitalism itself.[29]

Although not a Party organisation, Party members also played a leading role in the National Unemployed Workers' Committee Movement, set up in 1921, for which Wal Hannington, a prominent communist, became National Organiser.[30] The history of the Movement is part of the history of the Public Order Act 1936, to which we return in Chapters 5 and 6.

The Special Branch

Pelling records that throughout its early years the Communist Party had 'to grow accustomed to the bitter hostility of public opinion and the close surveillance of the police'.[31] For those on the Left this was not unusual, as the war-time experience of the Clydeside socialists and others makes clear. Nevertheless, the formation of the Party was viewed with some concern by the Special Branch which evidently allocated considerable resources to counteract the threat which it was perceived to present, a responsibility which it shared with the secret service.[32] The Special Branch had been established in 1883 in order to track down Irish nationalists who were planting bombs in London, though before the war its activities extended also to assisting the secret service in the hunt for German spies. In 1913 it was given a 'new and dynamic head' in the form of Sir Basil Thomson, son of the provost of Queen's College Oxford and Archbishop of York. Educated at Eton and New College Oxford, Thomson had a varied career, serving in the colonial service in Fiji, Tonga (of which he was Prime Minister) and British New Guinea, followed by a spell as governor of a number of prisons which included Dartmoor and Wormwood Scrubs.[33] As assistant commissioner of police from 1913 it 'fell to his lot to combat suffragettes and, even before the outbreak of war in 1914, enemy espionage'.[34] Indeed it has been said that 'such was the completeness of the preparations made to meet that

---

[29] MacFarlane, ibid, p 117.

[30] See J Stevenson and C Cook, *The Slump: Society and Politics during the Depression* (1977), ch 9. See also Chapter 5 below.

[31] Pelling, n 5 above, p 27.

[32] On the role of the secret service and the tensions between it and the Special Branch, see C Andrew, *Secret Service* (1986), chs 5, 7, 9 10 and 11. The relationship between MI5 and the Special Branch generally, and in relation to the surveillance of the CPGB in particular, is obscure. In 1914 Viscount Haldane acknowledged that the former worked closely with the Metropolitan Police and in particular with the 'Special Branch of the Criminal Investigation Department': H L Debs, 25 November 1914, col 145.

[33] *Dictionary of National Biography 1931–1940*, p 857.   [34] Ibid.

emergency that it was possible for the police to lay their hands on almost all enemy agents'.[35] It is open to question whether this success was due to MI5 rather than the Special Branch, though it is clear that Thomson brought an extraordinary degree of enthusiasm to his work in combating communism, writing on one occasion that since the Armistice he had been 'concerned with the Red propaganda from Moscow which had fascinated the Labour extremists in England'.[36] In cynical and offensive vein, he continued by asserting that there was a 'yearning appetite for a share of the Bolshevist fund which was being spent in western Europe to foment the "world revolution" so ardently desired by the Moscovite Jews in Moscow'.[37] Such is the nature of the people we have in the past employed to defend our liberty.

From the time of the Armistice, Thomson provided the Cabinet with regular reports 'on the progress of revolutionary organisations', these being produced on a weekly basis from May 1919.[38] In 1920, some time before the Communist Unity Conference, he also prepared a paper on 'Revolutionaries and the Need for Legislation' which was circulated by the Home Secretary to the Cabinet.[39] Here he argued that it was remarkable that 'with the example of the special Anti-Revolutionary Legislation found necessary in Canada and the United States, it is still not illegal in England to advocate the abolition of Parliament and the setting up of Soviet Government, to circulate Bolshevik literature, to accept money from abroad for revolutionary agitation, and to be a secret representative of the Russian Soviet Government, provided that one does not advocate acts of violence or armed rebellion'. The paper, together with its recommendation for legislation, was considered at a Conference of Ministers on 25 February 1920 at which a Committee was appointed to prepare a draft Bill for consideration by the Cabinet.[40] But it was not until May in the following year that the first draft of the misnamed Preservation of Public Order Bill 1921 was considered by the Home Affairs Committee of the Cabinet.[41] Under the Bill which for the most part was not intended to 'create any new offences',[42] it was proposed to make sedition a statutory offence, and also to make it an offence to

[35] Ibid.

[36] B Thomson, *The Scene Changes* (1939), p 387.   [37] Ibid.

[38] Andrew, n 32 above, p 337.

[39] PRO, CAB 24/97, Special Report No 14, 2 February 1920. See T Young, *Incitement to Disaffection* (1976), p 31.

[40] PRO, CAB 23/20, Conference of Ministers.

[41] For a note of the conclusions of the Committee (with a draft Bill) see PRO, CAB 24/125, CP 3007, 1 June 1921.

[42] PRO, CAB 23/25, Cabinet Home Affairs Committee, 27 April 1921.

import literature the publication of which would be an offence under the Bill. Equally important was the proposal that prosecutions could be instituted by solemn or summary procedure, a response to the concern that prosecuting under indictment for the existing common law of sedition was too cumbersome. By this time, however, a national coal dispute was underway and it was thought inexpedient to legislate until it was over. But in any event the Home Affairs Committee was divided on the wisdom of legislation, with the Chairman of the Committee expressing himself 'very reluctant to advertise that the country was subject to real danger from revolutionary agitation', preferring 'to trust to the common sense of the working classes, who, in his experience, were generally contemptuous of the revolutionary speeches of street-corner orators'.[43] The Bill was presented to the Cabinet without any policy recommendations.[44]

Thomson was not to see his proposals come to fruition, some members of the Home Affairs Committee concerned also that 'the powers in the Bill would lend themselves to the possibility of great abuse, and would be regarded by many as an attack on the liberty of the subject'.[45] The pressure for legislation was, however, maintained by his successor who was appointed following Thomson's enforced resignation in November 1921. Although he was 'not in the least bit keen'[46] to assume this particular mantle, contemplating business, the bar or politics, Major General Sir Wyndham Childs (who had been a staff officer in the War Office since 1910) did not appear to need much persuasion, claiming that the Communist Party was composed of 'some three thousand wasters, workshies, half-wits and professional agitators'. There is little doubt that Childs saw the Party as being very dangerous and little doubt also that he saw the solution as being to 'smash the organisation'.[47] Indeed he claims that 'it was impressed upon [him] by the particular representative of the Government concerned with these matters that here actually lay the most important part of [his] work'. Childs was to lament, however, that he spent the seven best years of his life 'trying to induce various Governments' to allow him 'to use the full force of the Law, or if the Law was not sufficiently comprehensive, to give [him] legislation'. But he 'wasted' his time in a 'fruitless endeavour', unable to comprehend 'why the successive Governments [he] served always refused to strike one overwhelming and final blow against the Communist organisation'.[48] Although he had 'never been blind to the difficulties of trying the

---

[43] PRO, CAB 23/26, Cabinet Home Affairs Committee, 31 May 1921.   [44] Ibid, p 4.
[45] PRO, CAB 23/25, Cabinet Home Affairs Committee, 27 April 1921.
[46] Sir W Childs, *Episodes and Reflections* (1930), p 185.   [47] Ibid, p 209.   [48] Ibid.

leaders of the organisation for seditious libel or seditious conspiracy', in his view 'these difficulties have never been insuperable' and could have been overcome 'with a little energy and determination'.[49]

It is clear that along with others in the intelligence business, Childs lobbied for legislation with which to attack the communists, offended it seems by the 'sedition' which 'poured forth' from its bookshop 'at sums varying from 2s 6d to 1d'.[50] He applauded the attempt by a few backbenchers who introduced private members Bills which would have given him the power he sought, but despaired when 'these bills died the usual death from want of milk from the Government cow'.[51] He must have been particularly scornful of the 1924 Labour government under which he served,[52] for it is clear that it tended to underplay the communist 'menace', though paradoxically it was this which was to prove its undoing not once but twice in 1924. True, the activities of the CPGB were considered by the Labour Cabinet and indeed a Cabinet Committee on Industrial Unrest was appointed to investigate the extent of communist activity in strikes and industrial disputes.[53] But no doubt to the alarm of the Special Branch it was reported that 'while the Communist party have undoubtedly intervened in recent industrial disputes with a view to their prolongation and extension and have done their best to persuade workers to reject the advice and instructions of the Trade Unions concerned, there is little evidence (save perhaps in one or two cases) that the Communists have actually themselves initiated a dispute'. Indeed the Committee appeared firmly of the view that 'the importance and influence of the Communists in these matters may be and is often greatly exaggerated and their misguided activities are credited with consequences which in fact are attributable to quite different causes'.[54] It is hardly surprising then that 'after careful consideration' the Committee should have concluded that 'no useful purpose would be served by, and considerable harm might result from, any attempt by the Government to take legal proceedings against the Communists', though 'the possibility of so doing must not . . . be altogether excluded'.[55]

In view of the attitude of the short-lived Labour administration, Childs was clearly cheered when the Conservatives were elected to government in 1924 'with a colossal majority'; it was at this point that he confessed that

---

[49] Childs, n 46 above, p 210.   [50] Ibid, p 209.   [51] Ibid, p 210.
[52] On which see T Barnes, 'Special Branch and the First Labour Government' (1979) 22 *Historical Journal* 941.
[53] PRO, CAB 23/48, Cabinet 27 (24), 15 April 1924.
[54] PRO, CAB 24/166, CP 273 (24), n 15 above.   [55] Ibid.

his hopes 'ran high', for two reasons. In the first place 'pledges had been given before the election that if the existing Law was not strong enough to deal with Communism, legislation would be taken', while secondly Childs 'recognised in the person of Sir William Joynson-Hicks, the incoming Home Secretary, a man who had the courage and energy to deal with the menace of Communism'. Childs (nicknamed 'Fido' for the obvious reason) claims never to have received 'greater support' from any Home Secretary than from Joynson-Hicks, whose 'enthusiasm almost exceeded' his own, and who 'had he had his way' would have ensured that 'there would be no Communist Party in England today'. Yet despite this political support, and despite having written 'countless memoranda' and having 'put forward countless proposals', looking back over the period of the Baldwin government, Childs saw 'no milestones showing progress'. True, the matter was revisited by the Cabinet in October 1925 when on the advice of the Attorney General,[56] a small committee was established to consider the matter.[57] But again the Committee (whose members included Joynson-Hicks) recommended against legislation at that time on the ground that it would serve 'no useful purpose' while simultaneously arguing that it was 'desirable to formulate legislation on the general lines of the draft Preservation of Public Order Bill [1921]'. Correctly anticipating problems which were to arise in the following decade, the Committee observed that 'except in moments of national crisis, the passage through Parliament of proposals for dealing with sedition presents exceptional difficulties, and there is every reason to believe that future attempts to legislate would meet with even greater opposition and obstruction'. Concern was expressed that to proceed with any Bill would be extremely contentious and could even 'precipitate an industrial crisis'.[58]

But although Childs was disappointed about the lack of any special powers taken to deal with communist subversion, this is not to say that his political masters were indifferent to the problem.[59] Indeed the contrary is the case, with a number of sometimes brutal steps being taken throughout the 1920s in what appears to have been a sustained, relent-

---

[56] PRO, CAB/175, CP 420 (25). Memorandum by the Attorney General on The Present Law in Regard to Sedition and Strikes, 9 October 1925.

[57] PRO, CAB 23/51, Cabinet 48 (25), 13 October 1925.

[58] PRO, CAB/179, CP 136 (26). Report of the Public Order Committee, 25 March 1926.

[59] The Labour Government of 1924 is interesting in this respect. Although MacDonald (himself the subject of surveillance earlier in his life) was not over-concerned by the communist threat and hostile to the intelligence services, this was not a position adopted by all members of the Cabinet, and not by the Home Secretary (Arthur Henderson) in particular. Indeed a Cabinet committee was established in April 1924 to determine to what extent the incidence of industrial action was due to communist activity. See Barnes, n 52 above, p 945. See also Andrew, n 32 above, pp 428–30.

less, and withering campaign against the organisation, culminating in the great sedition trial of 1925. Indeed it was this successful prosecution of communist leaders that helped to persuade the Cabinet Public Order Committee that there was no immediate need for legislation. In the remainder of this chapter we trace some of the developments in the campaign against communism, beginning with the prosecution of senior party officials during the great lock-out of miners in 1921: this was done under the Defence of the Realm Regulations 1914 and Emergency Regulations 1921 for activity which did not seem obviously related to either the war or the dispute in the coal mining industry.[60] In the pages which follow we also examine allegations and incidents of surveillance and infiltration of the Party, which self-evidently took place in the light of the weekly reports by Thomson and Childs (which Ramsay MacDonald refused to circulate to the Cabinet as his predecessors had done). This leads in turn to an examination of the way in which the authorities cracked down on Communist Party literature, meetings and assemblies, leading to not one but two important trials, each of which was a major political event with far-reaching implications. What emerges quite clearly from these developments is that so far as the Communist Party was concerned there was no freedom of association, no freedom of assembly and no freedom of expression, a conclusion reinforced by the censorship of Russian films and newspapers.[61] On the contrary the Party was in its own terms the victim of a vendetta by a 'nervous and angry' but 'unflagging' government,[62] whose officials regarded communism as 'the one barrier standing between us and commercial prosperity, between class good feeling and class hatred'.[63]

'Police Terrorism' and the *Inkpin* Case

'Barely a few weeks had elapsed since its formation in January, 1921, when the Party was made acutely aware that its activities were engaging

---

[60] *Inkpin v Roll* (1922) 86 JP 61.

[61] In 1925 the Home Secretary announced that steps were to be taken to ban the entry of *Pravda* into the country (H C Debs, 11 June 1925, col 2265 (WA)). It was subsequently confirmed that *Inprecorr* (a 'publication of the Communist International' which 'circulated all over the continent') was also banned 'under the authority of a Secretary of State's warrant to the Postmaster General on the ground that its circulation in this country would be contrary to the public interest' (H C Debs, 6 March 1930, col 628). The British Board of Film Censors banned a number of revolutionary films, including 'The Battleship Potemkin', 'The End of St Petersburg', 'Mother October', and 'New Babylon'. See generally, N M Hunnings, *Film Censors and the Law* (1967), p 97. The censoring of 'The Battleship Potemkin' is covered in the *Workers' Weekly*, 16 July 1926.

[62] *The Communist*, 7 May 1921.   [63] Childs, n 46 above, p 214.

the special attention of the Government'.[64] The opportunity to attack the Party was provided by the Emergency Regulations 1921, made after the proclamation of emergency on 31 March 1921,[65] in response to the national lock-out of the miners.[66] Described by Ronald Kidd as 'a constant menace to our civil rights',[67] the Emergency Powers Act 1920 authorised the King to declare a state of emergency in the face of industrial action 'calculated, by interfering with the supply and distribution of food, water, fuel, or light, or with the means of locomotion, to deprive the community, or any substantial portion of the community, of the essentials of life' (s 1(1)). Under the Act, Parliament must be informed of the Proclamation (s 1(2)), which once made authorises the government to make regulations 'for securing the essentials of life to the community' (s 2(1)), and these regulations must then be approved by Parliament.[68] Said by *The Times* to be 'extraordinarily complex and drastic',[69] the Emergency Regulations of 1921 bore an uncanny resemblance to many of the war-time regulations made under the Defence of the Realm Consolidation Act 1914:[70] the government was authorised to take possession of property (subject to an obligation to pay compensation), while other regulations empowered the Minister of Transport to regulate traffic, and authorised the Board of Trade to regulate the use of ports, and to prohibit exports. The Board of Trade could also give directions as to the supply of gas, water and electricity, while the Postmaster General could direct that 'telegraphic messages . . . shall not be accepted for transmission'.[71]

Particularly significant for our immediate purposes were regulations 19 and 20, these being very similar to Defence of the Realm regulations 42 and 9A. Regulation 19 dealt with incitement to sedition and mutiny (of the armed forces, police forces, fire brigades or civilian population), as well as measures designed to impede, delay or restrict the supply and dis-

---

[64] CPGB, *Report of the Executive Committee 1921*, p 2.　　　　[65] See (1921) 65 *Sol Jo* 457.

[66] For background, see R Page Arnot, *The Miners: Years of Struggle* (1953), ch 10.

[67] R Kidd, *British Liberty in Danger* (1940), p 48. A harsher judgment claimed that the Act 'authorises the setting up of a capitalist dictatorship whenever His Majesty in Council, that is to say the capitalist class, thinks that it should be done': J R Campbell, *My Case* [n d], p 13.

[68] Though as was pointed out Parliament's 'right to review the situation' arises only 'after the Act has been in operation for a period of 7 days': Campbell, ibid, p 13. For a full account of the Act, see G S Morris, 'The Emergency Powers Act 1920' [1979] PL 317. See also Chapter 4 below.

[69] *The Times*, 5 April 1921. But it did concede that the government would have 'no difficulty in defending them'.

[70] The regulations (which are remarkably omitted from S R & O 1921 on the ground that they were 'spent') are reproduced in the *Board of Trade Journal*, 7 April 1921, pp 385–8.

[71] The code of regulations formed a blueprint for those introduced in 1926 and are considered in some detail in Chapter 4 below.

tribution of a number of essential services. Consistently with the terms of the Emergency Powers Act 1920, however, it was expressly provided not to be an offence to take part in a strike, or peacefully to persuade others to do so. Regulation 20 dealt with public meetings and processions, authorising the Home Secretary (and magistrates or chief officers of police if authorised by the Home Secretary) to ban such gatherings. The power could be exercised where there was reason to believe in the case of a meeting that it would give rise to 'grave disorder', and in the case of a procession that it would lead to a breach of the peace or promote disaffection. Where a meeting or procession was held or attempted to be held in breach of any ban, the police were empowered to do what was necessary to disperse it or prevent it from taking place. Other regulations gave the police extensive powers of arrest and search of individuals, as well as entry and search of private property, powers which could be exercised even though no offence had been committed. Thus, the police could arrest without a warrant 'any person who so acts to endanger the public safety, or who is guilty, or is suspected of being guilty of an offence' under the regulations.

The 'elastic and accommodating'[72] regulations thus armed the authorities with 'extensive powers', so much so that they 'put every trade unionist at the legal, as formerly he was at the illegal, mercy of the police, the agent provocateur, and those professional bullies, the magistrates'.[73] It has been said that 'the first prosecutions to follow on the 'emergency' were 'of course, prosecutions of Communists',[74] and there were in fact over fifty communists arrested while the regulations were in force, though not all of them were arrested for breach of the regulations.[75] Nevertheless there were many arrests for sedition in breach of regulation 19, and reports of homes being searched and literature being removed, and the possession of Communist Party membership cards being offered as 'damnatory evidence' in legal proceedings. The prosecutions under regulation 19 included those of W H Bishop, charged with statements uttered at a public meeting in the course of which he offered to put the King in the mines 'with his shirt off and make him do the same as the miners, and get corns on his shoulders picking coal'.[76] They also included the case of James Matthews who was arrested for remarks expressed at a meeting at Hyde Park in which he discouraged trade unionists from signing up as reservists, saying 'You workers have nothing to lose. Now

---

[72] *The Communist*, 25 June 1921.   [73] *The Communist*, 16 April 1921.   [74] Ibid.
[75] Campbell, *My Case*, n 67 above, p 9 claims that 71 were arrested.
[76] *The Communist*, 30 April 1921.

is the time to throw over the rotten Government system and the capitalist class'.[77] Other cases included that of James Stewart, the Midland
organiser of the Party, charged in connection with a speech to the unemployed in Wolverhampton in which he was alleged to have urged a
crowd to 'get up a demonstration' for food and blankets, in proceedings
which hotly disputed the police version of events based on statements
written in an officer's notebook after the meeting 'from memory'.[78]

The Communist was convinced that there was a 'vigorous vendetta' being
waged against the Party and its members by the secret service and the
Special Branch.[79] Any such thoughts were likely only to be reinforced by
the raid on the Party's offices on 7 May 1921 (the 'culminating point of
the persecution')[80] as a result of which Albert Inkpin, the General
Secretary, was arrested under regulation 19 in connection with the publication of the Theses and Statutes of the Communist International,[81]
thereby challenging the very 'basis on which the united Party had been
created'.[82] Police officers then 'proceeded to ransack' the offices, 'strip-
ping them of practically everything that was moveable',[83] leaving only
the ashes of Eleanor Marx Aveling, 'reposing in an urn ready to be conveyed to Moscow'.[84] According to J R Clynes who raised the matter in
Parliament, 'the police carried away almost everything they could lay
their hands on, including pictures on the walls, money in the safe, and a
gold watch, filling a large motor lorry and two taxi-cabs'.[85] Both the
arrest and the search were without the authority of a warrant which
police officers informed Inkpin was not necessary under the regulations.[86]
But although he was arrested under the Emergency Regulations, Inkpin
was also charged under regulation 42 of the Defence of the Realm
Regulations, the measure, it will be recalled, which was aimed at sedition and disaffection. The charges in relation to the latter (the Defence
of the Realm Regulations) concerned offences allegedly committed
between 25 November 1920 and 31 March 1921, while the charges
under the former (the Emergency Regulations) concerned offences committed since 1 April, when these regulations had come into force. All the

---

[77] *The Communist*, 16 April 1921.   [78] *The Communist*, 23 April 1921.
[79] *The Communist*, 30 April 1921.   [80] CPGB, *Report of the Executive Committee 1921*, p 2.
[81] The incident is graphically described in *The Communist*, 14, 21 May 1921. The Acting National
Organiser, Robert Stewart, was also arrested.
[82] CPGB, *Report of the Executive Committee 1921*, p 2.
[83] *The Communist*, 14 May 1921. They 'removed all papers connected with *The Communist*—circulation books, paper, pencils, files, books, everything—down to the pictures on the walls and the
unused envelopes on the tables' (ibid).
[84] *The Communist*, 21 May 1921.   [85] H C Debs, 9 May 1921, col 1514.
[86] *The Communist*, 21 May 1921.

charges related to 'certain literature' which had been issued from Party headquarters, including the Theses and Statutes of the Communist International, *Communist International* Nos 1 and 13, *German Spartacists*, and *Communist Review* No 1.

So far as the Defence of the Realm Regulations were concerned, one of the two charges under these provisions related to the Theses and Statutes of the Communist International which had been ordered in November 1920. The contrived nature of this charge was teased out with commendable restraint by defence counsel who claimed that 'it seems remarkably strange that if there had been really an offence committed by the defendant under the Defence of the Realm Regulations, assuming these regulations were in force and capable of being enforced, that this would have been going on in November 1920, and deliveries taking place in January and February 1921, without any notice being taken whatever of the matter or anything said at all'. Turning to the Emergency Regulations, in relation to which there were now three charges, it was argued that much of the material in question (such as various copies of the *Communist International*) was seized from premises not in the occupation of Inkpin. They were not in his possession any more than they were in the possession of the rest of the staff.[87] He did not order the material, nor was there evidence that he had given instructions for it to be ordered, and nor did he take delivery of it. 'In the absence of evidence showing personal responsibility for a crime', submitted his counsel, Inkpin was entitled to be acquitted. But more than this would be required to convince the Lord Mayor (who heard the case). He was satisfied not only that publication of the material was calculated and likely to cause mutiny, sedition and disaffection, but also that Inkpin had ordered the printing of the material, his complicity being demonstrated by the fact that 'it was paid for by cheques drawn upon an account opened by him for and on account of the Communist Party, the bodies of which cheques were in his handwriting', though crucially 'the cheques were not signed by [him]'. Inkpin was found guilty and sentenced to six months' hard labour for three offences under the Defence of the Realm Regulations (despite claims that they had ceased to apply) and three months with hard labour for two offences under the Emergency Regulations, the two sentences to run concurrently.

The *Inkpin* prosecution in fact gave rise to the first reported case relating to the campaign against the communists.[88] In an appeal against the

---

[87] For a full account of the trial, see *The Communist*, 9 July 1921.
[88] *Inkpin v Roll* (1922) 86 JP 61.

Lord Mayor's decision, two points were taken, the first a matter of procedure, and the second a matter of substance. The former related to the fact that Inkpin had been brought before the court after having been arrested without a warrant (under the Defence of the Realm and the Emergency Regulations) but without written information or summons in relation to any of the charges specifying 'precisely the nature of the charge': in the appellant's view it was insufficient that the charges were entered in the police charge sheets and duly read over to him. The appeal on this ground was dismissed with the elderly Lord Chief Justice, Lord Trevethin (appointed in April 1921 at the remarkable age of 77)[89] noting that no objection had been taken until the fifth day of the proceedings before dismissing the point on the ground that there was no authority imposing such an obligation. Citing *R v Hughes*,[90] the Lord Chief Justice pointed out that the authorities 'show that, when a person is brought before a justice, the charge may be formulated before the justice; it must be formulated so that the prisoner has an opportunity of understanding it, and opportunity ought to be given him, if he desires it, of an adjournment, if there is anything like surprise, and if he wants time in order to prepare his defence'. In a similar vein Avory J held that there was 'nothing in this objection at all', and echoing points made by the Lord Chief Justice he claimed that 'it does not appear that the appellant was in any way prejudiced in his defence by the absence of any written information or summons'. But this hardly seems the point.

The substantive issue in the appeal raised more difficult questions of statutory interpretation and as such related only to the conviction on two charges under the Defence of the Realm Regulations 42, 48 and 48A in

---

[89] The appointment was attacked by *The Nation* (16 April 1921, p 85) as 'a perversion of patronage', though applauded by the *Solicitors' Journal* which noted that he had never been a law officer nor sat in Parliament, 'so that his selection creates a precedent': (1921) 65 *Sol Jo* 465. In fact he resigned in March 1922 (in his 79th year), though he lived to 92. He had previously been known as A T Lawrence J, having been elevated to the Bench in 1904, but overlooked for higher office. For a full account of the disgraceful circumstances of his appointment and resignation/removal, see R Jackson, *The Chief: The Biography of Gordon Hewart Lord Chief Justice of England 1922–1940* (1959), pp 126–46. Trevethin was appointed following Reading's move to India as Viceroy. The existing Attorney General (Hewart) coveted the position of Lord Chief Justice but was needed by the Prime Minister (Lloyd George) for political work (being 'one of the two great successes of the administration'). A deal was struck where the position would be offered to one of the existing elderly judges who would vacate the position on request by the Prime Minister in order to make way for Hewart. Trevethin was preferred to Darling (an appointment which 'would be condemned unanimously by his colleagues and the two professions' (Jackson, ibid, p 142), though it was thought that Lawrence's qualities as a 'sound lawyer' were not enough to 'atone for the circumstances of the appointment' (ibid). He was 'abandoned without ceremony' and read of his own resignation in *The Times* (ibid, p 144).

[90] (1879) 4 QBD 614.

respect of offences between November 1920 and March 1921.[91] These regulations had been made under the authority of the parent Act of 1914 which authorised regulations to be made 'during the continuance of the present war'. Although the Armistice had been signed, the war had been prolonged as a matter of law by the Termination of the Present War (Definition) Act 1918 which provided that the war did not terminate until 31 August 1921. In the meantime, however, the War Emergency Laws (Continuance) Act 1920 provided by section 2 that the Defence of the Realm Regulations referred to in Schedule 2 would continue in force until 31 August 1920 'and as so continued shall have effect as if enacted in this Act'. From this it was argued that the effect of the 1920 Act was that the Defence of the Realm Regulations had come to an end, for although the Defence of the Realm Consolidation Act 1914 authorised the making of regulations for the duration of the war, this was impliedly repealed by the 1920 Act which clearly provided that the regulations would expire on 31 August 1920.[92] But perfectly predictably, the Divisional Court was having none of this either, the Lord Chief Justice taking the view that 'the rule of law is that a subsequent statute repeals a prior one where the second is inconsistent with the first, where the two cannot stand together'. This is clearly unexceptionable, but where the reasoning breaks down is in the conclusion that 'in saying that the regulations shall continue until the termination of the war, and further saying that they shall continue until August 31st, 1920, the statutes are not inconsistent but stand together'! It is surely torturing language and logic to say that 'the two statements do not in the least conflict the one with the other'.

It is difficult to avoid the conclusion that this prosecution and the conviction of Inkpin represented a cynical use of statutory powers for a purpose for which they can scarcely have been intended. The charges related to material such as the *Communist International*, *Communist Review*, and the Theses and Statutes of the Communist International, without any specification of how their publication affected the war effort on the one hand, or indeed how it was specifically directed to the dispute in the coal industry on the other. In other words, the emergency provided the government with an opportunity rather than a reason to move against the

---

[91] Regulations 48 and 48A dealt with attempts and the soliciting or inciting of others to commit an offence against the regulations.

[92] Although not raised in argument this is a view reinforced by the doubts expressed by the Leader of the House (Bonar Law) during the enactment of the Emergency Powers Act 1920 when he said that the war-time powers were 'not now available' and that in any event the government should not rest its powers in a national emergency 'upon an Act framed to deal with the common enemy'. See H C Debs, 25 October 1920, col 1401.

Communist Party, the very existence of which (in view of the fact that the prosecution was based on the Theses and Statutes of the Communist International) would appear to have been seditious. The difficulty for the government, however, was that with the expiration of the Defence of the Realm Consolidation Act 1914 it was denied a 'convenient weapon against incitement to revolutionary violence'.[93] It was principally for this reason that a number of Cabinet ministers had supported the Preservation of Public Order Bill, with the Home Secretary explaining in Cabinet Committee that when the Defence of the Realm Regulations lapsed, it would be possible to proceed for sedition only by way of 'the cumbrous and old fashioned procedure of an indictment for sedition'.[94] As a result, when the war-time legislation ceased to operate on the formal conclusion of the peace, 'there would be no adequate powers of dealing promptly with offences of this character'.[95] This was a danger which in the view of the Solicitor General was not 'fully appreciated', the Solicitor General expressing concern that the 'country would be much more unprotected than it should be', while protesting 'strongly against the fiction of continuing war legislation' on the ground that 'the continued use of the Defence of the Realm Act and regulations to obtain convictions on the strength of the legal fiction that the war was still continuing was wrong'.[96] But this was no Pauline conversion to free speech on his part.

Special Branch Surveillance and Infiltration

Notwithstanding the failure to proceed with the Preservation of Public Order Bill, with the 1921 prosecution the government provided a sharp warning of the strong tactics that would be used to crush dissent. It did so in a manner which betrayed no liberal tolerance for a competing political ideology whose adherents at the time were relatively small in number but whose revolutionary potential was undoubtedly profound, particularly if they had been able to retain a home in the Labour Party. But this would not be the last time the Communist Party would find its offices raided and cleared by the police, and it would not be the last time that it would find its senior officers imprisoned. In the meantime, it remained the subject of close attention by the Special Branch, with the activities of which it was to become wearily familiar. The *Workers' Weekly* claimed in May 1924 that:

---

[93] PRO, CAB 24/125, CP 3007, n 41 above.
[94] PRO, CAB 23/25, Cabinet Home Affairs Committee, 27 April 1921.   [95] Ibid.
[96] PRO, CAB 23/26, Cabinet Home Affairs Committee, 31 May 1921.

Scotland Yard's most important function is the protection of the supreme murderers, robbers and criminals—the Capitalist class itself. And for this purpose there exists parallel with the CID the 'Special Branch' under General Sir Wyndham Borlase Childes (sic), successor to the notorious Basil Thomson.

The methods of the Special Branch are many. *In addition to its own agents (paid up to £10 a week) members of working class organisations are regularly bribed to betray information.* Not only are individuals shadowed and the offices of organisations watched, but their correspondence is also opened in the post and photographed.

Telephone lines are tapped by means of 'dictaphones', which record conversations. 'Microphones' are concealed in meeting places when the 'Yard' cannot obtain access or eavesdrop by other means.[97]

Special Branch activity in fact took several forms. So far as the *interception of correspondence* is concerned, several allegations appear in the columns of the *Workers' Weekly*. Perhaps the most extraordinary is the claim that in February 1924 'a little girl picked up in the street a packet addressed to Sergeant Evans, who is head of the police in Pontycymmer'. According to the report, the packet contained about eight pages of foolscap, signed by Colonel Lindsey, the chief of the Glamorgan constabulary. The first page was marked 'Secret' with the instruction 'To be burned immediately', and was accompanied by an explanation that the information came from a very delicate source. The package was said to reveal details of the Blaengarw branch of the Communist Party, and to give the name and address of every member, together with an exact account of the branch's financial position. Other information dealt with the position of Party members 'in their various Works' Committees', and included the accurate figure of the quantity of *Workers' Weekly* being sold. The report continued: 'Now there is only one Comrade in the local who knew all these particulars, and the latter were sent to Sergeant Evans just after that Comrade had sent in by post his February report, *which included a special report dealing with industrial nuclei.* Only in this report had the facts regarding the position of Party members on Works Committees been given, and such information could have been obtained from no other source'.[98] This led the *Workers' Weekly* to the conclusion that 'practically all correspondence between the South Wales Organiser and the various locals is being tampered with'.

Whether or not there is any substance in this story, it is almost certainly the case that CPGB correspondence was interfered with.[99]

[97] *Workers' Weekly*, 2 May 1924. Emphasis in original.
[98] Ibid. Emphasis in original.
[99] On the huge expansion of postal censorship during the war, see Public Record Office, *MI5: The First Ten Years, 1909–1919* (1997), pp 1–5. Almost 5,000 people were employed on this activity by November 1918.

Allegations were to appear in the columns of Hansard, and were the subject of exchanges between Party officials and the Home Office. In a letter to the Home Secretary on 12 February 1924, the General Secretary of the Party wrote in the following terms:

Ever since the formation of the Communist Party, nearly four years ago, correspondence addressed to our Party headquarters has been systematically tampered with. The same applies to correspondence to the private residences of members of our Central Executive Committee and other active workers of our Party. That our correspondence should be opened and inspected under the administration of a Conservative, Liberal or Coalition Government is understandable. We naturally expected, however, that the assumption of office by the Labour Party would at once lead to its discontinuance. Such, in fact, has not proved to be the case.[100]

The Home Secretary replied that 'it would not be possible for a Minister to enter into discussions' on these points, and he was subsequently unprepared to say one way or the other whether there had been a change of policy on the part of the government.[101] If there was a change of policy (and the *Workers' Weekly* was to claim that the Party's mail was arriving by the first post for the first time in years),[102] it was shortlived.[103] In December 1925, Shipurji Saklatvala claimed in the House that six days previously, ninety-four items of correspondence addressed to the CPGB were examined at the West Central District Post Office. His demand to know under whose instructions the examination was conducted was met with the usual response that it would not be in the public interest to provide such information.[104]

Although important, the interception of correspondence was not the only way by which the Special Branch obtained information about the Party and its activities. Perhaps the best known example of Special Branch *eavesdropping and attendance at meetings* related to the meeting of the London District Congress of the Party which was held at the Rehearsal Theatre, Bedford Street, in the centre of London.[105] When the meeting, which was held on 13 April 1924, was breaking up for lunch, the chairman with a number of others examined the platform from under which suspicious noises had been heard. When the trap door was flung open, a

---

[100] *Workers' Weekly*, 7 March 1924.   [101] H C Debs, 20 March 1924, cols 617–18.
[102] *Workers' Weekly*, 7 March 1924.
[103] In fact the 'Labour government in effect sanctioned the interception of Communist and Comintern communications: Andrew, n 32 above, p 430.
[104] H C Debs, 15 December 1925, col 1230 (WA).
[105] See *Workers' Weekly*, 18 April 1924 from which this account is drawn. A good account is also to be found in the *Daily Herald*, 14, 15 April 1924.

spiral metal staircase was revealed leading to a room below. Inside the room were found two men, later identified at Bow Street police station as Special Branch officers Gill and Hopley, 'the two most expert political secret service agents of Superintendent McBrian' of Scotland Yard. The officers left behind three notebooks which were retrieved by members of the Communist Party present, and were said to be 'the most damning evidence that has ever fallen into the hands of the working class organisation in this country of the means whereby the Capitalist State maintains its rule'. Photographs of the notebooks appeared in the *Workers' Weekly* of 18 April 1924, along with a number of extracts. These tended to show 'that these men had been continually employed spying at all Communist meetings, and sneaking into hotels to watch and listen to Communist delegates to conferences'. One of the books (that of Sergeant Gill) contained records of the movement of persons being watched and of previous conferences as well as the names, addresses and movements of delegates to those conferences. It also contained a verbatim record of the proceedings of the conferences, and a transcript of reports by Gill to McBrian. In a wonderful passage the *Workers' Weekly* reported that the notebooks 'will be precious exhibits in the future Museum of British Revolution', but that 'At present they are in safe keeping; they are being held in trust for the whole of the Labour Movement, and as soon as a responsible Labour Committee of Inquiry into the Secret Service is established, they will be handed over for their inspection'.[106]

It is not known what became of the notebooks. But the demands for a Committee of Inquiry fell on stony ground even though the Bedford Street case had 'proved all the allegations of the Communist Party against the Secret Political Police beyond dispute', and even though the police notebooks revealed 'a systematic tracking and shadowing and spying on delegates and representatives of working class organisations'. The matter was, however, raised in the Commons by George Lansbury,[107] forcing the (Labour) Home Secretary (Arthur Henderson) to concede that two police officers were in fact found on the premises, as claimed, despite the fact that 'The Communist Party as such, is not illegal'. But because 'the declared policy of certain of its leaders would, if carried out by the methods proposed, involve breaches of the ordinary law of this country', a 'certain amount of vigilance on the part of the police [was] called for if they are to discharge their duty to the rest of the

---

[106] Most of these details were confirmed by Hopley under cross-examination during the course of the communist trial, below, pp 136–44. See *The Times*, 19 November 1925.

[107] H C Debs, 14 April 1924, cols 928–30.

community'. Not all members of the House shared Lansbury's indignation. Viscount Wolmer asked 'why any political party should object to police officers being present', while Mr Ormsby-Gore questioned whether it was in order to accuse the police of spying. After consulting the Metropolitan Police Commissioner (who had been 'out of town') at the time of the incident, Henderson later reported to the House that there was no likelihood of a recurrence of the Bedford Street affair, though 'the police [would] continue to show the necessary vigilance'.[108] This was more than could be said for the press, which for two days had made the most of the story until 'as if by magic, a sudden silence' descended. By whose command, teased the *Workers' Weekly*, did the newspapers (with the exception of the *Manchester Guardian*)[109] ignore the invitation to reproduce photographs of the notebooks and a verbatim record of their contents?[110]

So far as the use of *paid informers* is concerned, there is some evidence, apart from the regular claims in the *Workers' Weekly*, to support the belief of the Party that this tactic was used by the Special Branch to infiltrate the organisation. Although evidence of this kind is obviously difficult to secure, Sir Basil Thomson refers in his autobiography to the Special Branch infiltration of Sinn Fein,[111] which seems almost certainly to have been mirrored by similar infiltration of the Communist Party in view of the seriousness with which the communist threat was taken. Clearer evidence of infiltration of the Party was provided in a Commons exchange in 1927 which referred to events which had allegedly taken place several years earlier.[112] The matter was raised by Oswald Mosley of all people, before his defection to the forces of evil, after having been approached by 'a very well known solicitor', who 'considered it was a matter of public duty' to bring the matter to public notice. According to Mosley, the solicitor held two statements, one from the wife and the other from the mistress of a man named Henry Johnstone, who had committed suicide. Both alleged that he was 'in the pay' of the police and the Home Office, that he had been engaged to spy on the National Unemployed Workers' Committee Movement, and that he had committed suicide after having been exposed as a spy. Mosley then read from one of the statements in which it was claimed that Johnstone was 'in the pay of Scotland Yard, and had been submitting reports to them on what happens in the work-

[108] H C Debs, 1 May 1924, col 1854.　　[109] *Manchester Guardian*, 21 April 1924.
[110] *Workers' Weekly*, 25 April 1924.　　[111] Thomson, n 36 above, pp 388–9.
[112] H C Debs, 28 July 1927, cols 1539–42.

ing class Movement, particularly the National Unemployed Workers' Committee Movement, for at least three years'.

It was also claimed that Johnstone was paid £3 a week and that additional special payments were made, as when he embezzled £14 belonging to the Lewisham Branch of the NUWCM following which:

he told the police that he was to be expelled from the Movement over this, and they paid him £20 in order that he could pay the money back and prevent his expulsion. He paid back the £14, but was expelled from the Lewisham branch of the NUWCM, and also from the Communist Party. He had, however, regained his connection with the Movement by establishing a branch of the NUWCM at Bromley, Kent, and taken on secretaryship. It was from this branch that he continued to sit upon the London District Council of the NUWCM.

A special grant of £8 was also paid for a report in 1926 of a special conference of the NUWCM, and another for attending a reception at Holborn Town Hall given to the communists released from prison in 1926. The statement also claimed that 'on occasions when he did not have sufficient spicey material for his reports', Johnstone 'wrote it up out of his own imagination, very often giving statements and extracts from speeches that were never made'. His main contact was 'an officer of the yard' named MacBrien, though he also knew a Sergeant Gill, and had been led to believe by the former that 'in the event of the Movement discovering his connections he would receive from MacBrien a lump sum of roughly £100 down to enable him to clear out of the district or abroad if necessary'.[113] Needless to say Mosley thought this to be 'a very grave matter', 'a little beneath the dignity of a great country . . . so as to degrade itself as to use an instrument which at the end is so ruthlessly and callously cast aside'. But when challenged 'entirely to refute these allegations', the Home Secretary refused 'to say whether the man is a spy or not', repeating the mantra that 'If there is a Secret Service, it must be secret', and asserting that so long as he was 'responsible for the administration of any portion of the Secret Service', it would remain 'secret'.

There is little cause to doubt any of these allegations. For even if they are a bit fruity in the telling, they are nevertheless symptomatic of an extraordinary degree of surveillance and infiltration which must have taken place.[114] It is openly acknowledged in Cabinet conclusions that

[113] This is presumably the same MacBrien as the McBrian referred to above by the *Workers' Weekly* and the *Manchester Guardian*.

[114] It seems to be widely acknowledged that the Party was infiltrated. See for example, Andrew, n 32 above, p 454, and A J P Taylor, *English History 1914–1945* (1965), pp 289–90. See also the cross-examination of Detective Hastings in the sedition trial below (infiltration of the YCL): *The Times*, 18 November 1925.

arrangements were made by the Home Secretary 'for keeping under observation the activities and speeches of Communists in this country'.[115] Furthermore it was conceded in the course of the sedition trial of Communist Party officials in 1925 (on which see below) that the police had been keeping a close watch upon the CPGB head office 'for years' (entering the premises to buy copies of the *Workers' Weekly*),[116] and that 'spying upon the C.P. *and other Labour organisations* was part of the normal routine work of the police'.[117] It would in any event have been impossible for the authorities to have compiled the volume of information about the Party on such a regular basis and in such detail without fairly elaborate and sophisticated methods of surveillance and infiltration. As already pointed out, the head of the Special Branch prepared weekly reports for the Home Secretary which, until the election of the Labour Government, were circulated to the Cabinet. These were not insubstantial documents, with Childs' last effort running to sixteen pages, some of which appears to be based on intercepted correspondence.[118] Apart from the weekly reports produced by the head of the Special Branch, special reports were produced periodically on specific events. An example is a detailed memorandum prepared in 1925 by the Home Secretary on the forthcoming annual congress of the Party in Glasgow. This included an account of the agenda of the meeting, and reports of recent meetings, together with an account of the fraternal delegates who were expected to attend from overseas.[119] Again this information could have been obtained only by some form of surveillance or infiltration or both.

Freedom of Expression: the Campbell Case of 1924[120]

In his autobiography Wyndham Childs wrote that the evidence against the communists has 'never been the spoken word but the published

[115] PRO, CAB 23/51, Cabinet 47 (25), 7 October 1925.

[116] See *The Times*, 18, 19 November 1925.

[117] T A Jackson, *Trials of British Freedom* (1940), pp 192–3. Emphasis in original. Jackson wrote for the *The Communist* and the *Workers' Weekly*.

[118] PRO, 24/164, Report No 238 (!), 10 January 1924.

[119] PRO, CAB 24/173, CP 224 (25), 2 May 1925. In fact one of the issues raised by the document was whether foreign delegates should be denied entry to the country in order to attend. The recommendation that they be refused entry was made after consulting with Arthur Henderson which was said to be 'highly confidential'. The Home Secretary's proposals were accepted: PRO, CAB 23/50, Cabinet 25 (25), 13 May 1925.

[120] For a full account see J Ll J Edwards, *The Law Officers of the Crown* (1964), pp 199–225, and *The Attorney General, Politics and the Public Interest* (1984), ch 11. Also F H Newark, 'The Campbell Case and the First Labour Government' (1969) 20 NILQ 19. A good account is also to be found in R W Lyman, *The First Labour Government 1924* (1957). See also Klugmann, *History*, n 10 above, pp 342–6.

document'.[121] Yet there were no special measures on the statute book to deal with the dissemination of communism, despite requests for such measures having been made from time to time by the military authorities and the secret service.[122] In fact the nearest we came to the enactment in the 1920s of special powers to deal with communism was the bizarre Seditious and Blasphemous Teaching to Children Bill, passed by the Lords in 1924.[123] The Bill (which got as far as the Report Stage in the Commons in 1927)[124] proposed to make it an offence to teach seditious or blasphemous matter to children under the age of sixteen or to sell or distribute any such matter to children. The target appears to have been Proletarian Sunday Schools and journals such as the *Young Comrade* and *Young Worker*. Happily the country was spared such nonsense, despite its support by the Archbishop of Canterbury and seven Dukes. This is not to say, however, that the authorities were powerless to punish those responsible for the publication of communist literature.[125] It is true that the war-time offences of sedition and incitement to disaffection had been revoked, and that similar measures in Emergency Regulations operated for a limited period only. But there were other measures which could be deployed as the occasion arose, including the common law felony of seditious conspiracy[126] and the statutory offence of incitement to mutiny,[127] limited in scope though the latter may have been.

Under the Incitement to Mutiny Act 1797 it was a felony maliciously and advisedly to endeavour to seduce any member of the armed forces from his duty and allegiance to the Crown or to incite mutiny. Although never repealed, the Act lay dormant between 1804 and 1912, revived to deal with the emergence of militant trade unionism and the publication in *The Syndicalist* of an 'Open Letter to British Soldiers'. The possibility that striking workers might be killed by the intervention of the troops was not fanciful, with striking miners having been killed by troops at Featherstone in 1893 and troops having been deployed to support the police at Tonypandy in 1911 (when in the course of disturbances a miner

[121] Childs, n 46 above, p 209.   [122] See Young, n 39 above, pp 28–9.

[123] See H L Debs, 3 July 1924, col 158 (Second Reading); 17 July 1924, col 688 (Committee); 5 August 1924, col 434 (Third Reading).

[124] See H C Debs, 11 March 1927, col 1525 (Second Reading); 1 July 1927, col 845 (Report).

[125] See Aliens Restriction (Amendment) Act 1919, s 3 and Police Act 1919, s 3. For background see respectively H C Debs, 22 October 1919, cols 153–66; and H C Debs, 18 July 1919, col 795 and 1 August 1919, col 2458.

[126] For a contemporary account of the law of sedition, see Sir James Stephen, *A Digest of the Criminal Law* (1877), pp 55–6.

[127] On the 1797 Act, see Williams, n 1 above, pp 179–80.

was killed).[128] The offending article in *The Syndicalist*, for which the printer and publisher were indicted under the 1797 Act, urged the troops not to kill workers engaged in a strike, even when called upon to do so by their officers. The men were each convicted and imprisoned for periods of six and nine months with hard labour. This followed the rejection by Horridge J of the argument for the defence that the indictment was bad because it revealed only a general appeal by the accused rather than any specific attempt 'to tamper with some specific person or persons serving in the forces of His Majesty'. It also followed the rejection by the jury of the argument that the article was 'merely a comment upon armed military force being used by the State for the suppression of industrial riots'. The jury, it seems, preferred the view that the article was designed 'to induce soldiers to disobey their officers in the event of a strike'.[129]

Following its successful deployment in the *Bowman* case, the 1797 Act was to become an important weapon in the response to the rise of communism. Against a 'background of mounting attacks on the [minority] Labour Government' which had assumed office in January 1924,[130] the Act was wheeled into service in the controversial Campbell case. The occasion for the deployment of the Act was a campaign which the CPGB had organised to coincide with the tenth anniversary of the beginning of the Great War. As a prelude to 'war week' the *Workers' Weekly* on 25 July 1924 carried an Open Letter in which it called upon soldiers, sailors and airmen 'to begin the task of not only organising passive resistance when war is declared, or when an industrial dispute involves you, but to definitely and categorically let it be known that, neither in a class war nor a military war, will you turn your guns on your fellow workers, but instead will line up with our fellow workers in our attack upon the exploiters and capitalists, and will use your arms on the side of your own class'. The article also urged the formation of 'committees in every barracks, aerodrome, and ship', these to be the 'nucleus of an organisation that will prepare the whole of the soldiers, sailors and airmen not only to refuse to go to war, or to refuse to shoot strikers during industrial conflicts, but will make it possible for the workers, peasants and soldiers, sailors and

---

[128] On Featherstone, see Report on the Disturbances at Featherstone, C 7234 (1893–4). On Tonypandy, see H A Clegg, A Fox, and A F Thompson *A History of British Trade Unionism since 1899*. vol 2: 1911–33 (1985), p 29. And see the interesting account by Childs, n 46 above, ch 9, who was there as a War Office staff captain. Tanks were also deployed in Glasgow in 1919 during a strike by engineering workers, as an over-reaction by authorities who misread it as a Bolshevist uprising. See I McLean, *The Legend of Red Clydeside* (1973), chs 10 and 11.

[129] *R v Bowman* (1912) 76 JP 271.   [130] MacFarlane, n 8 above, p 106.

airman, to go forward in a common attack upon the capitalists, and smash capitalism forever, and institute the reign of the whole working class'. In bold type soldiers were implored to 'Refuse to shoot down your fellow workers', 'Refuse to fight for profits', and to 'Turn your weapons on your oppressors'.

According to MacFarlane, there was 'something faintly ludicrous in the Communist Party issuing a call of this nature when it would probably have found it hard to muster a couple of dozen members in the whole of the armed forces'.[131] Nevertheless, J R Campbell, the acting editor of the *Workers' Weekly*, was arrested on 5 August following a police raid of Party premises and charged under the 1797 Act with 'attempting to seduce from loyalty to the King members of the Navy, Army and Air Force'.[132] The *Daily Herald* reports that six detectives arrived at Party headquarters at 2.00 pm but they left immediately after discovering that J R Campbell had been editorially responsible for the offending article. They returned an hour later with a warrant for the arrest of Campbell who was taken by two officers to Bow Street while the others remained to search the premises. When asked what right they had to search without a search warrant, the police officers 'replied that they had arrested a suspect and were looking for evidence'.[133] But although they had 'no other authority',[134] police officers admitted under cross-examination that 'cheque books, paying in books, a cash book, receipt books, and correspondence were taken away from the premises'.[135] It is perhaps unsurprising that the Communist Party should think that 'the police seized more than evidence relating to the offence for which Campbell had been arrested'.[136] Indeed the removal of 'all the branch files of the Communist Party',[137] simply serves to confirm the suspicion that it was 'evidence against the Party that they were looking for'.[138] In fact the search lasted for over two hours after which a lorry was called for to remove all copies of the *Workers' Weekly* for 25 July and 1 August together with a pile of other documents.

As the *Workers' Weekly* pointed out, the case was of 'the utmost importance' in view of the fact that 'a Labour Government is in power'.[139] On

---

[131] MacFarlane, n 8 above, p 106.

[132] *Workers' Weekly*, 8 August 1924. The full charge is at *Workers' Weekly*, 15 August 1924.

[133] *Workers' Weekly*, 8 August 1924.

[134] *Daily Herald*, 7 August 1924. The power to conduct searches of this nature was to arise for consideration in *Elias v Pasmore* [1934] 2 KB 164 following a raid of the National Unemployed Workers' Movement. See Chapter 5 below.

[135] *Daily Herald*, 7 August 1924.   [136] *Workers' Weekly*, 8 August 1924.

[137] *Daily Herald*, 6 August 1924.   [138] *Workers' Weekly*, 8 August 1924.

[139] Ibid. The Labour Party had complained in 1921 about the sedition prosecutions as violating free speech, 'the birthright of every citizen and the fundamental condition of democracy': PRO, CAB/125, CP 3006, 2 June 1921.

the day after the arrest the matter was raised in Parliament by a number of concerned Labour backbenchers who were strongly critical of the government's decision to prosecute.[140] James Maxton (Glasgow Bridgeton) rose to ask the Prime Minister if he had read the article and if he was aware that it contained 'mainly a call to the troops not to allow themselves to be used in industrial disputes', a point of view 'shared by a large number of the Members sitting on these benches'.[141] The Attorney General (Sir Patrick Hastings) is reported as having replied that his attention had been called by the Director of Public Prosecutions to an article in *Workers' Weekly* which in the opinion of the Attorney 'constituted a breach of the law'. Following a ruling by the Speaker that the matter was *sub judice* and could not be the subject of debate, George Buchanan (Glasgow Gorbals) rose on a point of order to complain that the matter raised 'the whole right and liberty of the Press', pointing out that the article 'largely express[ed] the views and findings of Labour Party conferences' as well as of 'some of the men who are are at present sitting on the Front Bench'. But his plea that the issue was one of 'extreme public importance' which the House should consider fell on deaf ears, though it was not finally disposed of on this occasion until Thomas Dickson (Lanark) rose to ask the Attorney General whether Members of the House would also be subject to prosecution if in the course of speeches to their constituents they were to express similar opinions to those expressed in the offending *Workers' Weekly* article. For if so, he continued, the government would 'probably lose half their party', himself doubtless included.

The Campbell case was considered later that day (6 August) by the Cabinet, the Attorney General having been summoned to attend for part of the proceedings.[142] But to add spice to the drama, the Prime Minister questioned the accuracy of the Cabinet Conclusions of that meeting which at his insistence were then complemented by notes taken by the Principal Assistant Secretary to the Cabinet.[143] The latter reveal that a number of members of the Cabinet who had seen the offending article had taken a strong view as to its content. It was variously described as

[140] H C Debs, 6 August 1924, cols 2928–9. It tends to be forgotten that at the time of the arrest members of the CPGB were permitted also to be members of the Labour Party and to be adopted as Labour Party candidates, even though affiliation of the CPGB to the Labour Party had been denied. It was not until later that year that the Labour Party moved decisively against the communists. See pp 98–9 above, and p 124 below.

[141] It is unclear how carefully Maxton can have read the article, if at all!

[142] See Edwards, *The Law Officers of the Crown*, n 120 above, p 204.

[143] See PRO, CAB 23/48, Cabinet 48 (24), 6 August 1924, and PRO, CAB 23/48, Cabinet 55 (24), 9 October 1924 (from note of meeting of 6 August by Tom Jones).

'criminal' (Home Secretary), 'calculated to sow sedition' (War Secretary), a 'bad criminal offence', (Attorney General), and 'tripe' (Colonial Secretary). Stephen Walsh (the Secretary of State for War) in fact thought that it was the 'worst' article he had 'ever read', describing it also as 'atrocious'. But it was also clear that the prosecution had been instituted without the knowledge of the Prime Minister who insisted that he 'must be informed before action [of this kind is] taken', and that political cases should come to him in advance in accordance with a well established convention. Although he is reported cryptically as preferring to 'go through once started than show white feather', MacDonald also made clear that 'If put to me I should not have sanctioned it. I know the men and the game'.[144] Faced with what reads like a very censorious Cabinet, the Attorney General (who accepted full responsibility and ought to have resigned)[145] offered 'a possible way out' if this was desired, whereby Campbell would write a letter saying that he was only acting temporarily as editor while someone was on holiday. The Attorney General would accept the letter, the contents of which he would have 'to take cognisance reluctantly', thereby allowing steps to be taken not to press the prosecution. It was agreed that 'in the particular case under review the course indicated by the Attorney General should be adopted'.

It is clear that some Cabinet members shared the doubts reported by the Prime Minister about withdrawing the prosecution. According to Thomas it would 'create lively situation. Think they'd got us on the run'. Nevertheless when Campbell appeared in court after having been remanded on bail for a week, Mr Travers Humphreys QC for the prosecution stated that 'since process was issued in the case it had been represented that the object and intention of the article in question was not to endeavour to seduce men in the fighting forces from their duty and allegiance, or to disobey lawful orders, but that it was comment on armed military forces being used by the State for the suppression of individual disputes'. 'If that was a correct description of the article', he continued, it would be a complete defence in view of the judgment of Horridge J in the *Bowman* case 'seeing that the offence, to be complete, must be done maliciously, which meant intentionally and advisedly'. According to Humphreys it was easier to accept this rather benign interpretation of the article in view of the fact that Campbell was a man of 'excellent

---

[144] It is not clear what 'game' of theirs he had in mind, though the CPGB was later to claim that Campbell had intended to call MacDonald and others as witnesses, as they had been 'identified with resolutions opposing the use of soldiers in industrial disputes' (*Daily Herald*, 14 August 1924). These threats were dismissed by Childs, n 46 above, p 243.

[145] See also Taylor, n 114 above, p 289.

character' with 'an admirable military record':[146] he had in fact been seriously wounded during the war and had been awarded the Military Medal, though as the *Daily Herald* pointed out on 6 August his communist credentials were also beyond reproach; he was 'well-known in Glasgow as the late editor of the *Worker*, the Communist organ in that city'. The course proposed by the prosecution was accepted by the magistrate,[147] and the police agreed to return the books and documents which had been seized, these being said to comprise 'a whole heap of papers which had nothing to do with the case'. By this time of course the haul would no doubt have been recorded and fully digested by Childs and his chums in the Special Branch.[148]

The decision to withdraw the prosecution was greeted by the Political Bureau of the CPGB as 'a victory for the workers', the result of 'severe pressure' brought to bear on the government by the Labour movement.[149] But it was a strange kind of victory which was to lead within two months to the fall of the government, and within a year the imprisonment of virtually the entire leadership of the CPGB following the Conservative victory at the ensuing general election. The government was accused of being soft on communism and of being guilty of political interference in the administration of justice, charges which were particularly powerful at a time when it was already courting unpopularity because of its diplomatic links with Soviet Russia, one of the great achievements of the short-lived administration.[150] Resignation of the government after only nine months followed a defeat on a Liberal amendment to a Tory censure motion,[151] the amendment calling for an investigation of the Campell affair by a Select Committee, unacceptable because 'it proposed to put the honour of the Government in the hands of a partisan committee composed of seven opponents of the Government and only three supporters'.[152] At the heart of the debate

[146] *Workers' Weekly*, 15 August 1924.

[147] Thereby confounding the anticipation of the Special Branch which had concluded that because the case had so 'clearly established itself' he would 'refuse to allow the proceedings to be withdrawn'. See Childs, n 46 above, p 243.

[148] The foregoing account of proceedings is based on the report in the *Daily Herald*, 14 August 1924. See also *Workers' Weekly*, 15 August 1924. For a fuller explanation by the Attorney General, see H C Debs, 30 September 1924, col 8. [149] *Daily Herald*, 14 August 1924.

[150] Paradoxically the Labour Party was simultaneously taking steps to exclude communists. Indeed on 7 October 1924 (the day before the censure motion) Party conference voted to prevent Communists from being Party candidates or members. See pp 98–9 above.

[151] H C Debs, 8 October 1924, cols 581–704. On the previous day the Labour Party conference had voted communists ineligible for membership. See Klugmann, *History*, n 10 above, pp 309–24.

[152] PRO, CAB 23/48, Cabinet 52 (24), 6 October 1924. For an account of the position adopted by the Liberals, see E A Jenkins, *From Foundry to Foreign Office: The Romantic Life Story of the Rt Hon Arthur Henderson MP* (1933), p 111.

was the constitutional role of the Attorney General who has wide discretionary powers relating to the administration of justice, in the exercise of which 'he is not subject to direction by his ministerial colleagues or to control and supervision by the Courts'.[153] The Campbell case did, however, reveal genuine uncertainty concerning the extent to which the Attorney General was permitted to consult Cabinet colleagues about the authorisation of a prosecution, as well as about whether a prosecution should be withdrawn. Both the Attorney General and the Prime Minister were clearly of the view that the Law Officers were entitled to seek the views of other ministers 'in a case where the public interest may conflict with the strict exercise of [their] duty'.[154]

During the censure debate on 8 October the Attorney General, Sir Patrick Hastings, had asserted the right to 'have received instructions from the Government' on a matter such as the prosecution of communists.[155] In the course of doing so, he effectively cited recent precedents involving Attorneys General, F E Smith and Sir Gordon Hewart, which tended to support his view, and indeed went some way to suggest that it was the established practice for the prior sanction of the Cabinet to be obtained before prosecutions of a political nature were commenced.[156] In the same vein the Prime Minister asserted as a matter of principle that 'every Law Officer who is undertaking a prosecution in the interests of the State' must be advised on whether 'the prosecution will be harmful or beneficial to the State in whose interests it has been undertaken'.[157] There was little dissent from this position.[158] There was, however, a distinction drawn between consulting colleagues in advance of a decision to prosecute on the one hand and consulting colleagues in advance of a decision to withdraw a prosecution, a distinction which Sir Patrick clearly did not accept. Sir John Simon had never heard of a case in which a prosecution had been withdrawn in such circumstances, while Sir

[153] *Gouriet v UPW* [1978] AC 435, at p 487 (Viscount Dilhorne).
[154] H C Debs, 8 October 1924, col 598. [155] Ibid, col 614.
[156] These are fully considered by Edwards, *The Law Officers of the Crown*, n 120 above, pp 208–11. See also H C Debs, 8 October 1924, cols 598–9.
[157] H C Debs, 8 October 1924, col 629.
[158] Except, it seems from Childs, n 46 above, pp 241–2 who thought the matter 'perfectly simple', and saw no reason why the government should have been consulted. Shortly after the election in 1924 Baldwin replied to a parliamentary question by saying that 'it is the duty of the Attorney-General, in the discharge of the responsibilities so entrusted to him, to inform himself of all relevant circumstances which might properly affect his decision: when the proposed prosecution is of such a character that matters of public policy are, or may be, involved, it is the duty of the Attorney General to inform himself of the views of the Government or of the appropriate Minister before coming to a decision': H C Debs, 18 December 1924, col 1214. In other words the Attorney General must seek the views of the government but is not bound by them, in the sense that he must still exercise an independent judgement in deciding whether to prosecute or not.

Douglas Hogg 'never took advice or counsel, or brooked interference from any Minister or anybody else in the question whether [a prosecution] should be withdrawn'.[159] That was a decision for the Attorney General to take 'judicially and uninfluenced by any outside person'[160] but which in this case had been taken in response to backbench pressure. Such a distinction has a rather disingenuous ring to it, particularly if there is a duty on the part of the Attorney General to be kept informed of the public interest;[161] even more absurd is the claim that by its conduct the government had departed from 'the most essential bulwark of our liberty', namely 'the freedom of the judiciary from any executive interference'.[162]

J H Thomas had thus been proved to be perfectly correct when he predicted a 'lively situation', though not even he could have anticipated that a 'trivial matter of domestic politics' would lead to the defeat of the government.[163] This is not to say that Sir Patrick was blameless and not deserving of the strongest censure.[164] Had he secured the advice of his colleagues before consenting to proceed (as his successor Sir Douglas Hogg did less than a year later before commencing proceedings for sedition against a number of leading communists),[165] the whole affair could have been avoided:[166] having given his consent, he exposed the government to the charge that they had reacted to political pressures in their own interests rather than the public interest, a perception not helped by the triumphalist response of the CPGB.[167] But for all that the Campbell case provided an opportunity rather than a reason to remove the minority government, with a sanctimonious but hypocritical appeal to consti-

---

[159] H C Debs, 8 October 1924, col 686.　　　　　　　　　　　　　[160] Ibid.

[161] Is the acknowledged duty of the Attorney General to have regard to public interest considerations before authorising a prosecution not a continuing obligation?

[162] H C Debs, 8 October 1924, col 686.

[163] H Pelling, *A Short History of the Labour Party* (11th edn by A J Reid, 1996), p 54. According to Arthur Henderson's biographer, 'Nobody in his wildest moments imagined in the summer that the prosecution of an obscure and war-wounded Communist in a London police court would lead to the downfall of a Socialist Government' (E A Jenkins, n 152 above, p 110). Campbell defiantly denied responsibility for the fate of the government: J R Campbell, *My Case*, n 67 above.

[164] See also J Ll J Edwards, *The Attorney General, Politics and the Public Interest*, n 120 above, pp 313–14. Nor is it to suggest that the Cabinet should have the right to instruct the Attorney General about prosecutions, though this does not appear to have happened here, the Attorney General having taken a decision to withdraw which was subsequently endorsed by the Cabinet. See Edwards, ibid, p 315.

[165] H C Debs, 1 December 1925, col 2171.

[166] It ought nevertheless to be noted that Sir Patrick's speech in the censure debates was widely praised, and that he was formally thanked by the Cabinet: PRO, CAB 23/48, Cabinet 53 (24), 8 October 1924.

[167] See especially *Daily Herald*, 14 August 1924, and also *Workers' Weekly* 22 August 1924 which hailed the withdrawal of the prosecution as a 'triumph' for 'outside political forces'.

tutional principle failing to disguise more base political motives. The real sacrifice of constitutional principle to political expediency in this sorry affair was freedom of expression, with only the *New Statesman* of the mainstream press prepared to defend 'complete freedom of the press', arguing that it was time 'the police authorities were informed that prosecutions for "sedition" are out of date and will not be officially supported'. Going further the *New Statesman* urged the Home Secretary to 'circulate a Minute to this effect and thus save the Public Prosecutor from the necessity of such a palpable climb-down as he has had to make'.[168] Perhaps predictably it was left to the *Workers' Weekly* to call on the government to repeal the various laws on the statute book 'which are being continually used for the suppression of working class opinion', referring to 'musty sedition laws which are used only against working class agitation'.[169] The Party was soon to feel the full blast of these laws, musty or not.

Meetings and Assemblies

Following the Campbell case, the harassment of the Party developed another dimension, relating to the difficulty encountered in holding meetings and assemblies, notwithstanding the fact that the evidence against the Party 'has never been the spoken word'.[170] Two problems in particular arose: the first was the problem of prior restraint; and the second was the problem of police powers in relation to things said or done in the course of a meeting or assembly, there being 'hardly a meeting held in any part where the Home Secretary does not post his men'.[171] So far as prior restraints are concerned, the first source of difficulty related to *private property* in which to hold meetings, a problem illustrated by the circumstances surrounding the Lenin memorial campaign, 'organised on a larger scale than any preceding'[172] by the Party for Sunday, 18 January 1925. In one well-publicised example Mr Charles Gulliver, as occupier, had given permission for a meeting to be held in the New Oxford Theatre, a decision which apparently had caused much opposition.[173] Three days before the meeting was due to be held, Gulliver

---

[168] *New Statesman*, 16 August 1924. The *Daily Herald* (14 August 1924) was also critical of the decision to prosecute, but not expressly on free speech grounds.
[169] *Workers' Weekly*, 22 August 1924. See also Campbell, *My Case*, n 67 above, p 4.
[170] Childs, n 46 above, p 209.   [171] H C Debs, 11 July 1928, col 2374 (S Saklatvala).
[172] CPGB, *Report of the Seventh National Congress 1925*, p 153.
[173] This account is drawn from the *Workers' Weekly*, 23 January 1925. See also *The Times*, 17–19 January 1925.

received a letter from O & P Productions Ltd informing him that the superior licensors of the theatre had not consented to the meeting being held and instructing him 'to cancel the arrangements immediately'.[174] Gulliver replied that he knew of no agreement which would prevent the meeting being held during his tenancy and that in the absence of an injunction to restrain the meeting from being held, he had no power to cancel the arrangement. He also pointed out that 'the same people' (the communist organisers) had already held a meeting on another of his properties, that they had also held a meeting at the Royal Albert Hall, and that they had 'supplied satisfactory bankers' references, solicitors' references and a policy of insurance covering any possible damage to the property'.

On receiving a copy of O & P Productions letter, the Communist Party advised Gulliver that they wanted to proceed with their meeting. He agreed to carry out his contract and an injunction (on grounds unknown) was applied for at 4.00 p.m. on Friday, 16 January, to restrain Gulliver from allowing the meeting to go ahead. The case was adjourned until 10.30 a.m. the following morning (Saturday) to allow Gulliver to be present and to make representations. According to the *Workers' Weekly*, 'Dry as dust legal argument' ensued on the Saturday morning, with 'fortune veering first this way then that. It appeared that thousands of pounds were at stake on the verdict, and the point was at last put that to disappoint the Communist Party would be far and away cheaper than disappointing certain other people'. The injunction was granted by Finlay J to restrain the present occupier from permitting any political meeting to be held at the New Oxford Theatre, drawing the predictable but perhaps not unjustifiable response that 'the powers that be have made up their minds that the Communist Party shall hold no meetings to express their views, and are prepared to use any weapon, fair or foul, to accomplish their purpose. So much again for the vaunted English tradition of Free Speech'. According to the *Workers' Weekly*, the case demonstrated 'with pitiless clearness the way in which the censorship of the British ruling class acts in relation to the revolutionary workers' Party'. In other words 'Free Speech—for all except those who are dangerous to capitalism'. Mr Gulliver was thanked for his 'gallant attempt to stand by

---

[174] This was by no means the only example of steps being taken to prevent meetings from being held. Halls were unobtainable in several Midland centres, Newcastle and elsewhere, while in Bradford advertisements were refused for display by the municipal authorities at the last minute. See CPGB, *Report of the Seventh National Congress 1925*, p 153.

the contract', and his open advocacy of the rights of the Communist Party to be heard along with everyone else.

Faced with difficulties in securing premises for the holding of meetings, an obvious response would be to hold assemblies in the open-air—in the streets, parks or seashore. But without wishing to suggest that communists were forbidden from meeting,[175] here too the Party encountered trouble, not the least of which was caused by *local bye-laws* requiring the permission of the magistrates before meetings or assemblies could be held in public places. One example of this was Glasgow where the bye-laws required the prior consent of the magistrates for meetings to be held on Glasgow Green.[176] Another example was Greenock where permission was required for street processions.[177] An unsuccessful attempt to challenge the legality of the first of these measures was made in 1925 by Guy Aldred 'a lecturer in socialist politics' who although not a member of the CPGB referred to himself as a 'non-parliamentary communist'. In upholding his conviction for an unauthorised meeting on Glasgow Green, the High Court of Justiciary sitting in Edinburgh found the bye-laws neither arbitrary nor unfair.[178] Dealing specifically with the claim that the bye-law was 'an unwarranted violation of the rights of free speech and public meeting', the Court held first that there was 'no interference with the right of the speaker to express any opinion he pleases', and secondly that it merely regulates but does not prevent the holding of public meetings. Admittedly, the court did deprecate the magistrates' practice of 'sporadic enforcement' of the bye-law on the ground that this does not 'make for its respect or due observance'. But it was held nevertheless that the magistrates were free to enforce it when they saw fit.

The use of bye-laws as a way of prohibiting communist meetings and assemblies was a matter of particular controversy in Greenock where it seems that the magistrates had rigidly refused permission for communist marches, though other organisations—the Boy Scouts, the Boys' Brigade and the Salvation Army—were free to march with relative impunity. As early as 1921 five 'comrades' were charged with addressing an assemblage of persons without the permission of the magistrates. A crowd of several thousand people had assembled, but were met by a large

---

[175] See for example the communist demonstration held in Trafalgar Square in July 1924, addressed by Shipurji Saklatvala and M Henriet, communist member of the French Chamber of Deputies. See *The Times*, 28 July 1924.

[176] See *Aldred v Miller*, 1925 JC 21.

[177] Difficulties encountered by communists in Greenock are reported in *The Communist*, 23 April 1921.

[178] *Aldred v Miller*, 1925 JC 21.

number of police, some of them mounted. Those charged with breach of the bye-law pleaded guilty, although one of their number explained that he was a stranger to the town and unaware of the bye-law, while another pointed out that he had been making speeches for over fourteen years without a permit and had never encountered any trouble. They were each sentenced to forty shillings or twenty days.[179] Further difficulties in Greenock were encountered in June 1925 when the Communist Young Pioneers defied a refusal by the magistrates to grant permission for a street procession, and marched through the town with a band playing and banner flying, followed by a large crowd. A great meeting of protest was then held in the town, at which several young communists spoke, including 'Comrade' Taylor, a twelve-year-old who conveyed greetings from the Glasgow Party Congress. The meeting was dispersed by the police and a number of protesters were arrested, including 'Comrade Murphy' who was playing the big drum. Also arrested was the woman who took over the drum after the arrest of Murphy.[180] The Secretary of State for Scotland later informed the House of Commons that permission to hold the demonstration had been refused because the magistrates 'considered as a result of previous experience that it was not desirable in the public interest to grant such permission'. The matter was one 'entirely in the discretion of the magistrates'. So far as claims about police brutality were concerned, the Minister was again unable to comment in light of 'legal proceedings . . . pending in connection with the arrests'.[181]

Turning to the question of police control of the conduct of meetings, this too had a number of dimensions, one being the *police power to prevent meetings from being held, and the police power to stop meetings*. It is true that more specific powers of this kind were, as we have seen, contained in the Emergency Regulations 1921 and that a number of Communist Party activists fell foul of these restrictions. But the repeal of the regulations did not remove the powers of the police, with the courts refusing to recognise as early as 1924 the individual's private right 'to make use of any

---

[179] *The Communist*, 23 April 1921.

[180] *Workers' Weekly*, 19 June 1925.

[181] H C Debs, 29 June 1925, col 2044 (WA). Further evidence of difficulty is revealed by the case of Councillor Canning (a communist member of Greenock Town Council) and John Porter (chairman of the Greenock Trades and Labour Council) who were charged with contravening a magistrates' order forbidding a procession in the town. In spite of the order the accused issued leaflets to workers urging them to join the Communist Party and to rally to the demonstration, with the result that thousands turned up to see what would happen. A large force of police was also present (*The Times*, 15 September 1925).

public street for the holding of public meetings'.[182] In that case Guy
Aldred (again) appealed to the High Court of Justiciary against his conviction by the Maryhill Police Court under the Glasgow Police Act 1866
whereby it was an offence to cause an obstruction in any road or street
or to hinder or prevent the free passage along the highway. Aldred had
regularly held open air meetings near the Botanical Gardens in Glasgow,
the meetings being 'well known to the police' and drawing large crowds.
On one occasion, however, a crowd of 300 gathered, blocking one of the
pavements, and causing traffic to slow down. When a car was brought
to a standstill until a passage was cleared, the driver complained to a
police officer who asked Aldred to stop lecturing, a request which was
denied on the ground that he was 'not going to give up his right to
address a public meeting'. In dismissing the appeal against conviction
(despite the fact that Aldred 'was conducting himself in a perfectly
orderly manner in the exercise of his right of speaking in public and
addressing the lieges on his political views'), the High Court of Justiciary
denied the right of public protest, and held that an obstruction of the
highway 'is not any the less objectionable because the author of it is a
person who advertises or otherwise convenes a public meeting in order
that it may stand on the street and listen to his speeches'.[183]

The case is important for indicating the extent to which the police
could move against those preaching a communist or socialist message in
public, the oppressive use of the power being indicated by the evidence
that it was used selectively, with evidence that the police appeared to tolerate larger gatherings by other organisations.[184] But there is no suggestion in the report that this thereby gave the police the power to stop a
meeting from taking place or continuing, or indeed to arrest the organiser or speaker. In this case Aldred (who had offered the police officer his
name and address) had been cited to answer the complaint (in other
words summonsed to appear in the local police court), though convictions of this kind could well have had a chilling effect in respect of similar such meetings in the future. There are however other cases, more
specifically directed at communists who wished to hold public meetings,
in which the police appear to have assumed the power to ban the
meeting or assembly from being held. One example of this is the case of
Harry Webb from Sheffield, who complained about the police stopping

---

[182] *Aldred v Miller*, 1924 SLT 613, at p 615.   [183] Ibid.
[184] For evidence of the power being used against communist speakers, see *The Times*, 11 July 1924
where it is reported that 'At Govan Police Court, 12 well known Communist leaders and sympathisers were fined sums varying from £1 to £6 for obstruction at a street meeting on Sunday
evening'.

a factory gate meeting in the city on 8 March 1926, without asking the purpose of the meeting or stating their authority to suppress it. Webb was told that he would not be permitted to speak and was 'jostled' away by police officers (of which there were nineteen present, including two on horseback) when he announced his intention to do so. The aborted meeting was to be held outside Hadfields where meetings had been held regularly for twenty years, the company having erected a special platform for the purpose. The freedom of communists to hold meetings at this spot was only restored following a deputation to the Acting Chief Constable from members of the Party and employees engaged at Hadfields.[185] This incident—which anticipates the famous decision of the Divisional Court in *Duncan v Jones*[186] by some ten years—highlights the de facto power of the police to license an assembly, even where, as here, the legal authority for the exercise of such a power was far from clear and perhaps not really very important.

Apart from these powers relating to the very fact of a meeting being held, the other power was the *police power to restrain what could be said or done at a meeting*. This was perhaps a more significant and more frequent ground for police action. In one case involving three prominent members of the Communist Party in Birmingham, Arthur Swain, Forbes Robertson, and James MacDonald, the defendants were charged with 'inciting' by 'inflammatory speeches' a crowd of some 250 assembled at a meeting of the central branch of the National Unemployed Workers' Committee Movement being held at the city's Bull Ring.[187] Swain was reported as having said that 'They gave you rifles and bayonets to kill the enemy class, as they told you; but let me tell you, the enemy is here, and you have got to get the rifles and bayonets to use them where your enemies are'. Later he said 'You will get nothing without bloodshed, and it rests with you whose blood it is to be. You have got to see it is their blood. They have all the rifles and bayonets. You have got to get possession of these things and use them on those people who are out to shed your blood'. Later still Swain is reported as having said that 'There is enough food in this country for all. It is only waiting for you to go and take it. You have got to rise up in your might and attack these people'. These statements were said to have been received with great cheering and the police who were present (two of whom were taking shorthand notes) 'became apprehensive that violence would break out'. According to the prosecution, the speeches were 'likely to incite to acts of violence

---

[185] *Workers' Weekly*, 26 March 1926. [186] [1936] 1 KB 218. See Chapter 6 below.
[187] *The Times*, 22 August 1924.

and to thefts from shops. They were addressed to unemployed men down on their luck and rather bitter against life, and were therefore of a highly mischievous nature'. In fairly defiant terms one of the accused claimed that he had no intention to incite the public to violence, but was out to change the system 'and would use any means, either the Army, the Navy, or the Air Force to effect this'; another proclaimed that 'he would take his stand in the fight against capitalism, and it would not worry him if his remarks caused a disturbance of the peace'.

The three accused were dealt fairly leniently by the stipendiary magistrate, who concluded that 'there was no doubt the speeches were calculated to cause a breach of the peace'. The three were bound over to keep the peace, with the option of prison sentences of three months for Swain, six weeks for Robertson, and one month for MacDonald. Although the threat of imprisonment was hardly surprising in view of the facts, there are nevertheless important questions which are raised by the binding over power, and in particular the affront which it creates for fundamental principles such as the Rule of Law or the principle of legality, given that it permits the imposition of restraints on individuals without there necessarily being proof that the individual committed an offence.[188] Nevertheless the power is one of great antiquity, being referred to by Blackstone as suitable for use in a number of different cases, including 'for words tending to scandalise the government',[189] and as such it was widely used against those who engaged in radical politics, including George Lansbury who urged the suffragettes to 'break the law on every possible occasion'.[190] Other evidence of binding over orders being used against communists is provided by the case of Ernest Woolley, described as the leader of the Young Communist League, who was bound over for twelve months at Manchester in September 1925. In this case it was alleged that in Ogden Street, Higher Openshaw, Woolley and another man had set up a platform 'without necessary police permission' (the source of the need for which was unclear) to hold a meeting in the street. When warned by a police constable, Woolley is alleged to have called to the crowd 'This is the dirty specimen of a Britisher who tries to prevent free speech', whereupon he was arrested.[191] As we shall see in Chapter 4 below, the refusal to be bound over in the early days of the General

---

[188] See Law Commission, *Binding Over*, Cm 2439 (1994), and Law Commission, Working Paper No 103, *Criminal Law. Binding Over: The Issues* (1987), pp 45–55.

[189] Blackstone, *Commentaries on the Laws of England* (7th edn, 1775), iv, p 256.

[190] *Lansbury v Riley* [1914] 3 KB 229.   [191] *The Times*, 2 September 1925.

Strike led to the imprisonment of Shipurji Saklatvala following a speech made at Hyde Park in May 1926.

There were in fact very few *specific offences* for which speakers at communist meetings could be charged. There was the possibility of obstruction of the highway or breach of the bye-laws for holding a meeting without the consent of the appropriate local authority. Yet at least ostensibly these were concerned with the fact that a meeting or assembly was being held at all, rather than with the substance of what might have been said at the meeting. But apart from the possibility of imprisonment for breach of the peace for refusing to be bound over (as in the case of Saklatvala who was imprisoned for two months), there were very few offences which could be enlisted to challenge the substance or content of the communist message, though admittedly the binding over power was potentially as effective as it was constitutionally offensive. With the revocation of the Emergency Regulations there was no general police power to arrest for sedition or disaffection, though this is not to say that the authorities were completely naked in the face of communist speeches. Admittedly the Army Council was disappointed that regulation 42 of the Defence of the Realm Regulations was not made permanent 'to deal with propagandists';[192] but there were nevertheless two statutory provisions introduced in 1919 aimed at those seeking to promote disaffection. The first was the Aliens Restriction (Amendment) Act 1919 which by section 3 provided that it was an offence for an alien to do anything to cause sedition or disaffection amongst the armed forces or the civilian population. But in practice this measure played little part in the regulation of communist meetings and assemblies in the 1920s, one reason perhaps being the determination with which aliens with communist sympathies were excluded from the country in the first place.[193] As the biographer of Sir William Joynson-Hicks pointed out, vindicating concerns raised during the Report stage of the 1919 Act,[194] one of Joynson-Hicks's aims as Home Secretary was 'to keep out undesirable political agitators who sought to enter the country to foment trouble'.[195]

---

[192] Young, *Incitement to Disaffection*, n 39 above, p 29.

[193] These powers were exercised, for example, in the case of foreign delegates to the CPGB annual congress in 1925. See PRO, CAB 24/173, CP 224 (25), 2 May 1925. Memorandum by the Home Secretary. Also PRO, CAB 23/50, Cabinet 25 (25), 13 May 1925 (Cabinet approval for course proposed by Home Secretary).

[194] Concern had been expressed (by Colonel Wedgwood) that 'this Clause may be read so as to make it impossible for any person of well-known Socialistic politics in any of the countries of Europe or America to remain on these shores without grave danger to himself. [HON. MEMBERS: Hear, hear!]' (H C Debs, 22 October 1919, col 153).

[195] H A Taylor, *Jix—Viscount Brentford* (1933), p 181. So notorious was this campaign that even

The other measure designed to combat sedition was the Police Act 1919, passed at a time of discontent in the police force and in the aftermath of the only strike by British police officers. The Act provided for the establishment of the Police Federation and also prohibited police officers from being members of trade unions. So far as disaffection is concerned, this was dealt with in section 3 which made it an offence to cause disaffection amongst the members of any police force. It was explained during the Second Reading debate that this measure was designed to protect police officers from 'the doctrines of men of very wild and extreme views',[196] and later that it was 'the agent of disaffection and of revolution and the agent of real mischief which is aimed at' in section 3.[197] But although it does not appear to have been widely used in the campaign against communism, there are a few cases in which it features prominently. One of these is the case of the Greenock councillors, 'Comrades' Hinshelwood and Gillies who were convicted for breaching the Police Act 1919 for words spoken while addressing a communist meeting on 13 September 1925, where they were reported as attempting to induce members of the police force to go on strike, use their batons against their superior officers, and organise themselves as workers' defence corps. They were each sentenced to sixty days' imprisonment and fined £10, with another thirty days in the event of default.[198] Inciting disaffection in members of the armed forces was also still an offence notwithstanding the lapsing of the Defence of the Realm Regulations 1914 and the Emergency Regulations 1921. Under the Incitement to Mutiny Act 1797, as we have seen, it was an offence for any person maliciously and advisedly to endeavour to seduce a member of the forces from his or her duty of allegiance to Her Majesty. Yet there is no evidence to suggest that this was regularly, if ever, used against speakers at communist meetings or assemblies, even though penetration of the military was an important part of communist strategy.[199] But notwithstanding the setback for the authorities in the Campbell case, the 1797 Act was to become a key weapon in the planned attack on Communist Party publications.[200]

---

the *New York Times* had commented on his 'barring the British Isles in the most vigorous fashion to all alien Communists and Bolshevist agents' (ibid). See pp 207–9 below.

[196] H C Debs, 18 July 1919, col 795.   [197] H C Debs, 1 August 1919, col 2458.

[198] *The Times*, 9 October 1925.

[199] And even though the preamble to the Act clearly contemplates that it was a response to 'malicious and advised speaking' as well as 'the publication of written or printed papers'.

[200] Another problem which was beginning to appear in the 1920s was the problem of fascist disruption at meetings. See for example *The Times*, 20 July 1925 (fascist disruption at a Communist Party meeting in Fulham). (See also *The Times*, 4 May 1925, 25 May 1925, 8 July 1925—burglary of Party offices in Glasgow.) See generally, Chapter 7 below.

The Sedition Trial of 1925

Following the resignation of the MacDonald government in 1924, the Conservatives were returned at the general election winning 419 of the 615 seats, helped in the process by the complicity of the secret service[201] (though not it seems the Special Branch)[202] in publicising the notorious Zinoviev letter which is thought to have played some part in determining the outcome of the general election.[203] The campaign against com-

---

[201] Andrew, n 32 above, p 438.

[202] See Barnes, n 52 above, p 949. Wyndham Childs successfully sued for libel 'a certain journal' which accused him of playing 'a large part in the infamous affair' (Childs, n 46 above, p 246).

[203] It is widely acknowledged that the election was dominated by the Labour Government's diplomatic recognition of Soviet Russia, which included the conclusion of a General Treaty and a Trading Agreement. The Conservatives fought a campaign which was strongly anti-Russian, in the course of which they sought to show that Labour and Communism were closely connected and that 'Labour's mildness was traceable wholly to its minority position'. According to one Conservative leaflet, in a communist Britain, 'the monarchy will be ended and a Bolshevik Republic set up. Religion will be stamped out. The Home will be destroyed . . . Children will be taken from their mothers and made the property of the State'. Into this cesspit was thrown the infamous 'red letter', alleged to have been written from the headquarters of the Third International in Moscow to the Communist Party of Great Britain, and bearing the names of Zinovieff (the president), Kuusinen (the secretary), and MacManus (a member of the Presidium). The letter, bearing the date 15 September 1924, drew attention to the fact that the Anglo-Soviet Treaty was due to be considered for ratification by Parliament and called upon the proletariat to 'show the greatest possible energy' in the struggle for ratification in light of the fierce campaign against ratification being 'raised by the British bourgeoisie'. These provisions were no doubt unexceptionable, though this was not true of subsequent terms of the letter which were about developing 'the propaganda of ideas of Leninism in England', about the need (as a precondition of 'armed warfare', to 'struggle against the inclinations to compromise which are embedded among a majority of the British workmen', and about the need to improve 'agitation-propaganda work in the Army', and to develop the military section of the 'British Communist Party', the 'future directors of the British Red Army'. The text of the letter, the contents of which were 'no novelty' (E H Carr, 'The Zinoviev Letter' (1979) 22 *Historical Journal* 209) is reproduced in the *Workers' Weekly*, 31 October 1924. See also Cmd 2895 (1927), p 30. Copies of the letter became available to Conservative Central Office (which 'paid handsomely' for its copy) (R Blake, *The Conservative Party from Peel to Churchill* (1970), p 225) and the *Daily Mail*. When the newspaper announced its intention to print the letter, it was published by the Foreign Office (which had received a copy of the letter on 10 October), together with a strong note of protest to the Soviet Charges d'Affaires which had been drafted by the Prime Minister but released without his consent. The note, bearing the name of an official J D Gregory, was also damaging, accusing the Russians of a breach of faith in failing to curb the Comintern's propaganda, or alternatively of making agreements which 'it knows it cannot carry out'. Either way the government stood condemned: 'either MacDonald knew all along that the Soviets were in the habit of signing agreements with no intent to keep them, or he has only just learned this by the bitter experience of the Zinoviev letter; if the former, he should never have negotiated the Anglo-Soviet treaties; if the latter he stands convicted of incompetence' (Lyman, n 120 above, p 259). A Cabinet Committee appointed on 31 October was unable to come to any conclusion on the authenticity of the letter, the original having been neither produced to nor seen by any government department (PRO, CAB 23/48, Cabinet 58 (24), 4 November 1924). But although the letter contributed to the 'general atmosphere' of the election (Lyman, n 120 above) the Labour vote remained remarkably solid; losing 64 of its 191 seats but in the process winning another 24 and increasing its share of the popular vote, though the Party fought more seats than in previous elections. The real victim of the election was the already declining Liberal Party, reduced to a rump of 40 seats. So far as the Zinoviev letter is concerned, it is widely thought to have been a forgery: see now G Bennett, '*A Most Extraordinary and Mysterious*

munism continued apace, culminating in the arrest of twelve of the Party's senior officials in October 1925.[204] Inevitably, government ministers played a key part in the proceedings, the leading players being the Home Secretary (Sir William Joynson-Hicks, or 'Jix' as he was sometimes known) and the Attorney General (Sir Douglas Hogg, later Lord Hailsham). History records that Sir William acquired information 'through those who are charged with the carrying out of law and order in this country' which he 'put before' the Attorney General and the Director of Public Prosecutions 'to decide whether there is a case or not'.[205] He subsequently denied that there was a Cabinet decision 'to proceed with the prosecution in the first place', though the impact of this denial was reduced by his concession that there was complete unanimity of his colleagues on the matter. How widely they had been consulted can only be speculated from a rather opaque response in a parliamentary exchange in which he said that he was in touch with his colleagues 'with very many matters, day by day and all day long' as a result of which he was 'prepared to say' that his colleagues, 'if there had been a Cabinet decision, would not have disavowed the action taken'.[206]

This suggests that the communist threat was taken more seriously by the Conservative administration than by its predecessor. Although Arthur Henderson had also referred material to the Attorney General in 1924 before the Campbell prosecution, presumably from the same Special Branch source, there is no evidence that he consulted colleagues in the Cabinet before doing so. Nor is there evidence that Sir Patrick Hastings had consulted the Cabinet before giving the Director of Public Prosecutions the authority to proceed. In this case, however, Christopher Andrew claims that:

On 13 October the Attorney General, Sir Douglas Hogg, informed the Cabinet that there was enough evidence 'to justify the arrest and prosecution of nine of the leading British Communists on a charge of sedition, and that in his opinion a prosecution was likely to result in convictions'. The Cabinet was asked whether there were 'any factors in the national or industrial situation which rendered a prosecution undesirable' but said that it had 'no objection'.[207]

Business': The Zinoviev Letter of 1924 (1999). It is to be noted that the British were also in the business of forgery, with false copies of *Pravda* being dispatched to Finland in 1921, a fact revealed when the printer's name appeared on the paper! See H C Debs, 8 March 1921, col 272 (WA).

[204] Those arrested were 10 members of the central committee of the Party and two others: CPGB, *Report of the Eighth Congress 1926*, p 2.

[205] H C Debs, 1 December 1925, col 2095.   [206] Ibid.

[207] Andrew, n 32 above, pp 454–5. In so responding, the Cabinet formally acknowledged 'the constitutional responsibilities of the Attorney General' (PRO, CAB 23/51, Cabinet 48 (25), 13 October 1925).

There was, of course, nothing constitutionally improper about this course of action, the Attorney General merely consulting rather than taking instructions from the Cabinet. Although the distinction between the two may not always be clear, as a result of this case Cabinet consultation was nevertheless elevated into a constitutional duty rather than a constitutional right of the Attorney General. In a famous speech Sir John Simon asserted that a good Attorney General would be 'a fool' if he were 'to start on his own motion prosecutions which involve grave matters of public concern—treason, sedition, corruption, and the like—. . . without knowing that, in the view of his colleagues, public policy was not offended by undertaking such a prosecution'.[208]

According to the *Daily Herald*, although the warrants had been issued on the morning of 14 October (the day after Cabinet 'approval' had been given), 'the police waited until as many of the officers and prominent members of the Party as possible were on the premises. Then they acted'.[209] In fact, it is clear that the police raided several premises in London, including the headquarters of the CPGB, the offices of the Red International of Labour Unions, the Young Communist League and the National Minority Movement.[210] It is clear too that the premises which were raided were also ransacked again. Thus, 'Every room [of the Party's premises] was invaded and every scrap of paper and all the files, including the cabinets, were removed in two lorries, which returned several times. The office was absolutely cleaned out, even the pictures being taken off the walls. The whole of the books, periodicals and other publications were removed in 20 vans to Scotland Yard. All the back numbers of *Workers' Weekly*, as well as those for publication . . . and other Communist publications were also confiscated'.[211] Much the same appears to have happened at the simultaneous raid of the National Minority Movement's premises, with Harry Pollitt complaining that the police not only ransacked his room but also seized 'every single document they could lay their hands on, although it had no relation to the charge'.[212] A police officer later claimed that 'he had the power to take whatever he liked, and he took whatever he thought necessary', while the Home Secretary thought the procedure perfectly regular even though conducted without the authority of a search warrant.[213] It is true that at

---

[208] H C Debs, 1 December 1925, col 2106. Further light may be shed on this issue by the closed Home Office file 'Activities of the Communist Party of Great Britain. The relative responsibility of Attorney General and Home Secretary in instituting political prosecutions' (PRO, HO 144/4684).

[209] *Daily Herald*, 15 October 1925.   [210] *The Times*, 15, 16 October 1925.

[211] *Daily Herald*, 15 October 1925.   [212] *The Times*, 18 November 1925.

[213] H C Debs, 17 February 1926, col 1960.

common law police officers could 'search the dwelling of a person for whose arrest a warrant has been issued, whenever it seems likely that any material evidence . . . can be obtained'.[214] But it is unclear how this would support the removal of furniture or other materials 'without regard to their possible relevance to the case'.[215]

This was not the only note of controversy in the wake of the arrests. On the same evening the Home Secretary addressed the Hounslow Amateur Dramatic Society. In what was described by *The Times* as 'a most improper whoop',[216] he is reported as having said that 'the greater part of the audience will be pleased to hear that warrants were issued, and in the majority of cases have been executed, for the arrest of a certain number of notorious Communists'.[217] Describing this as an 'outrageous statement', the *Daily Herald* pointed out that here we had 'a Minister closely associated with the administration of justice asking an audience to be pleased over the arrest of certain of the King's subjects, men who may possibly have to stand their (sic) trial before a jury'.[218] Yet the Home Secretary's was not the only 'extraordinary lapse'. An article in the *Westminster Gazette* on 15 October alleged that the aim of the communists was 'to instil terror into the minds of the public by means of criminal outrages in the hope that the path would be clear for undermining the confidence of the people in the strength of the Constitution'.[219] The *Evening News*, encouraged by the Home Secretary's speech, also 'defied' the law by publishing a leading article headed 'Well done "Jix" ' and a cartoon directed to the case. It was fined £100 for contempt of court by Avory J for publishing material likely to prejudice the fair trial of the accused.[220] Perhaps unsurprisingly the *Workers' Weekly* thought the amount of the fine 'surprisingly small', in view of the fact that the *Evening News* was a high circulation newspaper.[221] There is no record of contempt proceedings being brought against the Home Secretary,[222] who in the following week also read to the Cabinet 'a number of documents which had been seized in connection with the [raid]'.[223]

---

[214] H C Debs, 17 February 1926, col 1960. See *Bessell v Wilson* (1853) 20 LT (OS) 233, and *Dillon v O'Brien and Davis* (1887) 16 Cox CC 245. See subsequently *Elias v Pasmore* [1934] 2 KB 164. See generally, Chapter 5 below.

[215] H C Debs, 17 February 1926, col 1960.   [216] *The Times*, 30 November 1925.

[217] *Daily Herald*, 16 October 1925.   [218] Ibid.

[219] As reported in the *Workers' Weekly*, 23 October 1925.

[220] As reported in the *Workers' Weekly*, 30 October 1925.   [221] Ibid.

[222] The matter was raised at the subsequent trial in the course of which counsel for the accused claimed that the minister's remark 'was very near' a contempt of court. The Home Secretary subsequently claimed in Parliament that he had been misquoted. See H C Debs, 1 December 1925, col 2088.

[223] PRO, CAB 23/51, Cabinet 50 (25), 23 October 1925.

The trial itself—'one of the principal political trials of modern times'[224]—opened before Swift J on 16 November.[225] The accused faced three charges to which they all pleaded not guilty: conspiracy to publish and utter seditious libels and words; conspiracy to incite persons to commit breaches of the Incitement to Mutiny Act 1797; and conspiracy to endeavour to seduce from their duty persons serving in His Majesty's Forces to whom might come certain publications, book, pamphlets, to wit, the *Workers' Weekly* and certain other publications, and to incite them to mutiny. Opening the case, the Attorney General, Sir Douglas Hogg, claimed that the twelve defendants were the heads in this country of an illegal organisation, the Communist Party of Great Britain. It was controlled from Moscow, being an international party, the supreme head and working power of which were based there. Moscow was also the location of the World Congress and the Executive Committee, the decisions of which were binding on all branches of the Party in whatever part of the world they might happen to be. The Party was allegedly 'illegal' because it had as its object 'the forcible overthrow by arms of the present existing state of society, and, as a means to that end, the seduction from their allegiance of the armed forces of the Crown'. The Attorney General did not deny that in Britain everyone had the right to free speech. Indeed, 'every man was entitled to try to persuade his fellow-citizens that the government ought to be overthrown or that this constitution ought to be changed'. But it was essential to do so within the law rather than by seeking 'forcibly to overthrow the rule of the majority and government as by law established'.

Much of the evidence was provided by 'printed documents' which the defendants were said to have kept and sold 'as being their avowed purpose' and used also as propaganda. The Attorney General dealt 'at great length' with the aims and objects of the Communist International to show that it was an illegal body. The earliest document to which he referred was the Report of the Communist International held at Moscow in 1920 which contained the statutes of the CI and stated that its aim was 'to organise an armed struggle for the overthrow of the international bourgeoisie and the establishment of an international Soviet Republic as a transition to the complete abolition of the capitalist state'. According

[224] CPGB, *Report of the Eighth Congress 1926*, p 2.

[225] The trial and the background to it are poorly served by the literature. The fullest accounts we have been able to find are in Jackson, n 117 above, ch 14, and J Klugmann, *History of the Communist Party of Great Britain*, vol 2 (1969), pp 67–79. The Communist Party also published a number of pamphlets in connection with the trial. These included *The Communist Party on Trial. Harry Pollitt's Defence* (1925); the same, *J R Campbell's Defence* (1925); and the same, *William Gallacher's Defence* (1925). The following account is drawn from the full report in *The Times*, 17–26 November 1925.

to the Attorney General, while the defendants were free to advocate the complete abolition of the capitalist state, 'they were not entitled to advocate the use of force or illegal means to attain that purpose'. Yet apart from 'a scheme to organise an armed struggle for the overthrow' of the international bourgeoisie, one of the other themes of the literature was that 'a persistent and systematic propaganda was necessary in the Army, where Communist groups should be primed in every military unit'. There were references throughout the documents 'to armed revolt and civil war and the conquering of the state if only the Army and Navy could be won'. Soldiers were to be persuaded that they were ill-treated as compared with officers, 'in order that the foundations of capitalist rule might be undermined and to provide that when the revolution took place there would be plenty of men with military training and with weapons to carry on the civil war'.

In a six-hour speech for the defence, Sir Henry Slesser (Labour Member of Parliament for Leeds South East and Solicitor General in the 1924 Government) began by emphasising that the charge was not one of seditious conspiracy but of conspiracy to publish seditious libels, which was not necessarily the same thing. In his view, the jury had to consider not whether there was a seditious conspiracy, but whether it had been proved that the accused had conspired to publish seditious libels. He continued by submitting that 'nothing short of a direct incitement to disorder and violence was a seditious libel' which in turn must 'obviously tend to provoke people to commit a definite crime'. The circumstances of the moment would have to be taken into account, and the test was whether the language used was calculated to bring about violence and disorder, 'not as a remote contingency, but then and there as a natural consequence of the language used'. This test was not satisfied by literature reproducing the ultimate objects of the international communist movement which failed to establish that the defendants had incited anyone to disorder or crime. Nor did the mere fact that the literature was published by the CPGB make it seditious. The essence of the Crown's case, argued Slesser, was that 'these things are seditious because they are published by the Communist Party', and 'the Communist Party is a seditious body'. But Slesser urged the jury to begin by asking if the material was seditious, a question which could not be answered affirmatively simply because of the identity of the publisher.

Turning to the literature itself, Sir Henry began by referring to the Theses of the Communist International, as adopted by the second Congress in Moscow in 1920. Here he claimed the document was

simply an account of the theses on which the Russian Revolution proceeded, and 'contained no new discovery or unearthing of any plot or
secret design'. As such it dealt with the theory and philosophy of the
Russian Revolution and did not incite to violence the British Communist
Party much less any other British subject. Yet quite apart from their content, it was established that no copy of the documents had been sold since
1 January 1924; that only three copies of one particular document had
been found, it no longer being in circulation; and that the document in
question could not as a result produce disorder, violence, or anything else
which constituted a seditious libel. Turning to the charges relating to the
1797 Act, these were based on general appeals to soldiers not to shoot
strikers which had been published in the *Workers' Weekly*. In Slesser's
view, this aspect of the case was equally ill-conceived in the sense that
the articles had appeared when a trade dispute had been feared, but had
not yet materialised. Because no dispute had yet arisen, the use of the
troops was at best contingent with the result that the soldiers were being
asked not to shoot a group of persons whom there was no reason to
believe they would shoot anyway. So even if Horridge J was correct in
the *Bowman* case to rule that a general appeal to the troops, not addressed
to a particular person, was enough to constitute an offence under the
1797 Act (a ruling which Slesser did not accept), there was no offence
here because the incitement was too remote.

The trial lasted for eleven days in the course of which several of the
accused conducted their own defence. According to one of their number,
William Gallacher (already encountered in Chapter 2 above), this
'arrangement was come to so that we could have the full benefit of political and legal arguments'.[226] In his summing up on the last day, Swift J
(whose conduct of the trial deserved 'nothing but praise')[227] began by
asking the jury to discount a number of considerations, including criticism of police methods. Thus, it had been admitted by Special Branch
officers in cross-examination that the Party's premises had been watched
(though they never witnessed any of the fascist defacement of these
premises); that they sometimes bought propaganda material from the
shop in King Street; and on at least one occasion had passed themselves

---

[226] W Gallacher, *The Rolling of the Thunder* (1947), p 82 (Gallacher records at p 81 that George
Bernard Shaw had stood surety for him before the trial). It has been reported that 'the speeches
made by our comrades from the dock were worked out in consultation with the Party, and have
been universally recognised as effective statements of the Party case': CPGB, *Report of the Eighth
Congress 1926*, p 2.

[227] (1925) 60 *Law Journal* 953–4. But the journal did appear slightly critical that a prosecution
had been brought in the first place.

off as Party members to gain greater access to the organisation. It was admitted also that Special Branch officers had burgled Communist Party premises and allowed the fascists to take the blame. Swift J regretted that such methods had to be adopted, but appeared consoled by the view that 'if crime was committed in secret, secret methods had to be adopted to detect it'. That being the case, 'it had nothing to do with the jury if detectives had represented themselves to be Communists or had hidden beneath a platform', an obvious reference to the Bedford Street incident several years earlier.[228] Turning to the charges themselves, he reminded the jury that all three related to conspiracy, which was 'an agreement to do an unlawful act or an agreement to do a lawful act in an unlawful way'. There was little doubt that the accused had entered into an agreement (though in the case of Gallacher that was established by rather dubious police methods), but 'that was a long way from saying that they were in unlawful agreement'. So while the twelve men were clearly carrying on the work of the CPGB (ten of the accused were members of its executive committee), the jury had to be satisfied beyond reasonable doubt that the accused had conspired to publish seditious libels or to incite persons to breach of the 1797 Act.

On the substance of the conspiracy to publish seditious libels, Swift J instructed the jury to apply their minds to three tests: Was the object of the documents to lead to civil war? Did the language used imply that it was lawful and commendable to employ physical force in any manner or form against the government? Did the language used tend to subvert the government and the laws of the Empire? Later, he said that the jury must look at the documents and ask themselves whether the CPGB was a political party which was merely preparing for the inevitability of revolution, or whether they were 'inviting or inciting persons to join them with the object that there should be a revolution for the overthrow of the State'. So far as the 1797 Act was concerned, it was no answer to the charge to say that 'this was a musty old Act of Parliament'. The Act was essential to the maintenance of an Army or Navy. In his view, it would be laughable, if it were not so serious, to imagine that anyone would be allowed to persuade soldiers and sailors not to carry out the orders of their officers. The jury was sent off with the message that it would be 'a bad day for the country' if the government 'was not strong enough to bring those suspected of [treason, insurrection, tumult, and sedition] before a Court of law' or if there was 'the slightest faltering either on the part of the jury

---

[228] See pp 114–16 above.

or the Judge in putting down the offence'. After no more than ten minutes the jury returned a verdict of guilty against all the defendants on all counts.

The Aftermath: the Communist Papers

The sentencing of the twelve defendants brought to an end an extraordinary chapter in the history of civil liberties in Britain. In the eleven days of the trial, the jury was told of remarkable police practices and was informed that much of the information which formed the basis of the prosecution had already been published as a Command Paper. In 1921, a Political and Economic Report by a government-appointed Committee to Collect Information on Russia advocated 'a close study of events in Russia' and reproduced part of the Theses of the Communist International, as well as a full translation of chapter 8 of Trotsky's *Terrorism and Communism*, the whole of which was said to be 'worthy of study'.[229] Where were the public to get access to this material, if not from the Communist Party, asked Sir Henry Slesser? The jury was also to hear, however, of allegations of Russian money to the Party, it being alleged that the salaries of a few key personnel came from money provided by Moscow. The allegations (for which there was 'very little evidence') were not insignificant, with the jury being invited to consider whether the Communist Party in Russia would be likely to send money to people in England to preach any other doctrines than they themselves held. Allegations of Moscow gold—which as we have seen were not without considerable substance[230]—were to recur, and indeed led eventually to the introduction of emergency regulations to stem the flow of money during the General Strike.

The Communist leaders were sentenced to periods of six to twelve months' imprisonment. The higher sentence was reserved for five of the twelve who had previous convictions, mainly for seditious speeches in the past, most probably in breach of Defence of the Realm or Emergency Regulations. Although denying strongly that the men were convicted for political offences, Swift J acknowledged that they were 'not of the ordinary criminal class', and would not be dealt with in the ordinary way but would be put in the second division (though not in the first division as

---

[229] Report (Political and Economic) of the Committee to Collect Information on Russia, Cmd 1240 (1921).
[230] See pp 97–8 above.

requested by counsel on their behalf).[231] This meant that they were not to be treated as 'political prisoners' (first division) or as 'depraved or . . . usually of criminal habits' (third division).[232] More remarkable perhaps was the treatment of the remaining seven, none of whom had any previous convictions. Given the option of renouncing communism or imprisonment, they all defiantly chose the latter after having been observed 'to consult hurriedly among themselves'.[233] They were each sentenced to six months, 'not for sedition', wrote Gallacher in typically sardonic vein, 'but for refusing to leave the Communist Party'.[234] The men were driven off to Brixton from where they were transferred to Wandsworth, five at least taken out of service until after the General Strike.[235] It has, however, been doubted whether the government had this in mind when the prosecutions were undertaken. According to MacFarlane, the administration's handling of the miners' dispute in 1925–1926 'suggests incompetence and improvisation rather than clever scheming. Competent schemers would have ensured that all twelve Communist leaders were imprisoned throughout the whole period of the crisis'.[236]

The defendants were sentenced on 25 November 1925. *The Times* seemed satisfied, thundering that the 'trial was conducted with the perfect fairness which is happily associated with the administration of justice in this country'.[237] The *Workers' Weekly* was less pleased, proclaiming that the prosecution was 'the greatest political trial in modern British history'.[238] The opposition in Parliament was also uneasy with a censure motion debated on 1 December condemning 'the action of the Government in initiating the prosecution of certain members of the Communist Party [as] a violation of the traditional right of free speech

---

[231] This was slightly odd for the Prisons Act 1877, s 40 provided that the Prison Commissioners 'shall see that any prisoner under any sentence inflicted on conviction for sedition or seditious libel shall be treated as a misdemeanant of the first division within the meaning of s 67 of the Prisons Act 1865, notwithstanding any statute, provision or rule to the contrary'. (Section 40 was repealed by the Criminal Justice Act 1948, Sch 10.) First division offenders were not to be 'deemed a criminal prisoner' (Prisons Act 1865, s 67). Under the Prison Act 1898, s 6(2), however, the trial judge was empowered to direct that a prisoner be treated as a prisoner of the first or second division, in the absence of which the prisoner was to be treated as a prisoner of the third division.

[232] See L W Fox, *The Modern English Prison* (1934), p 70. For an account of the triple division of offenders (under the Prison Act 1898, s 6), see Fox, ibid, ch 5.

[233] *The Times*, 26 November 1925.   [234] Gallacher, n 226 above, p 82.

[235] For an account of the prison life of the 12, see Gallacher, ibid, pp 84–94.

[236] MacFarlane, n 8 above, p 138. For its part the Party believed that the aim of the trial was to take those convicted out of action 'in preparation for the capitalist offensive in May' (CPGB, *Report of the Eighth Congress 1926*, p 2). In response to MacFarlane, the authorities were highly unlikely to have been able to predict the relatively light sentences for offences so grave.

[237] *The Times*, 26 November 1925.

[238] *Workers' Weekly*, 27 November 1925.

and publication of opinion'.[239] Leading the attack was Ramsay MacDonald who reminded the House that the trial had been preceded by a general search. It was, he said, 'none of your old-fashioned, stilted pieces of constitutional rectitude, when the search took place for a specific thing, and, if that specific thing was not found, nothing else was disturbed'. This 'old habit', this 'old prejudice' of British constitutionalism was 'torn up like a scrap of paper'.[240] The Home Secretary was attacked also for his own seditious activities during the Home Rule crisis in Ireland in 1912–1914 when it was alleged that he had 'not merely published pamphlets, books and theses. He had taken part in a definite conspiracy to create mutiny'.[241] The twelve communists 'were mere babies in their sedition and mutiny compared with the robust adult stage the Right Hon. Gentleman reached in 1912 and 1913'.[242] Yet devastating though this may be, the Home Secretary was also roundly condemned on grounds of principle, in the sense that 'whoever holds opinions, whoever brings into the light their ideas, ought to be left alone, so far as the law is concerned'.[243] For not only is liberty the only defence between reaction on the one hand and revolution on the other, to punish people for their ideas is likely only to be counter-productive, generating sympathy and support. Criticism was also directed at the government from the Liberal benches, notably by Sir John Simon, later to serve as Lord Chancellor in the government of Winston Churchill, having held many of the senior offices of State beforehand.[244]

Although he was satisfied that the men had had a fair trial, and although he found communist views abhorrent, Sir John was nevertheless 'profoundly disturbed at the way in which this matter has been bungled'.[245] His first concern related to the decision to prosecute in the first place, drawing attention to the fact that sedition is a charge that can be made against 'all sorts of people who are asserting all sorts of unpopular opinions'.[246] By the prosecution the government had made clear that certain opinions were to be pilloried, 'and that there must be a new campaign sweeping through the country in favour of Conservatism against everybody else'.[247] The service of democracy would be better served, he

---

[239] H C Debs, 1 December 1925, cols 2075–189, from which the following account is drawn.
[240] Ibid, col 2076.   [241] Ibid, col 2079. See Chapter 7 below.
[242] Ibid.   [243] Ibid, col 2077.
[244] In the course of his career, Simon had been Attorney General (1914–15), Home Secretary (1915–16, 1935–7), Foreign Secretary (1931–35) and Chancellor of the Exchequer (1937–40). He served in Liberal, National and Conservative Governments and was a noted 'anti-socialist'.
[245] H C Debs, 1 December 1925, col 2108.   [246] Ibid, col 2107.
[247] Ibid, col 2108.

argued, by leaving matters of this sort to be dealt with openly, rather than driving them underground. But although thus clearly troubled by the decision to prosecute, Sir John Simon's greater concern was with the role of the Home Secretary after the arrests took place, claiming that three of Joynson-Hicks's speeches 'give a handle to people who desire to suggest that justice is unequal'. 'Is it really the way to satisfy a possibly suspicious, credulous, biassed opinion in this country that justice is fairly administered between all sorts of people', asked the future Lord Chancellor, that after making his announcement of the prosecution, the Home Secretary 'goes on to say in effect, in another speech, that he can hardly contain himself until the verdict is out, and then he will say what he wishes to say, and in a third speech that what is wanted is a touch of Mussolini?'[248]

The Home Secretary responded to this criticism, first by apologising for his pre-war speech on Irish Home Rule (though claiming that it was not seditious), and secondly by denying that he had said anything improper to the Hounslow Amateur Dramatic Society on the evening of the arrests. On the question of free speech, *The Times* had previously attacked as 'spurious' the claims of those who saw the prosecution as 'an attack on the liberty of speech and publication to which the people of this realm are traditionally and deeply devoted'. Even on the assumption that revolution in this country was most improbable, it continued, 'the abuse of the great and unparalleled freedom of speech and publication which we enjoy retards the national recovery from the stress of the war'.[249] The Home Secretary's starting point was that there can be 'no such thing as a general right of free speech. There must be limits to the freedom'.[250] In fact 'the right of freedom of speech' was 'a compendious term which means really a limited right within the law of the land'.[251] What this means in turn is that 'there is complete freedom of discussion' provided that 'the opinions are not expressed in such terms and in such circumstances as to incite to the crime of violence or to crimes against the community'.[252] That principle remained unaffected by the communist trial in which the defendants were not convicted for their opinions. While the men were free to advocate 'a complete alteration of the basis of our constitution' and free to advocate the setting up of different principles, they were not free to attempt to do so by 'violent and unconstitutional means'.[253] In an extraordinary passage the Home Secretary explained that he wanted 'to put before the House clearly the real

---

[248] H C Debs, 1 December 1925, col 2106.
[249] *The Times*, 26 November 1925.
[250] H C Debs, 1 December 1925, col 2089.
[251] Ibid.
[252] Ibid.
[253] Ibid, col 2090.

necessity for preserving the right type of freedom of speech',[254] by which he meant, when pressed, 'freedom of speech as allowed by law', and 'freedom of speech which gives the right to a full propagation of your opinion, provided you do not try to damage the Constitution'.[255]

Turning to the prosecution the Home Secretary argued that he was 'bound to have regard to the reports of speeches and documents which came to [him], week by week and month by month, in regard to this agitation', which he did not specify. He was bound, he argued, 'to have regard to the efforts which were made to incite the public at various places like Hyde Park Corner'.[256] At the heart of the prosecution, however, was the government's concern that 'any portion of the body politic should be carrying out an organisation in this country and receiving money from another country and instructions from another country in order to destroy the Constitution'.[257] He then read from a number of documents,[258] purporting to make the connection between Moscow and the activities of the CPGB, evidence he hoped would show that 'this is a conspiracy with foreign money, with foreign instructions to do harm in this country'. But the evidence was not wholly convincing, with Sir John Simon subsequently remarking that 'it was very natural and appropriate' that the Home Secretary 'should have made his references to Communists at a comic opera society'. For the impression left on Sir John's mind by the evidence was 'not so much that they are criminals, but that they are lunatics'.[259] Yet although clearly bruised by the experience, the government easily survived, with the House in fact approving an amendment applauding the prosecution as 'a timely vindication of the duty imposed upon all British Governments to safeguard the State against sedition' and that 'it is undesirable for the legislature to interfere in the administration of justice'.[260]

In the course of the debate the Home Secretary undertook to publish some of the material which had been seized during the Special Branch raids. The undertaking was given in response to criticism that he was making sweeping allegations about the Communist Party, without any evidence.[261] A command paper was eventually published on 22 June 1926,[262] the frontispiece explaining that:

[254] H C Debs, 1 December 1925, col 2093.
[255] Ibid.　　　　　　　　　　[256] Ibid, col 2094.　　　　　　　　　[257] Ibid, col 2096.
[258] Ibid, cols 2096–102.　　　　　[259] Ibid, col 2104.　　　　　　　　[260] Ibid, col 2125.
[261] He was criticised in particular by Sir John Simon (at col 2104) for 'regaling' the House with a number of extracts from intercepted correspondence which the Attorney General had not thought it appropriate to put before the jury.
[262] Communist Papers. Documents Selected from those obtained on the Arrest of the Communist Leaders on the 14th and 21st October 1925, Cmd 2682 (1926).

On the arrest of the Communist leaders on the 14th and 21st October 1925, a mass of documents was seized at the Headquarters of the Communist Party of Great Britain (16 King Street, Covent Garden) and of the National Minority Movement (38 Great Ormond Street), and at other addresses. From the documents so seized, those printed within have been selected for publication as being of general public interest.

Although the *Workers' Weekly* claimed that it was a 'futile bombshell', an 'abject fizzle', and carried a cartoon bearing the legend 'The cupboard was bare',[263] the initial print run of 2,500 sold out within a week (according to the government), due to 'unexpectedly heavy demands'.[264] A second edition was duly prepared, but it was never established by what legal authority the Home Office were acting in taking this step. It is true that the police may seize evidence while lawfully searching the premises of an arrested person.[265] It is also the case that in certain circumstances the courts were to assert the principle that 'the interests of the State must excuse the seizure of documents, which seizure would otherwise be unlawful'.[266] But where is the authority for the police to hand over seized material for publication and display by the Home Office, when that material was not even used as evidence in the criminal proceedings?

The volume of published documents was priced at 3 shillings and ran to 110 pages, plus an appendix and glossary. The fifty-two documents were divided into five categories:

(1) the first were designed to illustrate the relationship between the CPGB and the Third International;
(2) the second were designed to illustrate the participation of the Russian Trade Delegation in the affairs of CPGB;
(3) the third illustrated the finances, including receipts and expenditures of the CPGB;
(4) the fourth illustrated the nature of the political work undertaken by the Party, the Young Communist League, and the National Minority Movement;
(5) the fifth dealt with the activities of organisations affiliated to the Third International in British Dominions and Colonies.

Of these five categories, which significantly did not include much of the literature (such as the Theses and Statutes of the Communist International) relied on at the trial, perhaps the most interesting were the

---

[263] *Workers' Weekly*, 2 July 1926.   [264] H C Debs, 8 July 1926, col 2243.
[265] See the cases cited at n 214 above.
[266] *Elias v Pasmore* [1934] 2 KB 164, at p 173. See the arguments in that case, which were not pursued, relating to the ownership of documents alleged to be seditious. See Chapter 5 below.

first and the third, with the documents in the latter category indicating a high degree of dependence on Russian money.

Concern about Russian money was never far from the surface (replacing war-time concern about German-funded subversion).[267] Indeed in the (unpublished) Preservation of Public Order Bill 1921 it was proposed to prohibit the importation of 'money, securities, or valuable property' intended to be used for seditious purposes,[268] a similar measure being proposed in a private members' Bill in the following year.[269] As already indicated, the issue of Moscow gold had been raised at the trial where Swift J was prepared to draw adverse inferences and to encourage the jury to do the same. The flow of Russian money appears to have been confirmed by the published papers which include a copy of undated shorthand notes for a letter to 'Comrade Bennett', the Third International representative in Britain, on the financial crisis in the Party. This revealed that the Party had been allocated £16,000 from the Communist International for 1925. Apart from this allocation, it seems that the normal weekly income of the party was only £20. As MacFarlane has pointed out, this indicates that in 1925 the Communist Party expected to receive £1,000 from its own members and £16,000 from the Comintern. Clearly, he continues, 'this meant their complete reliance on the Comintern to finance the organisation and activity of the party, in particular to finance the full-time officials, the various subsidiary organisations and their publications'.[270] By the time the documents were published a lapsed amendment to the Emergency Regulations introduced during the General Strike had given the Home Secretary the power to 'prevent the payment, transfer or dealing in money, securities or credit coming from abroad where there was any reason to believe that it would be used for any purpose prejudicial to public safety or the life of the community'.[271]

The publication of the documents attracted little adverse comment, perhaps predictably in view of the fact that it coincided with a state of

---

[267] See Public Record Office, *MI5: The First Ten Years*, n 99 above, p 8.

[268] See above, pp 97–8.

[269] See H C Debs, 24 May 1922, col 1209 (Seditious Propaganda Bill 1922, designed to prevent the importation from overseas of money, valuable securities and property intended to be be used for seditious propaganda).

[270] MacFarlane, n 8 above, p 139. A Home Office inquiry in 1928 was in little doubt that substantial sums of money had found their way from the Moscow Narodny Bank in London to Communist organisations in this country. See Russian Banks and Communist Funds. Report of an Enquiry into certain Transactions of the Bank for Russian Trade, Ltd., and the Moscow Narodny Bank Ltd., Cmd 3125 (1928).

[271] Emergency Regulations (No 2), S R & O 1926 No 556, Regulation 13A. See H C Debs, 17 June 1926, cols 2466–71. But see Chapter 4 below.

emergency. Although the matter was raised in the Commons, this was not to question the legal basis of the government's action, but principally to complain that the first print run had sold out and that people were unable to buy it. The only notes of censure related to alleged mistakes and misrepresentations. Thus Captain Wedgewood Benn asserted that the claims made in the preambles to each document (for which the Home Secretary was responsible) were 'not borne out by the document', referring in particular to a document said to illustrate 'the participation of the Russian Trade Delegation and of The All-Russian Co-operative Society (Arcos), London, in the affairs of the Communist Party of Great Britain'.[272] (Arcos was itself to be raided in highly controversial circumstances within a few months,[273] precipitating a rupture in Anglo-Soviet relations and the publication of the fruits of that particular raid.)[274] On a lighter note, Shipurji Saklatvala asked whether the government would be prepared to reduce the price and make a public edition 'if the Communist Party are prepared to take over a certain number'.[275] This was consistent with the line adopted by the Party to publication, with an article in the *Workers' Weekly* mocking the government for the high price of the document, as evidence that it was intended only to scare a middle-class audience.[276] More seriously, Saklatvala may well have had some cause for complaint, given that the published volume included correspondence by him to the Political Bureau of the Communist Party of Great Britain (admittedly very damaging) as well as details of his election expenses (showing that the bulk of his funding came from Party headquarters, and by implication from Moscow).[277]

Conclusion

We have seen that the formation of the Communist Party of Great Britain drew a vicious response from the public authorities, as had earlier socialist initiatives. The action of the authorities challenged the very foundations of the Party: its ideology, its organisation, and its means of

---

[272] H C Debs, 8 July 1926, col 2243.

[273] The affair is well covered by the *Daily Herald*, 13–27 May 1927, and by the *Manchester Guardian* for the same period.

[274] Documents illustrating the Hostile Activities of the Soviet Government and Third International against Great Britain, Cmd 2874 (1927).

[275] Ibid, col 2244. [276] *Workers' Weekly*, 9 July 1926.

[277] The publication of Communist Party papers was all the more remarkable for the reticence of both the Conservative and Liberal parties to publish details of their internal affairs. See H C Debs, 7 December 1926, col 1922 where a private member introduced a Political Subscriptions (Publication) Bill 'to compel the publication by all political parties, organisations and associations of income and expenditure duly certified and audited by chartered or incorporated accountants'.

communication. We have also seen that the campaign was waged without the need to take extra powers; the existing legal and administrative structure was adequate, with emergency powers available to deal with the consequences of large-scale industrial unrest. It is true that the possibility of introducing additional statutory measures was considered from time to time. But it was not until the Incitement to Disaffection Act 1934 that any such legislation was introduced to deal specifically with the activities of communists. And even that—despite the controversy which surrounded it—was aimed at only one activity of the Party (the subversion of the military) which was in any event already unlawful. By the time the legislation was introduced, the problem which inspired it appears largely to have passed. At any rate, with the rise of fascism on the streets of Britain there were now more important battles for both the Party and the public authorities to fight.

So far as *constitutional principle* is concerned, the experience of the 1920s reveals the fragility of the Rule of Law as a governing principle of British constitutionalism. Partly this was because of the heavily diluted quality of the concept, as inherited from Dicey, to mean no more than that the State must not violate the legal rights of its citizens in its dealings with them. As the campaign against communism was clearly to demonstrate, however, this gave a lot of scope for oppressive conduct without government agents having to meet the charge that they were acting unlawfully. But in part the fragility of the Rule of Law as a governing principle is its compliance and flexibility in times of expediency, as in the case of several examples referred to in this chapter. This is not the behaviour of a government strongly committed to the principle of legality, any more than is the unwarranted publication of tittle tattle improperly obtained in the course of the raid. What we see in the 1920s is a single minded campaign against a threatening and deeply challenging political ideology, in the conduct of which all the forces of the State were deployed as necessary, and in the campaign against which due legal propriety was observed where it was possible or expedient to do so. But in no sense is there a feeling that agents of the State felt constrained by law or indeed embarrassed by the absence of specific measures of control.

What the experience of the 1920s reveals above all is the flexibility of the response of the authorities. There was no need for legal authority, for in much of the area under discussion individuals had no rights to violate: the State could therefore act with complete impunity. In areas where there was a need for legal authority, it could readily be provided, in one of a number of ways. This is not to say that constitutional principle had no role to play in the campaign against communism. But constitutional rectitude was discovered, in the shape of the Independence of the Judiciary (an admittedly essential feature of legality) only as a stick with which to beat the first Labour government, and then only to meet what was at best incompetence of practice rather than corruption of principle. Paradoxically the stick was used in response to a decision which had the effect of preserving political freedom (in the sense that the government pulled back from prosecuting Campbell for what he was alleged to have published) and promoting tolerance by a government which was clearly perceived as 'soft' on the 'Red peril'. But this was merely a symptom of the abuse of constitutional rectitude which was employed as an engine for the oppression of the communists, behaviour which was justified, explicitly or implicitly, in the interests of liberty, the Rule of Law and constitutional government by political actors who by their deeds and sometimes their words demonstrated only a limited commitment to the principles by which they claimed to have been moved.

The absence of relative integrity in British constitutional theory in the 1920s had important implications so far as *constitutional practice* is concerned, as has perhaps being adequately indicated already. However, a revealing and disturbing feature of the decade was what might be referred to as the absence of legality and the denial of civil liberties. The former is revealed most clearly by the fact that the secret service was largely unaccountable, operating without a statutory mandate quite consciously to frustrate rather than to serve the democratic process, as demonstrated by its involvement in publicising the Zinoviev letter at a crucial point before the 1924 General Election. Although steps were taken to bring the Special Branch into line and to remove Sir Basil Thomson, the evidence provided by his successor suggests that it had become little more than the private political police force of the Home Secretary for the time being in power, anxious to please and particularly willing to engage in the battle with communism and Soviet Russia. Admittedly Thomson was to write in his autobiography in celebration of the British constitution, and Childs was to echo similar sentiments. But this was a constitution which was to eschew genuine political freedom for what the Home Secretary, Sir William Joynson-Hicks was to refer to with such astonishing arrogance and authoritarianism as the 'right kind of freedom of speech', and by extension the 'right kind' of freedom of assembly, and the 'right kind' of freedom of association.

Apart from the fact that there existed an unaccountable secret service and a barely accountable Special Branch, a matter of equally compelling concern is the denial of civil liberties, in the sense that there was no political freedom in Britain save that which the authorities were prepared to tolerate. In one of the greatest challenges to the depth of the liberal commitment to civil liberties, that commitment was found easily to yield under pressure. It is true that the communist message was calculated to shock, and that it raised the spectre of revolutionary rather than (bourgeois) democratic change. But nothing can begin to justify the relentless effort which was undertaken to suppress and crush what remained a relatively small political movement. Nor can anything begin to justify the manner by which this was done. In some respects officials of the State acted without legal authority but not unlawfully (as in the case of the different methods of surveillance and infiltration), while on other occasions they acted with doubtful legal authority but with the complicity of the courts where this was necessary, as in the sedition cases in 1921 and 1925: the former was an unjustifiable use of the different emergency regulations, and the latter a ridiculous abuse of the common law offence of sedition at a time when there was not the remotest likelihood of insurrection or revolution. In some cases too, as we shall encounter in the following chapter, they acted openly in clear defiance of the law.

4

The General Strike and its Aftermath

In 1926 a new challenge was presented to established order when between one and two million trade unionists responded to a call by the TUC to strike in support of the miners who had been locked out by the coalowners. The miners had refused to accept a cut in wages and an extension of working hours. This was the first time that industrial action had been employed on such a scale, and although the TUC claimed consistently that its motives were purely industrial (to help the miners), it was portrayed (and may even have been believed) by the government as being a direct challenge to the constitution. But it was not the first time that action of this kind had been threatened: it was the fear of large-scale industrial action on an earlier occasion that led to the enactment of the Emergency Powers Act 1920. Although the General Strike was not the first occasion for a State of Emergency to be declared under the Act, there is no other dispute before or after in which a State of Emergency has been in operation for so long. As a result the events of 1926 provide a fascinating insight into how emergency powers were used in peacetime to deal with large-scale labour unrest. The experience was not a happy one, leading to a breakdown of established constitutional principle, particularly the Rule of Law. It is true that in the narrowest of senses law and order were maintained, but it was at a terrible cost to civil liberties in the coalfields in particular.

The General Strike and the miners' lock out gave rise to important legal issues. While the six months generated only two reported cases, one of these was of great importance, and gave rise to a great deal of controversy and was much written about. In practice, however, the General Strike did not greatly involve the members of the senior judiciary, with the most important case being presided over by the otherwise obscure Astbury J and the other (a case of no lasting or general significance) by the Lord Chief Justice. It is true that senior judicial figures took part in parliamentary debates to condemn the Strike, as in the example of Lord Buckmaster who referred to the General Strike as 'one of the most wanton and most reckless exercises of tyrannical power that this country has been called upon to meet for centuries'. 'Everyone who values the ordered progress of this country and the removal of grievances by the use of honoured and constitutional means', he continued, 'is bound to lend all the power and support he can to the Government in the difficult position in which they are placed'.[1] But like the other Law Lords, he was not called upon to adjudicate in any dispute arising out of the Strike, and for the most part the real legal story of the General Strike and its aftermath was not to reach the Law Reports. Rather it related in part to the use of the Emergency Powers Act 1920 and the regulations made thereunder, and in part also to the central management of local policing which allowed the emergency to be dealt with (sometimes amicably and sometimes brutally) without the need to deploy the military to assist the civil power.

The Chronology of Events

In 1925, the British coalowners demanded that the miners accept reduced wages and an extension of the working day, in the face of increased international competition and a changing international market. The Miners' Federation of Great Britain refused to comply with these demands, but in view of the large stockpiles of coal were in no position to take effective industrial action without the support of other unions. This was promised by both the railwaymen, the transport workers and the seamen who all agreed not to move coal from 31 July 1925. Faced with this prospect the government intervened by appointing a Royal Commission on the Coal Industry, under the chairmanship of Sir Herbert Samuel, its recommendations to form the basis of future negotiations. In the meantime the government introduced a subsidy to operate until 30 April 1926, to allow wages and conditions to remain unaltered pending a new settlement. But to the dismay of the miners' unions, the Royal Commission (on which they were not represented), recommended that wage reductions were 'essential to make the industry profitable',[2] a recommendation which was wholly unacceptable. As no agreement could be reached between the owners and the miners before the subsidy was to end, the employers posted notices stating that new terms, including a cut in wages, would take effect from 1 May 1926. A State of Emergency was declared on 30 April and the miners were duly locked out on the following day.

Negotiations were also taking place between the government and the TUC General Council. While these negotiations were taking place a

[1] H L Debs, 5 May 1926, col 55. See also H L Debs, 30 August 1926, cols 525–32.
[2] M Morris, *The General Strike* (1976), p 173.

special conference called by the TUC on 1 May voted overwhelmingly in favour of sympathetic action in support of the miners. The conference, attended by 800 to 1,000 delegates of unions affiliated to the TUC and representing 3,653,537 members in 137 unions, voted overwhelmingly in favour of strike action, the only note of dissent being from the National Sailors' and Firemen's Union with less than 50,000 members. The initial plan was for 'a selective strike on a national scale, not a universal stoppage',[3] with workers in certain key industries only being called out. These were transport, printing, productive industries, building, gas and electricity supply (to industry only). A number of unions were thus not called upon to take part while, with a view to inflicting 'the maximum pressure upon the Government whilst doing the least harm to the community', workers in 'the health and sanitary services and those responsible for distributing food were expressly excluded from the strike and all unions were asked to help to ensure that milk and food continued to reach the whole population'.[4] Those unions which were called upon to support the miners were asked to give full authority to the TUC General Council to call and organise the action, which 'in many unions . . . meant setting aside . . . rule books and normal strike procedures', which might, for example, require the holding of a ballot before industrial action was authorised.[5] In other cases this would mean the calling of action in breach of collective agreements between unions and employers which required notice to be given in advance of a strike.

Negotiations continued between the General Council and the government until 3 May when they were discontinued by ministers following a refusal by the compositors at the *Daily Mail* to print an anti-union editorial. This incident was referred to as an interference with the freedom of the press by the Prime Minister when he rose to address Parliament on the same day to give an account on behalf of the government.[6] Baldwin also launched a fierce attack on the decision of the General Council, complaining that there had not been 'anything like a thorough-going consultation with the rank and file before this despotic power was put in the hands of a small executive in London'. This 'irresponsible power', he continued, 'is a gross travesty of any democratic principle',[7] even though

---

[3] Ibid.　　　　　　　　　　　　　　　　　[4] Ibid, pp 22–3.

[5] Ibid, p 24.　　　　　　　　　　　　　　　[6] H C Debs, 3 May 1926, col 69.

[7] Ibid, col 71. The Prime Minister had earlier complained that the unions 'did not consult their members by ballot before taking this momentous step, when their rules required such consultation' (ibid, cols 70–1). He also complained that the TUC had secured 'plenary powers to order a strike without notice' (ibid, col 71).

'nearly all trade union members who were asked to strike, did strike'[8] and even though as many as two million workers demonstrated solidarity with the miners. In the course of a speech in which 'his mood grew angrier',[9] Baldwin charged the trade union leaders with 'threatening the basis of ordered government, and going nearer to proclaiming civil war than we have been for centuries past'.[10] He also referred to the strike as an attempt 'to challenge the existing Constitution of the country and to substitute the reign of force for that which now exists'.[11] This was a theme which the government was quite happy to exploit, thereby raising considerably the gravity and seriousness of the TUC action. These claims were not confined to Parliament, being reproduced in the pages of the *British Gazette*, 'the propagandist sheet of capitalism . . . masquerading under the title of a national newspaper'.[12] Edited by Winston Churchill, the 'official organ' cost £16,000 to produce,[13] money which was allocated evidently without the need to secure parliamentary approval.[14]

The first issue, published on 5 May 1926, reproduced much of the Prime Minister's speech of 3 May, under the heading 'The Constitution or a Soviet'.[15] It also carried a lengthy article claiming that there were 'at present two quite different disputes which are holding up the country', the first of which was the trade dispute between the miners and the coalowners, and the second being the dispute between the TUC and the government 'to compel the Government to grant an indefinite prolongation of the subsidy to the coal trade at the expense of the general taxpayer'. This theme was maintained as the circulation of the *British Gazette* allegedly grew, from 232,000 on 5 May to 2,209,000 a week later, with the second issue carrying a message from the Prime Minister claiming that 'Constitutional Government is being attacked', and that the 'General Strike is a challenge to Parliament and is the road to anarchy and ruin'.[16] An editorial in the same issue carried the headline 'Constitution to be

[8] Morris, n 2 above, p 28.   [9] J Murray, *The General Strike of 1926. A History* (1951), p 113.
[10] H C Debs, 3 May 1926, col 71.
[11] Ibid, col 72.
[12] H C Debs, 6 May 1926, col 507 (Mr E Thurtle). It was also described as a 'miserable little sheet of news that was the object of much ridicule'. See D Kirkwood, *My Life of Revolt* (1935), p 233.
[13] H C Debs, 14 July 1926, col 404. The £16,000 did not include the costs of distribution by air 'which was regarded by the Air Ministry as taking the place of experimental and practice flying'. The *British Gazette* was published from the premises of the *Morning Post*, though the *Daily Mail* and the *Daily Express* 'both placed their resources entirely at the Government's disposal, and many other leading newspapers, like the *Daily Telegraph* were also willing to give whatever assistance was required' (H C Debs, 20 May 1926, col 425).
[14] The cost was borne by the Treasury vote: H C Debs, 5 May 1926, col 278.
[15] *British Gazette*, 5 May 1926.   [16] *British Gazette*, 6 May 1926.

Vindicated' and conceded that the trade union leaders 'did not intend, when they launched the General Strike', to raise the constitutional issue.[17] But whatever they intended or thought, insisted the *British Gazette*, 'a national issue has been raised of supreme magnitude', and 'the responsibility of these Trades Union leaders is grievous'. It was also 'a personal responsibility', the article claiming not only that the action had been called without the authority of a ballot (though why this was relevant is not quite clear),[18] but also in breach by workers of contracts and engagements 'to which their good name was pledged'. The columns of the *British Gazette* were also used to encourage workers to return to work, the government teasing trade unionists about not having been consulted and promising that those who went back would not stand to lose any trade union benefits as a result of victimisation by their unions.[19]

The General Strike lasted for nine days. It was widely supported by those unions which took part, and as a result presented difficulties for the government particularly in terms of distributing food and other supplies. But it has been said that the government was extensively and thoroughly well prepared,[20] having used the period since 31 July 1925 'to examine, lubricate and tighten up the emergency machinery'.[21] The country was divided into eleven districts 'each under the administration of a Commissioner. These eleven Commissioners were to work directly under a Chief Commissioner in London',[22] and had extraordinary powers 'to maintain essential services, distribute food and prevent violence'.[23] The whole operation was under the control of the Home Secretary, who also chaired the Cabinet's Supply and Transport Committee which met daily to co-ordinate the government's response to the Strike. Although no new legislation was passed in preparation for the emergency, it appears that legislation was contemplated and that concern was expressed about the fact that the Emergency Regulations 'made no provision in regard to the prevention of peaceful picketing'.[24] Consideration was also given to

---

[17] The TUC emphasised that there was no constitutional crisis and that this was simply a trade dispute. Statements to this effect were carried daily in the columns of the *British Worker*, the TUC's newspaper (see p 168 below). On 6 May it was proclaimed that there was 'No Attack on the Constitution'.

[18] But it was referred to also by the Prime Minister when he addressed the Commons on 3 May. See H C Debs, 3 May 1926, cols 70–1.

[19] See especially *British Gazette*, 7 May 1926.

[20] See G M Young, *Stanley Baldwin* (1952), pp 116–17.

[21] A Mason, 'The Government and the General Strike, 1926' (1969) 14 *International Review of Social History* 1, at p 7.

[22] H A Taylor, *Jix—Viscount Brentford* (1933), p 193. Full details of the Commissioners are to be found in *British Gazette*, 5 May 1926.

[23] J R Clynes, *Memoirs 1924–1937* (1937), p 83.   [24] Mason, n 21 above, p 10.

the possibility of legislation to remove immunity from trade union funds, an immunity which been conferred by the Trade Disputes Act 1906,[25] as well as to make picketing illegal. Such measures were, however, to prove unnecessary, with existing legal powers in the Emergency Powers Act 1920 and elsewhere proving to be more than adequate. Indeed by 7 May the government's only concern about its handling of the dispute related to alleged intimidation which had already been carried out, or which had been threatened.[26] But this too was met by the swelling of police ranks by the special constabulary from 98,000 to 226,000 by the end of the Strike, a number which 'far outnumbered the regular police force'.[27]

It thus soon became clear that the Strike, for which the TUC was 'totally unprepared'[28] would not succeed, and the government was to insist on nothing less than an unconditional surrender with the 'whole crux of the struggle' having been 'skilfully shifted by propaganda from a sympathetic protest at the unfair treatment of the miners to a Constitutional struggle between Parliament and anarchism'.[29] By 7 May the TUC General Council was looking for a settlement, stung by a controversial claim made in Parliament by Sir John Simon that the action was illegal,[30] a claim reinforced five days later by an equally controversial decision of Astbury J in *National Sailors' and Firemen's Union v Reed*.[31] But in seeking a settlement the TUC was impaled on the horns of a dilemma: on the one hand the miners would not agree to any settlement which contemplated wage cuts, while on the other the government (at

[25] For a stinging attack on these measures, see Birkenhead, *Frederick Edwin Earl of Birkenhead* (1933), pp 162–9. The Act was said to have opened the way 'to new and graver controversies and encourage[d] the wilder Socialists to promote strikes with political aims on a larger and larger scale until in the General Strike of 1926 they found their Waterloo' (p 169).

[26] Mason, n 21 above, p 16.

[27] See J Morgan, *Conflict and Order. The Police and Labour Disputes in England and Wales, 1900–1939* (1987), p 120.

[28] Mason, n 21 above, p 14.

[29] Clynes, *Memoirs*, n 23 above, p 88. But for a defiant defence of the 'national strike' as it was referred to by the TUC, see Arthur Pugh's Presidential Address to the 1926 Annual Congress of the TUC. See TUC, *Annual Report 1926*, p 74.

[30] H C Debs, 6 May 1926, col 582. For the effect of his remarks on the TUC see Morris, n 2 above, p 259. For a strong criticism by Sir Henry Slesser see H C Debs, 10 May 1926, col 793.

[31] [1926] 1 Ch 536. An interim injunction was granted on 6 May (*British Gazette*, 7 May 1926). The case was concerned with whether one branch of the union could call its members out to support the strike without the authority of the national executive council. In so far as it touches on the question whether the Strike as such was 'illegal', it was widely thought to be wrong. See especially A L Goodhart, 'The Legality of the General Strike' (1927) 36 *Yale L J* 464, and W S Holdsworth, 'The Legality of the General Strike', *The Architect and Building News*, 21 May 1926, p 445. See also (1926) 70 *Sol Jo* 625.

the mercy of its own intransigents—Churchill, Joynson-Hicks and Birkenhead) refused to negotiate without such a declaration from the miners.[32] An attempt by Sir Herbert Samuel to mediate a settlement foundered on the miners' unwillingness 'even to consider anything in the nature of wage cuts',[33] but his proposals were nevertheless ultimately accepted by a negotiating committee of the General Council (which did not include any of the miners' leaders). On 12 May the TUC leaders waited on the Prime Minister to inform him that it was over, a total and unconditional defeat which led to the victimisation of strikers by employers in its wake, and to retribution on the part of the government in the form of the Trade Disputes and Trade Unions Act 1927 which introduced a more restrictive legal framework within which trade unions had subsequently to operate. Yet although the General Strike ended on 12 May, it did not resolve the dispute in the coalfields where the lock out continued, as did the State of Emergency which was to be renewed on no fewer than seven occasions. In fact the dispute was not resolved until the end of November when the last of the miners' unions instructed its members to return to work on the employers' terms.[34]

The General Strike and the State of Emergency

A State of Emergency was proclaimed on 30 April 1926 and emergency regulations were made on the same day.[35] The Emergency Powers Act 1920 not only conferred wide powers on the executive, but also imposed a number of restraints, in a way quite unlike the Defence of the Realm Consolidation Act 1914. Thus although a proclamation of emergency is made effectively by the government, the Act requires that it should be communicated 'forthwith' to Parliament which if adjourned or prorogued, must be summoned within five days.[36] Similarly, although the Act authorises the government to make emergency regulations 'for securing the essentials of life to the community',[37] these may be made only where a proclamation of emergency is in force which means that regulations would be effective for no more than one month, though they may

---

[32] Morris, n 2 above, p 265.   [33] Ibid, p 267.
[34] R Page Arnot, *The Miners: Years of Struggle* (1953), p 506.
[35] For the text of the Proclamation, see H C Debs, 3 May 1926, col 35.
[36] Emergency Powers Act 1920, s 1(2). On 3 May 1926 the House voted on a resolution moved by the Prime Minister that a humble Address be presented to His Majesty, thanking His Majesty for His Most Gracious Message communicating to the House that His Majesty had deemed it proper by Proclamation made in pursuance of the Emergency Powers Act 1920 and dated 30 April, to declare that a state of emergency exists. See H C Debs, 3 May 1926, col 36.
[37] 1920 Act, s 2(1).

be renewed in the event of a fresh proclamation being made. Regulations made under the 1920 Act must also be laid before Parliament 'as soon as may be after they are made', and may continue in force for only seven days unless 'a resolution is passed by both Houses' providing for their continuance.[38] The regulations may confer on the government or any other person 'such powers and duties as His Majesty may deem necessary for the preservation of the peace, for securing and regulating the supply and distribution of food, water, fuel, light, and other necessities, for maintaining the means of transit or locomotion, and for any other purposes essential to the public safety and the life of the community'.[39] It is further provided, however, that regulations may not impose any form of compulsory military service or industrial conscription, or make it an offence to take part in a strike 'or peacefully to persuade any other person or persons to take part in a strike'.[40]

On 5 May 1926, the Home Secretary (Sir William Joynson-Hicks) moved that the Regulations made by His Majesty in Council by Orders dated 30 April and 3 May 'shall continue in force'.[41] Predictably the powers were wide ranging, though the code which the government introduced was based on earlier measures introduced during states of emergency in 1921 and 1924, the latter by a Labour Government, as ministers were happy to remind the Opposition on a number of occasions.[42] The regulations fell into eight distinct categories,[43] the first and second of which dealt with *the compulsory acquisition of property*, and *the regulation of the supply and distribution of food* respectively. Regulation 1 empowered the Army Council, the Board of Trade, the Commissioner of Works or any other authorised person, 'where it appears necessary to do so' to take possession of 'any land, buildings or works (including works for the supply of gas, electricity or water and of any sources of water supply) and any

---

[38] Emergency Powers Act 1920, s 2(2).　　　　[39] Ibid, s 2(1).　　　　[40] Ibid.

[41] The first code of regulations appear as S R & O 1926 No 451. They were not published in Statutory Rules and Orders 1926, which does however include the second code (S R & O 1926 No 556).

[42] Significantly, however, the 1924 Code did not include the controversial limitations on civil liberties to be found in Regulations 21 (sedition) and 22 (public meetings and processions) of the 1926 Code. It did, however, include provisions similar to Regulations 20 (injury to property) and 33 (arrest without warrant). But the 1924 Regulations were neither published nor brought into force, the dispute (involving transport workers) being settled the day after the Prime Minister announced a proclamation of emergency (G S Morris, 'The Emergency Powers Act 1920' [1979] PL 317, at pp 351–2). The 1924 Code is printed at PRO, CAB 23/47, Cabinet 23 (24), 27 March 1924, Appendix. It consisted of 24 regulations in contrast to the 39 in the much more expansive 1926 Code.

[43] Cf Morris, n 42 above.

property (including plant, machinery, equipment and stores) used or intended to be used in connection therewith'. Property owners were to be compensated in respect of 'any property which is requisitioned or of which possession is taken', with compensation to be determined by arbitration in the absence of agreement.[44] Regulation 2 then provided that the Board of Trade, or any other authorised person, could, by order, take possession of 'any food, forage, fuel, material or stores, and any articles essential for the life of the community', while regulation 3 authorised the Board of Trade by order to regulate or give directions with respect to 'the production, manufacture, treatment, use, consumption, transport, storage, distribution, supply, sale or purchase' of food, forage, fuel, material or stores. In order to stop profiteering the Board of Trade was also authorised to fix maximum prices for any foodstuffs.[45]

The third category of regulations gave extensive powers to regulate *the operation of transport*, while the fourth dealt with *the production and distribution of coal*. So by regulation 4 the Minister of Transport was empowered to 'regulate, restrict, or give directions with respect to, the use for the purposes of road transport . . . of any horses or vehicles in use or capable of being used for the purpose of road transport'.[46] Under regulation 7 the Minister of Transport was empowered to take possession of 'any harbour, dock, pier, railway, light railway or tramway' and to give directions as to the management of any such property, while by regulation 8 the Minister could take possession of any canal, and any person 'concerned in the management or working thereof' was under a duty 'to comply with the directions of the Minister as to the management and user of the canal'. Other regulations dealt with ports, harbours and rivers (regulation 10), and shipping (regulations 11 and 12). So far as the powers relating to the production and distribution of coal are concerned, regulation 14 authorised the Board of Trade to take possession of buildings and property used for the purpose of storing, distributing or supplying coal, as well as empowering the Board to take possession of any coal,

[44] S R & O 1926 No 556, Regulation 31. The Law Officers had advised that anyone whose property was taken under the 1920 Act would be entitled to compensation anyway so that Regulation 31 was unnecessary, and that it was ultra vires to the extent that it cut down the compensation to which the property owner would otherwise be entitled. The advice is contained in PRO, LO 3/816 (Emergency Powers Act 1920. Emergency Regulations). The government took possession of Hyde Park for food and milk distribution. See S R & O 1926 Nos 530 and 531. For the position under the war-time code, see Chapter 2 above, p 52.

[45] See H C Debs, 2 June 1926, col 768.

[46] It was not necessary to ration petrol, though parking restrictions were removed! See *British Gazette*, 5 May 1926.

'wheresoever situate and by whomsoever held'.[47] Directions could also be given, as to the 'production, manufacture, treatment, transport, storage, distribution, supply, shipment, disposal or use of any coal', as well as for the 'fixing of prices of coal'. The Coal (Emergency) Directions 1926,[48] made under the authority of regulation 14, limited domestic consumers of coal to one cwt a week and industrial consumers to half their weekly average consumption; in both cases these maxima could be increased with the written consent of a local authority, though in the latter case only where it was expedient in the public interest to give such consent.

The fifth category of regulations dealt with the *public utilities*, with regulation 15 authorising the Board of Trade, the Minister of Health and the Minister of Transport 'to require the owners of any undertakings for the supply of gas, water and electricity to comply with any directions given . . . as to the supply thereof'. Powers were also given to the Board of Trade to control the use of lights (regulation 16) and to prohibit and regulate the sale and distribution of motor spirit (petrol) (regulation 17). More controversial were the provisions of regulation 18 which authorised the Postmaster General 'to direct that telegraphic messages of such classes or descriptions as he may prescribe shall not be accepted for transmission'. Unlike the other regulations in this category, regulation 18 was discussed in Parliament where the Attorney General insisted that the power could be required where it was necessary to send, for example, 'a large number of telegraphic orders with regard to food supplies, or with regard to stopping ships from leaving, or for a variety of other matters'. Suppose, he continued, that a race meeting was being held at the same time 'and a number of betting telegrams were likely to be transmitted'. In these circumstances thought the Attorney General, it was quite reasonable that the Postmaster General should have the power not to take betting telegrams.[49] But this did little to overcome suspicion that regulation 18 was designed to stop unions sending instructions to their branches,[50] and it was for this reason that an unsuccessful attempt was made to omit it.[51] The importance of the telegram system is perhaps dif-

---

[47] For Labour attempts to amend Regulation 14 to compel the government 'to take possession of the coal mines, open them and work them in the interests of the miners and in the interests of the country', see H C Debs, 30 July 1926, col 2587. See also H C Debs, 28 September 1926, col 489.

[48] S R & O 1926 No 452.

[49] H C Debs, 5 May 1926, col 373.   [50] Ibid, col 381.

[51] Ibid, col 369. Further discussion was frustrated by the Speaker: H C Debs, 2 June 1926, col 797.

ficult to fathom at the end of the twentieth-century. But as Margaret Morris points out, 'Very few trade union secretaries had telephones in 1926',[52] with the result that it was necessary to rely on telegrams to maintain contact with branches and local officials. In the case of the National Union of Railwaymen alone (with 1,640 branches), no fewer than 41,000 telegrams were dispatched from Unity House in the first fortnight in May 1926.[53]

The sixth category of regulations imposed *restrictions on civil liberties*, and in particular freedom of expression on the one hand and freedom of assembly on the other. Reflecting the terms of the Defence of the Realm Regulation 42, Emergency Regulation 21 provided that it was an offence for any person to attempt or to do 'any act calculated or likely to cause mutiny, sedition or disaffection among any of His Majesty's forces, or among the members of any police force, or any fire brigade, or to cause sedition or disaffection among the civilian population, or to impede, delay or restrict the supply or distribution of food, water, fuel, light or other necessities, or the means of transit or locomotion, or any other service essential to the public safety or the life of the community'.[54] This was subject to a proviso, itself reflecting the terms of section 2(1) of the parent Act, that 'a person shall not be guilty of an offence under this regulation by reason only of his taking part in a strike or peacefully persuading any other person to take part in a strike'. Regulation 21 was complemented by regulation 22 which was concerned with public meetings and processions. Where it was apprehended that the holding of a meeting or procession would 'conduce to a breach of the peace' and would thereby cause 'undue demands to be made upon the police' or would 'promote disaffection', an order could be made (by the Home Secretary, or a mayor, magistrate, or chief officer of police (or by any two of them acting together)[55] authorised by the Home Secretary) prohibiting the meeting or procession. Any meeting or procession which was held in breach of a banning order could be duly dispersed by the taking of 'such steps as may be necessary'. This power 'to prohibit a particular

---

[52] Morris, n 2 above, p 78.   [53] Ibid, p 26.

[54] According to the Home Secretary this was 'merely an adaptation of the existing Common Law', there being no difference between the common law and the new statutory offence. The aim was simply to allow cases to be dealt with summarily rather than by indictment (H C Debs, 5 May 1926, cols 293–4). This explanation was, however, contradicted by the Attorney General, Sir Douglas Hogg, claiming that although disaffection was 'very nearly' the same as sedition, nevertheless there could be cases where something could go so far as to be disaffection and yet not constitute sedition (H C Debs, 6 May 1926, col 496).

[55] According to the Attorney General 'so as to ensure that it shall not be exercised without due deliberation': H C Debs, 6 May 1926, col 515.

assembly, meeting or procession'[56] was condemned on the Labour benches as effectively taking away 'the right of public meeting and the right of participating in a procession'.[57]

The seventh category of regulations dealt with *mutual aid*, that is to say the movement of police officers from one area to another to permit the national co-ordination of policing. Two measures facilitated this process, the first being regulation 26 which applied where 'it appeared expedient' to the Home Secretary that one police force (the aided force) should be 'temporarily strengthened' by officers from another force (the aiding force). The Home Secretary was thus empowered by order to direct that as many as ten per cent of the total number of members of the aiding force be transferred, though this could be increased by up to twenty per cent where 'in the opinion of the Secretary of State the force is not immediately affected by the emergency'. The officers transferred in this way would be deemed to be members of the aided force and would have 'the like powers, duties and privileges'. In addition to these measures, regulation 27 empowered the Home Secretary, where it appeared to him to be 'expedient that a body of police should be available for duty outside the police district of the force to which they belong otherwise than by way of transfer to another force', to direct that members of another police force should be employed on such duty. Again the numbers deployed in this way could not exceed ten per cent of the number of officers in the aiding force, though also again this could rise to twenty per cent on the same basis as under regulation 26. Unlike regulation 26, the financial burden of such officers (in terms of 'any expenses' incurred by reason of their employment) would be borne by the police force to which they belonged rather than the force to which they were deployed, though such officers would have 'all the powers, duties and privileges of a member of the police force of the district in which [they] may for the time being happen to be'.[58]

Finally, the eighth category of regulations were those which dealt with *police powers*. These were mainly contained in regulation 33, 'one of the least defensible of the whole of these Regulations',[59] which conferred

---

[56] H C Debs, 6 May 1926, col 515 (Attorney General). Compare the Public Order Act 1936, s 3. See Chapter 6 below.

[57] H C Debs, 6 May 1926, col 507.

[58] See Regulation 27(4). See generally Morgan, n 27 above, esp ch 5. It is to be noted that troops were not used for public order purposes. But they were used for other activities, for example naval ratings to keep power stations open. See H C Debs, 5 May 1926, col 296.

[59] H C Debs, 30 July 1926, cols 2581–2 (J Westwood, Labour Member for Midlothian and Peebles).

extensive powers of arrest, search and seizure. So far as arrest was concerned, a police officer was empowered to arrest without a warrant 'any person who so acts to endanger the public safety, or who is guilty or is suspected of being guilty, of an offence' against the Regulations.[60] It was thus possible for the police to arrest, even though the arrested person had not committed and was not suspected of committing an offence under the Regulations or otherwise: it was enough that they were acting to endanger the public safety. So far as the powers of search and seizure were concerned, there were separate powers in respect of premises, persons and vehicles. The power to search premises was a power to search without a warrant, though it did require the authorisation of the chief officer of police, which, if given, authorised a police constable to 'enter, if need be by force, any premises or place suspected of having been, or being used for any purpose endangering the public safety or otherwise contrary to [the] regulations', to 'search any part of such premises or place', and 'seize or detain anything found therein' which was being used or intended to be used for a prohibited purpose. In the case of an alleged offence 'in connection with a registered newspaper', these powers (condemned as authorising the government 'to raid any printing press in the country which ventures in any way whatever to criticise their activities')[61] could be exercised only with the consent of the Home Secretary, who had also to determine how to dispose of any seized or detained printing press or other plant used for printing or publishing the newspaper.[62] In addition to this power to search property, a police constable could also search any person believed to be in possession of any article, the possession of which was an offence against the Regulations.[63] There was also a power to stop and search vehicles.[64]

The General Strike and the Emergency Regulations

The 1926 Regulations were thus wide-ranging, and at times very controversial, 'giving to the Government, and under them to the armed forces and the police, the powers exercised in the world wars beginning in 1914 and in 1939—with this difference only, that the Royal Proclamation had to be renewed from month to month'.[65] The same author was to write of 'drastic' regulations, 'sweeping' in their 'abolition

---

[60] For an account of police powers of arrest at the time under the general law, see H C Debs, 29 November 1926, col 908 (Captain Hacking, Under Secretary of State for the Home Department).
[61] H C Debs, 6 May 1926, col 561 (T Johnston MP).
[62] See Regulation 33(2).
[63] See Regulation 33(3).
[64] See Regulation 33(4).
[65] Page Arnot, n 34 above, p 422.

of customary civil liberties',[66] while others were to claim with somewhat less restraint that with 'all the fierceness of a police State, with all the evil maliciousness of fascism, the British Government of the day, by invoking the Emergency Powers Act, was able to use terror tactics to intimidate the workers'.[67] This might have been written with particular reference to regulations 21, 22 and 33, the principal measures empowering the police to control the right to freedom of expression, the right to hold meetings and demonstrations, and the right to picket and disrupt the supply of goods and materials. The use of the Regulations was extensive, and unlikely ever to be repeated (even if the 1920 Act is invoked again) for the simple reason that many, though admittedly not all, of these measures made their way into the regular law in the 1930s and thereafter,[68] so that it was not necessary in the Regulations made after the Second World War to include provisions of this kind.

The main source of irritation during the nine days of the Strike was unquestionably regulation 21 ('perhaps the most contentious one of the whole of the Regulations'),[69] the first limb of which (sedition and disaffection) was used mainly against inflammatory speeches and publications, largely by the Communist Party.[70] But the widely drafted second limb (impeding supplies and services) was also a potentially serious threat to freedom of expression, as was revealed by the raid of the premises of the *Daily Herald*. During the Strike, the printers were called out which meant that the national newspapers were effectively closed down. As we have seen, a government newspaper, the *British Gazette*, was produced throughout, using the *Morning Post* premises and equipment, and non-union labour. The TUC responded with the *British Worker* which was printed at the *Daily Herald* with the help of *Daily Herald* staff, running to eight pages compared to the four page *British Gazette*.[71] But before the first issue was printed, the *Daily Herald's* premises were visited on 5 May 1926 by 'a force of police about 60 strong, armed with a warrant' signed by the Home Secretary,[72] presumably under the authority of regulation 33. The

---

[66] Page Arnot, n 34 above, p 422.   [67] Murray, n 9 above, p 119.

[68] See Chapters 5 and 6 below.

[69] H C Debs, 2 June 1926, col 814 (Sir W Joynson-Hicks).

[70] 'Take the case of those men who . . . were guilty of inciting by speech or by printed documents; many of them were known to me and to the police for months past as carrying on an active and hostile propaganda against the leaders of the Labour Party. . . in order to force them over to the Left. The moment the strike began those men and women sought to make things worse by incitement' (Sir W Joynson-Hicks, H C Debs, 2 June 1926, col 826).

[71] But on 7 May 1926 (issue 3) the *British Worker*, was reduced to four pages after the Cabinet stopped its supply of paper.

[72] H C Debs, 6 May 1926, col 556 (T Johnston MP).

building was entered by a number of plain-clothes officers, headed by a detective-inspector, who ordered that the machines should not be started, producing the warrant which authorised him to 'search for and seize all copies of the *Daily Herald* of May 4, all material used in producing it, or which *might be used* in producing *any document* calculated to impede measures taken for the maintenance of essential services'.[73] It was quickly made clear, however, that what really interested the police was not the *Daily Herald* of 4 May, but the *British Worker* of 5 May, and that the raid was merely a pretext for obtaining copies of the *British Worker*.[74]

The police inspector requested that a dozen copies of the latter should be run off for submission to the 'City Commissioner' whose decision would determine whether publication could go ahead.[75] While waiting for the decision of the City Commissioner, Ramsay MacDonald and Arthur Henderson were both informed of what had taken place. Henderson immediately got in touch with the government, and while these conversations were taking place 'the word came that the ban had been lifted'.[76] 'After a while', writes Margaret Morris, 'a telephone message came saying the paper could be printed', and just before midnight on 5 May the first issue was on the streets.[77] The matter was raised in the House on the following day by Thomas Johnston the Labour Member for Dundee who not only had been present in the *Daily Herald* building when the police arrived, but as editor of *Labour Leader* in 1915 had himself been at the centre of a similar incident some ten years earlier. The Attorney General was asked which passages in the *Daily Herald* had justified the police action to which he replied that he had 'not had an opportunity of making an exhaustive study of the newspaper'. He did explain, however, that the government was concerned by passages which advised trade unionists to pay no attention to 'any [government] statement that may be broadcast by wireless or circulated in any other form', and by an article which had claimed that the government was

---

[73] Murray, n 9 above, p 129. Emphasis in original. [74] Morris, n 2 above, p 242.
[75] On the role of the Commissioners, see p 159 above.
[76] *British Worker*, 6 May 1926.
[77] Ibid. There were, however, allegations that shopkeepers who displayed the *British Worker* were threatened by the police that their shops would be closed unless the paper was removed. See H C Debs, 12 May 1926, col 880. But it was not only the *British Worker* which attracted the attention of the authorities. Local bulletins were also vulnerable to attack, as in the case of the Birmingham Joint Trade Union Emergency Committee which published a daily strike bulletin. Following a police raid on the committee's offices, some 20 leading Labour representatives concerned in the publication of the bulletin were charged under the Emergency Regulations with publicising a false statement likely to cause disaffection, namely that the government had been defeated in the House of Commons. Those charged included three justices of the peace, one of whom was the secretary of the Birmingham Trades Council, as well as John Strachey who was later to be a minister in the Attlee government (*British Gazette*, 12 May 1926).

worried about the risk of oscillation interfering with its broadcasts. This was a document, insisted the Attorney, which 'is obviously not only calculated, but intended to impede, delay, restrict and hamper the measures which the Government have taken for the safety of the public',[78] contrary to regulation 21(1).[79]

Although it thus had a role in regulating speech, the main impact of the second limb of regulation 21 related to picketing, aimed at both the disruption of the supply of food and other materials on the one hand, and persuading workers to refrain from working on the other. The ordinary law at that time was governed by the Conspiracy and Protection of Property Act 1875 and the Trade Disputes Act 1906.[80] By virtue of the former a number of offences were enacted in respect of conduct designed to compel another person 'to abstain from doing or to do any act which that person has a legal right to do or abstain from doing', where this was done 'wrongfully and without legal authority'. The conduct in question covers the use of violence or intimidation, persistently following the other person, hiding the tools, clothes or property of the person, watching or besetting the house or other place where that person resides, works, carries on business or happens to be, and following that person in a disorderly manner. As interpreted by the Court of Appeal these provisions operated to make even peaceful picketing unlawful on the ground that the attendance of pickets was in itself 'wrongful and without legal authority' and as such violated the restriction against watching and besetting.[81] Under the 1906 Act it was expressly provided that—in contemplation or furtherance of a trade dispute—it was lawful to attend at or near a place of work or a place where a person happens to be for the purpose only of peacefully persuading a person to work or abstain from work, or for the purpose only of obtaining or communicating information. As a result, peaceful picketing was protected from potential liability under the 1875 Act, though there was no immunity for the consequences of intimidatory picketing.[82] This was still punishable by three months' imprisonment or

---

[78] H C Debs, 6 May 1926, cols 569–70.   [79] See also Morris, n 2 above, p 242.

[80] See now Trade Union and Labour Relations (Consolidation) Act 1992, ss 241 and 220 respectively.

[81] *J. Lyons & Sons v Wilkins* [1896] 1 Ch 811; [1899] 1 Ch 255.

[82] It is to be noted that a narrower approach was taken to the scope of the right to picket, a Home Office circular in December 1925 having reminded chief constables that 'in any future dispute in which the country may become involved, they should take all possible steps, so far as their resources will permit, to repress any proceedings, on the part even of properly constituted pickets, which pass beyond peaceful persuasion and assume any form of compulsion'. See 'Intimidation and Molestation', Home Office Circular, 30 December 1925, addressed to chief constables of England and Wales, as to the provisions of the law relating to intimidation and molestation, Cmd 2666 (1926).

a fine of £20, though there was no power to arrest without a warrant, and cases proceeded on indictment rather than summarily before a magistrate.

There was great concern on the Labour benches during the debates on regulation 21 about its effect on peaceful picketing as protected by the ordinary law, and indeed as protected by section 2(1) of the Emergency Powers Act 1920 which had provided clearly that the regulations must not make it an offence for a person to take part in a strike or peacefully to persuade any other person or persons to take part in a strike,[83] a measure which, as we have seen, was included expressly in the Regulations as a proviso to regulation 21. The point was well made by the former Solicitor General, Sir Henry Slesser, who asked whether it would be an offence for a person peacefully to persuade another person to take part in a strike, if it results in 'the impeding, delaying or restricting of measures taken for maintaining the supply of necessities'.[84] The issue was raised when the Regulations were presented to Parliament for the first time, and on several occasions thereafter, but was never satisfactorily resolved, leading to the conclusion that the Home Office was quite content with the uncertainty created and the possibility that the regulation might well be used against pickets in some cases despite the statutory guarantees. It is true that the Attorney General accepted that 'where it is solely a matter of peaceful persuasion to strike, although that persuasion may impede the supply of necessities, it would not be an offence'.[85] The Attorney General also emphasised, however, that 'if any pickets have been interfered with . . . it must be because their ideas of peaceful persuasion differ considerably from those of the Government'. But as Sir Henry Slesser pointed out in a dogged campaign against regulation 21, intimidatory picketing was already unlawful under the Conspiracy and Protection of Property Act 1875, section 7, leading him to conclude that there was no need to address picketing in the Regulations and 'nothing to justify the existence of an extraordinary law'.[86]

The main object of picketing during the General Strike was to stop the distribution of goods and materials throughout the country, and to ensure also that public transport was immobilised. A problem was caused, however, by the arrangements for the distribution of food which the TUC had no wish to prevent, partly in order to avoid the charge that it was responsible for the starving of women and children. As a result a system was introduced to allow the free passage of drivers who had first

---

[83] H C Debs, 5 May 1926, col 473 (Mr G Lansbury). [84] Ibid, col 483.
[85] Ibid. [86] H C Debs, 28 September 1926, col 424.

obtained a permit from the local trade union organisation.[87] For its part, however, the government refused to accept the co-operation of the TUC and was determined to show that it could secure the free movement of food without trade union assistance under the direction of the Cabinet's Supply and Transport Organisation. One consequence of the government's response was that some police authorities adopted the attitude that the permits were illegal,[88] so that requests to drivers for permits, or the refusal to grant permits, could lead to prosecution under regulation 21. One example is provided by Margaret Morris of the carter who was sentenced to two months with hard labour for impeding the loading of foodstuffs at a flour mill. He claimed that he had merely asked the drivers for their Carters' Union permits, but was told by the magistrate that 'People can use the King's Highway without permits from unions'.[89] There are, however, instances where a failure to issue a permit led to prosecution, most famously in the cases of the Northumberland miners' leader Will Lawther, and the Chairman of Blaydon UDC, Henry Bolton. They had been called out to investigate an unfounded report of a police baton charge on pickets at Blaydon and on their way home saw two lorries and a number of police officers outside a public house. On stopping to investigate, both Lawther and Bolton were arrested after refusing to give a permit for the lorries which had been stopped by pickets. Ostensibly carrying groceries and provisions for miners and their families, on closer inspection the vehicles were discovered to be laden with birdseed, inviting the retort from Lawther that it would be a pity 'if the canaries died because of the General Strike'.[90] They were refused bail and sentenced to £50 or two months' imprisonment.[91]

So far as the conduct of the picketing was concerned, the TUC gave instructions that it expected 'every member taking part to be exemplary in his conduct and not to give any opportunity for police interference . . . The [General] Council asks pickets especially to avoid obstruction and to confine themselves strictly to their legitimate duties'.[92] It is clear, however, that not all pickets complied with these instructions to the letter, and that steps were often taken to immobilise vehicles by letting down tyres, removing vital pieces of equipment, or overturning them.[93] It was

[87] For an account of the permit system, see Morris, n 2 above, pp 57–69.
[88] *British Worker*, 7 May 1926.   [89] Morris, n 2 above, p 65.
[90] The matter was raised in Parliament on 12 May 1926. See H C Debs, 12 May 1926, col 879.
[91] For a full account see Morris, n 2 above, pp 56–7.
[92] *British Worker*, 5 May 1926.
[93] The *British Gazette* in particular regularly drew attention to excess of zeal on the part of pickets. The issue of 6 May refers to an incident in which coal was thrown at a tramcar in Leeds, and

admitted in the columns of the *British Gazette*, however, that '[n]o very serious disorder has occurred in any part of the country' during the first week of the strike.[94] But that was to change in the second week, with the government announcing that 'Intimidation both by disorderly crowds and picketing has occurred in many places, and may soon occur in many more'.[95] There is evidence of much more heavy-handed policing in the second week, often associated with the transfer of police officers into one area from another,[96] and with the enlistment of special constables, some of whom were said to be fascist sympathisers.[97] There were in fact disturbances, and sometimes allegations of indiscriminate brutality on the part of the police, in places as diverse as Glasgow,[98] Edinburgh, Hull, Newcastle, Middlesbrough, Leeds, Doncaster, Preston and London. In one incident in Poplar (the only one of its kind to be referred to in the *British Worker* which was remarkably silent on the civil liberties dimension to the strike) it was alleged that the police first drove a lorry through a crowd of people causing injury as people scattered to get out of the way. The vehicle then stopped and police officers charged the crowd striking blows indiscriminately, and then followed members of the fleeing crowd into private property, including a nearby pub where the beatings were said to have continued. When a complaint was made to the Home Secretary he agreed to receive a deputation of local councillors but refused to sanction an inquiry unless witness statements were handed over to the police, a demand which was resisted for fear of retribution. As it was, one complainant, a vicar, was visited at home in the early

to another in London where a bus was 'held up' and its passengers required to walk to their destination. The issue of 7 May refers to an incident in Aberdeen in which student bus drivers were attacked by a mob and 'roughly handled', and to others in which missiles were thrown at cabs and tramcar drivers were assaulted. The issue of 8 May refers to an incident in which nails were scattered on the road to immobilise traffic, and of missiles being thrown at a bus at the Elephant and Castle in London, leading to the death of a pedestrian. In the same issue it is reported that four men waited behind a hedge and rushed a bus, pulling the driver off, and damaging the engine. There are also reports of vehicles being overturned by pickets, and of attempts being made to pull drivers from their vehicles.

[94] *British Gazette*, 8 May 1926.   [95] Ibid.

[96] As pointed out above (p 166), the Emergency Regulations provided that police officers could be transferred from one force to another where it was 'expedient' that the latter should be 'temporarily strengthened', and also that members of a police force could be directed to be 'available for duty outside the police district of the force to which they belong otherwise than by way of transfer to another force' (Regulations 26 and 27). In practice, however, 'the Home Office found that the necessary measures for national co-ordination could be adopted without any recourse to the compulsory powers' in the Regulations (Morgan, n 27 above, p 129).

[97] From 11 May until 1 June 1926 no fewer than 142,000 special constables were recruited. See H C Debs, I June 1926, col 597. Some of the specials were said to be 'boys hardly out of school, dressed in the most unsuitable manner, . . . swaggering about the streets with special constables' armlets on their arms' (H C Debs, 5 July 1926, col 1829).

[98] See H C Debs, 2 June 1926, cols 881–2.

hours of the morning by a group of thugs thought to be from a far-right organisation who claimed that they had authority to take him to 'Whitehall'.[99]

According to information released by the Home Office there were in total 1,760 prosecutions under the Regulations in England and Wales alone, of which 150 related to 'incitement by speech or by printed documents', and 1,389 to 'violence and disorder', the great bulk of these being concerned with 'men who were guilty of actual disorder—who stopped the traffic, who used violence to the drivers of motor lorries or other vehicles'.[100] Some of the cases in the last category would almost certainly have proceeded under regulation 20 as dealing with damage to property, though it is likely (on the basis of information relating to prosecutions between May and December) that the majority were taken under regulation 21. According to the *British Gazette* 'sharp sentences' were imposed by magistrates on a number of arrested people for disorder and intimidation,[101] though in fact only about half of those convicted of offences under the Regulations relating to violence and disorder were imprisoned. A number of these are reported in a rather menacing way in the *British Gazette* of 9 May 1926 where William Carver was charged under regulation 21 with preventing the proper working of a motor transport van by attempting to overturn it. There is also the case of James Clements charged with preventing the use and working of vehicles by trying to pull a driver from his cab. But although regulation 21 was thus an important instrument for dealing with picketing, it was as we have seen in addition to the established powers under the general law which were resorted to from time to time. Indeed in the case of two Bermondsey pickets fined 40 shillings for 'booing and insulting men while on their way

---

[99] H C Debs, 2 July 1926, cols 1521–6. Also H C Debs, 30 July 1926, cols 2572–4. On the question of compensation in relation to the Poplar incident, see H C Debs 15 July 1926, col 593. There is a closed Home Office file dealing with Poplar: 'General Strike, 1926: police baton charge at Poplar' (PRO, HO 144/6903). The other incidents were just as alarming. The Doncaster incident was raised in the Commons on 30 July by the Labour Member for Don Valley who read a letter he had received from the secretary of the local branch of the National Union of Railwaymen. Here it was alleged that on 12 May during a melee between miners and police, the police ran amok, with one of his members being struck while standing at his own front door. According to the letter, 'the police showed no mercy to man, woman or child' (H C Debs, 30 July 1926, cols 2545–6).

[100] H C Debs, 2 June 1926, cols 823–6 (Sir W Joynson-Hicks). See also H C Debs, 1 June 1926, col 598 where it is revealed that there were 604 arrests without a warrant between 3 and 12 May for offences in the Metropolitan area arising in connection with the emergency. But not all of these were proceeded with under the Emergency Regulations. Some were brought under the Metropolitan Police Act 1839, the Offences against the Person Act 1861, the Malicious Damage Act 1861, the Conspiracy and Protection of Property Act 1875, the Prevention of Crimes Amendment Act 1885, and the Larceny Act 1916.

[101] *British Gazette*, 12 May 1926.

to work', the magistrates were heard to lament that 'For some reason the police prefer to put the charge in the old form of "insulting words and behaviour" under which the magistrate's power is limited to a penalty of forty shillings', warning the defendants that it was open to the police to prefer a 'much more serious charge' in which case they would 'certainly' have been sent to prison.[102]

After the General Strike: Renewal of the State of Emergency

As we have seen the end of the General Strike did not mean an end to the dispute in the coal industry which had provoked it in the first place, and the miners remained locked out until the end of November 1926 when they were forced back to work on the employers' terms. So although the General Strike came to an end on 12 May 1926, the State of Emergency was not discontinued, nor were the Emergency Regulations revoked. Indeed a fresh regulations were issued on that same day empowering the government to confiscate money sent from abroad during the Strike,[103] and although these were never laid before Parliament, they were invoked to prevent the transfer from and require the return to Moscow of £200,000.[104] The continuation of the dispute was thus used as a pretext by the government for continuing to invoke the Emergency Powers Act 1920, thereby renewing the State of Emergency and the Emergency Regulations made thereunder. In fact eight proclamations were made, and the regulations were in turn renewed seven times, with the last set of regulations being reintroduced in a heavily amended form after the return to work. The powers were thus invoked until December and were not revoked until the miners returned to work. This is not to say, however, that the exercise of these

---

[102] *British Gazette*, 10 May 1926. The Emergency Regulations carried three months' imprisonment, or a fine of up to £100, or both. See p 182 below.

[103] See Regulation 13A. The Charges d'Affaires in Moscow was also instructed to inform the Soviet Government of Britain's concern about this support for the General Strike which according to the Foreign Secretary was 'an illegal and unconstitutional act constituting a serious threat to established order'. See H C Debs, 14 June 1926, col 1956. The TUC had earlier refused to accept a Russian donation of £26,000. See Morris, n 2 above, p 264.

[104] H C Debs, 17 June 1926, cols 2466–7. Russian contributions continued to be made to the miners after the General Strike ended, but these were not stopped by the government because the miners were 'engaged in a genuine trade dispute' and such donations clearly stood 'on a different footing'. See H C Debs, 20 May 1926, col 421. By 11 November 1926 some £1,1087,000 is reported as having been transferred from Russia for the relief of the miners. See H C Debs, 11 November 1926, col 1226. See also on Russian funds, *Workers' Weekly*, 28 May 1926. There are also a number of closed Home Office files which may be relevant: 'Miners' Strike, May 1926: Russian money, telegrams and letters from abroad' (PRO, HO 144/6891), and 'Payments from Russia in aid of the General Strike' (PRO, HO 144/7985).

powers was uncontroversial or that questions were not raised about the exercise of a provision which was designed to deal with action 'of such a nature and on so extensive a scale as to be calculated, by interfering with the supply and distribution of food, water, fuel, or light, or with the means of locomotion, to deprive the community, or any substantial portion of the community, of the essentials of life'.

The place for raising these concerns and for scrutinising the conduct of government was Parliament. Indeed in the early days three opportunities were provided to examine the conduct of ministers, though as we shall see the government soon wearied of constitutional propriety, with the Home Secretary referring on one occasion to the 'tiresome necessity of summoning Parliament'.[105] First, when a Proclamation was made by His Majesty the Act required that it be communicated to Parliament 'forthwith', and this would be done in the form of a Message which was read by the Prime Minister (in the case of the first proclamation) or the Home Secretary (in the case of subsequent proclamations) at the Bar of the House, a Minister of the Crown then moving that it be taken into consideration.[106] As was later explained by Captain Wedgewood Benn, the Liberal Member for Leith who took a keen interest in constitutional questions, this was more than an act of courtesy, but rather an occasion which provided the Commons with an opportunity 'for debate and control',[107] though in practice no debate took place at this stage. Secondly, a humble address thanking His Majesty for his message, would then be moved by the Home Secretary, 'in order that a further Debate might take place',[108] in the course of which the House would have a full opportunity to consider the case for making the Proclamation. Although this gave rise to the bizarre spectacle of the Home Secretary effectively 'asking for a Vote of Thanks to Himself',[109] the procedure nevertheless enabled the House to consider whether the exercise of the statutory power was justified. This would then be followed thirdly by a debate on a motion to continue in force the Regulations made under the Act after the proclamation of emergency had been issued. This might take the form of a general debate on the merits of the code as a whole, followed by a consideration of various amendments to omit particular regulations,

---

[105] PRO, CAB 24/180, CP 278 (26). Memorandum by the Home Secretary, 20 July 1926. This was all the more remarkable for the fact that the most vocal defender of Parliament when the Bill was being passed was none other than Sir William Joynson-Hicks, now Home Secretary. See his powerful contribution at H C Debs, 25 October 1920, cols 1422–3.

[106] H C Debs, 26 November 1926, col 724. See for example H C Debs, 1 June 1926, col 588.

[107] H C Debs, 26 November 1926, col 724.   [108] Ibid.

[109] H C Debs, 2 June 1926, col 756 (J Batey, Labour Member for Spennymoor).

usually 21, 22 and 33. This had to be done within seven days of making the regulations which would otherwise lapse.

The government's decision to issue a second Proclamation on 29 May was condemned in measured terms by the Leader of the Opposition who accepted that 'a Government faced with conditions such as the Government was faced with a week or two ago is bound to ask for emergency powers'. Indeed had Labour been in government at the time, admitted MacDonald, they would have done the same, 'whatever view' they might have taken of 'the matters that brought about the emergency'.[110] However, there was no justification for the fresh Proclamation and the continuation of the Regulations, having regard in particular to 'the state of the country' and the 'experience of the last Proclamation', referring here in particular to the arbitrary nature of the system of summary justice meted out by the local magistrates. In a spirit of conciliation, the Liberal Member for Hull Central, Lieutenant Commander Kenworthy argued that there was a difference between those regulations which put emergency powers in the hands of the government for securing fuel, light and other necessaries of life 'in the face of a possible continuation of the coal stoppage', and those 'which are, broadly, classed amongst those for the supposed preservation of public order—arrest without warrant, search without magistrate's order and all the rest of it'.[111] So far as the first category is concerned, he did not wish 'to deny those powers to any Government', but argued that the second category of regulations were unnecessary, particularly 'after the experience of the last month'. Urging that these 'more contentious penal clauses' should be dropped, Kenworthy pleaded that if they were renewed, 'it will show a want of trust in the good sense and constitutionalism of our people'.[112]

The occasion of the third Proclamation of a State of Emergency led to a Labour Motion of Censure 'regretting the policy pursued by His Majesty's Advisers, which has been an impediment in maintaining and restoring peace in the coal industry and, consequently, a menace to public order'.[113] In moving the motion for the Opposition, J R Clynes contended that the 'ordinary agencies of the law . . . are quite sufficient for the purpose of maintaining law and order' and that the continuation of the emergency powers were 'a provocation to disorder rather than a means of preventing it'.[114] For its part the government tossed aside its critics with the Chancellor of the Exchequer (Winston Churchill)

[110] Ibid, col 743.
[111] Ibid, col 746.
[112] Ibid, cols 746–7.
[113] H C Debs, 2 July 1926, col 1485.
[114] Ibid, col 1489.

arguing that when 'a great stoppage has been in progress for so long', it is 'obviously the duty of the Government to arm itself with the necessary powers, however mildly or moderately they may be used, to carry out the essential services, and to maintain public order'.[115] When the House returned to the matter several days later to consider the third presentation of the Emergency Regulations Labour renewed its attack, arguing mainly that the experience of the previous month was such that there was now clearly no need for the regulations, and no state of emergency. Particularly deeply regretted was regulation 21, not only because it gave to magistrates ('which does not even mean a stipendiary magistrate but any two county magistrates who happen to be sitting on any Bench in some rural area')[116] the power to deal with serious allegations of sedition ('a matter that requires the trained mind of a judge to direct the jury very carefully'),[117] but also because it 'creates a new offence', disaffection, which is 'greater in extent than sedition itself'.[118] Again, however, the government was uncompromising, despite conceding 'the peaceful character of the population', and the fact that only sixty-eight prosecutions had been brought under the Regulations in the previous month, all of these for a breach of either regulation 20 or 21.[119] In a speech which was frequently interrupted, and in the course of which he confessed difficulty in keeping his temper, the Home Secretary revealed that the public order regulations were nevertheless necessary in view of the fact that 'there are people who are trying to stir up trouble'.[120]

By the time the fourth and fifth Proclamations were made, the government discontinued the practice of moving the humble address, thereby denying the House the opportunity to consider whether the Proclamations were a proper exercise of the statutory powers.[121] The role of Parliament was restricted to no more than giving approval to the regulations, the bare minimum required by the 1920 Act. A casual explanation was offered by the Home Secretary when he said that the government 'did not think it necessary at this time, this being the third renewal of the Proclamation, to put down an Address in reply to His

---

[115] H C Debs, 2 July 1926, col 1543.
[116] H C Debs, 5 July 1926, col 1772 (Sir H Slesser).   [117] Ibid, col 1773.
[118] Ibid, col 1774.
[119] No meetings had been banned under Regulation 22 in the previous month: H C Debs, 5 July 1926, col 1797.
[120] Ibid, col 1798.
[121] It ought to be said that the 1926 government was more conscientious than that in 1921 which also declared a state of emergency. See H C Debs, 4 April 1921, col 28, and 5 April 1921, col 129 (no debate on the address); H C Debs, 2 May 1921, col 681, and 4 May 1921, col 1079 (no address); and H C Debs, 30 May 1921, col 601, and 2 June 1921, col 1277 (no address).

Majesty'.[122] But as was pointed out earlier, the debate on the address is an important one which raises issues separate from the debate on the motion to continue in force the Regulations for another month. The former provides the House with the opportunity to consider the decision to issue a proclamation of emergency and in particular whether that decision can be justified in the light of the statutory criteria. The latter in contrast provides an opportunity to consider the code of regulations and in particular whether they are both collectively and individually a proper exercise of a quite separate statutory power. The matter was picked up by Captain Benn who noted that for the first time a Royal Message had been received but that no minister had seen fit to move that it be taken into consideration, and 'deeply regret[ted]' the fact that the Address in reply to His Majesty had been abandoned, partly because of the loss of 'a vital opportunity' for discussion and partly because the debate on the Address 'was debated in the daylight' whereas the Resolution on the Regulations 'might perfectly well be moved at 12.30 or 1 o'clock in the morning'.[123] Benn was in fact left to fight a solitary campaign, and it is a matter of considerable shame that he should be left to regret, again 'deeply' that 'no support was forthcoming' for his 'plea that the old procedure should be retained'.[124]

On the substantive points arising during the debates on the fourth and fifth set of Regulations, the point was again made by the Opposition that there was now no need for special powers, that there was no national state of emergency, and that the ordinary law was perfectly capable of dealing with any disorder that might arise.[125] The government had already conceded that 'since the conclusion of the general strike the coal stoppage has not resulted in any very great trouble'.[126] Developing another line of attack which had been made less forcefully in earlier exchanges, the former Solicitor General, Sir Henry Slesser, condemned the government for going much further than was ever intended when the

---

[122] H C Debs, 30 July 1926, col 2510. When Benn tried to move that the message be taken into consideration on the occasion of the fifth Proclamation, he was told by the Speaker that this could be done only by a minister. See H C Debs, 30 August 1926, col 6.

[123] H C Debs, 30 July 1926, col 2519. He had raised the matter for the first time a few days earlier. See H C Debs, 28 July 1926, col 2112.

[124] Ibid.

[125] See especially H C Debs, 30 July 1926, cols 2527–34 (R MacDonald). The government's view was that the emergency powers were necessary for when there was a return to work, at which point 'there is almost certain to be fresh trouble, and persons with Communist or extremist views will do their utmost to make difficult the position of those men who are willing to work'. It was also said that common law proceedings would be 'quite ineffective as a check on such persons'. See PRO, CAB/24/180, CP 278 (26), n 105 above.

[126] H C Debs, 30 July 1926, col 2510 (Sir W Joynson-Hicks).

Emergency Powers Act 1920 was introduced. In his view 'the Legislature contemplated that in times of emergency the Government should have the power to commandeer materials, to control prices, and secondly, to take the necessary steps to preserve the peace'. But he very much doubted 'if the steps which were to be taken to preserve the peace were ever intended to include the creation of a vast mass of new offences such as we find here catalogued'.[127] Slesser also complained about the government bringing forward the same Regulations for approval month after month. In his view, 'the amount of regulation which is made under this Statute ought not to be a hard and fast amount. It ought to vary with the necessities of the case. Instead of repeating month after month the same stereotyped Regulations, the amount of coercive legislation required ought to be varied and modified from month to month according to the necessities of the time'. The intention of the Legislature in asking Parliament to review and and renew these Regulations from month to month, he claimed, was that 'intelligence should be brought to bear upon them each month in accordance with the conditions which had arisen during that month'. If the same Regulations are to be presented to Parliament every month, not only is the intention of Parliament defeated but the whole process 'becomes something not much better than a farce'.[128]

Farce or not the process was repeated at the end of September when the government bounced back a sixth time with a fresh Proclamation and a request for authority to continue the Regulations for another month. By this time, however, the Home Secretary could point to an increase in the number of prosecutions, associated with the beginning of a trickle back to work in some of the mining areas: 'as a larger number of men are going back to work, there has been an increase in the cases occurring under the Emergency Regulations'.[129] Thus from 22 August until 22 September there were 309 cases under the regulations (including 212 under regulation 21), of which 191 (compared with only eleven in the previous month) were brought in four counties—Nottingham, Derbyshire, Staffordshire, and Warwickshire—where the return to work

[127] H C Debs, 30 July 1926, col 2540.

[128] Ibid, cols 2540–1. In the light of these arguments it is to be noted that the matter had been considered by the government. The Home Secretary expressed the view in a memorandum to Cabinet colleagues on 20 July that Regulations 21 and 22 were 'absolutely necessary' and that there was 'no advantage in attempting to shorten the code', even though there were 'certain Regulations of which no use [was] now being made'. These were Regulations 1–9, 17, 18, and 23–5. See PRO, CAB 24/180, CP 278 (26), n 105 above.

[129] H C Debs, 28 September 1926, col 412 (Sir W Joynson-Hicks).

was greatest. According to the Home Secretary, on 24 September there were 17,678 miners back in Nottingham and twenty prosecutions under the Regulations, compared with only 600 in the previous month when there were no cases at all. As if to indicate that the real purpose of the Regulations was to facilitate a peaceful return to work and the breaking of the strike, the Home Secretary contended that in the light of this and other information he had adequately disposed of 'the suggestion that there was no need for these Regulations'.[130] But still Labour was unconvinced, with Ramsay MacDonald leading the charge on this occasion. Although it could not be argued in light of the return to work in some areas and in view of the disorder which it provoked that the Regulations were now irrelevant, the Leader of Opposition maintained that the problem could be contained by the ordinary law, returning to another of the several points which had been made before. In a powerful and persuasive speech, MacDonald conceded that the Home Secretary had made out a case for the ordinary law. He had made out a case for policemen, magistrates, fines and imprisonment. But 'he has got to make out a case for special law, special administration, special sentences, and special arrests', and this he had failed to do.[131]

The government nevertheless returned a seventh and then an eighth time with additional Proclamations, seeking authority to maintain the Regulations for further periods of a month. By the time of the seventh Proclamation there had been a decline in the number of prosecutions, there being only three under regulation 20 and sixty-six under regulation 21. Clearly on the defensive about the government's desire to continue the Regulations for another month, the Home Secretary repeated more forcefully a point that had been made some time in the past, the argument that 'it was in the interest of all classes that there should be a short and quick punishment under the provisions of these Regulations', rather than have the cases 'prosecuted in the ordinary way and go to trial at the Assizes and possibly involve longer sentences'.[132] For this explanation the Home Secretary was teased mercilessly by Sir Henry Slesser who felt that at long last he was being offered an explanation why the common law was not sufficient to deal with offences which might arise in the course of the dispute. But needless to say Slesser was unconvinced by the explanation, which provided 'no justification for refusing to allow cases to be dealt with by the ordinary processes of law',[133] and which was undermined by a number of telling arguments. In the first place some of the

---

[130] Ibid, cols 410–12.
[132] H C Debs, 26 October 1926, col 732.
[131] Ibid, col 417.
[133] Ibid, col 746.

Regulations introduced new offences which were not recognised by the common law, an example of this being the offence of disaffection in regulation 21. In these cases, argued Slesser, it could hardly be claimed that people got more lenient treatment under the Regulations than they would according to the ordinary legal process, 'because the offences could never have been created at common law'. Secondly, it was not the case that the ordinary legal process was less favourable to the accused than the system of magisterial justice under the Regulations. He cited as an example section 7 of the Conspiracy and Protection of Property Act 1875 breach of which, as we have seen, was punishable on indictment by a £20 fine or a maximum of three months' imprisonment. Breach of the regulations in contrast was punishable by a fine of up to £100 or three months' imprisonment.

The eighth request for Regulations was preceded by another illustration of constitutional indifference on the part of the government. Under the 1920 Act a proclamation of emergency is to be communicated 'forthwith' to Parliament. As was pointed out, 'That is an order made by the House in respect of its own business, and it is in the Statute'.[134] On this occasion, however, on Tuesday 23 November the ever alert Mr Benn drew attention to the fact that the Proclamation had been issued on the previous Saturday but had not yet been communicated to Parliament despite having been reported in the press. The matter was raised in the House, but without much success, dismissed by the Speaker in the most casual terms. Thus although it was claimed that he had 'clearly expected a Message to be received on Monday'[135] (a day on which the House sat), the Speaker informed Captain Benn, having raised the question, that 'If it be a breach of the Statute, the remedy does not lie with me'.[136] Perhaps unsurprisingly the Message was delivered to the House that day, the Speaker being so informed in the course of his exchange with Benn. A debate on the Regulations took place three days later on Friday 26 November, but had to be continued until the following Monday 29 November, more than the stipulated week after the Proclamation was made, which meant that the Regulations 'would cease to be operative on Sunday',[137] though the point was alluded to only briefly. Needless to say Captain Benn (rightly) saw this as 'a further invasion of the rights of the House', though it is a matter of astonishment again that no other voices were raised in protest at the propriety of the government's conduct, par-

---

[134] H C Debs, 26 November 1926, col 724.   [135] Ibid.
[136] H C Debs, 23 November 1926, col 189.
[137] H C Debs, 26 November 1926, col 725 (Captain Benn).

ticularly in view of the earlier steps which had been taken to undermine the standing of Parliament. For as he pointed out this was not only an example of 'of the ingrained contempt of the Government for the rights' of the House, but it was also 'a flat defiance of the order made by the House and which is in the Statute' that a Proclamation should be communicated forthwith.

The occasion of the eighth request for the renewal of the Regulations was extraordinary for other reasons, which highlighted the inadequacy of a debate on the Regulations alone and reinforced the need for a debate on the decision to issue a fresh Proclamation. Although there had been a slight increase in the number of prosecutions under the Regulations in the previous month (to 511), more than half the miners had returned to work and the dispute was now in its dying days. Nevertheless the Home Secretary requested the renewal of the Regulations 'as a matter of precaution' in order that 'there may be no difficulty whatever about preserving the peace', undertaking to dispense with them 'at the very earliest possible moment',[138] though this too was to give rise to constitutional difficulties which need not be explored here.[139] But as was pointed out forcefully by a number of members on the Opposition benches, there was no authority for the government to declare a state of emergency on such grounds, the Act being restricted to circumstances where the essentials of life were threatened. In a very effective speech Sir Henry Slesser claimed that the Regulations were thus 'utterly illegal', partly because they were made under the authority of an 'unfounded' Proclamation, but partly also because they went beyond what was necessary for the 'preservation of the peace'.[140] When the debate was resumed on the following Monday (by which time almost all of the coalfields were back at work) Slesser returned to the charge with even greater effect in a devastating speech, taunting the Home Secretary who in the meantime had tried unpersuasively to show that the essentials of life were still threatened. Asserting that 'at the present moment there is no actual menace to the life of the community: none whatever', Slesser asked rhetorically how could it be claimed that the life of the community is in peril 'when we have imported coal, when we have foodstuffs, and when our normal processes are going on?'[141]

---

[138] H C Debs, 26 November 1926, col 725 (Captain Benn), col 715.
[139] Ibid, cols 727 (Captain Benn) and 740 (Sir H Slesser).   [140] Ibid, cols 740–1.
[141] H C Debs, 29 November 1926, col 886.

The 'Iron Heel' in the Coalfields

So much then for Parliament. The longer the dispute went on the more marginalised it allowed itself to become, eventually confined to endorsing the pro forma Regulations which the government brought forward on a monthly basis. Despite the strength of opposition to some of the Regulations, and despite concerns that they were unnecessary, overbroad, or even unlawful, the government won every vote to renew the Regulations, and not a single regulation was omitted as a result of parliamentary opposition. Moving from form to substance, we turn our attention now to consider how the Regulations were deployed in the coalfields while the emergency continued after the end of the General Strike. Sir Henry Slesser complained that the government had effectively suspended the common law and introduced 'what is really martial law',[142] while even Ramsay MacDonald was heard to complain about 'this extraordinary drift' towards 'a police state'.[143] Claims of martial law may be difficult to sustain, particularly if we are to adopt the definition of martial law as being 'the suspension of ordinary law and the temporary government of a country or parts of it by military tribunal'.[144] Even after the enactment of the Emergency Powers Act 1920 it remains true that martial law in this sense, the 'true' sense, is 'utterly unknown to the Constitution',[145] and in fact this is a dispute in which the military played a residual (if not insignificant) role, with the primary responsibility for public order, for example, resting throughout with the civilian authorities.[146]

But martial law is a term which is not always used in this true sense. Indeed Dicey was to acknowledge that 'by martial law [may] be meant the power of the government or of loyal citizens to maintain public order, at whatever cost of blood or property may be necessary'.[147] Using the term in this sense Slesser may not have been wide of the mark, with the *Workers' Weekly* writing in typically evocative terms not of the coalfields being under the influence of constitutional principle, but 'under the Iron Heel' of 'police terror', which intensified as the strike was prolonged when in 'desperate' efforts to 'stampede the miners back to work' min-

---

[142] H C Debs, 26 October 1926, col 745.   [143] H C Debs, 30 July 1926, col 2533.

[144] A V Dicey, *Introduction to the Study of the Law of the Constitution* (10th edn, 1959), p 287. It has also been referred to as a situation where 'Instead of habeas corpus you would get post mortems': Jack London, *The Iron Heel* (1971 edn), p 91. For a genuine example of martial law, see Chapter 7 below.

[145] Dicey, n 144 above, p 293.

[146] See Morgan, n 27 above, pp 117–19, 123–4.

[147] Dicey, n 144 above, p 290.

ing communities experienced a 'frenzied application of the EPA'.[148] Quite how far such hyperbole was justified is of course impossible to tell from our relatively comfortable contemporary vantage point, though there is evidence of a number of different but interconnecting character- istics which are both singly and (even more powerfully) cumulatively evi- dence at least to sustain MacDonald's claims about a drift towards a police state. These are as follows:

(i)   arbitrary police powers;
(ii)   the suspension of civil liberties;
(iii) excessive and unaccountable policing;
(iv)   techniques of summary justice;
(v)   judicial bias in the operation of the law;
(vi)   exemplary sentencing;
(vii) the limited scope for appeal, and the nature of the appeals.

It is to a consideration of each of these matters that we now turn, focus- ing for the most part on events in the coalfields after 12 May 1926.

(i) *Arbitrary police powers*

As we have seen the Regulations conferred wide powers of summary arrest on the police. It was not necessary for the exercise of these pow- ers that an offence should have been committed, the police being author- ised to arrest anyone 'who so acts as to endanger the public safety', as well as anyone suspected of having offended against the Regulations. Although these measures were strongly condemned,[149] there are many reports in Hansard and elsewhere of their being widely used. There are allegations of people being arrested and not charged, including the case of the Derbyshire man talking to his friends by the side of the road when told to move on by the police. When he refused to do so he was arrested and taken into custody, but he could not then be bailed because the arresting officer had left without specifying a charge. The case was brought before the magistrates in the morning at which point the arrested man was released without any charges being laid.[150] There are allegations also of people being assaulted in police custody until they pro- vided evidence which could then be used in the prosecution of others, as in the case of the 'young boy' in Bonnyrigg, Midlothian, who was taken

[148] *Workers' Weekly*, 12 November 1926. See also *Workers' Weekly* (Supplement), 19 December 1926.
[149] H C Debs, 2 June 1926, col 804 (G Lansbury).
[150] H C Debs, 28 September 1926, col 483.

to the local police office where he was 'brutally treated' by six police officers until 'certain evidence was forced from him' which was then used to
imprison seven men on a charge which the Sheriff admitted was not 'very
strong'.[151] There are allegations further of people being arrested and
prosecuted on whimsical grounds, and of such cases then being withdrawn by the prosecution. Frank Lee (Labour Member for Derbyshire
North East) gave as an example the case of the woman in her sixties who
admitted saying to two young fellows who were coming from a colliery
'You do look nice coming home in your pit clothes'. She was arrested,
taken to a lock-up some four miles away and charged, but the case was
withdrawn after the prosecutor was unable to believe the testimony of
the witness for the prosecution.[152] Much less fortunate was the Yorkshire
householder visited by the police at night 'to inquire whether a certain
gentleman they wanted was there'. The householder 'presumed to give
[the police] some advice', along the lines 'that the policeman might be
engaged on better work' and was 'promptly arrested'. He was subsequently convicted and sentenced to three months' with hard labour.[153]

Related to the foregoing were the arbitrary powers of entry, search
and seizure, with the Regulations permitting any police constable to
enter, if need be by force, any premises or place suspected of having
been, or being, used for any purpose 'endangering the public safety' or
otherwise contrary to the Regulations. Once on the premises the police
were empowered to search them and to seize or detain anything which
might be used for any purpose contrary to the Regulations. Condemned
by George Lansbury as a 'monstrous injustice', these powers could be
used, as we have seen, to search a man's (sic) house without the need for
a warrant, 'and without the man being there to see for what they are
searching and what they find, and getting a receipt for it'.[154] They were
in fact used much more extensively, with complaints in Derbyshire that
the police were claiming 'the right to enter the branch rooms [of trade
unions] where purely branch meetings are being held'.[155] There were
complaints also of the raiding of newspaper premises, as in the case of
the *Daily Herald* discussed above. Although it was true that the authority
of the Home Secretary was required in such cases there was no need for
such authority unless the newspaper was registered, and as we shall see
there were a number of allegations of the police entering and searching
premises occupied by members of the Communist Party and seizing

[151] H C Debs, 26 November 1926, col 793.
[152] H C Debs, 28 November 1926, col 483.
[153] H C Debs, 2 June 1926, col 847.
[154] Ibid, col 804.
[155] H C Debs, 26 October 1926, col 793.

equipment used in the production of propaganda. There were further complaints of the raiding of homes in Pontypridd, South Wales on the day after the end of the General Strike. Those subjected to this treatment included the secretary of the local strike committee, a man who had been secretary of the local trades council for many years, a very active and prominent member of the urban district council, an active member of one of the local churches, and a promoter of the YMCA. They also included another miners' leader, 'a man who serves in several public capacities, who was asked and assisted to keep law and order', in this case the police 'very carefully' searching cupboards and bookshelves for seditious material. This was done, claimed the local MP, Mardy Jones, 'in towns where there was no disturbance', and significantly, 'against individuals who are not Communists, but known by their public record in the towns to be anti-Communists'.[156]

(ii) *The suspension of civil liberties*[157]

The main power to restrict civil liberties was the power in regulation 22 authorising the Home Secretary to ban meetings and demonstrations where it was anticipated that there would be a breach of the peace which would in turn cause undue demands to be made on the police or would promote disaffection. Although it appears to have been accepted that these rights of public meeting and demonstration could not be unlimited, it was also argued that the common law, in the landmark case of *Beatty* v *Gillbanks*,[158] had 'devised a carefully balanced principle to deal with this question relating to all meetings which are apt to irritate other people and promote disorder'.[159] According to Sir Henry Slesser, 'good sound principles' were laid down in that decision, 'as to which assemblies were lawful and which were not'.[160] Although it was impossible to 'tell beforehand whether a meeting is going to cause disaffection',[161] the authorities nevertheless presumed to use the power on a number of occasions, one reported casualty being a meeting and procession due to be held in South Wales on 8 September 1926, to be addressed by Shipurji Saklatvala. The meeting was advertised in late August and was to take place under the management of the South Wales Miners' Federation, not the Communist Party. On the late afternoon of 7 September the local official of the miners' union was informed by the police superintendent that the meeting

---

[156] H C Debs, 2 June 1926, cols 858–60.
[157] See also pp 200–7 below, 'Emergency Powers and the Communist Party'.
[158] (1882) 9 QBD 308.   [159] H C Debs, 30 July 1926, col 2543 (Sir H Slesser).
[160] Ibid.   [161] Ibid, col 2544.

would be cancelled and that notices to this effect were being printed. Apart from the predictable and legitimate concern about the short notice, questions were also raised about the vagueness of the ban which prohibited any meeting at or in the vicinity of Hoelycue, the location of the banned meeting. It was only after being wired by Saklatvala that the Chief Constable of Glamorgan announced that this meant that a meeting should not be held within five miles radius of Hoelycue.[162]

From 1 May until 19 October 1926 the Home Secretary had authorised the prohibition of meetings or processions on twenty-two occasions.[163] Particularly controversial, however, was the fact that on 19 October he gave a blanket authority to chief constables to make an order prohibiting the holding of any meeting or procession in connection with the dispute in the mining industry where they had reason to apprehend a breach of the peace or that the meeting would promote disaffection.[164] It is not clear whether such delegation was a lawful exercise of the powers granted by regulation 22, a point taken up by Sir Henry Slesser who argued that the conferring of a general discretion of this kind was both undesirable and a 'straining' of the regulation.[165] In his view 'the intention of the words of [regulation 22] was that whereas a mayor and magistrates, by virtue of their office, have power to proclaim a meeting, a chief officer of police can be vested with that power by the Secretary of State, but is vested only for the purpose of making a particular order for a particular meeting'.[166] Yet despite the uncertain legal status of this general delegation of power, it was invoked by the Chief Constable of Staffordshire to prohibit meetings to be addressed by the miners' leader

---

[162] See H C Debs, 28 September 1926, cols 451–7. See now Public Order Act 1986, s 14A, as inserted by Criminal Justice and Public Order Act 1994.

[163] H C Debs, 17 November 1926, cols 1847–8.

[164] See H C Debs, 25 October 1926, cols 634–5. Between that date and 14 November 1926 (that is to say within a period of less than a month) the power had been exercised by chief constables on no fewer than 63 occasions in England and Wales alone (H C Debs, 17 November 926, col 1848). See pp 204–6 below.

[165] The point was made also by G Thorne who argued that the Home Secretary should 'not only take the technical but the direct responsibility' for the exercise of power under Regulation 22. See H C Debs, 26 October 1926, col 768.

[166] Ibid, col 769. There are also suggestions that the police not only required organisers to inform them about the existence of meetings, but effectively required them to seek police permission before a meeting could be held. The point is alluded to by T Williams, the Labour MP for Don Valley who referred to a meeting to be addressed by Herbert Smith, the President of the MFGB. According to Williams, 'the local people who were organising the meeting had to do all manner of things before they could secure the final permission of the superintendent of police for that meeting to take place'. Not surprisingly, he was to insist that 'this Regulation ought [not] to be continued if the local superintendents of police are going to insist upon permission being sought in this way'. See H C Debs, 30 July 1926, col 2546.

A J Cook,[167] a matter which was said to have 'surprised many people, and to have disconcerted some'.[168] In responding to these concerns in the course of a Commons debate on the Coal Trade Dispute on 25 October 1926 the Home Secretary announced that he did not consider himself bound to give reasons for the banning of a meeting or to say any more than it was prohibited in accordance with regulation 22.[169] On this occasion, however, he was prepared to make an exception, announcing that the meeting had been banned because Cook had made an inflammatory speech several months earlier, the Chief Constable taking the view that a breach of the peace would be caused by a speech of that kind delivered in the same place when there was 'a bitter feeling in the district'.[170] But as was pointed out in the House on the following day, there was no reason why 'the meeting should be banned because of one particular speaker'.[171]

(iii) *Excessive and unaccountable policing*

Turning to the question of the police conduct during the dispute, the main concern here was the excessive use of force,[172] often associated with the presence of police officers drafted in from another locality, the phenomenon of 'flying squads of police'[173] which was deeply resented the length and breadth of the country.[174] Complaints were made of abusive

[167] H C Debs, 26 October 1926, cols 634–42. This was not a coincidence. On 18 October (the day before the Home Secretary's delegation of authority) the Cabinet had discussed the problems caused by the speeches of A J Cook, appointing a committee to consider whether the Home Secretary had adequate powers to deal with Cook's campaign against the return to work. See PRO, CAB 23/53, Cabinet 53 (26), 18 October 1926.

[168] Anon, 'Chief Constables and Apprehended Disturbances' (1926) 90 JP 593, which contains a detailed consideration of some of the legal issues surrounding the ban. For a different perspective see *Workers' Weekly*, 29 October 1926 ('Under the Iron Heel').

[169] H C Debs, 26 October 1926, col 636.

[170] Ibid, col 638. The delegation of authority was not revoked until 26 November when the Home Secretary announced that with immediate effect there would be no banning of any meeting or procession unless by himself personally, and he would 'be responsible by question and answer in this House for any exercise of [this] power'. H C Debs, 26 November 1926, col 715. For other examples of meetings banned by chief constables under the general authority delegated by the Home Secretary, with an account of the reasons for the bans, see H C Debs, 22 November 1926, cols 21–2; 25 November 1926, cols 515–17.

[171] H C Debs, 26 October 1926, col 758.

[172] But it was not the only concern. There are also allegations of unauthorised entry into premises, the excessive and unprovoked use of force, and the imposition of restrictions on literature which mining trade unionists were free to circulate, these other complaints often being made about police officers drafted into areas where they were unknown, largely unaccountable for their behaviour during the dispute. [173] H C Debs, 26 October 1926, col 796.

[174] According to Morgan, n 27 above, '[s]ome hundreds of men were borrowed by Derbyshire (595), Nottinghamshire (385), the West Riding (350), and Glamorgan (447), and small contingents by two or three other forces' (p 129). For various accounts of the problems, see H C Debs, 2 June 1926, col 839 (Durham), H C Debs, 28 September 1926, col 468 (Nottingham), and H C Debs, 26 November 1926, col 748 (Durham).

language, threats of violence, and excessive force on the part of the police.[175] There was particular concern about the use of baton charges, as there was during the General Strike, in connection with which we have already referred to the incidents at Poplar and elsewhere. Complaints were made of violent police conduct towards crowds in places as diverse as Doncaster, Wigan, West Fife, South Wales and Durham, it being claimed in the last case that the police had unleashed 'a veritable reign of terror'. Some of these complaints related to what appeared to be the gratuitous use of violence, as in those from West Fife where police baton charges were said to arouse 'bitter feeling in the mining villages'.[176] According to Page Arnot, '[i]n the third week of September 1926 there had been a night raid and batoning by the police, with a number of casualties, at Glencraig. On September 20 a similar incident took place at Lochore' where it was alleged that 'a woman was batoned down, and had to get four clasps in her head'. The woman in question 'was away for chips', and to 'make things worse, this woman is within a fortnight of a very critical period of her life'.[177] A meeting of several hundred miners in the nearby town of Lochgelly (the scene of an earlier baton charge which was said 'to have had a soothing effect on the locality') was held on the following evening, leading to the arrest, prosecution and conviction under regulation 21 of Bailie James Stewart, thought at the time to be the only magistrate in Scotland to be a communist.[178]

In other cases the concern related more specifically to the lack of opportunity which the police provided to enable large crowds to disperse before a baton charge took place. A good example of this are the complaints made by Adwich-le-Street Urban District Council about 'the action of the police in batoning innocent men, women and children in a most callous and cowardly way' at Bullcroft Colliery on the evening of 15 September.[179] Although the police announced that a charge would be made in two minutes if the crowd of between 200 (according to the local MP who was present) and 2,000 (according to the Home Secretary who was not) did not disperse, 'the two minutes were not allowed, but the

---

[175] There are also allegations of drunkenness on the part of the police and of imported police officers being billeted in pubs and hotels. See for example H C Debs, 26 November 1926, col 766. See also the complaints of police officers terrorising communities: H C Debs, 26 November 1926, cols 862–4.

[176] R Page Arnot, *A History of the Scottish Miners* (1955), p 178.

[177] Ibid, pp 178–80.   [178] Ibid, pp 179–81.

[179] H C Debs, 28 September 1926, col 431. It seems that the police had been provoked by booing from the crowd when some of the strikebreakers left work. The Home Secretary had earlier informed the House that 'Booing is not legal': H C Debs, 30 August 1926, col 17.

charge was made almost immediately after the intimation, and as a result many men and boys suffered grievous bodily injury'.[180] They included a man who was 'going home with a child, nine weeks of age, in his arms' who received injuries which required several stitches. Other victims were a sixteen-year-old boy returning from the cinema who was 'struck twice on the back of the head, knocked down, and left unconscious on the road', with a 'huge scar over his eyes and on his nose and down the whole of his cheekbone where the flesh had been scraped off'. There was also the case of the 65-year-old man, 'almost blind', out for a casual walk with his sons, and 'struck several times by the police'.[181] Perhaps predictably the Home Secretary resisted parliamentary calls for a public inquiry and defended the police conduct. He accepted that a number of people had been injured but was content to remind the House that 'You cannot make a baton charge without people being hurt'.[182] His only concern was whether 'the baton charge was justified, or whether, in the case of a justified charge, the police used greater force than was proper to meet the needs of the case'.[183] He had not heard any evidence to suggest that the police had acted improperly in either respect.[184]

Sadly this was by no means an isolated incident, as events in a village near Wigan were to make clear in the following month. It was alleged that on 15 October, the Chief Constable 'ordered the constables to charge the crowd and use their batons after he had told the [group] that he would give them five minutes to clear'. In fact a baton charge took place after a minute, in the course of which 'men, women and children', including an eleven-year-old girl, 'were struck and knocked down indiscriminately'. After the crowd had dispersed, the police were alleged to have gone through the village 'and struck people who had not been within half a mile of the place when the charge was ordered'.[185] It was claimed that '[w]omen were struck while standing in their own doorways' and that ' a man returning from his work on the railway was struck down by the police'. Again, however, the Home Secretary refused to take any further action, defending the police decision to charge the crowd and denying that women or children had been batoned. This was followed a week later by concerns raised in the House about a disturbance in

---

[180] H C Debs, 28 September 1926, col 432.

[181] These incidents are taken from a dossier of Mr Wilf Paling, Labour Member for Doncaster, who raised them in the House on 28 September: H C Debs, 28 September 1926, cols 431–5. See also *Workers' Weekly* (Supplement), 24 September 1926.

[182] H C Debs, 28 September 1926, col 458.   [183] Ibid.

[184] On the question of accountability see further Morgan, n 27 above, p 212.

[185] H C Debs, 11 November 1926, cols 1229–31.

Abercwmboi, South Wales, the Home Secretary being asked whether his attention had been drawn to a police baton charge on 9 November 'at which charge a boy, 13 years of age, suffering from epilepsy, a disabled soldier in receipt of 100 per cent disablement pension, and other men, women, and children were struck and knocked down indiscriminately', and whether he was 'aware that serious complaints are being made by the inhabitants against the behaviour and language of the imported police', and whether he would 'order an inquiry to be made into the circumstances of the baton charge and the conduct of some of the police now stationed in that area'.[186] Yet again the Home Secretary saw no reason 'for any further inquiry', though he did in fact send Leonard Dunning, an Inspector of Constabulary, to make an inquiry.[187] But according to Morgan, '[t]he outcome, inevitably, was that Dunning "afterwards expressed satisfaction at the general conduct of the police" '.[188]

(iv) *Techniques of summary justice*

Quite apart from the conduct of the police, the quality of justice dispensed by the magistrates under the Regulations appears to have been far from the ideal. The first problem related to the speed with which cases were processed. In one case in Northumberland, a group of young miners 'not much more than boys' were 'seized at 4 o'clock in the morning. No one knew where they were until 10 o'clock, and they were before the Bench at noon that day'.[189] In another case in South Yorkshire, a group of pickets disarmed a lorry driver who had pointed a revolver at them. The police arrived and proceeded to baton the pickets, fifteen of whom were arrested. According to Tom Williams, Labour Member for Don Valley, they 'were taken to Court that same morning. They had nobody to defend them and no chance of securing any legal assistance at all'. Apparently, 'without any discrimination, every person who was unfortunate enough to receive a blow of a baton was taken to court and they each got three months' hard labour'.[190] Not all those brought before the magistrates knew the details of the charges against them, a fact revealed in the prosecution of David Kirkwood, the Labour Member for Dumbarton Burghs, summonsed to appear in court at Renishaw in

---

[186] H C Debs, 18 November 1926, col 1935.   [187] H C Debs, 29 November 1926, col 881.

[188] Morgan, n 27 above, p 212, citing an article in *Police Review*, 10 December 1926.

[189] H C Debs, 2 June 1926, col 849.   [190] Ibid, col 854.

connection with speeches he had made in Derbyshire.[191] The summons simply stated that he had delivered speeches which were calculated to put a stop to the production of fuel.[192] Thereupon Kirkwood immediately wrote to the Superintendent of Police for details of the passages of his speeches which were to be relied upon by the prosecution, so that he might get his witnesses and his defence ready. But although the case was to begin only a few days later, he received a reply intimating that the matter had been referred to the local Chief Constable to be dealt with. Raising the matter in the Commons, Kirkwood was particularly indignant that a Member of Parliament should be treated in this way, and complained that he had been 'pushed off' and that he 'had no evidence of what they are going to put against me'.[193] He was supported from the Labour front bench by J R Clynes who asked courteously whether 'a Member of this House is not entitled to be in possession, before he enters the court on Monday, of the terms of the charge to be preferred against him'.[194] If this is how Members of Parliament were treated by the police, we can only speculate about the treatment meted out to those who had no way of ventilating their grievances.[195]

In light of the fact that cases were often brought before legally unqualified magistrates, it is perhaps no wonder that complaints should be made about the marked inconsistency in the disposal of defendants. The Labour MP for Westhoughton in Lancashire, Rhys Davies, referred to a case in which five young people in Openshaw, Manchester were arrested 'because they dared to have a printed statement in their possession that the working class organisations of this country ought to come to the aid of the miners'. According to Davies 'the magistrate declined to convict and actually rebuked the police for bringing the cases forward'. In the neighbouring town of Salford, however, a man was 'brought into Court

---

[191] Failures of this kind served to compound the mischief that by no means all of those charged under the Regulations had the benefit of legal representation, with even the Home Secretary conceding that only the 'bulk' rather than all cases leading to imprisonment were defended by lawyers. See H C Debs, 2 June 1926, col 826. There were also concerns raised about the poor quality of the evidence which was used to convict and imprison defendants. See H C Debs, 2 June 1926, col 847.

[192] In his autobiography, Kirkwood, n 12 above, p 235 claimed that the offending passage was as follows: 'if my country treated my wife and family as the miners were being treated I'd "blow the whole thing to babarags" '.

[193] H C Debs, 11 November 1926, col 1409. Kirkwood in fact alleged that he had been summonsed not because of his speeches to the Derbyshire miners but because of an earlier attack on Chief Constables which he had made in the Commons.

[194] Ibid, col 1414.

[195] The point was also made in Parliament by the member for Glasgow Gorbals (George Buchanan). See H C Debs, 26 November 1926, col 756. Kirkwood was found guilty and fined £25 by a bench of 'very imposing County people' (Kirkwood, n 12 above, p 236).

for possessing exactly the same document', and he was sent to prison.[196] Undoubtedly the problem was due partly to the drafting of the Regulations which at times seemed contradictory, and partly due to the nature of the statutory offences which gave no guidance as to their meaning and so encouraged inconsistency. Thus 'in one part [of the Regulations] we find it is set out that it is lawful to persuade other persons not to work, and then we come to [another part] in which it is made an offence to impede in any way the production and supply of certain commodities'.[197] In asking where the line was to be drawn, Sir Henry Slesser pointed out that 'If I persuade somebody not to work, I do impede the production of commodities'.[198] This issue in fact occupied a considerable amount of parliamentary time though it was never satisfactorily resolved by the Home Secretary.[199] So far as difficulty about the nature of the offences is concerned, Slesser pointed out that many of the Regulations dealt with 'offences which have never been defined by a court of law' with the result that it was hardly surprising that the magistrates had some difficulty in knowing what they mean. Magistrates were hardly likely to have been guided by the rather unhelpful comments of the Attorney General who explained when pressed on the meaning of disaffection that it 'is very nearly the same thing as sedition, but I do not like to say that you might not get something which went so far as to cause disaffection and yet not to be sedition. I think that is so'.[200] If the legal officer of the Crown did not know what his legislation meant, how were lay magistrates expected to cope?

(v) *Judicial bias in the operation of the law*

But the magistrates stood condemned of more than inconsistency. Also important were the allegations of political and personal bias, though Labour Members had to show some ingenuity in raising these matters in the House in view of the rules of parliamentary procedure which forbid criticism of the judiciary except on a substantive motion, a rule that was applied by the Speaker to include the magistracy.[201] It was claimed by the highly respected Labour Member (and former Cabinet minister), Ellen Wilkinson, that 'according to the custom of this country' people are 'very largely made Justices of the Peace because of political services' and

---

[196] H C Debs, 5 July 1926, col 1803.

[197] H C Debs, 26 October 1926, col 750.   [198] Ibid.

[199] It also gave rise to the only reported case to arise out of the dispute, with the Divisional Court under Hewart LCJ intervening to restrain one example of magisterial excess. See *Smith v Wood* (1927) 43 TLR 179.

[200] H C Debs, 5 May 1926, col 496.   [201] H C Debs, 2 June 1926, cols 833–6.

are 'chosen largely for political considerations'. As a result, the 'Benches throughout the country are largely manned by Members of the party opposite, which took good care in the past to see that this should be the case'.[202] A specific example of this was provided in the case of Durham where, according to one of its MPs, Labour held nine of the eleven parliamentary seats and the county council was held by Labour, as were most of the other elected bodies locally. Yet 'of the magistrates in Durham, over 300 are opposed to Labour and about 30 are in favour of Labour'.[203] Perhaps the most startling example of the problem related to the prosecution of David Kirkwood in Derbyshire where it was claimed that the 'chairman of the bench was the Conservative candidate at the last Election',[204] a man who 'not many months ago was saying what he would do with the "Reds", what he would do with the extreme people, and how he would deal with them if he had the power'. Now, it was complained, 'he comes on to the bench as chairman to judge a political opponent'.[205] Raising the matter in the House, George Buchanan, the Labour Member for Glasgow Gorbals, exclaimed (with the Kirkwood case clearly in mind): 'Just imagine the Home Secretary being charged under a Labour Government with a seditious speech, in contravention of the Emergency Powers Act, and I happened to be Chairman of the Justices!'[206]

So far as personal bias is concerned, it was claimed 'that nearly every Justice on the benches before which these cases come is interested in the coal industry'.[207] More specifically, allegations were made that in one case in Durham men were sent to prison by a coalowner[208] and that in Warwickshire 'coalowners are sitting upon the benches of magistrates'.[209] Indeed the problem was so serious that the question was raised whether it would be possible to adopt in the Regulations the provisions of the Coal Mines Act 1911 which enacted by section 103(2) in effect that anyone with a personal interest in the mining industry should not sit in a court of summary jurisdiction to deal with an alleged offence under the Act, unless both parties agreed. It appears, however, that an amendment providing that 'Justices with a financial interest in the coal industry shall not try . . . cases' under the Regulations was rejected by the Under Secretary of State at the Home Office who is said to have replied that 'practically all the Justices had a financial interest in the coal industry'

---

[202] Ibid, col 890.
[204] H C Debs, 26 November 1926, col 755.
[206] Ibid.
[208] H C Debs, 2 June 1926, col 757.

[203] Ibid, 2 June 1926, col 757.
[205] Ibid, col 756.
[207] H C Debs, 28 September 1926, col 419.
[209] H C Debs, 30 July 1926, col 2558.

and that if the House passed the amendment, it would be 'impossible in some cases to fill the bench'.[210] There is thus no evidence of any magistrate being disqualified because of personal interest as a coalowner or because of a financial interest in the dispute, despite the case law at the time which stressed the 'fundamental importance that justice should not only be done but should manifestly and undoubtedly be seen to be done'.[211] This contrasts with the fate of trade unionists who also happened to sit on the bench, with claims being made of 'another great injustice' that 'Labour leaders, justices of the peace', were 'prevented from sitting' on cases under the Regulations. George Spencer cited the example of a 'Labour justice' in his district,who had been told 'by the clerk to the magistrates that it is *ultra vires* for him to sit and adjudicate on these cases'.[212]

The problems facing Labour magistrates were not related only to the refusal to permit them to sit. There is also evidence of trade union officials being removed from the Bench because of their activities during the dispute.[213] The matter was raised at Question Time on 27 July 1926 when the Labour MP for St Helens, James Sexton asked about communications sent from the Chancellor of the Duchy of Lancaster seeking 'an explanation as to their conduct as trade union officials and representatives during the general strike'.[214] It was replied on behalf of the government that 'allegations' about magistrates had been 'received' from unspecified persons (itself a source of controversy) 'that in connection with the general strike they committed breaches of the law or took action incompatible with their position as magistrates'. The issue was revisited on 24 November when the Attorney General replied to a question asking what action was to be taken against justices of the peace who 'either by word or deed, prevented, or endeavoured to prevent, any person, or persons, from carrying out their lawful work since or during the general strike'.[215] The Attorney General announced that the Lord Chancellor

---

[210] H C Debs, 28 September 1926, col 419 (Captain Benn).

[211] *R v Sussex Justices, ex parte McCarthy* [1924] 1 KB 256, per Hewart LCJ.

[212] H C Debs, 28 September 1926, col 470. The chairman of the West Riding Quarter Sessions was advised by the Lord Chancellor's Department that justices who were members of the MFGB ought not to sit: PRO, LCO 2/915 (Justices of the Peace).

[213] See H C Debs, 15 July 1926, cols 593–4 for the well documented case of Henry Bolton, chairman of Blaydon Urban District Council in Northumberland, 'excluded from the exercise of his functions as a justice by the Lord Chancellor in consequence of his conviction for a serious offence under the Emergency Regulations' (Sir Douglas Hogg, Attorney General). See p 172 above.

[214] H C Debs, 27 July 1926, col 1902.

[215] It is unclear whether this was the test used to discipline magistrates. It was announced on 7 June, however, that mere participation in the General Strike (albeit in breach of contract) would not be grounds for removal. See H C Debs, 7 June 1926, col 1110.

had received complaints about the conduct of sixty-one magistrates, only four of whom had been convicted of any offence, though three others had been bound over, and another had been discharged under the Probation of Offenders Act. Although this was thought to be 'creditable',[216] following investigations no fewer than thirteen magistrates were cautioned (4), removed from advisory committees (3), or removed from the Bench (6). It was also revealed that in the Duchy of Lancaster another five magistrates had either been cautioned (4) or removed from the Bench (1), although there were no convictions of magistrates in Lancashire.[217] Whether the government was even-handed in its treatment of this issue is a matter of some dispute. It was claimed, for example, that a prominent Conservative was fined for breach of the coal regulations issued under the Emergency Regulations. He was not, however, removed from the list.[218]

(vi) *Exemplary sentencing*

It is not altogether clear just how many people were arrested, prosecuted and convicted under the Regulations between the end of the General Strike and the end of the lock out in December. Historians of the mining unions claim that 'it was not dozens, but hundreds, of miners who were arrested under the Emergency Powers Act and clapped into gaol',[219] and this is borne out by the (partial) information provided by the Home Secretary on a monthly basis. Information released in 1927, after some of the dust had settled, reveals that no fewer than 7,960 people were charged with offences arising out of the General Strike and the mining dispute. At least 1,760 of these related to the period of the General Strike itself,[220] and not all of the cases arose out of the Regulations, the figures including both people charged under the Emergency Regulations (3,304) and the ordinary law (4,656).[221] So far as prosecutions under the Regulations are concerned, it seems that the bulk of cases were brought in connection with regulations 20 (damage to property) and 21 (seditious

---

[216] (1926) 90 JP 688.

[217] H C Debs, 24 November 1926, col 392. Details of the removals and the reasons are to be found in PRO, LCO 2/918 (Justices of the Peace. Improper Conduct). Three had been convicted under Regulation 21, while the other three had participated in the strike, for example by issuing permits or by picketing. But not all of those who were active in the strike suffered this fate, as is evident in the case of three Wallesey magistrates whose case is considered in PRO, LCO 2/918, ibid.

[218] H C Debs, 26 November 1926, col 755.

[219] Page Arnot, n 176 above, p 181.

[220] H C Debs, 10 June 1926, col 1678. 632 sentences of imprisonment were passed in these cases.

[221] The figures are drawn from Morris, n 42 above, at pp 340–1.

speeches and literature, and disrupting supplies, wide enough to cover the actions of pickets).[222]

Regardless of total numbers, a matter of great controversy were the sentences imposed by the magistrates. Here a number of concerns were raised, including the fact that the imposition of even the smallest fine of £5 was too much for people who had been without income since May. Of even greater concern, however, was the use of imprisonment on what looked like a routine basis, often for 'offences of the most trivial character',[223] leading one Member of Parliament to complain that 'because of these extraordinary Regulations', 'many magistrates all over the country feel that they have imposed upon them a duty of inflicting the most harsh sentences imaginable'.[224] Examples of the 'brutal' sentences complained of include the man sentenced to a month for pulling a government notice off a wall;[225] the lead miner sentenced to three months' hard labour for advising workers not to enlist as special constables;[226] the trade unionist sentenced to three months' hard labour with a £50 fine for telling workers 'what he conceived to be their duty to their trade union';[227] and the teenage pickets from Northumberland each given a month 'for a very paltry offence'.[228] A matter of just as great resentment was the failure of the Home Secretary to entertain the idea of an amnesty for the prisoners, arguing that the 'great bulk of these cases concerned men who were guilty of actual disorder—who stopped the traffic, who used violence to the drivers of motor lorries or other vehicles'.[229] He was, however, willing to remit a fine of 14 shillings imposed on a coal company which had been convicted under the Regulations for selling coal without a permit.[230]

(vii) *The limited scope for appeal, and the nature of the appeals*

The final issue for consideration here relates to the right of appeal to the Quarter Sessions for those unhappy with the magistrates' decision. The main difficulty here, of course, would be the cost of embarking upon such a journey by people impoverished by the dispute, dependent for the most

---

[222] For example, 398 of the prosecutions between 17 October and 17 November were for breach of either Regulation 20 or 21, though the vast majority related to the latter. See H C Debs, 7 December 1926, col 1938.

[223] Ibid, col 1827.   [224] H C Debs, 2 June 1926, col 854.

[225] Ibid, col 863.   [226] H C Debs, 7 June 1926, col 1110.

[227] H C Debs, 30 July 1926, col 2547. [228] H C Debs, 2 June 1926, col 850.

[229] Ibid, col 826.

[230] H C Debs, 26 November 1926, cols 730–1. It was claimed as a result that 'There is certainly no justice at all in the Courts of Britain for working class people while these Regulations exist'. See H C Debs, 29 November 1926, col 865.

part on charity and hand-outs.[231] There were, however, also a number of irregularities with the appeal procedure which further conspired to undermine its impact. These included the allegation that the Doncaster magistrates demanded a deposit of £100 each from two miners' wives who wished to appeal against being sentenced to two months' imprisonment for intimidation. As was pointed out in a private notice question to the Home Secretary, this was 'equal to depriving these women of their inalienable right of appeal'.[232] Even more remarkable was the allegation that in at least one case in Doncaster, 'the presiding Magistrate who, at the original hearing inflicted the sentence', attended the Quarter Sessions to give evidence in the appeal. Counsel for the accused is reported as having commented that it was 'rather unusual for a magistrate to come and give evidence in a case in which he was chairman'. The Home Secretary was 'astonished' on hearing this 'most extraordinary' and 'very serious' charge, and asked for full details. In fact the magistrate (Mr George Cooke—Yarborough) had been called for the sole purpose of proving by reference to his notes exactly what the appellant had said,[233] though the magistrates in question had never been asked before to come to the Quarter Sessions to give evidence in an appeal from their own decision.[234] Perhaps even more extraordinary still was the fact that the Lord Chief Justice, Lord Hewart, accepted appointment as a trustee of a voluntary fund collected by *The Times* 'on behalf of the police force, in recognition of their services during the general strike'.[235] Two of the remaining five trustees were the Home Secretary and the Secretary of State for Scotland.[236]

It is difficult to know just how many magistrates' decisions were appealed, but only one made it to the Law Reports. In *Smith v Wood*[237] an agreement had been reached at the beginning of the dispute between the South Derbyshire Miners' Association and the coalowners whereby coal could be raised where this was necessary to preserve the safety of the mines. It was suspected, however, that this agreement was being broken and that 'the concession was being employed not only for safety, but to allow other men to get coal'.[238] As a result, William Smith, a union

---

[231] See H C Debs, 2 June 1926, col 838.   [232] H C Debs, 26 October 1926, col 693.

[233] *The Times*, 7 August 1926 (letter from Joynson-Hicks to Paling). A full account of the affair is to be found in PRO, LCO 2/915 (Justices of the Peace).

[234] H C Debs, 30 July 1926, col 2575.

[235] For details of the fund, see (1926) 90 JP 304, 316, 340, and 388.

[236] H C Debs, 28 June 1926, col 818.   [237] (1927) 43 TLR 179.

[238] (1927) 43 TLR 179, at p 180. The problem of safety cover was a continuing issue throughout the dispute. Allegations of breach of another agreement led to the disturbances at Bullcroft Colliery ending with the police baton charge: see pp 190–1 above. Disputes about safety cover led

official, was instructed to write to the owners and the managers to warn them that if the agreement was not observed, all safety cover would be withdrawn from the pits. He was then charged with having violated regulation 21 for distributing a document which was calculated or likely to impede, delay or restrict the supply or distribution of fuel! Smith was found guilty by the Derbyshire justices, though his conviction was quashed by a Divisional Court presided over by Hewart LCJ, who held that the communication fell outside the scope of regulation 21, first because it was designed to preserve a safety agreement rather than impede the supply or distribution of fuel, and secondly because the letter to the owners did not constitute the 'distribution' of a document within the terms of the regulation. But in case he was wrong on these points, the Lord Chief Justice also held that the matter fell within the proviso, on the ground that the regulation was not intended 'to fetter the liberty of the persons engaged in a strike to endeavour to increase it in a direction where it had hitherto been diminished'. But taking a narrower view of the matter, Salter J held that here was a publication which 'was clearly calculated to restrict, and, indeed, to stop altogether, the supply of fuel at the pits in question'. And although he was prepared to concede that the proviso applied, this appears to have been only because 'the resolution was a communication sent by one organisation through its secretary to inform the other that unless the agreement was kept the safety men would lawfully terminate their engagements'. In his view that was 'taking part in a strike' and on that ground he was prepared to grant the appeal.

Emergency Powers and the Communist Party

Predictably, the Communist Party played an active part in both the General Strike and the dispute in the coalfields thereafter.[239] Members

to notices being posted by the police throughout the Yorkshire coalfields reminding people of s 4 of the Conspiracy and Protection of Property Act 1875 by which it was a criminal offence for any person wilfully to break a contract of service where to do so would endanger human life or expose valuable property, real or personal, to the risk of destruction or serious injury. The police notice claimed that it would be an offence to incite or induce safety men to break their contracts. See H C Debs, 26 October 1926, cols 740–2. The matter was also discussed by the Cabinet on 27 October where it was agreed that the Home Secretary should confer with the Attorney General and that they should take appropriate action if it were found that safety men had come out in Yorkshire (or elsewhere) in violation of the law. See PRO, CAB 23/53, Cabinet 54 (26), 27 October 1926. The issue of safety cover also led to the ban on communist meetings. See pp 205–6 below.

[239] For a full account (relating to the General Strike only), see J Klugmann, *History of the Communist Party of Great Britain*, vol 2 (1969).

of the Party executive were dispersed throughout the country, in an attempt to provide in their terms 'the drive and leadership which the workers were now demanding',[240] leaving only a skeleton staff in London,[241] the energy of Party members no doubt serving to fuel the suspicions of those in government that this was a 'deep-laid plot' which 'had been hatched in Moscow'.[242] Although the Home Secretary's 'vast conspiracy theory'[243] was born of fantasy,[244] from the very beginning of the dispute Party members found themselves at the sharp end of the law, leading to claims that the Party had effectively been proscribed by the authorities. Its publications were suppressed, its meetings were banned, and its members were arrested in large numbers.[245] Indeed it has been estimated that between 1,000 and 1,250 members of the Communist Party were arrested during the strike, leading to the conclusion that as many as a third of the estimated 3,000 arrested were communists.[246] One of those arrested was Shipurji Saklatvala, the Communist MP for North Battersea who was arrested on Monday 3 May on a warrant charging him with inciting the public to commit a breach of the peace during a speech which he made on May Day in Hyde Park in the course of which he had called upon the army to 'revolt and refuse to fight'.[247] The prosecution asked the magistrate to take the same course as in *Lansbury v Riley*,[248] and explained that the defendant could have been charged under the Emergency Regulations, but that it was 'decided not to adopt this course, since these are the first proceedings to be in during the present state of affairs'.[249] Saklatvala refused, however, to be bound over and was jailed for two months.[250]

The different forms of harassment sent many communists underground: 'the leading members changed their address every night so that

---

[240] Murray, n 9 above, p 123.

[241] L J MacFarlane, *The Communist Party: Its Origin and Development until 1929* (1966), p 163.

[242] C Andrew, *Secret Service* (1986), pp 456–7.   [243] Ibid, p 457.

[244] But he was not alone. The same fantasies were shared by the head of the Special Branch. See Sir W Childs, *Episodes and Reflections* (1930), p 214.

[245] See Klugmann, n 239 above, pp 163–9.   [246] Morris, n 2 above, p 87.

[247] On the same day as his arrest, he attended the Commons to hear the Prime Minister who interrupted his speech to attack Saklatvala: see H C Debs, 3 May 1926, col 71. It seems that Saklatvala was a known target of the government, as suggested by the closed Home Office file: 'Political activities and subsequent imprisonment of Shapurji Saklatvala, MP' (PRO, HO 144/6099).

[248] [1914] 3 KB 229. See Chapter 3 above.   [249] *British Gazette*, 5 May 1926.

[250] *British Gazette*, 7, 8 May 1926. An unsuccessful attempt was made by David Kirkwood to protect Saklatvala by parliamentary privilege, an attempt met with the frosty response of the Speaker that a member of the House 'is, with regard to the criminal law, in exactly the same position as any other person'. See H C Debs, 7 May 1926, cols 601–2, where there is also reproduced the contents of the letters to the Speaker from C Biron, the Chief Stipendiary Magistrate at Bow Street who dealt with the case.

they could avoid arrest and continue to produce their bulletins'.[251] These were distinguished from the TUC publications by the 'inclusion of two political demands on top of the call to unite behind the miners: first, for the nationalization of the mines without compensation and their operation under workers' control; and, secondly, for the resignation of the Government and the formation of a Labour Government'.[252] So far as Party publications are concerned, various steps were taken to prevent their production and distribution. It had been decided to produce a daily edition of the *Workers' Weekly* during the strike, but on 5 May the police raided the party's offices in King Street and removed vital parts of machinery necessary for its printing, presumably exercising powers under regulation 33(2).[253] This led to the *Workers' Daily* being replaced by a duplicated *Workers' Bulletin* which was 'widely distributed and used in many areas to produce local strike papers'.[254] Yet this too was likely to be frustrated, there being evidence that typewriters used to produce the strike bulletins were seized and detained by the police, also acting under the authority of regulation 33. One such example was the raid on 8 May of a communist club which occupied premises in Islington, North London. The matter was raised in Parliament on 2 June by which time the equipment had not been returned, despite repeated requests to the police, even though 'the necessity for the issue of any bulletins' about the General Strike had long since passed.[255]

The other line of attack against publications was the arrest of Party members involved with the distribution and sale of communist materials. An early example was the arrest of William Stocker, a leading Manchester communist, who was given two months in the second division for having 'attempted to do an act calculated to cause disaffection

---

[251] Morris, n 2 above, p 87.   [252] Ibid.

[253] See Murray, n 9 above, p 125. This led to the prosecution of Bob Stewart, Acting General Secretary. See *Workers' Weekly*, 21, 28 May 1926 for details of the raid and the prosecution. There is also said to have been a nationwide raid of Party premises: *Workers' Weekly*, 21 May 1926. Although the *Workers' Weekly* reappeared after the Strike, it continued to run into trouble and was eventually closed down as a result of a libel action which was heard before Acton J in late November 1926. See *The Times*, 25 November 1926, and *Workers' Weekly*, 26 November 1926, 21 January 1927. The proprietor and editor of the *Workers' Weekly* were also convicted of the criminal libel of the Durham police by the Lord Chief Justice for a report on 15 October 1926 on the death of a bandsman at a demonstration in Chester-le-Street. Although neither had any previous convictions, they were each sentenced to four months' in the second division. See *Workers' Weekly*, 17 December 1926, and *The Times*, 5 March 1927.

[254] MacFarlane, n 241 above, p 163. Circulation of the *Workers' Bulletin* was thought to be around 15,000, and of communist papers (typescript) generally to be 100,000. See R Page Arnot, *The General Strike* (1926), p 193.

[255] H C Debs, 2 June 1926, col 880. For full details of raids on Party premises and on the homes of Party members, see *Workers' Weekly*, 21, 28 May 1926.

among His Majesty's Forces and civilian population and to impede, delay or restrict measures essential to the public safety'.[256] According to press reports Stoker's 'high powered car' was found by the police outside the Socialist Hall in Manchester with 1,600 copies of the General Strike edition of the *Workers' Daily*, which the prosecution alleged Stoker knew contained seditious matter.[257] This was no isolated incident, it being claimed that 'Many of those arrested for producing or distributing bulletins containing "sedition" or "false rumour" were Communists involved in handling the Communist Party's *Workers' Bulletin* or local versions of it',[258] such as the *Birmingham Worker* (a type-written sheet).[259] One of the most notable examples of such arrests was that of Marjorie Pollitt following an incident on 5 May when a police officer saw a number of people reading copies of the *Workers' Bulletin*. The offending passage claimed that according to the 'Government wireless', a number of soldiers 'refused to entrain for an industrial centre', but that from another source 'it was nearly a whole battalion'. The article continued by claiming that 'the Welsh Guards are confined to barracks at Chelsea for insubordination', the trouble arising 'from an order to prepare for departure for South Wales'.[260] Pollitt's name appeared on the *Bulletin* as its publisher, and she was visited by the police three days later and charged under the Emergency Regulations.

Pollitt was holding a copy of the *Workers' Bulletin* when she was arrested by Inspector Frost of the Special Branch, at the premises of the Young Communist League. According to the *British Gazette*, Frost (in the company of other officers) thereupon 'subsequently proceeded to the prisoner's residence' in Highgate, where, upon 'searching her rooms, in the kitchen they found in a drawer, among a quantity of linen, a document headed *Workers' Bulletin*. On a further search of the room they found a copy of the same paper dated May 5'.[261] Apparently unconcerned by the niceties of the law relating to contempt of court the report continues by claiming that 'In this paper false and misleading statements were printed which were the subject of the charge'. Too bad if her defence was that the statements were true! Nevertheless, she was remanded by the Bow Street magistrates for a week and bailed. According to the *Workers' Weekly*

[256] According to the *Workers' Weekly* he appealed and was at large on bail (21 May 1926).

[257] See *British Gazette*, 7 May 1926.

[258] Morris, n 2 above, p 86. Compare Morgan, n 27 above, p 209. According to the *Workers' Weekly*, 21 May 1926, most communists arrested during the strike were arrested for disaffection.

[259] See *British Gazette*, 12 May 1926, regarding the prosecution of five members of the CPGB for circulating in the *Birmingham Worker* false statements likely to cause disaffection.

[260] *British Gazette*, 12 May 1926.   [261] Ibid.

(which continued to report such cases long after the demise of the *British Gazette*) she was subsequently found guilty and fined £50 with the alternative of three months' imprisonment. The magistrate, Sir Chartres Biron, found the whole document 'disgraceful and outrageous'.[262] Other cases reported by the *Workers' Weekly* include those of George Miles for publishing *The Young Striker* (fined £20) and Sarah and Bessie Span for copies of *The Young Striker* found in their flat (bound over, being 'of an age when folly was not surprising').[263] The last case tends to confirm the suggestion that 'mere possession of a copy of [communist bulletins] was deemed sufficient grounds for prosecution, although not all of them carried appeals to the army or police but merely urged support for the strike'.[264] There are in fact several cases reported in the *Workers' Weekly* on 28 May 1926 of people convicted (and on some occasions imprisoned for up to three months) for mere possession.[265]

Apart from its publications, the Communist Party was also having difficulty organising meetings and demonstrations. In what appears to be the first recorded exercise of regulation 22 the Home Secretary prohibited a mass procession into the heart of London organised by the Deptford Branch of the Communist Party, the National Unemployed Workers' Committee, and the International Class War Prisoners' Aid. The procession, scheduled to take place on 5 May, was banned on police advice that 'anything of that kind at the moment would be likely to lead to a breach of the peace'.[266] There are in fact a number of examples of meetings being banned by the authority of the Home Secretary under the powers taken in regulation 22, including a meeting of the Battersea workers organised by the National Minority Movement 'to discuss the lessons of the general strike'.[267] They also included a meeting of Communist Party sympathisers scheduled to be held in Battersea in early July and to be addressed by the local MP, Shipurji Saklatvala. The organiser received notice from the Metropolitan Police Commissioner ninety minutes before the meeting was due to start, informing him that

---

[262] *Workers' Weekly*, 28 May 1926.

[263] Ibid. They were evicted from their accommodation as a result of the case. The hardship suffered by those who were convicted should not be overlooked. The Communist Party organised the International Class War Prisoners' Aid to provide legal defence, to help the families of people in jail, and to ensure that miners did not lose their homes because of the non-payment of fines. Those imprisoned were also struck off the electoral roll. See *Workers' Weekly*, 24 September 1924.

[264] Morris, n 2 above, pp 86–7.

[265] In one case in Rotherham the magistrate offered to pay the fine of one Comrade 'if he would leave the Party'. He refused, and on leaving the dock was rearrested for other charges.

[266] H C Debs, 5 May 1926, col 229.

[267] H C Debs, 3 June 1926, col 947. No reason was given for this initiative.

it had been banned by the authority of the Home Secretary, for which the latter was subjected to a blistering attack in the Commons by Saklatvala who pointed out that regulation 22 can be activated only where 'there appears to be reason to apprehend', and not 'If there appears to be reason in the opinion of unreasonable beings to apprehend'. In his view the remedy was very simple, namely that if 'the Home Secretary will order the police not to go near any meetings or processions organised by the working classes of this country there will be no undue demand on them, no disturbance of the peace, and no apprehension in the mind of anybody as to what might happen'.[268]

As we have seen, the power to ban particular events was delegated by the Home Secretary to chief constables on 19 October 1926, a power which was used with Home Office approval to ban the holding of public meetings under the auspices of the Communist Party in South Wales.[269] More sinister, however, was the fact that the Home Secretary had sent to the chief constables in England and Wales 'the published list of speakers taking part in the campaign organised by the Communist Party', interpreted by one Opposition backbencher as 'a list of speakers who are not to be allowed to address public meetings in mining areas'.[270] But in fact it was much more serious. In the course of an Adjournment Debate on 18 November 1926, the Home Secretary came to the House to explain that he had in fact invoked a ban on communist meetings, acknowledging also that he had no legal authority for such a step. This was done at a time when attempts were being made by a number of labour leaders to secure peace in the coal industry and a return to work. The initiatives were opposed by the Communist Party which represented these efforts as a surrender and a betrayal, urging the miners to fight on.[271] Although it was 'not acting illegally', the Communist Party was nevertheless acting 'in such a manner as would be exceedingly detrimental to the efforts that are being made on all hands, and have been taking place during the last fortnight to arrive at a settlement', by sending speakers into the districts to 'work up a strength of feeling which will prevent anything in the nature of a peaceful settlement of the dispute'. As a result the Home Secretary, in his own words 'wrote to all the chief

---

[268] H C Debs, 5 July 1926, cols 1820–1.
[269] H C Debs, 10 November 1926, cols 1085–6.   [270] Ibid, col 1933.
[271] The Home Secretary was later to explain that the ban had been imposed 'because the Communists were to start a campaign in order to bring out the safety men and induce men to leave the pits' at a time when negotiations were going on and many hoped that the stoppage was coming to a conclusion: H C Debs, 29 November 1926, col 877. This brought a stinging rebuke from Sir Henry Slesser (ibid, cols 890–1).

constables calling their attention to this campaign of the Communists and quite definitely and distinctly authorised them to ban all the Communist meetings during this period at which these speakers were announced to speak'. He did it, not merely in the interests of the country, 'but of the Labour Party as a whole'.[272]

It is unclear whether the ban was imposed in consultation with Labour Party and TUC representatives: there was no criticism of the Home Secretary from the Opposition front benches,[273] extraordinary if for no reason other than the fact that the minister assumed responsibility for the interests of the Labour Party.[274] But such involvement would serve simply further to condemn rather than commend conduct by the government which was both inexcusable on grounds of its clear threat to free speech as well as (by the government's own admission) being illegal. Yet the only effective criticism was from George Lansbury who complained rightly that the Home Secretary had admitted that at a critical point in the dispute he had used the 'whole power of the forces of the Crown, and his extraordinary legal powers under the Emergency Powers Act, not to preserve order, but to suppress Communist propaganda'. 'Those powers were not given him for that purpose', continued Lansbury, asserting also that the Home Secretary had 'abused his power and the trust the House of Commons placed in his hands'.[275] Nevertheless the ban was widely invoked and was the main reason why there had been a significant increase in the number of meetings banned under regulation 22. It seems that the sixty-three meetings banned since 19 October (compared with only twenty-two before then) had nothing to do with the fact that the Home Secretary had delegated power to the chief constables, but mainly with the communist ban which was a Home Office rather than a police initiative 'communicated to the chief constables, telling them that . . . at this juncture these meetings would not be conducive to a peaceful state of the mining areas'. The minister 'suggested to' the chief constables that 'they should ban' the meetings 'and they did'.[276]

---

[272] These extraordinary passages are taken from H C Debs, 18 November 1926, cols 2086–7. For details of banned meetings in Derby and Yorkshire (where the ban was 'heavily applied') see *Workers' Weekly*, 12 November 1926.

[273] Lack of notice is no excuse, as the Home Secretary had indicated earlier in the day that he intended to raise the matter in the evening debate. See H C Debs, 18 November 1926, col 1934.

[274] It is not until 29 November that specific objection was taken to the Home Secretary's remarks, by which time the dispute was all but over. See H C Debs, 29 November 1926, col 899.

[275] H C Debs, 19 November 1926, cols 2107–8.

[276] H C Debs, 18 November 1926, col 2090. For further examples of communist meetings being banned in this way under Regulation 22, see H C Debs, 25 November 1926, cols 516–17. There is a closed Home Office file on the application of Regulation 22: 'Prohibition of meetings or processions: Orders under Regulation 22 of the Emergency Regulations 1926' (PRO, HO 144/7983).

Yet apart from these restrictions on the institutional activities of the Party, known communists were also the target of special treatment by the police and the magistrates. There are allegations of Party members being visited at home by police officers threatening them with arrest unless they made a statement[277] and there is evidence of raiding of premises occupied by Party members, including those of David Evans in South Wales. A police search for seditious matter on 15 May (after the end of the strike) led to the confiscation of 118 books and documents. The great bulk of these had been sold openly for several years, but as if to emphasise that there is no such thing as sedition in the abstract, the prosecution under regulation 21 was based on passages from *The Communist Manifesto*, a Communist Party training manual, a document entitled 'Moscow's Reply to the ILP', and the *Communist International*. The prosecution laid great emphasis on *World Revolution* by Walter Gorter, which demanded 'A minimum standard of living for the workers; Work to be obligatory to all; Repudiation of national debts; Confiscation of war profits; Confiscation of banks; Confiscation of large businesses; Confiscation of land; [and] Judicial power to be wielded by the proletariat'. Together with the fact that the Communists were endeavouring to establish factory nuclei this was enough to prove that it was the intention to spread dangerous and poisonous stuff among factory workers. In the course of the trial before magistrates in Swansea, the following exchange took place between the representative for the defence and a police witness (Inspector Thomas):

Mr Samuel (for the defence): I find in the list of books put in a novel by William Morris, entitled 'News From Nowhere'. Is that seditious?
Inspector (Thomas): I don't know. It was difficult at the time of raid to say what was seditious.
Mr Samuel: And there is Darwin's 'Origin of Species'. Do you suggest that is seditious?
Witness: I don't know.
Mr Samuel: Do you know anything of the Minority Movement?
Witness: No.

A pamphlet was then handed to the Inspector, 'with the request that he single out a seditious statement. After a good deal of searching, a passage dealing with international unity was read'.

It was argued that the case was 'flimsy' and that the accused was being attacked because he was a communist. He was found guilty and fined

---

[277] H C Debs, 28 September 1926, col 434.

£10, despite a plea by his lawyer that the magistrates should not allow political prejudice to colour their judgment.[278] The plea betrays a more general concern about bias on the part of the magistrates, who were said to be 'fiercely class-biassed' and to have 'left the bounds of decency in inflicting penalties'.[279] The matter was raised in the Commons by Morgan Jones, the Labour Member for Caerphilly, who complained that 'the fact that a man was known to belong to a Communist organisation was stated in Court as if it were a statement of a heinous offence'. He continued by claiming that when communists have appeared in court, 'over and over again, we have had *obiter dicta* from the magistrate here, there and everywhere, up and down the country, concerning Communism and other subjects of public discussion—statements utterly irrelevant to the issue, utterly unnecessary and indeed, doing nothing except proving the political bias of the person sitting for the moment on the magisterial bench'.[280] Complaints were also voiced about Sir Chartres Biron, the Chief Magistrate, said to be 'notorious for senile hatred of the working class'.[281] Biron, who was to play a part in many of the subsequent cases against communists and their supporters,[282] did nothing to endear himself to his political enemies by sentencing the Acting Secretary of the Young Communist League to three months for distributing a leaflet in mining areas calling for mass pickets to stop the scabs.[283]

The most significant impact of the alleged anti-communist bias of the magistrates was felt by aliens who faced deportation if convicted. The point was raised in Parliament on 10 June when the Home Secretary was asked about the number of alien communists in this country, whether their whereabouts were known, and whether they would be returned to their native countries. In reply Sir William was reluctant to give information about the number of alien communists, but was content to reassure the House that 'the doings of all Communists, alien or otherwise, receive all necessary attention'. He also said that he did not hesitate, whenever he was 'satisfied that an alien is undesirable, and opportunity offers, to order his deportation to his own country'.[284] The power to deport was contained in the Aliens Order 1920 which enabled the Home

---

[278] *Workers' Weekly*, 18 June 1926.   [279] *Workers' Weekly*, 21 May 1926.

[280] H C Debs, 5 July 1926, col 1807.   [281] *Workers' Weekly*, 1 October 1926.

[282] In his autobiography, he reveals a close professional relationship with successive Home Secretaries since his appointment in 1920. He saw most of Joynson-Hicks and 'never enjoyed working with anyone so much'. See Sir C Biron, *Without Prejudice: Impressions of Life and Law* (1936), p 303. See further Chapter 5 below.

[283] *Workers' Weekly*, 1 October 1926.   [284] H C Debs, 10 June 1926, col 1668.

Secretary to issue a deportation order in any case 'he thinks fit',[285] and although it is uncertain just how extensively the power was used it is nevertheless clear that it was used on a number of occasions,[286] sometimes to visit great hardship on those concerned, to say nothing of the destitute families left behind. Some of the cases were raised in the Commons, including that of Anton Opulsky convicted under the Regulations and due for deportation to Lithuania. The question was raised about 'his position as regards the pension of £2, which he was drawing for disability as the result of war service in the British Army'.[287] Another case to attract some attention was that of Luca Cecchini, an Italian subject who had been in this country some twenty-three years, married with four children. He was also convicted under the Regulations and sentenced to three months' hard labour, although he had never been 'charged with any offences against the law before his conviction'.[288] Although 'not a recognised leader of the strike or the trade union movement'[289] as a communist Cecchini was also deported. After wandering about Europe for a while, he committed suicide in 1926.[290]

Conclusion

The General Strike and the lock out in the coalfields introduces a different dimension to our understanding of civil liberties in peace-time. As in the previous chapter when we examined the response of the public authorities to the emergence of the Communist Party, the response to the General Strike and its aftermath raises fundamental questions about the nature of constitutional principle and the integrity of constitutional practice. But the issues are different from those which occupied our attention in Chapter 3, for here at least the authorities were purporting to act with the authority of legislation, and with due accountability to Parliament. Nevertheless the different legal environment which we encounter in this chapter continues to expose as risible Dicey's intuition about the Rule of

---

[285] S R & O 1920 No 448, Regulation 12, on which see *R v Leman Street Police Station Inspector, ex parte Venicoff* [1920] 3 KB 79.

[286] There were, however, obstacles to be overcome in some cases, as in the case of Michael Prooth whose deportation to Russia was frustrated initially because the skipper of a Russian ship refused to take him without a visa. See *Workers' Weekly*, 30 July 1926. Compare S R & O 1920 No 448, Regulation 12(5) (duty on part of skippers to take deportees).

[287] H C Debs, 8 July 1926, col 2285.

[288] H C Debs, 27 September 1926, col 246 (Sir W Joynson-Hicks).

[289] I MacDougall (ed), *Militant Miners* (1981), p 96.

[290] Ibid. Further light on the position of aliens may be shed by the closed Home Office file: 'Dangerous alien Communists and activities of the Communist Party of Great Britain' (PRO, HO 144/5318). Also 'Aliens engaging in communist activities' (PRO, HO 144/17711).

Law, particularly in view of the fact that what was done was under the authority of legislation conferring extraordinary power to make and apply extraordinary regulations which were some steps removed from the ordinary law of the land. So much for 'the absolute supremacy or predominance of regular law as opposed to the influence of arbitrary power'.[291] But before having another laugh at Dicey's expense, it is as well to acknowledge here too that the experience from May to November 1926 was to call into question that other great principle of the British constitution, namely the sovereignty of Parliament, at least to the extent that it was the duty of a sovereign legislature to scrutinise the administration and to prevent the enactment of unjust laws and the unjust application of the law by ministers purporting to act under the authority of Parliament.

So far as *constitutional principle* is concerned, the experience of the General Strike and the miners' lock out is such as to reinforce the conclusions reached in Chapters 2 and 3 about the fragility of legality as a governing principle of the constitution. It is true that much of what was done by the government and others had the authority of legislation, on this occasion the Emergency Powers Act 1920 which authorised the state of emergency and the controversial Regulations made thereunder. Yet despite the scope of these powers it is also true that much of what was done during the dispute was done without legal authority, and indeed that much that was done in the name of the constitution was little better than executive lawlessness. Government without the law was all-pervasive, but most notable in the extraordinarily frank admission by the Home Secretary that he was seeking to introduce the Regulations for an eighth time despite the fact that there was no longer any need for them; they were merely a matter of precaution, something for which the Act makes no provision. But it was equally evident in the acknowledgement of the Home Secretary that he had earlier used his powers under the Regulations to ban meetings by the Communist Party, not because they were acting 'illegally', but simply because they were acting in a way that would be 'exceedingly detrimental' to the efforts that were being made to secure a peace settlement. Not only is such a blanket ban almost certainly one which in other circumstances would be an unlawful fettering of discretion,[292] there was in any event no power to ban a meeting on the ground that such a meeting would make a government objective more difficult to secure.

---

[291] Dicey, n 144 above, p 202.
[292] *R v Port of London Authority, ex parte Kynoch* [1919] 1 KB 176.

But as we have seen the principle of legality requires more than a formal deference to law: government according to law requires not only that there should be legal authority for the actions of government, it also requires that the authority should not confer unlimited powers on agents of the State to determine the boundaries of their own power. Otherwise we might have government with legal authority, but it would hardly be government by law. Here too the experience of the General Strike and its aftermath reveals problems with legality, even when the government and its officials were purporting to act with lawful authority. Virtually unlimited discretion was all-pervasive, from the declaration of a state of emergency, to the content of the Regulations, to the way in which they were applied locally by the police and magistrates. The point was made forcefully when the Bill was in Parliament by Lord Buckmaster (who was later stoutly to defend the use of the Act in 1926), referring to decisions under what is now the 1920 Act being a matter for the 'uncontrolled opinion of the Government', and complaining of a failure to provide 'any definite protection against an unreasonable or excessive use of its powers'.[293] But the point was made even more forcefully by experience in the coalfields in 1926 where the legal regime was consistent with 'a system of government based on the exercise by persons in authority of wide, arbitrary, [and] discretionary powers of constraint'.[294] This led one backbencher to complain that 'the police and the magistrates seem to think they are quite absolute, that they can do almost anything they wish'.[295]

Turning from matters of constitutional principle to matters of *constitutional practice*, questions may be asked about the role of both Parliament and the courts during the period of the dispute, and in particular about their role in defending civil liberties. So far as the former is concerned, it is to be recalled that Parliament had a critical role to play: under the 1920 Act it had to approve on a monthly basis the regulations which were the source of so much difficulty. But in truth this did not seem unduly to trouble the government, which could rely on a majority in both Houses to assent to the continuance of regulations even when there was no emergency within the terms of the Act. No fewer than eight Proclamations were made, with the Regulations also being endorsed on no less than eight occasions (albeit to be greatly amended within a short time on the eighth occasion). Some regulations, for example regulation 13A, were allowed to lapse before being considered by Parliament. In the other cases the approval of the Regulations would be preceded by a

---

[293] H L Debs, 28 October 1920, col 110.   [294] Dicey, n 144 above, p 188.
[295] H C Debs, 30 July 1926, col 2552 (J Lawson, Labour Member for Chester le Street).

lengthy debate on the merits of the Regulations with a debate on a series
of amendments. But as pointed out above, the fact is that on each occasion the code of regulations was approved by Parliament. Moreover,
despite the strength of opposition to some of the regulations and the allegations of abuse in their operation, not one was omitted as a result of
parliamentary opposition. Indeed the government won every vote in relation to the Act from the first declaration of emergency on 30 April until
the expiry of the last in December.[296] It is true that the exercise did provide an opportunity for the Opposition to argue, sometimes effectively,
that the Regulations were unnecessary, that they were overbroad and
inflexible, and that at least on the occasion of their renewal in November
for the last time, that they were unlawful. But ultimately Parliament
showed itself indifferent to serious concerns relating to personal liberty
and police powers, freedom of expression and the liberty of the press, and
freedom of assembly and the right of public meeting.

Turning our attention from Parliament to the courts, it is true that the
role of the senior judges was limited, and that primary judicial responsibility fell upon the magistracy who (with a few exceptions) were a credit
to their political masters. As such the experience of the General Strike
and its aftermath helps to shine a light on areas of the judiciary which
usually escape attention. The result was to expose serious problems in the
administration of justice which went a long way to reveal the 'inevitably
biased fashion in which magistrates work in cases when political or other
prejudice is involved'.[297] So much for the assertion that the 'constitution
is pervaded by the rule of law' in the sense that there were 'general principles of the constitution (as for example the right to personal liberty, or
the right of public meeting)' which were respected by public officials.[298]
But although the role of the senior judges was limited, it was nevertheless important, particularly in the *NSFU* litigation where the interim
injunction was delivered at a critical time in the General Strike. While it
is difficult to assess the impact of the judgment, it at least reinforced the
devastating legal blow delivered by Sir John Simon in the House of
Commons on 6 May. The case is particularly important because it was
so obviously wrong (and regarded as such by those like Holdsworth who
were by no means sympathetic to the Strike), highlighting once again the

---

[296] The amended set of Regulations was issued on 2 December 1926. These contained only
Regulations 10–15 and were designed 'to control the export of coal and the supply of gas, water and
electricity, pending the return to normal working in the coalfields'. See H C Debs, 9 December 1926,
col 2418.

[297] D N Pritt, *Law, Class and Society. Book 2: The Apparatus of the Law* (1971), p 67.

[298] Dicey, n 144 above, p 195.

extent to which the courts will unquestioningly fall into line behind the administration in times of national stress. Had there been confidence in the judgment it would not have been necessary for the government to introduce a Bill—which became the Trade Disputes and Trade Unions Act 1927—declaring general strikes to be illegal. It is true that the Act (which also protected trade unionists from discipline or expulsion for failing to take part in an illegal strike, and imposed restrictions on 'intimidatory' picketing) made organising and participating in such industrial action a criminal offence (section 1): but if the judgment of Astbury J was right it was a criminal offence anyway in view of the fact that the immunity from criminal liability in the Conspiracy and Protection of Property Act 1875, section 3 would not have applied.

5

The National Unemployed Workers' Movement

The scale of the national economic collapse that occurred at the start of the 1930s led to hardship of extraordinary severity and breadth. The situation was greatly worsened by the exceptionally harsh and blinkered reaction to the crisis displayed in Autumn 1931 by the incoming National Government. It is with the protest engendered by the decisions taken by that administration that this chapter is primarily concerned. The worst consequences of the National Government's rigour on taking office in 1931 were imposed upon the very poor and the unemployed, and it is with the mass movement of popular protest that was sparked off by these severe cutbacks in welfare provision that our chapter begins. This takes us once again into a discussion of the contribution of the Communist Party to the development of civil liberties law in Britain, since it was Party members who were mainly responsible for the enormous success enjoyed by the National Unemployed Workers' Movement (NUWM), particularly in the first half of the 1930s, with its 'hunger marches' and vast petitions of Parliament. The first and second parts of this chapter are concerned with tracing the origins and rise of this movement and with the State's response to its activities. The questions raised related mainly to the freedoms of assembly and association, though it was a 1920s-style police raid on the headquarters of the Movement that was to lead to the famous decision of Horridge J in *Elias v Pasmore*.[1] As we shall see, the reaction of the government, the police and the courts to the NUWM shows how far from reality was the nation's ostensible commitment to liberty, at least as far as the communication of radical views was concerned.

The hand of the Communist Party, and the opportunity afforded by the economic crisis of 1931, are also to be seen in the second great civil liberties issue of the early 1930s, the enactment of the Incitement to Disaffection Act 1934. The decision by the incoming National Government to impose pay-cuts in the public service in addition to the cutbacks in welfare led to general discontent, most seriously in sectors of the armed forces. After the widely publicised 'Invergordon Mutiny' involving service members on many of the ships of the Atlantic fleet,

---

[1] [1934] 2 KB 164.

which occurred in September 1931, the government was persuaded that it was the Communist Party which had been largely responsible, a view from which the Party did not energetically dissent. In fact, the Party's campaign of inciting disaffection in the armed forces had been ongoing for some years without any great success before Invergordon, and it was not the primary cause behind the short-term revolt there in any event. But Invergordon inflamed the government into further and more strenuous action against a Party which, despite all the measures taken against it in the 1920s, had refused to disappear but had instead sought to attack the most sensitive point in the State's armoury: the willingness of the armed forces to defend the power structure at the apex of which the executive stood. Such anxieties led eventually to the Incitement to Disaffection Act 1934, and it is with the origins and enactment of this hugely controversial piece of legislation that we are concerned in the third and fourth parts of this chapter.

The final two sections of this chapter take us back to the NUWM and to its renewed street protests in the mid-1930s against further State efforts to cut back on the entitlements afforded to the unemployed and their dependants. It is at this point that we see the emergence of another organisation of great importance. The National Council for Civil Liberties (NCCL) was formed primarily in an effort to control the excesses of police violence that had invariably accompanied NUWM protest on the streets, but in its first year as the then Council for Civil Liberties it had also enjoyed great success in its parliamentary campaign against the Incitement to Disaffection Bill. The organisation's non-revolutionary personality asserted itself in its confidence that the rhetoric of the Rule of Law could be deployed via the courts to curb executive excess. This belief led to the famous case of *Duncan v Jones*[2] which like *Elias v Pasmore* before it grew out of the State's attempt to hinder the efforts of mainly Communist Party members to agitate on behalf of the unemployed, a campaign of control that had reached its height late in 1931, when a clampdown had been imposed on political speech outside employment exchanges in London. Both *Elias* and *Duncan* added to the ordinary common law, just as the Incitement to Disaffection Act 1934 was a permanent addition to the stock of ordinary legislation. The same trend towards the expansion of the ordinary law is also evident in the chapter that immediately follows, when we trace the rise of fascism in the mid-1930s and the enactment of a new national Public Order Act 1936.

---

[2] [1936] 1 KB 216.

The National Unemployed Workers' Movement

Even before the National Government came to power, the level of unemployment benefit had been 'the central feature of an intense debate about public finance' which had led to the disintegration of the previous Labour Administration.[3] The MacDonald Government of 1929 to 1931 had been notably more generous than its predecessors as far as the provision of State aid for the unemployed had been concerned, and this meant that in the first half of 1931 the value of benefits had sharply increased. The rises were widely believed to be unsustainable at a time when financial stringency was thought everywhere to be required. It is easy in retrospect to be more relaxed about the figures than were the politicians of the day. The controversial benefits in question amounted in total to no more than about seven per cent of all public spending and we now know that it was likely that even this seven per cent benefited the economy by raising average consumption at a time when demand was heavily constrained. But the mood of these pre-Keynesian times did not allow for such far-sighted rationality. Starting in September 1931, the National Government introduced a series of measures designed to curb spending in this area and thereby (so it was believed) to compel the economy to return to an even keel. The National Economy Act 1931, which received the Royal Assent on 30 September 1931, empowered the executive to make Orders in Council for 'the purpose of effecting economies' in the fields of education, national health insurance, police, unemployment insurance and roads. Benefits were reduced and a 'family means test' was introduced.[4] Regulations were implemented, the effect of which was to deny benefit to many married women by ignoring their premarital national insurance contributions. Applicants for the dole were henceforth to be means-tested by local poor law authorities, with the savings as well as the income of entire households being taken into account. The result was that the income of relatives and even of lodgers could now be deducted from benefits.[5]

The cumulative effect of these changes was greatly to impoverish the already desperately poor, and to give a new lease of life to the National

---

[3] S Glynn, *No Alternative? Unemployment in Britain* (1991), p 88. Much of the economic data that follows is drawn from this work. Also helpful to understanding the background is F M Miller, 'The Unemployment Policy of the National Government, 1931–1936' (1976) 19 *Historical Journal* 453.

[4] Among the Orders in Council made under the Act were the National Economy (Unemployment Insurance) (No. 1) Order (S R & O 1931 No 814) setting out new rates of contribution and benefit and the National Economy (Unemployment Insurance) (No. 2) Order (S R & O 1931 No 853) dealing with transitional payments to replace benefits in certain cases.

[5] Glynn, n 3 above, p 89.

Unemployed Workers' Movement. The organisation had been formed in April 1921 at the International Socialist Club in London as the National Unemployed Workers' Committee Movement, becoming the NUWM in 1929. Initially the movement functioned as an amalgam on a national level of the seventy to eighty committees of unemployed that had sprung up across the country after the war.[6] The organisation's purpose from its inception was to campaign on behalf of the unemployed, and it was established in the aftermath of a shocking episode in October 1920, when some 20,000 unemployed marchers had been indiscriminately set upon by the police in 'the Battle of Whitehall'.[7] Led by skilled engineers and 'intimately connected with the Communist Party',[8] the future NUWM organised the first national hunger march to London in Autumn 1922. Despite almost hysterical denunciation in Parliament and the press,[9] an estimated crowd of some 50,000 turned out,[10] and the protests continued on and off until the following January, with a further high-point being 'a day of national demonstration . . . known as "Unemployed Sunday" ' which took place on 7 January.[11] This was to be something of a high

[6] See J Klugmann, *History of the Communist Party of Great Britain*, vol 1 (1968), pp 121 et seq.

[7] The *Daily Herald* observed of the event that 'the manner in which the police in a mad frenzy were ordered to charge up and down Whitehall running down and clubbing men, women and children is only on a par with the sort of outrage committed by the Black and Tans in Ireland': *Daily Herald*, 19 October 1920. Wal Hannington, who estimated the crowd at 40,000 in his autobiography, *Never on our Knees* (1967), p 80, described the police action as a 'merciless and unprovoked attack': ibid, p 81. For a full account of the disorder, and for the similar consequences that followed a demonstration in Liverpool the following year, see J Morgan, *Conflict and Order. The Police and Labour Disputes in England and Wales, 1900–1939* (1987), pp 234–7. Morgan's work is a valuable source for many of the details of the activities of the police and the NUWM during the 1920s and 1930s. The relevant Home Office file on the October 1920 disturbances is however closed for 100 years: 'Demonstration by the unemployed in October, 1920—made the occasion of rioting by an unruly mob' (PRO, HO 144/1692).

[8] Morgan, n 7 above, p 237. See P Kingsford, *The Hunger Marchers in Britain 1920–1940* (1982). 'The leadership of the unemployed movement was taken, from the beginning, by the Communist Party, along with a number of militants of the I.L.P., local Labour Parties and the trade union movement': Klugmann, n 6 above, p 128.

[9] The national organiser of the NUWCM from its inception, Wal Hannington, described some of this press coverage in his autobiography: 'The day before this demonstration several leading daily newspapers launched a vicious front-page campaign of lies and slanders against the marchers and the leaders of the movement. They declared that 100,000 armed men intended to march on Downing Street. They invented scare stories about the bloody consequences. They alleged—completely untruthfully—that there were men with criminal records in the leadership of the marchers. Here are some of the banner headlines which appeared in these papers: *Daily Express*: "Great Communist Plot Exposed"—"Whitehall Riot Plan"—"Notorious Criminals as Leaders"—"Revolutionary Attempt . . .". *Daily Mail*: "Downing Street and a Red Plot"—"Whitehall Riot Scheme". *Pall Mall Gazette* (evening paper): "Communist Plot in London"—"Organised Plan to Provoke a Riot at Dictation of Moscow"—"Incitement to Violence" ': Hannington, n 7 above, p 142.

[10] Hannington, ibid, p 143, claimed 70,000. The *Daily Sketch*, 23 November 1922 estimated 50,000.

[11] Hannington, n 7 above, p 151. See Klugmann, n 6 above, pp 125–8.

point in the early phase of the organisation's history, with no further large-scale marches to London taking place until 1929, and even then the two that occurred in that and the succeeding year were small, tame affairs.[12] It seemed that most potential demonstrators were prepared to place their trust in the then still functioning minority Labour Government.[13]

The mood changed almost immediately after the formation of Ramsay MacDonald's new National Government, with the NUWM now receiving a large influx of members and greatly increased support. There were at this point nearly two million unemployed workers from whom the organisation could draw support. The protests began with the resumption of Parliament after the 1931 Summer recess. A huge crowd which had congregated to view the flood-lighting around Westminster found itself joined by a gathering of about 900 or so unemployed protestors who proceeded to sing and to shout slogans abusive of the new government. Mounted and foot police promptly swooped on this group, separating it from the rest and driving it away from the larger crowd. To complaints in Parliament about this 'wholly unnecessary and most provocative display of force',[14] the newly appointed Home Secretary Sir Herbert Samuel responded that the 'crowd had to be dispersed in order to maintain the public highways for the use of the population in general'.[15] When one MP interjected that the Home Secretary had spoken 'tonight the comfortable words which were given to him by superintendents and chiefs of police',[16] Samuel fell back on the annual sessional order, passed by Parliament almost a year before, on 28 October 1930, the intention of which was to secure free passage around the House when Parliament was in session.[17] There was however no answer forthcoming to the assertion of another Member that 'unemployed men and women have as much right to be in that crowd as anyone else'.[18] The mood of many members of the House was one of anxious foreboding as to the

---

[12] There were however a number of marches in Scotland during this time. See for example National Unemployed Workers' Committee Movement, *Scottish Miners' March to Edinburgh* (1928).

[13] Morgan, n 7 above, pp 241–3. A further demonstration at Temple underground station in London on 16 December 1930 was outnumbered two to one by the police because it was 'much smaller than was anticipated' (H C Debs, 18 December 1930, col 1406 (Mr Clynes)). Note that the public do not have access to the relevant Home Office file in the PRO: 'Unemployed miners' march to London in 1927'. 'March of the Unemployed to London in 1929'. 'Hunger march to London in 1930' (PRO/HO/144/12143). The file is closed for 100 years. Also closed for 100 years is 'Communist Party and National Unemployed Workers' Movement: demonstrations and speeches, 1930–1' (PRO, HO 144/22581).

[14] H C Debs, 9 September 1931, col 254 (J J McShane).   [15] Ibid, col 252.

[16] Ibid, col 257 (Miss E C Wilkinson).   [17] Ibid, col 263.

[18] Ibid, col 249 (C J Simmons).

way the police would handle the protests that were bound to take place as the true effect of the new government's policies began to be felt.

Given that Britain's commitment to the right to demonstrate was then widely perceived within the country to be both historically rooted and absolutely genuine,[19] it is quite remarkable how little protection the law actually afforded the unemployed during the Autumn of 1931. Time and again police assertions that they had been subjected to violence were unquestioningly believed by the authorities and accepted as justifying the most extreme and at times brutal counter-measures. The law was largely irrelevant to these police actions. Insofar as it did impact on events, the Rule of Law functioned as a powerful enemy against the expression of the views of the NUWM and its supporters, with local bye-laws, local Acts of Parliament, the sessional order, the binding over jurisdiction available to the justices, and the power of the police (both in relation to arrest and in respect of the power that flowed from their apprehension of breaches of the peace) all conspiring to make the effective communication of their point of view next to impossible. Typical in this respect was the arrest, on 3 October 1931, of one of the NUWM leadership, Wal Hannington, who was subsequently charged with inciting breaches of the peace. After a finding of guilt, the Bow Street magistrates made a binding over order, with two sureties required of £100 each. When Hannington refused to come up with the sureties, he was imprisoned for one month.[20] Thus could a key activist be almost effortlessly removed from the scene, a pattern that we shall see repeated during many NUWM campaigns.[21] It was in the twilight world of unreported cases and barely noticed procedural ruses and obscure laws that the flimsy rhetoric of a nation's largely only theoretical commitment to political

---

[19] This may seem slightly surprising in view of the events discussed at length in Chapters 3 and 4 above, but consider how a problem with detention on remand in Buenos Aires in 1930 provoked a highly critical *Justice of the Peace* into the following encomium of the position in the United Kingdom: 'In a country where the liberty of the subject is really guarded with the utmost jealousy, an unwarranted detention or a high-handed arrest, whether at the instance of a responsible Government Department or a humble police constable would always provoke a popular outcry, and judges have always been quick to check the least encroachment upon the individual's rights, so that today such infringements of liberty are almost unknown': 'The Liberty of the Subject' (1930) 94 JP 358. Such fine sentiments did not prevent the same journal defending the dispersal of the unemployed around Westminster on 8 September, remarking that the 'crowd has its safety valve in Hyde Park' (1931) 95 JP 626.

[20] Hannington, n 7 above, pp 239–40. Hannington had been jailed with five Coventry leaders of the unemployed in 1922, having refused to be bound over on that occasion as well: *Daily Mirror*, 7 April 1922. His personal Home Office file ('Walter Hannington: subversive activities': PRO, HO 144/20618) is closed for 100 years.

[21] See also *Aldred v Langmuir*, 1931 SLT 603, and generally Chapter 3 above for earlier examples of the control of meetings.

liberties came up against the immovable reality of State repression. In 1932, this became clearer than at any time since the General Strike.

The year started with a 'national day of struggle' against both unemployment in general and the reviled means test in particular, set for 23 February. The day was marked by high tension across the country, particularly in London, where police 'guarded the entrance to the House of Commons while uniformed and plain-clothes police patrolled the streets and broke up groups of demonstrators'.[22] On the following day, the *Daily Sketch* devoted its front page to a graphic photograph of running battles between police and demonstrators under the headline '30 hurt in street battle'.[23] In the Spring and Summer months, violent clashes took place between the police and unemployed protestors in Merseyside, Manchester, Birmingham, Cardiff, Coventry, Nottingham, Oldham, Porthcawl, Stoke, Wigan, Preston, Bolton and Belfast. After a couple of encounters with unemployed protest, the Bristol Chief Constable began privately to agitate for an end to all NUWM-inspired demonstrations.[24] In September, the tension increased even further with running battles between police and protestors, hundreds of arrests, and many serious civilian injuries in Birkenhead and Liverpool, where the police use of 'intimidatory violence and arrests . . . reached an extraordinary pitch'.[25] Even bloodier scenes occurred in Belfast in the second week of October where two workers were shot dead by police.[26]

This was the atmosphere in which the NUWM set about planning that year's national hunger march, which the organisation scheduled to begin on 26 September and to arrive in London just before the day fixed for the opening of Parliament, 27 October, with a view to the presentation of a petition. In her detailed study of the period, Morgan

[22] Morgan, n 7 above, p 246. Even before the 'national day of struggle', nine men had been charged with disorderly and riotous conduct at Kilbirnie in Scotland on 8 February, amid allegations that the police had unnecessarily batoned a crowd that had gathered after a deputation had made representations to the public assistance committee for the area. All nine were convicted: H C Debs, 8 June 1932, cols 1931–2 (Sir A Sinclair, Secretary of State for Scotland). There was particular concern about the behaviour of the police in Scotland towards the NUWM protestors: see the supply day debate in the Commons at H C Debs, 28 June 1932, cols 1741–57.

[23] *Daily Sketch*, 24 February 1932.

[24] See correspondence between the Chief Constable and his counterpart in Manchester in the Bristol Record Office, cited by Morgan, n 7 above, p 246. The key Home Office file is closed for 100 years: 'Demonstrations by Bristol unemployed workers between 12 April and 28 October 1932' (PRO, HO 144/22587).

[25] S Bowes, *The Police and Civil Liberties* (1966), p 29. For a description of the violence in both places, see Hannington, n 7 above, pp 252–4. One of the key Home Office files is however closed for 100 years: 'Police arrangements to prevent disorder at public meetings in Liverpool, 1931–8' (PRO, HO 144/21037).

[26] Hannington, n 7 above, p 255. See 'Belfast's night of terror': *News Chronicle*, 12 October 1932.

describes the extensive efforts that the authorities made to undermine its success:

The Ministry of Health told its local authorities to pursue a tough line with the marchers, while the Ministry of Labour gave instructions that persons taking part in the march were not to be given facilities to draw unemployment benefit at Unemployment Exchanges which they might pass *en route*. The Home Office primed the local police with details of the march programme, routes, and assembly points. It added, as usual, that 'strict insistence on the conditions attaching to the grant of relief to the marchers may give rise to disorder'. The police must, therefore, prevent any breaches of the peace, especially near casual wards. The Home Office itself had been fully warned, through 'civil security intelligence', about the activities of the unemployed, the Communists, and the League against Imperialism.

The Metropolitan Police made particularly careful preparations for the marchers' arrival and stay in London. In August 1932 efforts were made to ascertain the names of local leaders; subsequently, particulars of the more notorious of them, with photographs and details of any previous convictions, were forwarded to the divisions. Both the Special Branch and police informers were active at an early stage. Several of these had infiltrated the council of the NUWM and NUWM branch meetings.[27]

Local police chiefs in London were reminded by Scotland Yard of section 21 of the Metropolitan Police General Orders, dealing specifically with meetings and processions. The instructions laid down there were more reminiscent of a military campaign than of policing a democratic society:

161 Meetings etc. likely to become dangerous should be carefully watched and the leaders identified if possible with a view to obtaining proof of the same persons acting as ring leaders on various occasions. Notes should if possible be made of the speeches either by uniform or plain clothes constables who will prepare a brief report quoting any inflammatory language used. In special cases authorised by the Commissioner short-hand may be employed but not otherwise.[28]

The instructions also reminded officers that:

Persons guilty of violence or of uttering threats should be at once arrested and charged with one or more of the following offences: Assaulting or resisting or obstructing police on due execution (sic) of duty (Offences against the Person Act 1861, Section 38). Using threatening, abusive or insulting words or behaviour

---

[27] Morgan, n 7 above, p 248. For a heartbreaking example of how far the authorities were prepared to go to harass hunger marchers, so severe that it was even too much for the Scottish judges who heard the appeal in the case, see *Wilson v Mannarn*, 1934 JC 92.

[28] Morgan, n 7 above, pp 249–50, citing MEPO 2/3039.

with intent to provoke a breach of the peace or whereby a breach of the peace may be occasioned (Metropolitan Police Act 1839, Section 54(13)). Wilfully obstructing the free passage of any highway (Highways Act 1835, Section 72).[29]

The deployment of these various laws, together with the desperation of some of the unemployed and the rigorous way in which the police were clearly prepared to respond to little more than a hint of trouble, guaranteed that October 1932 would not be trouble-free. Serious clashes between the unemployed and the police in Liverpool, Birkenhead and North Shields[30] were matched by further violent disorder in South London, when the police dispersed a crowd of 10,000 which had gathered to support an NUWM deputation to the London County Council. The trouble was so severe in the London episode that it was raised the following evening in an adjournment debate in the Commons by no less a figure than the leader of the Labour Party, George Lansbury. The veteran activist concluded his moving and emotional speech by going beyond the bloody events of the night before to call on the government to 'organise hospitality for [the marchers, who were shortly to arrive in the city] and send them back home with a message that the damnable means test is to be revoked, and that you are going to treat them not on a uniform basis of the lowest level to which you can cut them down, but as human beings, as the victims of a system which . . . is responsible for their condition'.[31] After such a flight of rhetoric, it must have seemed rather beside the point even to his own supporters for the Home Secretary to have responded by asserting yet again that it was 'quite clear . . . that the National Unemployed Workers' Movement, a Communist organisation, or in the main, a Communist organisation, has been at the root, and has been the instigator, of these difficulties'.[32]

Given this background, it was not surprising that the arrival of the marchers in London, on 26 October as scheduled, should have led to more trouble, though who was responsible for what happened was the subject of bitter dispute. The arrangement that had been made was for all the marchers to converge on Hyde Park, where a welcoming demon-

---

[29] Morgan, n 7 above, pp 249–50, citing MEPO 2/3039. We can only surmise about how much we might learn from: 'Powers and duties of the police at meetings, processions and demonstrations, 1932–3' (PRO, HO 144/18294), since the Public Record Office file is closed for 100 years.

[30] See H C Debs, 18 October 1932, cols 4–5; H C Debs, 27 October 1932, col 1187 (WA). The new Home Secretary Sir John Gilmour refused in each case to order an inquiry into the behaviour of the police.

[31] H C Debs, 19 October 1932, col 269. The whole debate is at ibid, cols 264–90.

[32] Ibid, col 275. Another deputation to the LCC the following week was accompanied by no fewer than 1,000 police and special constables: H C Debs, 2 November 1932, col 1796 (Sir J Gilmour) (WA).

stration had been organised by the NUWM. A contemporary account records what happened on the Edgware Road after the protest in the Park had got under way:

There was a good deal of booing and banter going on between some of the unemployed gathered on the pavements and the police, when suddenly, without the slightest provocation and for no apparent reason, the mounted police started to race up and down the roads flourishing huge staves in their hands, smashing their way in and out amongst the traffic, scattering people gathered on the pavements and even pushing and heaving their horses down upon the innocent citizen who happened to be just going about his ordinary business. From Edgware Road they galloped their horses into the Park, still brandishing their staves at people . . . .

Up to this the marchers and the unemployed had behaved in an orderly manner but it was not to be wondered at that a few of them immediately lost their temper and seized a few branches of trees lying about and flung them at the police . . . The police immediately lost complete control of themselves and proceeded to sweep their horses into the crowds, slashing out indiscriminately both at spectators and marchers. Their behaviour fell a long way behind even the disgusting conduct of the Indian Police, who freely baton down the followers of Mr. Gandhi.[33]

The *Daily Herald* reported that '[s]creaming women fled before the prancing horses, windows were smashed, and stones, bricks and other missiles were hurled about'.[34] Even the Home Secretary Sir John Gilmour was forced to concede that there had been a 'general melee, lasting about twenty minutes', though he predictably claimed that the police, both 'mounted and foot', had been 'obliged to draw their truncheons' only after 'stones and bolts' had been thrown in their direction, albeit hailing mainly from 'a number of men who were straggling in the rear of the procession'. Sir John ended his Commons' statement on the incident by issuing a warning to ordinary members of the general public that by their presence 'they contribute[d] greatly to the difficulty of maintaining order both in the streets and the parks by assembling in unnecessary numbers and swelling the crowds'.[35] Given that on the government's own figures fifty-eight of the demonstrators had been injured (as against nineteen police officers), it may well be that the casualty list would have been

[33] J L Grant, 'The Hunger Marchers and the Police' [1932] *Socialist Review* (Winter) pp 243–4, quoted in Morgan, n 7 above, p 251. For another contemporary account from the same perspective, see Hannington, n 7 above, pp 262–5.

[34] *Daily Herald*, 28 October 1932. See further the *Daily Worker*, 28 October 1932.

[35] For the full statement, see H C Debs, 28 October 1932, cols 1315–17.

much higher, at least on one side, had not the general public been around to impose a restraining influence.

Further trouble erupted three days later when a meeting in Trafalgar Square attended by a crowd estimated by the government at about 8,000 provoked a police response which involved the use of horses and truncheons to clear the streets.[36] The culminating event of the whole campaign was scheduled for the following day, 1 November. This was the date on which the NUWM planned to present Parliament with its petition against the means test, signed by no fewer than one million people. Meetings were arranged in about ten locations in London, and a huge protest was held at Clerkenwell Green, from where it was proposed to send a deputation to present the petition to Parliament. Members of the government were determined that the petition should not be accepted, and the police went to extraordinary lengths to prevent the deputation getting through. The whole of Parliament Square was sealed off[37] and so many reinforcements were drafted into the area that ordinary policing for the rest of London had to be left to the special constabulary. A leaflet issued by the NUWM calling on the police not to turn on the demonstrators so inflamed the Metropolitan Police Commissioner Lord Trenchard that he gave instructions that anybody seen distributing it was to be arrested.[38] The NUWM petition itself was seized 'on the instructions of the local Superintendent of Police, as a precautionary measure in view of imminent disorder'.[39] Unsurprisingly, this police action caused that which it was (supposedly) designed to prevent. After the confiscation, disorder quickly broke out across Trafalgar Square, spreading into Whitehall and Victoria Street. The *Daily Herald* reported how a huge force of police then moved to clear the crowd (by now estimated to be between 20,000 and 30,000 people), with mounted and foot-patrol officers carrying out an operation of almost military precision.

Removing the NUWM Leadership

The government was beginning to lose patience with the hunger marchers, with the Home Secretary being frequently required to go

[36] See H C Debs, 31 October 1932, cols 1442–4 (Sir J Gilmour). The total number of injuries sustained as a result of the disorder on 27 and 30 October was 93 (public) and 32 (police): H C Debs, 9 November 1932, col 340 (Sir J Gilmour). See also *Daily Worker*, 31 October 1932.

[37] See the complaint about his access to the Commons voiced by Earl Winterton: H C Debs, 3 November 1932, cols 1952–4.

[38] *Evening News*, 1 November 1932.

[39] It was returned to the NUWM on 3 November 1932: H C Debs, 14 November 1932, cols 743–4 (Sir J Gilmour, from whom the quote in the text is also drawn).

down to the Commons to fend off allegations of police brutality. The newspapers were also piling pressure on Gilmour, with one *Daily Telegraph* editorial on 29 October 1932 identifying Wal Hannington as the cause of all the trouble and calling on the 'authorities not merely to take precautions to deal with the Marchers when they arrive but to put an end to the Marches themselves'. The newspaper went on to assure the Home Secretary that '[s]entimental weakness in handling this situation [would] only issue in more disturbances and a longer list of casualties'. On 1 November, the same paper's editorial was headed 'Why Tolerate These Demonstrations?'[40] Responding to the concerns of a Conservative colleague about the continuing protests, Sir John declared that 'the House and the country realise[d] the iniquity of these proceedings and we will consider any means by which we can bring them to an end'.[41] In fact the State had already begun the process of reining in the NUWM,[42] which according to Bowes was being watched ceaselessly by the Special Branch, its leaders shadowed, mail intercepted and speeches recorded, in a manner with which we have become familiar.[43]

Just before the 1 November protest got under way, and on the eve of the remarks of the Home Secretary quoted above, the police had raided the headquarters of the NUWM. The purpose of the raid was ostensibly to execute an arrest warrant against Wal Hannington and he was duly arrested. But the police, who had waited patiently until Hannington was in the building before making their move, also took the opportunity to cart away a vast quantity of documents relating to the business of the Movement. According to Hannington, an attempt had been made the previous day by an agent provocateur to pass to him a plainly incriminating document, and it may have been this evidence that the police had been so keen to find. In fact Hannington had burnt the material on receiving it from an innocent third party.[44] The immediate effect of the raid was the jailing of Hannington, first on remand and then on 8

---

[40] For further details of the press campaign, see Hannington, n 7 above, pp 265–7. In an editorial headed 'Moscow's game' which appeared on 1 November, the *Evening News* castigated the leadership of the NUWM for being 'under the orders of Moscow'. Five days later, on 6 November, the *Sunday Dispatch* 'revealed' in a front page lead story that the hunger marchers had been 'backed by red gold'.

[41] H C Debs, 2 November 1932, col 1785.

[42] The key Home Office files on these episodes are closed for 100 years: 'Communist Party and National Unemployed Workers' Movement: demonstrations and speeches, 1932–3' (PRO, HO 144/22582); 'Demonstrations by unemployed in London, 1931–2' (PRO, HO 144/16355); 'National Unemployed Workers' Union: march to London in protest against means test, 20 September–31 October 1932' (PRO, HO 144/18186); 'National Unemployed Workers' Union: march to London in protest against means test, 1 November 1932–2 January 1933' (PRO, HO 144/18187).

[43] Bowes, n 25 above, p 110.   [44] Hannington, n 7 above, pp 268–9.

November for a period of three months, on a charge of attempting to incite disaffection among the police in contravention of the Police Act 1919.[45] The evidence was based on certain remarks in Hannington's speech at Trafalgar Square, made two days before his arrest. The case was heard by the celebrated Bow Street Magistrate Sir Chartres Biron, a man whom we encountered in Chapter 4 above and who was distinguished for his unqualified commitment to public tranquillity.[46] A few days later, the Chairman of the NUWM, Sid Elias (who had taken over responsibility for the petition in Hannington's absence) was also proceeded against on a charge of soliciting and inciting two of his colleagues (Hannington and another) to 'cause discontent, dissatisfaction and ill-will between different classes of His Majesty's subjects and to create public disturbance'. The evidence against him was collated from the mountain of material seized by the police on 1 November.[47] He was duly jailed for two years.

It may well be that, by the end of November, Sir John and his colleagues in the National Government felt entitled to relax, believing that the NUWM threat had been finally seen off by the infinitely superior forces of coercion that they had deployed to their advantage. If so it was a misplaced hope, as was made abundantly clear in a letter sent to the Prime Minister on 9 December. Hannington and Elias, together with the NUWM treasurer Tom Mann and its secretary Emryhys Llewellyn, announced the Movement's intention to invite the Prime Minister to receive a further petition (also signed by a million people) from a new deputation on 19 December. The official reaction to this unwelcome news seems to have been one of panic. Ignoring (or perhaps forgetting) the constraints that usually inhibited any public exposure of the intimacy of the connection between politics and the law, the Home Secretary later admitted to Parliament that what he then did was to draw the attention

[45] The authorities may have been particularly sensitive about the police in view of the pay cut that was being imposed on the force at exactly this time: *Reynolds News*, 6 November 1932. The 1919 Act had previously been used against two Greenock councillors for words spoken while addressing a communist meeting on 13 September 1925: see Chapter 3 above.

[46] Sir Chartres's enthusiasm for the preservation of public order may be deduced from the following comments made from the Bench in the course of one of the many cases he dealt with arising out of the disorders on 1 November: 'I should like it to be generally known that if any citizens are present when any disorder arises it is their duty to help the police. If they are called upon to help the police and they do not do it, they are guilty of an indictable offence': (1932) 96 JP 733. In making this remark, Biron was perhaps intending to achieve the same end result as that desired by the Home Secretary when he had earlier warned that ordinary people should stay away from the marches and demonstrations: see text at n 35 above.

[47] (1932) 96 JP 736. Further details are to be found in the *Daily Worker*, 9 November 1932.

of the two men (Mann and Llewellyn) 'in the ordinary course to the Director of Public Prosecutions who, after considering the available evidence and with the approval of the Attorney-General, applied to the chief magistrate [Sir Chartres Biron] for process against the persons concerned'.[48] In the circumstances it was hard to resist one MP's assertion that these 'proceedings [were] political prosecutions'.[49] Indeed, no allegations of substantive offences were even attempted. Instead, it was said that as the two men were planning to organise 'mass demonstrations which were calculated to cause breaches of the peace and breaches of Section 23 of the Seditious Meetings Act, 1817', it was therefore necessary to issue warrants 'to bring these persons before the court to show cause why they should not be ordered to enter into recognisances and to find sureties for their good behaviour and to keep the peace'.[50] This was tantamount to saying that the planned protest was by definition unlawful.

Even for the National Government, such a procedural ruse was scraping the bottom of the barrel. The 'evidence' supporting these 'charges' of imminent disorder was fairly meaningless, being rooted more in the men's membership of the Communist Party and in a vague connection with an article in the *Daily Worker* (a permitted newspaper) for which neither had been responsible.[51] A Detective Pasmore spoke of the trouble that had occurred the previous November, but neither he nor any other witness appear to have produced any evidence pinning any blame for that trouble on either defendant. Both men protested to the presiding magistrate, Sir Chartres Biron, that they had never been involved in any violence but were merely engaged in the matter of expressing their political views. But declaring that there 'had been a misapprehension as to the nature of these proceedings', Biron emphasised that all that was required was that both men be bound over to be of good behaviour. A

---

[48] H C Debs, 23 February 1933, col 1886. Compare H C Debs, 19 December 1932, col 754. Hannington and Elias were already in jail at this stage of course. There are two files in the Public Record Office under the tantalising title, 'Two organisers (Tom Mann and another) of a proposed mass demonstration of unemployed, imprisoned for refusing to enter into recognisance to keep the peace and be of good behaviour. Correspondence between the Prime Minister and the Home Secretary; approval of the court proceedings invoking an Act of 1360' (PRO, HO 144/19835 and 19836), but both are closed for 100 years.

[49] H C Debs, 23 February 1933, col 1885 (F S Cocks).

[50] H C Debs, 19 December 1932, col 754 (Sir J Gilmour).

[51] *Daily Worker*, 5 December 1932, See the adjournment debate in the House of Commons at H C Debs, 22 December 1932, cols 1268–300. The newspaper was itself also attacked by the State in a more direct fashion. In December, the individual responsible for the *Daily Worker* as editor, publisher and proprietor was tried at Leeds Assize on a charge of libelling the police. A term of imprisonment of six months was handed down: see (1932) 96 JP 838.

contemporary account of the Chief Magistrate's words captures the evidential uncertainty that pervaded his application of the law:

It was clear that there was a mass meeting announced and arranged for Monday, which was to present a petition to the House of Parliament [sic]. In his view there would be a mass mob within the vicinity of the House of Commons. There is nothing to prevent anyone presenting a petition to the House of Commons but it is most undesirable that such a petition should be presented by an organised mass of people marching on the House of Commons. It is common knowledge that this mass of people were meeting on Monday to make this mass demonstration under exactly the same conditions as a meeting in October, when there was great disorder. He did not say that the present defendants were responsible for that. But it showed what such meetings were likely to produce and against which he had sworn to preserve the peace.[52]

When, inevitably, the men refused to be bound over as though they were criminals, they were both promptly dispatched to prison for two months. These proceedings took place on 17 December, just a couple of days before the planned petition was to have been presented. The Home Secretary had 'no illusions that the arrest of two men [would] entirely prevent disorder, but it [was] clear that it must be brought home to those who organise disorder, that certain penalties are bound to fall if they will not give definite undertakings which are simple and direct and which they can give if they so desire'.[53] The arrests and speedy imprisonments seem to have done the trick; 19 December passed off peacefully and without the embarrassment of having to use force to reject a NUWM petition.[54]

This attack on the leadership of the NUWM was a crucial blow for an organisation which in 1933 saw a majority of its executive committee in jail.[55] But it was a plight from which it recovered, taking a leading part in the organisation of hunger marches in 1934 and 1936, as well as mounting 'quite large rallies' in London 'on several occasions'.[56] It is also

[52] See George Lansbury's speech in the adjournment debate at H C Debs, 22 December 1932, col 1287, from where the quotation in the text is taken.

[53] H C Debs, 19 December 1932, col 755.

[54] At the end of the month, the Eton and Cambridge-educated Sir Chartres Biron retired from the Bench, with the acclaim of the legal and political élite ringing in his ears. The contrast with Tom Mann, aged 76, the veteran activist, who had been imprisoned for incitement to mutiny in 1912, starting yet another term in jail—this time over Christmas—could not have been more stark. For a particularly fulsome tribute to Sir Chartres, see (1933) 97 JP 33. Mann's two part Home Office file is available to be perused at the Public Record Office: see 'Activities of Tom Mann, agitator' (PRO, HO 144/7062).

[55] J Stevenson and C Cook, *The Slump: Society and Politics During the Depression* (1977), p 164.

[56] Ibid, p 190. Stevenson and Cook's volume is a valuable, if sceptical, account of the NUWM and the marches and demonstrations of the period. On the leadership of the Movement in 1936 see N Branson, *History of the Communist Party of Great Britain, 1927–41* (1985), p 156.

one which led to a notable legal victory for the Movement, this arising directly from the raid of its premises on 1 November 1932. Hannington recalls in his memoirs that while in Pentonville Prison, he was:

visited by a well-known solicitor, Harry Thompson, who was renowned in trade union circles for his expert legal services in claims for compensation in respect of industrial accidents.[57] He had the right as a solicitor to meet me in a room without the presence of a warder. He told me that after my arrest it had been clearly established that the police had no search warrant when they seized the loads of documents from the N.U.W.M. offices.[58]

He said there were strong grounds for a prosecution against the police.[59] He had discussed the matter with eminent lawyers whom I knew and they were ready to fight the case in the courts on behalf of myself and other national officers of the N.U.W.M. if I was willing to authorise the commencement of proceedings. He was very confident that we were on a winner and that the other side would have to meet all the legal costs. I needed no persuasion about such a proposition and I readily gave my consent. I went back to my cell very happy that day.[60]

Thompson's optimism was not misplaced. The extent of the State's power of search and seizure, whether with or without an arrest warrant, had long been controversial, and the epoch-making decision of *Entick v Carrington*[61] had made clear as early as 1765 that the executive had no general right to seize documents on its own authority. Hannington's legal advisers were quick to realise that the enormous amount of material seized from the NUWM made their case look suspiciously like *Entick*, albeit one that was disingenuously disguised by the figleaf of an accompanying arrest warrant.

In an earlier chapter we saw how this precise issue of the seizure of documents upon arrest had arisen on several occasions in the 1920s in the context of the arrest of members of the Communist Party.[62] In July 1921, the then Home Secretary Edward Shortt could do no more by way of identifying the legal basis for such conduct than declare that it had 'from time immemorial been the practice for police officers to search the dwelling of an accused person whenever it is thought likely that any material evidence, for or against the prisoner, [was] likely to be so

---

[57] This was W H Thompson, author of *Civil Liberties*, published in 1938, arguably the first text on civil liberties in Britain.

[58] D N Pritt later claimed in the Commons that a hundredweight of documentation had been taken by 11 police officers: H C Debs, 10 July 1936, col 1563. The *Evening Standard*'s contemporaneous report on 1 November stated that five hundred-weights of material had been seized.

[59] As we shall see it was in fact a civil claim that Thompson was contemplating.

[60] Hannington, n 7 above, p 278.   [61] (1765) 19 St Tr 1030.

[62] See Chapter 3 above.

obtained'.[63] Shortt had gone on to say that the 'practice [was] brought to the cognizance of courts almost daily, and ha[d] never . . . been adversely commented on by a Judge—much less [been] held to be illegal'.[64] The assumption in this and other similar replies in the 1920s[65] clearly was that there should first have been an arrest and that then the search should relate only to the case of the arrestee and not to that of any other individual and should be of his or her dwelling rather than any other place. The potential unlawfulness of such a practice was recognised by the Royal Commission on Police Powers and Procedures, which reported in the following terms in 1929:[66]

We are . . . informed that it has long been the practice of the Police to search the dwelling of a person for whose arrest a warrant has been issued, and, in cases of arrest without warrant, to search premises as well as the arrested person, in cases of serious crime, whenever it seems likely that any material evidence can be obtained. In normal cases, the Police obtain the consent of the occupiers before carrying out a search in such circumstances. But it appears that, in the event of a refusal to consent, the Police, if they proceed with the search, may be faced with the risk of a subsequent action for trespass. This is a risk which is commonly taken by the Police and the practice seems to have had the tacit approval of the Courts for so long that, in the opinion of the Home Office, it has become part of the common law.

Even if the Home Office's version of the law was correct, it was clear that the raid on the NUWM, like earlier raids on the Communist Party in the 1920s, had gone far beyond even that to which it could be claimed the courts had given their tacit approval, a matter which had been pointed out in the Commons by Sir Stafford Cripps.[67]

The case finally came on for trial before Horridge J whom we have already encountered in Chapter 3 above. The action, in the names of

---

      [63] H C Debs, 14 July 1921, col 1458.   [64] Ibid.

   [65] For example, when the issue arose again four years later, in the context of the raid on the Communist Party which had preceded the 1925 prosecutions, the then Home Secretary Sir William Joynson-Hicks had used an almost identical formula: H C Debs, 17 February 1926, col 1960 (WA). For the background to this raid, see Chapter 3 above.

   [66] Cmd 3297 (1929).

   [67] When the Under Secretary of State at the Home Office, O F G Stanley assured the Commons in February 1933 that the 1 November search had followed a 'practice . . . [that] . . . has constantly been brought to the notice of the Courts, and was recognised as necessary and proper by the Royal Commission on Police Powers', he made no mention of, much less made an effort to justify, the seizure power that had accompanied that search. When Sir Stafford Cripps intervened to ask whether the police now had a right 'to search offices in which a man is employed, when the warrant is against the man alone and not against the body which employs him', Stanley's defensive reply was that if 'on any occasion the police in a search of this kind exceed their powers the remedy lies in the civil courts': H C Debs, 9 February 1933, cols 341–2.

Elias, Llewellyn and another tenant James, was against the two police officers in charge of the search, Pasmore and Kitchener, with Baron Trenchard and the Receiver for the Metropolitan Police District also added to the list of defendants. Damages were sought for trespass to premises and to goods and for the wrongful retention of the still withheld documents, together with an order for the delivery of these back to the plaintiffs. To put the NUWM case, Thompson briefed the well-known barrister D N Pritt. Looking back, Hannington was later to describe the proceedings as a 'very keen and erudite legal battle, involving numerous quotations from dusty old law books, that went on throughout many days'.[68] Pritt naturally focused on the weakest element in the police defence, which related to their having taken so much irrelevant documentation. Addressing the judge in oral argument, Pritt:

desired to make it clear that, if it had been a mere case of the police, when they came to arrest Hannington, seeing on a desk a document which might be evidence against Elias, and seizing that, this action would not have been brought. What they desired to stop—and what many other people possibly viewed with alarm—was the practice of sending 11 people to enter the offices of a perfectly lawful organisation and make what Mr Justice Charles at the Central Criminal Court described as a 'clean sweep'. For a country which had hitherto prided itself on the rule of law, that was a shocking thing both in fact and law. It was more than ever necessary that the rule of law should be strictly observed in dealing with persons who were members of an unpopular movement.[69]

No less a figure than the Attorney General Sir Thomas Inskip presented himself in Horridge J's court and he set about defending all aspects of police behaviour during the search. But when asked by the judge whether there was 'any answer to the case so far as it related to documents which were found to be irrelevant to any proceedings and were returned to the plaintiff', Inskip could do no more than explain that 'it was manifestly more convenient for everyone that the documents should be taken away and sorted than that a police officer should stop in the offices of the National Unemployed Workers' Movement for hours or days to do the work'. The judge replied to the submission that he did 'not think that that will do' and went on to declare that 'on that part of the case . . . there must be some damages, however small'.

---

[68] Hannington, n 7 above, p 279.
[69] See the report of argument in the case in *The Times*, 17 January 1934, from which the interchange between the Attorney General and the judge that follows is also taken.

Another weak link in the police case emphasised by Pritt related to the failure to return outstanding NUWM documentation to the Movement at the end of the two trials, and here again the court was sympathetic to the plaintiffs, brushing aside the suggestion by the Attorney General in argument that there could be 'no property in seditious documents and . . . [t]here could not be property in any article which it was a crime to possess'.[70] But although the award of £30 damages with costs was not to be sneezed at, this was in reality a phyrric victory. It is true that it would be difficult after *Elias v Pasmore* for the police ever again to ransack premises in the way that they had those of the NUWM and the Communist Party in the preceding decade.[71] The case also served indirectly to highlight the dubious legality of the decision of a decade before to publish Communist Party documentation as a command paper.[72] Yet in truth neither of the points on which the NUWM was victorious was of central importance as far as future police practice was concerned. In this respect, what really mattered was the excusability of the police seizure of papers on the basis of their materiality to later criminal proceedings, involving not just the arrestee Hannington but also his colleague Elias. There was little doubt that, to the extent that the seized documentation had been deployed in the trial of the arrestee Hannington, then that seizure would be held excusable in law, and this was what Horridge J duly found.[73] But the stakes were far higher as regards the seized items which were claimed to be material to or which had been used in Elias' trial. If such seizures were excusable, then new legal ground would undoubtedly be broken, with the police being able, pursuant to an arrest warrant, to make general searches with a view to uncovering evidence material to as yet unknown crimes involving as yet unnamed individuals. The relevance of this sort of police power in the context of political prosecutions must have been readily apparent, involving as it did the sort of executive power which had been the true target of the famous rhetoric of Lord Camden CJ in *Entick v Carrington*.

As already suggested, Horridge J found in favour of the State on this crucial point. In doing so he held in a very controversial passage that:

the interests of the State must excuse the seizure of documents, which seizure would otherwise be unlawful, if it appears in fact that such documents were evi-

---

[70] The Attorney General dropped the submission 'for the purposes of this case only': see [1934] 2 KB 174. The point is not dealt with in the judgment.

[71] See Chapter 3 above.   [72] Ibid.

[73] In fact only one letter, signed 'P C', a copy of which was found on Hannington, fell into this category.

dence of a crime committed by any one, and that so far as the documents in this case fall into this category, the seizure of them is excused.[74]

So the documents which were seized in the raid of the premises to arrest Hannington were held to have been legitimately seized because 'they were capable of being evidence in the case against Elias, who was convicted of unlawfully soliciting and inciting Emrys Glunf Llewellyn and Walter Hannington to commit the crime of sedition'.[75] Needless to say, this remarkable extension of the common law—which justified the legality of the action of the police by what happened subsequently—had no secure base in precedent. Indeed none of the three cases cited by Horridge J remotely supported such a position,[76] and he himself openly acknowledged that there was no 'direct authority'[77] in English law to sustain the principle that 'though the seizure of documents was originally wrongful, if it in fact turned out that the documents seized were documents which might be properly used in a prosecution against any one, then the seizure would become excused'.[78] But it was not until 1969 that the Divisional Court's mistake was accepted, with the Court of Appeal in *Ghani v Jones*[79] holding that Horridge J had gone 'too far',[80] particularly by suggesting that an unlawful seizure would be justified if the document in question revealed 'evidence of a crime committed by anyone'.[81] In seeking to narrow the scope of the decision, Lord Denning said that *Elias v Pasmore* could be justified only 'on the ground that the papers showed that Elias was implicated in the crime of sedition committed by Hannington. If they had only implicated Elias in some other crime, such as blackmail or libel, I do not think the police officers would have been entitled to seize them' for that would have been a flat contradiction of *Entick v Carrington*.[82]

In a powerful restatement of the principles of *Entick v Carrington*, Lord Denning declared in *Ghani v Jones* that:

The common law does not permit police officers, or anyone else, to ransack anyone's house, or to search for papers or articles therein, or to search his person, simply to see if they have committed some crime or other.[83]

---

[74] [1934] 2 KB 164, at p 173. For an interesting summary of the common law as it was believed to be pre-*Elias v Pasmore*, see Anon., 'Police Seizures of Property' (1931) 95 JP 98.

[75] Ibid.

[76] See respectively *Pringle v Bremner and Stirling* (1867) 5 M (HL) 55; *Dillon v O'Brien* (1887) 20 LR Ir 300; and *Crozier v Cundey* (1827) 6 B & C 232.

[77] [1934] 2 KB 164, at p 172. [78] Ibid, at p 171. [79] [1970] 1 QB 693.

[80] Ibid, p 706. [81] Ibid. [82] Ibid. [83] Ibid.

This revision of this aspect of *Elias v Pasmore* was of course some time after the case itself had been decided. Although many of the initial comments on the decision focused on the award of damages,[84] Pritt wrote many years later that, though 'generally hailed as a substantial victory for civil liberty', it was clear that 'in reality, to those who knew the law, the judgment seemed actually to narrow the restrictions on the activities of police invaders'.[85] An anonymous but prescient note in the *Police Journal* observed that the 'much discussed' decision of Horridge J 'generally has been regarded as limiting [the police] right of search and seizure when effecting a warrant of arrest' but that '[c]onsideration of the effect of the judgment [did] not, however, lend much support to that view of the case'. On the contrary, 'the decision, though in some respects it create[d] new difficulties for the police, may be of assistance in clarifying a branch of the law on which there ha[d] hitherto been some doubt'.[86] The anonymous reviewer of judicial decisions in 1934 in *Law Notes* was surely right to advise the journal's readers that 'if you had to select a yearling having some pretensions to the classics do not summarily dismiss *Elias v Pasmore* from your deliberations. There is classic blood here'.[87] That this 'classic blood' threatened to dog the present and subsequent generations of radical activists was the central point of E C S Wade's powerful attack on the decision, published in the *Law Quarterly Review* in July 1934:

How can the public enjoy the protection to liberty of person and property secured by the General Warrant Cases if the existence of a warrant for the arrest of A enables the police to hunt for information throughout the building where A happens to be at the time of his arrest and use material thus discovered to prosecute, say, D, who alone out of B, C, D, E and F is thus shown to have committed a crime? Is not D, as well as B, C, E and F, presumed to be innocent and immune from invasion of his private property by the police, unless and until charged with an offence connected therewith, or in the case of the statutory exceptions reasonably suspected of the commission of, such an offence?[88]

The Communist Party and the Armed Forces

Horridge J gave his judgment in *Elias v Pasmore* on 23 January 1934. A few months later, in April 1934, the government suddenly opened a new

---

[84] See *New Statesman and Nation*, 27 January 1934, p 107. But cf *Manchester Guardian*, 24 January 1934.

[85] D N Pritt, *The Autobiography of D N Pritt, Vol 1: From Right to Left* (1965), p 139.

[86] (1934) 7 *Police Journal* 144, at p 146.   [87] (1934) 53 *Law Notes* 374.

[88] E C S Wade, 'Police Search' (1934) 50 LQR 354, at pp 359–60.

and more direct line of attack against the activities of the Communist Party. The rationale for the extensive inroads into civil liberties proposed by the Incitement to Disaffection Bill lay in the Party's somewhat desultory efforts at propaganda within the armed forces. Despite its weakness, the Party had nevertheless embarked at the end of the 1920s on a campaign of political persuasion aimed at members of the armed forces that was eventually to provoke the 1934 Bill.[89] In June 1928, four miners were convicted of sedition by a Scottish jury for having circulated to four soldiers a pamphlet which advocated trade unionism in the forces. For this act, 'calculated to excite disaffection, commotion, and resistance to lawful authority among His Majesty's lieges, and particularly among His Majesty's Forces', the defendants were each jailed for one month.[90] Despite both their organisational weakness and the deterrent effect that such sentences must undoubtedly have had, the communists' tactic of leafleting army barracks with political messages nevertheless intensified during 1929. In September of that year, the first edition of *The Soldiers' Voice* emerged. Claiming to be the organ of the communist members of the armed forces, it found at least one section of its readership willing to take it seriously; for the always anxious Army Council, the journal seemed finally to confirm what its members had long feared, that their men were being radicalised under their noses by seditious propaganda.

The content of the leaflets put out by the communists varied from place to place. Those distributed to soldiers leaving Chelsea barracks on 17 March 1930, for example, called on the troops to protest against compulsory church parades and to defend Soviet Russia. Perhaps of more immediate concern to the Army Council, those left at Fenham barracks in Newcastle on 24 May 1930 advised soldiers to refuse to go to India if so ordered.[91] The difficulty lay in determining the right way to respond to such provocation. A couple of distributors of *The Soldiers' Voice* were prosecuted under a local bye-law and this severely disrupted the paper's distribution in Manchester for a time, and the pamphleteers outside the Chelsea barracks mentioned above were successfully prosecuted under a local measure (almost certainly section 54(13) of the Metropolitan Police Act 1839) for 'insulting behaviour'.[92] The main legal weapon available

[89] See Branson, n 56 above, ch 5.

[90] T Young, *Incitement to Disaffection* (1976), pp 49–50.

[91] H C Debs, 6 June 1930, cols 2564–5 (WA) (Sir J Simon). It is not clear from the parliamentary record what, if any, action was taken against those distributing the material.

[92] See the description of the case in these terms given to Parliament by the Home Secretary, J R Clynes at H C Debs, 7 May 1930, col 1036. Each of the three defendants was fined £2. There was a similar prosecution arising out of an incident at Hounslow on 12 April.

on the national stage was the antiquated blunderbuss of the Incitement
to Mutiny Act 1797 which we have already encountered. During 1930,
two Party members were jailed under the Act for distributing anti-war
leaflets to soldiers at Brecon,[93] and another received an eighteen-month
sentence under the Act from Swift J for handing out leaflets at
Aldershot.[94] When the *Daily Worker* published a strong attack on the latter's sentence, four of those most closely involved with the paper were
convicted for conduct 'calculated to bring the learned judge into contempt and lower his authority'.[95] A number of arrests followed a mutiny
aboard the *HMS Lucia* at Plymouth in December 1930,[96] and a couple
of months after this event, a communist was convicted under the 1797
Act in Bristol, apparently for doing nothing more than making an inflammatory speech to an audience which does not seem even to have
included any servicemen among its number.[97]

Despite these convictions, the Labour Government then in power
appeared to take the pamphleteering issue somewhat less seriously than
did the Army Council and certainly less than a few backbench
Conservative MP's might have wanted.[98] Through the summer of 1930,
the government resisted pressure to act against those responsible for the
many leaflets of the day addressing the morality of the army's role in
India.[99] The lack of any publishing details on the pamphlets made it difficult to proceed against those directly responsible for them. Even when
action was taken, the Home Secretary's critics were not satisfied. After

[93] *Daily Worker*, 5 January 1931. One of the men had been in 'his younger days a champion
wrestler and an idol of the fans in Wales'.
[94] The pamphlet concerned was contained in an envelope marked 'Lee's Tip for the Derby' and
was left close to barracks at Chatham, Aldershot, Yorkshire, Newcastle, Edinburgh and Wellington.
Only the distributors of the pamphlet at Aldershot and Brecon were caught, with the two persons
convicted at the latter assize under the 1797 Act being sentenced to 12 and 8 months' imprisonment respectively. There was no indication on any of the pamphlets as to who had printed or published them: see the remarks of the Attorney General, Sir William Jowitt, at H C Debs, 7 July 1930,
cols 35–6.
[95] Swift J had presided over the communist sedition trial in 1925, a fact that did not go without
notice in the columns of the *Daily Worker*. A partner in the Workers' Press was later jailed for six
months on the same charge: *Daily Worker*, 19 January 1931; ibid, 24 January 1931. See also (1930)
94 JP 470.
[96] *Daily Worker* 6 January 1931; ibid, 21 January 1931; ibid, 22 January 1931.
[97] Young, n 90 above, p 51. The defendant was bound over to keep the peace for 12 months.
[98] The Labour Home Secretary, J R Clynes, found himself frequently required in the Commons
politely to decline to declare outright war on the communist leafleteers. It was 'not necessary' to
appoint 'a committee to investigate the question of Communist propaganda in Great Britain', he
assured one MP who had expressed in Parliament an enthusiasm for the idea: H C Debs, 29 May
1930, cols 1505–6 (WA).
[99] An example of one such leaflet was the one distributed to the forces in May 1930 headed 'We
must not murder the workers and peasants of India': H C Debs, 26 June 1930, col 1349. It is
reprinted in full in Branson, n 56 above, p 72.

the convictions of the defendants in the Chelsea barracks case, Sir Kingsley Wood opened a supply day Commons debate in May 1930 with a speech on the issue, inquiring why, '[h]aving regard to the well-known principles of British justice . . . these three comparatively humble individuals have been proceeded against while the people who are mainly responsible, namely, the printers and publishers of the leaflets, who undoubtedly gave them the leaflets, have not'. Wood went on to wonder aloud 'whether it [was] sufficiently realised what a large number of centres there are in this country under the direction not of people in this country, but of what is called the Comintern, who are daily issuing, or issuing as often as they can, subversive and certainly disgraceful periodicals and leaflets in this country'.[100] When Clynes wryly suggested that the 'Communists will thank [Wood] for the wide advertisement which he has given to their literature and their efforts',[101] the victim of the jibe intervened to remark, quite accurately, that the minister was 'hardly dealing with the cases seriously'.[102] In what could not be described as a ringing endorsement of free speech, the Home Secretary concluded his remarks by assuring the House in a more sober vein that in deciding whether or not to prosecute such conduct, the government would 'have regard to the interests of the State and, incidentally, to the rights of individuals freely to hold opinions which are not in themselves offensive'.[103] But he did at least go on to declare that it was 'none of our business to try to make new offences while we are in office'.[104]

The fall of the Labour Government in August 1931 led to the formation of the National Government under Ramsay Macdonald, and one of its very first acts was to propose the making of deep cuts in the salaries of many public officials. These were to average about ten per cent, but they were to hit the navy particularly hard with some classes of seamen being expected to suffer a drop in their income of as much as twenty-five per cent. What made these proposals even more controversial was both that they contradicted a series of assurances given by earlier administrations and that they were expected to take effect almost immediately. Shortly after their announcement, 'discussions took place in the large Navy canteen at Invergordon, where most of the ships of the Atlantic Fleet were engaged in training exercises. On 15 September, 12,000 men refused to obey orders to fall in for work and the "Invergordon Mutiny" hit the headlines'.[105] After the trouble had been brought under control, thirty-six of the alleged ringleaders were immediately dismissed without charges being

[100] H C Debs, 7 May 1930, col 990.   [101] Ibid, col 1034.   [102] Ibid, col 1035.
[103] Ibid, col 1037.   [104] Ibid.   [105] Young, n 90 above, p 52.

brought against them. The criminal law was reserved for the usual scape-goats, the members and supporters of the Communist Party, though it must be admitted that the Party's public celebration of Invergordon had left it vulnerable to State reaction, whether or not it had in fact been involved in inciting or planning the mutiny. On 25 September the offices of the Party's paper, the *Daily Worker*, and its printer Utopia Press were searched by Special Branch without a warrant.[106] The managing direc-tor of the Press W T Wilkinson was duly charged and bailed on condi-tion that 'no matter [was] to appear in [the *Daily Worker*], while you are on bail, in any way touching or concerning the armed forces of his Majesty'.[107] Wilkinson was later convicted under section 1 of the 1797 Act, receiving a sentence of nine months' imprisonment from Hawke J.

In vain did the sixty-eight-year-old Wilkinson plead that the printing firm could not be held responsible for the contents of the journal it pub-lished. The judge's response, that the case was solely about the 'offence of inciting sailors to disobey orders' and had nothing to do with free speech, might have been less incredible had the defendant before him had any responsibility for writing the words that were the subject of the charge.[108] In a subsequent prosecution, Wilkinson's alleged co-conspirator Frank Paterson was charged with incitement to mutiny. The presiding judge at his trial was Humphreys J, whom we have earlier seen as Travers Humphreys QC, chief prosecution counsel in the 1924 Campbell case and the 1925 sedition trials,[109] and whom we will encounter again in the course of this chapter.[110] On this occasion, a senior police officer's enthu-siasm for his brief caused this usually reliable judge to engage in mild crit-icism of police practice:

A police inspector called at the offices of the *Daily Worker* and asked Paterson and others who was responsible for the issues of the paper. One man replied that he understood they were not required to make any reply unless a charge was preferred; upon which the inspector said that it would be to their advan-tage if they were not responsible.[111]

---

[106] *Daily Worker*, 26 September 1931. Bowes, n 25 above, p 110: detectives 'ransacked the offices and printing plant and employees' personal belongings and, censoring the paper, did not allow it to go to press until a number of deletions they had ordered had been made'. See the brief exchange on the affair between W J Brown and the Under Secretary of State for the Home Department, O Stanley, at H C Debs, 30 September 1931, cols 358–60. Stanley refused to go into any details on the basis that the 'matter ha[d] culminated in criminal proceedings' and was therefore *sub judice*: ibid, col 358.

[107] *Daily Worker*, 28 September 1931.

[108] See the report of the judge's remarks in (1931) 95 JP 674.   [109] See Chapter 3 above.

[110] See p 263 below.

[111] See (1931) 95 JP 738, from which the quotations that follow are also taken.

Humphreys J observed of this sequence of events that the officer had been 'endeavouring to induce this man to make a statement as to whether he was the person or not who had in the view of the prosecution committed a crime'. Anything said as a result of this inducement was to be regarded as inadmissible. But any optimism that such remarks might have generated that Paterson would be leniently dealt with were dashed by Humphreys' imposition of a sentence of two years with hard labour. The police officers had apparently no 'personal blame' for what had happened, explained Humphreys.[112]

After Invergordon, the incidents of disaffection in the forces do not seem markedly to have increased, or even to have increased at all. Though the new Home Secretary appointed after the National Government assumed office, Sir Herbert Samuel, felt able to claim in the Commons in May 1932 that there had been 'some increase in the output of Communist literature',[113] no evidence of this was offered and there was certainly no indication that any of the alleged increase was aimed specifically at the military. Indeed the campaign of circulating leaflets at army and navy bases seems to have been wound down, or if it did continue it attracted no parliamentary attention. This was except for one curious incident in the summer of 1933, when AA road signs leading to an RAF display at Hendon were covered by 'anti-war and Communist notices'. Showing (whether intentionally or not is unclear) a Clynes-like sense of proportion, D H Hacking, the Under Secretary of State for Home Affairs assured the House that no action was necessary since the 'handbills [had been] destroyed by passers-by and the action of the weather'.[114] The civil liberties focus in the early 1930s was on the hunger marches and on the rise of the British Union of Fascists,[115] and only one prosecution of any note (Humphreys J again presiding) seems to have taken place under the 1797 Act after the Invergordon furore had died down; even this seems to have been more about persecuting the South Wales communist leadership than about incitement to mutiny

---

[112] *Daily Worker*, 24 November 1931. Public anxiety at the conduct of the authorities after Invergordon centred on the use of agent provocateurs, and one particularly unpleasant case arose out of an elaborate trap set for two defendants by a couple of sailors taking their instructions from their superiors. In sentencing the two (who were, perhaps inevitably, associated with the *Daily Worker*) to 20 months and 3 years imprisonment respectively for incitement to mutiny, Acton J felt compelled to declare that the witnesses for the prosecution were not provocateurs in the ordinary sense: see Young, n 90 above, pp. 55–6; (1931) 95 JP 754; *Daily Worker*, 5 October 1931; 27 November 1931. The Home Secretary, Sir Herbert Samuel, refused to intervene in the sentences of any of the three men: see H C Debs, 9 December 1931, cols 1861–2.

[113] H C Debs, 9 May 1932, col 1549.   [114] H C Debs, 6 July 1933, col 508.

[115] On the rise of the fascists, see Chapter 6 below.

(with the latter being merely a means to the former via the use of an agent provocateur).[116]

Notwithstanding the apparent decline in activity by the CPGB aimed at the military, the pressure for legislative action against disaffection in the armed forces began if anything (and somewhat paradoxically) to increase. The push for new law took place entirely in secret and came not so much from Members of Parliament as from various elements within the government itself. We have already noted that a Preservation of Public Order Bill had been prepared by a Cabinet committee in 1921[117] and that the issue was revisited as early as 1925 by another Cabinet committee (chaired by the Lord Chancellor, Viscount Cave), set up at the time of the sedition trial. Representations were made to that Committee 'respecting the highly objectionable and dangerous efforts made by the Communists to undermine the loyalty of and create disaffection among members of the Fighting Services'.[118] At that point however the Committee thought that the Cabinet would 'appreciate the difficulty of legislating against propaganda ostensibly directed towards the betterment of conditions in the Fighting Services'.[119] Though the Committee agreed that 'the sedition law needs codifying and strengthening', and to this end it appended a further draft Preservation of Public Order Bill to its Report, it nevertheless concluded that 'no useful purpose would be served by attempting to introduce such legislation at the present moment'.[120] In the early 1930s, renewed pressure for legislation came from first and most predictably the Army Council, which had long hankered after the transformation into permanent legislation of the wide protective regulations that it had enjoyed first under the Defence of the Realm Acts and subsequently under the Emergency Powers Act when regulations under it had been in force.[121] The Council had functioned as

[116] See Young, n 90 above, pp. 61–2. The Public Record Office is not as helpful in this area as might have been expected. The following files are closed for 100 years: 'Communist propaganda to incite His Majesty's Forces to mutiny. Sedition charges against John Gollan' (PRO, HO/144/22373); 'Communist propaganda: question of expediency in instituting prosecutions' (PRO, HO 144/9486); 'Communist propaganda: articles contravening the law, 1931–2' (PRO, HO 144/22588).

[117] See Chapter 3 above.

[118] PRO, CAB/179, CP 136 (26), Report of the Public Order Committee, 25 March 1926.

[119] Ibid.   [120] Ibid, para 8.

[121] For Regulations 27, 42 and 42A of the DORR, see Chapter 2 above. The attempt to insert versions of these Regulations into the annual Army Bill in 1919 had drawn fierce criticism in the House of Commons, with the proposals being withdrawn: H C Debs, 2 April 1919, cols 1252–76. The government had more success with the Aliens Restriction (Amendment) Act 1919, s 3(1), which was loosely based on Regulation 42: see Chapter 3 above. For similar Regulations, introduced during the General Strike, see generally Chapter 4 above.

a permanent lobby for legislative change throughout the 1920s and continued its efforts into the early 1930s.[122]

After Invergordon, a second important Whitehall player came over firmly onto its side. In October 1932, the secret service reported to the Home Office on 'the rising menace constituted by Communism to the Country and the inadequacy of the present law to deal with it'. The Service appended to its report a draft Public Security Bill which was broadly framed so as to prohibit:

Use or advocacy of the use of force, violence, intimidation, etc. for the purpose of procuring the alteration of the established law, form of Government, or constitution of the United Kingdom, or for the purpose of bringing into hatred or contempt the administration of justice, or for the purpose of interfering with the administration of the law, or with the maintenance of law and order.

To this attempt to introduce a statutory offence of sedition, it was proposed to add a measure which would have made it an offence to induce 'any member of H M Forces to fail in his duty, or commit a breach of discipline'. But although these proposals were again rejected by the government, the secret service 'did not give up', and in 1933 further information came to light of Comintern attempts to seduce members of the armed forces from their allegiance. Concern was also expressed by the First Lord of the Admiralty that 'nothing could be done' to stop the issue of pamphlets inciting the Fleet to mutiny: those proved to have issued such material could be punished but probably it would only be possible to secure evidence against a distributor who would be a mere hireling. The existing law did not make it an offence to prepare such a pamphlet or to hold it before publication.[123] It was probably in response to the promptings of both lobbies that a new legislative proposal, in the form of an Incitement to Disaffection Bill less extreme than that envisaged by the secret service, was drafted and this eventually appeared on the Cabinet agenda in October 1933.

At this stage, the third source of pressure for the legislation seems to have become involved. Since November 1931, the Metropolitan Police had been under the command of Baron Trenchard, a man already famous for having founded the Royal Air Force. The 'father of the air-force'[124] was extremely suspicious of even the mild-mannered Police

---

[122] 'Undaunted by this annoying but instructive set-back [i.e. the legislative defeat in 1919], the Army Council launched a political crusade for permanent measures to deal with propagandists which was to continue more or less uninterrupted until 1934': Young, n 90 above, p 29.

[123] This discussion draws heavily on C Andrew, *Secret Service* (1986), pp 517–18. Also helpful is Young, n 90 above, p 57.

[124] *Dictionary of National Biography, 1951–60* (1971), p 988.

Federation that had been put in place after the police union had been outlawed in 1919, referring in his annual report for 1932 to his having 'reason to be somewhat concerned by deliberate attempts that have been made to stir up discontent in the Force'.[125] This was probably a reference to the Police Federation, but with an Incitement to Disaffection Bill now circulating in official circles, Trenchard appears to have taken the opportunity to persuade the Home Secretary, Sir John Gilmour (who had replaced Samuel in 1932) that the proposed Bill should include the civil police.[126] Certainly this was the proposal that Gilmour put to Cabinet in February 1934, and it took all the powers of persuasion of the Prime Minister to force him to withdraw.[127] While the police lost this particular battle, much of the rest of the Bill that was eventually published bears the imprint of police influence. Indeed the controversy that the measure was to attract centred as much on its extension of ordinary police power as it did on its proposed broadening of the law on disaffection. Section 3 of the Police Act 1919 already made it an offence to cause disaffection amongst the members of the police force, and as such was widely drawn, much more so than the 1797 Act. Thus the 1919 Act applied not only to 'any act calculated to cause disaffection' but also to inducements to police officers to withhold their services or commit breaches of discipline. Nevertheless problems similar to those that affected the 1797 Act probably also arose in connection with the 1919 Act, particularly in relation to the preparation of offending material, though there is not much evidence of publications designed to cause disaffection in the police.

When the National Government's proposal for new legislation was finally published in Spring 1934, it was greeted with a mixture of

---

[125] Report of the Commissioner of Police of the Metropolis for the Year 1932, Cmd 4294 (1933), p 14. In a memorandum he compiled listing the deficiencies he had found in his first six months in office, Trenchard complained that the 'Police Federation was holding 480 meetings a year and this has been going on for some twelve years. The Police Act of 1919 only sanctioned twelve meetings a year of one day each': quoted by A Boyle, *Trenchard* (1962), p 608. The Commissioner does not return to his disaffection theme in his Report for 1933, published at the same time as the second reading of the Incitement to Disaffection Bill: Report of the Commissioner of Police of the Metropolis for the Year 1933, Cmd 4562 (1934).

[126] See Andrew, n 123 above, for the role of the police in the formulation of the legislation.

[127] See Young, n 90 above, p. 64. When Gilmour was asked in the Commons in May 1933 to comment on Trenchard's remarks about discontent in the Metropolitan Police, he replied: 'I do not think it would be in the public interest to enter into further details on this matter at this stage . . . I will shortly issue a White Paper for the information of the House and legislation, no doubt, will follow': H C Debs, 4 May 1933, cols 988–9. For the role of the Police Act 1919 in countering disaffection in the police, see Chapter 3 above.

incredulity, astonishment and anger.[128] It was during the early months of that year that Mosley's fascists were enjoying what was to prove to be the high point in their popularity with the British people[129] and it seemed a malicious eccentricity on the part of the government to choose this moment to propose, apparently out-of-the-blue, new legislation on what was by the Spring of 1934 already widely perceived as an old and largely non-existent problem. As we shall see, the extraordinarily hostile public reaction shown to the Bill led to a series of significant amendments being made to it during its passage through the Commons and these greatly diluted its breadth and range. In its original form, the measure represented a calculated attempt to render a whole segment of radical political opinion vulnerable to arbitrary police action. As we have seen earlier in this chapter, by 1934 the government had already been exposed to the pressures brought to bear on it by the hunger marches of the NUWM.[130] It probably knew exactly what it was doing when it attempted to give the police significant new powers with which to control this huge segment of contemporary political radicalism. That the plan was largely foiled stands as a tribute to the parliamentarians from all sides who opposed it, and as a reminder of the value of an open and accountable democratic process as a means of law-making, at least when it can be made to function properly. The caution of Cave's Cabinet Committee of 1926, which had warned that '[p]ast experience shows that, except in moments of national crisis, the passage through Parliament of proposals for dealing with sedition presents exceptional difficulties',[131] was spectacularly vindicated.

The Incitement to Disaffection Act 1934

Management of the Bill was left in the hands of the Attorney General, Sir Thomas Inskip. The son of a Bristol solicitor, Inskip had been Solicitor General in Bonar Law's Administration and was now in his second term of duty as Attorney General, appointed to the post in 1932 after having previously served for two years in 1928 to 1929. When opening the Second Reading debate, Inskip sought to defuse the tension that its publication had already caused by stressing that the proposed

---

[128] The relevant files on the Act in the Public Record Office are closed for 100 years: 'Incitement to Disaffection Bill 1934, 17 April–21 June 1934 and 25 June–4 November 1934' (PRO, HO 144/19701 and 19702).

[129] The infamous Olympia meeting was to follow a mere seven weeks after the Second Reading of the Bill: see Chapter 6 below.

[130] See pp 216–34 above.   [131] See n 118 above, para 5.

measure was 'of more limited scope than, if I may judge from some published comments, some persons think it to be'.[132] As this remark indicates, his tactic was to emphasise that the Bill involved little more than a procedural rationalisation of already well-established legal rules. The language of the Incitement to Mutiny Act 1797 was 'substantially reproduced'[133] in the Bill but with the added advantage that under the new measure summary prosecutions would now be possible, thus providing 'an easier, swifter and more suitable remedy and punishment for the comparatively humble persons who are caught distributing literature', while the 'cumbrous, slow-moving machinery of indictment'[134] with the possibility of a life sentence under the 1797 Act would remain for the 'somewhat sly and almost skulking breed of inciter' who was 'too shy or too cowardly to put . . . names and addresses to the literature which they [were] in the habit of producing'.[135] The Bill, which dealt with 'matters of real importance' and was 'not a panic Measure',[136] was commended to the House primarily on the basis that it was 'concerned wholly with the prevention and punishment of endeavours to seduce Members of His Majesty's Forces from their duty or allegiance'.[137]

The Attorney General's approach inflamed rather than conciliated the Opposition. The first and most obvious, but also the most powerful, objection to the Bill was that it was unnecessary. The Attorney General made a great play of quoting from passages in *The Soldiers' Voice* and its Navy equivalent, *The Red Signal*. It is true that the passages in question (which had also excited the secret service[138]) were inflammatory, inviting members of the armed forces to get in touch with 'that Communist or member of the Unemployed Movement you used to know at home' and proclaiming that '[i]f war does come, then it must be turned into a civil war against the capitalist war-mongers and their bankrupt system'.[139] But the most recent of the quoted passages was May 1933 (almost a full year before the Bill's introduction), while the Attorney General went on to undermine his own argument by declaring his confidence that 'these pieces of propaganda are an insult to members of His Majesty's Forces'

---

[132] For the Second Reading debate see H C Debs, 16 April 1934, cols 739–855. The Attorney General's comments are at ibid, col 739. The newspapers on the morning of the debate were almost uniformly hostile. In its editorial, the *Manchester Guardian* condemned the Bill in the following terms: 'It makes it easier to send people to prison for their opinions. It widens the scope of political offences and greatly increases the power of the police to interfere arbitrarily with the domestic liberties of the individual': *Manchester Guardian*, 16 April 1934.

[133] H C Debs, 16 April 1934, col 739.   [134] Ibid, col 743.   [135] Ibid, col 740.
[136] Ibid, col 749.   [137] Ibid, col 739.   [138] See Andrew, n 123 above.
[139] H C Debs, 16 April 1934, col 742.

who 'in general are inspired by a passionate loyalty to their Service'.[140] As the Liberal MP Isaac Foot asked, not necessarily rhetorically, 'I wonder what evidence there is that a single soldier has been influenced in his allegiance?'[141] No evidence was forthcoming. When Inskip sought support for the Bill by pointing out that during 1932 there had been seventeen different subversive pamphlets and twenty places of distribution, and eleven such pamphlets and such centres during 1933,[142] Members were quick to reply that these figures reflected a sharp decline in the problem over the two years, and that this was a powerful argument against rather than in favour of legislation. Requests for information about the propagation of such literature in the first months of 1934 met with no response from Inskip or any of his ministerial team.

The antagonism shown towards the Bill went beyond the question of its necessity. The actual provisions it contained conclusively refuted the Attorney General's claim that the Bill was substantially procedural in content. Clause one declared that 'If any person endeavours to seduce any member of His Majesty's forces from his duty or allegiance to His Majesty he shall be guilty of an offence under this Act'. This differed in two important respects from the 1797 provision which Inskip had said it was effectively duplicating. First, the phrase 'maliciously and advisedly' which qualified the phrase 'endeavour to seduce' in the old Act was nowhere to be found in the new.[143] Secondly and more importantly, where the 1797 measure had referred to seducing members of the forces from their 'duty *and* allegiance', the 1934 Bill proposed instead that the seduction be from their 'duty *or* allegiance'.[144] Manifestly the latter formula was far broader than the former, since it would be perfectly possible to invite a soldier not to do his duty in a way which did not challenge his allegiance. The importance of this change of phrase was brought home by the extraordinary clause 2(1) which the Attorney General put before the House:

[140] Ibid, cols 742–3. During July 1934, when the Bill was still going through the Commons it was claimed by the Financial Secretary to the War Office, Douglas Hacking, that there had only been two incidents of mutiny during the previous 10 years, the first at Jamaica in 1929 and the second in Singapore in 1932, though how 'far these cases [could] be ascribed to political propaganda or to political influence [was] a matter of conjecture on which [the Minister was] not prepared to pronounce': H C Debs, 25 July 1934, col 1763. Interestingly, no mention of Invergordon was made.

[141] H C Debs, 16 April 1934, col 763.

[142] Ibid, col 743.

[143] This point was made by Dingle Foot in the course of his speech in the Second Reading debate: see ibid, col 797.

[144] Emphasis added. This was the formula that had been deployed in later legislation on the navy (in 1866), the army (in 1881) and the Royal Air Force (in 1913), a point made by Inskip when defending the change in the wording: ibid, col 740.

If any person, without lawful excuse, has in his possession or under his control any document of such a nature that the dissemination of copies thereof among members of His Majesty's forces would be an offence under section one of this Act, he shall be guilty of an offence under this Act.

Inskip almost casually described this as being intended to put people off distributing the pamphlets,[145] but members of the House were not slow to pick up the fact that possession of a document would now be a crime if circulating it to the forces would be an offence under section one, and this was so even if there was no intention whatsoever of any such circulation taking place.[146] The effect of this would be to leave vulnerable to prosecution those who possessed almost any sort of literature of a radical or communist nature. Even more remarkable was the possibility, raised by a number of MPs, that the possession of pacifist material in, for example, the Friends' Meeting House in London or the Oxford Union (which had recently carried its famous pacifist motion), would henceforth very likely be an offence under the Act.[147] To make matters worse, clause 2(2) went on to provide that 'If any person does or attempts to do, or causes to be done or attempted, any act preparatory to the commission of an offence under section one of this Act, he shall be guilty of an offence under this Act'. Inskip justified this by talking vaguely of punishing '[a]n attempt . . . to engage some of these unhappy distributors or to enter into a contract for the printing'.[148] Neither eventuality was particularly likely, given the subterfuge nature of such propaganda operations. One MP was closer to the mark when he wondered 'what would be the position if I or some other person boarded a train for Aldershot, and it were contended that that was preparatory to our committing an offence under the Bill'.[149] Yet controversial though clauses 1 and 2(1) and (2) of the Bill were, the anger they generated was as nothing compared to the fury sparked by clause 2(3). Even Inskip recognised that it had 'quite rightly . . . attracted the attention of many Members with a view to seeing that we [were] doing nothing outrageous'.[150] In its original form, the sub-clause read as follows:

---

145 H C Debs, 16 April 1934, col 745.

146 Ibid, col 750. See in particular the comments of Major J Milner at ibid, col 789.

147 It might have been thought by some opponents of the Bill that the seizure by the police of anti-war material during a military pageant in Edinburgh in June 1934 (i.e. while the Bill was going through committee) was a sign of things to come, though in this case the police purported to rely on their powers under s 193 of the Edinburgh Corporation Order Confirmation Act 1933: see H C Debs, 14 June 1934, col 1907 (Sir G Collins) (WA).

148 H C Debs, 16 April 1934, col 746. 149 Ibid, col 789 (Major J Milner).

150 Ibid, col 747.

If a justice of the peace is satisfied by information on oath that there is reasonable ground for suspecting that an offence under this Act has been committed, he may grant a search warrant authorising any constable named therein to enter at any time, if necessary by force, any premises or place named in the warrant, and to search the premises or place and every person found therein, and to seize anything found on the premises or place or on any such person which he has reasonable ground for suspecting to be evidence of the commission of such an offence as aforesaid.

The inevitable complaint about this provision was that it amounted to the enactment of the right to obtain general warrants of a type that had been condemned in *Entick* v *Carrington*, the seminal decision which we have already encountered on several occasions.[151] The Attorney General attempted to defuse such a predictable objection as follows:

This Clause has nothing to do with general warrants. General warrants were objectionable to the law in those days because the law made no provision for them, and the fact that they were general was an objection. The fact that they were issued by a Secretary of State only and not by a magistrate upon information was another objection. This Clause is not an illustration of the general warrant.[152]

At a purely technical level, Inskip was undoubtedly correct. The problem with the warrant issued by the Secretary of State in *Entick v Carrington* had been more to do with its lack of a legal basis than with its content, and there remained a requirement in this clause that a crime be reasonably suspected of having been committed. But it was a very tenuous Rule of Law that allowed such a power on the basis of a crime so vaguely defined and by the authority of a single magistrate's warrant 'under which you do not need to specify anyone's name, and under which it is possible for a police officer to go and fish around for evidence upon which he can subsequently frame a criminal charge'.[153] MPs also pointed out that it contained 'no limit to the time or place' in which the search could be effected[154] and that it reposed far too much discretion in individual JPs, many of whom were 'so Conservative that nearly half the Conservatives in this House would repudiate [their] views'.[155] In 1925, an earlier government had sought to slip into a routine Criminal Justice Bill an even broader provision than what was now proposed, allowing magistrates to authorise general searches where an indictable offence had been or was

---

[151] See n 61 above.

[152] H C Debs, 16 April 1934, col 747.

[153] Ibid, cols 799–800 (D Foot).

[154] Ibid, col 758 (J J Lawson).

[155] Ibid, col 755.

about to be committed, but the ruse had been spotted by Sir Patrick Hastings, whose speeches against the proposal in the Commons had been so devastating that the initiative had been quietly dropped.[156] It looked as though the National Government, perhaps inspired by Trenchard, was trying its luck in the same way, no doubt to the embarrassment of the Prime Minister who as Leader of the Opposition had excoriated the 1925 proposal as 'monstrous' and as 'the most pernicious proposal that had been made in modern times for the undermining of personal liberty'.[157]

The Second Reading debate was little less than a six-and-a-half hour mauling of the Bill, with many Members remarking on the absence of government supporters willing to speak in favour of the measure. Particularly noteworthy was the fact that the Home Secretary, Sir John Gilmour, had carefully distanced himself from the measure, despite its manifest domestic importance.[158] The Solicitor General, Sir Donald Somervell (later to achieve high judicial office in the Court of Appeal and the House of Lords) put a face more brave than rational on the humiliation when at the end of the debate he professed both the Attorney General and himself to be 'satisfied with the reception which the Bill has received'.[159] Even more bizarrely, he then went on to declare that 'no argument of substance ha[d], on examination, been produced against the Bill'.[160] Despite such bravado, the government had been badly shaken. Opposition to the Bill continued to gain momentum and was in full flow through May, June and July when a parliamentary standing committee of some fifty members (with invariably thirty to forty in attendance) devoted no fewer than fifteen sittings to a minute consideration of its many controversial aspects. Opposition to the measure went beyond the precincts of the House of Commons. The newly formed Council for Civil Liberties (subsequently the NCCL) organised two demonstrations in Trafalgar Square and a deputation to the Attorney General. Its petition against the Bill as 'a grave menace to the fundamental liberties of the British people' was signed by 63,134 people.[161] A protest meeting in Oxford on 5 May, attended by such distinguished legal luminaries as the Vinerian Professor in English Law, Sir William Holdsworth, the Master

---

[156] See H C Debs, 11 May 1925, col 1599 (Sir W Joynson-Hicks) and the speeches of Sir Patrick Hastings QC, ibid, cols 1604–6 and H C Debs, 16 November 1925, cols 155–7.

[157] The point was exploited by opponents of the 1934 Bill: see H C Debs, 16 April 1934, col 754 (J J Lawson). MacDonald was also vulnerable in that his pacifism during the 1914–18 war would have brought him within the Bill's provisions had it then been in force, a point made by among others J McGovern, ibid, col 804.

[158] A point made by J J Lawson, ibid, col 751.   [159] Ibid, col 842.   [160] Ibid.

[161] H C Debs, 31 October 1934, col 177. The Communist Party of Great Britain, *The Sedition Bill Exposed* (1934) is a well-informed critique of the Bill.

of University College, Sir Michael Sadler, and the Warden of New College, H A L Fisher, was so vitriolic in its condemnation that the *Justice of the Peace*, which had earlier robustly supported the Bill, now coyly predicted that its 'prospects . . . [were] not very promising'.[162] By 4 June, the government admitted to having already received 161 resolutions against the Bill from trade unions and political and religious organisations.[163] A galaxy of leading writers and even military personnel entered into the fray in opposition to the government's plans.[164]

In view of all this, it was not at all surprising that Inskip and his colleagues should have felt obliged to accept a series of amendments in Committee. The phrase 'maliciously and advisedly' from the 1797 Act was added to clause 1, and clause 2(1) was greatly limited by the replacement of the vague defence of a 'lawful excuse' for the possession of the criminal material with a new requirement that the holding of the material be for the purpose of committing an offence under section 1.[165] Rather pathetically, Inskip was reduced to boasting to the Committee that 'Professor Holdsworth says that my Amendment "makes this section comparatively unobjectionable" '.[166] Even more dramatically, clause 2(2) was dropped in its entirety, with the Attorney General, 'putting all [his] cards on the table', admitting that 'it might be said that if a person of thoroughly bad character, a Communist, took a ticket at Waterloo for Aldershot, as has been suggested, that might be an act preparatory to the commission of an offence'.[167] Clause 2(3) was also the subject of numerous concessions, not the least of which were those which limited the police who could apply for warrants under the sub-section to inspectors or more senior officers and which replaced the single justice of the peace to whom applications could originally have been made for such warrants

---

[162] (1934) 98 JP 299. For the support which the journal (normally a good barometer of the temperature of the highly conservative legal professions) had given the Bill after its second reading, see ibid, pp 283–4. The anonymous writer who was probably responsible for both pieces had clearly been somewhat intimidated by the array of stars who disagreed with his (or her) initial assessment.

[163] H C Debs, 4 June 1934, col 265 (Sir D Somervell).

[164] See Young, n 90 above, pp 66–7 for further details. On one occasion during Committee discussion of the Bill, a clearly exasperated Inskip referred to 'all the letters [he had] received from groups of people in colleges or ecclesiastics in the dim darkness of a cathedral': H C Standing Committee A, 1933–4, 14 June 1934, Incitement to Disaffection Bill, col 473.

[165] As enacted, clause 2(1) now reads: 'If any person, with intent to commit or to aid, abet, counsel, or procure the commission of an offence under section one of this Act has in his possession or under his control any document of such a nature that the dissemination of copies thereof among members of His Majesty's forces would constitute such an offence, he shall be guilty of an offence under this Act'.

[166] H C Standing Committee A, 1933–4, 31 May 1934, Incitement to Disaffection Bill, col 346.

[167] Ibid, 5 June 1934, col 390.

to two justices or to a stipendiary magistrate. It might have been thought that these concessions, together with another amendment allowing defendants to choose jury trial if they so desired,[168] would have pacified the Bill's critics and allowed it to have negotiated its remaining parliamentary hurdles without difficulty.

But while this may have been Inskip's hope, it was not to be realised. Sir William Holdsworth for one was not convinced. In an astonishing attack on the Bill, published in the *Spectator* when the Committee debate on clause 2 was winding down, the Vinerian Professor welcomed the changes that had occurred which had 'removed some, but by no means all, of those features which [had made] [the Bill] the most daring encroachment upon the liberty of the subject which the Executive Government has yet attempted at a time which is not a time of emergency'.[169] But even as amended the Bill still showed that there was a danger that 'with the help of Parliament . . . the conception of the Rule of Law, and of liberties guaranteed by a supreme law, will disappear'. The opposition continued at such a pitch that the government felt compelled to agree even further dilutions after the Committee stage had concluded, the most important of which restricted the warrant procedure in the old clause 2(3) to a judge of the High Court, a change for which Holdsworth in particular had been pushing.[170] This was a major concession, for which there appears to have been no precedent; even the Official Secrets Act 1911 permitted warrants to be issued by magistrates, and indeed in some cases effectively by the police themselves. The Bill that limped from the Commons was thus a very different and tamer breed of legislative animal than the vicious beast that had been unleashed at Second Reading. But even the Lords only passed the measure after the peers had delivered another series of savage intellectual blows at Second Reading and had had a whole series of amendments successfully resisted by what must have been a deeply exasperated government.[171] The former Rufus Isaacs, now nearing the end of his life sitting in the House of Lords as the Marquess of Reading, emerged from retirement to launch a particularly wounding attack, asking a series of questions to which satisfactory

---

[168] H C Standing Committee A, 1933–4, 31 May 1934, Incitement to Disaffection Bill. This was achieved by increasing the punishment on summary conviction to a term not exceeding four months: clause 3(1).

[169] *Spectator*, 29 June 1934, p 990.

[170] For the debate on these latter stages of the Bill, see H C Debs, 30 October 1934, cols 47–176; 31 October 1934, cols 201–322 (Report); and 2 November 1934, cols 525–610 (Third Reading).

[171] See H L Debs, 6 November 1934, cols 96–162 (Second Reading); 8 November 1934, cols 201–374 (Committee); 13 November 1934, cols 379–91 (Third Reading).

answers were no nearer the public domain then than they had been at the start of the whole process, over six months before:

My difficulty throughout is to understand what is the good cause in this case. What is the necessity for this Bill? How came it to be introduced? Who was responsible for it? Who initiated it?[172]

But although wounded, the government was unbowed, with a majority in the Lords large enough to ensure a safe if sometimes stormy passage. There were nevertheless no fewer than fifteen divisions in Committee.[173] Among the more interesting of these was the vote on the proposal that clause 1 should be amended to reflect the 1797 formula: that an offence be committed only where the accused was guilty of conduct which seduced members of the forces from their duty and allegiance, rather than from their duty or allegiance, a controversial phrase which had survived intense Commons' scrutiny. It was in the course of these exchanges that a new twist emerged in the tale, with the Marquess of Reading complaining bitterly that the House had been misled by the War Secretary (Viscount Hailsham) who had given the impression that 'really there was no distinction'[174] between 'duty and allegiance' on the one hand and 'duty or allegiance' on the other. But although the government remained convinced that the formula 'made very little difference'[175] it was still not prepared to accept the amendment, the division on which attracted more of their Lordships into the voting lobbies than on any of the others. It remains the case, nevertheless, that the use of the disjunctive rather than the conjunctive in the 1934 Act must 'have been done for a reason', an argument accepted as 'sound' by the Court of Appeal some forty years later.[176] It is perhaps only the limited use which has been made of the 1934 Act since its enactment—thereby tending to confirm that the government was tilting at windmills after all—which has helped to ensure that the significance of this development has not been fully realised.

Having campaigned so long for an anti-disaffection Bill, the executive now found itself with a measure so truncated by Parliament that its anti-communist utility was sharply reduced. The Act was not used as the basis of a prosecution for three years and then only in a case in 1937, 'the impropriety of [which prosecution was] quite obvious from the facts'.[177]

---

[172] H L Debs, 6 November 1934, col 119.
[173] H L Debs, 8 November 1934, cols 201–374.   [174] Ibid, col 231.
[175] Ibid, col 235.   [176] *R v Arrowsmith* [1975] QB 678.
[177] Young, n 90 above, p 77. The details of the case may also be found in R Kidd, *British Liberty in Danger* (1940), p 67. See Young, n 90 above, pp 76–94 for the subsequent history of the

It may have been that, apart from the amendments that were achieved, it was the controversy itself which the measure aroused that made the executive reluctant to enforce it. That controversy was of course largely due to the offensive content of the legislation. It was clearly significant, and recognised as such at the time, that here was a Bill which was intended to be a permanent and ordinary part of the law and which was in this highly material way different from the Defence of the Realm Regulations and Emergency Regulations which had preceded it. That this was so widely recognised must in no small measure have been due to the organisational skills of the nascent NCCL which as we have earlier noted had arrived on the scene in February 1934, just before the Bill's Second Reading. Of equal importance to the Bill's emasculation was the fact that it was also opposed by so many establishment and conservative figures, of whom Sir William Holdsworth was the most well-known and the most strident. It was this coalition between left and right, both within and outside Parliament, which so effectively damaged the measure. That there was right-wing antagonism may at first sight seem mysterious, but it is more readily understandable when seen as part of a more general rejection of the role of government and as part of a distaste for bureaucracy which was then prevalent in many conservative circles.[178] An important symptom of just this sentiment was the well-known polemic of the Chief Justice, Lord Hewart, which we have already encountered.[179] But as we shall see, this did not mean that Lord Hewart was thereby a stout defender of political freedom. Indeed, far from it.

The NUWM and the Trenchard Ban

Protest against the National Government which as we have seen assumed office in August 1931 was restricted neither to the members of the armed forces who stood their ground at Invergordon, nor to the hundreds of thousands of hunger marchers who took to the streets. According to the *Daily Worker*, a total of 1,432 'workers' were prosecuted between 31 October 1931 and 28 February 1933 for crimes allegedly committed in

enforcement of the measure. As to whether s 2 was used to procure search warrants we have no clear information, but no such warrants had been obtained by 4 February 1935: H C Debs, 4 February 1935, col 796 (Sir T Inskip).

[178] For a flavour of the times, see Report of the Committee on Ministers' Powers, Cmd 4060 (1932). See D G T Williams, 'The Donoughmore Report in Retrospect' (1982) 60 *Public Administration* 273.

[179] See Chapter 1 above.

the course of their political activities. Of these, 480 were reportedly jailed, 734 fined, 130 bound over and the remainder (a mere eighty-eight) acquitted.[180] Not all of these would have been picked up in the great set piece marches. Many of them would have fallen foul of the law because of their participation in other flashpoints of protest in the early 1930s. One of the most inflammatory of these was the political meeting outside the local employment exchange. Though less spectacular than the marches, such meetings may well have had a greater impact on individual communities, particularly on those with high unemployment where 'signing-on' was a regular humiliation for many hundreds of local people. Such unemployed workers would have been particularly susceptible to an attractive and persuasive political message, and it was at such meetings that the NUWM gained much of its support, particularly in the autumn of 1931 when its membership was suddenly and dramatically swollen with new recruits, and when benefits were being cut by the new government.

From the start the National Government was extremely agitated by the targeting of employment exchanges and training centres by the NUWM. Frustratingly for the government, however, such gatherings appeared to fall full-square within the kind of peaceful political assembly which the British constitution was supposed to be committed fully to protecting. Serious incidents of disorder outside labour exchanges, whether independently of or following upon such meetings, appear to have been practically non-existent in 1931, with *The Times* carrying no reports of any such disorder for the first ten months of the year.[181] The temperature was heightened slightly in November, when the NUWM targeting began to have an effect. A curious episode occurred in Kentish Town on 13 November. *The Times* began its report on this north London affair in a way which perhaps reflected the authorities' view of this type of protest, observing that the 'first sign of trouble was when about fifty persons assembled in front of the exchange and held a meeting'.[182] After about twenty minutes, it appears that some of the men and women present at the meeting entered the employment exchange and tried to get into the boardroom on the first floor, where an appeal board was sitting. They were removed from the building by the police after what *The Times* called

---

[180] Cited in D G T Williams, *Keeping the Peace* (1967), pp 14–15.

[181] There were occasional reports of disorder within exchanges, but these were more the result of the desperate actions of stricken men than of political agitation. A typical example occurred in October 1931, with *The Times* reporting that one Herbert Morris, 'a heavily built man' had been jailed for two months with hard labour by Alderman Sir William Burton for assaulting the deputy manager of the labour exchange in Mansell Street, Aldgate.

[182] *The Times*, 14 November 1931 from which report the quotations that follow are also taken.

'a short struggle', at which point the protestors 'contented themselves by marching to the local headquarters of the organised unemployed in High Street, Camden Town, where they dispersed'. Four days later, a meeting addressed by Wal Hannington outside the labour exchange at Kingsland Road (also in London) was followed by efforts by those assembled to break into the local public assistance committee offices, an action that was only repelled by the use of police truncheons. On the same day a large crowd caused an obstruction at Camden labour exchange, with police action being once again required, leading on this occasion to one demonstrator being charged with an offence for allegedly causing cruelty to a police horse. On 24 November, a deputation from the St Pancras branch of the NUWM had to be forcibly ejected from a local public assistance committee office.[183]

These various events increased anxiety in the already nervous Ministry of Labour, the department responsible for the administration of employment exchanges and training centres. As early as 2 October, officials from the ministry had written to their counterparts in the Home Office warning about the danger of disturbances following upon the reduction of unemployment benefit. Now on 18 November, when the anticipated agitation seemed to be on the increase, ministry officials appealed to the Metropolitan Police Commissioner to keep the vicinity of employment exchanges clear of political meetings, pointing out in support of their proposal that the 'natural result of these meetings is to excite the temper of the crowd'. As we have seen the force had at this point just come under the control of Lord Trenchard, a man whose political and civil libertarian sensitivities were very much secondary to his military inclinations. The political temperature in London at this time was extremely volatile. Hannington and Elias had just been jailed and the NUWM was planning the renewal of its mass petition of Parliament, the threat of which was shortly to lead to the jailing also of Mann and Llewellyn. The apparent freedom with which radicals could preach their message across London must have been an affront to this RAF man. On 25 November, therefore, there emerged, 'wrapped in obscurity and secrecy',[184] what was to become known as the Trenchard ban. Though unannounced in Parliament or the press, and apparently only eventually becoming public knowledge through a leak in breach of confidence,[185] the ban was to

---

[183] These details together with many others that follow in the text are drawn from PRO, HO 144/20149. Prohibition of meetings held in the vicinity of employment exchanges.

[184] H C Debs, 10 July 1936, col 1551 (D N Pritt).

[185] Ibid, col 1552. No details of this supposed breach of confidence were given in the course of the debate in the Commons where it was mentioned. See, however, the contemporary news report,

have a profoundly repressive effect on popular protest in London and (though not mentioned in the case) was eventually to give rise to the famous High Court decision of *Duncan v Jones*.[186] The Commissioner's direction was that 'in future, no meetings are to be held by unemployed or other persons in close proximity to Labour Exchanges, irrespective of whether or not any actual obstruction is caused, on the ground that such meetings have been found liable to lead to breaches of the peace'.

The new rule was immediately implemented, with a meeting outside the St Pancras exchange being broken up by police on 26 November and with further police action on 27 November leading to 'some of the most bitter fights in London'.[187] The *Daily Worker*'s front page headline on 28 November was 'Unemployed fights with police all over London'.[188] On the second day following the ban's introduction, *The Times* reported on its imposition in the following way:

Fourteen men and a woman were arrested yesterday after struggles between police and unemployed agitators in several London districts. Several police officers were injured.

Instructions were recently issued by Lord Trenchard, the Commissioner of Police, forbidding the holding of meetings or demonstrations of unemployed persons near Labour exchanges. Police officers, both mounted and on foot, were accordingly posted near all the principal exchanges yesterday, and as soon as speakers began to address the unemployed they were ordered to go away.

The most serious disturbance occurred at Fulham, where bottles and other missiles were thrown at the police. There was a free fight, and before further help could be obtained three police officers had been roughly handled by the crowd. In another disturbance in Sulgrave Road, Shepherd's Bush, a policeman was struck on the head and had to be relieved of duty for the rest of the day. Arrests were made near the Labour Exchange in Kentish Town, and also in St. Thomas' Square, South Hackney, where a man, who is alleged to have attacked a policeman, was taken to the local police station. In other districts men who had assembled with the intention of holding meetings acted on the advice of the police and dispersed without causing trouble.[189]

Ten of the fourteen arrestees were subsequently charged before the West London magistrate with charges including obstruction and assault. Ominously for these defendants, all their cases were remanded so that charges of unlawful assembly could be brought. The police campaign continued in the days that followed. 'Day after day the London

at n 189 below, from which it would appear that there was public awareness of the fact that the Commissioner had issued a new instruction, even if the precise contents of the instruction might not have been known.

[186] [1936] 1 KB 218.
[188] *Daily Worker*, 28 November 1931.
[187] Hannington, n 7 above, p 248.
[189] *The Times*, 28 November 1931.

unemployed defied the ban and faced baton charges by the police to uphold their right to free speech and peaceful assembly outside the Labour Exchanges'.[190] On 1 December mounted police were used 'to clear the whole area around the exchange' at Shepherd's Bush after the police had prohibited a political meeting there.[191]

The following day, the legality of these various police actions was raised in Parliament. One possible source of legal authority, and one to which Trenchard may initially have been attracted, was the long-winded section 52 of the Metropolitan Police Act 1839, which authorised the chief of police 'to give directions to the constables for keeping order and for preventing any obstruction of the thoroughfares in the immediate neighbourhood of her Majesty's palaces and the public offices, . . . and other places of public resort, and in any case when the streets or thoroughfares may be thronged or may be liable to be obstructed'. Unaware of the precise formula deployed by Trenchard in his 25 November direction, one MP demanded of the Home Secretary that instructions be given 'that at places where traffic is not interfered with and where the proceedings are conducted in an orderly manner such meetings shall not be dispersed by the police'.[192] The Home Office had always considered that it was extremely unlikely that the 1839 Act could bear the full weight of a total ban on political activity around employment exchanges of the sort that Trenchard had decided to impose. In view of this, therefore, it was not altogether surprising that in replying to V La T McEntee, the Home Secretary, Sir Herbert Samuel, should have chosen not to mention the 1839 Act. Instead, drawing upon the precise instruction issued by the Commissioner, the Home Secretary asserted that Trenchard's action had been necessary 'since recent experience ha[d] shown that meetings held in such circumstances [were] liable to lead to breaches of the peace'.[193] The weakness in this assertion, of course, was that, the few episodes discussed above aside, there appeared to have been little or no such disorder until the police actions of 26–7 November. Yet, when asked whether 'the disturbances occurr[ed] before the police interfered or after',[194] Samuel replied:

The disturbances came first. There was interruption of the work at the Employment Exchanges, with disorder, and it was in consequence of that having occurred on several occasions that the Commissioner of Police, in the performance of his usual duties, thought it necessary that, at all events for the time

---

[190] Hannington, n 7 above, p 248.   [191] *The Times*, 2 December 1931.
[192] H C Debs, 2 December 1931, cols 1087–8 (V La T McEntee).
[193] Ibid, col 1088.   [194] Ibid, col 1089 (D Kirkwood).

being, meetings should not be held in the proximity of Employment Exchanges.[195]

It is not clear whether these disturbances were inside or outside the exchanges, or whether they flowed from or were independent of any political meetings that might or might not have been held. The Home Secretary offered the Commons no evidence of any of this, or of any of the disorder which he said had precipitated the ban. By the time of his annual report for the year 1931, Trenchard once again reiterated the public order rationale for the ban:

Owing to the assembly of hostile crowds outside labour exchanges, it became necessary to prohibit meetings in their immediate neighbourhood. Some cases of disorder occurred in consequence and Police Officers were injured. The moderation with which the Police behaved under trying circumstances was noteworthy.[196]

This explanation of the ban is revealing in that it appears to make clear that the problem with the crowds was that they were hostile rather than that they were violent, and that the disorder that did occur was a consequence of the ban, rather than the other way around, as the Home Secretary had asserted in the Commons the previous December. It was against this uncertain legal base for the ban that the newly formed Council for Civil Liberties sought to test it in the courts after it had been in operation for over two years.[197] The first step was a letter from the General Secretary Ronald Kidd on 29 May 1934, addressed to the Metropolitan Police Commissioner, objecting to the ban and demanding to know its legal basis. Having first been tempted to point to section 52, the Commissioner eventually replied only that he did not 'regard it as part of his duty to discuss with the Council for Civil Liberties the propriety of the measure or its legal sanction'.[198] The first concerted effort at a test case followed shortly afterwards, and was mounted at Stratford

---

[195] Ibid.

[196] Report of the Commissioner of Police of the Metropolis for the Year 1931, Cmd. 4137 (1932), p 31.

[197] Hannington, n 7 above, p 248 claims that the ban was withdrawn after two months but it is more likely that it was more or less rigorously enforced depending on the political atmosphere in the capital: see H C Debs, 2 May 1932, cols 877–8 (G Buchanan). Something like this ban may also have been in operation in other parts of the United Kingdom. In Paisley on 10 May 1935, for example two defendants who addressed a meeting of unemployed persons, and who refused to stop when required to do so, were successfully prosecuted on obstruction charges and jailed for 50 days without the option of a fine (they were released on 22 May after having launched an appeal): H C Debs, 23 May 1935, col 503 (N Maclean).

[198] See PRO, HO 144/20149), prohibition of meetings held in the vicinity of employment exchanges, n 183 above.

on 24 July 1934. The location of the labour exchange in that part of London was such that the protest meeting outside it could be held in a cul-de-sac, thereby minimising the opportunity available to the police to use obstruction of the highway as an effective (because well-established) legal cover with which to break up the meeting.

The Times reported the following day on what happened:

Several hundred people assembled near Stratford Labour Exchange yesterday for the purpose, it was said, of testing the validity of a ban imposed by the Home Secretary and Lord Trenchard on the holding of meetings in the vicinity of Labour Exchanges. The Chief Constable of the district and a number of plain clothes officers were present. The demonstration passed off in orderly fashion. The organisers attempted to place a movable platform in the street opposite the doors of the Labour Exchange, but they promptly agreed to a request of the Chief Constable to move to another spot in order not to cause any obstruction. Mr T. E. Groves, Labour M.P. for the Stratford Division said that the meeting would be the beginning of a campaign for the establishment of civic rights and the right to express their views.[199]

If what Groves and his colleagues desired was to be arrested, and this seems clearly to have been the case, then they were disappointed. The police contented themselves by allowing the meeting to continue. Groves' mistake seems to have been to have agreed to the alteration of location suggested by the police. Although the move was to a place only twenty yards away from the nearest door or window of the exchange, it gave the police an excuse not to act. The matter was raised in Parliament in the following week by Groves himself when he asked the Home Secretary to remove the Trenchard ban in view of the fact that the Stratford meeting had been 'of a very orderly character, necessitating no interference from the police and causing no annoyance or obstruction'. But the Home Secretary had no intention of having the ban revoked (even if he had the power), and explained that the meeting to which Groves referred had been 'held not outside the entrance to the exchange as was originally intended, but on another site . . . [at which no] disorder or obstruction occurred'.[200] The reality probably was that the authorities had no desire to arrest a Member of Parliament if they could possibly avoid it, particularly when the legal basis for any such action still seemed to hover

---

[199] *The Times*, 25 July 1934. For evidence that the campaign was inspired by the Council for Civil Liberties, see Groves' speech on the events in Stratford in the Commons adjournment debate: H C Debs, 31 July 1934, cols 2505–9. The *Daily Worker* reported the story on 25 July 1934 under the optimistic headline, 'The Trenchard dictatorship receives serious blow': *Daily Worker*, 25 July 1934.

[200] The interchange between Groves and the Home Secretary, Sir John Gilmour, is at H C Debs, 31 July 1934, cols 2471–2.

uncomfortably in an uncertain no-man's-land somewhere between obstruction and breach of the peace.[201]

A less benevolent response from the authorities was in evidence two days after Groves' Stratford meeting, when the campaign that the MP had there signalled against the ban tried to move into second gear. The focus was once more the Stratford exchange. Two men, Humphrey Slater and Albert Oram, set-up a portable platform at 10.30 am at exactly the same spot as Groves had planned to speak two days before. Once again the Chief Constable was in attendance and once again he asked that the meeting be moved twenty yards from the entrance, on the basis not of any anticipated breach of the peace but because this would prevent 'obstruction to persons going into or leaving the Labour Exchange'.[202] Unlike Groves, the two men did not comply with the police request. Slater began to address a meeting from his platform in a position which was a mere six yards from the entrance to the women's department of the exchange. When he resisted efforts to make him move, Oram came to his assistance and both men were promptly arrested, apparently for obstructing the officer in the execution of his duty. When the case reached the magistrates' court, the Chief Constable, Major George de Chair, explained his action by saying that he 'had received instructions from the Commissioner of Police to prevent any meetings outside labour exchanges, because such meetings had caused disorder'. Thus breach of the peace rather than obstruction of the highway had once again become the prominent factor in the exercise of the police dis-cretion, though here clearly it was less a matter of discretion than it was of obedience to superior orders, a point which raises its own questions of legality.[203] It was also open to question whether the power of arrest could be exercised before a breach of the peace had been witnessed by the arresting officer, or before the arresting officer had reason to believe that

---

[201] Thus explaining the nature of the ban in the course of his reply to a written parliamentary question, ibid, Gilmour asserted as its rationale that 'experience shows that meetings held in such circumstances are likely to lead to disorder and obstruction': ibid, col 2472.

[202] *The Times*, 27 July 1934. The quotes from this case that follow are drawn from *The Times* report. Further information can also be obtained from the comments of Sir John Gilmour in reply to questions at H C Debs, 30 July 1934, cols 229–33 and from the adjournment debate on the Stratford meetings the following day: H C Debs, 31 July 1934, cols 2505–12. A full account is also to be found in the *Daily Worker*, 27 July 1934; ibid, 28 July 1934.

[203] The exercise of a discretionary power should not be effectively transferred to another by unquestioningly accepting that other's opinion as to how it should be exercised. The then contem-porary authorities, rooted in statutory discretions vested in local authorities, were *Ellis v Dubowski* [1921] 3 KB 621 and *Mills v London County Council* [1925] 1 KB 213. From a slightly different point of view, see now *O'Hara v Chief Constable of the RUC* [1997] 1 All ER 129.

a breach of the peace was a real possibility.[204] For this purpose, it is now clear that there must exist 'proved facts from which a constable could reasonably have anticipated such a breach'.[205]

Slater and Oram both made strong efforts to turn their prosecution into a test case but they were foiled by the court and by the government's lawyers. Before their hearing commenced, the defendants applied for an adjournment three times. The dual purpose behind the first two of these requests was to enable them to obtain legal aid and to contact witnesses who would be able to give evidence that their meeting had caused no obstruction. The first request for an adjournment was for a week, the second was for a morning, and the third was for no more than ten minutes, to enable the defendants to make contact with the witnesses they wanted, who were just outside the courtroom as the case came on for hearing. Each of these three requests was opposed by the Crown and rejected by the court, the prosecution's lawyer being Travers Humphreys, a future judge and son of the High Court judge of the same name whom we have already frequently encountered and whom we are shortly to see in action once again. Deprived of his adjournments, Oram made no defence to the charge against him. Slater in contrast asserted that there had been 'no real obstruction' and that at the earlier meeting, Groves had spoken 'with the intention of being arrested in order to bring before the Court a test case as to whether meetings could not be held outside labour exchanges, so long as they did not cause obstruction'. Both men were convicted with the Chairman of the magistrates' bench observing that the 'accused must realise that every precaution should be taken for the safety of those attending labour exchanges'. Slater was fined 40 shillings with £2 2s costs. Oram was fined 20s with £1 1s costs. An obviously embarrassed Groves pleaded in Parliament with the Under Secretary of State for the Home Department, Captain Crookshank, for remission of penalty for both men. This was unsuccessful, with the Captain rather superciliously declaring that 'to put it mildly', it was 'inconvenient . . . [and] hardly fair to the officials in the Exchanges [to have] . . . the pandemonium of a public meeting just outside'.[206]

It was against this background of failed attempts at a test case, and of other deliberate transgressions of the Trenchard ban that also occurred at this time,[207] that Mrs Katherine Sinclair Duncan made her famous

---

[204] See now *Piddington v Bates* [1960] 3 All ER 660; *Moss v McLachlan* [1985] IRLR 76.

[205] *Piddington v Bates*, n 204 above, at p 663.   [206] H C Debs, 31 July 1934, col 2509.

[207] See *Daily Worker*, 3 August 1934 for the case of Claud Cockburn from the Council for Civil Liberties, charged with a colleague from the NUWM with obstruction for having attempted to hold a meeting outside Battersea labour exchange on 1 August.

decision to address a meeting outside the Nynehead Street training centre on 30 July 1934, a mere three days after Slater and Oram had been convicted and fined. Mrs Duncan was a well-known radical and a leading member of the NUWM with a long history of political activism, having been jailed for a month in 1932 for refusing to be bound over to be of good behaviour.[208] The evidence against her was supplied mainly by a solicitor named Clayton who heard her speak at a public meeting in Bermondsey Town Hall in 1931, with vital corroborative support being provided by a Detective Inspector Jones of the Special Branch, who had also been present at the meeting and who supplied the court with details of what he had written down from memory shortly after its conclusion.[209] Now, three years later, Jones was back on Duncan's path, literally. Like the Stratford protests, the meeting at Nynehead Street took place in a cul-de-sac with houses on one side and the training centre on the other. It was specially contrived to make it impossible for the authorities not to act if they were at all serious about enforcing the Trenchard ban. The meeting was advertised by chalkmarks on the roadway headed 'sedition' and was called in order, it was said, to 'defend the right of free speech and public meeting'.[210] Those present and planning to speak included the general secretary of the Council for Civil Liberties, Ronald Kidd, the barrister A Bing and E Hanley from the Amalgamated Engineering Union. Inspector Jones and the local chief constable were also hovering in the background, together with an acting superintendent, another inspector, a sergeant and no fewer than ten constables.

Freedom of Assembly: the High Court's Decisive Blow

When Mrs Duncan commenced proceedings by mounting her soap box and beginning her address to the crowd (which by now numbered about

---

[208] Mrs Duncan had her own dedicated Home Office file, but it is closed for 100 years: Kath Sinclair Duncan, Communist: obstruction of police and breach of the peace, 1932–4 (PRO, HO 144/19284).

[209] See George Lansbury's account of these 1932 proceedings at H C Debs, 22 December 1932, cols 1275–81.

[210] Chalkmarks were a favourite device in the 1930s for advertising political meetings. Perhaps inevitably therefore, the authorities were antagonistic to the creators of such markings. In early 1934, a man was bound over for 'defacing a church wall with a notice about "hunger marchers" ': (1934) 98 JP 66. The issue had provoked a strong editorial line from the *Justice of the Peace* the year before, after two men had been convicted at the West Ham police court for chalking words which the magistrate described as insulting within the meaning of s 54(13) of the Metropolitan Police Act 1839. Under the heading 'The Chalk Nuisance', the journal declared that the 'highway [was] not the proper place on which to propagate political or economic theories by means of the written word': (1933) 97 JP 18.

thirty), Inspector Jones intervened, and requested that Mrs Duncan switch the location of the meeting to a spot on another street some 175 yards away. This was a far more draconian request than Groves, Oram and Slater had had to face, and it was inevitable that it would be rejected. When Duncan refused to comply, she was immediately arrested and charged with the obstruction of a police officer in the execution of his duty, contrary to the Prevention of Crimes Act 1871, section 12, as amended by the Prevention of Crimes Amendment Act 1885, section 2. The case came before the magistrate a week later, and astonishingly no mention appears to have been made of the Trenchard ban. Neither was any attention drawn by the prosecution to section 52 of the Metropolitan Police Act 1839, which as we have seen had been considered by the police to be one of the legal bases of the ban when it had been contemplating its response to Kidd's letter. The irrelevance of this provision to Duncan's small meeting in a cul-de-sac must have been immediately obvious to Crown counsel. Instead, like Sir Herbert Samuel nearly three years before, and reflecting the original terms of the Trenchard ban, the whole emphasis in the case was on Jones having acted as he did to prevent a reasonably apprehended breach of the peace. The magistrate was informed that the 'superintendent at the training centre had asked for the police in consequence of a riot that [had] followed a meeting held outside the centre once before', and that it had been this earlier incident which had underpinned Jones's perfectly legitimate (so it was said) apprehension about the consequences of the meeting now. The secret police report to the Home Office in the immediate aftermath of the incident makes no mention of any such disorder, but it was enough to sink the test case. Duncan was duly convicted, and fined 40s with five guineas costs.

This talk of riot was heady stuff and it was hardly surprising that in light of it the magistrate had felt compelled to convict. When the case was taken on appeal to the London sessions, however, the riot had mysteriously disappeared, and had been replaced by allegations of a much milder protest of a quite different sort. A report in *The Times* throws the following interesting perspective on the factual basis for Jones' supposed fears:

On May 25, 1933 . . . a meeting had been held opposite the entrance to the training centre which Mrs Duncan addressed, and after that meeting a disturbance took place at the training centre. The superintendent of the training centre, who attributed the disturbance to the meeting, sent for the police to prevent a breach of the peace. Subsequently Mrs Duncan made one or more attempts to hold a meeting at the same spot, which attempts were frustrated by the police. Before July 30, 1934, the superintendent of the training centre, who feared a repetition of the previous disturbance, communicated with the police, and, by reason of that communication and of reports made by the police, the chief constable of the district and the Inspector apprehended that a breach of the peace would result if the meeting of July 30, 1934, were held.[211]

The continuing absence of any reference to the Trenchard ban adds a dimension of the surreal to such a careful recounting of fact. Even accepting this version of events, Jones' fears of an imminent breach of the peace would seem to have been rather overstated. The trouble that had occurred previously had been inside rather than outside the centre and two former employees gave evidence to the appeal court to the effect that it had arisen 'in the centre from discontent and not because of a meeting outside'.[212] There was even doubt as to whether it had been at Nynehead Street or at a neighbouring centre that this supposed disturbance had occurred.[213] The London sessions, however, dismissed Duncan's appeal, with the deputy chairman Sir Herbert Wilberforce observing that 'the only point was whether the police had reasonable cause to believe that a breach of the peace was likely to [have been] caused'.[214] Clearly the bench was disposed to accept Jones' word. The case was then taken to the Divisional Court on a point of law about the extent of the power of the police in respect of political meetings. The platform for the test case had been finally erected.

The case came on for argument on 16 October 1935, before a Divisional Court composed of Lord Hewart LCJ, Humphreys J and Singleton J. We have already met two of these judicial personalities on several occasions. As Travers Humphreys QC, the second had been chief Crown prosecution counsel in the communist trials nearly ten years before.[215] He had also been involved in some of the disaffection cases that preceded the enactment of the Incitement to Disaffection Act 1934. The Lord Chief Justice, Gordon Hewart, had an even longer record of involvement in the issues discussed in earlier chapters. In 1916, as the then Liberal MP for Leicester, he had been knighted and appointed to the post of Solicitor General in Lloyd George's war-time administration. As such he would certainly have been required to take a view on the draconian controls on freedom of assembly that were promulgated under the Defence of the Realm Acts in that year.[216] When the time came for the

---

[211] *The Times*, 17 October 1935.
[212] Ibid. See further H C Debs, 10 July 1936, cols 1559–60 (D N Pritt).
[213] See Kidd, n 177 above, p 23.   [214] *The Times*, 17 October 1935.
[215] See Chapter 3 above.   [216] For the details see Chapter 2 above.

enforcement of a similar regulation under the state of emergency proclaimed in 1921, Hewart had progressed to the Attorney Generalship
and a place in the Cabinet.[217] In such a position of seniority he would
have been intimately involved in the application of this and of all the
other emergency regulations of the day. Indeed so valuable an ally to the
Prime Minister was he that Lloyd George was prepared to flout convention in order to ensure that he did not take the Lord Chief Justiceship
immediately upon Reading's assumption of the Viceroyalty of India in
1921.[218] There can be little doubt that so political a figure as Hewart
would have quickly recalled the resemblance between the police action
in *Duncan* and the Regulations he had earlier patrolled on behalf of the
State; it is also not unlikely that he would have been aware of the
Trenchard ban and of the public controversy that had surrounded it in
the years since its imposition.

This was the presiding judge before whom D N Pritt and the Liberal
MP Dingle Foot launched their oral argument in *Duncan v Jones*. These
two distinguished civil libertarians concentrated their rhetorical fire on
the leading Victorian authority of *Beatty v Gillbanks*.[219] Such a tactical
decision was hardly surprising. This famous and frequently cited case
appeared to reflect a common law commitment to just the sort of freedom of assembly that was in issue in the case before the court, and as we
have seen it had been treated by no less an authority than Professor
Dicey as exemplifying what he considered to be the civil libertarian
strength of the common law.[220] And as we saw in Chapter 4 above, it
was frequently cited in Parliament during the debates about the emergency legislation in 1926: such was its political and legal significance. It
will be remembered that in *Beatty*, the appellants (who were members of
the Salvation Army) had been held by the Divisional Court to be entitled to assemble for a lawful purpose, despite there having been good reason to suppose that the effect of their gathering would have been to cause
their opponents (the 'Skeleton Army') to commit breaches of the peace.
Pritt and Foot accepted that the precise charge in that case differed from
the one before the court, but they confidently submitted that the same
principle governed both situations. The attraction of the precedent from
their point of view was that it could be said to protect Duncan even if

[217] For the details of the relevant regulation, Regulation 20, see Chapter 2 above.
[218] For further details on the extraordinary story of his eventual appointment see Chapter 2 above.
[219] (1882) 9 QBD 308. See Chapter 1 above.
[220] Counsel cited Dicey's, *Law of the Constitution* (8th edn, 1915), p 508.

(and it was never admitted) there had been a disturbance which had resulted from an earlier meeting which she had held, since, applying *Beatty*, she could not be taken to be 'responsible for those who caused it, and the bad conduct of another person cannot make that wrong which is otherwise innocent'.[221] For once, therefore, it was the mainstream of the English common law tradition, rather than some cleverly worked nook or cranny, that was being deployed in the defendant's favour in a political case. Quite simply, the police should have moved against those acting or proposing to act unlawfully, not those acting lawfully.

It might have been thought that the author of *The New Despotism* would have had a sympathetic ear for arguments rooted in the old common law about police excess which were put before him on Mrs Duncan's behalf. In fact Hewart's 1929 polemic had not given any very great impression of being concerned with excessive State power except insofar as it operated to the detriment of the wealthy in society.[222] Indeed the *Scots Law Times* had commented of the book that 'Lord Hewart might have done better service if he had not weakened his case by unfortunate illustrations and by a somewhat intemperate and violent use of language more suited to his former role of politician than to the judicial calm expected of a Lord Chief Justice'.[223] But whatever his political skills, Hewart is now more frequently remembered as 'perhaps the worst Chief Justice since the seventeenth century, not as being dishonest but as lacking dignity, fairness and a sense of justice'.[224] It was distinctly Hewart the former law officer rather than Hewart the (selective) scourge of the executive that Pritt and Foot found listening impatiently to their submissions. Counsel for the police had barely got into his stride when he was stopped by the court, which then invited Pritt to sum up the arguments for his side. Having heard these out, the court then unanimously dismissed Duncan's appeal, without bothering even to reserve judgment so as to be able further to reflect either on what the result should be or on how the decision should be phrased. The result of such speedy adjudication was a decision which is as noteworthy today for the vacuity of its reasoning as for its long term deleterious effect on civil liberties. The case is well known for the latter, and frequently applied by the police, though its historical context has long been forgotten. Also neglected has been the mode of legal

---

[221] *Duncan v Jones* [1936] 1 KB 216 at p 221, citing *R v Londonderry Justices* (1891) 28 LR Ir 440.

[222] But see the following passage, not further developed, which appeared to support the principle in *Beatty*: '[A] public meeting, if otherwise lawful, does not become unlawful merely because it is prohibited by a Secretary of State or magistrate, or by the police': Lord Hewart, *The New Despotism* (1929), p 32. Of course the statement begs the question as to when a meeting can be characterised as unlawful.

[223] 1930 SLT (News) 36.   [224] D M Walker, *Oxford Companion to Law* (1980), p 565.

reasoning deployed by the three judges who heard the case, and it is to these judgments that we now turn. There are few better illustrations in the law reports of the political dimension to the supposedly autonomous common law.

The leading judgment was that of the Chief Justice, though this seems an odd way of describing fifty-five lines in four paragraphs dealing with a matter of this political and legal significance. Hewart commenced by making clear what he considered the case not to be about:

There have been moments during the argument in this case when it appeared to be suggested that the Court had to do with a grave case involving what is called the right of public meeting. I say 'called,' because English law does not recognise any special right of public meeting for political or other purposes. The right of assembly, as Professor Dicey puts it, is nothing more than a view taken by the Court of the individual liberty of the subject. If I thought that the present case raised a question which has been held in suspense by more than one writer on constitutional law—namely, whether an assembly can properly be held to be unlawful merely because the holding of it is expected to give rise to a breach of the peace on the part of the persons opposed to those who are holding the meeting—I should wish to hear much more argument before I expressed an opinion. This case, however, does not even touch that important question.[225]

It is true that this may not have been the precise issue raised by the case; there were no hordes of antagonistic workers waiting to beat up Duncan if she continued to speak, thereby fortuitously bringing the issue of her protection full square within Lord Hewart's 'important question'. But simply on that account to dismiss the whole notion that the case had anything at all to do with the right to hold a public meeting is remarkable. The right of public protest must include, if it is to mean anything at all, the liberty to speak to people who want to hear you, whether or not there are others present not inclined to let you communicate. If anything, the simple matter of addressing a crowd without hindrance raises a far more obvious and simple issue of free speech than the more complicated situation where a speaker's communication is causing opponents to resort to violence. It is hard not to resist the conclusion that the only purpose of Hewart's distinction was to enable him to dispense with the precedential power of *Beatty v Gillbanks*, and he may indeed have had a point in wanting to do this.

---

[225] [1936] 1 KB 216, at pp 221–2.

It would have been well known to Hewart that the police had in the past regularly and without legal challenge acted in precisely the way that Mrs Duncan and her civil libertarian colleagues now thought both obnoxious and unlawful. Quite apart from the Trenchard ban, we shall see in the next chapter how frequently the police deployed a *Duncan v Jones* power in advance of the case itself to limit the liberty of anti-fascist protestors in the early 1930s.[226] In a case from Sheffield in 1926 to which we have referred in Chapter 3 above, one Harry Webb had been prevented by the police from speaking to a crowd outside a factory gate despite the lack of any violence and the fact that meetings had been regularly held at that precise spot for some twenty years.[227] It may be that it was this informal world of *de facto* police power that Hewart had in mind when he turned to *Beatty v Gillbanks*:

Our attention has been directed to the somewhat unsatisfactory case of *Beatty* v *Gillbanks*. The circumstances of that case and the charge must be remembered, as also must the important passage in the judgment of Field J., in which Cave J. concurred. Field J. said: 'I entirely concede that every one must be taken to intend the natural consequences of his own acts, and it is clear to me that if this disturbance of the peace was a natural consequence of acts of the appellants they would be liable, and the justices would have been right in binding them over. But the evidence set forth in the case does not support this contention; on the contrary, it shows that the disturbances were caused by other people antagonistic to the appellants, and that no acts of violence were committed by them'. Our attention has also been directed to other authorities where the judgments in *Beatty v Gillbanks* have been referred to, but they do not carry the matter any further, although they more than once express a doubt about the exact meaning of the decision. In my view, *Beatty v Gillbanks* is apart from the present case. No such question as that which arose there is even mooted here.[228]

This is the common law at its least persuasive. The decision is 'somewhat unsatisfactory' (for reasons not explained); its 'circumstances . . . and . . . charge must be remembered' (though neither is explicitly recalled); 'the important passage' in Field J's judgment is in fact a casual concession to counsel and wholly obiter; the 'other authorities' which 'more than once' doubt *Beatty*'s meaning are not referred to. All this is designed to attach a kind of spurious credibility to the extraordinary conclusion that *Beatty* is 'apart from the present case'.

---

[226] See in particular Chapter 6 below.

[227] *Workers' Weekly*, 26 March 1926. The freedom of communists to hold meetings at this spot was only restored following a deputation to the acting chief constable from members of the Party and employees engaged in the factory. See Chapter 3 above.

[228] [1936] 1 KB 216, at p 222.

Freed of this key precedent, Hewart devotes his penultimate paragraph to an obscure *dictum* from a case dealing with licensed premises, which he erects to the level of a principle:

The present case reminds one rather of the observations of Bramwell B. in *Reg. v Prebble*,[229] where, in holding that a constable, in clearing certain licensed premises of the persons thereon, was not acting in the execution of his duty, he said: 'It would have been otherwise had there been a nuisance or disturbance of the public peace, or any danger of a breach of the peace'.

Armed with this quotation, Hewart then returns with confidence to the facts before him, concluding his judgment in the following way:

The case stated which we have before us indicates clearly a causal connection between the meeting of May, 1933, and the disturbance which occurred after it—that the disturbance was not only post the meeting but was also propter the meeting. In my view, the deputy-chairman was entitled to come to the conclusion to which he came on the facts which he found and to hold that the conviction of the appellant for wilfully obstructing the respondent when in the execution of his duty was right. This appeal should, therefore, be dismissed.[230]

Like the Chief Justice, Humphreys J also saw the decision as 'a plain case' having 'nothing to do with the law of unlawful assembly'.[231] This part of the common law was so obvious that discovery of it did not require evidence of case law in the ordinary way: 'It does not require authority to emphasise the statement that it is the duty of a police officer to prevent apprehended breaches of the peace'.[232] Armed with this awareness of the law, Humphreys J could naturally 'conceive [of] no clearer case within the statutes than' the one before him.[233] Singleton J was similarly emphatic in his seven line concurring judgment, remarking with *Beatty* probably primarily in his mind that '[a]uthorities in other branches of the law do not carry the matter any further'.[234]

Much of the academic scholarship on *Duncan v Jones* has been devoted to attempts to reconcile it with *Beatty v Gillbanks*.[235] Contemporary critics of the decision were less interested in its technical virtues or vices than in its effect on the powers of the police. One treatise, published in 1934, commented that before the case 'it was taken for granted that the powers of the police authorities to prevent the holding of a meeting on a pub-

---

[229] (1858) 1 F & F 325, at p 326.   [230] [1936] 1 KB 216, at p 223.
[231] Ibid.   [232] Ibid.   [233] Ibid.   [234] Ibid, at p 224.
[235] Williams, n 180 above, pp 120–3; H Street and R Brazier (eds.), *de Smith's Constitutional and Administrative Law* (4th edn, 1981), pp 504–6; T C Daintith, 'Disobeying a Policeman—A Fresh Look at *Duncan v Jones*' [1966] *Public Law* 248.

lic highway were limited to cases of obstruction, breaches of the peace and disorderly conduct' but that *Duncan v Jones* now showed that 'much greater powers' were in fact available to them.[236] The disappointed General Secretary of the Council for Civil Liberties Ronald Kidd thought the decision 'perfectly clear':

It establishes the precedent that the police have power to ban any political meeting in streets or public places at will: no matter that such meetings are held in blind alleys where they cannot interfere with traffic; no matter that they are peacefully conducted; no matter that they are local people's only means of ventilating their opinions or pressing for redress of grievances. The police are set up by this judgment as the arbiters of what political parties or religious sects shall and shall not be accorded the rights of freedom of speech and freedom of assembly—two civil rights which even the judges of earlier times were jealous to protect.[237]

Writing in a similar vein in the *Cambridge Law Journal*, E C S Wade considered that since *Duncan v Jones*, 'the net has closed entirely upon those who from lack of resources, or for other reasons, desire to hold meetings in public places'.[238] Wade understood that the Home Office was 'satisfied that the powers of the police to deal with disorder at public meetings [were] sufficient'.[239] This was surely correct. The last thing the authorities now wanted was statutory clarification, a point made with typical acumen in the pages of the *Police Journal*:

[T]here is often uncertainty as to the meaning of an Act of Parliament and its application to particular facts. Indeed it is manifest that the police are better served by the common law—with all its elasticity and adaptability—than they would be by any rigid statutory code; and in our view at any rate their existing powers at common law, including the power of taking preventive action in connection with apprehended breaches of the peace and the power of dispersing an unlawful assembly or a riot, are sufficient to enable the police to discharge effectively their responsibilities.[240]

It would appear from the Home Office files that this article was in fact contributed by a departmental official. The department's chief anxiety about *Duncan* when it was decided was with whether or not it required evidence of a previous disturbance before the police could be said to be justified in breaking up a meeting. Having carefully perused the decision,

---

[236] J Baker, *The Law of Political Uniforms, Public Meetings and Private Armies* (1937), p 75.
[237] Kidd, n 177 above, p 24. But see now *Redmond-Bate v DPP*, The Times, 28 July 1999.
[238] E C S Wade, 'Police Powers and Public Meetings' (1936–9) 6 CLJ 175, at p 179.
[239] Ibid.
[240] Anon. (1936) 9 *Police Journal* 18. See *Davies v Griffiths* (1937) 30 Cox's CC 595.

an official minute recorded that evidence of such earlier disorder was not required, and had merely been evidence of the reasonableness of the police apprehension in the case before the court. The departmental minute ended with an assurance to colleagues that 'We may sleep in our beds'.[241]

When Pritt sought to raise the case in the Commons during a Home Office supply debate, the Home Secretary, Sir John Simon, intervened to enquire in mock horror whether he was being asked to 'champion the view of the Lord Chief Justice against the view of the hon and learned Gentleman'.[242] The deputy-chairman overseeing the debate promptly intervened to remind Pritt that '[w]hat is laid down by a competent court of law we must regard at the moment as being the law of the country. On Supply we must not discuss matters involving legislation'.[243] Pritt duly conformed, stressing that he had had 'no intention whatever of discussing the court' and that his only concern was that:

the law is in such a difficult state that it is extremely easy for the police to take repressive measures and find that often they are approved of by the courts as acting in accordance with the law. I am criticising the police alone.[244]

It was, however, a matter of great concern to Pritt that 'the moment [he began] to attack the police the right hon. Gentleman, having one of the acutest minds in England, thinks naturally and inevitably that [he] must be attacking the court instead'.[245] Nevertheless there can be no better illustration of the covert nature of judicial law-making. Like *Elias v Pasmore* before it, the legal status of *Duncan v Jones* insulated it from political criticism, and this was regardless of the novelty of its repressiveness, the obviousness of its political bias or the faultiness of its reasoning. At least the Emergency Regulations which were the forefathers of *Duncan v Jones* had required the Lord Hewarts of the political world to defend their content in Parliament, explaining their necessity and what was required to be done under their authority. Now as Lord Chief Justice, no elected representative was allowed even to discuss, much less criticise or condemn, Gordon Hewart's draconian law-making.

---

[241] See (PRO, HO/144/20149). Prohibition of meetings held in the vicinity of employment exchanges, n 183 above.

[242] H C Debs, 10 July 1936, col 1561.   [243] Ibid.   [244] Ibid.

[245] Ibid, col 1562. Pritt in fact mounted a damning attack on the police and their failure to intervene 'to restrain breaches of the peace and not to restrain other people from pursuing perfectly lawful activities'. He compared the *Duncan* case with the willingness of the police to spend thousands of pounds to give a platform to Mosley 'however many breaches of the peace might follow': ibid.

Conclusion

In this chapter we have seen a continuation of the deployment of the full force of the law against the Communist Party, directly in respect of the Incitement to Disaffection Act 1934 and indirectly in respect of the action against the NUWM. Even if our earlier chapters had not prepared us for such a conclusion, the sheer inappropriateness of Dicey's approach to the Rule of Law would have been made unavoidably clear by the events and cases that we have discussed. Indeed it is hard to say which of the limbs to Dicey's three-pronged definition is the more fatally undermined by the circumstances we have chronicled. The binding over orders used to clear the political leadership of the NUWM out of the way at critical moments could hardly be said to have endorsed Dicey's claim that 'no man is punishable or can be lawfully made to suffer in body or goods except for a distinct breach of the law established in the ordinary legal manner before the ordinary courts of the land'. While Dicey's second principle might indeed be true, that 'here every man, whatever be his rank or condition, is subject to the ordinary law of the realm and amenable to the jurisdiction of the ordinary courts', the clear message to flow from this chapter is that some men (and women) were a great deal more amenable than were others, a point that will be made even clearer when we discuss the treatment of the fascists by the law in the following chapter. But perhaps the principle most mocked by this chapter is Dicey's third, in which he claims that 'the general principles of the constitution (as for example the right to personal liberty, or the right of public meeting) are with us the result of judicial decisions determining the rights of private persons in particular cases brought before the courts'. To put it at its very mildest, the decisions discussed in this chapter sit uneasily with such a grandiose, civil libertarian claim.

From the perspective of *constitutional principle*, the events dealt with in this chapter reinforce earlier conclusions about the fragility of the Rule of Law in times of State anxiety or perceived emergency. This chapter more closely recalls part of the story told in Chapter 3 than it does those recounted in Chapters 2 or 4 because here, just as in the mid-1920s in respect of the actions taken at that time against the Communist Party, the State found itself conducting its campaign of oppression through the medium of ordinary rather than emergency law. The overriding impression is of all three branches of government joined in hostile action against a radical minority. This might be expected from a government that was for much of the period of discussion in this chapter dominated by the Conservative Party, and therefore by many of the political actors who had been closely involved in the anti-communist actions of the 1920s. As we have seen, however, this process also involved both the legislative and the judicial branches of the State. As far as the first of these is concerned, the enactment of the Incitement to Disaffection Act 1934 marked the introduction into the law in a permanent form of police powers and substantive offences that had hitherto been regarded as unacceptably broad and therefore permissible only in exceptional circumstances. Indeed it was an understanding of this dimension to the Bill that underlay much of the hostility with which it was greeted when first introduced in Parliament. Though Parliament was eventually persuaded to pass the measure, it was during the debates on the Incitement to Disaffection Act that the legislative body came closer than it has yet done in the course of this book to appreciating that its function was the double-sided one discussed in Chapter 1, namely to hold the executive to account as well as to legislate at its invitation.

As far as the judiciary is concerned, the story is very much grimmer. The cases discussed here achieved the transformation of what had been emergency law into the mainstream of the common law. But *Elias v Pasmore* and *Duncan v Jones* go even further than this, in that they represent what amounts to the retrospective according of judicial legitimacy to executive acts previously considered of, at the very least, doubtful legality. Nothing more explodes the idea of a judicial branch ever-vigilant on liberty's behalf than the casually restrictive judgments of Horridge J in *Elias v Pasmore* and Hewart LCJ and his colleagues in *Duncan v Jones*. After the latter decision in particular, it becomes impossible to view *Beatty v Gillbanks* as other than the eccentric exception that it truly was, whatever Dicey may have thought of it when compiling his Oxford lectures on the constitution in 1885. The senior judiciary's particular contribution to the history of civil liberties in the 1930s was to extend the executive's repressive power into the ordinary law, without any of the publicity, accountability or clarity that had been so damaging to the executive during the passage of the 1934 Act. But what was also troubling about the common law development was the sheer scale of discretion which was conferred as a result on the police, whether it be to seize papers in the course of a raid (a practice which could be justified by what was found), or equally significantly, in the power simply to ban a political meeting on the flimsiest of grounds. This will become much clearer in the following chapter.

Turning now to the lessons for *constitutional practice* from this chapter, we see once again in this book the spectacle of a State mobilising all its branches to control forms of political speech and public protest of which it vehemently disapproved. It might be expected that the police would view with distaste the mass meetings and processions that marked the era of the hunger marches in Britain, but it still comes as something of a surprise to learn of the extent of the lawless violence that they meted out to such protestors, apparently without fear of punishment or subsequent legal proceedings. As was the case in Chapter 3, once again we see the secret service engaged in predictable canvassing for further repression, this time in relation to the Incitement to Disaffection Act. Most depressing of all, however, is the enthusiastic willingness of successive governments and the courts to go along with, and indeed occasionally to amplify, such reflexive repressiveness. The values of liberty and freedom to which many senior figures in British politics and law declared themselves genuinely committed during this period seem to have had no connection whatsoever in their own minds with the clamping down on the civil liberties of members of the CPGB and the NUWM in which so many of them were at exactly the same time so actively involved. As that emblematic figure from the 1920s, William Joynson-Hicks, had so precisely put it during that earlier period of State coercion, the problem with the exercise of traditional civil liberties in such contexts was that they did not involve 'the right kind of freedom of speech'.[246]

One of the most significant new developments during the period recorded in this chapter was the establishment of the NCCL.[247] Its moving spirit, Ronald Hubert Kidd, had campaigned for women's suffrage and lectured for the Workers' Educational Association before going into service in the First World War. Having subsequently been employed as a civil servant and an actor, his background made him in some ways an unexpected but in others an ideal head of a national movement for the protection of liberty. His rise to prominence had been triggered by a public exchange of views in August 1933 with the well known writer A P Herbert on the use of agents provocateurs by the police, a dialogue which Kidd had cleverly widened to embrace this sort of police activity in the context of the hunger marches. Early in 1934, a provisional committee was set up with representatives drawn from the arts, literature, journalism, medicine and the law. A circular letter drawing attention to the new Council for Civil Liberties dated 1 February 1934 drew still wider support, and the Council's effective interventions in the debate about the Incitement to Disaffection Bill that then ensued guaranteed its successful

---

[246] See Chapter 3 above.
[247] The details that follow are drawn from B Dyson, *Liberty in Britain, 1934–94* (1994), ch 1.

establishment as part of British civil society. But its strategy of using the courts to secure better protection for political freedom did not prove successful, with *Duncan v Jones* having long outlived the Trenchard ban as a source of open-ended police power to restrict civil liberties. The organisation's tactical use of the courts raises full-square the question of whether the Rule of Law can function as a guardian of civil liberties, a point of central importance to this book, and one to which we shall return in the chapters that follow.

6

The Rise and Fall of Fascism

In this chapter, our central concern is with the rise of the British Union of Fascists (BUF) and with the crisis of disorder that the movement's style of political campaigning provoked.[1] In our first section, we trace the origin and growth of British fascism before then proceeding to consider in detail the political and civil libertarian context of one of the most dramatic occasions of the inter-war period, the June 1934 BUF meeting in Olympia and the disorder which it both caused and provoked. In our third section we examine *Thomas v Sawkins*,[2] an important case which belongs with *Elias v Pasmore*[3] and *Duncan v Jones*[4] to that trilogy of Divisional Court decisions for which the 1930s has always been remembered by public lawyers. But its significance lies principally in the context of partisan policing practices, a point that is further developed in our fourth part when we discuss the policing of fascist meetings and demonstrations in the post-Olympia period. At exactly the time that the police were cracking down on the Left in ways that we have earlier discussed, they were also choosing to devote considerable time and resources to protecting the right of fascists both to march and to hold public meetings. It was in the exercise of their discretion in respect of these right wing groups that the police were invariably able to rediscover a nineteenth century style dedication to political liberty and to free speech that had been and continued to be totally lacking in their approach to the Left.

In the remaining sections of this chapter we deal with the political and extra-parliamentary pressure for legislation against the fascists which culminated in what became known as the 'Battle of Cable Street', and with the legislation—the Public Order Act 1936—which this disorder helped at least in part to bring about. In a way that mirrored the support shown to the fascists by the police, the government had for years excused its own legislative inertia in this field by deploying a rhetoric of freedom and tolerance that had rarely if ever surfaced when it was NUWM or communist-inspired agitation that was being attacked. The main effect of the Public Order Act was not only to control fascism (explicit support for

---

[1] For a general account see G D Anderson, *Fascists, Communists, and the National Government: Civil Liberties in Great Britain, 1931–37* (1983).

[2] [1935] 2 KB 249.   [3] [1934] 2 KB 164. See Chapter 5 above.

[4] [1936] 1 KB 216. See Chapter 5 above.

which was already on the wane by the end of 1936) but also to impose a further clampdown on radical protest in London and across the country. But we will also see how the old, tried and trusted means of dealing with dissent were by no means superseded by the Act. The overarching theme of this chapter is therefore the extent to which a Rule of Law that is based on little more than official discretion can be speedily debased by the prejudices and predispositions of those in power.

The Rise of Fascism

Though now inevitably connected in the public mind with the character and ambitions of one man, Sir Oswald Mosley, British fascism started as early as 1923, with the establishment of the Fascisti by the twenty-six-year-old Miss R L Lintorn-Orman, the daughter of a major and the granddaughter of a field-marshal.[5] The organisation's political roots were mainly in middle-class pressure groups such as the British Empire Union, the Middle-Classes Union and the National Citizens' Union. These were bodies which had 'evolved at the end of the war to protect property against the alleged socialist menace'.[6] There was some working class support from the start, with H Havelock Wilson of the Seaman's Union, a stalwart of working class anti-socialist movements,[7] having addressed an anti-Bolshevik meeting stewarded by 600 fascists at the Royal Albert Hall as early as 1926.[8] In the 1920s, fascism also attracted the support of a range of establishment figures who hoped that it might become a populist bulwark against what was still seen as the lively threat of communism. The official attitude to the far Right was even then substantially more tolerant than it was to the Left, a point well illustrated by the Home Secretary Sir William Joynson-Hicks's admission to the Commons in 1925 that there was no bar on police membership of the British Fascisti (though he did at least go on to assure the House that 'it would not be considered desirable for a constable to join this body').[9] There were some curious incidents of fascist violence in these early years, such as the kidnapping of Harry Pollitt in 1925[10] and an attack on a *Daily Herald*

---

[5] R Benewick, *The Fascist Movement in Britain* (1972), p 27. See also S G Payne, *A History of Fascism, 1914–45* (1995), R Griffiths, *Patriotism Perverted: Captain Ramsay, the Right Club and British Anti-Semitism 1939–40* (1998).

[6] R Thurlow, *Fascism in Britain, A History, 1918–85* (1987), p 51.

[7] See *Cotter v NUS* [1929] 2 Ch 58.   [8] Thurlow, n 6 above.

[9] H C Debs, 24 June 1925, col 1552 (Sir W Joynson-Hicks) (WA).

[10] On which see H C Debs, 16 March 1925, cols 1858–60; H C Debs, 17 March 1925, cols 2075–7; H C Debs, 19 March 1925, cols 2447–8.

delivery van in the same year,[11] but the fascist movements of the period were generally too fragmented and divided to be other than a peripheral nuisance. Certainly they did not attract the same attention from the Special Branch as did the Communist Party, a matter which was raised by the defendants during the 1925 sedition trial.[12]

This situation changed with the formation by Mosley of the BUF in the Autumn of 1932, at exactly the time when the radical agitation of the NUWM, discussed in the preceding chapter, was coming to its first political climax. The movement was established after the calamitous performance of Mosley's New Party in the 1931 general election, and was initially comprised of followers both of Mosley and of Lintorn-Orman. According to Mosley, fascism 'was in essence a national creed' and his version of it in Britain presented it as 'an explosion against intolerable conditions, against remediable wrongs which the old world had failed to remedy'.[13] Lord Nuffield had given £50,000 to Mosley when he had launched the New Party,[14] and the BUF attracted the financial support of Lord Rothermere and of '[i]industrialists and merchants of more moderate stature [who] used also to support [the Party's] headquarters'.[15] Mosley claims to have given some £100,000 of his own money to the organisation[16] and although the question of foreign funding is in the words of his biographer 'impenetrably obscure', it is highly probable that Mussolini was an important financial patron in the critical early years.[17] As we shall see, the BUF enjoyed a meteoric rise in popularity during 1933 to 1934, until the controversy over Olympia set it back somewhat, with numbers stabilising at around 16,000 by late 1936. During this post-Olympia hiatus, membership became temporarily more restricted than previously to working class supporters drawn from the north of England and the East End of London, but by the following year the middle class had returned in sufficient numbers to give back to the organisation much of its earlier social base.[18] While it never returned to the levels of support it enjoyed in the first two years of its existence, the BUF represented a challenge to the established order throughout much of the 1930s

---

[11] See H C Debs, 16 November 1925, cols 25–7; H C Debs, 3 December 1925, cols 2487–8. After this incident, Joynson-Hicks issued 'personal instructions to one of the Commissioners of Police that if there was reason to think that any Fascist organisation had, in fact, instigated this action, every effort should be made to obtain evidence which would lead to the conviction of those responsible, since, of course, the law must be administered with complete impartiality': ibid, col 2487.

[12] On which see Chapter 3 above.   [13] O Mosley, *My Life* (1968), p 287.
[14] Or so at least Mosley claims: see ibid, p 345.   [15] Ibid, p 348.
[16] Ibid.   [17] R Skidelsky, *Oswald Mosley* (1975), pp 463–4.
[18] See generally G C Webber, 'Patterns of Membership and Support for the British Union of Fascists' (1984) 19 *Journal of Contemporary History* 573.

and remained an irritant even when it began its sharp decline after the coming into force of the Public Order Act 1936 and in the run-up to the Second World War.

Some sense of the nature of the organisation and its beliefs are to be found in the pages of its newspaper, *The Blackshirt*, which first appeared in February 1933.[19] In an article in the first issue, Mosley wrote of the BUF as being 'an altogether different organisation from the old political parties', which he collectively denounced as the 'Old Gang'. It was, he proclaimed, 'a political movement carrying on propaganda for revolutionary changes by peaceful means', and to this end it sought to 'penetrate every element and institution in national life', including Parliament itself, which was to be transformed to 'different purposes'. Indeed it was proposed that after the election of the first fascist Parliament, the electoral system would be changed so that subsequent Parliaments would be elected on an occupational rather than geographical franchise, with people voting within industries in such a way that every interest of national life would be represented in a 'technical' rather than a 'political' Parliament. This would reflect the proposed reorganisation of the economy on the basis of the Corporate State—the answer to the problems of unemployment and poverty—whereby industry would be governed by representatives of employers, workers and consumers under the auspices of a Ministry of Corporations within a fascist government.[20] On another occasion, it was reported that all interests which operated against the nation would be 'rigorously suppressed',[21] and the intolerant nature of the movement was further reflected in its proposals for the repatriation of aliens who were allegedly occupying British jobs. The BUF gave strong support to the fascist regimes in Italy and Germany,[22] and despite claiming initially not to be against the Jews it became progressively more virulently anti-semitic, with *The Blackshirt* carrying some deeply offensive material which would not be lawful today.

[19] See also J Drennan, *BUF: Oswald Mosley and British Fascism* (1934), especially ch 8.

[20] *The Blackshirt*, 9 February 1934. The corporations would settle disputes between workers and employers, and systematically raise wages as science, rationalisation and industrial technique increased the power to produce.

[21] *The Blackshirt*, 2 December 1933. The same issue contained the following statement of the Party's ideals: 'All shall serve the State and none the Faction; all should work and thus enrich their country and themselves; opportunity shall be open to all, but privilege to none; great position shall be conceded to great talent; reward shall be accorded only to service; poverty shall be abolished by the power of modern science released within the organised State; the barriers of class shall be destroyed; and the energies of every citizen devoted to the service of the British nation . . . which by our own exertions shall be raised to its highest destiny—the Great Britain of Fascism'.

[22] This included an extraordinary defence of Hitler's concentration camps: *The Blackshirt*, 4 November 1933.

The BUF's initial outing was a public meeting in Trafalgar Square addressed by Sir Oswald Mosley fifteen days after the announcement of its establishment,[23] and this was soon followed by a demonstration in the Strand in central London. This incident was to lead to the first reference to the BUF in Parliament, the Home Secretary being asked to prohibit the holding of such demonstrations in view of the fact that their objective was the 'creation of an anti-Semitic war in this country'. But the Home Secretary thought the police 'fully competent' to deal with that incident and saw no reason to issue any special directions.[24] In November, a fascist meeting in Kentish Town, north London, was apparently the first of such occasions to result in disorder, with a couple of members of the BUF suffering injuries. Shortly after the launch of *The Blackshirt*, Mosley made a highly publicised visit to Rome in April 1933 where he celebrated a fascist commemoration of the birth of the city in the company of Mussolini.[25] The black shirt was from the start the movement's uniform, and it was in such dress that Mosley's paid national defence force accompanied him on his many speaking tours around Britain, acting as stewards at his public meetings. The 'blackshirt' was an item of clothing 'which anyone could buy or have made at home for a few shillings . . . Soon our men developed the habit of cutting the shirt in the shape of a fencing-jacket, a kindly little tribute to my love of the sport'.[26] These events, through which Mosley and his supporters achieved national prominence, were invariably noisy and often rowdy affairs, with disorder constantly being threatened by the combination of robust heckling on the one hand and strong stewarding by the defence force on the other. According to Mosley, '[o]ur men were always forbidden to use weapons, but they were later trained to fight in organised units under clear command, and were practised in judo and boxing'.[27]

One of the first illustrations of what was to become the pattern of disorder with which BUF meetings were to be associated occurred in the spring of 1933, at a high profile BUF meeting at Manchester's Free Trade Hall. At the start of the proceedings, Mosley stood alone on the platform, drawing attention to his 140 black- and grey-shirted stewards, and explaining that while he did not want violence, these men from his defence force were present to ensure that his right to free speech would be upheld. Shortly afterwards, trouble broke out between the stewards

---

[23] R Benewick, *Political Violence and Public Order* (1969), p 88.

[24] H C Debs, 27 October 1932, col 1137 (Sir J Gilmore). The questioner was E Doran MP.

[25] The visit is fully covered in *The Blackshirt*, 1 May 1933.

[26] Mosley, n 13 above, p 302.   [27] Ibid, p 301.

and members of the audience, with hecklers being set upon with rubber truncheons, while factions of the audience competed with rival renditions of the 'Red Flag' and 'God Save the Queen'. Such was the level of fighting and disorder that the police were obliged to intervene.[28] There was an element of inevitability about the outbreak of such violence. From the start, Mosley's meetings were targeted by opponents who attended in the hope of causing the maximum of disruption, and it was for their aggressive and frequently violent attitude towards these opponents that members of Mosley's defence force quickly became controversial.[29] In October, another Manchester venue featured two departures in style which were soon to become standard fare at the larger gatherings of the BUF. At a rally in Belle Vue in the city, attended by some 2,000 blackshirts,[30] spotlights trained on Mosley during the meeting were switched to focus on any scuffle or on any heckler in the audience who dared to intervene, with the individuals concerned being immediately descended upon, in the full glare of the lights, by uniformed members of the defence force, whose ejection of them was then both highly visible and extremely robust.[31] The second new departure involved the fascists mustering into ranks after the meeting and marching away in army-style formation, their military authenticity being given added credibility by their common uniform. At Belle Vue this procession was set upon by its opponents, and such disorder after BUF meetings was also quickly to become a regular feature of Mosleyite rallies.[32]

The number, scale and intensity of BUF meetings reached its highest point in the Spring and early Summer of 1934. This was when the movement was at the height of its popularity, attracting about 50,000 members from the middle and working classes and being strongly backed by Rothermere's *Daily Mail*.[33] During the year as a whole, there were eighty-

[28] For further details on this and other violent meetings in Manchester during this period, see Memorandum prepared for the information of members of the deputation appointed by the Manchester city council to interview the Home Secretary on the question of political demonstrations in PRO, HO 144/21059. Manchester had a large Jewish population and as a result it was always a favourite target of the Mosleyites. A predictably different version of the Manchester meeting, under the headline 'Police used to Protect Red Flag', is to be found in *The Blackshirt*, 18 March 1933.

[29] Similar disorder to that at Manchester followed at meetings held during the summer and autumn of 1933. These details are from Benewick, n 23 above, pp 87–90.

[30] 8,000 according to *The Blackshirt*, 21 October 1933.

[31] See *The Blackshirt*, 21 October 1933. As to who was responsible for the lighting of BUF meetings see n 48 below.

[32] In the first six months of 1933, there were 11 disturbances in the London metropolitan area which were attributed by the police to the provocation caused by the wearing of political uniforms. For the second six months of the year, the comparable figure was 22: H C Debs, 20 February 1934, col 174 (Sir J Gilmour).

[33] See generally Webber, n 18 above.

nine meetings, at no fewer than fifty-eight of which disturbances were reported.[34] Between 1 January and 16 July, nineteen fascist meetings in London alone deteriorated into disorder when they were made the focus of anti-fascist anger.[35] Whereas there were no casualties at fascist meetings in the capital in 1932, and only ten in the whole of 1933, no fewer than forty-five men and three women were seriously injured in London in the first five-and-a-half months of 1934 alone. At a fascist meeting in Colston Hall, Bristol, protestors were ejected 'in such a way that half the audience had no idea of what was happening . . . yet, in such a way that it will be a long time before they again attempt to break up a Blackshirt meeting'.[36] On that occasion bitter fighting occurred after the meeting, when 400 to 500 fascists in uniform engaged in running battles with a hostile crowd.[37] On 26 April 1934, there were disorderly scenes at the corn exchange in Plymouth, when anti-fascist disruption of a speech by the former Labour MP John Beckett caused the police to enter 'with drawn truncheons'.[38] In the north-east, a BUF meeting in Newcastle-upon-Tyne on 29 April resulted in two injuries,[39] and a meeting two weeks later at the same location, at which Beckett was again scheduled to speak, had to be abandoned in chaos, so successful were the disruptive tactics deployed by the anti-fascists present.[40] At a Gateshead meeting the following day, also due to be addressed by Beckett, the fascists took no risks, arming their stewards with India rubber tubing and knuckle dusters.[41] A BUF meeting at Bedminster, Bristol was closed on the advice of the police in early June,[42] the same day on which fascists and anti-fascists clashed after a BUF meeting in the Usher Hall, Edinburgh.[43] Two days later, the park authorities at Finsbury Park were compelled to invite the police onto their property to restore order at a BUF meeting,[44]

---

[34] S M Cullen, 'Political Violence: The Case of the British Union of Fascists' (1993) 28 *Journal of Contemporary History* 245, at p 249. This article provides an excellent survey of the violence surrounding the BUF during the 1930s.

[35] H C Debs, 16 July 1934, col 785 (Sir J Gilmour) (WA). During the same period, two anti-fascist meetings were disturbed by political opponents. These were both CPGB meetings, held on 23 April at Shepherd's Bush and Uxbridge: Cullen, n 34 above, p 252.

[36] *The Blackshirt*, 6 April 1934.

[37] H C Debs, 9 April 1934, col 15 (Sir J Gilmour).

[38] Three men and a woman were taken to hospital and the police escorted the fascists from the area after the meeting: *News Chronicle*, 27 April 1934.

[39] H C Debs, 7 May 1934, cols 739–40 (Sir J Gilmour).

[40] H C Debs, 16 May 1934, cols 1759–60 (Sir J Gilmour).

[41] H C Debs, 17 May 1934, col 1923 (W J Thorne).

[42] H C Debs, 6 June 1934, col 931 (Sir J Gilmour).

[43] Ibid, cols 1054–5 (Sir G Collins, Secretary of State for Scotland).

[44] H C Debs, 6 June 1934, cols 930–1 (Sir J Gilmour). Ten people (including two police officers) were injured in the operation.

and in the following weekend, fascist meetings throughout London raised the tension in the capital to even greater heights.[45]

Olympia

In this atmosphere, it was perhaps inevitable that the large fascist rally at Olympia scheduled for 7 June should quickly have come to be seen as a showdown between these rival forces. The Olympia meeting was planned as one of three huge events in London that Spring and Summer which were designed to capitalise on Lord Rothermere's 'massive press campaign in support of the BUF which [had] suddenly thrust it from comparative obscurity into the limelight'.[46] The Communist Party became involved in a coherent way for the first time, and set about putting in place what was a highly effective plan of disruption. The Party printed counterfeit tickets for the event and arranged for hecklers to be placed at strategic points around the hall.[47] The idea was to combine this disruption of the meeting itself with a large demonstration outside. For its part, the BUF had long been schooled in the rhetoric of anti-communism, and it was more than ready for the interruptions that it knew would be attempted. Mosley began the meeting some thirty minutes late, entering to the loud fanfares and dramatic pageantry that were typical of his movement. In the two-and-a-half hours that followed, any interruptions to his speech caused Mosley to pause dramatically while the spotlights previously focused on him switched to the intervenor, who was then inevitably and promptly set upon by the blackshirted stewards. Such 'stewarding' was of course standard BUF procedure by now, but what seems to have been unusual about Olympia was Mosley's extraordinary readiness to treat all interventions as hostile. The very first interruption 'was one still, small voice calling out something like the ordinary remark we hear in a meeting, "How would you like to live on 15s 3d a week?" Immediately the leader stopped and the searchlight was turned on that individual, who was then dealt with and ejected'.[48] Such extravagant sensitivity, particularly unnecessary in light of the fact that the speaker's words were amplified by no fewer than twenty-four loudspeakers, led

[45] H C Debs, 13 June 1934, col 1693 (Sir J Gilmour).

[46] Skidelsky, n 17 above, p 365. The first of the meetings at the Albert Hall on 22 April had already taken place. The third was scheduled for White City in the August.

[47] 'For three weeks before the meeting, incitements to attack it were published, and maps were printed to show how to get to the meeting': Mosley, n 13 above, p 297.

[48] H C Debs, 14 June 1934, col 1953 (T J O'Connor). Skidelsky, n 17 above, p 376 denies that the spotlights were arranged by Mosley. Mosley himself says that they belonged to the newsreel companies and were not under his control, n 13 above, p 299.

many who were at the meeting to conclude that its real purpose was to demonstrate the strength of the fascist defence force as a means of securing free speech for Mosley and his followers, a sentiment to which Mosley gave explicit expression in the course of his speech.[49]

A second way in which standard BUF procedures were toughened up even further at Olympia was in the extremely brutal handling by the stewards of the members of the audience on whom they descended. While leaving the question of culpability open, Mosley's biographer accepts that there was 'no doubt that fighting took place inside Olympia, and that the Blackshirts used very violent methods'.[50] Many were severely beaten by upwards of ten or twenty stewards before being ejected from the hall. This was all done without any attempt at disguise, despite the fact that included in the audience were many well known or highly regarded individuals who, being by no means necessarily predisposed to fascism, were present as observers or merely out of curiosity. In a letter to the *Manchester Guardian*, seven members of London University who had been in the hall gave evidence as to nine incidents which they had personally witnessed. In one of these, a man had been 'thrust out of the Blyth Road gates convulsed and fainting, streaming with blood from a number of wounds and gashes in the head'. In another, 'a semi-conscious man was thrown out, wearing only a torn shirt. He was deeply cut in the face, and collapsed almost immediately'.[51] Terence O'Connor, a Member of Parliament, reported to the Commons that he had seen a young heckler 'thrown to the ground by at least six people. Some four or five other people came down, and while he was securely held and unable to do anything they struck him with their fists

[49] Looking back on the event years later, Mosley described it as a 'victory for free speech' but one which had not been won 'without bitter experience': n 13 above, p 296.

[50] Skidelsky, n 17 above, p 372. Skidelsky argues that the violence was not pre-planned and only increased as the seriousness of the disorder became apparent, but even allowing for this he accepts that 'some deterrent motive of a "teaching them a lesson" kind was probably present': ibid, p 377.

[51] *Manchester Guardian*, 12 June 1934, quoted by Isaac Foot in the supply day debate on the incident that took place on 14 June: see H C Debs, col 1916. A Council for Civil Liberties commission into the events at Olympia, chaired by Aylmer Digby KC and held on 10–11 July, placed the blame for the disorder squarely on the fascists: see B Dyson, *Liberty in Britain, 1934–94* (1994), pp 13–4. The weekly *Justice of the Peace* took a different but entirely characteristic line, declaring that the 'fact is that in England we enjoy the rule of law, and that rule is exercised with absolute impartiality as was well demonstrated by the reports of proceedings in metropolitan police courts arising out of the Olympia incidents'. As for the disturbances themselves, while it might have been true that the stewards had been somewhat robust, '[w]hat would have happened in any other country than ours may well be imagined!': (1934) 98 JP 387. (Nazi Germany may however have been an exception: in an earlier issue the same year, the same journal said of the Reichstag fire trial that 'German justice [which] has been under the fierce glare of world-wide interest' has 'come through the ordeal with honour' (1934) 98 JP 2.)

as he was on the ground'.[52] In the supply day parliamentary debate that followed shortly after the meeting, a number of MPs reported similar incidents. The perceived viciousness of the BUF stewards was even troubling to parliamentarians who might otherwise have considered themselves inclined to support the cause. W J Anstruther-Gray, Unionist MP for North Lanark, confessed to the Commons that 'if anybody had told me an hour before the meeting at Olympia that I should find myself on the side of the Communist interrupter, I would have called that man a liar', but this had been the effect of the stewards' over-zealousness as far as he was concerned.[53]

Hundreds of persons appear to have been injured in the course of the meeting, with fourteen individuals being so severely affected as to require hospital treatment.[54] A question that immediately arose in the aftermath of such disorder was as to the action, or more accurately the inaction, of the police. At the Manchester Free Trade Hall meeting the year before, officers had entered the hall after similar disorder on a far less serious scale had broken out. Indeed on that occasion, the police had gone so far as to require the uniformed Blackshirts to leave before they would allow the meeting to continue, causing Mosley and his supporters subsequently to view the evening as a victory for their communist opponents. It was probably this evening in Manchester the year before that Mosley had in mind when he set about asserting his right of free speech with such single-minded brutality and without police assistance at Olympia.[55] Whether because of complaints made by the BUF after Manchester and other later meetings which had also been successfully disrupted by the Left, or because Trenchard's Metropolitan Police would have taken a different line in any event, the police were nowhere to be seen at any stage within the Olympia meeting. The closest they got to the action was when a small group of uniformed officers entered the precincts (but not the actual meeting) to tend to a man whom the police had been explicitly called upon to assist. Immediately they arrived, these officers saw Blackshirt stewards in the process of beating up other individuals, though the stewards all ran off when they saw the police arrive. Despite this, the constables confined their response to quickly removing both the injured

---

[52] H C Debs, 14 June 1934, col 1955.   [53] Ibid, col 2003.

[54] H C Debs, 14 June 1934, cols 1970–1 (Sir J Gilmour). For a good account, see I Montagu, *Blackshirt Brutality. The Story of Olympia* (1934). A rather different story is told in *The Blackshirt*, 15 June 1934.

[55] In Skidelsky's opinion, it was Mosley's 'experience at Manchester on 12 March 1933 [that] convinced him that the police would try to stop the stewards doing their duty': Skidelsky, n 17 above, pp 375–6. See 'Police used to Protect Red Flag', *The Blackshirt*, 18 March 1933.

man and themselves from what was manifestly a conflict zone. Extraordinarily, no action followed upon this eye witness discovery by police officers of the activities that were going on probably within and certainly in the environs of the meeting.

Faced with allegations of police indifference to the plight of these protestors at Olympia, the Home Secretary, Sir John Gilmour, sought refuge in what he presented as the majestic inevitability of the law. Citing an earlier departmental committee report,[56] Gilmour declared in the Commons four days after the event that:

it is no part of the ordinary duty of the police to deal with interrupters at public meetings held on private premises, and they have no legal authority to enter the premises except by leave of the occupier or the promoters of the meeting or when they have good reason to believe that a breach of the peace is being committed. Nor again is it any part of the duty of the police to act as stewards at a meeting, but the police have been advised by the Home Office that, on extraordinary occasions when there is a definite reason to apprehend disturbance of a serious character, they should make arrangements for policing the meeting inside as well as outside if they are asked to do so by the persons responsible for convening the meeting.

On the present occasion, the British Union of Fascists informed the Commissioner that the fascists did not require the assistance of the police inside the building and at no stage was any request made for police to enter the meeting.[57] But even on the version of the law provided by the Home Secretary, the police should have intervened when the fact of ongoing violence had become apparent to them. Although the law was genuinely uncertain, it is unclear whether the Home Secretary gave a full account of the contemporary position. Returning to the departmental committee report, it was recognised as early as 1909 that the police 'may and indeed are bound to intervene in the case of an actual breach of the peace; and they may arrest without warrant a person whom they have seen committing a breach of the peace, and even if they have not seen any such breach committed they may arrest without warrant a person charged by another for such breach, if there are reasonable grounds for apprehending the continuance or immediate renewal of such breach'.[58]

[56] Report of the Departmental Committee on the Duties of the Police with respect to the Preservation of Order at Public Meetings, Cd 4673 (1909). Particular reliance was placed on para 8.
[57] The full statement of Sir John Gilmour is at H C Debs, 11 June 1934, cols 1343–8. The remarks quoted in the text are at cols 1343–4. The language was similar during the supply day debate three days later: see H C Debs, 14 June 1934, col 1968.
[58] See n 56 above, para 8, citing *Stone's Justices' Manual* (1908), p 136. See also the evidence provided to the Committee by the private secretary to the Metropolitan Police Commissioner, George

This would appear to cover the circumstances of the brutal treatment of hecklers by the stewards, with even Gilmour acknowledging that 'the law does not allow undue violence to be used'.[59] But the possibility that 'the question whether unnecessary force was used may come before the courts' meant that the Home Secretary considered that it would 'not be proper' for him 'to make any comment' on the allegations of excess by fascist stewards.[60] In his first version of events offered to Parliament, Gilmour admitted that 'the advice as regards police action ha[d] been based on the assumption that the stewards of a meeting in dealing with interrupters [would] act without undue violence and [would] themselves avoid illegal acts', and he had then gone on to suggest that if 'this assumption should be found to be unwarranted as regards meetings promoted by any particular organisation, the whole policy of police action inside such public meetings [would] have to be reviewed'.[61] This seemed to suggest an operational decision taken at a high level rather than the course of action required by law to which he had also referred during the same statement in the Commons. During the supply day debate three days later, the Home Secretary took the view that while a change in the law may be desirable, 'of course, [this] would entail legislation'.[62] Between these two parliamentary events there occurred two meetings of the principal State actors in the Home Secretary's room in the House of Commons, on 12 and 13 June. At the first of these, the Attorney General was firmly of the opinion that 'the law was explicit that the police could not go in [to a meeting] except on the invitation of the promoters, unless they knew that an offence had been or was being committed'. It was presumably this advice that led to Gilmour's emphasis on the need for legislation in the supply day debate.[63]

The suspicion of deliberate police partisanship towards the BUF was increased by what went on around Olympia while the meeting was in

---

Edwards: Departmental Committee on the Duties of the Police with respect to the Preservation of Order at Public Meetings. Volume 2: Minutes of Evidence, Cd 4674 (1909), pp 9–13.

[59] H C Debs, 11 June 1934, col 1344. [60] Ibid. [61] Ibid.

[62] H C Debs, 14 June 1934, col 1968.

[63] See 'Note of a conference held in the Home Secretary's room at the House of Commons, 12 June 1934' in PRO, HO 45/25386. Note that this formula is different from what the Home Secretary had said in the Commons the previous day, in that it refers to offences rather than to a breach of the peace. On 14 June, Gilmour asserted in the Commons, in accordance with this advice, that the Commissioner had instructed his officers 'not to go into the hall unless they had reason to believe that something contrary to the law was taking place'. But having said this he then in the subsequent discussion reverted to his earlier use of the language of breach of the peace: H C Debs, 14 June 1934, cols 1967–8. This may be a difference without a relevant distinction for present purposes, however, since the actual occurrence of a breach of the peace invariably also involves the commission of at least one offence, e.g. an assault.

progress, when a force of about 760 officers kept in check an anti-fascist crowd of some 5,000, making some twenty-three arrests (on suspicion of assault, obstructing the police and insulting behaviour). In the tense weeks that followed, the evidence of police partisanship seemed to mount, with those who were prepared to take a public stand against fascism appearing invariably to attract the repressive instincts of the authorities while the fascists themselves continued to be carefully protected. In Plymouth on 13 June, a crowd of 1,000 demonstrators which congregated to protest outside the fascist headquarters in the town was broken up by the police, whose clearance of the streets led to two of those present being afterwards jailed for three months for assaulting officers in the execution of their duty.[64] A protest at an open-air fascist rally in Bristol led to nine arrests, all apparently of demonstrators rather than of fascists.[65] In contrast, a relatively small scale BUF meeting in West Ham, typical of the period, attracted the protective solicitude of no fewer than thirty-four foot and four mounted police officers.[66] When serious disorder was threatened at a Mosleyite meeting planned for the City Hall Sheffield on 28 June, with a range of anti-fascists (organised under the banner of the 'Sheffield United Action Committee') planning Olympia-style direct action, the authorities appeared willing to risk a repetition of the disorder that had occurred in London, with the Home Secretary reiterating just two days before the meeting the constraints on police action that he had first formulated in the wake of the Olympia melee.[67] Significantly, no attempt appears to have been made to prohibit the meeting on the ground that its occurrence was likely to provoke a breach of the peace, for which there was far more evidence than was later to underpin the police intervention in *Duncan v Jones*.[68] (In the event the City Corporation resolved the impasse by making the attendance of the police a condition of the letting contract, with the result that when the meeting finally took place the audience of 2,500 was encircled not only by 300 blackshirt stewards but also by 100 police officers. Despite a hostile crowd of no fewer than 10,000 outside the building, the meeting passed off with no reports of serious disorder, inside or out.[69])

[64] H C Debs, 18 June 1934, col 14 (Sir J Gilmour).

[65] H C Debs, 27 June 1934, cols 1122–3 (Sir J Gilmour). Interestingly, the charges included disorderly conduct, an offence apparently similar to s 54(13) of the Metropolitan Police Act 1839, a provision frequently deployed in London.

[66] H C Debs, 25 June 1934, cols 800–1 (D H Hacking, Under Secretary of State for Home Affairs).

[67] H C Debs, 26 June 1934, col 968 (Sir J Gilmour).

[68] See n 4 above. See generally Chapter 5 above.

[69] H C Debs, 2 July 1934, cols 1564–5 (Sir J Gilmour) (WA).

Despite Olympia and the provocative effect both of the blackshirt uniform and of the military-style conduct of Mosley's defence force, the government determinedly and consistently refused to propose in public any change in the law that might lead to a clampdown on these fascist activities. In private however there was intense pre-legislative activity. A Uniforms Bill had been drafted early in 1934 but had been allowed by Cabinet decision on 30 May to 'stand over for the present',[70] probably on account of the difficulty of definition as much as anything else.[71] Now after Olympia the issue returned briefly at the top of the government's private agenda, with a Bill being put before Cabinet in July 1934 which would have empowered the police to enter private premises without authority if there was 'reason to believe that disorder [was] likely to occur'.[72] No further progress was achieved however.[73] As far as Mosley's military pretensions were concerned, the Home Secretary was content merely to continue to draw attention to the Unlawful Drilling Act 1819, which prohibited 'unauthorised meetings and assemblies of persons for the purpose of training or drilling themselves, or for the purpose of practising military exercise, movements of evolutions'.[74] It was also asserted that there was no need for legislation to make illegal the possession of knuckledusters and India rubber truncheons (the favourite weapons of the blackshirt stewards) because these could already be dealt with under

[70] In PRO, HO 144/20158 the issue of banning fascist uniforms was frequently raised in Parliament in the first half of 1934: see H C Debs, 20 February 1934, cols 173–4 (Sir J Gilmour) where the Home Secretary said that the 'whole question [was] engaging [his] serious consideration'. This led the *Express* the following day to lead its front page with the news under the headline 'The Home Secretary has his eye on black, green, khaki, red and blue shirts': *Express*, 21 February 1934. For subsequent parliamentary responses to the same pressure for change, all of a holding nature, see: H C Debs, 1 March 1934, col 1249 (Sir J Gilmour); H C Debs, 15 March 1934, col 562 (Sir J Gilmour); H C Debs, 2 May 1934, col 312 (Sir J Gilmour). A short debate on the topic initiated by Commander Oliver Locker-Lampson (H C Debs, 16 May 1934, cols 1765–72) proved counter-productive for the proponents of change, with the commander presenting 'his case so violently that he converted a friendly House of Commons to opposition to his proposed prohibition of uniforms': *News Chronicle*, 15 May 1934.

[71] The comment of one Home Office official, expressed on 12 March in PRO, HO 144/20158, may well be representative of the informal departmental view of the proposal: 'There is not the slightest doubt that there will be plenty of opportunity in Parliament for the legal brain to find amusing points to tear to pieces. People of the A P Herbert type will get some amusement out of it!'

[72] See the Home Secretary's paper to Cabinet, Preservation of Public Order CP 189 (34) in PRO, HO 144/20158.

[73] The government was as a result still defending its refusal to act in Parliament in October 1934 (H C Debs, 30 October 1934, col 11 (Sir J Gilmour), and again in February 1935 (H C Debs, 13 February 1935, col 1931 (Sir J Gilmour)).

[74] H C Debs, 31 January 1934, col 360. In June 1934, the Home Office considered launching prosecutions under the 1819 Act, and on 6 June obtained counsel's opinion (supplied by Eustace Fulton) to the effect that such prosecutions would be within the Act. At a meeting between the Home Secretary and the Attorney General it was however decided that no proceedings should be launched. See PRO, HO 144/20158.

section 4 of the Vagrancy Act 1824, which condemned as rogues and vagabonds any person 'armed with any gun, pistol, hanger, cutlass, bludgeon or other offensive weapon, or having upon him or her any instrument, with intent to commit any felonious Act'. But whether this law had ever been deployed in the way suggested was not made clear.[75] The government's inaction would have been more convincing had it not been deeply embroiled at exactly this time in securing the legislative passage of an Incitement to Disaffection Bill that was as hostile to certain political opinions as it seemed disproportionate, unnecessary and over-reactive.[76] The suspicion that two different codes of law operated for the Right and the Left was soon to be given further substantiation, in a famous Divisional Court decision to which we now turn.

Thomas v Sawkins[77]

Sir John Gilmour's claim that the law had compelled the police to forbear from entering the BUF meeting at Olympia on 7 June had been greeted with a degree of scepticism from the moment that it was made. The problems with Gilmour's statement of the legal position went beyond any dispute as to the facts, however. The main difficulty was that it did not appear to be in accord with past police practice. In earlier chapters we have encountered examples of unwanted police attendance at public meetings. To take just one example among many, the evidence given by Inspector Jones on the occasion of the binding over of Mrs Duncan in 1932 (discussed in Chapter 5 above) had been based on what he had heard at a meeting which she had addressed, and it is a fair bet that he had not revealed his status and asked permission to enter before taking his place in the audience. When asked about just this sort of situation in the Commons, Gilmour had explained that there was 'a distinct difference between uniformed police going to a meeting, which is not proper unless they are asked to go, and the police taking such steps as they think are desirable to have the fullest information of these meetings'.[78] But even this version of the appropriate police conduct was at odds with past practice, in which on at least one occasion Sir John Gilmour himself had been intimately involved. In 1928, a meeting in Glasgow which was addressed by two radical MPs had been attended by

[75] See H C Debs, 26 February 1934, col 757 (Sir J Gilmour).
[76] See Chapter 5 above.   [77] See n 2 above.
[78] H C Debs, 11 June 1934, col 1347. For examples of police surveillance of Communist Party members in the 1920s, see Chapter 3 above.

no fewer than eleven detective officers. When the legitimacy of their presence was afterwards queried, it had been the Home Secretary himself (in
his then capacity as Secretary of State for Scotland) who had justified
their presence, not this time as information gatherers, but as officers who
would be in a position 'to detect the persons responsible for any outbreak
of disorder that might take place'.[79] On that occasion, Gilmour had gone
on to declare that he was 'not aware' whether permission to attend had
been asked of the organisers; clearly such permission was not thought to
carry the legal weight that was to be accorded to it by the same man in
more controversial circumstances six years later.

In August 1934, a mere couple of months or so after Olympia, the
police practice of entering public meetings without permission was
revived, notwithstanding the Home Secretary's apparently unequivocal
statement in the Commons that the law—or at least invariable police
practice—made it impossible. The occasion for the police action was a
series of meetings which were held by the Communist Party in the South
Wales coalfields during that summer month. The principal speaker on
each occasion was Alun Thomas[80] and the authorities were assiduous in
keeping a careful eye on him. At Nantymoel on 9 August, the police
declined Thomas's request that they withdraw from his meeting. At
Caerau on 14 August, Thomas retaliated by telling his audience that he
would have the police ejected if they insisted on attending, uninvited, the
meeting he had planned for the same town three days later. At Maesteg
on 15 August, he declared that if it were not for the presence of the
police, he would tell his audience 'a hell of a lot more'. When the Caerau
meeting came around on 17 August, the agenda before the large crowd
in the local library may have been ostensibly concerned with a protest
against the Incitement to Disaffection Bill and with a call for the resignation of the local chief constable, but the real issue was whether

---

[79] H C Debs, 17 July 1928, col 202 (Sir J Gilmour). At the turn of the decade, meetings of anti-
vivisectionists were regularly disrupted by their political opponents. It seems to have been assumed
that the police were entitled to be at these meetings, though presumably the organisations involved
were anxious to have them present, to deter their opponents from acting in a disruptive manner:
see the comments of the then Secretary of State for the Home Department, J R Clynes, at H C
Debs, 18 July 1929, col 596. According to A Short, the Under Secretary of State at the Home
Department, the police were 'not responsible for seeing that speakers at public meetings secure an
uninterrupted hearing'. Their 'only duty' on such occasions was 'to intervene, if called upon by the
promoters, to prevent a breach of the peace': H C Debs, 17 December 1930, col 1289 (WA).

[80] This account of the background to the case is largely drawn from D G T Williams, 'Preventive
Action and Public Order: The Principle of *Thomas v. Sawkins*' (1985) 16 *Cambrian Law Review* 116. It
is likely that useful background information is contained in the Home Office file, 'Industrial unrest
and communist activities in South Wales, 1933–36' (PRO, HO 144/20132) but the file is closed for
100 years.

Thomas would seek to make good his threat of three days before. At the start of the meeting, three police officers (including Inspector Parry and Sergeant Sawkins) entered the hall, despite protests at the door. The organiser of the event, Fred Thomas, who had just successfully defended himself against an obstruction charge in Maesteg police court arising out of a street meeting in July,[81] immediately went to the local police station to complain, and on his return he informed the three officers that they were to be ejected, placing his hand on Parry's shoulder for added emphasis. At this point, Sawkins (with 'the loyal cry of "I won't allow you to interfere with my superior officer" '[82]) immediately pushed away Thomas's hand, whereupon a large body of officers suddenly swarmed into the hall, where they insisted on remaining for the rest of the meeting.

The police brought no charges arising out of the events at the meeting, and the episode would probably have been quickly passed over (as yet another example of the lawless hostility of the State to Communist Party agitation), had it not been both for the nascent Council for Civil Liberties enthusiasm for litigation and for the Home Secretary's post-Olympia statement of the law the previous June, which seemed to give the lawyers grounds for optimism that they had a sustainable legal case. There being no prosecution or even binding over order to fight, the mode chosen to get the issue into court was a private prosecution against Sergeant Sawkins for assault contrary to section 42 of the Offences Against the Person Act 1861. This was an unusual but not unprecedented device, its value lying in the fact that it allowed the promoter Fred Thomas to argue in court that all he was doing when he was 'assaulted' by Sawkins was seeking to remove trespassers from what was (for the relevant period at any rate) his property. When the case came before Bridgend magistrates in September, Thomas' legal representative, W H Thompson,[83] naturally sought to demonstrate that Sir John Gilmour's statement in the Commons accurately stated the law. But the police claimed in reply that their presence was required because they were regularly attacked by communists, pointing out that forty-five members of the audience had a total of 390 convictions between them, and also that Caerau was a distressed area. Such extra-legal appeals to class hostility worked with the magistrates, who found in Sawkins' favour, albeit after a hearing which lasted for no less than nine hours. It is clear,

---

[81] *Daily Worker*, 23 July 1934.

[82] Williams, n 80 above, at p 121. See the account in the *Daily Worker*, 20 August 1934.

[83] Thompson was also involved in *Elias v Pasmore*: see Chapter 5 above.

however, that the police would need more legal meat than this before the Divisional Court of the King's Bench, to where Thompson now took the case on appeal, arguing an error of law on the part of the magistrates.

We have seen several times in the course of this study how, in moments of crisis, the malleable concepts of sedition and of breach of the peace are the chosen legal vessels into which are poured, for the benefit of an appeal, the bias and class antagonism that is presented to magistrates as straightforwardly honest issues of fact. Sergeant Sawkins now informed the court that he and his fellow officers had insisted on remaining in the hall 'because, in the judgment of himself and the other officers (based on their experience and knowledge of previous meetings organised by the Community Party at Caerau), it was to be anticipated that the meeting would become an unlawful assembly or a riot, or that breaches of the peace would take place, to the alarm of the residents of Caerau, and that seditious and inflammatory speeches were likely to be made at the meeting'.[84] To counter this submission, Thompson recruited two heavyweight political lawyers: Sir Stafford Cripps QC and Dingle Foot. The strict rules of court prevented the lawyers from making any reference to Gilmour's statement of the law in the Commons, without which they were reduced to relying upon general legal principle as evidenced in the authoritative legal texts.[85] It was readily conceded that 'the general duties of a constable are to preserve the King's peace and with that object to keep watch and ward and to bring criminals to justice'.[86] But it was also argued that to 'perform those duties', the constable may enter private premises without a warrant only to take a felon, where felony has been committed and a particular person is reasonably suspected to be the offender; where a felony is likely, or about, to be committed; where he hears an affray on the premises; or to preserve and arrest those who have taken part in an affray.[87] There was, however, 'no authority empowering a constable to enter private premises merely because he has a reasonable belief that an offence or a breach of the peace *may* be committed therein'.[88]

Neither the eminence nor the loquacity of Thompson's legal team could compensate for the negative judicial reaction to their submissions.

---

[84] Williams, n 80 above, at p 121.

[85] *Thomas v Sawkins* [1935] 2 KB 249, at pp 252–3.　　　[86] Ibid, p 252 (argument of counsel).

[87] Ibid, citing *Stone's Justices' Manual*, n 58 above, p 208, and Burn's *Justice of the Peace*, 30th edn, vol 1 (date omitted), pp 301 and 303. See in relation to the former, the Report of the Departmental Committee on the Duties of the Police with respect to the Preservation of Order at Public Meetings, n 56 above.

[88] Ibid, pp 252–3 (our emphasis). The case is distinguishable from Olympia on the ground that while there was almost certainly a breach of the peace at Olympia, there was not yet one here.

Presiding over the three-man court was the Lord Chief Justice, Lord Hewart, whose political and judicial background we have earlier discussed when considering his ruling in *Duncan v Jones*.[89] With him on the Bench in *Thomas v Sawkins*[90] were Avory J, already well into his eighties and a veteran of similar cases from earlier eras of popular protest,[91] and Lawrence J, a relative newcomer who was later to become famous as the British judge at Nuremburg. The brevity and peremptory nature of the court's unanimous dismissal of Thomas' appeal foreshadows the line that the Lord Chief Justice and two of his other judicial brethren were to take in *Duncan v Jones*[92] the following year. To Cripps' claim that the power for which the police now argued represented 'an unheard-of proposition of law', the Lord Chief Justice replied in the course of his judgment that there was in fact both academic support for it, in a passage from the work of the eighteenth-century scholar Blackstone,[93] and judicial support, in the form of *dicta* to be found in two nineteenth-century Irish cases. In the first of these, a police constable had removed an orange lily from the clothing of a woman who had been wearing it in a provocative fashion in a Catholic neighbourhood; and in the second (which we have encountered in Chapter 1) a meeting by the Land League was banned for fear of violence by local Orangemen.[94] Lord Hewart also drew attention to 'certain observations' supportive of the police line which had been made from the bench some thirty years before—by none other than the octogenarian beside him, Avory J.

All of this was highly unpersuasive. None of the passages relied on were actually quoted by the Lord Chief Justice, who was content to do no more than to refer to counsel's arguments. Blackstone had merely been referring generally to the need to 'keep the King's peace and to keep watch and ward'.[95] The Irish cases were themselves open to question, and appeared to be inconsistent with English authority on the key

---

[89] See Chapter 5 above.
[90] See n 2 above.
[91] See most notably *Lansbury v Riley* [1914] 3 KB 229.
[92] See n 4 above.
[93] Blackstone's *Commentaries on the Laws of England* (7th edn, 1775), i, p 356, referred to by Hewart LCJ [1935] 2 KB 249, at p 254. Avory J also relied on this passage: ibid, at p 256.
[94] Respectively *Humphries v Connor* (1864) 17 Ir CLR 1; *O'Kelly v Harvey* (1883) 14 LR Ir 105. Avory J invoked yet another Irish case: *R v Queen's County Justices* (1882) 10 LR Ir 294: [1935] 2 KB 249, at p 256.
[95] As summarised by Avory J, [1935] 2 KB 249, at p 256. To quote the Blackstone extract in full is perhaps to explain why none of the judges felt it opportune to refer to it other than in the vaguest of terms: 'The general duty of all constables, both high and petty, as well as of the other officers, is to keep the king's peace in their several districts; and to that purpose they are armed with very large powers, of arresting, and imprisoning, of breaking open houses, and the like: of the extent of which powers, considering what manner of men are for the most part put upon these offices, it is perhaps very well that they are generally kept in ignorance': Blackstone, n 93 above, p 356.

point of principle.[96] Avory J's remarks in 1914 (also rooted in Irish case law) had occurred in *Lansbury v Riley*,[97] which had been a highly controversial decision on the breadth of the binding over jurisdiction, handed down in a case involving the campaigner for votes for women George Lansbury at the height of the suffragette agitation. Yet this was the evidence on the basis of which the Lord Chief Justice felt able to conclude that 'there [was] quite sufficient ground for the proposition that it is part of the preventive power, and, therefore, part of the preventive duty, of the police, in cases where there are such reasonable grounds of apprehension as the justices have found here, to enter and remain on private premises'.[98] Hewart's version of this executive power went substantially beyond what had been envisaged by the Bridgend magistrates, however. It was a power which the police officer could exercise 'ex virtute officii' whenever 'he ha[d] reasonable grounds for believing that an offence [was] imminent or [was] likely to be committed'.[99] It went 'without saying' that the 'powers and duties of the police [were] directed, not to the interests of the police, but to the protection and welfare of the public'.[100] Legitimising such police action whenever 'an offence', apparently of any sort, was anticipated, took the author of *The New Despotism*[101] into a fresh realm of judicial deference, at least where this brand of executive excess was concerned.

The judgment of Avory J was not clear on this key point of the breadth of the police power. At one stage, echoing the Lord Chief Justice, the vital element seemed to be that the police were present 'for the express purpose of preventing a breach of the peace or the commission of an offence'.[102] At the end of his judgment, however, Avory J appeared to regard the reasonable belief that 'seditious speeches would be made and/or that a breach of the peace would take place' as necessary to underpin the lawfulness of the police action, the police being 'entitled to enter and to remain on the premises . . . [t]o prevent any such offence or a breach of the peace'.[103] In his short concurring judgment, and inso-

---

[96] In particular *Beatty v Gillbanks* (1882) 9 QBD 308.

[97] [1914] 3 KB 229, at pp 236–7. Avory J also referred to the decision, making clear that the origin of the relevant dicta for the case before him lay in *R v Queen's County Justices*, n 94 above.

[98] [1935] 2 KB 249, at p 254.   [99] Ibid, at p 255.   [100] Ibid, at p 254.

[101] See Chapter 5 above.

[102] Ibid, p 255. A textbook published shortly after the decision considered that it permitted the police 'to enter and remain on private premises against the will of the owner or those who are lawfully in possession of the premises whilst a public meeting is being held there, . . . whenever the police have reasonable grounds for believing that an offence *is likely to be* committed': J Baker, *The Law of Political Uniforms, Public Meetings and Private Armies* (1937), p 42 (emphasis in original).

[103] Ibid, pp 256–7.

far as he expressed any view (something which is in itself hard to divine), the newcomer Lawrence J seemed to assume that the police power should be restricted to situations where it was 'in the execution of [a police officer's] duty to preserve the peace'.[104] More important than these uncertainties about the exact ratio of the decision was the unequivocal message of support that it sent to the authorities. The *Police Journal* thought the case to be 'most helpful to the police' because it gave them the 'right to attend and remain at a public meeting if they think it necessary to do so in the interests of public order'.[105] Less favourably disposed critics were affronted both by the vacuity of the legal reasoning and by the obvious partisanship of the police when their conduct in South Wales was compared with their inactivity at Olympia.[106] Yet when the decision was drawn to the attention of ministers, all that the Under Secretary of State for Home Affairs Captain E Wallace would say was that it 'definitely clear[ed] up a rather obscure situation, and the police do know the extent of their powers, which they will exercise with complete impartiality'.[107] This was not an obscurity or uncertainty that had preoccupied the Home Secretary in June 1934.

Police Partisanship and Partiality

In the absence of new legislation, but strengthened after 30 May 1935 by the decision in *Thomas v Sawkins*[108] which removed one of the main engines driving the desire for legislative action in 1934, the police felt under no compulsion to depart from their usual approach to matters pertaining to public order. This meant that the suspicion that the police were partisan towards the fascists, which had been present since the formation of the BUF, became more deep-rooted than ever. In a way, it was almost impossible for the police not to be considered partial. A peculiarity of fascist subversion was a highly selective but nevertheless ostentatious commitment to the Rule of Law. Fascists frequently launched their own private prosecutions and wore their uniforms in the witness box when giving evidence.[109] When a police constable was shot in Sussex in 1934, fascists from London

---

[104] Ibid, p 257.　　　　　　　　　　　　　　　　[105] (1935) 8 *Police Journal* 398–9.

[106] See in particular A L Goodhart's powerful indictment: 'Thomas v. Sawkins: A Constitutional Innovation' (1936–8) 6 CLJ 22.

[107] H C Debs, 16 July 1935, col 1016. The matter was raised by E L Mallalieu, col 949, in the context of the police role in relation to a BUF meeting at the Albert Hall, on which see p 297 below.

[108] See n 2 above.

[109] H C Debs, 15 March 1934, col 562 (W J Thorne). For evidence that the occasion there referred to was not a 'one-off', see H C Debs, 11 April 1934, col 324 (Sir J Gilmour).

and elsewhere came down to the area to join in the police search that followed, many of them proudly wearing their blackshirt regalia.[110] Stewarding their own meetings was of a piece with this BUF fantasy of themselves as a law enforcement body, working in conjunction with rather than in opposition to the police. Naturally this appeared attractive to the police, as it did to many members of the magistracy.[111] Whether such pleasure at the solicitude offered to the police by this branch of the citizenry extended also to police support for the aims and ideas of the BUF is more debatable. Incidents such as the blatant leniency shown by the police towards virulently anti-Jewish remarks at a public meeting in Hampstead in May 1936[112] may or may not have been as frequent as critics suggested, but at the very least such episodes showed a disturbing deployment of police discretion in a highly selective way.[113]

We have already seen many examples of the stark contrast between the police anxiety to protect the civil liberties of the fascists on the one hand with their utter disregard of exactly the same rights when other political activists from a different perspective sought to express them on the other. Two events a mere three days apart at two different locations in March 1935 made the point with disturbing clarity. The first of these occurred at Blaina in Monmouthshire on 21 March. A demonstration before the local public assistance committee in the town had been arranged as a means of expressing opposition to the new scales of unemployment relief which had been introduced. The action came at the end of a campaign of protest that had been underway around the country for some time,[114] but the Chief Constable of Monmouthshire considered for

---

[110] H C Debs, 12 June 1934, cols 1523–4 (Sir J Gilmour).

[111] See the account of a tithe dispute in Suffolk in the central criminal court: (134) 98 JP 214 (7 April 1934).

[112] The remarks had been so strong that the audience had been 'roused to indignation', according to V Adams, H C Debs, 26 May 1936, cols 1859–60. The Home Secretary Sir John Simon could merely say by way of an explanation for the police failure to act under s 54(13) of the Metropolitan Police Act that 'one of the police officers present heard a very offensive remark used but at the moment his attention was divided between the speaker and the noisy crowd and he is not in a position to say on oath by whom the expression was used': ibid, 1860 (WA).

[113] One historian of the BUF has somewhat cautiously concluded that '[i]f one were seeking an institutionalised bias in the Metropolitan Police in these years it would be better to characterise it as "anti-left" rather than "pro-fascist" ': J Stevenson, 'The BUF, the Metropolitan Police and Public Order', in K Lunn and R C Thurlow (eds), *British Fascism. Essays on the Radical Right in Inter-War Britain* (1980) 135, at p 147. While this may have been true both of London and the provinces, it is equally clear that the protestors on the receiving end of police militancy saw little difference between the two.

[114] A crowd of 10,000 had earlier protested in Sheffield (H C Debs, 11 February 1935, cols 1581–2) and a large number of unemployed workers had also gathered at a public meeting in Dundee on 13 February 1935, after which ten arrests were made: H C Debs, 27 February 1935, col 1131 (Sir G Collins) (WA). See on this campaign, F Miller, 'The British Unemployment Assistance Crisis of 1935' (1979) 14 *Journal of Contemporary History* 329.

some reason that its only purpose in Blaina was what he described as 'intimidation by numbers'. As a result, he determined that 'it could in no circumstances be allowed'. The official account of what then happened was that 500 people from Abertilly and 5,000 from Natyglo who tried to enter Blaina on the appointed day were turned back by the police, who were then 'compelled to draw their truncheons' in order to run back a crowd from the town which refused to obey an order to disperse. Despite the 200 men whom he admitted were the victims of police truncheons, the Home Secretary afterwards declared himself 'satisfied that the police dealt with a difficult situation with firmness but with their usual forbearance'.[115]

The significance of Blaina lies not only in the severe way that the police, even on their own admission, chose to deal with the demonstrators but also in the almost casual way in which they assumed the power to ban this public manifestation of political opinion. Three days later, in contrast, a large and entirely solicitious police presence ensured that the BUF was able to hold without mishap a public meeting at the Royal Albert Hall in central London. Indeed an anti-fascist procession that day which attempted to proceed from Hyde Park Corner to the meeting in order to register its opposition to the fascists was stopped by the police, senior officers having chosen to impose a *cordon sanitaire* of a half mile radius around the hall, so as to ensure that no protestors got within sight or sound of the fascists. When the matter was raised in Parliament, it emerged that the police had acted in exactly the same way when a similar meeting had occurred in the Royal Albert Hall the previous October. The rationale behind both actions was said to be the prevention of disorder and of breaches of the peace 'arising from the contact of opposing factions',[116] though why it should be the Left rather than the Right that was automatically controlled was not explained. When the Home Secretary was asked in the Commons about the legal basis for this arbitrary police action, his somewhat cavalier response was that it was 'a matter of judgment and common sense'.[117] The police actions at both Blaina

[115] H C Debs, 25 March 1935, col 1585 (Sir J Gilmour). The other quotes in this paragraph are also drawn from the Home Secretary's statement to the House. See 'Police and unemployed in hand-to-hand fight', *Western Mail and South Wales News*, 22 March 1935. The Home Office file, 'Blaina rioters: resolutions and protests against sentences, 1935' (PRO, HO 144/20032) is closed for 100 years.

[116] H C Debs, 2 April 1935, col 204 (Sir J Gilmour) (WA). The matter was raised by Aneurin Bevan MP. In execution of the October 1934 order, a procession of about 50 demonstrators was required to be dispersed at a point near Kensington police station. One person who chose to make a stand was arrested for obstructing the police in the execution of their duty and was subsequently bound over in his own recognisance to be of good behaviour for three years: ibid.

[117] H C Debs, 28 March 1935, col 2068 (Sir J Gilmour).

and around the Royal Albert Hall reflected a routine exercise of just the kind of police discretion that was afterwards to be legitimised in *Duncan v Jones*, and it may be that the automatic way in which the power was regularly deployed against the Left at this time (undetected in the academic textbooks) explains Lord Hewart's otherwise curious remark at the start of his judgment in that case that the facts before him had 'nothing to do' with the right to hold a political meeting.[118] To add to the Left's sense of grievance, the Royal Albert Hall was routinely available to the fascists at this time, but equally consistently denied to any organisation of even a vaguely radical nature, something for which 'no Government has any responsibility', as Sir John Gilmour informed Edward Williams MP when he raised the matter in the Commons.[119]

Police partiality towards the fascists went further even than the protection of their meetings from outside hostility and extended to a remarkably passive interpretation of *Thomas v Sawkins*[120] within the meeting itself. Clearly, it was no longer possible after this decision for the police to rely on the law as an alibi for refusing to interfere with how the fascists policed their own meetings. One of the first big tests for the new police practice post *Thomas v Sawkins*,[121] was a large BUF meeting held in Stratford on 24 July 1935, at which twenty-four uniformed police officers were engaged within the hall. Their presence did not in the least inhibit Sir Oswald and his cohorts from the usual robust response to non-compliant interventions and questions. According to an account of the meeting published contemporaneously in the local newspaper:

A man was putting a question, the purport of which was not clear, when Sir Oswald Mosley said: 'I have seen men like you get behind a policeman and shout insults to Fascists'. The man was ejected, and he struggled and later on appeared in the hall with his shirt in tatters.[122]

An eye-witness account supplied to the local MP provided further details of the behaviour of the stewards:

[118] In the sense that if the police reasonably apprehended disorder on the basis of past violent events, then it was clearly the case that their decision to act had plenty of historical precedents if not an actual legal decision on their side. See Chapter 5 above.

[119] H C Debs, 2 April 1935, cols 195–6. For details of the partisanship of the corporation of the Royal Albert Hall, see Dyson, n 51 above, pp 14–15. Even the British section of the women's world committee against war and fascism was thought too dangerous to be allowed a meeting (in April 1936). The problem of securing space for meetings was one with which the Communist Party was well familiar: see Chapter 3 above.

[120] See n 2 above.   [121] Ibid.

[122] The details of this affair appearing here are drawn from the short adjournment debate on the meeting in the Commons: H C Debs, 2 August 1935, cols 3076–87.

A young man (with a girl) who was sitting in front of me was attacked by a group of Fascists who still went on hitting him whilst he was lying on the floor. He was carried out bleeding from the face. The splashes of blood on the stairs were further evidence of their brutality.

Throughout all this, according to the local newspaper:

[t]he police in the hall watched with cold dispassionate gaze the ejectment of interrupters and seemed more or less bored with the whole proceedings.

Outside the hall, before the meeting, it had however been a somewhat different story, with an enthusiastic and proactive police force working in tandem with the fascists. An account published in the same paper by a local man drew attention to how his entry to the meeting had been achieved:

Instead of being allowed to walk right in as I have hitherto done when I have attended public meetings there, I was stopped by a policeman, who, before allowing me to pass the door, said to a gentleman in a blackshirt uniform, 'Is he all right'. On receiving an affirmative answer from the gentleman in the black shirt, I was allowed to pass up the stairs.

When challenged as to why the police should have allowed themselves to be so completely identified with the BUF in this way, the Home Secretary could only say that the exercise had been designed 'as a precautionary measure to deal with any breaches of the peace that might occur',[123] an explanation that might have been marginally more credible had the police not subsequently stood idly by while exactly this violence was occurring within the hall before their very eyes, and had they not, after the meeting, employed mounted and foot patrols to drive back with some brutality the large anti-fascist crowd that gathered around the hall in the course of the evening. Matters came to a violent head when the sequence of events that had taken place at Stratford was repeated with depressing exactitude at the next great set-piece occasion for the BUF in London, a meeting in the Royal Albert Hall scheduled for 22 March 1936. Incredibly, the fascist procession to the hall was allowed to proceed along Constitution Hill, past Buckingham Palace and along Birdcage Walk, a route more frequently used for royal processions, and one which the First Commissioner of Works, W G A Ormsby-Gore, was afterwards forced to admit should not be used by the fascists as a general rule.[124] Their opponents meanwhile were once again restricted by police instruction to Hyde Park, with another half mile exclusion zone

[123] H C Debs, 30 July 1935, col 2475.   [124] H C Debs, 30 March 1936, cols 1609–10.

of dubious legality having been thrown up around the Albert Hall itself. Despite this, John Strachey from the London district council of the Communist Party issued a circular calling for 'an overwhelming demonstration to take place outside the Royal Albert Hall at 7 pm to be followed by a public meeting in Exhibition Road at 8.30 pm'.[125] When the fascist meeting finally got under way, an audience of some 7,000 was packed into the hall to hear Mosely. Despite this vast number and the freedom of manoeuvre they had been handed by *Thomas v Sawkins*,[126] the police positioned a mere thirty uniformed officers within the hall itself, with a further one hundred men being posted at the doors leading from the meeting to the surrounding corridors. The police instruction unambiguously required total passivity on their part, with their only permitted function being to receive hecklers as and when they were ejected from the hall.[127] The officers within the hall itself were denied even this role, being reduced to the disinterested spectators they had been in Stratford the previous July.

It was an outrageously minimalist interpretation of *Thomas v Sawkins*,[128] and Mosley's blackshirted stewards had a field day.[129] The gallery of the hall was packed with uniformed stewards with heavy buckled belts and many of them were also wearing gloves. Before Mosley arrived on stage, they patrolled the hall in groups, seeking out and reporting on the whereabouts of suspected anti-fascists. These unfortunates were then surrounded by up to twelve stewards, so that before Mosley had even begun it was clear that there was very likely to be trouble. Within half an hour, disorder began to break out in different parts of the hall. Blackshirts removed their belts and attacked suspected anti-fascists with the metal buckles. A number of members of the audience had their faces cut open. One man was ejected by being thrown through a solid glass exit door, smashing it in the process. Another was struck with a blow of such ferocity, by a steward who came up to him from behind, that he was knocked unconscious and afterwards taken to St George's Hospital where he was

---

[125] Strachey's determination to challenge the authorities on this matter may have been partly because his co-ordinating committee against fascism had had at least two requests for use of the Albert Hall as a venue turned down, in September 1934 and again in March 1935: see Dyson, n 51 above, p 14.

[126] See n 2 above.

[127] See the new Home Secretary, Sir John Simon's statement in the House of Commons three days later: H C Debs, 25 March 1936, cols 1227–32.

[128] See n 2 above.

[129] The following account of the meeting and the disorder in Thurloe Square that took place at the same time is drawn from Ronald Kidd's discussion of it in *British Liberty in Danger* (1940), pp 126–30. Kidd was in the Albert Hall at the BUF meeting.

detained for a fortnight with a suspected fractured skull. There were many lesser acts of violence. During this disorder the police within the hall consistently refused to intervene, resisting the many desperate calls made to them by explaining that they had not been instructed to act to preserve order and that they would not do so. The senior police officer within the hall was approached by an NCCL observer and confirmed that the police had no intention of becoming involved. The contrast with what was happening outside could not have been more stark. While the 130 or so officers lounged about in the hall or its surrounding corridors, no fewer than 2,500 police had been deployed to deal with the threat to public disorder posed by the anti-fascist groups, and many of these officers were now on duty outside the hall itself, as some 2,000 to 3,000 people heeded Strachey's call for a counter-demonstration in defiance of the police on Exhibition Road. The crowd gathered in Thurloe Square (which faced the end of Exhibition Road), where they were addressed by Strachey and others, including a clergyman, a prospective Liberal parliamentary candidate and a member of the Labour Party. After this meeting had been underway for about an hour, it was attacked without warning to the organisers or chairman by mounted police who rode their horses into the thickly packed crowd, forcing men and women against street railings, where they were then unceremoniously batoned by both mounted and foot patrol officers.

The Home Secretary's version of these events was as predictable as it was highly tendentious:

Before the arrival of the police there was disorder at the bottom of Exhibition Road, and members of the crowd were stopping motor cars. A bottle was thrown at a police officer, but missed the officer and broke a shop window. In order to prevent the approach of the police to Thurloe Square, a number of persons round the meeting linked arms and appealed to the crowd to stand fast. The police were informed by a member of this body that they had better not approach the crowd, or the police would get more than they anticipated. The officer in charge of the police replied that the assembly was in the prohibited area, and was, moreover, causing serious obstruction, and he appealed for the meeting to be closed and for the crowds to disperse. The crowd refused, and some of them threw stones and earth. The officer in charge ultimately instructed the mounted police to disperse the crowd; they advanced, and, in view of attempts made to unseat the riders, truncheons had to be drawn and in some cases used. The crowd was dispersed in about 10 minutes and order was thereafter restored.[130]

---

[130] H C Debs, 25 March 1936, col 1229 (Sir J Simon).

The speed with which 'order was . . . restored' does not suggest a crowd spoiling for a fight. An investigation by the NCCL into the events, chaired by Professor Norman Bentwich, afterwards concluded that the action of the police was unprovoked, and that the Home Secretary's statement to the House had been 'based on substantially inaccurate information, and on confusion of incidents which happened elsewhere'.[131] The meeting's peaceful flouting of the police prohibition zone was probably the reason such brutally robust action was taken against it when the opportunity arose.[132] As with so many similar statements to the Commons in the 1930s, the Home Secretary's parliamentary explanation of what had happened—disorder already occurring; attacks on the police; provocative words from the crowd, etc.—contained all the ingredients which made the police action next to impossible for commentators or politicians in retrospect thoroughly to gainsay, unless like the NCCL they were prepared to call the police liars. The honest choice lay therefore between supporting the authorities or risking isolation as an 'extremist'. Not surprisingly, many parliamentarians preferred the safety of intellectual confusion, deploring the behaviour of the police without rejecting their argument as to why they had had to act.

The Battle of Cable Street

Against the background of events such as the Thurloe Square baton charge, it should not surprise us that the police did not feel an urgent need after 1934 to push government for new public order legislation. The existing law seemed fine as far as attacking the Left was concerned, while the issue of fascist marching was simply not perceived as a problem worthy of legislative intervention. For its part, the government was disinclined to resurrect the draft legislation which had been circulating in or around Whitehall for some four years. This led it inevitably into frequent

[131] Kidd, n 129 above, p. 130. The evidence to support the NCCL conclusion was supplied to Parliament by Dingle Foot, in an adjournment debate on 25 March 1936: H C Debs, cols 1361–78. The report itself was afterwards sent to the Home Secretary: H C Debs, 30 July 1936, col 1766 (Sir J Simon) (WA). Its call for an official public inquiry into the conduct of the police was not heeded.

[132] But note the newly appointed Metropolitan Police Commissioner, Sir Philip Game's subsequent private admission that a 'prohibited meeting will probably try to meet elsewhere and will either get their way or have to be broken up by the police. I made this mistake through inexperience in connection with the fascist meeting at the Albert Hall last March with the result of the unfortunate clash between the crowds and the police in Thurloe Square' (PRO, HO 144/20159). Observations from the Metropolitan Police Commissioner on the necessity for new legislation, 12 October 1936, para 10. For the strange affair of Captain A O J Hope's car, which may have played its part in sowing seeds of confusion on the day, see H C Debs, 25 March 1936, cols 1364–7 (Captain Hope).

parliamentary defences both of legislative inertia during 1935 and 1936[133] and of the sort of police conduct, albeit on a lesser scale, that had generated such controversy at Stratford and Thurloe Square. It seemed that—short of donning the blackshirt itself—there was nothing that the police could do that would not afterwards be officially defended or explained in Parliament or elsewhere.[134] One particularly glaring incident occurred in 1936 in Walthamstow where the police forcibly concluded a traditional NUWM meeting so as to allow a meeting of fascists to take place. The Home Secretary was provoked into describing the police decision as 'an error of judgment'. He was clear however that 'the error [had been] due not to any element of favouritism but solely to the mistaken belief that, because the Fascists had publicly advertised their intention to hold a meeting . . . on that evening and had informed the police of their intention, the Fascists had a prior right to the meeting place'. The minister went on to assure the Commons that 'steps [were] being taken by the commissioner to give further directions to his force which it is hoped will avoid the repetition of any similar incident in future'.[135]

Other reasons for having considered legislative change as a matter of urgency in 1934 were also not as prominent two years later. Radical NUWM activity had declined somewhat from its 1932 to 1934 heyday, and left-wing protest generally was not worrying the police to the same extent as it had in the past. As we have seen, such protest had been the main concern of police chiefs when it had come to pressurising government in earlier years. While it was true that, after Olympia, there had been a perceived need to enact more effective statutory controls on the holding of public meetings, it was now the case that after *Thomas v Sawkins*[136]—however minimally applied in practice—this too was no longer a burning issue. In the course of resisting calls for legislative action after a particularly controversial BUF meeting in Edinburgh in May 1936, the Secretary of State for Scotland, Sir Godfrey Collins, was able to explain that he was 'advised that under the existing law the police

---

[133] The position with regard to uniforms was still being 'carefully watched' in May 1936: H C Debs, 7 May 1936, col 1895 (G Lloyd, Under Secretary of State for Home Affairs) (WA). The following month, the 'difficulty would be to define what is a uniform': H C Debs, 22 June 1936, col 1427 (Sir J Simon).

[134] See the incident at Paddington in April 1936, raised in Parliament by William Gallacher MP: H C Debs, 6 April 1936, cols 2424–6. For a first hand account of the police conduct during these years from an NCCL perspective, see S Scaffardi, *Fire Under the Carpet. Working for Civil Liberties in the 1930s* (1986), ch 7. Another first-hand account is J Jacobs, *Out of the Ghetto. My Youth in the East End, Communism and Fascism 1913–39* (1978).

[135] H C Debs, 14 May 1936, cols 573–4 (Sir J Simon) (WA).   [136] See n 2 above.

[were] entitled to enter and remain in a hall during a meeting, if they are requested by the promoters to do so; also, if they have reason to believe that a breach of the law is being committed; or further, if they have reasonable grounds for apprehending that a breach of the law is about to be committed'. Given this interpretation of *Thomas v Sawkins*,[137] a case that was not even formally part of the law within the jurisdiction, it was hardly surprising that the Secretary of State should have gone on to assure his audience that '[f]urther powers to prevent or deal with any breach of the peace' were 'unnecessary'.[138] The common law breach of the peace power was also widely believed to be available to control open air meetings and this was confirmed in *Duncan v Jones*[139] in October 1935.[140] Its utility as the basis for the imposition of draconian conditions on processions had been clearly in evidence in the *cordon sanitaire* that had been erected around the Royal Albert Hall (presumably on its basis) on at least three occasions after Olympia. As Trenchard's successor as Metropolitan Police Commissioner, Sir Philip Game was privately to admit to the Home Office in October 1936, '[w]e have, or anyhow have assumed, considerable powers already to proscribe [the] routes [of processions], to direct them for traffic or other reasons and even to forbid them, if likely to lead to a breach of the peace'.[141]

The truth was that if the government was determined not to act on the genuine problems posed by the uniforms worn by and the paramilitary activities of the BUF, then there was little or no reason for legislative intervention of any sort. BUF uniforms and military formations apart, the grievance felt about the law at this time centred not so much

---

[137] See n 2 above. See also H C Debs, 14 May 1936, cols 573–4 (Sir J Simon) (WA).

[138] H C Debs, 26 May 1936, col 1807. In practice the law was construed far more widely than this Commons statement would suggest. See the Home Secretary Sir John Simon's revealing version of *Thomas v Sawkins*, volunteered in the course of the Second Reading debate on the Public Order Bill in November 1936, that 'if anybody takes a hall and invites the public to come in, he has no right whatever to object to the presence of somebody just because he is a policeman or a soldier': H C Debs, 16 November 1936, col 1365. Simon went on to say that the practice in London was for the police to be present inside meetings 'not because they have been sent for or because there is a riot, but because the authorities think that . . . it might be convenient to have a policeman there': ibid.

[139] See n 4 above.

[140] An example of the similar jurisdiction in Scotland is provided by a case in Paisley where two men addressed a meeting of the unemployed. They refused to stop when required to do so by the police, with the result that they were charged and convicted of both breach of the peace and obstruction. Astonishingly, the men were then jailed for 40 days' hard labour without the option of a fine. It was this bizarrely harsh sentence that drew attention to the case, and the men were released shortly after an appeal was launched on their behalf: H C Debs, 23 May 1935, col 503 (N MacLean).

[141] Observations from the Metropolitan Police Commissioner on the necessity for new legislation, 12 October 1936, n 132 above, para 10. Lord Trenchard had been even more certain that he had a power to ban processions: see his recorded comments at a conference held in the Home Secretary's room in the House of Commons, 13 June 1934, in PRO, HO 45/25386.

on its content as on its selective enforcement. As this and the preceding chapter have demonstrated, the authorities were spoilt for options if they decided to repress the expression in public of a political sentiment that they chose to deem unacceptable. Apart from the breach of the peace jurisdiction and the simple application of superior force of dubious legality, which seems to be what occurred in Blaina, a myriad of (lawful) procedural ruses were always also available to the authorities, such as the binding over orders and the tactical arrests—so favoured by the then Attorney General, Sir Thomas Inskip—that had been engineered against the NUWM in 1932 and 1934.[142] A valuable dimension to this binding over jurisdiction from the authorities' point of view had been revealed in an otherwise obscure exercise of the power in 1931.[143] A defendant was found to have disturbed the peace and to have incited a breach of the peace, his offence having been to have made two speeches in reference to ejectment proceedings in which the Staveley Coal and Iron Company were then engaged. He was duly bound over, and in default of providing surety for good behaviour was committed to prison for three months. Unusually, the defendant then appealed the case to his local quarter sessions which held however that, as he had not been convicted, no appeal was possible. In this way the magistrates' binding over jurisdiction—no matter how absurdly or arbitrarily applied—appeared to be entirely insulated from scrutiny.[144]

Apart from the foregoing, the authorities could also invariably fall back if they so desired on obscure local legislation or local bye-laws[145] to achieve their chosen ends. We have already seen examples of how section 52 of the Metropolitan Police Act 1839 was interpreted to empower the authorities to impose sweeping conditions on processions in London, and there was a similar provision in the Town Police Clauses Act 1847,[146] available in various forms in most urban centres in England and

---

[142] The tactics predate the NUWM agitation. The binding over jurisdiction can be seen in operation in *Lansbury v Riley*, n 91 above, and it was used extensively against members of the Communist Party in the 1920s: see generally Chapter 3 above.

[143] The details that follow are drawn from (1933) 97 JP 255.

[144] A right of appeal was not in fact introduced until the Magistrates' Courts (Appeals from Binding Over Orders) Act 1956.

[145] Liverpool's bye-laws are reproduced in PRO, HO 144/20159, n 132 above. An example of the attempted application of a local bye-law to prohibit the occurrence of a public procession occurred in Birmingham in January 1931, when a public procession to Council House was prevented by the police after the Lord Mayor indicated that he would not receive a deputation from the group: see (1931) 95 JP 43. The magistrate found that the police action had not been warranted by the bye-law.

[146] See s 21.

Wales.[147] London had its annual sessional orders as well, available if required to protect Whitehall from unwanted political truths. For its part, Scotland had the Burgh Police Act 1892 and various local measures underpinning the kind of bye-law that had been applied so effectively in *Aldred v Miller* in 1925.[148] Given this kind of background, the only unusual or surprising thing about the decision of the Cardiff Chief Constable to prohibit all processions to and from a BUF rally in Cathays Park in November 1936 would have been the organisation that was thereby restricted.[149] Sometimes formal legal action was not even required, with officials able to rely on informal powers of persuasion, backed by the threat of the application of one or other of these myriad laws. Thus in July 1936, Manchester Town Council, apparently in consultation with the local chief constable, allowed the fascists to march only on condition that they did not wear their uniforms, a stipulation to which they reluctantly acceded.[150]

As late, therefore, as the end of Summer 1936, the government appears to have had no definite plans to introduce public order legislation of any sort, nor any good reason to do so, if action against BUF uniforms and paramilitary activities was still being ruled out. Two events then occurred which appear together to have altered the official mind, or at least that of the Home Secretary, Sir John Simon, fresh to the job

[147] In 1912 Liverpool had procured private legislation which went further than the Town Police Clauses Act, and Bolton had achieved a similar result in 1925. However these legislative initiatives were unusual. Efforts by local councils to expand their powers in respect of the control of public protest were usually unsuccessful, with the Home Office being generally opposed: see PRO, HO 144/20158. Provisions requiring advance notice of processions were in contrast 'freely allowed in Private Bills in recent years', ibid, Home Office note, 4 July 1934.

[148] 1925, JC 21. See pp. 129–30 above. There is a very good account of the legal position in Scotland given in the course of the Second Reading of the Public Order Bill in 1936 by T M Cooper, the then Lord Advocate: see H C Debs, 16 November 1936, cols 1413–18. For some of the many local provisions in Scotland governing the control of processions, see PRO, HO 144/20158 and 20159.   [149] Cullen, n 34 above, p 255.

[150] *Manchester Guardian*, 17 July 1936. The fascist meeting duly took place on 19 July, with over 5,000 people crowded into an open space near the Jewish quarter' (*The Times*, 20 July 1936). There was little trouble and only eight arrests were made, all of hecklers who interrupted the meeting: *Manchester Guardian*, 25 July 1936. See further H C Debs, 27 July 1936, cols 1095–6 (Sir J Simon). The Home Secretary was uncertain as to whether there was a legal basis for the council's action, though presumably the police could have relied if they had chosen to do so on their breach of the peace jurisdiction. The fascists had first sought permission to process because of s 213 of the Manchester Police Act 1844, a provision similar to s 21 of the Town Police Clauses Act 1847 and s 52 of the Metropolitan Police Act 1839. The powers in the Act were therefore concerned more with keeping the thoroughfare clear than with political protest and were as a result 'not so valuable as they may on the surface appear to be' in PRO, HO 144/20159. Memorandum prepared for the information of members of the deputation appointed by the Manchester City Council to interview the Home Secretary on the question of political demonstrations. The Cardiff police took similar action in respect of a BUF meeting in November 1936: see Cullen, n 34 above, pp. 255–7, where the background to the policy is discussed.

but a politician of long standing, with experience in the control of domestic dissent that went back to the First World War.[151] Perhaps predictably, the events that changed the political climate both involved assertive action by the Left. The first was the 'Battle of Cable Street' on 4 October. During 1936 as a whole, no fewer than fifty-seven of the BUF's 117 meetings were disrupted by their communist opponents.[152] In early October, the fascists planned a large march in the East End of London to mark the culmination of the long and violent summer campaign that they had waged against the Jewish community resident in that part of the capital. The procession was to be followed by no fewer than four large-scale open air rallies, each to be addressed by Mosley himself. There was no doubt that the BUF viewed the occasion with deadly seriousness and huge posters advertising it appeared throughout the East End. Efforts at persuading the authorities to prohibit or control the procession having proved unavailing, members of the local community organised by the Communist Party and the Independent Labour Party mounted a massive campaign of direct action against the BUF plan.[153] So vast and well organised was the throng that gathered to oppose the fascists that the large police presence that had mustered to support their right to march was not sufficient to achieve its and the fascists' goal. This was not before the occurrence of a succession of running battles between police and anti-fascist protestors. A series of baton charges managed slowly to clear some streets for the march, but the police finally came to grief at Cable Street, where the crowd held its ground and saw off the best aggressive efforts of both mounted and foot patrol officers. Windows were broken, a lorry was commandeered by the crowd and sticks and stones were rained upon the police.

[151] See Chapter 2 above.   [152] Cullen, n 34 above, p 249.

[153] The *Daily Worker* produced a special supplement on 3 October, under the banner headline, 'Save the East End of London from Fascism'. One of the participants in the day's events has left the following description of preparations for the resistance: 'The big fascist posters were torn down and replaced with a fresh appeal: "Bar the Road to Fascism!", "They Shall Not Pass!", "Remember Olympia!", "Aldgate Sunday 2 pm!". The message was spread in whitewash, and reinforced with leaflets, at propaganda meetings, appealing to trade unions, trades councils, Labour Parties. The call was for a mass rally at Gardiner's Corner Aldgate, to block the key junction commanding the main routes into the East End, and to face Mosley with an impassable human barrier if he attempted to march in through the main stream and not creep in at the back door. Cable Street—another possible route into the East End—was to be secured as an advance line of defence by putting up street barricades. A disused lorry in a yard nearby was earmarked to be overturned, together with piles of timber, junk, old furniture, bedsteads and mattresses. Dockers living in the Cable Street area were called on to co-operate. Riders on motorbikes and bicycles were to report back to headquarters the latest moves "from the front". First-aid posts with doctors and nurses in charge were set up in shops and houses in the neighbourhood': Scaffardi, n 134 above, pp 153–4. See also 'Wild Scenes in the East End', *News Chronicle*, 5 October 1936, p 1.

At 3.30 pm, the Metropolitan Police Commissioner, Sir Philip Game (who was present during most of the day) felt compelled to direct Mosley and his cohorts to disperse.[154] There was to be no march, and—more to the point—no inflammatory rallies afterwards. 'Victory was in the air with a feeling of sober jubilation' was how one NCCL observer later remembered the atmosphere that afternoon as the enormity of what had been achieved gradually sunk home.[155] The views of those in government were naturally rather different. The main effect of the events of 4 October was to add a massive political impetus to the case for legislative intervention. The anti-fascist opposition had long hankered after new controls on overt displays of fascist power. The annual conference of the Labour Party opened the following day, and an emergency resolution was passed, urging the government to 'institute an immediate inquiry into the recent disturbances and into the activities and finances of the Fascist Organisations'.[156] A conference of the Party's London MPs, mayors and London County Council members later met to express further concern, authorising Herbert Morrison to write to the Home Secretary on its behalf calling for 'effective action' in respect of the recent disorders in the capital. The NCCL and the London trades council added their voices to the push for reform. Even Ramsay MacDonald, now out of power, called for measures to prevent 'deliberate planning to create disorder under the cloak of freedom of speech . . . to insult the Jews and arouse unnatural passions'.[157] The tension was heightened by the events that happened in the days that followed Cable Street, with a series of attacks by disgruntled and vengeful fascists in the East End, and two further large demonstrations by both sides, the one triumphal, the other defiant. On 14 October, the general secretary of the TGWU and chairman of the TUC, Ernest Bevin, telegrammed the Prime Minister Stanley Baldwin from Geneva that his union viewed 'with grave concern [the] renewed disturbances in East London'. Pointedly drawing attention to the risk of 'grave industrial unrest and serious dislocation of industry' if the 'government permit[ted] fascist provocation to continue', Bevin

---

[154] Sir Philip banned the Mosleyite march in the exercise of his common law power to prevent a reasonably apprehended breach of the peace: see the note by the Metropolitan Police Commissioner to the Home Secretary, 9 June 1937 in PRO, HO 144/21086.

[155] Scaffardi, n 134 above, p 156 et seq: Jacobs, n 134 above, pp 235–58 also has a lively account. The events of 4 October led to 146 charges being brought against demonstrators, 133 of which had been proved by 10 November with another 10 cases pending: H C Debs, 10 November 1936, col 703 (Sir J Simon) (WA).

[156] Labour Party, *Annual Report 1936*, pp 164–6.

[157] Quoted in Scaffardi, n 134 above, p 159.

urged the Prime Minister to 'take immediate action to protect peaceful citizens against uniformed fascist attack'.[158]

It is probable that the reaction to Cable Street alone would have been enough to have forced the government finally to act against fascist provocation, providing one of the clearest examples in the history of British civil liberties of the effectiveness of proportionate political violence in achieving a desired legislative aim. Cable Street had however moved the debate beyond uniforms and private armies into the whole question of marching per se, with the Labour Party now taking a broader line on the possibility of tightening the law on both marches and assemblies. Speaking to his constituents in Cleckheaton Town Hall on the Wednesday after Cable Street, with the Labour Party conference now in full swing, the Home Secretary, Sir John Simon, saw the opportunity to extract some political advantage from the pressure to which he was being subjected:

The Home Secretary is not a dictator with power to allow or prohibit processions as he thinks fit, and it is very characteristic of Socialistic mentality that Mr Morrison should imagine that a Home Secretary, by prohibiting a meeting or procession, would make it unlawful. That may be so in Russia, and might be so in a Socialist State, but it certainly is not so in free England. . . . If the law is to be changed it must apply all round—to the demonstrations of the Left just as much as to the demonstrations of the Right.[159]

There was more than Party point-scoring in these remarks. After a period of quiet, the government was once again about to be subjected to the intense moral pressure brought about by that emotional weapon in the hands of the unemployed and impoverished, the national hunger march. In July, revised UAB scales and means test regulations had been published which were certain to entail severe cuts for large sections of the unemployed. The date for the introduction of these changes was to be 16 November, and a large autumn campaign had been launched by the NUWM in protest against their imminent implementation. Apart from the NUWM campaign, which was planned to include a series of marches converging on London's Hyde Park on 8 November, an autonomous group of protestors had also become involved, setting out from Jarrow in the north-east just a day or so before the Home Secretary's Cleckheaton

---

[158] These quotations are from Scaffardi, ibid, pp 156–8.
[159] *The Times*, 8 October 1936. Sir John appears to have recycled the speech a number of times. It was loyally filed away by officials in the Home Office and may now be found in the Public Record Office under the title, ' "Liberty and Liberalism". A speech by Sir John Simon in Spen Valley, 7 October 1936' (PRO, HO 144/20159).

speech. This small band of men was intent on drawing attention to the terrible poverty in their own town in particular, caused both by an exceptionally high rate of unemployment and by the closure of the local shipyards.[160]

There was something about the poignant independence of this small group of 'Jarrow Crusaders'—no more than a couple of hundred men— that led to them attracting ever-increasing public support from the moment of their departure from Jarrow. This was not something of which the authorities took immediate notice. One week after Cleckheaton, on 14 October, the Cabinet indicated after its regular meeting that the government 'had under consideration the fact that a number of marches on London are in progress or in contemplation' but that such 'marches . . . [were] altogether undesirable' and that 'Ministers cannot consent to receive any deputation of marchers'.[161] Such calculated aloofness was too much even for *The Times*, which noted in an editorial that the Jarrow marchers at least 'had enlisted a large amount of public sympathy' and that the government's declaration was 'liable to be construed or misconstrued as a discouragement of this march in particular and as a refusal of Ministers to meet the spokesmen of a forlorn community'.[162] (The decision was afterwards reversed, and meetings did take place with various marchers' representatives which achieved some alleviation of the regulations as originally envisaged.[163]) It was at this 14 October meeting—a mere ten days after Cable Street, and the very day on which Baldwin had received Bevin's ominous telegram—that the Cabinet finally decided to proceed with new public order legislation. The Home Secretary told his colleagues that what was 'wanted, however, in the present connexion [was] not an Emergency Regulation but a strengthening of the ordinary law of the land'.[164] In the King's Speech to mark the opening of the new Parliament on 3 November—the very week the

---

[160] See the book by the local MP, E Wilkinson, *The Town that was Murdered* (1939). For the author's involvement in the Crusade, see B D Vernon, *Ellen Wilkinson, 1891–1947* (1982), pp 141–7.

[161] *The Times*, 15 October 1936.

[162] Ibid.

[163] See W Hannington, *Never on our Knees* (1967), pp 318–20. The two Home Office files on the marches, 'Hunger March 1936' in PRO, HO 144/20696–7 are closed for 100 years.

[164] The meeting of 14 October had before it a memorandum by the Home Secretary on the preservation of public order (PRO, CP 261 (36)), from which the quotation in the text is drawn. The Home Secretary admitted that the question had been 'brought to a head by the attempted fascist demonstration in the East End of London on Sunday, 4th October'. According to the minute, the Cabinet was 'very strongly in sympathy with the desire of the Home Secretary to strengthen the existing law'. A Cabinet sub-committee was established to consider the kind of legislation that should be put before the House. For these and further details on the origin of the 1936 Act see generally PRO, HO 144/20158.

Jarrow Crusaders finally left London—a Bill for 'strengthening the law without interfering with legitimate freedom of speech or assembly'[165] was promised. The new Public Order Bill was introduced on 9 November, the day after the NUWM's own protest march in London. The Bill's main target may have been the fascists, but it would never have reached Parliament as a legislative proposal had not the anti-fascists asserted themselves in typical fashion at a peculiarly opportune time. Much of its content made the proposed measure very much a double-edged sword as far as radical protest was concerned, though this fact was somewhat obscured by the directness of its assault on fascism. It is to this legislation that we now turn.

The Public Order Act 1936

The Bill commended to the House by Sir John Simon at its second reading on 16 November 1936 could not have received a reception more different from that which had so effectively ambushed the Incitement to Disaffection Bill two years before. The Labour opposition gave it 'a general welcome'[166] and it enjoyed a brisk and relatively untroubled passage through both Houses, receiving the Royal Assent on 18 December.[167] The atmosphere of the Commons was very different for Donald Somervell, now Attorney General and the recipient of much parliamentary wrath as Solicitor General at the time of the Incitement to Disaffection Bill, but able on this occasion to say with confidence that the government had 'every reason to be satisfied with the course the [second reading] debate [had] taken'.[168] From the perspective of the Labour Party, Herbert Morrison expressed himself in the following terms in the course of the Second Reading debate:

---

[165] H C Debs, 3 November 1936, col 12 (King's Speech).

[166] H C Debs, 16 November 1936, col 1368 (J R Clynes). But see the critical appraisal of many of its provisions by D N Pritt in *New Statesman and Nation*, 14 November 1936, pp 761–3. In its final form, parts of the Act were to be subjected to a swingeing attack from W Ivor Jennings, 'Public Order' (1937) 8 *Political Quarterly* 7.

[167] The parliamentary debates are to be found at: H C Debs, 16 November 1936, cols 1349–473 (Second Reading); H C Debs, 23 November 1936, cols 49–193 and H C Debs, 26 November 1936, cols 581–710 (Committee); H C Debs, 7 December 1936, cols 1659–756 (Report); H C Debs, 7 December 1936, cols 1756–1785 (Third Reading); H L Debs, 11 December 1936, cols 741–73 (Second Reading); H L Debs, 15 December 1936, cols 837–93 (Committee); H L Debs, 16 December 1936, cols 961–71 (Report); H L Debs, 16 December 1936, cols 971–2 (Third Reading). The Commons accepted each of the few amendments made in the Lords: H C Debs, 17 December 1936, cols 2781–4.

[168] H C Debs, 16 November 1936, col 1466.

A political organisation which has the purpose of destroying freedom of action and freedom of political organisation cannot itself very well plead the cause of freedom to do exactly as it likes. Consequently, if there be a political organisation in the State which is seeking by methods which have been successful in other countries to destroy the liberty of our people, to destroy the liberty of expression, to destroy the liberty of political organisation . . . then a State which desires to preserve liberty has a right to take action with a view to checking action which is calculated to destroy the liberty we wish to preserve.[169]

It seems that Labour would have gone further to attack fascism, for in addition to the measures proposed by the government, Morrison also expressed concern about the funding of the fascists, and in particular about the suspicion 'that money is coming from foreign countries, whether Germany or Italy, or both of them', contending that 'the situation is unhealthy' and 'no British political party ought to be dependent upon it'.[170]

Whatever the shortcomings of the Bill, particularly welcomed on all sides of the Commons were those clauses which at last dealt with political uniforms and the quasi-military organisation of political parties. As far as the first of these was concerned, clause 1 prohibited any person from wearing in any public place or at any public meeting a 'uniform signifying [his][171] association with any political organisation or with the promotion of any political object'. A proviso allowed a chief officer of police (with the consent of the Secretary of State) to exempt from the full rigour of the Act uniforms worn on any 'ceremonial, anniversary, or other [special][172] occasion' which the senior officer was satisfied was not 'likely to involve the risk of public disorder'. This, together with a requirement that the Attorney General consent to proceedings under the clause, was as far as the government was prepared to go by way of limiting the reach of the new offence. Where once the liberties of the fascists

---

[169] H C Debs, 16 November 1936, cols 1454–5.

[170] Ibid, cols 1461–2. Foreign funding was strongly denied by Mosley: see *The Blackshirt*, 14 November 1936, and also a leader in the same paper on 21 November 1936. On 12 November, James Griffith MP asked the Home Secretary whether 'his Department [kept] any check upon sums of money which are sent from abroad to the British Union of Fascists and National Socialists', and if so, 'whether he [could] give any indication of the amount and origin of foreign subsidies to Fascist propaganda and organisation in Great Britain'. In response, Sir John Simon was unwilling to make a detailed statement, but he did say that information had reached him 'which goes to show that, both in the case of Fascist and Communist organisations, their funds have been supplemented from abroad'. When asked what steps were being taken 'to try to stop that practice' in relation to the fascists, he replied that he had nothing to add: see H C Debs, 12 November 1936, cols 1029–30. It is true that financial problems were certainly evident for the fascists in 1938, when it was felt necessary to make an appeal for funds and to assure potential donors of their anonymity: see *The Blackshirt*, 29 January 1938.

[171] Added at the Report stage in the House of Commons.

[172] Added in Committee in the House of Commons.

had been pre-eminent, now it was 'their organised rowdyism' which was 'threatening to undermine essential British liberties'.[173] Whereas previously the problem of defining a 'uniform' for the purposes of penal legislation such as this had been one of the insuperable barriers to its introduction, now there was, according to the Home Secretary, to be 'no statutory definition because we are satisfied that it is better to take what is, after all, a perfectly well-known English word and use it in the connotation here appearing'.[174] Indeed, writing on the Bill in the *New Statesman*, even the noted civil libertarian D N Pritt was to be found arguing that clause 1 was the least unsatisfactory part of the Bill, it being 'far wiser to leave the question of what amounts to [a] uniform to the courts (even to courts of summary jurisdiction) than to attempt to frame a definition'.[175] This was an important concession from the leading contemporary foot-soldier in the battle for civil liberties, who was otherwise concerned by the 'low co-efficient of certainty' in the Bill.[176]

The problem of quasi-military organisations was dealt with in the 'necessarily long'[177] clause 2, the central effect of which was however laid out clearly enough in sub-clause 1:

If the members or adherents of any association of persons, whether incorporated or not, are—

(a) organised or trained or equipped for the purpose of enabling them to be employed in usurping the functions of the police or the armed forces of the Crown; or

(b) organised and trained or organised and equipped either for the purpose of enabling them to be employed for the use or display of physical force in promoting any political object, or in such manner as to arouse reasonable apprehension that they are organised and either trained or equipped for that purpose;

then any person who takes part in the control or management of the association, or in so organising or training as aforesaid any members or adherents thereof, shall be guilty of an offence under this section.

It was mainly through paragraph (b) that it was hoped to address the fascists, with the Home Secretary being quite prepared to admit that paragraph (a) was designed as a bulwark of principle against 'a danger which

---

[173] H C Debs, 16 November 1936, col 1350 (Sir J Simon). The Home Secretary went to some lengths to stress that the section was not directed against the Blackshirts alone, however.

[174] Ibid, cols 1352–3.   [175] Pritt, n 166 above, p 761.

[176] Ibid. As we shall shortly see, Pritt had many other critical points to make in respect of the measure.

[177] H C Debs, 16 November 1936, col 1355.

might develop in the future'.[178] Though the consequential sub-clauses in clause 2 were the subject of a variety of amendments in both the Commons and the Lords, both this sub-clause and the whole of clause 1 on uniforms emerged unscathed from the parliamentary process.[179] An entirely new sub-clause to clause 2 was added to the Bill on Report in the Commons and this change did prove highly controversial. Acting on the basis of a suggestion made by a backbencher during earlier Committee discussions,[180] the government now proposed to add that:

(6) Nothing in this section shall be construed as prohibiting the employment of a reasonable number of persons as stewards to assist in the preservation of order at any public meeting held upon private premises, or the making of arrangements for that purpose or the instruction of the persons to be so employed in their lawful duties as such stewards, or their being furnished with badges or other distinguishing signs.

While it was of course true that there did need to be some means of keeping order at BUF meetings which did not require resort to the police, this late addition to the Bill nevertheless had the potential to unravel many of the anti-fascist gains that had been achieved in the rest of the clause and in clause 1. Despite a strong attack from Aneurin Bevan, who warned that the Commons was 'now re-importing into the Bill the possibility of an organised, disciplined and semi-military force',[181] the government held firm, secured support for its proposal, and the sub-section duly appeared in the finished measure. The criticism of the new sub-clause in clause 2 was all the more vehement because of another proposal already in the published Bill which, while appearing just as innocuous and impartial, was in reality particularly helpful to the fascists. This was the extraordinary addition to the Public Meeting Act 1908 that the government tried to slip through as a merely technical change, with Sir John Simon proposing that if any constable reasonably suspected an offence under the 1908 Act, he was to be empowered to require the disrupter—on pain of criminal penalty—to reveal both his or her name and address. Incredibly the Bill then went on to require that the officer concerned 'report the name and address to the chairman of the meeting or

---

[178] H C Debs, 16 November 1936, col 1355.
[179] The proviso to cl 2(1) (which appears in s 2(1) of the enacted measure, 'allowing a defence to the charge in certain, narrowly defined circumstances, was added at the Committee stage in the Commons. A minor addition to what was enacted as s 1(2) was also made at the same stage in the parliamentary process.
[180] See H C Debs, 23 November 1936, cols 104–17 (O Lewis).
[181] See H C Debs, 7 December 1936, col 1674.

to some other person responsible for calling the meeting together'. Clearly the idea here was to facilitate private prosecutions under the 1908 Act, since this was to remain the only means of proceeding under it. While not objectionable in theory, the application of such a procedure at fascist meetings would have been an invitation to retaliatory violence against hecklers after a meeting had long concluded, of a far more brutal sort than could be meted out at a public meeting, even one with aggressive stewards and passive police officers. It took an intervention from no less a figure than the Labour leader Clement Attlee before the government was finally persuaded to drop the reporting requirement,[182] though the offence remained, leaving open the possibility of constables volunteering the dangerous information to the fascist organisers of a disrupted meeting.

The double-edged nature of the new Bill, already apparent from its provisions on stewarding and heckling at public meetings, was brought further to the fore in clause 3. This was the overarching national measure on public processions for which senior police officers in particular had long argued. As introduced, sub-clause (1) was as follows:

If the chief officer of police is of opinion, having regard to the time or place at which and the circumstances in which any public procession is taking place or is intended to take place and to the route taken or proposed to be taken by the procession, that there is ground for apprehending that the procession may occasion serious public disorder, he may give directions imposing upon the persons organising or taking part in the procession such conditions as appear to him necessary for the preservation of public order, including conditions prescribing the route to be taken by the procession and conditions prohibiting the procession from entering any street or public place specified in the directions.

In view of the breadth and range of powers already available to control processions, Simon could hardly claim that this new provision added much to the powers already enjoyed by many authorities across the country, and he did not try to do so. Indeed, just eight days before the Second Reading debate on the Bill, an NUWM-sponsored march (the 'National Procession of Unemployed and Employed Workers to Hyde Park') had been prohibited in advance from processing through the Strand, Piccadilly, Oxford Street and Edgware Road, the Under Secretary of State for Home Affairs, Mr Geoffrey Lloyd, explaining to Parliament that as 'a result of the experience of processions, the whole

---

[182] H C Debs, 26 November 1936, col 687. The clause disappeared at the Report stage: H C Debs, 7 December 1936, cols 1751–3.

question of the routing of processions [had been] reviewed by Scotland Yard some years ago, and it [had been] decided that a certain number of the main arterial thoroughfares of London . . . should not be used for the purposes of large processions'.[183] In this case the Metropolitan Police Commissioner purported to act under section 52 of the Metropolitan Police Act (which gave him, he claimed, the 'power to prevent the obstruction of streets at all times of public processions')[184] and it was this measure, together with the motley of local pieces of legislation earlier referred to, that underpinned the Home Secretary's assertion that the sub-clause enacted 'what, to a very large extent, [was] the present power to control the route that a procession takes'.[185] The justification for its enactment now lay merely in its national reach, its clear empowerment of the police rather than the local authorities,[186] and its clarity when compared to the 'somewhat archaic words' in 'some rather ancient Statutes' dating from 'before the full establishment of modern police forces'.[187] In Committee, the government accepted that the subjective discretion of the chief officer should be changed so as to require a 'reasonable ground' and with a new proviso on the display of flags added later in the Commons[188] and a further minor change in the Lords,[189] this was the form in which the sub-clause emerged as law.

The real meat in clause 3, indeed in the whole Bill, was to be found in its second and third sub-clauses, to which Sir John Simon—amazingly—made no mention at all in the course of his Second Reading speech. These provisions, which survived parliamentary scrutiny with no substantive modifications, gave the authorities the formal power to ban

---

[183] H C Debs, 5 November 1936, col 254.

[184] Ibid. Another example of the routine application of the same power at around this time occurred in Barking on Saturday, 14 November, when a peace procession was postponed for two hours by the Metropolitan Police Commissioner on account of the traffic congestion it would have caused had it taken place at the prearranged time of 7 pm. The matter only became controversial because of the lack of notice of the postponement given to the organisers; the legitimacy of the power was not otherwise questioned: H C Debs, 18 November 1936, col 1795 (G Lloyd).

[185] H C Debs, 16 November 1936, col 1359.

[186] See generally the Towns Improvement Clauses Act 1847 and the rather limited s 21 of the Town Police Clauses Act 1847.

[187] H C Debs, 16 November 1936, col 1359 (Sir J Simon). Note that a similar argument underpinned the proposed cl 5 of the new Bill (prohibiting offensive conduct conducive to breaches of the peace) which was also based on local provisions, though the penalty envisaged in the new Act was more severe than had typically been the case in such local measures and bye-laws: see p 318 below.

[188] 'Provided that no conditions restricting the display of flags, banners or emblems shall be imposed under this subsection except such as are reasonably necessary to prevent risk of a breach of the peace.' The fear was that the conditions power would be used arbitrarily to deprive processions of much of their (harmless) political colour.

[189] The omission of the word 'street' in the last line of the sub-clause as originally published.

processions in advance. As enacted, subsection (2), covering the country outside London,[190] provided that:

If at any time the chief officer of police is of opinion that by reason of particular circumstances existing in any borough or urban district or in any part thereof the powers conferred on him by the last forgoing subsection will not be sufficient to enable him to prevent serious public disorder being occasioned by the holding of public processions in that borough, district or part, he shall apply to the council of the borough or district for an order prohibiting for such period not exceeding three months as may be specified in the application the holding of all public processions or of any class of public procession so specified either in the borough or urban district or in part thereof, as the case may be, and upon receipt of the application the council may, with the consent of a Secretary of State, make an order either in terms of the application or with such modifications as may be approved by the Secretary of State.

Subsection (3) extended a similar power to the Commissioners of the City of London police and the Metropolitan Police, except that in each case the local authorities were bypassed in favour of direct applications from these police chiefs to the Home Secretary. Resisting all attempts to omit the subsections altogether, or at the very least to redefine the police discretion in them in objective rather than subjective terms, the government stressed how unlikely it was that the powers in them would ever be used. They were, according to Sir John Simon, present merely to provide for 'a perfectly exceptional case'[191] and the Home Secretary 'hope[d] that no occasion [would] arise for this power to be exercised'.[192] Using even stronger language, Simon's colleague, the Lord Advocate, T M Cooper, asked the Commons' committee 'to consider whether it [was] possible to conceive of a situation of emergency in this country so extreme as to justify the total banning of public processions and demonstrations throughout the City of London, without their being a grave matter of public importance such as to justify the most extreme Parliamentary action'.[193]

There was little controversy about section 4 (said by Pritt to be 'wholly praiseworthy')[194] which provided that it was an offence for any person who 'while present at any public meeting or on the occasion of any public procession, has with him any offensive weapon' without legal authority. According to the Home Secretary, this was an 'entirely reasonable' provision about which he hoped there would 'not be much

---

[190] Including Scotland: see ss 8(5) and 8(6), but excluding Northern Ireland: s 10(2). For the situation in Northern Ireland at this time see Chapter 7 below.
[191] H C Debs, 23 November 1936, col 172.   [192] Ibid, col 173.
[193] H C Debs, 26 November 1936, col 615.   [194] See n 166 above.

difference of opinion'.[195] It is perhaps surprising that as the law then stood, 'no sort of wrong is done if the people in a procession, however much heat and excitement there may be, whatever may be the risk of a clash, are in the possession of weapons which, in certain circumstances, they might be tempted to used'.[196] According to Simon, 'the evil which is contemplated is not an imaginary evil', the records of both Scotland Yard and the Home Office providing ugly cases 'which explain the need for a provision of this sort'.[197] Of greater long term significance was clause 5, which did not purport to make new law 'so much as it sets down in simple terms a rule which applies in some districts and which . . . ought to apply generally'.[198] Based on the Metropolitan Police Act 1839, section 54(13), the new clause 5 provided that it was an offence for anyone in a public place to use:

any threatening, abusive or insulting words or behaviour with intent to provoke a breach of the peace or whereby a breach of the peace is likely to be occasioned.

Although this measure would not significantly change the law in London, it was nevertheless welcomed by the Opposition, with Clynes highlighting the need to deal with racial abuse in particular, 'perhaps the most provoking and improper of all' such conduct.[199] But this too was a double-edged sword, with clause 5 being also clearly capable of being deployed against the Left. The Bill's overall purpose being very much to the liking of those traditionally most vigilant on behalf of civil liberties, it is perhaps not surprising that the repressive potential in this provision received less attention than its nationwide potential warranted. But the subsequent history of the use of the section was to see it being frequently directed against left-wing protest.[200]

Although the Bill was swiftly passed, it was not without its critics, who included but were not limited to the fascists.[201] Amongst the strongest attacks came from D N Pritt, whose comments on clauses 1 and 4 we have already encountered, and Ivor Jennings, who wrote a typically waspish comment which appeared shortly after Third Reading in the Commons.[202] Indeed Pritt went so far as to claim that the Bill 'gives the very clear impression that the mentality of the Government is reactionary, and indifferent to the rule of law and indifferent to freedom'.[203]

---

[195] H C Debs, 16 November 1936, cols 1361–2.   [196] Ibid.   [197] Ibid.

[198] Ibid, col 1362.   [199] Ibid, col 1370.

[200] See generally A T H Smith, *Offences Against Public Order* (1987), ch 7.

[201] See *The Blackshirt*, 14 and 21 November 1936.

[202] Jennings, n 166 above, at p 19.   [203] Pritt, n 166 above.

These strong words were inspired mainly but not solely by section 3—
said by Jennings to contain a 'dangerous innovation'—with its powers to
impose conditions and ultimately to prohibit processions. As to the first
of these, Pritt wrote:

This provision has a superficial plausibility and reasonability; and its defenders
may say that, whilst it goes in some ways far further than the Metropolitan
Police Act or the Town Police Clauses Act, 1847, it gives little power beyond
what already exists at common law. But, as I read it, there is one tremendous
difference. At common law, the police who are responsible for keeping order
may prevent a procession proceeding in any particular direction if that is the
only way of preventing a breach of the peace; but the legitimacy of their prohibition may be tested in the Courts. In this clause, however, as I read it, the whole
power is placed in the hands of the police, without challenge or appeal. The
mere opinion of the chief officer creates the right to impose such conditions as
he thinks necessary; the Courts cannot interfere, except, of course, to punish
those who do not obey. This is the birth of the Police State; the police are to be
the sole judges of what is needed, and the Courts are excluded.[204]

But these powers to impose conditions were thought to be only 'objectionable', in contrast to the power to ban processions, which was declared
to be 'extremely objectionable'. According to Pritt:

Here again, the common law power, with its liability to being checked by the
Courts, is ignored, the Courts are excluded, and the executive is supreme. If at
any moment public indignation at the Means Test, or at some new breach of
faith in foreign or home affairs, becomes sufficient to embarrass this or some
other Government, some high officer of police may quite conveniently be
alarmed, and within a day or two the populace will not even be allowed to
demonstrate. It is the Police State, more clearly and more crudely than ever.[205]

Perhaps somewhat overstated, these concerns were not without substance, as successive governments found forbearance less easy to practice
in the privacy of executive office than in the public and accountable
debating chamber in Westminster.

The Effect of the 1936 Act

The 1936 Act came into force on 1 January 1937. The BUF was particularly and immediately hurt by the attack on the wearing of political uniforms in section 1 of the Act. That this was perceived to be the central

---

[204] Ibid, p 762.
[205] Ibid, pp 762–3. Pritt had not recanted from his concern about the Act even by 1971: see
D N Pritt, *Law, Class and Society. Book 2: The Apparatus of the Law* (1971), p 45.

thrust of the Act can be seen from the fact that a treatise on public order published the year the Act came into effect was entitled *The Law of Political Uniforms, Public Meetings and Private Armies*.[206] Section 1 was viewed by Mosley as an attempt to deprive his organisation 'of a novel method of propaganda which is now regarded as too successful by opponents who previously derided it'.[207] They were also concerned, however, by section 2, while simultaneously claiming that its prohibition of quasi-military organisations would in no way affect the BUF, the long declared object of which was to win 'power by the capture of a majority at a General Election by constitutional methods'. Indeed by 1936 it had 100 parliamentary candidates in place. But a matter of acute concern, presumably to Mosley personally, was section 2(4) which aimed the criminal law at 'any person who takes part in the control or management' of quasi-military organisations. Guilt could be established by 'proof of things done or words written, spoken, or published by persons appearing to be members or adherents' of such a group. This provision, complained Mosley, erodes 'the well known principle of British law that the onus of proving guilt rests on the prosecution and that the onus of proving innocence does not rest upon the accused'. The main concern—whether fanciful or not— was that the provision enabled 'any opponent to put agents into an organisation for the purpose of contravening this law and thus securing the conviction of the principals of the organisation and the confiscation of its property'. The measure was, in short, an invitation to 'political corruption and the police methods of a South American Republic'.

Sections 1 and 2 clearly struck a chord, with the latter section being returned to in the columns of *The Blackshirt* in the following weeks.[208] There was in contrast no concern expressed at that time about the restrictions on marches: this is perhaps perfectly understandable given that the measures did not present a challenge to the very survival of the organisation. So far as section 1 is concerned, counsel's opinion was to the effect that the blackshirt uniform was illegal; that an ordinary shirt of black colour with a tie worn under an ordinary suit was legal; and that the BUF was not otherwise affected.[209] Defiantly, however, *The Blackshirt* proclaimed:

The British Union uniform will not disappear for long. The day will come, and it will not be long now, when the streets of Britain will rejoice and take pride in

---

[206] Baker, n 102 above. The author, the barrister Joseph Baker, described the prohibition on uniforms as probably the 'most important provision in the new Act': p vi.

[207] See *The Blackshirt*, 14 and 21 November 1936, from which issues the quotations in this paragraph are drawn.

[208] See particularly the issues for 21 and 28 November 1936.

[209] *The Blackshirt*, 2 January 1937.

the sight of tens of thousands of young men and women pledged to the building of a greater Britain and wearing a uniform designed to show the new outlook, methods and objective.[210]

But despite its claims to be a law-abiding Party, the BUF was soon in conflict with the police, the Metropolitan Police Commissioner having written to the BUF exhorting the organisation to 'advise its members to discontinue wearing [a uniform signifying association with the British Union]'. A representative immediately replied seeking clarification that 'an ordinary shirt of black colour worn with a tie under ordinary suits of normal and diverse pattern was not a uniform within the meaning of the Act'.[211] This was how the BUF proposed to comply with the Act, effectively by modifying the wearing of the blackshirt rather than giving it up altogether. But the Metropolitan Police Commissioner refused to co-operate, with an anonymous barrister writing in *The Blackshirt* of 'the edifying spectacle of a law-abiding organisation trying to obey a vague and indefinite Statute, while the institution responsible for the maintenance of law and order stood by, refusing guidance or instruction'.[212]

With the Act's implementation came allegations in *The Blackshirt* that it gave the police an opportunity to intimidate BUF members. Thus it was claimed that on 1 January 1937 (the day the Act came into force) a member of the organisation was threatened with arrest by a police officer 'for wearing an armlet bearing the symbol of a flash and a circle', while on the following day a police inspector at Walthamstow 'took the names of two members who were wearing the undress black shirts and of one member who was wearing a black polo sweater'. The anonymous barrister continued by claiming that the BUF had been advised (by the same barrister?) that 'the police have no right, either at common law or under Statute, to interfere with members in this way'. Apparently the Metropolitan Police Commissioner was duly informed that if the Act continued to be used in this fashion, 'individual Fascists will take proceedings in the High Court for the protection of their personal and traditional liberties'. It is not known whether this threat was carried out. But as the case law was to make clear, it would appear that the BUF members were being poorly advised by the lawyers. By April 1937, the Commissioner was able to assure the Home Office that 'the wearing of the political uniforms previously in use has been discontinued',[213] and there was no reason to doubt that this also reflected the experience of other senior police officers across the country. Indeed so effective was the

---

[210] Ibid. [211] *The Blackshirt*, 9 January 1937. [212] Ibid.
[213] See H C Debs, 12 April 1937, col 634 (G Lloyd) (WA).

law that the BUF prohibited the wearing of the blackshirt at a carnival dance attended by Mosley in December 1937.[214] How much the willingness or otherwise of the police to prosecute offenders played a part in this process is difficult to say. But apart from the complaints of harassment, there were six convictions under section 1 in the first month of its operation, thereby showing a determination on the part of the police to address the question, with few prosecutions being launched thereafter.

There is also evidence to suggest that the local magistrates in different parts of the country were not prepared to fall for the sophistry of the BUF's attempt to circumvent the law. In *R v Wood*,[215] the defendant had been offering fascist newspapers for sale while wearing 'a black shirt, a black tie and a peaked cap with a leather chin strap'. The defendant gave evidence that he had received the uniform as a result of a contract to sell papers to a certain value per week. Despite this, the stipendiary magistrate rejected the argument that the clothing was merely 'the livery of a news vendor' and imposed a fine of 40 shillings, a mild punishment said to reflect the fact that this was 'a test case'. In *R v Charnley*,[216] it was 'black trousers, a black belt with a fascist badge on the buckle, a dark navy blue woollen pullover, and a red brassard [*ie* badge]' that led the magistrate to find that in the circumstances of the case a uniform was being worn. He rejected the defendants' argument that only the badge and brassard signified association with a political object and that neither could be said to be a uniform. But it was not only the fascists who were proceeded against under the new Act. In *R v Taylor, Ward and Hawthorne*,[217] the defendants were found to have been wearing 'green shirts, green collars and green ties and armlets of green with the emblem of the Social Credit Party on them'. The defendants sought to distinguish *Wood* by showing that in that case the accused had been wearing all black, and it may have been this point that persuaded the Luton magistrates to dismiss the case without retiring. (The defendants had come to court dressed in exactly the same 'uniform' as had given rise to the prosecutions and it may also have been that this high risk strategy had paid off.) In a later Lambeth case in contrast, the stipendiary magistrate found the green shirt, green tie and armlet of the defendant to constitute a uniform, but nevertheless dismissed the summons under the Probation of Offenders Act on payment of a sum for costs.[218]

---

[214] *The Blackshirt*, 4 December 1937.

[215] (1937) 81 *Sol Jo* 108. This and the other cases discussed in this paragraph are considered in more detail in E R H Ivamy, 'The Right of Public Meeting' (1949) 2 CLP 183, at pp 184–7.

[216] Ibid. See also *R v Irvine* (1937) 81 *Sol Jo* 509.   [217] (1937) 81 *Sol Jo* 509.

[218] Mentioned without name in Anon, 'What is a Uniform?' (1937) 81 *Sol Jo* 509. The case is *R v Wright*: see Ivamy, n 215 above, pp 186–7.

The other provisions of the Act were not as immediately effective as section 1,[219] and it was not until June 1937 that section 3 was deployed for the first time.[220] The BUF planned a meeting for 4 July in Pigott Street, Limehouse, which was to be followed by a march to Trafalgar Square, via one of two routes, both of which would have taken the marchers through the main Jewish quarter of the East End of London. Because it was felt that no type of condition would have prevented the march from finding a provocative area through which to process, with a consequent threat of serious public disorder (hardly unrealistic in the light of Cable Street), the Metropolitan Police Commissioner sought and obtained the consent of the Home Secretary for an order under section 3(2) banning all political processions for a period of six weeks in a large part of the East End of the City.[221] Though the fascists defiantly went ahead with a procession outside the banned area on 4 July, culminating in a demonstration in Trafalgar Square, the banning order itself was not breached, and the 2,383 police officers on duty ensured that the protest that did occur passed off relatively peacefully.[222] This banning order was twice extended over the summer and autumn of 1937 and was then extended for a further three months in December 1937.[223] Two further banning orders covering the same area followed in March and June 1938.[224] It remained therefore, even in London terms, very much a local ban. In the first ten months of the Act's operation, there were no fewer than 110 fascist and sixty-one anti-fascist or communist marches in the Metropolis and many of these would have taken place after the banning order had come into effect, but outside the proscribed area.[225] Within the area itself, the ban seems largely to have held firm, with the important consequence that the problem of provocative fascist marching in Jewish areas in particular was finally being successfully and effectively

[219] Of which little was heard thereafter, though it was later to be used against Irish republicans in the early 1970s: see *O'Moran v DPP* [1975] QB 864.

[220] For the operation of the 1936 Act in relation to fascist demonstrations, see PRO, HO 144/21086 and 21087. The fascist response is to be found in *The Blackshirt*, 26 June 1937, declaring 'that whenever Socialists and Communists decide to organise a riot in order to prevent their opponents' propaganda, they will receive the assistance of the government to achieve their purpose'. See also *The Blackshirt*, 3 July 1937.

[221] See the statement by the Home Secretary, Sir Samuel Hoare, at H C Debs, 21 June 1937, cols 846–9. The area embraced within the banning order included the boroughs of Stepney, Bethnal Green, Poplar, Bow and Bromley, Shoreditch and parts of Finsbury, Hackney and Islington.

[222] The details of the police manpower at the 4 July march are at H C Debs, 15 July 1937, cols 1456–7 (Sir S Hoare). See also *The Blackshirt*, 10 July 1937.

[223] H C Debs, 13 December 1937, col 814 (Sir S Hoare).

[224] H C Debs, 14 March 1938, col 26 (Sir S Hoare); H C Debs, 20 June 1938, col 721 (G Lloyd) (WA).

[225] See H C Debs, 11 November 1937, cols 1837–8 (Sir S Hoare).

tackled. This was not the least of the many enduring legacies of the Cable Street disorders.

The 1936 Act did not of course extend to stationary meetings,[226] whether indoors or open air, and these remained a focus of tension after enactment of the measure, particularly in those areas where the opportunity to march was denied to the fascists (and incidentally to all other political groups as well) after the June banning order came into effect.[227] Thus after a BUF meeting held in Stepney Green shortly after the ban became operative within the district, there was serious disorder resulting in eight arrests.[228] The atmosphere of the day was not helped by a new policy embarked upon by the fascists at this time of turning up at and heckling the meetings of their political opponents.[229] Inevitably, in such a climate, the old allegations about police partisanship occasionally resurfaced. In June 1938, Sir Percy Harris asked the Home Office Minister, Geoffrey Lloyd, whether he was 'aware that a procession of 150 persons was permitted to march down the Bethnal Green Road in spite of its being an area in which processions are prohibited?' The minister pointed out in reply that there had been a fascist meeting in the area, opposition to which had been so widespread and so hostile that, '[i]n order to get the fascists away [after their meeting] the police [had] arranged to escort them down Bethnal Green Road, and it [was] no doubt this arrangement which [had] given rise to the suggestion that a procession [had been] permitted'.[230] There were also the usual complaints about the discriminatory nature of the policing of BUF meetings, with allegations that inflammatory language from the platform was being ignored in favour of action against members of the audience provoked on account of it. A particularly bad example of this occurred at a meeting in Stratford in

---

[226] Although s 5 could be deployed against persons seeking to disrupt such meetings, as occurred in Harlesden on 21 May 1937 when six people were arrested and charged with s 5 offences after a Mosleyite meeting had flared into disorder: *Telegraph*, 22 May 1937.

[227] See the letter written by Mosley to the Home Secretary and published in *The Blackshirt*, 4 September 1937: 'The Government by the Public Order Act has deliberately deprived us of all means of defending ourselves at open-air meetings. By that Act the right to use stewards at an indoor meeting is preserved and as a result serious disorder at our indoor meetings is now practically unknown. But at outdoor meetings the duty of preserving order rests with the police alone and we are forbidden by law to "organise and train or organise and equip" in readiness to defend ourselves'.

[228] H C Debs, 19 July 1937, cols 1794–5 (G Lloyd) (WA).

[229] A typical example of this sort of activity occurred at a Labour Party meeting in Stoke Newington Town Hall on 27 April 1938, when 30 members of the audience persisted in shouting and singing fascist slogans, leaving only when the police entered to restore order at the invitation of the chairman: H C Debs, 5 May 1938, col 1066 (Sir S Hoare) (WA). At an earlier meeting in Stepney, a series of fascist interruptions at a communist meeting had resulted in charges for obstruction of the police in the execution of their duty being brought against both the speaker and the organiser of the meeting: *Evening Standard*, 6 March 1937.

[230] The exchange is at H C Debs, 20 June 1938, cols 706–7.

February 1938 when two speeches referred to members of the audience in offensive anti-semitic terms. The speakers were not arrested, unlike four members of the audience who were charged with insulting words and behaviour.[231]

It would be easy to get the problem out of proportion, however. The disorder surrounding the marches that did take place was less serious than before, though there continued to be a stark contrast in the prosecution of communists on the one hand and fascists on the other.[232] Nevertheless, after violent clashes at a BUF march from Millbank to Bermondsey had led to many arrests in October 1937, there were no incidents of a similar type to report in London in the ensuing four months.[233] The police action at political meetings has to be seen in the context of the enormous number of potentially dangerous occasions that needed to be watched. In the year following enactment of the Public Order Act, there were no fewer than 12,011 meetings in the metropolitan police district alone, 3,094 of them fascist, 4,364 of them anti-fascist with a further 4,553 connected with neither political position.[234] This frenetic activity should not be allowed to hide the decline of the BUF during this period, which was precipitious. In the March 1937 elections to the London County Council, Mosley threw all his resources behind six fascist candidates in Bethnal Green, Stepney, Limehouse and Shoreditch. The campaign was nakedly racist, with Mosley himself writing the Party's manifestos, one of which rejoiced in the title 'Our Challenge to Jewry'. In the event, all six fascists were unsuccessful, with Labour being returned for each of the available six seats. None of forty BUF candidates who stood in subsequent local borough elections managed to secure victory. Mosley was forced to cut his salaried staff from 143 to thirty. Dissent quickly followed and the Party split a number of ways with two

---

[231] See the exchange between Thomas Groves and Sir John Simon's successor as Home Secretary, Sir Samuel Hoare, at H C Debs, 3 March 1938, cols 1273–4.

[232] Between January 1936 and the end of October 1937, there were 104 cases of assault on or violent resistance to police by communists or communist sympathisers during fascist demonstrations but only two equivalent cases brought against fascists in the same period: H C Debs, 11 November 1937, col 1838 (Sir S Hoare).

[233] H C Debs, 3 March 1938, cols 1297–8 (Sir S Hoare) (WA).

[234] H C Debs, 15 December 1937, col 1283 (G Lloyd). Between 1 July 1936 and 1 December 1936, the police asked on 20 occasions for meetings in London to be brought to a close because the audience was getting out of hand and because there was an imminent danger of a breach of the peace. Thirteen of these meetings were fascist and 7 were anti-fascist: H C Debs, 15 December 1937, col 1284 (G Lloyd). In the 12 months to 1 July 1937, there were 320 prosecutions for offences in connection with public meetings and demonstrations. These were mainly for assault, obstruction of a constable in the execution of his duty and insulting words and behaviour: H C Debs, 7 July 1937, col 350 (Sir S Hoare).

of his former associates, John Beckett and William Joyce, setting up a rival body and with another two of his more publicly acceptable colleagues disowning him in a fanfare of adverse publicity.[235]

The Public Order Act could not of course take all or even a large part of the credit for this collapse of fascism in Great Britain, even though it was seen by the BUF as 'the Government's great contribution towards the attempted defeat of National Socialism in Britain by the Capitalist-Socialist-Communist alliance'.[236] The decline had probably set in as early as June 1934 when the true nature of the BUF had been laid bare by the courageous provocation of the hecklers at Olympia. But there can be no question that the Act played its part in deflating the malevolent exhibitionism of the fascists. Its carefully targeted sections 1 and 2, together with the restrained application of section 3, signalled a societal antagonism at an important moment. Unhindered by any ideological commitment to free speech at any cost, British law was able to rise, however belatedly, to a challenge to its very basis, the full seriousness of which was to be made profoundly obvious in the years of war that were to follow. That the legislation should have been so slow in coming, and that the final acts that broke the executive's commitment to inaction should have been those of the Left rather than the Right, should not be allowed in themselves fully to obscure the Act's overall effectiveness. The legislation did not, however, apply only to fascists, as Pritt had pointed out. Its grave implications for the civil liberties of other than the fascists were to become particularly apparent to a later post-war generation of political activists, but those dangers were evident from the outset. Introduced to deal with a menace from the Right, it was the Left which was also to feel the full force of its restrictions. It was nevertheless to provide a useful tool in the campaign against the re-emergence of fascism as a political force in the 1970s. The Act quickly joined the pot pourri of procedural, judicial and legislative tactics that had always been available to the authorities when challenged by the exercise of political freedom in a manner that was deemed inimical to the forces of the State.

Conclusion

The way in which the military activities and the uniforms of the BUF came to be controlled in the 1936 Act serves as the closest approximation to the Diceyean ideal of the Rule of Law that we have yet encoun-

---

[235] See Scaffardi, n 134 above, pp 161–2.   [236] *The Blackshirt*, 24 July 1937.

tered, or will encounter, in this book. It is important to recognise that
Dicey never argued for the absolute inviolability of his 'general principles
of the constitution' (which principles would certainly have encompassed
the freedoms of association and assembly). It is reasonably safe to assume
that sections 1 and 2 would not have been offensive to him simply on
account of the fact that they restricted these civil liberties to some
degree.[237] What mattered to Dicey was the process, and on this point the
constitution excelled itself. The executive seemed genuinely sensitive to
the liberties of those upon whom such legislation would impact, and
indeed we have seen how determinedly resistant to change successive
Home Secretaries were from 1932 to 1936. When Parliament did eventually intervene at the invitation of the executive, it was to enact the carefully targeted and well prepared provisions now to be found in sections
1 and 2. These were in turn then sensitively but firmly enforced, with
police action being preceded as we have seen by communication with the
BUF and with the few prosecutions that were brought being scrupulously
overseen by the lower judiciary. Here then was law that was clear,
grounded in legislation and guarded by a predisposition to principle on
the part of the courts. In this context it is important to note that groups
other than the BUF were vulnerable to prosecution, and indeed were
prosecuted, as we have seen with the Social Credit Party. The BUF may
have been the main reason behind the enactment of sections 1 and 2,
but the organisation was not the only body within their restrictive ambit.
Every person therefore remained, as Dicey required, 'subject to the ordinary law of the realm and amenable to the jurisdiction of the ordinary
courts'.

What rather spoils this image, of course, is that it tells only part of the
story of this chapter. The main theme thrown up from the perspective of
constitutional principle has been not so much the excellence of this commitment to the Rule of Law in respect of the fascists, as the baldness of its
selectivity. Leaving the issues of uniforms and quasi-military organisations to one side, the deployment of the various local laws and bye-laws
in the years before 1936 shows how much flexibility the police really had
when it came to a question of whether or not to control public protest.
The point is well illustrated by section 3 of the 1936 Act, dealing with
the imposition of conditions upon, and the banning of, public processions. D N Pritt was perfectly right to characterise this section as effec-

---

[237] At least when viewed from the theoretical perspective. Whether Dicey's views would have
been distorted by his political perspective in the 1930s is of course impossible to know because Dicey
died some time before the decade commenced.

tively insulating the police from review by the courts in an area of intense civil libertarian sensitivity.[238] After enactment of section 3, the police could choose whether to permit or to prevent a march without much fear of having to account for their actions, in either a legal or a political forum.[239] As we have seen, conditions could be imposed on specific marches based on a police judgement as to the future, and it was entirely possible for these conditions to be so stringently constructed that their effect would be not dissimilar to that achieved by an outright ban. The best that could be said for section 3 was that its banning power could not be deployed against a particular march, being required to be either general or applicable to an ascertainable class of processions. In this way some residue of Dicey's emphasis on equal treatment before the law was retained.

Not even this crumb of respect for principle was true of the common law powers discussed in this and the preceding chapter. These were developed without regard to Parliament and they permitted just the kind of discrimination against certain subjects that Dicey's version of the Rule of Law appeared designed to prevent. After *Thomas v Sawkins*[240] and *Duncan v Jones*,[241] the police could effectively choose which meetings to permit, which to inhibit and which wholly to prevent, apparently on an ad hoc and entirely unprincipled basis, with the only constraint being the requirement for a suspicion about future behaviour which though required to be on reasonable grounds was almost impossible in retrospect to gainsay. This fatal blow to the principle of legality effectively gave to the police an unlimited power subject to minimal scrutiny by the courts which in the process also selectively undermined political freedom. Time and again we have seen the police act in a way wholly hostile towards the Left while preserving an impressive constitutional rectitude in relation to the Right. The protection of fascist meetings sits uneasily with the brutal treatment so regularly meted out both to the groups who gathered to oppose fascism and to those others from the Left who sought to demonstrate in support of their own particular causes. No better illustration exists of the 'wide, arbitrary, or discretionary powers of constraint', untrammelled by any real political or judicial accountability, about

---

[238] It is true that police decisions could technically be challenged, but this was never likely in the era of judicial restraint in which Pritt was writing. Indeed not even the post-war renaissance in public law has penetrated this realm of police discretion: *Kent v Metropolitan Police Commissioner, The Times*, 15 May 1981.

[239] It would not seem that the involvement of the Home Secretary in the decision-making process had much inhibiting effect on police practice in this area in respect of the early banning orders in London that were in place from 1937.

[240] See n 2 above.   [241] See n 4 above.

which Dicey had warned so eloquently in 1885. The 1930s is good evidence for the general assertion that the freedom of operational manoeuvre that comes with total freedom of discretionary action can easily descend into the management of institutional prejudice.

It is this flagrant discrimination against the Left which gives rise to the most interesting and telling points of *constitutional practice* in the period discussed in this chapter. We have seen in previous chapters how the different branches of government were deployed against the CPGB and related organisations. But in this chapter the process of persecution and discrimination was brought into even sharper focus by the stark contrast between the treatment of the fascists and the communists before the legislation of 1936. It is not clear what were the reasons for this, or why the fascists were so openly tolerated when the communists were viewed with such suspicion, for there is no question that fascism represented as great a threat to liberal democracy, albeit of a qualitatively different form. Nevertheless the fascists were shown a remarkable indulgence by the police, both in terms of their ability to hold meetings and processions, and in their ability also to police and regulate these demonstrations themselves. This was despite the fact that the fascists resorted to great violence, and despite the fact also that there was no want of legal authority for police intervention, partly as a result of case law which had been developed with other disturbers of the peace in mind. Thus it could fairly be said that so far as political freedom was concerned, it was the British Union of Fascists who were the principal beneficiaries of the continuing official commitment to the ideals of *A V Dicey*. It was in the conduct of the State towards the BUF that we see Dicey's principles in obvious operation as a matter of practice, and it is in the response to the BUF that we see *Beatty v Gillbanks*[242] being followed in all its glorious spirit. But it was not only the police who were prepared to go to considerable lengths to protect the freedom of the fascists: the government also went to great lengths by its inaction to tolerate their activities and the disorder which they caused, a deliberate lassitude that was unmoved by the reports of brutality at Olympia and elsewhere.

The government in the end was forced to act against the fascists only by the weight of popular opposition to them and the message of Cable Street which was uncompromisingly that without regulation there would be serious violence, at a time when the dreaded unemployed marchers were about to appear on the scene once again. So just as the law was

[242] See n 96 above.

used in a vain effort to crush the communists in the 1920s and 1930s, so it was used in 1936 to crush the fascists. But on this occasion the government's hand was forced by popular resistance. The legislation which resulted was much more carefully targeted and much more effective than the measures which had been aimed at the communists. As Mosley was to find out, life is full of strange paradoxes: who for example would have predicted as the police stood back at Olympia that within three years the BUF would have been the victim of such carefully directed legislation (even if it did bring noxious consequences in its wake)? And who would have thought that when the fascists were being openly tolerated while the communists were the transparent targets of all three branches of government, that it would be the CPGB rather than the BUF which would continue to play a significant part in the political life of the country? The Second World War was soon to reveal just how much more dangerous were the fascists to Dicey's rosy view of political freedom in Britain, though by then, as we have seen the BUF was already well in decline. The fortunes of the CPGB, however, were to brighten considerably, particularly after 1941 when the USSR joined the side of the Allies, with Party membership rising from 7,700 in 1935 to 56,000 in 1942.[243] But this is not to say there was an outbreak of tolerance of communists and their Party: the struggle for liberty in Britain was to continue, and is part of the story of the Cold War a narrative that is beyond the remit of this volume.

---

[243] H Pelling, *The British Communist Party: A Historical Profile* (1958), p 192.

7

Civil Liberties: the Irish Dimension

So far in this study we have been concerned exclusively with the law and practice of civil liberties in Great Britain. Throughout our period, however, the United Kingdom embraced all or part of the island of Ireland, and it is to this dimension of our story that we now turn. The constitutional and legal relationship between Britain and Ireland was a fraught one in the first half of this century, and the various crises to which it gave rise generated many issues of principle relevant to civil liberties and the Rule of Law. In particular what the engagement of British law in Ireland lays bare is the extreme vulnerability of the Rule of Law in times of perceived or genuine emergency. Of course this is a point which has to some extent been made time and time again in the course of our preceding chapters. But Ireland takes this discussion to deeper levels. Consideration of the nature of the conflict with militant Irish separatism and (after 1922) with nationalist dissent in Northern Ireland involves a further sapping of confidence in the integrity of the principle of the Rule of Law. Indeed we do not need to look to the future to challenge Dicey's assumptions about his times. For even when he was writing, the way that Ireland had been governed in the eighty or so years since its union with Britain in 1801 already offered strong contemporary evidence against his theory of the constitution.

As far as the common law is concerned, the case of *O'Kelly v Harvey*,[1] with its casual rejection of the authority of *Beatty v Gillbanks*, has already been referred to.[2] The briefest of looks at the kind of statutes that were deemed necessary to keep the island in check during the nineteenth century evinces a clear pattern of consistent coercion. The Union was itself born into a state of martial law[3] and the fourteenth and fifteenth statutes passed by the new United Kingdom Parliament were designed to keep in force this draconian state of affairs, together with the courts-martial and the suspension of habeas corpus that came along with it.[4] In the

---

[1] (1883) 15 Cox CC 435.   [2] See Chapter 1 above.

[3] See the Suppression of Rebellion Act 1798, revived with amendments in 1799.

[4] The Suppression of Rebellion Act 1801 and the Habeas Corpus Suspension Act 1801. A very good study is C Townshend, 'Martial Law: Legal and Administrative Problems of Civil Emergency in Britain and the Empire, 1800–1940' (1982) 25 *Historical Journal* 167. See also C Townshend, *Political Violence in Ireland. Government and Resistance since 1848* (1983), pp 55–6.

years of repression that both accompanied and followed the Napoleonic era, there flowed from the Westminster legislature an apparently unending stream of laws loosely gathered under the umbrella title of the Coercion Acts.[5] In the early 1880s, yet another crackdown[6] produced what Dicey in his then newly published *Introduction* described as these 'extraordinary powers which [have been] conferred by comparatively recent enactments on the Irish executive'.[7] But despite his awareness of the draconian content of such legislation, Dicey does not appear to have considered the extent to which such laws undermined civil liberties, presumably because they were oriented against those with whose opinions he was in profound disagreement, in a part of the Kingdom that happened not to be England.[8] Two years after publication of the first edition of the *Introduction* came another legislative initiative of doubtful legitimacy which, as we shall see, was to have a major influence on the exercise of state power in Ireland in the turbulent second decade of the twentieth century. Though unlimited as to time and wide-ranging in its effect on the criminal process, the right to jury trial and freedom of association, the Criminal Law and Procedure (Ireland) Act 1887 (known as Balfour's Crimes Act) went completely unnoticed by Dicey in his later editions.

In this chapter we develop what might be described as this weak link in Dicey's model of the constitution, examining how these and later laws continued to affect civil liberties in the series of crises that were to come in the first half of the twentieth century. We consider first the effect on civil liberties of Britain's rule in Ireland during the First World War and in particular how the events of Easter 1916 affected its government of the island. As we shall see, the application of the defence of the realm regulations, already considered in Chapter 2, had a very particular importance in Ireland, both before and immediately after the Easter Rising. Secondly, we examine the civil libertarian implications of that period of acute crisis between 1918 and 1921, when Britain's engagement with nationalist Ireland came closest to one of open war, and when

---

[5] See in particular the Coercion Act 1833 and the Crime and Outrage Act 1847.

[6] Precipitated in particular by the Phoenix Park assassinations of the Lord Lieutenant Lord Cavendish and his chief secretary T H Burke in 1882. See the Prevention of Crimes (Ireland) Act 1882.

[7] A V Dicey, *Lectures Introductory to the Study of the Law of the Constitution* (1885), pp 245–6 (footnotes omitted).

[8] See his *England's Case Against Home Rule* (1886). For the general background to Dicey's attitude to Ireland, see R A Cosgrove, *The Rule of Law: Albert Venn Dicey, Victorian Jurist* (1980), ch 6, and for further discussion of the Irish dimension specifically, see H Tulloch, 'A V Dicey and the Irish Question: 1870–1922' (1980) 15 *Irish Jurist (n s)* 131 and also J F McEldowney, 'Dicey in Historical Perspective—A Review Essay' in P McAuslan and J F McEldowney (eds), *Law Legitimacy and the Constitution: Essays Marking the Centenary of Dicey's 'Law of the Constitution'* (1985), p 39, esp pp 47–9.

military efforts to defeat a separatist guerrilla campaign led to the explicit jettisoning of many of the principles of the rule of law. In the third part of the chapter, we examine the impact on civil liberties of the Special Powers Act that was passed by the new Northern Ireland Parliament in 1922, as almost its first legislative act. This legislation put in place a structure of executive power profoundly inimical to civil liberties and the rule of law which was nevertheless to survive for over fifty years and to enjoy the passive support of successive British governments. If it is true that commitment to principle can only be tested properly under pressure, then Ireland offers a uniquely long-lasting laboratory experiment through which to evaluate the true health of British freedom in the period under consideration in this volume.

THE EASTER RISING

The years that followed enactment of the Criminal Law and Procedure (Ireland) Act 1887 gave no hint of the turmoil that was shortly to engulf Ireland. The period resembled in many ways the peaceful decades that had followed the lapse in 1835 of Lord Grey's infamous Coercion Act. For over two decades either side of the arrival of the twentieth century, the British administration ruled Ireland from Dublin Castle in an atmosphere of calm engendered by a set of conciliatory policies, relative economic prosperity and a fresh emphasis on positive change. The country enjoyed substantial land reform and an efflorescence of national sentiment, with the foundation of the Gaelic League in 1893 and the opening of the Abbey theatre in 1904 being only the two most obvious examples of the latter. The Peace Preservation (Ireland) Act 1881, which had given the government 'complete control over the importation and sale of arms and ammunition, and over the carrying of arms or the possession of ammunition',[9] was allowed to lapse in 1906. A few legacies of the coercive past remained on the statute books 'some of which [had been] passed by the Irish Parliament'[10] but they were not frequently used, and apart from the 1887 Act the tendency was increasingly to seek to rely when action was necessary on the common law or on UK-wide legislative measures such as the Explosive Substances Act 1883. The pressure for Home Rule that had dominated British politics in the last quarter of the nineteenth century remained bubbling beneath the

[9] Royal Commission on the Rebellion in Ireland, Cd 8279 (1916), p 4.   [10] Ibid, p 5.

surface, however, and the Liberal administration that was first elected in 1905 could finally avoid the issue no longer after the resolution of the parliamentary crisis of 1910 to 1911 had made it possible to proceed without necessarily procuring the consent of the Lords. This was particularly the case because the elections precipitated by the same crisis had greatly increased the strength in the House of Commons of John Redmond's Irish Parliamentary Party.

Defence of the Realm Acts 1914

The Home Rule Bill introduced by the Liberal Government in 1912 did not exclude the province of Ulster. Like its failed predecessors in 1886 and 1893, the measure anticipated an Ireland that was to have a single government and parliament which would exercise certain devolved responsibilities while remaining firmly within the United Kingdom. This latter security was not sufficient compensation for many Irish unionists, and protest against the Bill was not long in emerging. When the Government of Ireland Act 1914 reached the statute book, it was against a background of greatly increased tension, with 250,000 people having signed the solemn league and covenant in September 1912, pledging themselves to defeat the Bill which they saw as 'disastrous to the material well-being of Ulster as well as the whole of Ireland, subversive of our civil and religious freedom, destructive of our citizenship, and perilous to the unity of the Empire'.[11] Prominent supporters of the movement included William Joynson-Hicks and Edward Carson, both of whom we have encountered in earlier chapters of this book as champions in their later life of the deployment of sedition laws against members of the Communist Party.[12] By the end of 1913, tensions had escalated to the point where there were to be found no fewer than three paramilitary organisations on the island. The Ulster Volunteer Force (UVF) reflected the loyalist interest, the Irish Volunteers their nationalist opponents, with James Connolly's much smaller Irish Citizen's Army drawing support from a nonsectarian socialist base. The first two of these organisations achieved large-scale importation of arms into the country in 1914. With the benefit of hindsight, the Royal Commission which investigated the causes of the nationalist revolt in 1916 was surely accurate in its summation that 'the importation of large quantities of arms into Ireland after the lapse of the Arms Act, and

[11] The full text of the covenant is set out in B MacArthur, *The Penguin Book of Twentieth-Century Protest* (1998), p 41.
[12] See Chapter 3 above.

the toleration of drilling by large bodies of men first in Ulster, and then in other districts of Ireland created conditions which rendered possible the recent troubles in Dublin and elsewhere'.[13]

The immediate effect of the outbreak of war on 4 August 1914 was to defuse the mounting Irish crisis. The Irish Parliamentary Party immediately pledged its support and the Home Rule Bill was suspended prior to its enactment for at least the duration of the hostilities, thereby removing (albeit apparently only temporarily) the grievance felt by Ulster Unionists.[14] The draconian Defence of the Realm Regulations that emerged in their first consolidated form in November 1914[15] were designed to deal with the European war but they were also a convenient tool with which to counter the threat of Irish nationalist subversion, which continued to simmer away under the surface despite the loyalist euphoria which had been generated by the outbreak of hostilities. The prohibition on the importation of arms into Ireland was almost immediately brought explicitly within the new statutory framework.[16] The main problem for the authorities was initially not so much the use of such weapons as the threat that Irish nationalism posed to recruitment in the country. In the first ten months of the war some 27 people were arrested and detained for making statements at meetings designed to discourage recruiting, contrary to regulation 27.[17] The same regulation was also the main basis for the military authorities action in December 1914, 'with the full approval of the Irish Government,'[18] in seizing two newspapers, 'after a warning had been given to the printers of these and of other papers against contravening the Regulation forbidding the circulation of statements likely to cause disaffection or to prejudice recruiting'.[19] The *Irish Worker* was seized

---

[13] Royal Commission on the Rebellion in Ireland, n 9 above, p 13.

[14] Suspensory Act 1914: 'No steps shall be taken [to implement the Government of Ireland Act 1914] until the expiration of twelve months from the date [of its passing] or, if at the expiration of those twelve months the present war has not ended, until such later date (not being later than the end of the present war) as may be fixed by His Majesty by Order in Council'.

[15] See generally Chapter 2 above.

[16] The first Regulation, 12A, was introduced on 17 September 1914. It controlled the entry of arms into the United Kingdom as a whole, including Ireland. This was then promulgated as Regulation 31 in the consolidation that was effected on 28 November 1914.

[17] H C Debs, 21 June 1915, col 930 (A Birrell). One of these was Francis Sheehy Skeffington, who was afterwards shot in a controversial incident during the Easter rising: see n 44 below. A total of forty people were sentenced under Defence of the Realm Act to terms of imprisonment in Ireland during the ten month period mentioned in the text: H C Debs, 8 June 1915, cols 176–9 (A Birrell).

[18] This was a reference to the British administration in Ireland based in Dublin Castle.

[19] H C Debs, 8 February 1915, col 265 (A Birrell) (WA). The pressure on the authorities to suppress the nationalist press on this basis was present from the start of the war: see H C Debs, 23 November 1914, cols 816–17 (WA); H C Debs, 25 November 1914, cols 1120–1; H C Debs, 26 November 1914, cols 1289–92.

in February 1915[20] and three further papers were suppressed in March 1916.[21] In the first two years of the war, many journals appear to have been threatened in this way, though the authorities resolutely refused to give details of their actions to the House of Commons.[22]

As we know from Chapter 2, the Defence of the Realm Regulations gave the naval and military authorities wide police powers. These included the right to require an answer to questions (reg 53),[23] the power to authorise the search and seizure of property,[24] the power to declare curfew (reg 13) and the legal right to clear areas of their inhabitants (reg 9). From 10 June 1915 regulation 14B gave the authorities the power of internment,[25] though this does not appear to have been deployed in Ireland until after the Easter Rising. More relevant to the pre-1916 period were regulations 14 and 42. The first of these was the exclusion order power which was used in 1915 as a convenient way of keeping known nationalists away from their centres of influence.[26] By October 1915, twenty-one such orders were in place,[27] with the individual in each case said to have been 'suspected of acting in a manner prejudicial to the public safety or the defence of the realm', though invariably the government considered that 'it would be undesirable to give more precise details of the nature of the charge or of the evidence'.[28] The usual basis for the suspicion seems to have been the making of anti-recruiting speeches. It was under this regulation that the secretary of the Cork industrial development association was kept away from his place of work[29] and that the

[20] For more details, see the speech of Tim Healy MP during the debate on the suppression in Britain of the *Globe* newspaper: H C Debs, 11 November 1915, cols 1427–32. See pp. 47–8 above.

[21] They were *The Gael*, *The Spark* and *Honesty*: H C Debs, 30 March 1916, cols 876–8 (A Birrell).

[22] See for example the remarks of the Under Secretary of State at the War Office, H J Tennant at H C Debs, 5 May 1914, cols 1093–4.

[23] In early 1916, an Englishman and graduate of Oxford University, Claude Chavasse, was arrested for having 'failed to answer to the best of his ability questions reasonably addressed to him' when questioned by the police. It was subsequently alleged that he had been stripped, abused and held over night in a police cell. What he had done was to insist on answering the authorities in the Irish language, of which tongue the police officer in question had no knowledge: H C Debs, 22 February 1916, cols 562–3 (A Birrell). Another man, Padraig O'Conaire, was detained for a week for the same alleged offence some weeks later, though his prosecution was subsequently abandoned: H C Debs, 12 April 1916, cols 1736–7 (A Birrell).

[24] It was under the Defence of the Realm Regulations that, on 22 January 1916, the home of the Irish nationalist Countess Markievicz was searched by members of the Dublin Metropolitan Police, the warrant having been issued by 'the officer commanding troops, Dublin'. A printing press and 'a number of ballads and leaflets of an anti-British character were seized': H C Debs, 27 January 1916 col 1402 (W Rea, Lord of the Treasury).

[25] S R & O 1915 No 551.   [26] See *R v Denison* (1916) 32 TLR 528.

[27] H C Debs, 13 October 1915, col 1283 (A Birrell). At this point in time, two of these were suspended and six were not in force: ibid.

[28] H C Debs, 29 June 1915, col 1633 (A Birrell).

[29] H C Debs, 19 July 1915, cols 1166–8 (H J Tennant).

organiser of the Irish Volunteers, Ernest Blythe, was ordered out of Ireland.[30] Other distinguished victims included The O'Ràhilly, kept out of the counties of Kerry, Cork and Limerick,[31] and Desmond Fitzgerald, whose son Garret was later to serve as Taoiseach (Prime Minister) in the subsequently established Republic of Ireland. The way in which the regulation was deployed against Fitzgerald seems to have been typical. After making a nationalist speech in Kerry, he was ordered out of the county in January 1915. When he flouted that order, he was charged with the breach not only of regulation 14 but also of regulation 42, which penalised any attempt 'to cause mutiny, sedition, or disaffection among any of His Majesty's forces or among the civilian population'. The evidence for the regulation 42 offence appears to have been the same as gave rise to the exclusion order in the first place. Fitzgerald was duly brought before a Wicklow magistrate and jailed.[32]

With powers like these, there seemed to be no need to look to Parliament for new nineteenth century style coercive measures to meet what was still a potential rather than a real crisis of subversive revolt. But despite the main thrust of the war-time repression being to prevent anti-recruiting propaganda, by the start of 1916 enthusiasm for enlisting remained at a stubbornly low level outside loyalist Ulster. In Leinster province for example, which included Dublin, 29,186 men had enlisted, but government figures suggested that there were 167,492 available who had not. The statistics were even worse from the authorities point of view for the remaining two provinces: 15,190 enlisted in Munster with 133,237 suitable men left who had not yet done so, and a mere 3,939 enlistees in Connaught in the west of Ireland, where 80,330 suitable men were said to be available.[33] The alienation of large parts of Ireland from British rule was a reality with which the enforcement authorities had continually to deal, particularly when the impact of the 1915 amendment to

[30] H C Debs, 20 July 1915, cols 1317–18 (A Birrell). Along with three others, Blythe was later convicted and imprisoned by a resident magistrate for failure to comply with the order directed against him: H C Debs, 13 October 1915, cols 1283–4 (A Birrell). Eventually he was put on the Holyhead mailboat by the authorities and expelled from Ireland after having '[f]or months now last past . . . been busily and actively engaged in travelling about districts in Ireland organising meetings and other propaganda for the purpose of the promotion of sedition and anti-recruiting': H C Debs, 30 March 1916, col 876 (A Birrell).

[31] H C Debs, 6 July 1915, col 189 (A Birrell).

[32] These details are drawn from H C Debs, 26 October 1915, col 7 (H J Tennant) and H C Debs, 4 November 1915, col 817 (A Birrell). The case of Edward Moraghan was exactly the same. When he broke the order prohibiting him from residing in county Cavan he was tried under Regulation 42 for having made the speech prejudicial to recruiting which had been the basis of the original exclusion order: H C Debs, 21 October 1915, cols 1975–6 (A Birrell).

[33] H C Debs, 24 February 1916, col 787 (A Birrell).

the Defence of the Realm legislation, with its right to jury trial (discussed in Chapter 2) was taken into account. The disaffection of the country infected local justice as well as the local population from which juries were required to be drawn. One magistrate, a member of Kerry county council and the chairman of Killarney rural district council, was removed from his post after it had been established that he had been 'one of a party which [had] interfered with a recruiting meeting' in Killarney.[34] The magistrate who convicted Desmond Fitzgerald was a stipendiary, brought out of retirement to sit on the Wicklow bench.[35] A commissioner of the peace in Cork was suddenly removed from office after having opposed (in his capacity as a local councillor) a motion to give the freedom of the city to the Irish Lord Chancellor.[36] When it was desired to act against one Patrick Dyer for the 'doing of acts intended to prejudice recruiting' in Tubercurry, County Sligo, it was first deemed necessary to remove him to Dublin to be dealt with there by the dependable police magistrate.[37] Three 'respectable young men' who were jailed for refusing to be bound over for their part in an anti-recruiting fracas, found themselves before two stipendiary magistrates rather than their local Carrickmacross bench.[38]

Easter 1916: the Official Response

The Defence of the Realm Regulations really came into their own following the rebellion of 1916.[39] Launched in Dublin by the radical nationalist leader Patrick Pearse on Easter Monday, 24 April, the rebels' tactic of seizing important buildings was always a dubious one and uncertainty about whether the rising was to go ahead after the capture of Roger Casement and the loss of German weapons' support meant that it was probably

[34] H C Debs, 8 March 1916, col 1534 (A Birrell).

[35] H C Debs, 4 November 1915, col 817 (A Birrell).

[36] H C Debs, 23 March 1916, col 356 (A Birrell). The Chief Secretary, somewhat disingenuously, denied that this was the reason for the dismissal while at the same time asserting, without further explanation, that the man had 'made use in public of expressions [which were] inconsistent with the position of a magistrate': ibid.

[37] H C Debs, 6 December 1915, cols 995–6 (A Birrell).

[38] The three had been part of a crowd which had sung 'God Save Ireland' by way of a protest against 'a solicitor and two other gentlemen who had been present at a recruiting committee meeting': H C Debs, 11 January 1916, cols 1426–7 (H J Tennant).

[39] A good account is L O'Broin, *Dublin Castle and the 1916 Rising* (1966). See also Townshend, n 4 above, ch 6. Interestingly, on the very day of the Rising the authorities had taken the decision to arrest and intern in England the leaders of the Volunteers, their hostile association having been established two days before when the scale of Sir Roger Casement's involvement with the Germans on behalf of Irish nationalist interests had become apparent. This decision was of course overtaken by events: see Royal Commission on the Rebellion in Ireland, n 9 above, p 12.

doomed to failure from the start. While the insurrection never even got off the ground in the country at large, Pearse and his supporters did manage to hold out for five days in Dublin, forcing the British army into the dramatic counter-insurgency manoeuvres that were to wreck much of central Dublin.[40] The reaction of the authorities when they first began to come to terms with the depth of the crisis on 26 April was twofold. First, in an understandable but somewhat melodramatic move, the Lord Lieutenant Lord Wimborne proclaimed an immediate state of martial law in Dublin city and county.[41] Under this authority, the British army's commander-in-chief in the region, General Friend, promptly issued martial law regulations, which imposed a curfew and declared that any civilian carrying arms was liable to be fired upon without warning. On the following day, martial law was extended over the whole of Ireland, with the Prime Minister H H Asquith informing the Commons that this meant that General Sir John Maxwell was being 'given plenary powers under martial law over the whole country, [with] the Irish Executive [having] placed themselves at his disposal to carry out his instructions'.[42]

All of these dramatic declarations sounded tremendously aggressive and assertive, but in reality they achieved little more than a display of noisy confidence on the part of the authorities. Indeed this might well have been their main purpose. The Irish Attorney General subsequently recalled that the efficacy of these measures lay in the fact that 'undoubtedly the average civilian has an extraordinary belief in the magic term "Martial Law" and it therefore brings home to loyal and law-abiding people a great sense of security and safety, and upon the other hand the very indefinite knowledge of its powers spreads terror among the disaffected'.[43] The limited effect of these initiatives on the government's counter-insurgency tactics on the ground was admitted by Asquith in the House of Commons in July:

---

[40] The official casualty list arising from the insurrection was as follows: Crown forces: 124 killed; 388 injured: H C Debs, 9 May 1916, col 455 (H H Asquith); civilians: 180 killed; 614 wounded: H C Debs, 11 May 1916, cols 887–8 (H H Asquith).

[41] H C Debs, 26 April 1916, col 2483 (H H Asquith).

[42] H C Debs, 27 April 1916, col 2510. Maxwell's remit was set out in a letter sent the following day to Viscount French, field-marshal commanding-in-chief, home forces. In it, Sir Reginald H Brade, the secretary of the War Office, wrote that Maxwell was empowered to 'take all such measures as may in his opinion be necessary for the prompt suppression of insurrection in Ireland', and that he was to be 'accorded a free hand in regard to the movement of all troops': see H C Debs, 10 May 1916, col 675 (H H Asquith) (WA) where the full text of the letter is published. On 27 May, martial law was extended for an indefinite period. It was never formally revoked by proclamation, but simply ceased to apply when not judged essential: H C Debs, 26 February 1917, col 1688 (H E Duke).

[43] Quoted in Townshend, n 4 above, p 307.

I believe I am not travelling an inch beyond the truth when I say that there is no proceeding which has been taken by Sir John Maxwell or the military authorities in Ireland which is not taken under and which could not be justified by the Defence of the Realm Act. Martial law has never been put in force for any practical or effective purpose in Ireland.[44]

As Asquith here makes clear, the key to the irrelevancy of the martial law declaration lay in the availability of the Defence of the Realm Regulations. These equipped the authorities with the sort of powers that they would never have had available to them had the insurrection occurred in peace-time.

This was the second and infinitely more effective official response to the Rising. It was under the Defence of the Realm Regulations that extensive press censorship was imposed immediately after Easter Monday, so that 'news should not reach the neutral countries, and particularly our friends in America, which would be calculated to give them an entirely false impression as to the importance of what has taken place, important as that is'.[45] The regulations were now all the more attractive because the crisis meant that at last they could be enforced unhampered by jury trial. Recalling the state of the country in 1915 to 1916, a government inquiry was later to lament that as far as the Defence of the Realm Act was concerned, 'as regards Ireland, the teeth of this enactment were drawn by the Defence of the Realm (Amendment) Act 1915'.[46] The report lamented that during the passage of this Bill '[i]nsuf-

[44] H C Debs, 31 July 1916, cols 2142–3. Compare these comments in the Report of the Royal Commission on the Arrest and Subsequent Treatment of Mr Francis Sheehy Skeffington, Mr Thomas Dickson and Mr Patrick James McIntyre, Cd 8376 (1916): 'The effect, so far as the powers of military authorities are concerned, of a proclamation of martial law within the United Kingdom has often been expounded, but nevertheless, in the crisis which evokes such a proclamation, is not always remembered. Such a proclamation does not, in itself, confer upon officers or soldiers any new powers. It operates solely as a warning that the Government, acting through the military, is about to take such forcible and exceptional measures as may be necessary for the purpose of putting down insurrection and restoring order. As long as the measures are necessary, they might equally be taken without any proclamation at all' (para 55(3)).

[45] H C Debs, 26 April 1916, col 2484 (A Birrell). For further details, see the short adjournment debate on the topic at H C Debs, 27 April 1916, cols 2575–80. Sir John Maxwell's press officer Lord Decies was formally appointed to the post of press censor on 11 June 1916, but by then he had been doing the job for some weeks on an informal basis: H C Debs, 7 August 1916, col 653 (H W Forster, Financial Secretary to the War Office). The strength of the steps taken by the military to control criticism of the operation of the law in Irish newspapers is clear from the further debate that took place in the Commons on 1 August 1916: H C Debs, cols 161–8, the Home Secretary's reply to which is at cols 178–81 (H Samuel). The censor, whose office was 'open night and day for the convenience of the Press', was particularly concerned with the USA, regularly preventing the export there of Irish newspapers: see H C Debs, 14 August 1916, col 1431 (H W Forster) (WA) and H C Debs, 24 October 1916, col 932 (H W Forster), from which the above quotation is taken. The task of press censorship was transferred back to the civil authorities in November 1916: H C Debs, 30 November 1916, col 462 (H E Duke).

[46] Royal Commission on the Rebellion in Ireland, n 9 above, p 5.

ficient attention appear[ed] to have been paid to the state of affairs in Ireland in both Houses of Parliament'.[47] On the same day that martial law was declared, therefore, a further proclamation suspended the operation in Ireland of the relevant section of the 1915 Act.[48] The move had its roots in the statute itself, which by section 1(7) had set down that, 'In the event of invasion or other special military emergency arising out of the present war, His Majesty may by Proclamation forthwith suspend the operation of this section, either generally or as respects any area specified in the Proclamation, without prejudice, however, to any proceedings under this section which may be then pending in any civil court'.

The effect of this proclamation was now to bring into operation in Ireland regulation 58A,[49] which contemplated two types of military justice, a general court-martial and a field general court-martial, for persons charged with offences against the regulations. The general court-martial, already covered by regulation 57, was the normal form of tribunal in cases encompassing this type of military discipline and was quite formal in its approach. The field general court-martial provided for in regulation 58A, in contrast, was 'a particular form' of this general court-martial.[50] It was turned to 'in times of crises when it is impossible to have such a high degree of formalism as is observed at a general court-martial'.[51] The field general court-martial allowed for the more immediate dispensation of military justice by senior officers in the field. The jurisdiction of the body was exactly the same as for the general court-martial, and this included the death penalty where the intention of the accused had been to assist the enemy and, in other cases, extended to the imposition of terms of imprisonment of up to penal servitude for life. With these new powers, the authorities were able to escape from the constraints that had been achieved by Parliament in 1915 and henceforth to act in a way which was untrammelled by any need for the type of formal legality that was epitomised by the procedures of a standard criminal

---

[47] Ibid, p 7. The Royal Commission went on to provide a bleak assessment (from an official perspective) of law and order in the twelve months leading up to the Easter Rising: 'So seditious had the country become during 1915, that juries in Dublin, and magistrates in various parts of the country—through fear or favour—could not be trusted to give decisions in accordance with the evidence. The only tribunals which could be relied upon at this time were those presided over by resident magistrates in Dublin or Belfast, who had no power to impose a greater sentence than six months' hard labour'.

[48] See S R & O 1916 No 256.

[49] First introduced on 23 March 1915: S R & O 1915 No 235. A small drafting amendment in the Regulation was made on 26 April 1916 (S R & O 1916 No 257).

[50] *R v Governor of Lewes Prison, ex parte Doyle* [1917] 2 KB 254, at p 266 (Viscount Reading LCJ).

[51] Ibid, at 260, Sir F E Smith, Attorney General, putting the argument for the governor in the case.

trial. It was to the Defence of the Realm Regulations in general and to these informal tribunals of justice in particular that the State now turned in order to exact its legal revenge on those associated with the failed rebellion.

Questions of Legality

In the first weeks of May 1916, no fewer than 3,419 suspected Sinn Féin sympathisers were arrested under the internment and other provisions of the regulations, in a military operation that extended throughout the country. Five of the women and 1,836 of the men were subsequently interned in Britain, the majority at Frongoch in Wales.[52] A total of 183 civilians were tried by courts-martial for their alleged involvement in the Rising, and of these no fewer than 155 were convicted under regulation 50 (which carried the death penalty for acting with the intention and purpose of assisting the enemy).[53] The practice was for these tribunals to sit in secret. Death sentences were passed on ninety prisoners, with fourteen of these capital punishments being carried out in Dublin on 3, 4, 5, 8, and 12 May and a fifteenth taking place in Cork on 9 May. This gruesome sequence of executions was only brought to an end after an impassioned speech by the nationalist John Dillon in the House of Commons on 11 May which led the Prime Minster H H Asquith to order their immediate end.[54] No effort seems to have been made at this time to chal-

---

[52] These precise figures are from C Townshend, *Political Violence in Ireland*, n 4 above, p 308. Compare H C Debs, 4 July 1916, col 1357 (H Samuel) which estimated the number of internees at 1,800 and H C Debs, 6 July 1916, col 1637 (H Samuel) which indicates that an additional 1,200 suspects were arrested by the army in the first post-rebellion sweep but were later quickly released. Each internee had a right to have his or her incarceration considered by an advisory committee chaired by an English High Court judge, Sankey J. Some disquiet was initially expressed by Irish members of the House of Commons that no member of Sankey's committee was from Ireland: H C Debs, 31 May 1916, cols 2690–1 (H H Asquith). Within three weeks Pym J from the Irish bench had joined the panel: H C Debs, 20 June 1916, col 12 (H Samuel). The advisory committee allowed the internees access to legal advice but did not permit lawyers to act as advocates on their behalf: H C Debs, 29 June 1916, col 1006 (H Samuel). By the end of its first month of operation, a 'small number of recommendations for release [had] been made, and the men [had] been released': H C Debs, 5 July 1916, col 1510 (H Samuel). By the end of October 1916, a total of 547 internees remained in Frongoch: H C Debs, 24 October 1916, col 965 (W Brace, Under Secretary of State for the Home Department) (WA).

[53] See H C Debs, 30 April 1917, col 45 (H E Duke) (WA); H C Debs, 4 May 1917, col 617 (H E Duke). The leader of the Irish Volunteers, Professor Eoin MacNeill, had attempted to prevent the rebellion which had been planned by the militant Irish Republican Brotherhood without his knowledge, but despite this he was tried on eight charges of attempting to cause disaffection among the civilian population and on four charges of acting in a way likely to prejudice recruiting and was convicted and sentenced to penal servitude for life: H C Debs, 20 June 1916, col 15 (H H Asquith).

[54] The full parliamentary debate to which Dillon made his famous contribution is at H C Debs, 11 May 1916, cols 935–70. It has occasionally been alleged that James Connolly may have been

lenge the lawfulness of the executions but that the legal issues involved were not uncontroversial can be seen from the case of Gerald Doyle, a Dublin plasterer who had been taken prisoner at the start of the Easter rebellion when the hut that he had been occupying with other rebels was taken by government troops.[55] On 1 May he was duly charged with having taken part 'in an armed rebellion and in the waging of war against His Majesty the King, such act being of such a nature as to be calculated to be prejudicial to the defence of the realm, and being done with the intention and for the purpose of assisting the enemy'. His death sentence was afterwards commuted to three years' penal servitude and he was moved to Lewes prison from where, some months after the rising, he tried to escape by legal rather than heroic means.

His case rested in particular on two points. First, he argued that his conviction was bad because it related to offences committed before the dispensing of trial by jury had been proclaimed on 26 April (by which time Doyle was already in custody). The Lord Chief Justice (Viscount Reading) had no difficulty in rejecting the submission; the 'Proclamation certainly took effect from the time it was published, notwithstanding that the offence had been committed before the date of the Proclamation',[56] and this was because it dealt merely 'with procedure—with the mode of trial of the person'[57] rather than with matters of legal substance. Doyle's second and 'most substantial'[58] argument was that his trial was fatally defective because the proceedings had been wrongly held in secret. The fact that the field courts-martial after 1916 had all been held *in camera* had already provoked intense controversy, particularly after it was admitted by the Home Secretary Herbert Samuel in July that 'no civil legal authority [had been] consulted . . . beforehand', with the decision having been taken by the military authorities 'in the interests of public safety and the Defence of the Realm . . . while disaffection was still seething' in the country.[59] Doyle's counsel naturally pointed to the then recently decided and presumably well-known House of Lords decision of *Scott v Scott*,[60] which had

shot dead *after* the army commander Sir John Maxwell had received Asquith's orders to end the executions, though it seems clear from the debate in the House on 11 May that it was always intended that the two signatories of the 1916 Proclamation who were still alive, of whom Connolly was one, should be shot, whatever concessions might be made in respect of other prisoners.

[55] *R v Governor of Lewes Prison, ex parte Doyle* [1917] 2 KB 254.   [56] Ibid, at p 268.
[57] Ibid.   [58] Ibid, at p 265 (Viscount Reading LCJ).
[59] H C Debs, 3 July 1916, col 1194 (H Samuel). The Home Secretary went on to claim that the law officers 'entirely approved' of the decision: col 1195. Asquith's undertaking that the proceedings of the courts-martial would be published was not acted upon during his time as Prime Minister and was not honoured by the administration that followed his departure from office: H C Debs, 20 March 1917, cols 1842–54 (H E Duke).
[60] [1913] AC 417.

established that a court, assuming it had the discretion, had a duty to sit open to the public unless it could be shown that justice could not be administered except behind closed doors. Thus in that case the Lord Chancellor, Viscount Haldane, had asserted that 'the broad principle is that the Courts of this country must, as between parties, administer justice in public', and that this principle was subject to apparent exceptions though these in turn flowed from 'a yet more fundamental principle that the chief object of Courts of justice must be to secure that justice is done'.[61]

Doyle's lawyer asserted that in 'the present case no such circumstances ha[d] been made out'.[62] But this was always likely to be a difficult argument to sustain in light of Earl Loreburn's concession in *Scott* that 'tumult or disorder, or the just apprehension of it, would certainly justify the exclusion of all from where such interruption is expected'.[63] What chance had the applicant in Doyle where 'the court-martial which sat to judge [him] sat when an open rebellion was going on around the court'?[64] Yet his argument was further buttressed by the rules of procedure that applied to courts-martial, which provided in the relevant clause that such 'proceedings shall be held in open court, in the presence of the accused, except on any deliberation among the members, when the court may be closed'.[65] The Lord Chief Justice's answer to this submission was to assert simply that notwithstanding this rule, it was 'plain that inherent jurisdiction exists in any Court which enables it to exclude the public where it becomes necessary in order to administer justice'.[66] As for the House of Lords precedent, Viscount Reading considered that, having regard to the fact that the commander-in-chief of the army had formed the opinion that it was necessary for the public safety and for the defence of the realm that neither the public nor the press should be admitted to the trial, it was 'abundantly plain' that these *in camera* proceedings were well within the principle in *Scott v Scott*.[67] 'In the existence of such a state of circumstances' as then pertained in Dublin, it was 'quite possible to conceive a number of persons coming into court, if the public had been admitted, who might have terrorized, possibly even have shot, witnesses'.[68]

The Lord Chief Justice does not seem to have had very much confidence in the British army's ability to protect even its own courts-martial from attack, though in view of the surrender of the rebels before the trials

---

[61] [1913] AC 417, at p 437. See also the speech of the Earl of Halsbury at pp 440–3.
[62] [1917] 2 KB 254, at p 263 (Schiller KC).   [63] [1913] AC 417, at p 445.
[64] [1917] 2 KB 254, at p 274 (Darling J).
[65] Rule 119(c) of the Rules of Procedure 1907, made under the Army Act 1881.
[66] [1917] 2 KB 254, at p 271.   [67] Ibid, at p 272.   [68] Ibid.

had even commenced, it is difficult to state clearly who these notional attackers might have been. Interestingly, the court in *Doyle* expressly declined to pronounce upon the legality of the Proclamation, and counsel did not push the point, though it was at least arguable that the conditions in section 1(7) of the 1915 Act had not been met, namely that such a declaration could only be made in 'the event of invasion or other special military emergency arising out of the present war'. Neither factor was obviously to the fore in Ireland.[69] It is not probable however that any of the executed prisoners would have fared any better than Doyle had they thought to challenge the sentences imposed on them on this or any other basis. The court of seven was unanimous against him, with even Atkin J (later to become famous in another war-time case during the Second World War[70]) agreeing with Viscount Reading's judgment. Darling J probably caught the feeling on the Bench most accurately when he admitted to finding it 'incongruous that, before the echoes of this rebellion have died away, we should meet here solemnly to consider such points as have been argued before us'.[71] The court-martial had taken place while the 'ruins in Dublin were still hot cinders'[72] and it would have been 'grotesque . . . to do what would be equivalent to inviting the public to come and hear witnesses give evidence against rebels with whom a great many of that same public sympathised'.[73]

Conscription and its Consequences

Throughout 1917, the authorities continued half-heartedly to apply a policy of 'pin-pricking coercion'[74] against a still somewhat desultory Irish

---

[69] It has already been noted that the attempt to ship German arms to the rebels had been unsuccessful. Had arms got through, the Proclamation would have stood on firmer legal ground. That the government was alive, even before the Rising, to the need to root the suspension of the 1915 Act on firm legal ground is clear from the following remarks in a letter from Sir Matthew Nathan (then Under Secretary to the Irish government) to the Adjutant-General Sir Cecil Macready, written on 10 April 1916, some two weeks before the rising: 'I am advised that invasion of any part of the United Kingdom would justify the necessary Proclamation to suspend the trial by jury section of the Act in Ireland, and that any real rising in Ireland requiring the use of military forces for its suppression would also be a sufficient legal justification' (Royal Commission on the Rebellion in Ireland, n 9 above, appendix).

[70] *Liversidge v Anderson* [1942] AC 206. See Chapter 8 below.

[71] [1917] 2 KB 254, at p 273.   [72] Ibid.

[73] Ibid, at p 274. A delighted government, which had been relentlessly harried by Laurence Ginnell MP in the House of Commons on the point of the apparent unlawfulness of the secret nature of the courts-martial, welcomed the decision as establishing that the procedure at the courts-martial had been 'absolutely well founded': H C Debs, 20 March 1917, col 1849 (H E Duke).

[74] F S L Lyons, *Ireland since the Famine* (1971), p 386.

separatist movement.[75] We cannot now know for how long the slow growth in Irish separatism would have continued in the absence of the galvanising and pivotal crisis that was precipitated by the threat of Irish conscription in April 1918. After much hesitation, and against a background of enormous losses on the western front following the start of the German Spring offensive, the decision was finally announced on 9 April. The Cabinet was well aware of the almost total opposition to the move in the country and it steeled itself to impose its will.[76] On 11 May the appointment as Lord Lieutenant of Field-Marshall Viscount French of Ypres looked more like a military than a political move. At the same time Edward Shortt, a future Home Secretary at another critical juncture in British politics, was appointed Chief Secretary. In an atmosphere of growing political unrest but as yet only sporadic violence, the authorities embarked on a three-pronged policy of coercion. First, renewed use was made of the control inherent in the Defence of the Realm Regulations, but though the old powers were once again deployed,[77] the emphasis now was on such military regulations as 29B[78] which had been promulgated in the panic after the Easter Rising but which had never been used. Under its terms, a district could be designated a 'special military area' (or SMA) into which no person could enter without military permission. On 25 February, just such an SMA had been imposed on Clare. On the same day as conscription was announced, a second SMA was imposed on Limerick. Further SMAs were imposed on Tralee on 19 June and on the west riding of Cork county in September. In Tralee, permits to enter

[75] See generally C Townshend, *The British Campaign in Ireland 1919–1921. The Development of Political and Military Policies* (1975).

[76] See the adjournment debate at H C Debs, 15 April 1918, cols 180–4 and the numerous interventions by Irish members during the passage through the Commons of what became the Military Services Act 1918. The number of Irishmen, north and south, who were prepared to volunteer for service on the front had tailed off dramatically in both places in 1916 and 1917: the figures are at H C Debs, 15 April 1918, col 42 (J I Macpherson, Under Secretary of State for War). For a good overview of the situation, see A J Ward, 'Lloyd George and the 1918 Irish Conscription Crisis' (1974) 17 *Historical Journal* 107.

[77] Thus, in July 1918, Mrs Sheehy-Skeffington was prevented under Regulation 14E from returning to Ireland after a visit to the USA, being required instead to remain in Britain: H C Debs, 18 July 1918, cols 1213–5 (A W Samuels, Solicitor General for Ireland). On 4 July a new order prohibited all meetings, processions and assemblies in Ireland unless seven days notice was given and permission from the police was obtained: H C Debs, 11 July 1918, cols 482–3 (E Shortt). The new rule caught various Gaelic sporting events which were prohibited because the requisite notice had not been given: H C Debs, 1 August 1918, col 599 (E Shortt). An order was issued on 5 October 1918 under Regulation 9AA prohibiting the having, keeping or using of a motor-cycle in Ireland without a permit and on 9 October 1919, the Regulation was expanded to embrace motor cars: S R & O 1919 No 1445. The order was later described in Parliament in the course of a question to the administration as having 'roused indignation amongst all classes of the community in Ireland': H C Debs, 1 December 1919, col 51 (J Devlin).

[78] S R & O 1916 No 317, amended by S R & O 1918 No 540.

were supposedly 'only . . . refused to persons whom it was undesirable to allow in owing to their seditious and dangerous tendencies', though these were quite large categories to the embattled British administrators of the day.[79] According to Townshend, in the Cork SMA, 'troop strength was increased to two battalions, centred on Bantry and Macroom, with companies at Dunmanway, Skibbereen, Bandon, and Millstreet. Fairs and markets were prohibited without military permit, public houses were closed at 7pm, and a curfew was imposed on the very lawless town of Eyeries'.[80]

The authorities considered this Cork SMA to be 'a remarkable instance of the effect which a mild system of military control can have on a community'.[81] They were equally confident about the efficaciousness of their second coercive weapon against current and anticipated political unrest. This was Balfour's Crimes Act of 1887 which had been effectively deployed against an earlier generation of Land League agitators and which the government now resuscitated in the hope of achieving a similar success.[82] The accuracy of Darling J's remarks in *Doyle*, about the support the rebels were enjoying in early 1917, indicates how difficult it must have been even as early as this to get convictions against political offenders where juries or local magistrates were required by law to make guilty findings as a preliminary to incarceration, and the situation worsened substantially from the authorities' point of view in the following eighteen months. It was moreover a problem that was by no means solved by the suspension of the Defence of the Realm (Amendment) Act 1915 since the courts-martial thereby permitted applied only to offences against the regulations. Under the 1887 Act, the Lord Lieutenant was empowered to proclaim an organisation to be a dangerous association and once this was done he could then proceed to prohibit or suppress the same group. The proclamation of a whole district was also possible under section 5 of the Act, where it appeared to the Lord Lieutenant 'necessary for the prevention, detection, or punishment of crime and outrage'. Such a proclamation did not allow the suspension of habeas corpus, the creation of special courts or any such old fashioned coercion.

---

[79] H C Debs, 22 July 1918, col 1465 (E Shortt) (WA).

[80] Townshend, *The British Campaign in Ireland*, n 75 above, p 11.

[81] Ibid, p 12, quoting an intelligence note on the SMA in Cork. The SMA was lifted on 5 February 1919.

[82] In the second half of 1887, some 373 people had been imprisoned under the Act, and by 1890 the total had risen to 1,614: Townshend, *Political Violence in Ireland*, n 4 above, p 210. The Act had survived despite two House of Commons resolutions in favour of its repeal, in 1894 and 1907: see H C Debs, 12 February 1917, col 270 (H E Duke).

Instead, it provided a lawful basis for changes to the legal process, through special preliminary inquiries, the extension of summary jurisdiction, the establishment of special juries and the power to change the place of a trial. After resisting the pressure for a while, the government under the direction of Lord French changed tack, and on 14 June 1918, sections three and four of the 1887 Act were brought into effect in Clare, Cork county, Cork city, Galway, Kerry, King's county, Limerick, Limerick town, Longford, Mayo, Queen's county, Roscommon, Sligo, Tipperary, Tyrone and Westmeath.[83] These sections provided for special juries and for a change in the location of trials if this was judged necessary. By 25 July, fifteen cases had been transferred for trial by special juries to Cork city and five to Belfast.[84]

The 1887 Act was also now deployed in a direct assault on the fast growing Sinn Féin party. On 3 July 1918, five organisations, made up of Sinn Féin itself, the Sinn Féin Clubs, the Irish Volunteers, Cumann na mBan and the Gaelic League, were proclaimed to be dangerous under section six of the Act.[85] This 'very slight use' of the Act did not 'mean that anything [would] be done to those societies' but rather that it would function as 'a mere warning'.[86] It had been enough to help to decimate the Irish National League in 1887, but was less successful against these groups, with the number of people involved now vast compared with earlier eras of revolt: the Sinn Féin Clubs alone had a membership of more than 100,000. Undaunted by such levels of popular support, the authorities deployed their third coercive device against the republican leadership itself. This required an alteration to the Defence of the Realm Regulations. The internment power in regulation 14B was exercisable where it appeared to the authorities that 'for securing the public safety or the Defence of the Realm it [was] expedient in view of the hostile origin or associations of any person' to subject them to such an order. The problem lay in the doubt that Irish subversives could be presented as hostile, particularly as the German dimension to their conspiracy against the Crown had markedly receded from its 1916 highpoint. The answer lay in the following version of regulation 14B, promulgated on 20 April 1918, just two days after enactment of the Military Services Act:

In any area in respect of which the operation of Section one of the Defence of the Realm (Amendment) Act, 1915, is for the time being suspended, this regulation shall apply in relation to any person who is suspected of acting or

---

[83] See S R & O 1918 Nos 745–60.   [84] H C Debs, 25 July 1918, col 1977 (E Shortt).
[85] S R & O 1918 No 819.   [86] H C Debs, 29 July 1918, col 112 (E Shortt).

having acted or of being about to act in a manner prejudicial to the public safety or the defence of the Realm, as it applies in relation to persons of hostile origin or association.[87]

Mass arrests of the Sinn Féin leadership were duly carried out on the night of 17 May 1918.[88] The majority of the Sinn Féin leaders were detained. A story about a German conspiracy of some sort was pulled together so as to provide an accompanying political legitimacy for this dramatic State action.[89]

The Lessons for Civil Liberties

We now consider the implications for civil liberties of the operation of the rule of law in the years we have discussed in this first part of the chapter. The 1887 Act had been first deployed in a very different Ireland from that into which it re-emerged in 1918. The turn of the century saw Ireland relatively free of legislation restrictive of civil liberties, with the law that was used to control dissent, such as the 1887 Act and *O'Kelly v Harvey*,[90] being ostensibly part of the ordinary rather than the extraordinary law. The old legislation which had been used to manage Ireland through much of the nineteenth century was gradually allowed to die away, so that by the outbreak of the First World War the country had come thoroughly to enjoy the freedom that it had secured as an unexpected and hardly noticed beneficiary of Edwardian liberalism. This state of affairs did not survive the coming into effect of the Defence of the Realm Regulations, the repressive dimensions to which quickly moved sideways to encompass unacceptable expressions of Irish nationalist sentiment. The main focus was on the effect of the expression of nationalist sentiments on army recruitment but there can be no doubt that the

---

[87] S R & O 1918 No 462.

[88] 69 arrests were made with the detainees being subsequently interned in Great Britain: H C Debs, 30 May 1918, col 944 (E Shortt). No visits were allowed from relatives (H C Debs, 3 June 1918, cols 1230–1 (W Brace, Under Secretary of State for the Home Office)) but as in 1916–17, the internees were permitted to make representations to an advisory committee which was presided over by a High Court judge: H C Debs, 3 June 1918, col 1230 (A Samuels, Attorney General for Ireland). The committee received no such representations within the required time frame: H C Debs, 18 June 1918, col 183 (E Shortt) (WA). By the start of March 1919, all the internees had been released: H C Debs, 6 March 1919, cols 598–9 (J I Macpherson, Chief Secretary).

[89] See the statement by the Chief Secretary, followed by the Commons debate, under the heading 'German Plot and Recruiting' H C Debs, 25 June 1918, cols 905–1015. Shortt described the plot as 'a real imminent danger to this country', col 906, but the claim was greeted with both anger and scepticism. The controversy over the supposed plot simmered away in the background for years, culminating in a couple of White Papers published in early 1921, ostensibly laying out the facts: Documents relative to the Sinn Féin movement, Cmd 1108 (1921); Intercourse between Bolshevism and Sinn Féin, Cmd 1326 (1921).

[90] See n 1, above.

controls affected far more generally the expression of nationalist opinion as such. After the Easter Rising, the scale and intensity of these restrictions on what were (in Britain at any rate) traditional civil liberties deepened in several different respects, with the liberty of the person and the freedoms of association, assembly and expression being sharply modified by further executive action. The story of the war-time powers in Ireland up to this point was not unlike a more extreme version of the one with which we became familiar in the course of Chapter 2, with the executive branch deploying the enormously wide and uncontrolled powers which had been granted to it by the legislature to take action against certain groups and in certain ways that could hardly have been anticipated by the representatives who had voted the powers through.

Where Ireland was different was in the independence of the lower judiciary, particularly the lay magistrates. This refusal to fall into line with the executive was not something witnessed in Britain during the war. In Ireland, however, such independence as happened to exist was due not to any great commitment to the rule of law on the part of these part-time judges but rather to the fact that they tended not to be without some sympathy for many of the nationalist defendants that they found arrayed before them. It is hard to be very enthusiastic about a display of judicial autonomy that may have owed more to a shared political perspective with the accused person in the dock than it did to any commitment to the principle of legality as an idea governing his or her trial. It is the opposite kind of situation to that which we have frequently encountered in the course of this book; instead of the magistrates distorting the law to suit the prosecutors, they were frequently doing the same to please the defendants. In any event the executive was able to achieve its ends by reviving the 1887 Act, and by contriving to rely far more than would normally have been the case on the resident magistrates, so many of whom were drawn from former officers of the Royal Irish Constabulary. It should not be forgotten, either, that throughout this period the higher judiciary in both Dublin and London were consistently loyal to the executive and legitimised the operation of the Defence of the Realm regulations and other relevant restrictive legislation whenever litigation gave them the opportunity. The challenge for the judiciary became far graver with the escalation in the conflict on the island that began slowly in 1918 but which then grew into an increasingly bloody secessionist campaign. These violent circumstances put even more pressure on the courts to adhere to the Rule of Law at a time when they were confronted with an increasingly belligerent executive which was in turn having to deal with a situation of spiralling violence in a country which was becoming more hostile with every passing day.

BRITAIN IN IRELAND, 1919–1921

As we have seen, throughout 1917, the government's strategy was to use its powers of coercion greatly to inhibit the expression of nationalist sentiment. This had become an even more powerful imperative when the prospect of conscription became a firm one in April 1918. During the whole of this period, however, and also in the months after the announcement of conscription, there was comparatively little secessionist violence. There was a slight increase in such disorder during the Summer of 1918. In July of that year two RIC men were attacked in Ballingeary, county Cork and in the same county two months later a serious assault on the RIC was launched by nationalist rebels. But there were no fatalities in either of these skirmishes, and there was little sense of lawless panic in the country at large. When Lord French was appointed Viceroy in May 1918, he was advised by the government to concentrate his energies on the suppression of 'seditious' speech.[91] Whatever could be said about the moral basis for such a policy, and it may perhaps be put down to the repressive reflexes of a government at war, it was a catastrophic failure in practice. Sinn Féin achieved success in two bye-elections in Longford and Clare and then, in December 1918, the Party swept the boards in the post-war general election.[92] The following month, Sinn Féin MP's convened their own parliament in Dublin, and refused to attend the House of Commons at Westminster. On the same day as this 'Dáil Éireann' met for the first time, 21 January 1919, two RIC men were killed by members of the Irish Volunteers in an incident involving the seizure of gelignite in Soloheadbeg, county Tipperary. With these two events, the struggle between the Irish nationalists and the United Kingdom authorities entered a more violent phase.

[91] Townshend, *The British Campaign in Ireland*, n 75 above, p 9.

[92] When the general election was announced, the Chief Secretary on 4 November 1918 promised that the Regulation requiring police permits for political meetings and processions would be suspended, but nevertheless maintained that 'the wearing of what purports to be a military uniform and seditious speeches [would] remain illegal, and [be] subject to punishment': H C Debs, 4 November 1918, col 1784 (E Shortt). When the campaign got under way, the official harassment was sometimes very direct. In Belfast, for example, the offices of the local Sinn Féin branch were closed on 7 November, since they had allegedly been 'used as a centre for the distribution of seditious literature unconnected with electioneering purposes': H C Debs, 14 November 1918, col 2851 (E Shortt). Material judged by the authorities to be relevant to electioneering was returned to the Party.

The Conflict Escalates

The secessionist campaign of violence 'opened sporadically in the first six months of 1919'.[93] In the first seven months of 1919, there were a total of forty-seven attacks against magistrates and the police, involving seven fatalities and thirty-six injuries.[94] By the Summer the number of members of the armed forces present in the country had grown to 59,529.[95] The government found itself responding to the violence in a way that was merely reactive rather than strategically well-judged. Thus the Soloheadbeg killings[96] led to the immediate imposition of a special military area in the locality where the killings had occurred.[97] An SMA was also imposed on Westport on 4 April, and three days after this an order under regulation 9AA prohibited the holding of meetings in Dublin. After the killing of two RIC men during the rescue of a nationalist activist from a train in Knocklong, Limerick on 7 June, the decision appears to have been taken to ban Sinn Féin altogether. When District Inspector Hunt of the RIC was shot dead in broad daylight in Thurles ten days later, the five organisations previously declared to be dangerous under the 1887 Act, which included Sinn Féin, were prohibited and suppressed in both ridings of the county under the same Act.[98] On 13 August these five 'dangerous' organisations were also prohibited and suppressed in Clare.[99] Similar bans were subsequently imposed in Cork county and borough in September,[100] and in Dublin county and city in October.[101]

With the violence escalating, the partisanship of Irish juries was being further revealed at every opportunity. The killing of a member of the Shropshire light infantry in an ambush in Fermoy was described by the coroner's jury convened to adjudicate on it as 'an act of war' rather than as murder. The troops retaliated by attacking the property of the jurors, and the government had its say when, two days later, it introduced in Clare, Cork (city and county), Dublin (city and county), Limerick and

[93] C Townshend, 'The Irish Republican Army and the Development of Guerrilla Warfare, 1916–1921' (1979) 94 *English Historical Review* 318, at p 321.

[94] H C Debs, 14 August 1919, cols 1663–6 (J I Macpherson) (WA).

[95] H C Debs, 7 July 1919, col 1409 (W S Churchill, Secretary of State for the War Office) (WA).

[96] See p 135 above.

[97] It covered the south riding of Tipperary and was lifted on 14 June 1919, only to be reimposed on 29 September 1919.

[98] S R & O 1919 No 1252 and S R & O 1919 No 1253. The organisations involved are at text to n 85 above.

[99] S R & O 1919 No 1249.

[100] S R & O 1919 No 1250 and S R & O 1919 No 1251.

[101] S R & O 1919 No 1588.

Tipperary the draconian, continental-style investigative powers for designated resident magistrates that had been enacted in section 1 of the 1887 Act.[102] The defendants against whom murder charges were eventually brought arising out of the Fermoy incident found that their place of trial was switched from Cork to Londonderry, but the Irish Divisional Court—having heard evidence of earlier anti-Catholic rioting in the town—intervened to restore the original location.[103] The men accused of the Knocklong killings also found their trial relocated, on this occasion to Belfast. Once again the court intervened and Armagh was selected as the appropriate compromise venue.[104] Meanwhile the policy of the gradual suppression of nationalist sentiment came to its logical conclusion with the prohibition and suppression throughout Ireland of Dáil Éireann on 10 September.[105] The suppression throughout the country of the five 'dangerous' organisations followed on 25 November 1919.[106] Irish public opinion continued to be unpersuaded of the arguments marshalled in favour of the status quo by the forces of the Crown. This was despite continuing and increasingly harsh efforts at the control of the press[107] and widespread use of the regulatory power to ban meetings.[108] In the aftermath of a very nearly successful attempt on the life of the Lord Lieutenant at the end of the year, the Irish electorate contentedly gave Sinn Féin control of 72 out of 127 town councils in the municipal elections in January 1920, and the Party was even more successful in the rural elections that followed some months later.

---

[102] S R & O 1919 No 1240; S R & O 1919 No 1241; S R & O 1919 No 1242; S R & O 1919 No 1243; S R & O 1919 No 1244; S R & O 1919 No 1245; S R & O 1919 No 1246; S R & O 1919 No 1247; S R & O 1919 No 1248. Sections 3 and 4, already operative in many parts of Ireland, see text to n 83 above, were extended to Dublin cit.y and county on 24 October: S R & O 1919 No 1589. Between 1 November 1918 and 30 April 1920, 305 cases were dealt with by two resident magistrates under the 1887 Act: H C Debs, 6 May 1920, col 2217 (D Henry, Attorney General for Ireland).

[103] *R v Fitzgerald* [1920] 2 IR 428. The Spring and Summer of 1920 saw the start of a prolonged period of sectarian disturbances in Belfast.

[104] *R v Maher* [1920] 2 IR 440. [105] S R & O 1919 No 1254.

[106] S R & O 1919 No 1726.

[107] On 10 May 1919, the premises of the *Waterford News* were taken over by the police and the newspaper's printing plant was seized: H C Debs, 13 May 1919, col 1455 (J I Macpherson). At the end of 1919, the suppression of the *Freeman's Journal* caused great controversy: see H C Debs, 16 December 1919, cols 324–68 for an angry debate on the subject. In the 12 months to July 1920, 21 newspapers were suppressed, 12 of them on a temporary basis: H C Debs, 19 July 1920, col 49 (Sir H Greenwood, Chief Secretary for Ireland) (WA).

[108] In the 12 months to 30 October 1919, 71 meetings were prohibited in Ireland: H C Debs, 30 October 1919, col 863 (J A Macpherson). Between the first day of that year and 21 October 1920, no fewer than 127 meetings were prohibited: H C Debs, 21 October 1920, col 1053 (Sir H Greenwood).

It was from about this point that Sinn Féin's alternative structure of government began to take a firm hold on large parts of the island. As early as November 1919, the police had to step in to prohibit Monaghan county council from receiving a deputation from Dáil Éireann which was inquiring into the industrial resources of Ireland,[109] and in the months following the local elections, both Dublin Corporation and Dublin County Council pledged their allegiance to Sinn Féin.[110] On 26 May 1920, the Cork harbour board decided to fly the Irish flag on admiralty pier in Queenstown,[111] a decision that officials at the Cork court house emulated in July.[112] By the Summer of 1920, the Dáil courts were providing an alternative system of justice to that offered by the official authorities.[113] Emboldened by such displays of widespread popular support, the Irish Volunteers, or 'Irish Republican Army' as they were now increasingly coming to be called, sharply increased their commitment to the armed struggle. By the end of April 1920, the murder rate of police, army and government officials had risen steeply, and a total of forty such persons had now suffered violent deaths since the disorder had begun.[114] In response, the government still refused to countenance either full martial law or a credible political settlement, and it was therefore reduced merely to increasing the tempo of coercion. It was a case of more of the same, now more violently exercised. Curfews were imposed in Dublin in February[115] and in Cork in July. In January 1920, the military were authorised to exercise more widely their already extensive powers of search and arrest, with as many as 1,000 private homes being allegedly entered and searched in the course of one January night alone.[116] A new policy of internment was also embarked upon, with the legal basis being once again regulation 14B. In the course of January alone 1,955 arrests were made.[117] Inevitably the new policy brought in its wake the old problem of the prison hunger-strike, and

[109] H C Debs, 4 December 1919, cols 610–11 (D Henry, Attorney General for Ireland) (WA).

[110] For the details see H C Debs, 13 May 1920, cols 622–3 (D Henry); H C Debs, 15 July 1920, cols 2569–70 (Sir H Greenwood).

[111] H C Debs, 3 June 1920, cols 2022–3 (Sir H Greenwood).

[112] H C Debs, 21 July 1920, col 430 (Sir H Greenwood).

[113] See the statement of the Attorney General for Ireland, D Henry, at H C Debs, 17 June 1920, cols 1420–2 and the earlier interchange involving both Henry and the Chief Secretary Sir Hamar Greenwood at H C Debs, 3 June 1920, cols 2026–8.

[114] H C Debs, 28 April 1920, cols 1261–2 (D Henry) (WA). This escalation had a predictably demoralising effect on the police: between 1 June and 15 July 1920, there were no fewer than 250 resignations from the RIC: H C Debs, 15 July 1920, col 2624 (Sir H Greenwood) (WA).

[115] The prohibition was on being out-of-doors between 11.30 pm and 5 am: H C Debs, 4 March 1920, col 606 (J A Macpherson).

[116] H C Debs, 12 February 1920, col 198 (J A Macpherson). The Chief Secretary considered the figure 'grossly exaggerated', but clearly a great number of houses had been searched.

[117] H C Debs, 11 March 1920, col 1503 (J A Macpherson).

there were nearly 300 such protests under way in Wormwood Scrubs and Mountjoy prison by the start of May.[118]

Questions of Legality

An ambitious attempt to destroy the legal basis of this latest policy of internment proved unsuccessful.[119] On 14 January 1920, one Patrick Foy was arrested in Dublin and interned in Wormwood Scrubs prison in London. On 8 March, he sought a writ of habeas corpus from the King's Bench, his lawyers pointing out that the defence of the realm legislation hinged on the fact of the continuance of the war, and that the war was now effectively at an end, with peace with Germany having been formally signed four days before Foy's arrest. Appearing for the applicant, Sir John Simon QC argued that the war was 'practically at an end' and that the war-time legislation had not been 'intended to be used for the suppression of rebellion or the preservation of internal order even during the war, and still less at a time when the war was over'.[120] The weakness in this line of reasoning was that while the war was as a matter of reality over now that hostilities had ceased, it was far too convenient a state of affairs not to have continued in the eyes of the law. As we saw in Chapter 3, the Termination of the Present War (Definition) Act 1918 had reposed with the King in Council the power to declare when the war would come to an end, and no such declaration had at this stage been issued, a point which the Attorney General Sir Gordon Hewart emphasised in his argument before the court. In a decision which anticipated the outcome in *Inkpin v Roll* two years later,[121] the three judges hearing the case unanimously accepted the Attorney's submission, the Earl of Reading relying on the 1918 Act to declare that 'the war is not at an end; we are still in a state of war'.[122]

Unlike his first argument which raised questions of general interest, Foy's second line of argument was confined to conditions in Ireland. As we have seen, regulation 14B was expanded on 20 April 1918 to permit the internment of persons suspected of acting in 'a manner prejudicial to

---

[118] H C Debs 6 May 1920, col 2218 (E Shortt). See the adjournment and supply day debates at H C Debs, 12 April 1920, cols 1486–94 and H C Debs, 13 April 1920, cols 1538–91 respectively. By the middle of June, almost all the internees had been released: H C Debs, 10 June 1920, cols 576–7 (D Henry).

[119] *R v Governor of Wormwood Scrubs Prison, ex parte Foy* [1920] 2 KB 305. The report at (1920) 36 TLR 432 differs from the offical reports in a number of ways.

[120] [1920] 2 KB 305, at p 308. This is the same Sir John Simon whom we have frequently encountered in the course of this book.

[121] (1922) 86 JP 61. See Chapter 3 above.   [122] Ibid, at p 312.

the public safety or the defence of the Realm'. This expansion removed the need to connect the suspect with a 'hostile origin or association' and this was now more vital than ever as far as Ireland was concerned, the hostile foreign powers having all either surrendered or given up any interest (if they ever had any) in conspiratorial schemes with Irish nationalists. Crucially, however, under the amended form of the Regulation, the new expanded criteria only applied in those parts of the United Kingdom where the operation of the 1915 Act (with its guarantee of jury trial) had been suspended.[123] As we have seen, the only situation in which the Act's safeguards could be dispensed with was where there was an 'invasion or other special emergency arising out of the present war'.[124] This state of affairs had been purportedly the case in Ireland since 26 April 1916, but the legality of the expanded internment power now hinged on its continuing to be a valid description of the contemporary state of affairs in the country. Counsel argued that the proclamation that had then dispensed with the 1915 Act was no longer valid, since the 'occasion and condition of the making of that proclamation was the existence of a special military emergency [arising out of the present war] which had long since ceased to exist. With the cessation of that emergency the validity of the proclamation and with it the application of Regulation 14B to Ireland [in its expanded form] terminated. The internment order is therefore void'.[125]

This argument failed to convince the court. As the Lord Chief Justice put it in a predictably deferential passage, 'even if it is material to consider whether the military emergency has come to an end, it is not a matter which this Court can consider; whether the emergency continues to exist or not is for the executive alone to determine'.[126] It followed therefore that '[w]hen once the Court is satisfied that the proclamation was validly issued and that the war is still continuing, it has no power to interfere and to consider whether or not circumstances exist which justify the continuance of the proclamation'.[127] The Earl of Reading (as Isaacs had by now become) pointed out that the House of Lords had held in *R v Halliday*[128] that the question whether there is ground for suspicion that a particular person may be disposed to help the enemy is 'by the regulation thrown upon the Secretary of State', and that the 'same principle must apply to the question of the continuance of the military emergency'.[129] It was clear, therefore, that the 'effect of that decision is to

---

[123] The text of the addition to the Regulation is at text to n 87 above.
[124] Under s 1(7) of the Defence of the Realm Amendment Act 1915. See Chapter 2 above.
[125] [1920] 2 KB 305, at p 308 (Sir J Simon KC).
[126] Ibid, at p 311.   [127] Ibid.   [128] [1917] AC 260. See Chapter 2 above.
[129] [1920] 2 KB 305, at p 311.

place upon the executive the responsibility of determining whether the necessary facts exist, and to take away from the Courts the power which they would otherwise have had of dealing with such cases as the present'.[130] The Lord Chief Justice accepted that '[i]t is of course always to be assumed that the executive will act honestly and that its powers will be reasonably exercised'.[131] Avory J considered that '[i]f it were necessary for this Court to determine, which I do not think it is, whether the special military emergency, which undoubtedly arose in April, 1916, is still existing, I should have no hesitation, speaking for myself, upon the affidavits which are before us, in holding that it does. But in my opinion it is not for the Court to determine that as a question of fact'.[132]

The Drift towards Martial Law

Foy may have been one of the stimuli behind the enactment in the Summer of 1920 of the Restoration of Order in Ireland Act (ROIA),[133] but the new legislation's explicit rationale lay in the collapse of the jury system in the country at large, which meant that it was proving increasingly impossible to secure convictions for serious political crimes even when suspects were in custody with mountains of evidence capable of being marshalled against them.[134] The 1887 Act was not judged sufficient to cope with the level of alienation that was now being encountered. The ROIA came with its own set of regulations, similar to the old DORR, but somewhat expanded and now specifically designed with Ireland in mind.[135] Its successful (albeit guillotined) passage marked a fresh turn in the State's exercise of its coercive power. Section 1(1) was in the following terms: 'Where it appears to His Majesty in Council that, owing to the existence of a state of disorder in Ireland, the ordinary law

---

[130] Ibid.   [131] Ibid.   [132] Ibid, at p 315.

[133] The War Emergency Laws (Continuance) Act 1920, enacted on 31 March 1920, had also made special provision for the continuance of the Defence of the Realm Regulations in Ireland after the formal end to the war, but this measure was supplanted by the ROIA as far as Ireland was concerned. The war was finally brought to a legal end in the United Kingdom on 31 August 1921: S R & O 1921 No 1276.

[134] For the House of Commons debates on the Bill, which was guillotined through, see H C Debs, 5 August 1920, cols 2723–807 (Second Reading); H C Debs, 6 August 1920, cols 2847–961 (Committee). The allocation of time order debate is at H C Debs, 5 August, cols 2689–723. By the end of July, there were 76 prisoners awaiting trial for serious political crimes.

[135] See S R & O 1920 No 1530; S R & O 1920 No 2120; S R & O 1921 No 182; S R & O 1921 No 264; S R & O 1921 No 354; S R & O 1921 No 596. On the application of the ROIA internment power in England, see *Brady v Gibb* (1921) 37 TLR 975, a case noticeable for a powerful dissent from Scrutton LJ.

is inadequate for the prevention and punishment of crime or the maintenance of order, His Majesty in Council may issue regulations under the
Defence of the Realm Consolidation Act, 1914 . . . for securing the
restoration and maintenance of order in Ireland'. Under section 1(3),
provision was made for regulations which would ensure that where ordinary courts continued to hear cases involving offences against regulations, such tribunals would be constituted of at least two resident
magistrates, thereby reducing the risk of perverse acquittals from a sympathetic bench.[136]

The main intention of the new Act was however that most serious
crimes would now be routinely subject to court-martial. The Act
extended the power of courts-martial and summary trial 'to the trial of
persons alleged to have committed, and the punishment on conviction,
of persons who have committed crimes in Ireland' (section 1(2)). The
expression 'crime' here meant 'any treason, treason felony, felony, mis-
demeanour or other offence punishable, whether on indictment or summary conviction by imprisonment or by any greater punishment', but it
did not include 'offences against the Defence of the Realm Regulations
or these regulations', for which similar draconian provision was of course
already made.[137] These 1920 Act military tribunals were to be empowered by regulations to bind over persons before them (section 1 (3)(b)), to
summon witnesses in the same way as an ordinary court (section 1(3)(c))
and to impose fines (section 1(3)(d)). The tough way in which the legislation was initially enforced had an immediate effect on the nationalist
rebels, forcing many of them to go 'on the run', by which was meant that
they disappeared from ordinary society and formed 'flying columns' with
which to strike and harass their military opponents. This was a pivotal
moment in the deterioration of the Irish situation into something close to
an overt military conflict. From about August 1920, it becomes appropriate to describe what was happening in Ireland as a *de facto* guerrilla
war. The already tense and violent situation was made very much worse
by the policy of covertly authorised retaliation, or 'reprisals', which was
gradually adopted by the authorities during 1920 and which came into
its own in the Autumn of that year.[138] The auxiliary division of the RIC,
composed of former officers re-hired on double pay and stationed in the

---

[136] Section 1(3).   [137] See S R & O 1920 No 1530.

[138] For a flavour of the mood of British opinion at this time, see the (unsuccessful) vote of censure at H C Debs, 20 October 1920, cols 925–1040; an adjournment debate five days later at H C
Debs, 25 October 1920, cols 1467–508; and a third debate a month later: H C Debs, 24 November
1920, cols 487–602. Details of alleged reprisals are at H C Debs, 11 November 1920, cols 1345–8.

most disaffected areas, quickly earned a reputation for brutality, which was exceeded only by the levels of violence reached by the ex-servicemen specially recruited to the force, whose activities earned them a title that has become indelibly imprinted on the Irish historical consciousness, the 'Black and Tans'.[139]

As early as 28 June, the town of Fermoy had been wrecked after the IRA had succeeded in capturing three senior army officers who had ill-advisedly gone on a fishing holiday in the area.[140] The ROIA and the 'flying columns' now greatly exacerbated this tendency towards arbitrary retaliation. On 20 September, the town of Balbriggan was destroyed after an RIC officer there had been killed. On the day after the sacking of the town, the summary of official reports of outrages committed daily was suddenly made unavailable to the press with immediate effect, with the then head of the administration in Ireland, Sir Hamar Greenwood, describing the coincidence of the two events as 'only one of the many marvellous things that occur in Ireland'.[141] Further large-scale retaliation followed in Clare after the killing there of a district inspector.[142] On 4 November, the town of Granard was sacked and the local hotel burned down in retaliation for the killing of a district inspector in the town's hotel bar some days before. Greenwood denied any involvement on the part of the Crown's forces, although he admitted in the House of Commons that a 'mixed patrol of police and military' had left the town just before the fires appeared to have started.[143] When the nationalist leader Michael Collins had fourteen British intelligence officers shot dead in a co-ordinated and daring series of attacks on Sunday morning, 21 November, the authorities

---

[139] After a local pack of hounds in Limerick, where the men first drew attention to themselves by rioting indiscriminately in the city: see Townshend, *The British Campaign in Ireland*, n 75 above, p 94. For the terms of service of the Black and Tans, see the statement by the Chief Secretary Sir Hamar Greenwood at H C Debs, 25 October 1920, col 1332.

[140] Two of the three men were soon back with their own forces but one, Brigadier-General Lucas was held for some time by the IRA before eventually escaping: see H C Debs, 28 June 1920, cols 30–1 (Sir A Williamson, Parliamentary Secretary, War Office); H C Debs, 2 August 1920, col 1974 (W S Churchill). For a ministerial statement on the Fermoy disturbances, see H C Debs, 29 June 1920, col 245 (W S Churchill). Certain officers were later censured for their part in the affair: H C Debs, 21 December 1920, col 1494 (Sir A Williamson).

[141] H C Debs, 11 November 1920, col 1343.

[142] A county court judge, Judge Bodkin, later confirmed that extensive damage had been done by Crown forces: see H C Debs, 17 February 1921, cols 243–4 (Sir H Greenwood).

[143] H C Debs, 9 November 1920, col 992 (Sir H Greenwood). A vivid eye-witness account of Granard's destruction was provided by Hugh Martin for the *Daily News*: 'I found the town desolate, half deserted, and largely in ruins. Some of the ruins were still smoking. Eight of the largest places of business, together with the Town Hall, had vanished, leaving no trace but piles of rubbish. Six other buildings were badly damaged . . . Granard had been coolly, scientifically, methodically gutted by men who from first to last remained under some sort of discipline', quoted by T P O'Connor at H C Debs, 8 November 1920, col 830.

retaliated by shooting indiscriminately into the crowd at a Gaelic football match that was being held at Dublin's Croke Park the same day. Fourteen civilians died in what was to be Ireland's first 'Bloody Sunday'.[144]

Martial Law Proclaimed

Events finally came to a head with the killing of sixteen auxiliaries in an IRA ambush on 28 November. Over 500 nationalist sympathisers were immediately arrested, and two weeks later, large parts of the city of Cork were burned by auxiliary officers by way of reprisal.[145] The directors of the *Freeman's Journal*, by no means a radical paper, were detained under regulations 27(a) and (b) of the ROIR, charged 'with spreading a false report, and a report intended or likely to cause disaffection'.[146] Martial law was eventually proclaimed on 10 December, with Lord French's declaration covering the four south-western counties of Cork, Kerry, Limerick and Tipperary.[147] The phrases ringing through the proclamation seemed to come from a different age; there existed 'certain evilly disposed persons and associations' whose intent was 'to subvert the supremacy of the Crown in Ireland', and who had 'committed divers acts of violence' to achieve that end. Specific reference was made to the ambush on 28 November, a 'massacre and mutilation with axes of sixteen Cadets of the Auxiliary Division, all of whom had served in the late war, by a large body of men who were wearing trench helmets, and were disguised in the uniform of British soldiers, and who are still at large'.[148]

Two days after Lord French's proclamation, the general officer commanding-in-chief of the Crown forces, Sir Nevil Macready, issued his first martial law proclamation. This made into capital offences (after conviction by a military court) the unauthorised 'possession of arms, ammunition, or explosives'; the unauthorised wearing of military apparel; and the harbouring or assisting of any rebels who were 'levying war against

---

[144] The official version of events is at H C Debs, 23 November 1920, cols 199–202 (Sir H Greenwood). The dead were comprised of ten men, one woman and three children: H C Debs, 24 November 1920, col 454 (Sir H Greenwood) (WA).

[145] See H C Debs, 1 December 1920, cols 1239–40 for the details (from T P O'Connor MP) and the debate initiated by Lieutenant Commander Kenworthy at H C Debs, 13 December 1920, cols 149–94.

[146] H C Debs, 27 October 1920, col 1736 (Sir H Greenwood). See the adjournment debate at H C Debs, 7 December 1920, cols 2016–43, where it is alleged that it was an attack on the Prime Minister in the newspaper that had stimulated the prosecution.

[147] For the general strategic judgements that lay behind the declaration see the Prime Minister's statement at H C Debs, 10 December 1920, cols 2601–16 (D Lloyd George).

[148] The full text is in *R v Murphy* [1921] 2 IR 190, at p 198.

His Majesty the King'. As with French's document, the tone was gloriously colonial and old fashioned: 'Irishmen! understand this: Great Britain has no quarrel with Irishmen; her sole quarrel is with crime, outrage and disorder; her sole object in declaring Martial Law is to restore peace to a distracted and unhappy country'.[149] On 4 January, martial law was extended to counties Clare, Kilkenny, Waterford and Wexford. As had been the case in 1916, the question arose as to what difference these martial law proclamations made. The revival and massive application of the policy of internment that also occurred in the Spring of 1921 was solidly based in the ROIA.[150] Clearly, the biggest change lay in the vast expansion of capital offences, triable by the military, with the press now being 'almost invariably admitted' to such courts-martial (though it was generally requested that the names of witnesses, prosecuting counsel and the personnel of the court be omitted from any subsequently published reports).[151] Within the martial law areas, too, a policy of 'official reprisals' was vigorously followed, and this was a much more explicit version of the hooliganism of the Black and Tans that had been covertly sanctioned the previous year. It was this very honesty that was embarrassing to the government and it forced the abandonment of the policy after just five months.

But the fact remained that in the martial law areas, both the ordinary courts and the courts-martial under the ROIA continued to function. The authorities were faced with an ambiguous array of coercive weapons and the result was confusion and uncertainty. In particular there were powers under Defence of the Realm Consolidation Act 1914 as expanded by the 1920 Act to try offences under the Defence of the Realm Regulations by court-martial; secondly there were the punitive court-martial powers for serious crime generally in the Restoration of Order in Ireland Act 1920; and thirdly there were powers under martial law to try offences quite independently of these other statutory frameworks. So there were courts-martial operating under these three distinct systems each with their own powers and jurisdiction. This uncertainty and confusion led inevitably to the courts being drawn in. The first case

---

[149] For the full text see ibid, at pp 199–200. It would appear that General Macready had not always been so well disposed towards the Irish. When Ian Macpherson had replaced Edward Shortt as Chief Secretary in 1919, Sir Nevil had written to him, 'I cannot say I envy you for I loathe the country you are going to and its people with a depth deeper than the sea and more violent than that which I feel against the Boche': quoted in Townshend, *The British Campaign in Ireland*, n 75 above, p 20.

[150] By the end of June 1921, there were no fewer than 3,311 such detainees: H C Debs, 30 June 1921, col 2317 (Sir H Greenwood).

[151] H C Debs, 19 April 1921, cols 1682–4 (Sir L Worthington-Evans, Secretary of State for War).

involved a man sentenced to death at a general court-martial in Cork for
having been involved in an ambush in which a soldier had died. The trial
was held under the ROIA, however, and the Irish King's Bench
Divisional Court therefore found it 'unnecessary to consider the broad
question of the effect and application of martial law, as to which our
opinion would be in the nature of an obiter dictum'.[152] As far as the
ROIA tribunal was concerned, it had come to the wrong conclusion on
the admissibility of evidence against the accused but since this was an
error which did not go to jurisdiction, its verdict could not be disturbed
by the court. (The man had his sentence commuted to penal servitude
to life 'in view solely of the repeated postponements of his execution and
of the distress of mind which has been caused to him thereby'.[153])

The Question of Legal Legitimacy

The following month, February 1921, the same Divisional Court considered a case dealing with martial law proper. This was legally distinguishable from the ordinary law on breach of the peace and the like
which was always available to the authorities to deal with disorder of an
ordinary or predictable kind. As we have already observed, it was also
different from the special framework that had been introduced by the
Restoration of Order in Ireland Act and earlier by the Defence of the
Realm Regulations, though in each case reference was frequently made
to a form of martial law having been introduced. According to Dicey,
martial law proper was a term which was most accurately 'employed as
a name for the common law right of the Crown and its servants to repel
force by force in the case of invasion, insurrection, riot, or generally of
any violent resistance to the law'.[154] This was a 'right, or power' which
was 'essential to the very existence of orderly government, and is most
assuredly recognised in the most ample manner by the law of
England'.[155] As such it belonged in Dicey's view to the common law,
albeit a common law that was to be deployed only in the most extreme
of circumstances. Though Dicey appears to have been of the opposite
opinion, it would seem from the practical operation of martial law that
the steps permitted to the military under its terms could be 'accompanied by the creation of military tribunals to administer summary jus-

---

[152] *R v Murphy* [1921] 2 IR 190, at p 217 (Molony CJ).
[153] The press statement which contained this information is included in the law report.
[154] A V Dicey, *Introduction to the Study of the Law of the Constitution* (10th edn by E C S Wade, 1959),
p 288 and ch 8 generally. See also Chapter 4 above.
[155] Ibid, citing *R v Pinney* (1832) 5 Car & P 254.

tice'.[156] But any excessive action by the authorities over and above what was permitted by the common law was at least theoretically vulnerable to criminal prosecution.[157]

The case which gave rise to discussion of this form of martial law in the Irish courts involved one John Allen, who was sentenced to death by a military tribunal sitting in Cork for the 'possession of a revolver, some ammunition, and a book . . . purporting to be an official publication of the Irish Republican Army entitled "Night Fighting" '.[158] The sentence would not have been possible had Allen been dealt with under either the ordinary law or the ROIA framework. Giving the unanimous decision of the Bench, Molony CJ was clear about the judicial role:

It is the sacred duty of this Court to protect the lives and liberties of all His Majesty's subjects, and to see that no one suffers loss of life or liberty save under the laws of the country; but when subjects of the King rise in armed insurrection and the conflict is still raging, it is no less our duty not to interfere with the officers of the Crown in taking such steps as they deem necessary to quell the insurrection, and to restore peace and order and the authority of the law.[159]

Crucially, neither the assertions about the existence of a state of war contained in Lord French's proclamation nor the claim that such a state of disorder existed at the time of Allen's arrest were challenged. The court therefore considered that '[d]uring the continuance of such a state of affairs . . . the Government [was] entitled and, indeed, bound to repel force by force, and thereby to put down the insurrection and restore public order'.[160] Furthermore it was 'clear on the authorities that when martial law [was] imposed, and the necessity for it exist[ed], or, in other words, while war [was] still raging, this Court ha[d] no jurisdiction to question any acts done by the military authorities'.[161] The fact that for certain purposes, the ordinary courts were still functioning in the martial law areas did not affect the legality of the military courts that were also pronouncing judgements.[162] That the death penalty was not available for these offences under the ordinary law was an objection 'rather for the consideration of Parliament than for this Court, which cannot, *durante bello*, control the military authorities, or question any sentence imposed

---

[156] A W Bradley and K D Ewing, *Constitutional and Administrative Law* (12th edn, 1997), p 674. See *Re Clifford and O'Sullivan* [1921] 2 AC 570 for a discussion in the House of Lords of the legal status of such bodies.

[157] Subject to the enactment of indemnity legislation: see e.g. the limited indemnity in the Restoration of Order in Ireland (Indemnity) Act 1923.

[158] *R v Allen* [1921] 2 IR 241, at p 242.   [159] Ibid, at p 264.

[160] Ibid, at p 268.   [161] Ibid, at p 269.

[162] Ibid, at p 270, applying *ex parte Marais* [1902] AC 109.

in the exercise of martial law'.[163] There was to be no reprieve for Allen as there had been for Murphy: he was duly executed on 28 February, four days after the judgment was handed down, together with five others who had been caught in an ambush by the military authorities and whose fates were also sealed by the *Allen* decision.[164]

Writing to General Macready, the Under Secretary at Dublin Castle (and future Home Secretary) Sir John Anderson enthused that the decision in *Allen* was:

an enormous asset and puts us in an infinitely stronger position than if we had somehow contrived to dodge the issue . . . From the House of Commons point of view also the continuance of the civil courts guards one obvious line of attack.[165]

Macready was less delighted, seeing the cases that were now piling up in the courts as a source of delay and uncertainty which whatever their eventual outcome had largely 'nullified the effect of martial law'. The general did have a point. On 25 February writs were issued against two brigade commanders for damage which had been caused by official reprisals, tying up the military in a defensive and eventually successful legal manoeuvre to persuade the court to stay the action until such time as a state of war no longer prevailed.[166] In March death sentences imposed on seven men for levying war against His Majesty produced conditional writs of habeas corpus and certiorari on the basis that the military tribunal that had tried them had been improperly constituted. In discharging the order, and thereby upholding the convictions, the Chief Justice nevertheless asserted that the court had 'the power and the duty to decide whether a state of war exist[ed] which justifie[d] the application of martial law'.[167] The military only succeeded in this case because the court's independent evaluation of the situation coincided with that of the military and, this being the case, it would not then 'interfere to determine what [was] or [was] not necessary'.[168] On the same day as this decision, the court also rejected a root and branch attack on the

---

[163] *R v Allen* [1921] 2 IR 241, at p 272. As to what law should apply when peace is restored, see ibid, at p 273.

[164] H C Debs, 28 February 1921, cols 1408–9 (Sir H Greenwood).

[165] Quoted in Townshend, *The British Campaign in Ireland*, n 75 above, p 160. See also the references to various dicta of the Chief Justice made in the course of an adjournment debate on Ireland by the Attorney General for Ireland, D Henry: H C Debs, 13 May 1921, col 2408. There is an interesting account of Anderson's tenure in Ireland in J W Wheeler-Bennett, *John Anderson. Viscount Waverley* (1962), ch 3.

[166] *Higgins v Willis* [1921] 2 IR 386. The expectation was that an Indemnity Act would then be passed, protecting the military.

[167] *R (Garde) v Strickland* [1921] 2 IR 317, at p 329 (Molony CJ).   [168] Ibid, at p 332.

declaration of martial law which was based on the argument that, as part of the prerogative, the power to declare martial law had, as far as Ireland was concerned, been 'surrendered or released' by the Restoration of Order in Ireland Act. Molony CJ and his colleagues dealt with the submission in a single paragraph in a one page judgment, declaring that the submission had 'no foundation in law'.[169]

The Crisis of Legal Legitimacy

Even though they all resulted in victory, these cases were enormously exasperating to General Macready. At one point he went so far as to suspend unilaterally the jurisdiction of the civil courts over military matters in martial law areas.[170] Nothing can have prepared the general, or for that matter Sir John Anderson, for the astonishing decision of *Egan v Macready*.[171] The case was yet another challenge to a death sentence meted out by a military court, this time for the possession of ninety-seven rounds of revolver ammunition and five rounds of service ammunition. Its timing was immensely significant. The Government of Ireland Act, confirming the partition of Ireland, had passed into law on 23 December 1920 and the elections held under it in southern Ireland on 25 May 1921 had produced sweeping (albeit almost entirely unopposed)[172] victories for Sinn Féin, with the Party setting up a second Dáil Éireann on the basis of the results. Shortly after these election results became known, the Irish situation committee of the Cabinet decided that martial law should be extended throughout southern Ireland on 14 July, if by that date the Government of Ireland Act had not been made to work. The Cabinet subsequently agreed to the proposal. Argument in *Egan v Macready* was heard on the sixth, seventh and eight of July, just when this unpublicised clock was ticking towards its military denouement. Three days after Ireland's Master of the Rolls Charles O'Connor, sitting alone, had reserved judgment, and three days before the secretly agreed extension of martial law was to take effect, a truce was announced between the British forces and the Irish Republican Army. The agreement that was

---

[169] *R (Ronayne and Mulcahy) v Strickland* [1921] 2 IR 333, at p 334. For a useful account of another court martial case from the period see S Enright, 'Of courts martial and writs of *habeas corpus*' (1998) 148 *New Law Journal* 1368.

[170] Proclamation Number 3 by GOC-in C and military governor-general of Ireland, 14 April 1921. The political controversy is discussed by Townshend, *The British Campaign in Ireland*, n 75 above, p 161.

[171] [1921] 1 IR 265.

[172] See Lyons, n 74 above, p 423. Only Trinity College in the South stood against the republican tide, returning four *de facto* unionists to the legislature.

then tentatively concluded involved the suspension of the ROIA and a sharp reduction in military activities in martial law areas. For their part the Irish forces agreed to stop all attacks on British military and civilian targets.[173]

Whether because he thought the truce changed things, or because he was appalled at the severity of the penalty for such a relatively minor offence (which had in any event been only tenuously established on the facts), O'Connor MR decided that the power to declare martial law, being part of the prerogative, had been removed in Ireland with the enactment the previous year of the Restoration of Order in Ireland Act. This was the very line of reasoning that had been preemptorily rejected by the Chief Justice less than two months before. Though admitting that he may have 'gone grievously wrong' and that 'life as a Judge of the Chancery Division ha[d] left [him] unqualified for criminal cases',[174] O'Connor MR considered that the 'claim of the military authority to override legislation, specially made for a state of war, would seem . . . to call for a new Bill of Rights'.[175] If new powers were needed, Parliament was the place to get them: 'I cannot assume that Parliament is in a lethargic condition, incapable of energetic action'.[176] Strongly influencing the judge was the then very recent comprehensive statement on the prerogative *vis-à-vis* statute law to be found in the House of Lords decision in *Attorney General v De Keyser's Royal Hotel*.[177] Lord Atkinson's speech in particular had 'crystallized the law in language which ought to find its way into every textbook on constitutional law'.[178] But although O'Connor MR was clearly aware of the significance of *De Keyser's Royal Hotel*, it has been doubted whether he properly applied it in the case before him. Heuston claims that *Egan* 'has not met with approval', and appears 'to depend upon the view that the right to use martial law is a prerogative right'.[179] According to Heuston, the better view is that 'it is not a prerogative right but simply an extension of the ordinary common law power to meet force with force',[180] though O'Connor MR himself did not appear to have any doubts when he revisited the matter *obiter* the following year.[181] Indeed, Heuston's may be a distinction without a difference.[182]

---

[173] The full deal is set out and discussed by Townshend, *The British Campaign in Ireland*, n 75 above, p 198.

[174] [1921] 1 IR 265, at p 279.   [175] Ibid, at p 275.   [176] Ibid, at p 274.

[177] [1920] AC 508.   [178] [1921] 1 IR 265, at pp 275–6.

[179] R F V Heuston, *Essays in Constitutional Law*, 2nd edn (1964), p 159.   [180] Ibid.

[181] *R (Childers) v Adjutant-General of the Forces of the Irish Provisional Government* [1923] 1 IR 5 at p 15. The debate about the underlying basis of martial law has not been resolved: see C Campbell, *Emergency Law in Ireland 1918–1925* (1994), at pp 123–48.

[182] See *Council of Civil Service Unions v Minister of State for the Civil Service* [1985] AC 374.

But whether right or wrong in retrospect, O'Connor MR's judgment was right at the time in the narrow sense that it was law that had to be obeyed. The judge made the writ of habeas corpus returnable for 29 July. Macready was incandescent. Neither he nor Major General Strickland obeyed the order. A second writ in a case involving a man named Higgins, decided by O'Connor MR at the same time as *Egan v Macready* was also ignored. O'Connor duly issued writs of attachment against both Macready and Strickland, as well as against the governor of the prison in which the men were held, their obstruction having amounted to a 'deliberate contempt of Court—a thing unprecedented in this Court and the whole history of British law'.[183] The deadlock was only ended by the decision of the government, taken without consulting Macready, to release the two men involved. The action was described to Parliament as being 'based solely upon the existing situation in Ireland' and as being 'not due to any decision given by a Civil Court in Ireland' since such courts had 'no power to over-rule the decisions of the Military Courts in the martial-law area in Ireland'.[184] No doubt the authorities were anxious not to distract the country from the truce negotiations, which remained at a sensitive stage, and were equally keen that no precedent should have been set if hostilities were subsequently to resume. It is difficult to say what the outcome would have been had the fighting still been going on. Would O'Connor MR then have gone so far out of his way, to act, in such a diffident manner, to save two human lives? If so, would the Government have intervened 'to preserve the Rule of Law'?;[185] or would Macready have carried out his threat 'to arrest anyone, including the Master of the Rolls himself, who attempted to carry out the service of the writs'?[186]

Civil Liberties and the Rule of Law in Times of Military Crisis

We have now seen that during the years 1919 to 1921, the manifestation of British military strategy in Ireland went through three distinct though overlapping phases. First, there was the extensive application of the Defence of the Realm Regulations, which were robustly applied notwithstanding the practical ending of the war on which these regulations were

---

[183] [1921] 1 IR 265, at p 280. The Crown argued that it had the right to continue to hold the prisoners pending an appeal, citing in their favour *Re Clifford and O'Sullivan*, n 156 above, decided in the House of Lords the previous day. Argument started in that case on 7 July and ended on 14 July.

[184] H C Debs, 10 August 1921, col 437 (J A Chamberlain, Leader of the House).

[185] Heuston, n 179 above, p 160.

[186] N Macready, *Annals of an Active Life* (1924), vol 2, p 589, quoted in Heuston, n 179 above, p 161.

based. Then, when the termination of the European war could not much longer be denied, the deterioration of Britain's hold on law and order in Ireland was reflected in the enactment of the Restoration of Order in Ireland Act. As we have seen, this legislation was roughly based on the war-time regulations but was wider and more draconian in its effect, and was more carefully designed for the Irish situation to which it was exclusively applied. At the same time as the ROIA was being deployed for the first time, the commission of reprisals by Crown forces marked a further development in policy, this time into systematic lawlessness. These latter engagements outside the whole framework of law presaged the third phase in Britain's strategy during these years, which also involved the use of force outside the orthodox rule of law. Martial law was a form of authority rooted more in the exigencies of military necessity than in any autonomous code of law and as such it was hardly deserving of its description as law, whatever qualifying phrase might happen to be placed before it. That this never became clear in Ireland had less to do with any inherent limitations in martial law as such than with the fact that it was not fully implemented, with the ordinary system of justice coexisting uneasily alongside that of the military throughout the period under consideration. Though there were exceptions, the most obvious being *Egan v Macready*,[187] the higher courts in Ireland and (of course) Britain remained invariably supportive of executive authority and consistently disinclined to intervene in the defence of traditional civil libertarian principles. Even *Egan* can hardly be seen as a strong vindication of the rule of law, given the apparent inclination on the part of the military authorities simply to refuse to obey O'Connor MR's judicial orders.

It goes without saying that the extent of the executive's military engagement with Ireland in these years extended way beyond the boundaries of constitutional principle as articulated by Dicey, and also went further in terms of constitutional practice than anything that we have seen so far in this book. The extent of the emergency in Ireland during these years, however, makes it inappropriate to apply too rigorously a version of the Rule of Law that was never designed for such a situation. Dicey recognised as 'assuredly part of the law of England . . . the power of the government or of loyal citizens to maintain public order, at whatever cost of blood or property may be necessary'.[188] The bulk of the Irish people, together with the island's public authorities, juries and lower judi-

---

[187] See n 181 above, and see *R v Fitzgerald*, n 103 above, and *R v Maher*, n 104 above.
[188] Dicey, n 154 above, p 290.

ciary were combined in opposition to executive authority. In circumstances such as these, it was hardly an appropriate place properly to apply Dicey's principles relating to the Rule of Law, even assuming (which, as will be obvious by now, we do not necessarily do) that such a theory had any intellectual validity in the first place. But it was a singularly important test of Britain's commitment to legality: a test for which it was at best ill-prepared. This is what makes the period to which we are about to turn so important for traditional civil liberties and for the Rule of Law. The governing unit that was established as Northern Ireland in the Government of Ireland Act 1920 may have been born in the midst of extreme conflict but it did not continue for very long in such a severe situation of disorder. It was therefore a place to which the ordinary principles of the Rule of Law, as developed by Dicey, ought to have been capable of application. The extent to which they were in fact applied is the subject to which we now turn.

CIVIL LIBERTIES IN NORTHERN IRELAND, 1921–1945

The enactment of the Government of Ireland Act 1920 provided for the partition of Ireland, with (as we have seen) Sinn Féin securing a further electoral mandate in the elections in southern Ireland that took place under the Act's aegis in 1921. Events took a predictably different course in Northern Ireland, with the electorally dominant Unionist community displaying a willingness to take seriously the assembly provided for the Province under the Act. The State opening of the Northern Ireland Parliament on 22 June 1921 started an experiment in devolved government within the United Kingdom that was to last for just over fifty years. The occasion is now best remembered for the fact that King George V used the opportunity to make a placatory speech aimed directly at the nationalist leadership in the South. It was this Royal intervention, inspired by the Prime Minister David Lloyd George, which marked the start of a sequence of conciliatory gestures on the part of the British administration which was eventually to produce the IRA/British Army truce of 9 July discussed above. After this truce, and the Anglo-Irish Treaty that followed later the same year, it becomes appropriate to view the Irish aspect of British civil liberties in terms of Northern Ireland alone rather than the island of Ireland as a whole. The Irish Free State that was established pursuant to the treaty was from its inception outside the United Kingdom and in April 1949 it transformed itself, via a new written constitution adopted twelve years before, into a republic. Indeed, so marked was the jurisdiction's independence of Britain at this juncture that the departure from the Commonwealth which was then thought to be an inevitable part of such a radical change in status was viewed with equanimity by the vast majority of the State's inhabitants. The Irish Free State and its successor the Republic of Ireland have their own history of emergency and repressive legislation but it is not part of the British story.

The New Regime in Belfast

We turn therefore to that part of Ireland that remained within the United Kingdom, the new legal entity known as Northern Ireland whose Parliament the King was inaugurating when he made his visit to Belfast in 1921. There can be few public representatives now more reviled than those responsible for the government of the Province during its half-century of effective autonomy within the United Kingdom. In their defence it should not be forgotten that Northern Ireland came into being against a background of sectarian and political violence which was to continue on a sporadic basis throughout the Province's five decades of self-rule. Nor can it have been easy to govern a region whose right to exist was denied by a substantial minority of its own citizens, an attitude that was made all the more dangerous by the fact that the Province's only land neighbour was politically and (after 1937) constitutionally committed to its destruction. Despite all this, however, the main criticism levelled against successive governments of Northern Ireland, that they practised a form of religious apartheid as a matter of official Unionist Party policy, is hard to gainsay, even with the benefit of an historical perspective and an open mind. The most explicit legislative off-shoot of this sectarian domination was the Special Powers Act 1922, the full effect of which can only be understood by first considering the constitutional context in which it operated and the attitude of mind of those charged with the task of overseeing its application.

As far as the constitutional context was concerned, the abolition of proportional representation for local government elections in 1922 and for the Belfast legislature itself seven years later[189] had the effect of entrenching Unionist Party domination, and even extending it to those areas where there was no natural unionist majority. Thus under PR, non-unionist (mainly nationalist) Parties had controlled 32 per cent of the

---

[189] House of Commons (Method of Voting and Redistribution of Seats) Act (Northern Ireland) 1929.

local public bodies in the Province, but this had sunk to 16 per cent by 1927, after the reform in the electoral law had taken effect. The consequences of the change were sometimes startling: in county Fermanagh, for example, Nationalists had returned sixty-three members to the Unionists' fifty-seven, but after the abolition of PR the Unionists found themselves with seventy-four representatives to the Nationalists' forty-three. Similar incongruities resulted from the abolition of PR to the Belfast assembly. As regards both the local and the Provincial fora, matters were made even worse by changes to the electoral boundaries, which were so partisan as to lead the historian of the period to describe them as a 'major act of misgovernment'.[190] In the fifty years of their operation, many of the local authorities in Northern Ireland became heavily identified with sectarian practices. For its part, the Provincial legislature, 'ensconced from 1932 in the grandiose shell of Stormont',[191] never developed into the effective constraint on executive power for which the optimists among the drafters of the Government of Ireland Act might have hoped. Given the way in which its membership was contrived, and the fact that there was continuous one-party rule, this can hardly be considered surprising. The Parliament consisted of a House of Commons of fifty-two members and a Senate of twenty-six and, though it was carefully modelled on Westminster, it rarely met for more than a few months a year, and even then justified its existence by perpetual support of the government. A handful of Nationalist MPs were usually present to avoid a descent into total subservience, but these representatives hankered after the united Ireland they knew was unattainable and with a few isolated exceptions rarely dedicated themselves to the democratic task in hand. Given the structure of the democracy that they confronted, this was hardly surprising.

Turning now to the personalities of the members of the executive that enjoyed the perpetual confidence of these practically moribund legislative assemblies, it is not at all surprising to discover that the Unionism of successive Cabinets was as unrelenting as their confident Protestantism was divisive. The first Prime Minister, Sir James Craig, who ruled unchallenged until his death (as the first Viscount Craigavon) in 1940, on one occasion described the executive he headed as 'a Protestant Government for a Protestant People'.[192] His successor but one, Viscount Brookeborough, whose period as Prime Minister—twenty years—was

---

[190] P Buckland, *The Factory of Grievances. Devolved Government in Northern Ireland 1921–1939* (1979), p 228.   [191] R F Foster, *Modern Ireland 1600–1972* (1988), p 528.   [192] H C Debs (NI), 21 November 1934, col 73.

even longer than that of Craigavon's, had been 'deeply implicated' in the formation of the UVF[193] and had once controversially appealed to loyalists at a public meeting 'wherever possible, to employ protestant lads and lassies', a subject on which the future Prime Minister 'felt that he could speak freely . . . as he had not a Roman catholic about his own place'.[194] The average age of the first Cabinet when it came together in 1921 was fifty-four, despite which longevity in office was the norm. None served longer in a single post than the man entrusted with the sensitive task of heading the Ministry of Home Affairs with its particular responsibility for law and order. Sir Richard Dawson Bates was a solicitor and justice of the peace who had been co-founder of the UVF hospitals during the war and who had also helped to establish the UVF patriotic fund. He ran the ministry for twenty-two years, during which time his power was increased by the fact that Craigavon 'almost abandoned any responsibility for the administration of law and order'[195] from the moment he took office. Even by the standards of the unionist leadership at its unchallenged zenith, and certainly in comparison with Craigavon, Dawson Bates was an extreme and divisive voice. The nature of the man may be gauged from the fact that he (unsuccessfully) opposed allowing Catholics to work in the civil service when the matter came before the Cabinet in 1926 and in 1934, he refused to use the telephone for any important business after learning, 'with a great deal of surprise, that a Roman Catholic Telephonist has been appointed to Stormont'.[196] (The telephonist was transferred.)

The Special Powers Act

Dawson Bates' first legislative initiative as Minister of Home Affairs, and the measure for the enforcement of which he had ultimate responsibility for over two decades, was the Special Powers Act, or to give it its full title the Civil Authorities (Special Powers) Act 1922 (henceforth the SPA). This was the fifth Act passed by the new legislature, and it was to remain the source of all emergency law in the Province until its eventual replacement by the Westminster-enacted Northern Ireland (Emergency Provisions) Act 1973. The Bill came before the Northern Ireland House of Commons in Spring 1922, in an atmosphere of increasing anxiety, both about the rising levels of violence in Northern Ireland and about developments in the South, where the Anglo-Irish treaty of 1921 had been rejected by dedi-

---

[193] B Barton, *Brookeborough. The Making of a Prime Minister* (1988), p 20.   [194] Ibid, p 78.
[195] P Buckland, *James Craig* (1980), p 87.   [196] Buckland, n 190 above, p 22.

cated and apparently well-armed anti-partitionists. According to Dawson Bates' parliamentary secretary R D Megaw (who presumably had the IRA in mind), the SPA was needed 'to cope with the terrible conspiracy with which we are confronted at present'.[197] While it was true that there was IRA violence, with two members of the special constabulary being killed by the IRA on 23 March and with strong support for the organisation continuing to come from Michael Collins' embattled regime in the South,[198] the reality nevertheless was that much of the violence during 1922 was sectarian rather than secessionist in nature. Serious sectarian rioting was on the increase in Belfast, with 232 people being killed, a further 1,000 being wounded, and some £3m property damage being inflicted in the course of such disorder during 1992.[199] Originally designed to lapse after one year, the SPA was kept in force first by an annual vote, and then in 1928 for a further five-year period without the need for annual parliamentary renewal.[200] The violence from both sides was by this time substantially reduced, but despite this an effort in 1927 to force the expiry of the SPA failed by twenty-six votes to six in a Committee vote, with the Attorney General declaring that '[h]aving succeeded in restoring law and order, what the Government [was] now [being] asked to do [was] to throw away the weapon with which law and order was restored'.[201] The same logic led to the Act being made permanent in 1933.[202] By this time the Northern Ireland State had an armed police force which was overwhelmingly Protestant in composition and Unionist in political perspective.[203]

The original Act contained a schedule in which were set-out thirty-five regulations. As the 'civil authority', the Minister had an overriding power 'in respect of persons, matters and things . . . to take all such steps and issue all such orders as may be necessary for preserving the peace and maintaining order, according to and in the execution of this Act and the regulations' contained in it (section 1(1)). The powers given to the civil authority could be delegated to any police officer (section 1(2)), and in 1933 this power of delegation was expanded to include the Ministry's Parliamentary Secretary.[204] A more specific power was that which

---

[197] H C Debs (NI), 21 March 1922, col 91.

[198] E Phoenix, 'Michael Collins: The Northern Question 1916–22' in G Doherty and D Keogh (eds), *Michael Collins and the Making of the Irish State* (1998) is a good account.

[199] See Foster above n 191, p 529

[200] Civil Authorities (Special Powers) Act (Northern Ireland) 1928.

[201] H C Debs (NI), 12 October 1927, col 1963 (A B Babington).

[202] Civil Authorities (Special Powers) Act (Northern Ireland) 1933.

[203] See M Farrell, *Arming the Protestants. The Formation of the Ulster Special Constabulary and the Royal Ulster Constabulary, 1920–7* (1983). A contrasting work is that of Sir A Hellet, *The 'B' Specials. A History of the Ulster Special Constabulary* (1972).

[204] 1933 Act, s 1.

allowed the Minister to make additional regulations, '(a) for making further provision for the preservation of the peace and maintenance of order, and (b) for varying or revoking any provision of the regulations' (section 1(3)). Though notionally subject to the negative resolution procedure in the Belfast Parliament (section 1(4)), this power was subject to little or no effective democratic oversight. New regulations, of which as we shall see there were many, were never debated in the House and their promulgation is rarely even detectable from a perusal of the legislative debates. Yet it was this regulatory power that gave an ongoing momentum to the SPA and ensured that its overwhelmingly repressive character was always able to keep pace with its illiberal times. Though the SPA was ostensibly subjected to the self-denying proviso, which reflected the equally incongruous provisions of the Defence of the Realm Regulations,[205] that 'the ordinary course of law and avocations of life and the enjoyment of property shall be interfered with as little as may be permitted by the exigencies of the steps required to be taken under this Act',[206] the regime represented by the SPA was easily the most draconian applied in the United Kingdom in peacetime since the Great Reform Act of 1832.

It is not only the lack of parliamentary oversight which mocks Dicey; there was precious little evidence in the regulations themselves of a commitment to the Rule of Law. This would be true whichever of Dicey's principles we were to examine, and it would be true too of an understanding of the Rule of Law as a principle of legality in the manner which we have outlined in Chapter 1 above. The effect of the Act was to create a new array of permanent offences, involving breach of the regulations.[207] In so far as the requirement that people should be punished only for a breach of the regular law is concerned, this simple requirement was fatally undermined by the remarkable provision prohibiting any person from doing 'any act of such a nature as to be calculated to be of such a nature as to be prejudicial to the preservation of the peace or maintenance of order in Northern Ireland and not specifically provided for in the regulations' (section 2(4)). But it was the principle of equality before the law that was most conspicuously diminished by regulations transparently addressed to one section of the community in particular. The spirit of the time is perhaps best illuminated by the observations of one senior civil servant writing in the context of the Restoration of Ireland Act 1920,

---

[205] See Chapter 2 above. [206] 1922 Act, s 1(1).

[207] And note also the special punishment for offences, which involved private whipping (s 5) and the death penalty for any person convicted under ss 2 or 3 of the Explosive Substances Act 1883 (s 6).

but applicable with equal force to the SPA several years later. Thus S Watt doubted whether 'it was ever contemplated that these extraordinary powers should be used against those who are loyal to the Crown'.[208] It is quite clear that it is this principle of partisanship under, rather than the principle of equality before, the law which informed the way in which the coercive provisions of the Regulations were deployed: the sweeping police powers which we are about to encounter were used as instruments against the nationalist minority, as were the powers of internment. Although not powers restraining civil liberties (in the term in which we define that term in Chapter 1) directly, these measures were used almost exclusively against one section of the community in particular: this was a political law for a political police to be used against a political minority. But as might be predicted there are restrictions also on the classical civil liberties, though these too were deployed to silence and restrain those who would dare impertinently to challenge the Orange hegemony.

The Special Powers Act and Police Powers

The series of draconian actions that as we shall see were taken by the government in the Spring and Summer of 1922 must be seen against the backdrop of greatly increased disorder in the Province and a rapid deterioration in North–South relations. On 18 May the IRA launched 'a concerted campaign of arson and destruction by the Third Northern Division [of the IRA] throughout its three Brigade areas of Belfast, Antrim and north Down'.[209] Commercial property, police barracks and railway stations were attacked and on 22 May a Unionist member of the Northern Ireland Parliament, W J Twaddell, was assassinated. That same weekend, twelve Catholics were killed in 'an orgy of planned sectarian assassinations'.[210] One of the first actions taken under the SPA was the imposition on 25 May 1922 of a night-time curfew covering all of Northern Ireland except Belfast. Further orders followed covering various parts of Belfast and eventually Northern Ireland as a whole was included.[211] Other regulations were also available for immediate and forceful deployment against the IRA insurgency. These included the SPA's wide-ranging powers of police entry, search and seizure which

---

[208] Buckland, *The Factory of Grievances*, n 190 above, p 193.

[209] Phoenix, n 198 above, p 109. [210] Ibid.

[211] See Regulation 1, expanded by Civil Authorities (Special Powers) Act (Northern Ireland) 1922 Regulations (1922 No 31) (27 April 1922). The order applying the curfew Regulation to the whole Province (1923 No 72) took effect on 22 April 1923. For Sir Richard Dawson Bates's somewhat cursory defence of the curfew power, see the adjournment debate at H C Debs (NI), 13 November 1923, cols 1928–34.

were either ancillary to new offences (as with regulation 3 which prohibited the carrying of firearms or offensive weapons in public places) or which stood alone as general police powers. Of the latter, one of the more extreme was regulation 6, under which the 'civil authority, and any person duly authorised by him shall have right of access to any land or buildings or other property whatsoever'. Under regulation 19, the police were entitled to enter and attend any meeting if the civil authority or any superior officer (defined as senior to a constable) was 'of opinion . . . that an offence against these regulations may be committed thereat'. Regulation 21 was remarkably broad:

Any police officer or constable may stop any vehicle travelling along any public road, and, if he has reason to suspect that any vehicle upon any public road is being used for any purpose or in any way prejudicial to the preservation of the peace or maintenance of order, or otherwise unlawfully, may search and seize the vehicle and seize anything found therein which he has reason to suspect is being used or intended to be used for any such purpose as aforesaid.[212]

As far as the power of arrest was concerned, the main provision was in regulation 23, under which '[a]ny person authorised for the purpose by the civil authority, or any police constable, or member of any of His Majesty's forces on duty when the occasion for the arrest arises, may arrest without warrant any person whom he suspects of acting or of having acted or of being about to act in a manner prejudicial to the preservation of the peace or maintenance of order'.[213] The breadth of this already wide provision was greatly increased by the absence of any requirement for a pre-existing reasonable suspicion before action could be taken under it. An arrest power was also available in respect of any person 'upon whom may be found any article, book, letter, or other document, the possession of which gives ground for such a suspicion, or who is suspected of having committed an offence against these regulations, or of being in possession of any article or document which is being used or intended to be used for any purpose or in any way prejudicial to the preservation of the peace or maintenance of order'.[214] The purpose of such arrests under the SPA was never solely to press criminal charges.

---

[212] See also Regulations 8 and 18.

[213] See also Regulations 22 and 22A. Under the first, the civil authority could order a person 'to furnish him, either verbally or in writing, with such information as may be specified in the order'. Under the second, every person had a duty 'if so required by any member of any of His Majesty's Forces when on duty or by a police constable, to stop and to answer to the best of his ability and knowledge any questions which may reasonably be addressed to him'.

[214] This extract from the Regulation takes into account an amendment to it made on 6 July 1922: Civil Authorities (Special Powers) Act (Northern Ireland) 1922 Regulations (1922 No 41). See further, on the power of arrest, s 7 of the 1922 Act.

No time limit on the incarceration was set out, though if it was decided to bring a detainee before a court of summary jurisdiction, 'at least twenty-four hours' notice in writing of the nature of the charge' was required to be given to him or her. But men and women held under regulation 23 could be detained in prison 'or elsewhere, as may be specified in the Order, upon such conditions as the civil authority may direct'[215] and any person so detained could 'be removed . . . to any place where his presence [was] required in the interest of justice and [could] be detained in such place for such time as his presence [was] so required there'.[216] The impression that this regulation was designed to provide a covert form of internment was reinforced by further amendments to it, introduced on 23 and 24 June 1922, dealing with the compulsory photographing and fingerprinting of detainees[217] and with the conditions under which such persons were to be held whether in prison[218] or elsewhere.[219]

But by the time that regulation 23 had been beefed up in this way, a formal system of restriction orders and internment had already been introduced. These did not appear in the original SPA but were brought in very soon afterwards. As far as the first of these was concerned, under regulation 23A, introduced on 1 June 1922, a person 'suspected of acting, or of having acted, or of being about to act in a manner prejudicial to the preservation of the peace and the maintenance of order' could be 'prohibited from residing in or entering a certain area or areas' from which the authorities thought it 'desirable' to exclude him. Any such order could require the person affected by it to comply with any conditions 'as to residence, reporting to the police, restriction on movements, or otherwise as may be imposed on him'. He or she could also be required 'to report for approval his proposed place of residence . . . and not subsequently to change his place of residence without leave of the civil authority'.[220] A typical example of the way in which the regulation operated was that of J C Magennis, a trade union official from Dundalk in the Free State who was arrested while visiting his native town in Northern Ireland, held without charge for six months and on his release

---

[215] See Regulation 23 as amended by Civil Authorities (Special Powers) Act (Northern Ireland) 1922 Regulations (1922 No 34).

[216] See Regulation 23 as amended by Civil Authorities (Special Powers) Act (Northern Ireland) 1922 Regulations (1922 No 41).

[217] Civil Authorities (Special Powers) Act (Northern Ireland) 1922 Regulations (1922 No 39).

[218] Civil Authorities (Special Powers) Act (Northern Ireland) 1922 Regulations (1922 No 85).

[219] Civil Authorities (Special Powers) Act (Northern Ireland) 1922 Regulations (1922 No 86).

[220] Civil Authorities (Special Powers) Act (Northern Ireland) 1922 Regulations (1922 No 36).

prohibited from entering the six counties of Northern Ireland for a further two years.[221] By April 1926, despite the fact that most of the early disorder that had surrounded the formation of Northern Ireland had died away, fifteen orders under regulation 23A remained in force.[222] This was the regulation which kept Eamon DeValera out of nationalist parts of Northern Ireland for many years, despite the fact that he was, notionally at least, the South Down MP in the Belfast House of Commons until 1937.[223] In 1929, the MP Eamon Donnelly was arrested for breaching an order, made in October 1924, which prohibited him from entering the county of Armagh, despite the fact that this was the constituency he had been elected to represent.

The Special Powers Act and Internment

Internment was used in a similarly partisan fashion. The power was introduced at the same time as regulation 23A, as one of a much broader range of controls included in the new regulation 23B:

When it appears to the Minister of Home Affairs for Northern Ireland, on the recommendation of a Chief Officer of Police or of a Police Officer of higher rank [or of an advisory committee][224] that for securing the preservation of the peace and the maintenance of order in Northern Ireland it is expedient that a person who is suspected of acting or having acted or being about to act in a manner prejudicial to the preservation of the peace and the maintenance of order in Northern Ireland, shall be subjected to such obligations and restrictions as are hereinafter mentioned, the Minister of Home Affairs for Northern Ireland may by order require that person forthwith, or from time to time, either to remain in, or to proceed to and reside in, such place as may be specified in the order and to comply with such directions as to reporting to the police, restriction of movement, and otherwise as may be specified in the order, or to be interned as may be directed in the order.[225]

The regulation guaranteed that all internees would be able to make representations to an advisory committee 'presided over by a person who holds or has held high judicial office or is a Recorder or County Court

---

[221] H C Debs, 18 February 1924, cols 1369–70 (R J Davies, Under Secretary of State for Home Affairs) (WA).

[222] H C Debs (NI), 15 April 1926, col 526 (Sir R Dawson Bates).

[223] The restriction order had however been lifted by the time that DeValera was voted into power in the Free State in 1932: see H C Debs (NI), 10 March 1932, col 129 (G B Hanna).

[224] The words in square brackets were added by Civil Authorities (Special Powers) Act (Northern Ireland) 1922 Regulations (1923 No 58).

[225] Civil Authorities (Special Powers) Act (Northern Ireland) 1922 Regulations (1922 No 36). See the amendments to Regulation 23B in the Civil Authorities (Special Powers) Act (Northern Ireland) 1922 Regulations (1923 No 48).

Judge or a practising Barrister of at least ten years' standing'. But visits and correspondence were strictly controlled by the authorities[226] and the daily diet of the internees, set-out at length in an unusually detailed statutory instrument,[227] makes grim reading.

The authorities moved swiftly to deploy this internment power against those whom they judged to be their disaffected opponents. Between May 1922 and 24 December 1924, 728 men were interned at one time or another, with the highest number at any one time being 575 in May 1923.[228] In April 1924, there were still 280 internees, most of them held at Larne internment camp.[229] Despite the winding down of internment at the end of 1924, further arrests and detentions occurred during 1925, with one particular incident, in which in November 1925 thirty men were apprehended under regulation 23 and then interned under 23B, giving rise to questions and a bitter debate in the Northern Ireland House of Commons.[230] Even the Westminster Parliament became exercised over the issue, particularly on account of the fact that the authorities in Belfast had interned one of its own members, Cahir Healy, who was Sinn Féin member for Fermanagh/South Tyrone but who despite this spent from 22 May 1922 until 11 February 1924 interned on the prison ship *Argenta*.[231] After his release, he was briefly prohibited from entering his political base in Fermanagh, an action which drew the critical attention of the newly appointed British Prime Minister, Ramsay MacDonald.[232] The way in which internment operated, and the reluctance of the courts to become involved in its oversight, can be seen from the only reported case in which it was directly challenged, *R (O'Hanlon) v Governor of Belfast Prison*.[233] The applicant, an hotel proprietor from Portadown, was detained by the authorities on 10 June 1922 with no reasons being given to him as to why he was being held. In answer to his habeas corpus application made the following month, the police asserted that they were in possession of '[r]eliable information' that he 'was a member of an unlawful association'. What this reliable information was was not to be revealed to the court, however. It had 'not yet been possible to

---

[226] Civil Authorities (Special Powers) Act (Northern Ireland) 1922 Regulations (1922 No 41), adding Regulation 23C to the SPA Regulations; Civil Authorities (Special Powers) Act (Northern Ireland) 1922 Regulations (1922 No 87).

[227] Civil Authorities (Special Powers) Act (Northern Ireland) 1922 Regulations (1922 No 87).

[228] Buckland, *The Factory of Grievances*, n 190 above, p 210.

[229] H C Debs (NI), 10 April 1924, col 660 (Sir R Dawson Bates).

[230] H C Debs (NI), 8 December 1925, cols 1800–2; H C Debs (NI), 14 December 1925, col 1957; cols 1969–90.

[231] See H C Debs, 19 April 1923, cols 2246–7; H C Debs, 18 February 1924, cols 1305–6.

[232] See pp 385–6 below.   [233] (1922) 56 ILTR 170.

complete the investigations, and it would be prejudicial to the interests of justice and dangerous to the lives of others . . . to disclose the information . . . or to bring premature proceedings before the court'.[234] Without any hard evidence to rebut, O'Hanlon was reduced in an affidavit to declaring his innocence of any charge that might be brought against him, and asserting that '[a]ny information to the contrary . . . is absolutely false and malicious'.[235]

The Lord Chief Justice Sir Denis Henry was unmoved. The 'only question' before the court was whether O'Hanlon was legally held, and this he clearly was in light of regulation 23B of the SPA. The court had 'nothing to do with the consideration of whether there [was] any evidence against him'.[236] Thus there was no requirement on the part of the executive to supply reasons for their actions, either to the applicant or even to a court sitting *in camera*. The effect of the decision was to leave the question of internment entirely in the hands of the executive, with the courts having no role whatsoever, even where what was sought was the remedy of habeas corpus. Significantly, Henry LCJ drew support for his approach from the war-time House of Lords decision on internment, *R v Halliday*, which he presented as having 'decided that the Home Secretary had power to make such orders, and that the Court was prevented from interfering with them'.[237] That the Lord Chief Justice should have failed to distinguish these war-time and peace-time cases is perhaps not surprising. In an earlier life, Sir Denis Henry had been Attorney General for Ireland during the critical period, 1919 to 1921. In that capacity he had defended in the House of Commons the first instant execution of a rebel by drumhead court martial that had occurred in the Irish secessionist struggle of that period. The man involved had been tried, convicted and executed within twenty-six hours of his arrest. When asked in the House whether there had been 'any reasonable opportunity for those who were assigned to defend the accused to master and state the case', Henry had replied that he was 'sure that if any application were made, it would be duly considered by the court'.[238] There can be little

---

[234] Ibid, at p 170.

[235] Ibid, at p 171. In a vague stab at establishing his own innocence through proof of his elevated status in Northern Ireland society, O'Hanlon went on to assert that he had paid £8,000 for his hotel the year before, was a director of the Portadown gas company, had been 'financially interested in a number of English industrial concerns' and (somewhat pathetically) that he had been Irish chess champion in each of the preceding nine years.

[236] Ibid, at p 172. Wilson J concurred with the judgment of the Lord Chief Justice.

[237] Ibid. For a critique of this reading of *R v Halliday* [1917] AC 260, see Campbell, n 181 above, pp 334–6.

[238] H C Debs, 5 May 1921, col 1205.

doubt that the Lord Chief Justice's war had not ended in 1918, and that he was not the sort of man who had carved out his successful career by an over-robust scrutiny of the actions of the security forces.

The Special Powers Act and Civil Liberties

Our final substantive area of review takes us to the freedoms of association, assembly and expression. As far as *freedom of association* is concerned, we should first note Sir James Craig's assurance when the legislation was going through the House that the Act was 'not intended in any way to deal with trade disputes'.[239] Despite this, its drafters could not resist inserting an echo of the draconian DORR regulation 43C, which had been introduced at a time of industrial unrest in Great Britain after the end of the First World War.[240] Under SPA regulation 13A, strikes involving the government or a municipal body, or which affected the supply of electricity, gas or water to any city, town, borough or place, left those who had withdrawn their labour vulnerable to prosecution.[241] But as might be expected the main thrust of the association provisions was against the expression of republican solidarity. Apart from predictable prohibitions on military drilling,[242] and the unauthorised use of uniforms,[243] by a regulation added in May 1922, five organisations were deemed to be 'unlawful associations' so that membership of any of them or the promotion of their objects amounted to an offence against the regulations.[244] The organisations were the Irish Republican Brotherhood, the Irish Republican Army, the Irish Volunteers, the Cumann na mBan and Fianna na h'Éireann and these five were joined by Saor Éire in 1931,[245] the National Guard in 1933[246] and Cumann Poblachta na

---

[239] H C Debs (Northern Ireland), 23 March 1922, col 179.   [240] See Chapter 2 above.

[241] This was in addition to the Conspiracy and Protection of Property Act 1875 which through s 21 was applied to Ireland. The Industrial Courts Act 1919 which made permanent the defence of the realm regulatory code in relation to the electricity supply also applied in Ireland through s 12(2).

[242] See Regulation 5, brought into force on 28 October 1931 by the Military Exercise and Drill (Northern Ireland) Order 1931 (1931 No 120).

[243] See Regulation 3(1)(b) and the Civil Authorities (Special Powers) Act (Northern Ireland) 1922 Regulations (1922 No 37), Regulation 10A.

[244] Civil Authorities (Special Powers) Act (Northern Ireland) 1922 Regulations (1922 No 35), Regulation 24A. The regulation was to be the subject of a very controversial judicial interpretation nearly fifty years later: *McEldowney v Forde* [1971] AC 632. Cf Regulation 24 which dealt with promoting associations rendered unlawful by action taken under the 1887 Act and Regulation 24B which declared that if 'any person charged with any offence against these Regulations states in any Court before which he may be brought upon such charge that he is a member of an Association declared by these Regulations to be an unlawful Association or that he refuses to recognise the Court, he shall be guilty of an offence against these Regulations'.

[245] Civil Authorities (Special Powers) Act (Northern Ireland) 1922 Regulations (1931 No 119).

[246] Civil Authorities (Special Powers) Act (Northern Ireland) 1922 Regulations (1933 No 88).

h'Éireann in 1936.[247] Like the first five, these three groups were also nationalist in political complexion. The possession of a document relating to any of them was sufficient to establish guilt unless the accused could prove that 'he did not know or had no reason to suspect that the document was of any such character'.[248] Dawson Bates and his colleagues at the ministry were constantly vigilant least any expression of nationalist sentiment should escape their censorious reach. In 1931, Sir Richard assumed the power to ban 'the erection of any monument or other memorial' which he had 'reason to suspect . . . would be of a character calculated to promote the objects of an unlawful association, or to be prejudicial to the preservation of the peace or maintenance of order'.[249] Two years later, a further addition to the regulations prohibited the display of the Irish tricolour, in a memorably colourful display of repressive pedantry.[250]

The same attention to detail and the same political partisanship were evident in the way in which the SPA *controls on assembly* were applied by the authorities. The right to march has always been viewed by both communities in Northern Ireland as a vital aspect of the expression of their respective political and cultural identities. The SPA permitted the prohibition in any area of all 'meetings, assemblies . . . or processions in public places' without any need first to establish a likelihood or even a possibility of violence.[251] It also allowed the prohibition of specific meetings or processions where there appeared to the authorities reason to apprehend grave disorder or a breach of the peace or the promotion of disaffection.[252] Clearly these broad categories left much to the discretion

---

[247] Civil Authorities (Special Powers) Act (Northern Ireland) 1922 Regulations (1936 No 47).

[248] See Regulation 24A.

[249] Civil Authorities (Special Powers) Act (Northern Ireland) 1922 Regulations (1931 No 85), Regulation 8A.

[250] Civil Authorities (Special Powers) Act (Northern Ireland) 1922 Regulations (1933 No 127), Regulation 24C: 'Any person who has in his possession, or displays, or causes to be displayed, or assists in displaying or in causing to be displayed in any public place, or permits to be displayed on lands and premises in his occupation or under his control, any emblem, flag or other symbol consisting of three vertical or horizontal stripes coloured respectively green, white and yellow, purporting to be an emblem, flag or symbol representing the Irish Republican Army, or purporting to be an emblem, flag or symbol of an Irish Republic, or purporting to be an emblem, flag or symbol of any organisation declared to be an unlawful organisation, shall be guilty of an offence against this regulation, and any police constable may seize any such emblem, flag or other symbol so possessed or displayed contrary to this regulation'.

[251] See Regulation 3(1)(a). A totally arbitrary order under the Regulation would presumably have been vulnerable to challenge as ultra vires the SPA. Cf. Defence of the Realm Regulations, Regulation 9AA.

[252] See Regulation 4. The regulation was broadened by Civil Authorities (Special Powers) Act (Northern Ireland) 1922 Regulations (1933 No 80), Regulation 4. Note that the police were entitled to attend such meetings: Regulation 19.

of the authorities. As early as October 1925, a demonstration organised by the Irish Labour Party and various trade unions was proscribed, as was a march in Linenhall street, Belfast which was to have coincided with the official opening of Parliament.[253] The revolutionary and religious resonances of Easter week made it a very important commemorative time for the nationalist community and consequently a particular target of official vigilance. At an Easter gathering in Milltown cemetery in Belfast on 25 March 1928, eight men were arrested for refusing to take from their lapels a flower that the police present judged to be a nationalist emblem, with the men being subsequently held without charge for three weeks under the SPA. The following year, Easter processions in Belfast, Londonderry, Armagh and Newry were proscribed.

This pattern of banning Easter marches in important venues was repeated on an annual basis until 1935. On 20 April 1930, three men were arrested and detained under the SPA for wearing an emblem with the colours of the Irish Free State.[254] The following year, twelve months' hard labour was imposed on two men who were arrested after Easter week speeches in Newry, which was one of the proscribed areas.[255] From 1936, the authorities chose the more straightforward route of banning all marches anywhere in Northern Ireland during the whole of Easter week, a formula that was subsequently repeated every year until 1948.[256] Apart from these annual bans, the SPA was also invoked in an *ad hoc* way to prohibit public demonstrations, particularly in 1933 when gatherings in Belfast, Newry and Londonderry were proscribed in January and a seven-day ban on all meetings was imposed throughout Belfast the following October. Efforts to hold a nationalist meeting in Newtownbutler, county Fermanagh in November and December 1938 were persistently foiled by the authorities, with the town being made the subject of four such orders issued over a three week period and covering eight separate days. The particular sensitivity of the ministry may be explained by the fact that the purpose of the meeting was to have been to attack the Government of Ireland Act, with addresses on the subject expected from members of both the Stormont and Westminster Parliaments. '[W]e are

[253] See H C Debs (NI), 6 October 1925, cols 1131–70.

[254] H C Debs (NI), 7 May 1930, cols 1020–2.

[255] H C Debs (NI), 14 May 1931, cols 1654–705, especially at col 1673 (C Healy).

[256] A guide to the orders made under the SPA is at H C Debs (NI), 25 July 1950, cols 1438–43 (W B Maginess, Minister of Home Affairs). For a short adjournment debate on the issue, and Dawson Bates's vigorous defence of his action, see H C Debs (NI), 22 March 1932, cols 537–46. An invaluable work in this area will be L K Donohue, *Counter-Terrorist Law and Emergency Powers in the United Kingdom 1922–2000* (forthcoming), esp chs 1–2. (We are grateful to the author for allowing us to see the completed manuscript of her book.)

not going to tolerate disloyal meetings called in the name of politics with the object of bringing about the disruption of Northern Ireland', a clearly angry Dawson Bates told the Northern Ireland House of Commons[257] in the midst of the crisis.

Turning finally to *freedom of expression*, the constraints to be found in the SPA took two different forms. First, there were regulations, loosely based on earlier DORR, dealing with the protection of confidential information. Three of these may be referred to briefly here. Under regulation 10, it was prohibited, without lawful authority, to 'collect, record, publish or communicate, or attempt to elicit, any information with respect to the movement, numbers, description, condition, or disposition of any police force, or with respect to the plans or conduct, or supposed plans or conduct, of any operations by any such force, or any information of such a nature as is calculated to be or might be directly or indirectly useful to persons hostile or opposed to the preservation of the peace or maintenance of order'.[258] Under regulation 14, the civil authority could 'by order prohibit any person from approaching within such distance as may be specified in the order of any camp, barrack, work of defence or other defended work, or any work or place to which it is deemed necessary in the interest of the preservation of the peace or maintenance of order to afford protection'.[259] Regulation 27 prohibited the publication 'in any newspaper, periodical, circular or other printed publication, or in any public speech' of the contents 'of any confidential document belonging to, or of any document which has in confidence been communicated by, or any confidential information obtained from, any Department of the Government of Northern Ireland, or any person in the service of that Government'.[260]

Secondly, there were three regulations dealing explicitly with the control of expression. Regulation 25 declared that '[n]o person shall by word of mouth or in writing, or in any newspaper, periodical, book, circular, or other printed publication—(a) spread false reports or make false statements; or (b) spread reports or make statements intended or likely to cause disaffection to His Majesty, or to interfere with the success of any police or other force acting for the preservation of the peace or maintenance of order in Northern Ireland'.[261] The regulation also prohibited the spread-

---

[257] H C Debs (NI), 23 November 1938, col 2095.

[258] Cf. Defence of the Realm Regulations, Regulation 18.

[259] Cf. Defence of the Realm Regulations, Regulation 29.

[260] These offences were in addition to those to be found in the Official Secrets Act 1911, which extended to Northern Ireland.

[261] Cf. Regulation 16 of the SPA, which was based on Regulation 42 of the Defence of the Realm Regulations.

ing of reports or making of statements 'intended or likely to prejudice' recruitment into the 'police or other force enrolled or employed for the preservation of the peace or maintenance of order in Northern Ireland'. This regulation alone had the potential to exert a vice-like grip on the reporting of the politics of the Province but it was supplemented by the even wider regulation 26, under which the civil authority could 'by notice prohibit the circulation of any newspaper for any specified period'. Predictably the IRA newspaper *An Phoblacht* was banned, as was the less obviously subversive *Nation*.[262] The regulations were buttressed by a surveillance operation, supposedly legitimised by section 56(2) of the Post Office Act 1908, under which, it was said, 'correspondence for delivery to, or emanating from, persons in Northern Ireland suspected of engaging in seditious activities [was] liable to censorship'.[263] So much a part of the legal landscape did the SPA regulations become that by 1930, Dawson Bates felt able to promulgate a new regulation, 26A, under which 'the possession or exhibition of any cinematograph film' or 'the possession or rendering of any gramophone record' could be prohibited. The connection with 'making further provision for the preservation of the peace and the maintenance of order', as required by the SPA, was not made explicit.[264]

'There is no British Contribution'

Given the wide-ranging nature of the SPA and the partisan way in which it was applied, it might have been expected that a high level of criticism would have been forthcoming from the Westminster Parliament, particularly when it is remembered that, after 1921, Northern Ireland's repressiveness was a creature not of the United Kingdom executive but of a quasi-colonial regime theoretically subservient to Westminster's will. The facts however tell the very opposite story. In a Catholic Capuchin annual published early in the 1940s in the Irish Free State, an anonymous author writing under the pen-name 'Ultach' published an essay on 'The Persecution of Catholics in Northern Ireland'. It has been recently described as arguably 'still the most eloquent and concise condemnation of the discriminatory and oppressive features of the Unionist regime'.[265]

---

[262] H C Debs (NI), 24 March 1931, col 554 (Sir R Dawson Bates).

[263] H C Debs (NI), 28 April 1925, col 223 (Sir R Dawson Bates). On the legal basis, see H C Debs, 14 December 1925, col 1952. The censorship continued into the 1930s: see the short adjournment debate at H C Debs (NI), 14 May 1930, cols 1276–84.

[264] Civil Authorities (Special Powers) Act (Northern Ireland) 1922 Regulations (1930 No 58).

[265] P Bew, P Gibbon and H Patterson, *Northern Ireland 1921–1994: Political Forces and Social Classes* (1995), p 49.

'Ultach' did not then 'regard the present intolerable position of Catholics in the partitioned area as being a necessary consequence of partition as such, but rather [it was] the result of a particular form of administration'.[266] Correctly perceiving that the regime's weakness lay 'in the fact that it [could] be removed when England wishes',[267] the author went on to express puzzlement at why 'democratic' England had continued to support 'totalitarian' Unionism. That support was not only passive; it was evident also in the honours that the British nation accorded its Belfast leaders. In 1921, Dawson Bates was knighted and in 1937, he was created a baronet. James Craig was elevated to the peerage as Viscount Craigavon in 1927, the year before which he received an honorary DCL from Oxford University. His successor but one was later also raised to the House of Lords, as the first Viscount Brookeborough, in 1952.

While these honours may not have had much tangible meaning, they were a very clear indication, at the highest level, of the existence of no immense displeasure at the way in which the Unionist Party had chosen to govern their part of the United Kingdom. Britain's general non-interference with Northern Ireland could be explained by pointing to the implications that successive British Governments and Westminster Parliaments had chosen to draw from the constitutional status of Northern Ireland. We have already seen that internment and restriction orders against Cahir Healy MP had been lifted after direct pressure from the newly appointed Labour Prime Minister Ramsay MacDonald in 1924,[268] and it is also true that in both 1922 and 1925 the British Cabinet was involved in the sensitive task of securing the release through the Royal pardon of prisoners who had been convicted in Northern Ireland of offences of a political character.[269] But these examples of United Kingdom intervention, which appeared to contradict 'Ultach', were wholly exceptional. The normal response, almost from the moment of the establishment of the sub-State, was one of deliberate disengagement. A key reason for this was the analogy that was persistently drawn between the legislatures of the dominions (including the Irish Free State) on the one hand and the devolved legislative assembly in Belfast on the other.

---

[266] *Capuchin Annual 1940*, p 161.   [267] Ibid, p 174.

[268] See text at n 232 above. See H C Debs, 18 February 1924, cols 1305–6 (R MacDonald), and the brief parliamentary exchange at cols 2246–7.

[269] See the comments of the Secretary of State for the Home Department, Sir William Joynson-Hicks, at H C Debs, 9 March 1926, cols 2211–12. In 1922, it had been the Lord Lieutenant who had—on the British government's advice—overridden the Belfast government's view with regard to certain prison sentences: see Buckland, n 190 above, p 271.

The 1920s and 1930s was a time marked by important moves towards autonomy on the part of Britain's former colonies. The freedom that it was increasingly considered appropriate to accord to these dominion Parliaments was unthinkingly, almost instinctively, extended to Northern Ireland. Thus it was that the status against which the Unionists had fought so hard in 1920 came to be implicitly accorded to them and to function as a protective cover against any unwelcome British interest in their domestic affairs. As early as April 1923, an attempt to raise at Westminster the conditions aboard the prison ship *Argenta* on which many internees (including Healy) were then being held, was met by the official response that the Home Office had 'no information on this matter, which [was] entirely within the control of the Government of Northern Ireland'. Questions on it should therefore 'be addressed to that Government. There is no British contribution in this respect'.[270] Admitting that the MP's question 'had escaped [his] notice', the Speaker indicated from the chair that he considered it to be 'very desirable that we should not have questions on matters which we have delegated by Statute to the Irish Governments'. The last plural here is interesting in that it reflects a failure right from the start to make a constitutional distinction between the two parts of Ireland. The key Speaker's ruling on the Province came the following month: 'With regard to those subjects which have been delegated to the Government of Northern Ireland, questions must be asked of Ministers in Northern Ireland, and not in this House'.[271] This ruling quickly hardened into a constitutional convention, so much so that Sir Ivor Jennings felt able to pronounce in his leading treatise on constitutional law that 'it would be unconstitutional for Parliament to exercise its legal power of legislation in the matters delegated to the Parliament of Northern Ireland, except with the consent of that Parliament'.[272]

The effect of the Speaker's ruling was to stifle any effort even to raise issues, much less have them debated or considered, on the floor of the Westminster House of Commons. Thus the MP who sought in 1924 to raise the internment and restriction orders imposed on the trade unionist J C Magennis, discussed above, was informed that the matter was 'solely within the jurisdiction of the Government of Northern Ireland, and any representations thereon should therefore be addressed direct to

---

[270] H C Debs, 19 April 1923, col 2246 (W C Bridgeman, Secretary of State for Home Affairs).
[271] H C Debs, 3 May 1923, cols 1624–5.
[272] Sir Ivor Jennings, *The Law and the Constitution* (4th edn, 1952), p 158.

that Government'.[273] When the following year MPs tried to raise the fact that Northern Ireland prisoners were being held in Scottish prisons, away from their families and local communities, the inevitable reply from the Speaker was that 'where the duty of maintaining law and order has been transferred to another Government, it is not open to this House to discuss or criticise their action'.[274] The fact that this other government was making use of prisons within his jurisdiction did not dent the Speaker's determined detachment. By 1936, after discussion of the draconian regulation 22A had been routinely ruled out of order, the Labour Member Emmanuel Shinwell intervened to ask rhetorically, '[i]s it coming to pass that Northern Ireland is setting up what amounts virtually to a form of dictatorship?'[275] But by this time, efforts to get Northern Ireland debated had more or less ceased. The MPs who had previously tried to raise it on the floor of the House had more or less given up the ghost; throughout the 1930s, northern Rhodesia regularly received more entries in the annual sessional indexes than did Northern Ireland.

It is true that the House of Commons chamber was not the only place that pressure could be exerted, and we have already noted that the United Kingdom Government was not inactive behind the scenes in the case of prison releases in both 1922 and 1925. But ministers considered their room for manoeuvre to be very slight. A pivotal event had been the Northern Ireland Government's abolition of PR in local government in 1922. This had occurred in the teeth of objections both from Dublin and London, but while very hostile to the initiative the British Government had not been prepared indefinitely to withhold the Royal Assent for the measure, thereby precipitating a constitutional crisis the effects of which could not have been accurately foreseen.[276] By 1928, in contrast, when the question of the abolition of PR to the Belfast legislature had been put on the agenda by the Northern Ireland Government, the British Home Secretary, Sir William Joynson-Hicks, gave short shrift to an opposition deputation from the Northern Ireland Labour Party, writing to the Northern Ireland Prime Minister, 'I don't know whether you would care at any time to discuss the matter with me; of course I am always at your disposal. But beyond that "I know my place", and don't propose to interfere'.[277] It is hardly surprising that a critical report on the SPA from the

---

[273] H C Debs, 18 February 1924, cols 1369–70 (R J Davies, Under Secretary of State for Home Affairs) (WA).

[274] H C Debs, 3 March 1925, col 232.   [275] H C Debs, 27 May 1936, col 2020.

[276] The story is in Buckland, n 190 above, pp 267–75.

[277] Quoted ibid, p 266.

newly formed National Council for Civil Liberties (NCCL) should have been greeted in 1936 with confident derision from Stormont ministers. To Dawson Bates, it was merely the 'inaccurate and mischievous propaganda of the so-called Council of Civil Liberties'.[278] Viscount Craigavon considered it a 'grossly biased publication' which had emanated 'from a similar source to other propagandists whose sole ambition [was] to see the establishment of an All-Ireland Republic'.[279] Needless to say, the report received no attention whatsoever in the Westminster Parliament. Like its ministers, Britain's legislature also knew its place.

Civil Liberties in Northern Ireland: an Overview

The outbreak both of the Second World War and a new IRA campaign coinciding with it in 1939 led inexorably to an increased reliance on the SPA, with exclusion orders being more frequently relied upon[280] and a system of compulsory identity cards being introduced,[281] the latter being accompanied by a new provision requiring of visitors that they should be able to establish that their presence in the Province was 'not for any purpose detrimental to the preservation of the peace and the maintenance of order in Northern Ireland'.[282] The old standby of internment was also called into action, and by mid-October 1940 there were as many as 268 such detainees.[283] In 1943, a new Special Powers Amending Act permitted the prosecution of offences under the SPA to proceed by way of indictment but greatly increased the sentences that could be imposed where this mode of trial was chosen.[284] During this period, two rare legal challenges to the legality of police enforcement of the SPA and to Stormont's policies on law and order proved unsuccessful. The first of

---

[278] H C Debs (NI), 23 June 1936, col 1965. See Report of a Commission of Inquiry appointed to examine the purpose and effect of the Civil Authorities (Special Powers) Acts (Northern Ireland) 1922 and 1933 (London, 1936).

[279] H C Debs (NI), 26 May 1936, col 1766.　　　　　　　　　[280] Under Regulation 23A.

[281] Civil Authorities (Special Powers) Act (Northern Ireland) 1922 Regulations (1940 No 51), Regulation 1A(1).

[282] Civil Authorities (Special Powers) Act (Northern Ireland) 1922 Regulations (1940 No 61), Regulation 1B. For the earlier even more draconian version, see Civil Authorities (Special Powers) Act (Northern Ireland) 1922 Regulations (1940 No 54), Regulation 1A(2).

[283] H C Debs (Northern Ireland), 15 October 1940, col 2349 (W Lowry). Most of the internees were held for the duration of the war. Forty-five were released in July 1945, and the ensuing four months saw the release of a further 148. On 4 December 1945, 36 suspects were still interned, but these were released in the months that followed: see H C Debs (NI), 5 June 1947, col 875 (J E Warnock).

[284] To penal servitude for a minimum of three years and a maximum of fourteen years or a fine of up to £500 or both: Civil Authorities (Special Powers) Act (Northern Ireland) 1943, s 4 (the maximum under the old law had been two years or a £100 fine or both).

these cases was *Sweny v Carroll*[285] in which the High Court held that a general authorisation to the police was sufficient to meet the requirement under section 3(2) of the SPA that an 'offence against the regulations shall not be prosecuted except by such officer or person as may be authorised in that behalf by the Attorney General for Northern Ireland, and in accordance with such directions as may be given by the said Attorney General'. Making no reference to any presumption in favour of civil liberties that might have been assumed to have existed in the common law, Andrews LCJ noted only that 'expediency requir[ed] that the authorization should be of a general character'.[286] The same judge presided over the second legal challenge, in which the court refused to issue an order of mandamus requiring the Minister of Home Affairs to apply the 'Cat and Mouse' Act of 1913 so as to cause the release of a Republican prisoner who was on hunger strike and near death.[287] It was hardly a surprising result, but it cannot have been reassuring to the applicants both in this and in the *Sweny* case that the judge presiding over both courts should have been the brother of the man then just recently appointed Prime Minister of Northern Ireland.

To an extent the Second World War and the new IRA campaign provided further justifications for an official approach to civil liberties that had drifted in the years since partition into an intolerant authoritarianism that was as unreflective as it was hostile to criticism. Though notionally separate, the three branches of government in this tiny part of the United Kingdom seemed joined together in a common programme of resistance to unacceptable manifestations of Irish nationalism. The solidarity of the executive, legislature and judiciary in this regard resulted in a quite drastic curtailment of traditional freedoms for those on the wrong side of the sectarian divide, with the principles of legality and of equality under the law barely surviving even in a formal sense, much less as the constitutional paradigms celebrated by Dicey. That this system of law emerged from a culture which prided itself on its historical commitment to civil and political liberties demonstrates how dangerous power can be in the hands of a group or community consciously or unconsciously blinkered in its field of vision. This was a failure of awareness which permeated the Northern Ireland Government, from successive prime ministers via the courts and Parliament, down to its most blatant manifestation

---

[285] [1942] NILR 112.

[286] Ibid, at p 117. Brown J concurred with the judgment of the Lord Chief Justice.

[287] *R (Diamond and Fleming) v Warnock* [1946] NILR 171. The Act had been passed originally to deal with the suffragettes..

in the RUC and reservist police forces that imposed order on the streets. It was a failure which must bear at least part of the responsibility for the turmoil that was to engulf the Province in the last third of the twentieth century.

It is tempting to view Ireland's depressing history of civil libertarian restriction as wholly independent of that of the rest of the United Kingdom during the period under study. The very ambiguity of the description of the United Kingdom as Britain, an area of land that excludes the island of Ireland, seems positively to invite the erection of just such an intellectual *cordon sanitaire*. Certainly the breadth of the Defence of the Realm Regulations insofar as they applied to Ireland, the regulations brought into force by the Restoration of Order in Ireland Act and the post-1922 Special Powers' Regulations reflect an almost total disconnection from Dicey's principles or indeed from the principles of legality developed in Chapter 1. This departure from principle was far more extreme than anything that occurred in Great Britain during the period under study. The wide discretionary powers granted the executive and the discriminatory way in which these were then exercised nakedly breached *constitutional principle* at a multiplicity of levels and produced a regime that was both partisan and sectarian. The succession of police and military forces that we have encountered in the course of this chapter were all equipped with wide discretionary powers that amounted in certain cases to authorised banditry but which in all cases permitted little or no protection for the ordinary person. The adverse effect of this open invitation to the exercise of unaccountable power fell almost entirely on the nationalist community; during exactly the same period, other more quiescent elements in the community experienced a Rule of Law of a quite different and more benign sort, of a type which would have been easily recognisable to Dicey and his supporters.

The huge scale of the inequality of the application of the law as between communities and political groups is one obvious way in which the Irish experience did indeed differ from that of the rest of the United Kingdom. The occasional support shown by the judiciary for civil liberties, particularly outside Ulster in 1916 to 1921, is also an unusual aspect of Ireland's experience with the Rule of Law at this time, though we have suggested that this was less to do with principle than with the fact that many judges and magistrates were broadly nationalist in their politics. In terms of *constitutional practice*, the difference between Ireland and Britain, great though it was, was more one of degree than of substance. All that occurred on the island was a more deliberate, less restrained exercise of executive might than any we have come across in Britain in the course of this study. But this was an executive engagement in a struggle that used the same weapons as were deployed in Britain during the First World War and then against the Communist Party and the miners in the 1920s. There was simply more use of emergency law over a longer period and more executive excess in Ireland than in Britain. To this extent we can describe Ireland as an exaggerated version of the kind of activity to which the British system was also vulnerable, and to which, albeit in less dramatic fashion, it regularly succumbed during the first half of the twentieth century. The application of the Rule of Law in Ireland is not therefore in any sense the fatal flaw in Dicey's approach to the subject, for this is to suggest that his view of constitutional principle can be said to withstand critical scrutiny once Ireland is laid to one side. In reality however, as earlier chapters of this book have demonstrated, the problems in Dicey's theories are much deeper than those shown up by the application of the Rule of Law in Ireland. These defects would have been fully exposed had the United Kingdom never sought to embrace Ireland within its constitutional framework. Ireland is a serious flaw certainly, but it represents only one among many in a theory which was undermined by events across the Kingdom and not just in one, particularly recalcitrant, part.

8

Conclusion

In Chapter 1 we concluded that the Rule of Law as conceived by Dicey was an unstable basis for the protection of civil liberties in Britain. We saw that it was rooted in a political ideology of a very particular kind, and that this meant that it was bound to be hostile to the two central themes that were to come to dominate Britain's twentieth century public life, democracy and collectivism. Its conceptual redundancy was coming to be recognised even at the beginning of our era, when between 1906 and 1914 successive Liberal Administrations enacted collectivist and democratising legislation of a kind that was loudly abhorred by Dicey. Nowhere was Dicey more inaccurate than in his claim that the common law was the protector of political freedom within the framework of Britain's unwritten constitution. This was not even a true reflection of the Victorian era in which he had spent his formative years. We saw in Chapter 1 that by the start of the First World War, it had been Parliament which had secured the primary political liberties—notably the franchise—that were then available to the British 'subject', and that this had been achieved more in defiance of than in partnership with the courts. We also saw that secondary civil liberties, such as those of association, assembly and expression, were at this time largely unprotected by the common law, unless they happened to benefit indirectly from a judicial largesse that was being extended towards other more general, or property-based, interests. Thus at the onset of the Edwardian period, civil liberties were precariously rooted in English law.

In setting this scene in Chapter 1, we suggested that despite its faults the idea of the Rule of Law, recast in more modest but manageable form as a principle of legality, might be capable in principle of functioning effectively as a guardian (though not of course a guarantee) of civil liberties. The narrative with which this book has been largely concerned has been an exploration of the extent to which such a principle can be found to be operating in the law and practice of civil liberties in Britain in the first half of the twentieth century. In this final chapter we draw together the conclusions that we believe have emerged from the developments which we have encountered. In doing so, we also have regard to certain of the civil libertarian aspects of the anti-IRA legislation introduced in

1939 and to the emergency legislation that was enacted during the Second World War. The legislative, executive and judicial responses to the latter conflict in particular tend in terms of constitutional principle and practice to confirm the various judgements we have made about the Rule of Law in the period under study, and we refer to the evidence of why this should be so in the course of this chapter. Like the earlier conflict of 1914 to 1918, the Second World War involved emergency legislation and the promulgation of a wide range of regulations, governing many aspects of national life. It may be thought somewhat ironical that, after all the travails of the inter-war years, our volume should end where it began, with emergency regulations, wide executive discretion and the effective suspension of large tracts of the Rule of Law.

The Importance of Legality

At its most basic, the formal version of the Rule of Law that we discussed in Chapter 1 requires simply that the executive should have legal authority for whatever it does in the name of those on behalf of whom it purports to act. This has two aspects: in the first place the government must not act unlawfully in the sense of actually breaching the law; and in the second place it requires that the government must not act without authority, but may only act where it is formally empowered to do so. Without wishing to exaggerate the point, there can be little doubt that had it been properly understood and applied throughout our period, this principle would have provided greater protection for civil liberties in the period under study. Dicey appeared to presume that a rather different (and ultimately weaker) conception of legality was easily reflected by the demands of the common law, but if we turn from theory to practice, we find that one of the main features of the first half of the twentieth century is the extent to which the executive did not feel unduly constrained either by the principle of legality as we have defined it or even by the common law's prohibition on unlawful acts as epitomised by *Entick v Carrington*.[1] The fact is that time and again the executive engaged in actions which were of doubtful or of non-existent legality. The most obvious examples of State lawlessness of this sort arose in the context of public order and concerned the police and armed forces. At its bloodiest extreme this involved the authorities in a covert campaign of reprisals during the disturbances in Ireland in 1920. But in Britain too we have

---

[1] (1765) 19 St Tr 1030.

encountered many examples of unlawful police violence, such as during the General Strike and the miners' lock-out in 1926; in the course of dealing with the protests of the unemployed during the whole inter-war period; and in the context of repelling the marchers at Blaina in March 1935.

Such lawlessness has not been restricted to situations of sudden crisis brought on by spontaneous outbreaks of disorder, of the type that was in Dicey's mind when he distinguished martial law from his mainstream theory of the constitution.[2] The official breaches of the law of this sort have not always entailed a rejection of legality driven entirely and (it might be argued) somewhat excusably by the exigencies of the moment. On the contrary, there has been a calculated feel to many of these incidents. We have encountered allegations that the police entered the homes of anti-war activists without warrants in order to demand information during the First World War; examples of officers routinely ransacking property in the course of executing a power of arrest; Special Branch officers hiding under the platform at a Communist Party meeting in 1924; and the Metropolitan Police Commissioner imposing the 'Trenchard ban' on a sensitive form of public protest in London in the early 1930s. Nor has a relaxed attitude to the law been found only among the police. In this context we may recall the Home Secretary's action in 1926 in publishing as a command paper Communist Party documentation seized in a police raid and the decision in 1926 (admitted to be unlawful at the time) to ban all communist meetings under the emergency regulations in place for the General Strike. Home Secretary Joynson-Hicks's 'whoop of joy' and subsequent almost casual (but unpunished) contempt of court on hearing of the arrest of the Communist Party leadership in 1925 fell into a longer tradition than critics at the time were in a position to appreciate.

In a society with a properly functioning principle of legality it would be expected that these various actions would not have been allowed to have gone unpunished. Indeed we have seen that one of the central features of Dicey's version of the Rule of Law was that everyone was subject to the same rules regardless of their status in society. Whatever its theoretical qualities, the events recounted in this study seem to prove that such a view of the law had little or no foundation in reality, at least as far as civil libertarians were concerned. Of more confusing importance for the principle of legality are those handful of cases in which the courts,

---

[2] See Chapter 7 above.

confronted by apparent illegality on the part of the authorities, chose not to punish the wrongdoers (thereby occasionally vindicating the Rule of Law, however sporadically and inconsistently) but instead to legitimise their conduct as part of the common law. This was the consequence of the cases that were taken in the mid-1930s to test the legality of the Trenchard ban[3] and to counter police intimidation at communist meetings in South Wales.[4] It was also the effect of the decision in *Elias v Pasmore*,[5] though here the Rule of Law worked to the extent that damages were awarded against the police, albeit on an extremely narrow basis. In these cases, the principle of legality was deployed in a perverse way to sanction retrospectively the apparently illegal actions to which the police had earlier committed themselves. Such intellectual sleights of hand were facilitated by the open-textured nature of the common law but they were not restricted to it. The outstanding example of this sort of judicial legitimisation of apparent illegality occurred during the Second World War, and involved the interpretation of delegated legislation rather than the meaning of a common law rule.

The issue arose out of the internment of persons suspected to be of 'hostile origin or association' under regulation 18B of the Defence Regulations which had been promulgated at the outbreak of hostilities in 1939. As originally drafted, the power had been exercisable by the Secretary of State if he were 'satisfied . . . that it [was] necessary' to act, but this was quickly changed to a requirement to have a 'reasonable cause to belief' in certain facts after Parliament had made an issue about the repressiveness of the regulations and had forced a series of changes upon the executive.[6] At the time it was believed that the alteration to regulation 18B had imposed an objective test on the executive before it could intern suspects under the regulation, and the requirement remained in place despite a broadening of the regulation that occurred in the Summer of 1940.[7] During that Summer the power came to be exercised with greatly increased frequency and the executive grew into the habit of offering the most minimal of justificatory affidavits if any of its decisions to incarcerate happened to be challenged in court. These flimsy assertions of suspicion were found by the judges in a series of

---

[3] *Duncan v Jones* [1936] 1 KB 218.   [4] *Thomas v Sawkins* [1935] 2 KB 249.
[5] [1934] 2 KB 164.
[6] See the Commons debate initiated by Dingle Foot MP at H C Debs, 31 October 1939, cols 1829–902 and S R & O 1939 No 1681.
[7] S R & O 1940 No 770.

habeas corpus applications to amount to sufficient 'reasonable cause'[8] but when internees turned as an alternative to the tort of false imprisonment, the Home Office declined even to file such affidavits, lest it be drawn by the relevant rules of procedure (which were far more dynamic than those governing habeas corpus) into an evidential auction which it might then have been unable to control.

Matters eventually came to a head when one case, *Liversidge v Anderson*, came before the House of Lords.[9] By a majority of four to one their Lordships held that there was no need for any affidavit whatsoever from the Secretary of State by way of justification of his actions under regulation 18B. Effectively, the Law Lords were interpreting the 'reasonable cause to believe' criterion as requiring merely a belief in such a reasonable cause. It was because the words were reorganised in this subjective way that the majority felt able to dispense altogether with even the ostensible need for objective evidence which had been an ever-present element in the law since the very first of the regulation 18B cases had come along the year before. Lord Atkins' dissent was on the basis that some evidence was essential if the proper, objective meaning was to be accorded to the regulation. The regulation contained 'simple words [which] as it appears to me obviously give only a conditional authority to the minister to detain any person without trial, the condition being that he has reasonable cause for the belief which leads to the detention order'.[10] On the majority's interpretation, the Secretary of State enjoyed 'an absolute power which, so far as I know, has never been given before to the executive'.[11] In light of this, his Lordship had no inclination to 'apologise for taking some time to demonstrate that no such power is in fact given to the minister by the words in question'.[12] The emotional force of Lord Atkins' judgment is rather diminished by the fact that all he seemed to desire was to be shown an affidavit as facile and uninformative as the one that had enabled him quite contentedly in another case—decided at the same time—to keep a detainee in detention.[13] But his famous remark that in

---

[8] See the reported cases of *R v Secretary of State for the Home Department, ex parte Lees* [1941] 1 KB 72; *R v Home Secretary, ex parte Budd* [1941] 2 All ER 749 (in which, however, there is a powerful dissent by Stable J); *Greene v Secretary of State for Home Affairs* [1942] AC 284. See also *In re Shelmerdine and others* (1941) 85 Sol Jo 11.

[9] [1942] AC 206. The decision was predictably controversial at the time: see the broadly supportive notes from W S Holdsworth and A L Goodhart in (1942) 58 LQR at p 1 and p 3 respectively, and the more critical analysis by C K Allen, 'Regulation 18B and Reasonable Cause' (1942) 58 LQR 232. Cf. G W Keeton, 'Liversidge v Anderson' (1942) 5 MLR 162.

[10] [1942] AC 206, at p 226.   [11] Ibid.   [12] Ibid.

[13] *Greene v Secretary of State for Home Affairs*, n 8 above. Lord Atkin incorporated his judgment in the case into his speech in *Liversidge*.

this case he had 'listened to arguments which might have been addressed acceptably to the Court of King's Bench in the time of Charles I'[14] and that his colleagues had responded in a way which was 'more executive minded than the executive',[15] can stand as an observation not only on *Liversidge* but on successive judges' ability to absorb official illegality and turn it into part of the common law.

The Principles of Legality

The value of the principle of legality as we have so far discussed it in this chapter lies in its ideologically neutral character. Of course the law which the principle delivers and supports may itself be ideologically driven, but this does not diminish the apolitical character of the concept of the Rule of Law itself. Even at its most formalistic therefore, the Rule of Law would clearly have been a useful ally had it been adhered to by the executive and fairly applied by the courts. But as we saw in Chapter 1 it is possible to achieve a richer principle of legality than one which merely looks for formal legal authority for executive action. The construction of this more effective theory may be achieved by reflecting further on why we should put such store by the seemingly simple notion that government should act only with legal authority. This is not merely a piece of pedantic legal formalism. Legal authority has a purpose. Thus, as we saw in Chapter 1, the principle of legality also requires that a government must have a legal authority for its actions which is clear, published in advance and prospective only. In Chapter 1, we also suggested the requirement that the law should not be used to confer unduly wide discretionary powers. It is by the standards of this more complete principle of legality that much of the law and practice discussed in this study can also be found to be wanting. While it is certainly the case that the kind of lawbreaking discussed above has not been the norm, with the executive being generally able to point to enabling law by way of explanation for its repressive actions, it is nevertheless clear that the law to which it has had to turn for legitimation has in many instances been of a broad and general nature. As we have already pointed out, government may have had legal authority for what it did in many of these incidents, but it can hardly be said to have represented government according to law, particularly if exercised under common law or statutory powers without any effective review or restraint.

---

[14] [1942] AC 206, at p 244.   [15] Ibid.

This was certainly true of the power conferred by the common law which authorised important restraints on liberty by devices such as binding over orders and the preventive powers of the police, powers which could be exercised even where no offence had been committed. It is clearest of all in relation both to the Defence of the Realm Acts which the executive secured during the First World War and to the enactment of the Restoration of Order in Ireland Act. The emergency powers legislation passed after the First World War and Northern Ireland's special powers legislation also fit into this category. A contemporary writer castigated the effect of one provision in the Defence of the Realm legislation as 'characterised by a vagueness which puts public liberty entirely at the mercy of the executive'[16] but he or she could just as easily have been referring to the whole framework of emergency law. The Emergency Powers Act 1920 is an example of the same genre. So too is the Prevention of Violence (Temporary Provisions) Act 1939, hurriedly enacted as a response to an IRA bombing campaign in Britain.[17] The Act gave the executive wide powers to prohibit from entering Britain, to expel or forcibly to register persons involved in the preparation or instigation of acts of violence 'designed to influence public opinion or Government policy with respect to Irish affairs' (section 1(1)).[18] The police were empowered to arrest anyone whom they reasonably suspected 'to be a person concerned in the preparation or instigation of such acts of violence' and such suspects could be held for forty-eight hours and then for up to a further five days 'as may be authorised by the direction of the Secretary of State expressly given in each case' (section 4(1)).[19] These wide discretionary powers anticipated by more than thirty years the more well-known terms of the Prevention of Terrorism Act 1974 that was to be enacted as a response to IRA violence in 1974. The panic which had generated the 1939 measure was soon allayed by a reduction in IRA violence and was in any event soon superseded by the greater

---

[16] 'North Briton', *British Freedom 1914–1917* (1917), p 31.

[17] By the middle of July 1939, when the Act was introduced, there had been 127 incidents of which 57 had been in London and 70 in the provinces. The casualty rate had amounted to one man killed in Manchester and a national total of 56 injured, but there was little evidence of any inability to cope on the part of the police, particularly since by the middle of July no fewer than 66 suspects had been 'convicted by the ordinary processes of law' for their involvement in the campaign: see H C Debs, 24 July 1939, col 1049–51 (Sir S Hoare, Secretary of State for the Home Department).

[18] The only exemption was in respect of persons ordinarily resident in Great Britain throughout the last preceding 20 years.

[19] See generally O G Lomas, 'The Executive and the Anti-Terrorist Legislation of 1939' [1980] PL 16.

crisis of the outbreak of war with Germany which followed just weeks after its enactment.

Another example of legislation conferring wide and open-ended powers is the Emergency Powers (Defence) Act 1939. By virtue of section 1(1), His Majesty was empowered by Order in Council to make 'such Regulations (in this Act referred to as "Defence Regulations") as appear to him to be necessary or expedient for securing the public safety, the defence of the realm, the maintenance of public order and the efficient prosecution of any war in which His Majesty may be engaged, and for maintaining supplies and services essential to the life of the community'. The first set of regulations issued under the Act came the day after the enactment of the measure.[20] Referred to as code A, these 'comprised the regulations needed on the outbreak of war, but excluded the grosser violations of civil liberty'.[21] These latter provisions were to be found in code B, which was given legal effect on the day war was declared.[22] Introducing the primary legislation in the Commons, the Home Secretary Sir Samuel Hoare reminded the House of the long tradition of which he was now to form a part:

I am one of the comparatively small number of Members who remember the introduction of the first Defence of the Realm Bill in August, 1914. I remember very well Mr McKenna, my predecessor in office, coming to the House without a draft of the Bill, with only half a sheet of notes in his hand, and asking the House of Commons to give the Government the full powers required to meet the dangers with which the country was then faced.[23]

The effect on civil liberties of the kind of executive law-making that resulted from the enactment of broadly based emergency legislation of this nature has been one of the central themes of this study.

The implications for constitutional practice of both the anti-IRA and the war-time measures were immediate. As far as the Prevention of Violence (Temporary Provisions) Act was concerned, in the first two months of its operation, 113 expulsion orders, twenty-five registration orders and ten prohibition orders were issued,[24] and by the end of May

---

[20] Defence Regulations 1939 (S R & O 1939 No 927), promulgated on 25 August 1939. The Regulations were renamed the Defence (General) Regulations 1939 when they were reissued in a revised form on 23 November: S R & O 1939 No 1682, Regulation 11.

[21] A W B Simpson, *In the Highest Degree Odious: Detention without Trial in Wartime Britain* (1992), p 48.

[22] S R & O 1939 No 978.   [23] H C Debs, 24 August 1939, col 63.

[24] Report by the Secretary of State as to the Expulsion, Registration, and Prohibition Orders made during the period 28th July to 30th September 1939 (HC 173 of 1938–39) (12 October 1939). Six representations against expulsion orders were made, but no changes were made to the orders as a result. This report was published under s 1(7) of the Act, which had been a concession secured in

1940, a total of 167 expulsion orders had been issued.[25] Originally due to expire on 28 July 1941, the Act was kept in force until the end of that year by regulation under the Emergency Powers (Defence) Act[26] and did not disappear completely from the statute book until 1973.[27] As far as the war-time regulations proper were concerned, though initially exercised with restraint, the ease with which their discretionary powers could be exercised, allied to the escalation of the national crisis in the Summer of 1940, led to the promulgation of a series of vague and potentially repressive regulations reminiscent of the worst phases of the First World War.[28] Particularly noteworthy in this regard were regulation 2C, somewhat eerily entitled 'Corruption of public morale',[29] and regulation 2D[30] under which the Secretary of State took power to ban any newspaper which he was 'satisfied' was engaged in 'a systematic publication of matter which [was], in his opinion, calculated to foment opposition' to the war.[31] Under regulation 39BA, which was brought into force on 11 June 1940, it became an offence for any person to publish 'any report or statement relating to matters connected with the war which [was] likely to cause alarm or despondency'.[32] At the same time as these regulations were being pushed through, the internment power (the loose exercise of which we earlier saw being upheld by the courts in *Liversidge v Anderson*) was during 1940 to 1942 deployed with greater intensity and energy than ever.

It might be thought that the breadth and range of these war-time regulations would have led to their continuing into peace-time in the way that the Defence of the Realm Regulations had done after the First World War. It is significant, however, to note that, after the end of the

the Commons' Committee stage. No further reports appear to have been made, however. For further details of the operation of the Act, see S R & O 1939 No 1657.

[25] H C Debs, 23 May 1940, col 290 (Sir J Anderson). An independent adviser nominated by the Home Secretary was available to persons who objected to their treatment under the Act, with the adviser being required to report on his findings in each such case to the Secretary of State who was then required 'as soon as may be, [to] re-consider the case and either revoke the order or notify the person against whom it was made of his refusal to do so' (s 2(1)). Sir Walter Monckton KC was subsequently appointed: H C Debs, 1 August 1939, col 2167 (Sir S Hoare).

[26] S R & O 1941 No 1088.   [27] See Statute Law (Repeals) Act 1973, s 1.

[28] See generally N Stammers, *Civil Liberties in Britain during the Second World War: A Political Study* (1983); R Kidd, *British Liberty in Danger* (1940).

[29] S R & O 1940 No 680.   [30] S R & O 1940 No 828.

[31] It was under Regulation 2D that on 21 January 1941, the government banned both the *Daily Worker* and its sister publication *The Week*, at the same time using another Regulation to close down the printing presses where they had been produced: see Stammers, n 28 above, pp 104–8.

[32] S R & O 1940 No 938. A defence was set out of reasonable cause to believe that the report or statement was true and at the same time that the publication was 'not malicious and ought fairly to be excused'.

Second World War, it was thought possible quickly to remove those regulations thought most inimical in their impact on civil and political liberties.[33] The ordinary law was no longer the relatively empty vessel that it had once been. One of the more serious, because unprincipled, developments that we trace in this study has been the way in which various emergency regulations introduced during the First World War outgrew their origins and became, by the mid-1930s, part of the permanent legal landscape. This transformation was made possible by the enactment of the Incitement to Disaffection and Public Order Acts as ordinary legislation in 1934 and 1936 respectively, and by the broad common law rules formulated by the judges in *Duncan v Jones*,[34] *Thomas v Sawkins*[35] and *Elias v Pasmore*.[36] In Northern Ireland the key event was the making permanent, in 1933, of the previously temporary special powers legislation. The cumulative effect of these changes was that by the end of the 1930s, the executive's discretionary power in relation to the control of civil liberties had been greatly expanded without at the same time having been more carefully delineated or made more accountable in the manner of its exercise. Thus the many instances of the partisan application of police discretion against peace campaigners and Irish nationalists during the First World War and against the Communist Party in the mid-1920s find their echo in the similarly prejudiced deployment of police power against the hunger marchers and anti-fascists of the 1930s, with the vague legal framework once provided by the emergency regulations now having been supplanted by the similarly vague common law and by the provisions of the Public Order Act 1936. By the end of the period under discussion in this book, therefore, we see an executive power which has proved itself willing on occasion to act unlawfully, which has shown that it can still occasionally secure to itself draconian emergency power, and which can in any event always deploy to its advantage the flexible 'ordinary' law that was by the late 1930s to be found both in permanent statutes and in a reinvigorated, repressive common law. This was hardly a Rule of Law that Dicey would have recognised or applauded. What were the courts, Dicey's guarantors of the 'general principles of the constitution', doing in the face of such apparent executive excess? It is to this key question that we now turn.

---

[33] S R & O 1945 No 504, issued on 9 May 1945.
[34] See n 3 above.   [35] See n 4 above.   [36] See n 5 above.

Legality and the Role of the Courts

In Chapter 1 and again earlier in this chapter, we identified two meanings that we argued could be accorded to the principle of legality. We now recall our third requirement of the principle, a requirement which in Chapter 1 we considered brought us to the very boundaries of our principle of legality. This was for an autonomous and accountable legal process. It was because of his confidence in the judges that Dicey felt able to present the common law as the primary guardian of civil libertarian values in the English constitution. But so far as the data that have emerged in the course of this study is concerned, the results are stark indeed. It can be claimed with confidence that there is not a single example throughout the entire period of our study of a judicial decision in Britain at High Court or appellate level which can be said to have served to protect or to promote civil liberties against the hostile attentions of the State.[37] All that the advocates of the common law have to hold onto are a few judicial dissents, and even these are not necessarily unambiguously informed by any genuine commitment to the protection of civil liberties.[38] Indeed one of the startling lessons to emerge from our study is of the extent to which the senior judges simply failed to see the civil liberties implications of many of the cases with which they were dealing; Lord Hewart's denial at the start of his judgment in *Duncan v Jones* that the case before him had anything to do with the right to hold a public meeting was only possible from the man who had written *The New Despotism* because he genuinely could not believe or countenance the possibility that the English constitution provided any shelter for such radical activists.

The point is even clearer in the lower courts where antagonism and hostility was both closer to the surface and less restrained by the etiquette of legal discourse. The partiality of the magistrates was most obviously illustrated by the severity of the punishments that they meted out to the radical protestors brought before them. We have seen many examples of such harshness, particularly during the emergency of 1926 following the lock-out of the miners. Another extraordinary example of such excess occurred during the Second World War when Churchill himself had to intervene to order a review and a subsequent executive modification of the penalties being inflicted by justices of the peace on individuals brought before them charged with causing alarm or despondency under

---

[37] See now *DPP v Jones* [1999] 2 All ER 257.
[38] See for e.g. Lord Atkin in *Liversidge v Anderson*, n 9 above.

regulation 39BA, discussed above.[39] The executive had never felt compelled to act in this way before the war when it had been a Communist Party member or an unemployed protestor who had been brought before the local bench. Such activists were also vulnerable to punishment without ever being found guilty of any offence. Time and again we have seen procedural law being deployed against members of the Communist Party and other radical protestors, with the magistrates in every case being willing accomplices to such executive sleights-of-hand. It is not easy to see how the many binding over orders that litter the period, and through which it was possible to jail activists at key moments, can be reconciled with the principle of legality in even its narrowest form. Also controversial in this sense were such inhibiting devices as the denial of bail and the imposition of bail conditions, each of which was imposed at some point or another on protestors who found themselves entrapped within the legal process.

The sceptical conclusions that we might be inclined to draw from our scrutiny of the case law are further corroborated by evidence of the high degree of social solidarity that existed at this time between the executive and judicial branches of government. Complaints were frequently heard about the social composition of the local magistrates' courts, while the key post of chief stipendiary magistrate at Bow Street in London was for many years held by the Eton and Cambridge-educated Sir Chartres Biron. The handful of men from the higher judiciary who were invariably involved in the civil liberties cases of our period were certainly drawn from the same small élite as supplied the Cabinet and government ministers who ruled the country. A good example is Avory J, who in the first decades of the century confirmed the binding over order imposed on George Lansbury arising out of his suffragist activities in 1913,[40] upheld the legitimacy of police use of search powers during the First World War,[41] protected the power of internment in Ireland in 1920[42] and sanctioned the imprisonment of Communist Party general secretary Albert Inkpin in 1921.[43] The same judge also re-emerges many years later, in *Thomas v Sawkins*, where he is able to enjoy the satisfaction of seeing some

---

[39] H C Debs, 23 July 1940, col 598. For the results of the review see H C Debs, 8 August 1940, cols 407–8 (Sir J Anderson). A total of 28 cases were thought to require reconsideration. In one case a remission of part of a sentence of imprisonment was advised. In the remaining cases, the Secretary of State recommended the remission of substantial parts of the fines that had been imposed.

[40] *Lansbury v Riley* [1914] 3 KB 229.

[41] *Ex parte Norman* (1916) 114 LT 232. See Chapter 2 above.

[42] *R v Governor of Wormwood Scrubs Prison, ex parte Foy* [1920] 2 KB 305. See Chapter 7 above.

[43] *Inkpin v Roll* (1922) 86 JP 61. See Chapter 3 above.

of his remarks of twenty years before, in *Lansbury v Riley*, deployed by the Lord Chief Justice to the advantage of the police. Sir Horace Edmund Avory (1851–1935) was the second son of the clerk of the court at the Central Criminal Court, a post to which his brother succeeded in due course. He was educated at King's College London and at Corpus Christi College, Cambridge, where he took a third class in law and captained the College boat club. Twelve years as a prosecuting council at the Central Criminal Court led to the Inner Bar and then to the Bench, to which he was elevated in 1910. The honours came thick and fast throughout his long judicial career: honorary LLD from Cambridge in 1911; honorary fellowship at Corpus Christi College in 1912; fellow of King's College in the same year; treasurer of the Inner Temple in 1929; sworn in as a privy councillor while still a judge in 1932; member of the Garrick and United University Clubs. The only defence of personal liberty in which he appears to have engaged in the course of his long judicial career was that in the interests of the property owners who sought the return of their premises from munitions workers in *Chester v Bateson*.[44]

Avory J was not at all untypical of the kind of man on whom the judicial defence of civil liberties depended in the decades during and after the First World War. The *Dictionary of National Biography* records in a warm appreciation of his career that '[h]is judgement on any question of law [was] invariably treated as deserving the utmost respect'.[45] The encomium was penned by none other than his fellow Crown prosecutor Travers Humphreys, who was towards the end of Avory's career to join him on the Bench. Educated at Shrewsbury and Trinity Hall, Cambridge, and like Avory a member of the Garrick, Humphreys was prosecutor in the Campbell case[46] and he subsequently upheld the Trenchard ban when it came before him as a judge in *Duncan v Jones*. Other judges whose engagements with civil liberties issues have been noted in the course of this book invariably came from similar environments. These included: Richard Everard Webster, Viscount Alverstone (Charterhouse and Trinity College, Cambridge);[47] William Pickford, Baron Sterndale (Exeter College, Oxford and the Athenaeum and United University Clubs);[48] Sir John Sankey, Viscount Sankey (Lancing College and Jesus College, Oxford and the Oxford and Cambridge Club);[49] Sir Robert Younger, Baron Blanesburgh (Edinburgh Academy and Balliol College, Oxford and the Athenaeum);[50] Sir John Anthony

---

[44] [1920] 1 KB 829.
[45] *Dictionary of National Biography, 1931–1940* (1949), p 25.
[46] See pp 118–27 above.   [47] See p 33 above.   [48] See p 85 above and p 409 below.
[49] See p 409 below.   [50] Ibid.

Hawke (Merchant Taylors' School and St. John's College, Oxford and the Carlton and the Garrick);[51] Sir John Edward Singleton (Royal Grammar School, Lancaster and Pembroke College, Cambridge and the Oxford and Cambridge and the Athenaeum);[52] Thomas Walker Hobart Inskip, Viscount Caldecote (Clifton and King's College, Cambridge, and the Athenaeum and the MCC);[53] Gordon Hewart, Viscount Hewart of Bury (Manchester Grammar School and University College Oxford, and the Reform Club);[54] and Sir John Meir Astbury (Manchester Grammar School, Trinity College, Oxford, and the Garrick) whose judicially expressed views on the illegality of the general strike were to prove so helpful to the authorities of the day.[55]

The Home Secretaries whose actions or policies were directly or indirectly responsible for so much of our case law shared the same universities and clubs-circuit as the judges whose duty it was to sit in dispassionate judgment over them, and the police and other Crown servants for whom they were ultimately responsible. These included George Cave, Viscount Cave (Merchant Taylors' School and St John's College, Oxford and the Athenaeum and Carlton Clubs) who served as Home Secretary in 1916; Herbert Louis Samuel, first Viscount Samuel (University College School and Balliol College, Oxford and the Reform and National Liberal Clubs) whose various periods in the Home Office spanned from 1905 to 1932; Sir William Joynson-Hicks, first Viscount Brentford (Carlton and Constitutional Clubs) who was Home Secretary during the general strike; Sir John Gilmour (Trinity Hall, Cambridge and the Carlton Club) who served in the office from 1932 to 1935; and Sir John Simon, first Viscount Simon (Fettes and Wadham College, Oxford and the Reform Club) who was briefly Home Secretary during the First World War and who served in the post again between 1935 and 1937. Both lists reveal a shared success in securing the same high political honour either during or at the end of a politicians' or judges' career. The viscountcy seems to have been the traditional reward for this brand of State service. Of the foregoing, both Cave and Simon were also to serve as Lord Chancellor; indeed Simon had an extraordinary career as part lawyer and part politician, and in this he was not entirely untypical of the judges of the inter-war period, a point to which we now turn.

---

[51] See p 238 above.   [52] See p 263 above.   [53] See p 410 below.
[54] See pp 263–70 above.   [55] See pp 160–1 above.

The Politics of the Judiciary[56]

In our introductory chapter, we identified the value from the perspective of constitutional principle of a separation of the judiciary from the other two branches of government. Though we recognised the difficulties inherent in the whole concept of an independent judiciary, we considered that at its most basic this double insulation of the judges would have some value from the perspective of the principle of legality, even in a situation where there was generally a 'high degree of *ideological congruence*' between the various branches of government.[57] The patterns of social solidarity typified by this collection of political and judicial biographies might be thought to confirm our earlier suggestion that the best we can hope for is functional rather than genuine independence. There is some evidence that the judges did indeed see themselves as separate from the executive in this formal sense. A memorandum from all the judges of the Supreme Court of the Judicature presented to the Prime Minister on 4 December 1931 asserted that the judges were 'appointed to hold particular offices of dignity and exceptional importance' and that they occupied 'a vital place in the Constitution of this country', standing 'equally between the Crown and the Executive, and between the Executive and the subject'. The memorandum went on to assert that the judges had 'to discharge the gravest and most responsible of duties' for the proper discharge of which it had 'for over two centuries been considered essential that their security and independence should be maintained inviolate'. Equally impressively the judges declared that it 'was long ago said that there can be no true liberty in a country where the Judges are not entirely independent of the Government'. Had these sentiments been expressed in the context of the defence of civil liberties at a particularly divisive time, then it might be thought that here at last was valuable evidence of the importance of independence on the part of the judiciary. But the issue so exercising the higher judiciary was 'the recent reductions of the salary payable' to them which had raised 'certain considerations' which seemed 'to have escaped [the] notice' of the executive.[58] Certainly no functionally driven independence is detectable in the context of civil and political liberties. Indeed even the theoretical capacity for an autonomous

---

[56] The phrase is that of J A G Griffith, *The Politics of the Judiciary*, 5th edn (1997).

[57] The quotation is from R Miliband, *Socialism for a Sceptical Age* (1994), p 76. Emphasis in original. See p 16 above

[58] The memorandum is published at H L Debs, 27 July 1933, cols 1208–11.

legal process was undermined by a system of patronage which saw appointments to the Bench being made on political grounds, and which witnessed ministers of the Crown being elevated to the judiciary to adjudicate on disputes about legislation which they may earlier have had a hand in creating.

We have already noted in Chapter 1 Robert Stevens' view that for much of the period under consideration in this book, the most senior court in the country was 'highly politicized', this being true of both judicial decisions 'as well as in political activities'. As far as the judges who have had a direct impact on the law relating to civil liberties were concerned, we may begin by noting in this regard the case of Thomas Gardner Horridge, who as Horridge J presided over the jailing of the printers and publishers of *The Syndicalist* in 1912[59] and who was still around more than twenty years later to give the police their valuable dicta in *Elias v Pasmore*.[60] Horridge had been a Liberal MP for four years before his appointment to the bench and he was by no means untypical in having had a political past. John Astbury, who ruled (gratuitously) on the legality of the General Strike, had been Liberal MP for Southport for four years (1906 to 1910) before his appointment to the Chancery Division three years later. Both Hawke and Singleton JJ (the latter of whom sat with Hewart and Humphreys in *Duncan v Jones*)[61] had served as Conservative members in the House of Commons in the 1920s. The most notorious of these politico-judicial appointments, and one which had major civil liberties implications, involved the elevation of Charles John Darling to the bench after nine years as a Tory MP. As we saw in Chapter 2, the proposal was so outrageous that it excited the hostile attentions even of establishment opinion, with *The Times* publishing a strong leader seeking to preempt its occurrence. Yet as we have also seen, together with Lord Reading, Darling went on to adjudicate on most of the challenges to the Defence of the Realm Regulations that arose during and after the First World War and he decided all of them in favour of the government.

Like his colleague Avory J, Darling was made a privy councillor in 1917, but even his political partisanship pales by comparison with that of his senior colleague the Marquess of Reading, formerly Rufus Isaacs, Liberal MP for Reading from 1904 until 1913. It is Isaacs who more than any other judge during our period explodes even the formal divide between executive and judiciary, despite ironically being the son of a fruit

<hr/>

[59]　*R v Bowman* (1912) 76 JP 271　　　　[60] See n 5 above.　　　　[61] See n 3 above.

merchant in Spitalfields, and a pupil or student at neither an eminent private school nor a university of any sort. It might be thought that the position of the Lord Chief Justice in particular, to which Reading was appointed in 1913, raised important questions about independence even in the weakest sense of the term, but during his tenure in office Reading felt able, as we have already noted,[62] to undertake a variety of sensitive tasks on behalf of the government, included among which was a posting in 1917 as the government's special envoy to the USA. During his period in office, Reading was as we have seen frequently consulted by the very government whose actions he was from time to time adjudicating upon in the law courts in his judicial capacity. His was an unusual case, 'exceedingly anomalous' according to an admiring Lord Simon,[63] but examples of judicial involvement in executive functions are also to be found elsewhere. As we saw in Chapter 2, Pickford LJ, who was a member of the Court of Appeal which dismissed Zadig's habeas corpus application in 1916, was shortly afterwards invited to chair an inquiry into the origin and conduct of operations in the Dardenelles.[64] Two senior judges, Sir John Sankey and Sir Robert Younger, presided over an advisory committee which provided a veneer of legality for the internment power during the First World War, and Norman Birkett performed similar tasks in the course of the Second World War before his elevation to the bench in 1941.

There was yet another dimension to the appointment of Rufus Isaacs, however, which was if anything even more subversive of the weak notion of judicial autonomy described above than were his executive functions when on the bench. As we have seen in relation to both Avory and Humphreys JJ, many of the key judges of our period learned their trade as prosecuting counsel, but Isaacs went one further than this, since he had served as a law officer (Solicitor General followed by Attorney General) in Asquith's Liberal administration for nearly three years before his appointment as Lord Chief Justice. In the sixteen months immediately prior to his appointment he also sat in the Cabinet, so the many war-time cases on which Isaacs sat during this period need to be also seen in the light of this intimate connection with many of those over whom he was adjudicating. This startling interaction between the executive and judicial branches was by no means unique. Viscount Hailsham had

[62] See Chapter 2 above.

[63] *Dictionary of National Biography, 1931–1940*, n 45 above, p 466.

[64] This was on the death of Lord Cromer early in 1917. The report was published on 8 March 1917. Pickford was later appointed to the Mastership of the Rolls and elevated to the Lords as Baron Sterndale.

served two terms as Attorney General before his elevation as Lord Chancellor in 1928. Sir Edward Carson moved from a succession of senior positions in Cabinet to a position in the House of Lords as a Lord of Appeal in May 1921. Sir John Simon served as Attorney General as well as Home Secretary before eventually becoming Lord Chancellor in 1940. Many of the most important cases of our period were decided by men who were either still in the Cabinet (as was the case in *Zadig*[65] in which Lord Chancellor Finlay, another former law officer, presided in the Lords) or (which was more usual) by men who had previously served in high political office concerned with domestic affairs. The leading majority judgment in *Liversidge v Anderson*[66] was given by the former Lord Chancellor Lord Maugham, who had served briefly in Chamberlain's Cabinet before the outbreak of war. The 1911 trial of Max Schultz for the commission of a number of offences under the 1889 Official Secrets Act was presided over by Alverstone LCJ who as Attorney General Sir Richard Webster had introduced the Bill into the Commons twenty-two years before. The *Zadig* case was argued for the government by the then Attorney General F E Smith and the then Solicitor General Sir Gordon Hewart. Both men went on to high judicial office, Smith as Lord Chancellor, the first Earl of Birkenhead and Hewart as Lord Chief Justice.

We have already noted Hewart's pivotal role in the reception into the common law in the 1930s of many of the emergency powers which he had had a hand in drafting as Attorney General at the time of the enactment of the Emergency Powers Act 1920. As the first Lord Chief Justice of Northern Ireland, the former Attorney General for Ireland Sir Denis Henry was able to legitimise the internment power which the new administration in the Province had almost immediately introduced by way of delegated legislation, and which was not far removed from the internment provisions which he had as a member of the executive administered and defended throughout the whole island of Ireland just a couple of years earlier.[67] Viscount Caldecote presided over many of the challenges to the internment power in the Second World War, invariably finding in favour of the authorities. We have frequently come across him as the Attorney General Sir Thomas Inskip, advising the Cabinet on the breadth of public order powers available to deal with the hunger marchers and steering the unpopular Incitement to Disaffection Act 1934 through a hostile House of Commons. Extraordinarily, he had been in

---

[65] *R v Halliday* [1917] AC 260.   [66] See n 9 above.   [67] See Chapter 7 above.

the Cabinet which had the year before his elevation to the Bench decided upon the regulatory changes on internment over which as Lord Chief Justice he was later to preside so sympathetically. After he had found for the government in one habeas corpus case arising out of the war-time internment power, Caldecote wrote privately to the Secretary of State 'as a friend' expressing concern at the slowness of proceedings under the regulation and volunteering the view that many of the internees were 'wholly innocent and known to have the most friendly feelings towards this country'. This does not seem to have been an opinion that he allowed to influence himself in his judicial capacity.[68]

Civil Liberties and the Role of Parliament

Frequently disregarded by the executive and forsaken by the courts, those who sought to exercise their civil liberties had a third branch of government to which in theory they could turn for their defence. This was of course the legislative arm, on which as we have seen in Chapter 1 Dicey also placed great reliance. It will be remembered that in Chapter 1, we identified a paradox in the concept of parliamentary sovereignty, to the extent that a popularly elected assembly is required in the democratic age to perform two quite different and contradictory functions, the first being to legislate to carry out the wishes of the electorate with speed and efficiency, and the second being to scrutinise such proposed legislation and the conduct of the executive generally, so as to ensure that neither such laws nor any such government actions illegitimately erode civil liberties. Already somewhat unbalanced at the start of the twentieth century, a combination of the Party system, the control of parliamentary time by the governing Party and the lack of a clearly defined separation of the executive and legislative branches has meant that the scrutiny function of Parliament had not been allowed fully to develop during the first half of the twentieth century. Evidence of this failure can be seen in the rushed enactment of the Official Secrets Act 1911, in the wide powers given to the executive in the defence of the realm legislation in 1914 and in the breadth of the Emergency Powers Act 1920. Unlike the earlier war-time legislation, the last at least required some parliamentary oversight of the regulations made under its authority, but as we saw in Chapter 4 these parliamentary occasions were usually perfunctory, being

---

[68] The Lord Chief Justice went on to offer the Home Office some judges, possibly from the Court of Appeal, to speed the process up, but this was declined by the authorities. These details are in Simpson, n 21 above, pp 308–11.

frequently uncritical of the authorities that were supposedly being brought before Parliament to account for their actions.

The capacity of Parliament to oversee the executive in other than the purely lawmaking sphere was also frequently found wanting. Time and again there were parliamentary majorities in support of government action, no matter how damaging it might have been for the protection of civil liberties or subversive of the principles of the Rule of Law. The pressure that was mustered in the wake of the ill-fated Campbell prosecution in 1924, to precipitate the administration's collapse, was extremely unusual, reflecting the exceptional situation of a minority government. Just months later, the deposed Prime Minister Ramsay MacDonald was to reveal the more characteristic weakness of Parliament when a majority of its members were prepared to stand shoulder to shoulder with the government when he launched from the opposition benches a scathing attack on the new government's involvement in the 1925 sedition trials.[69] An extreme illustration of Parliament's failure to discharge its constitutional duty to hold the executive to account comes at the end of our period, with the rushing through, in the final week before the Summer recess, of all stages in both Houses of the Prevention of Violence (Temporary Provisions) Act 1939. The measure had only been considered for the first time by the Cabinet on 5 July, with legislative action being approved by the Cabinet's home affairs sub-committee as late as 19 July.[70] Nine days later, however, it was law, with neither the Commons nor the Lords having been able or inclined to halt or even delay a draconian Bill which had clear implications for civil liberties.[71]

The Home Secretary justified the government's decision to rush the 1939 Act into law on two grounds which were not as comprehensively explained to the Commons as they might have been. The first of these related to a 'very remarkable document'[72] uncovered by the police. Known as the 'S Plan',[73] the effect of the memorandum was to show the IRA in a deadly and efficient light, as an organisation which was deeply involved in preparations to attack the water supply, the drainage system, the fire service, the transport infrastructure and the electricity supply. According to Sir Samuel, the IRA had even 'been engaged upon a plan

---

[69] See p 146 above. The government survived.   [70] See O G Lomas, n 19 above.
[71] The debates in the House of Commons are at H C Debs, 24 July 1939, cols 1047–127 (Second Reading); H C Debs, 26 July 1939, cols 1502–602 (Committee); H C Debs, 26 July 1939, cols 1602–8 (Report, and Third Reading). For the debates in the House of Lords, see H L Debs, 28 July 1939, cols 644–55 (Second Reading); cols 655–64 (Committee); col 664 (Third Reading).
[72] H C Debs, 24 July 1939, col 1048 (Sir S Hoare).   [73] Ibid, cols 1047–8.

to blow up the Houses of Parliament'.[74] This dramatic aspect of the Minister's presentation had the desired effect, of both intimidating the House and ensuring favourable press coverage on the following day.[75] It also seemed to explain why action was needed so quickly that the Bill was required to be enacted in a matter of days just before the Summer recess. But little attention was paid to Sir Samuel's admission that the government had had this damaging document since 'about the beginning of the year',[76] in which case it could have been reasonably asked whether the authorities had not been culpably negligent in leaving action on such a supposedly vital document to such a late moment. There was, however, a second and even more dramatic reason for urgency. The Secretary of State went on to tell the Commons that 'we have in our possession reliable information that the [IRA] campaign is being closely watched and actively stimulated by foreign organisations'.[77] In the febrile atmosphere of the times, it was not surprising that the House should have immediately suspected German involvement, though the Home Secretary refused to elaborate further, asking Members on a number of occasions 'not to press me for details'.[78] Such reticence was understandable, since Lomas' study of the official papers relating to the Act has shown that the only foreign involvement of which the Cabinet was aware was Irish-American rather than European in nature.[79] The claim had nevertheless its desired effect.

Despite its neglected status, and the invariable quiescence of the vast majority of parliamentarians, it has however been the parliamentary branch which has done comparatively more to protect civil liberties in the course of our period than any other branch of government. The executive has been invariably able to drive its major policy initiatives through the Commons, but this has been occasionally only after a fight, and has sometimes even involved compromise and, on very rare occasions, defeat. The most significant victory for civil liberties that we have encountered was the emasculation of the Incitement to Disaffection Bill in 1934, and significant concessions were also secured from the executive

---

[74] Ibid, col 1052.

[75] *The Times* had the 'S' plan in headlines on the day after the debate: see Lomas, n 19 above, p 28.

[76] Sir Samuel Hoare admitted this in reply to a question from D N Pritt: H C Debs, 24 July 1939, col 1049.

[77] Sir Samuel Hoare asserted this in reply to a question from D N Pritt: H C Debs, 24 July 1939, col 1052.

[78] Ibid.

[79] See Lomas, n 19 above, p 29. In fact the advice to the Cabinet had gone even further than this, categorically declaring that there was no evidence of any other foreign involvement.

during the passage of the anti-civil libertarian parts of the Public Order Bill two years later. During both wars, a parliamentary backlash recovered some of the freedoms that had been given up in the panic at the start of war. In 1915 it was paradoxically the Lords who were to the fore in re-establishing the right to jury trial, just as it had been individual members of the Commons who had achieved a handful of significant changes to some of the more draconian regulations the year before. Though Parliament rushed emergency legislation through at the start of the Second World War, the Commons did engage in a wide-ranging and highly critical debate in the Commons just three months later, which led to the revision of many of the emergency regulations that had been previously promulgated, including the internment power (though we have already seen how the latter provision was subsequently expanded by the courts to the advantage of the executive). Indeed it is a bleak tribute to Parliament's power that in legislation passed both at the start and at the end of our period, the Official Secrets Act 1911 and the Prevention of Violence (Temporary Provisions) Act 1939 respectively, the executive felt the need to allow the legislative branch to be mislead as to the true need and breadth of the proposals before it.

Parliament's performance was not, therefore, always to be condemned. We saw in Chapter 1 how active the legislative branch was both before and during the period under review in securing the most basic freedom of political participation, the right to vote. There were other activities by Parliament which were also praiseworthy, and that these sometimes involved an apparent restriction on the liberty of some individuals or groups does not mean that for that reason alone they are automatically to be criticised. We should not be understood in this study to be suggesting that political freedom must always be without limits. One of the essential requirements of democracy is the need to constrain the liberty of some in order to enhance the liberty of others. That which appears as a restriction may on reflection, and viewed more generally, be a liberating measure. A good example of this in the period of this study is of course the Public Order Act 1936, and in particular those sections which were directed at the scourge of fascism which had appeared menacingly on the streets of London and elsewhere in the 1930s. It is true that this was a government bill, and that it would almost certainly not have been passed without government support. But on the other hand, Parliament's role was crucial, not only in demonstrating cross party support for the measure but also for acting as a focus for the popular agitation to restrict the activities of the fascists and to protect the targets of their harassment and abuse. The sections aimed at the fascists in the Public Order Act 1936 were a monument to the integrity of the parliamentary system and to the efficacy of political action rather than litigation as a strategy for change.[80] But for all that the 1936 Act was not an unequivocal triumph, being aimed not only at fascists but also the dispossessed, and containing in section 3 the type of unconstrained discretionary power which severely undermines the principle of legality. This was to come to be deployed against peaceful protest of a much more benign kind, and indeed contained executive powers which inevitably were to be extended in another decade of feverish political activity some fifty years later.

Conclusion

This inquiry into the protection of civil liberties in Britain in the first half of the twentieth century must end on a pessimistic note. Our conclusion is that neither the Rule of Law nor the principle of legality operated in the way that constitutional principle suggested that they should. In particular it cannot be said with any confidence that either operated as a constraint on executive power for the better protection of civil liberties. In every decade under examination, constitutional principle is not only undermined at the level of theory, but it is also further repudiated by constitutional practice. The executive was never wholly committed to legality, just as the legislature as an institution was largely uninterested in accountability, and the judiciary seemed more often than not positively hostile to the protection of civil liberties. Indeed, one of the most startling points to emerge is the degree to which emergency rather than ordinary law was the normal state of affairs in the Britain of our period. When we recall the Northern Ireland Special Powers Act as well as the war-time and Emergency Powers Act regulations in Britain, it becomes apparent that at no point from the onset of the First World War until the end of the Second was the United Kingdom wholly free of emergency law. The point is given added force when account is taken of the fact that, through their reception into the ordinary law in the 1930s, many erstwhile emergency powers became wholly normalised within a greatly expanded body of statute and common law.

As we saw in Chapter 1, the inter-war years were also those when the democratisation of Britain was completed, with the legislation of 1918

---

[80] In saying this we appreciate that one of the lessons to be drawn from the anti-fascist agitation which helped produce the Public Order Act is that legitimate political action may not always be, and historically has not been, restricted to the parliamentary sphere alone.

and 1928 finally achieving full adult suffrage. This is the deeper background against which to view the protection of civil liberties during these years. To an old order which had suffered the triple shock of the First World War, the Irish secession and the Russian revolution, the prospect of democracy must have seemed truly appalling, with its near certainty of a socialist parliamentary majority and (apparently inevitable) consequent radical transformation of society. The 'taming of the franchise'[81] that took place at this time took many forms. In the context of this study, we note that the series of crises of law and order that unfolded during our period bridged the gap between the old order and the new democratic society that was emerging, enabling the former to deploy the law in a rearguard, pre-emptive action against the changes that it was thought democracy was likely to bring. In this sense, the law was far from being a protector of civil liberties; rather it was an 'iron heel'[82] used to stamp out displays of energetic political activism on the ground. In this it enjoyed a high measure of success, with it being hard in retrospect to see how the Labour Administration of 1945 to 1951 could have emerged other than out of the radical turmoil caused by another savage war. The Britain of the late 1930s seemed to have successfully undermined, and certainly it had managed to control, the civil liberties of those whose political views threatened a radical transformation of that society.

Despite all its flaws and its patent detachment from reality on the ground, Dicey's rhetoric about constitutional principle, the Rule of Law and the protection of civil liberties was not entirely extinguished. Members of the executive certainly felt bound by it when they sought legislative legitimacy for their actions. No one who has read the long debates on the meaning of each word in the various clauses before the Commons Standing Committee which scrutinised the Incitement to Disaffection Bill could have doubted that, to the principal executive actors at least, what these proposed clauses precisely said did in an important sense matter. The same was true by extension of all the legislation passed during the period. It was not therefore a case of rule by the executive in a formal sense. The authorities did as we have seen frequently break the law, but they did not regard it as irrelevant that the law had been broken. Their preference was for legal power; hence the interminable confidential discussions in Cabinet and elsewhere through-

---

[81] C B Macpherson, *The Life and Times of Liberal Democracy* (1977), pp 64–9. See also R McKibbin *Class and Cultures. England 1918–51* (1998) for a valuable survey which shows clearly the extent to which the values of democracy were not internalised within Britain during these years.

[82] Jack London, *The Iron Heel* (1971 edn). The term was widely used by the *Workers' Weekly* in the 1920s.

out the period about the need for and the political advisability of further repressive legislation. In the same way, when the conduct of its police officers was impugned in court, the executive did not simply assert in response the requirements of executive will, but sought rather to root the impugned official behaviour in the law, a concept which the executive for these purposes certainly perceived as independent and autonomous. That these appeals to legal legitimacy invariably succeeded should not blind us to the significance of the fact that they were undertaken.

The principle of the Rule of Law mattered most of all however to those who sought to engage in radical politics under the protection it notionally afforded their civil liberties. It was these people, generally of the Left but also during the 1930s from the Right, for whom the rhetoric of civil liberties and the Rule of Law could be deployed to protective advantage. The mistake made by the NCCL was to confuse the rhetoric with reality. Its series of judicial defeats in the 1930s brought this message home. But to the political activists, unburdened by the ambitions of litigation, the established rhetoric of the Rule of Law could be, and frequently was, used to force government (however briefly) back on the defensive. Thus at the depths of each of the crises discussed in this study, it was always possible for every point of view to be expressed in the House of Commons, no matter how unpopular or radical it was, or how likely it was to be prohibited outside the House. These exchanges frequently involved invocation of traditional principles rooted in civil liberties and the principle of legality. We have seen for example how in 1926 the MP Shipurji Saklatvala was able to attack in the Chamber the fact that he had been banned from speaking outside it, and it was in the course of an adjournment debate around the same time that the Home Secretary, William Joynson-Hicks, was forced to admit that he had quite unlawfully imposed a ban on Communist Party meetings. When we speak of the scrutiny function of Parliament in this context, therefore, we are reminded that it is not the assembly as a whole that we have in mind but rather the dedicated involvement of a small band of tireless and fearless campaigners, men and women whose commitment to the protection of civil liberties led them frequently to suffer the wrath and the ill-informed contempt of the vast majority of the House. It was mainly through the early day motions, the adjournment debates, the constant stream of questions for ministers that campaigners like Charles Trevelyan, George Lansbury, Captain Wedgewood Benn, Dingle Foot, D N Pritt and Sir Stafford Cripps kept the protection of civil liberties an issue to the forefront of public concern during the dark decades from the start of the First to the end of the Second World War. Without these determined figures, Parliament would have quickly slunk into the complacent torpor that seemed to have engulfed the law courts on the Strand.[83]

The story of civil liberties that we have told is more than a history of the contribution made by the three branches of government. Outside the realms of official power, there is a more uplifting theme on which to end. That civil liberties survived during our period is ultimately due to the individuals who refused to give up their freedom, who were determined in their pursuit of a better life, for themselves, their families but most of all for their communities. These were the men and women many of whose goals have been vindicated by history but whose political campaigns were invariably conducted in the teeth of opposition from all official branches of the State. It was men and women like John MacLean, James Connolly, Albert Inkpin, William Gallacher, Wal Hannington, Tom Mann, Ronald Kidd and Katherine Duncan who kept the flame of liberty burning during these otherwise dark years. Nor should we forget the many thousands of men and women, whose names are now long lost, who stood in solidarity with their leaders, and who marched, protested, and sometimes battled for a better life. Some of these otherwise anonymous individuals live on in the law reports and legal journals as defendants in criminal actions, being jailed for their actions of commitment and of bravery in pursuit of their ideals: A J Thomas, jailed for eighteen months for handing out leaflets at Aldershot; W T Wilkinson, the sixty-year-old managing director of the Utopia Press jailed for nine months under the Incitement to Mutiny Act by Hawke J; the twelve defendants convicted after ten minutes of deliberation in the 1925 sedition trial; and many more. It is fitting that this long inquiry should end by celebrating the courage, idealism and tenacity of these civil liberties pioneers, to whom modern Britain owes so much.

---

[83] The tragedy is that so few of their colleagues were prepared to stand behind them to defend these fundamental principles.

Appendix

Public Record Office Files

In the course of this study it was discovered that a large amount of potentially relevant material is held at the Public Record Office (PRO). Under the Public Records Act 1958 (as amended by the Public Records Act 1967), public records are not made available for public inspection until thirty years after they were created. The Act provides, however, that the thirty-year period may be extended (s 5(1)), though no grounds for withholding access are set out in the Act. The Act also provides that some records may be retained by departments rather than transferred to the PRO where there is an again unspecified 'special reason' for doing so (s 3(4)). The procedures are explained at some length in the White Paper on *Open Government* (Cm 2290, 1993), ch 9.

In addition to the foregoing, there was issued in 1993 a Code of Practice on Access to Government Information, with a revised second edition being published in 1997. This is said to be designed to support the then government's policy of 'extending access to official information, and responding to reasonable requests for information' (Part I, para 1). According to the Code of Practice, the 'approach to the release of information should in all cases be based on the assumption that information should be released except where disclosure would not be in the public interest, as specified in Part II of the Code' (ibid). The Code is not legally enforceable, and is not intended to override statutory provisions on access to public records, whether over or under thirty years old (Part I, para 9).

On 16 October 1997 we wrote to the Home Office requesting that 101 pieces be opened. All but one are closed for 100 years,[1] and all relate to the period from 1908 to 1945. We were advised that although the Home Office is willing to consider applications to open individual files, the procedure requires a review of the material contained in them, in order to prevent the disclosure of information 'which ought not to be released: for example because it might cause substantial distress to a living individual or their close relatives, or because it still has a bearing on national security or intelligence'. We were also informed that a review of over 100 files was beyond the resources of the appropriate Home Office department, and our request was refused under the Code of Practice on Access to Government Information, 2nd edn (1997), Part II, para 9.

Part II contains categories of information which are exempt from the commitment to provide information set out in the Code, and para 9 applies to:

Requests for information which are vexatious or manifestly unreasonable or are formulated in too general a manner, or which (because of the amount of information to be

---

[1] The exception is closed for 75 years.

processed or the need to retrieve information from files not in current use) would require unreasonable diversion of resources.

It was not suggested that there was anything vexatious about our request for access, but that it was more than the Home Office could 'cope with in a reasonable time'. Although the department was willing to 'consider reviewing a selected sample of files to assist [our] research', it was pointed out that 'a review of the closure period of a single piece could take several months as it is likely that other government departments would need to be consulted'. We were nevertheless encouraged to 'identify one or two key pieces'.

It proved impossible to do so: the files to which we sought access were all identified because we thought they would be of value. Quite how much value they would be is impossible to say until we had examined them. So they remain closed (though it appears that one—relating to the activities of George Lansbury MP—has since been opened). We remain baffled why it is thought necessary to close for 100 years Home Office (not Security Service) files relating to matters such as: (a) disturbances at public meetings 1925–1936, (b) the activities and publications of the Industrial Workers of the World 1917–1925, and (c) the Law Officers' Opinion under the Emergency Regulations 1921 'as to recovery of expenses incurred by the Government in working Public Utility undertakings in default of the normal contractor'. We take this opportunity to list the pieces to which access was denied: the title of each is often in itself very revealing. The pieces in question are all held in the Home Office class HO 144 at the Public Record Office. They are as follows:

	HO 144	Date	Title
1	7044	1908–1927	Hyde Park: disturbance and annoying or insulting behaviour.
2	1650	1909–1921	Suppression of disturbances in the Metropolitan Area during war.
3	20069	1925–1936	Disturbances at public meetings.
4	22936	1911–1947	Military Aid to Civil Power: Law Officers' opinion.
5	8795	1917–1925	Industrial Workers of the World: activities and publications.
6	21188	1920–1939	Cyphers for emergency use in a period of industrial unrest.
7	4549	1919–1925	Government emergency arrangements in the event of a General Strike.
8	5992	1920–1926	Activities of Mr George Lansbury, MP.

	HO 144	Date	Title
9	7480	1921–1927	Emergency Powers Bill and Act 1920: Regulations 1921; Law Officers' Opinion as to recovery of expenses incurred by the Government in working Public Utility undertakings in default of the normal authority.
10	4663	1921–1925	Question of withholding passport facilities to notorious Communist (William Gallacher).
11	1746–1747	1921–1922	The Miners' Strike, 1921.
12	1703	1921	Persons attempting to cause disaffection among HM Forces. HO Circular to Police.
13	1705	1921	Offences connected with coal dispute. Cases dealt with at Swansea Assizes, July, 1921.
14	4684	1921–1925	Activities of the Communist Party of Great Britain. The relative responsibility of Attorney General and Home Secretary in instituting political prosecutions.
15	20097	1927–1936	Use of tear gas by police.
16	20618	1922–1933	Walter Hannington: subversive activities.
17	13544	1920–1931	Restrictions on the issue of passports to British subjects liable to cause disturbance abroad.
18	21356	1922–1939	Occurrences known or believed to have been caused by members of the IRA.
19	21357	1939	Ditto
20	21358	1939–1940	Ditto
21	6099	1923–1926	Political activities and subsequent imprisonment of Shapurji Saklatvala, MP.
22	6103	1923–1926	Subversive literature, etc.: policy as to prosecution.
23	6116	1923–1926	General Strike, 1926: emergency arrangements.
24	4775	1923–1925	British Fascists Movement.
25	5318	1925	Dangerous alien Communists and activities of the Communist Party of Great Britain.
26	21370	1924–1940	Communist activity: exchange of information with foreign powers.
27	6682	1925–1926	Communist Party: activities.

	HO 144	Date	Title
28	6707	1925–1926	Emergency Organisation: appointment of police liaison officers.
29	6751	1925–1926	General Strike, 1926: protection of convoys, vulnerable points, etc., by police with naval and military assistance.
30	22372	1925–1929	Communist propaganda to incite His Majesty's Forces to mutiny. Sedition charge against John Gollan.
31	22373	1930–1934	Communist propaganda to incite His Majesty's Forces to mutiny. Sedition charge against John Gollan.
32	6891	1926	Miners' Strike, May 1926: Russian money, telegrams and letters from abroad.
33	7983	1926–1927	Prohibition of meetings or processions: Orders under Regulation 22 of the Emergency Regulations 1926.
34	6894	1926	General Strike, 1926: local communist newspaper: police proceedings under Emergency Regulations.
35	9237	1926–1928	General Strike, May 1926: publications likely to cause mutiny, sedition, disaffection, etc.; Order under Emergency Regulations, 1926, dated 4 May 1926.
36	6896	1926	General Strike, 1926: conduct of certain Justices of the Peace.
37	6898	1926	Convictions arising out of the General Strike in Birmingham.
38	6900	1926	General Strike, 1926, formation of the Civil Constabulary Reserve.
39	7985	1926–1927	Payments from Russia in aid of the General Strike.
40	22377	1926	General Strike, 1926: Leniency of sentences passed by Ipswich Bench: complaint by Chief Constable; question of appointing temporary Stipendiary.
41	6902	1926	General Strike, 1926: situation reports.
42	6903	1926	General Strike, 1926: police baton charge at Poplar.

	HO 144	**Date**	**Title**
43	6904	1926	General Strike, 1926: proceedings under the Emergency Regulations, Yorkshire (West Riding).
44	12050	1926–1930	General Strike, May 1926: records of emergency proceedings and convictions and Home Office circulars; conduct of magistrates; amnesty for persons in prison for offences under Emergency Regulations; deputation to Lord Birkenhead.
45	9240	1926–1928	General Strike, May 1926: Emergency Services Vote, 1926–27.
46	7994	1926–1927	Proceedings under the Emergency Regulations 1926: Northumberland.
47	9486	1927–1928	Communist propaganda: question of expediency in instituting prosecutions.
48	12143	1927–1930	Unemployed miners' march to London in 1927. March of the unemployed to London in 1929. Hunger march to London in 1930.
49	22404	1927–1930	Communist activities in India. Merrut conspiracy trial: evidence as to intercepted mail, telegraphs, etc under Home Office Warrants.
50	17832	1929 Nov. 12–1931 Oct. 30	Interception of communist propaganda literature transmitted by post from abroad.
51	17833	1931 Nov. 14–1932 Apr. 25	Ditto
52	17834	1932 June 20–1933 Jan. 27	Ditto
53	22581	1930–1931	Communist Party and National Unemployed Workers' Movement: demonstrations and speeches.
54	22582	1932–1933	Ditto
55	12051	1926–1930	General Strike, May 1926: proceedings under Emergency Regulations at Durham.
56	10670	1926–1929	General Strike, May 1926: Councils of Action and Strike Committees.
57	8014	1926–1927	Trade Disputes and Trade Unions Bill, 1927.
58	10671	1926–1929	General Strike, May 1926: the Cramlington Miners convicted of derailing the 'Flying Scotsman'.

	HO 144	**Date**	**Title**
59	6939	1926	General Strike, 1926: conviction of city councillor who was also member of Hull Watch Committee.
60	17711	1925–1933	Aliens engaging in communist activities.
61	22381	1926–1927	Communist Party activities: consideration of proceedings against leaders; National Minority Movement.
62	8208	1926–1927	Tylorstown Riots: sentences passed at Glamorgan Assizes.
63	8226	1926–1927	Members of Monmouth County Council convicted of rioting at Pontypool.
64	22388	1927–1932	Communist activities amongst the population.
65	13821	1928 Mar.–May	Russian Banks and Communist Funds: investigations and inquiries.
66	13822	1928 May–1931 Mar.	Ditto
67	22587	1932	Demonstrations by Bristol unemployed workers between 12 Apr. and 28 Oct. 1932.
68	22588	1931–1932	Communist propaganda: articles contravening the law.
69	16355	1931–1932	Demonstrations by unemployed in London.
70	21037	1931–1938	Police arrangements to prevent disorder at public meetings in Liverpool.
71	16379	1932 Sept. 20–Oct. 31	Unlawful assembly at Mardy: conviction of Arthur Horner and others.
72	18186	1932 Sept. 20–Oct. 31	National Unemployed Workers' Union: march to London in protest against means test.
73	18187	1932 Nov. 1–1933 Jan. 2	Ditto
74	18294	1932–1933	Powers and duties of the police at meetings, processions and demonstrations.
75	21511	1932–1941	Allegations of the teaching of Communist doctrines at Dartington Hall Co-educational School.
76	21957	1938–1944	Communist publications.
77	19835	1932 Dec. 20–1933 Jan. 8	Two organisers (Tom Mann and another) of a proposed mass demonstration of unemployed, imprisoned for refusing to enter into recognisance

	HO 144	**Date**	**Title**
			to keep the peace and to be of good behaviour. Correspondence between the Prime Minister and the Home Secretary; approval of the court proceedings invoking an Act of 1360.
78	19836	1933 Jan. 12–May 17	Ditto
79	19284	1932–1934	Kath Sinclair Duncan, communist: obstruction of police and breach of the peace.
80	19838	1933/1935	'Daily Worker': scurrilous articles and cartoons.
81	20132	1933–1936	Industrial unrest and communist activities in South Wales.
82	19843	1933 Nov. 1–1934 Feb. 6	National Hunger Marches to London: Communist influence.
83	19844	1934 Feb. 6–13	Ditto
84	19845	1934 Feb. 15–22	Ditto
85	19846	1934 Feb. 26–1935 Jan. 29	Ditto
86	19701	1934 Apr. 17–June 21	Incitement to Disaffection Bill 1934.
87	19702	1934 June 25–Nov. 4	Ditto
88	2153	1932 Mar. 28–1936 Sept. 14	Spanish Civil War: Communist demonstrations.
89	21524	1936 Sept. 18–1941 Jan. 13	Ditto
90	20696	1936 July 29–Oct. 23	Hunger March, 1936.
91	20697	1936 Oct. 27–1937 Jan. 19	Ditto
92	23049	1937	Poster exhibiting hammer and sickle superimposed upon a crucifix: public indignation and demand for legal action.
93	21529	1936–1941	Reports on the activities of the 'Left Book Club'.
94	20058	1926–1935	Memoranda on problems of internal security prepared by the Home Office for the Committee of Imperial Defence.

	HO 144	**Date**	**Title**
95	21316	1939	Prevention of Violence (Temporary Provisions) Bill 1939.
96	22459	1939–1945	Stephen Lally: revocation of Expulsion Order made under the Prevention of Violence (Temporary Provisions) Act, 1939.
97	22462	1939–1944	Orders made under Regulation 39E of Defence (General) Regulations, 1939 prohibiting holding of public processions.
98	22474	1940	Subversive activities of Peace Pledge Union.
99	21991	1940–1944	Suppression of 'The Daily Worker'.
100	21635	1940–1942	Albert Harry Campbell: detained under Defence Regulations 18B; writ served upon Sir John Anderson and others.
101	8144	1926–1927	Question of the right to be registered as an elector whilst in prison.

Select Bibliography

ALLAN, T.R.S. 1993. *Law, Liberty, and Justice: Legal Foundations of British Constitutionalism* (Oxford: Clarendon Press).

ALLEN, C.K. 1942. 'Regulation 18B and Reasonable Cause' (58) *Law Quarterly Review* 232.

ANDERSON, G.D. 1983. *Fascists, Communists, and the National Government for Civil Liberties in Great Britain, 1931–37* (London: University of Missouri Press).

ANDREW, C. 1986. *Secret Service: The Making of the British Intelligence Community* (London: Heinemann).

BAILEY, S.H., HARRIS, D.J., and JONES, B.L. 1980. *Civil Liberties: Cases and Materials* (London: Butterworths), 4th edn. 1995.

BAKER, J. 1937. *The Law of Political Uniforms, Public Meetings and Private Armies* (London: H. A. Just & Co).

BARNES, T. 1979. 'Special Branch and the First Labour Government' (22) *Historical Journal* 941.

BARTON, B. 1988. *Brookeborough. The Making of a Prime Minister* (Belfast: Institute of Irish Studies, Queen's University of Belfast).

BATY, T. and MORGAN, J.H. 1915. *War, Its Conduct and Legal Results* (London: John Murray).

BENEWICK, R. 1969. *Political Violence and Public Order: A Study of British Fascism* (London: Allen Lane).

BENEWICK, R. 1972. *The Fascist Movement in Britain* (London: Allen Lane).

BENNETT, G. 1999. *A Most Extraordinary and Mysterious Business: The Zinoviev Letter of 1924* (London: Foreign and Commonwealth Office).

BERNSTEIN, E. 1993. *The Preconditions of Socialism* (Cambridge: Cambridge University Press).

BERRESFORD ELLIS, P. (ed.). 1973. *James Connolly: Selected Writings* (Harmondsworth: Penguin)

BEW, P., GIBBON, P., and PATTERSON, H. 1995. *Northern Ireland, 1921–1944: Political Forces and Social Classes* (London: Serif).

BIBBINGS, L. 1995. 'State Reaction to Conscientious Objection' in Loveland, I. (ed.), *Frontiers of Criminality* (London: Sweet and Maxwell).

BIRON, Sir C. 1936. *Without Prejudice: Impressions of Life and Law* (London: Faber and Faber).

BLACKBURN, R. (ed.). 1993. *Rights of Citizenship* (London: Mansell).

BLACKSTONE, W. 1775. *Commentaries on the Laws of England in Four Books* (1st pub. in 1765) (Oxford: Oxford University Press).

BLAKE, R. 1970. *The Conservative Party from Peel to Churchill* (London: Eyre and Spottiswoode).

BOWES, S. 1966. *The Police and Civil Liberties* (London: Lawrence and Wishart).

BOWMAN, H.M. 1916. 'Martial Law and the English Constitution' (15) *Michigan Law Review* 93.

BOYCE, D.G. and HAZELHURST, C. 1976–7. 'The Unknown Chief Secretary: H E Duke and Ireland, 1916–18' (20) *Irish Historical Studies* 286.

BOYLE, A. 1962. *Trenchard* (London: Collins).

BRADLEY, A.W. and EWING, K.D. 1997. *Constitutional and Administrative Law*, 12th edn. (London: Longman).

BRANSON, N. 1985. *History of the Communist Party of Great Britain, 1927–1941* (London: Lawrence and Wishart).

BRIGGS, A. and SAVILLE, J. (eds.). 1971. *Essays in Labour History 1886–1923. vol 2* (London: Macmillan).

BROWNE-WILKINSON, N. 1992. 'The Infiltration of a Bill of Rights' *Public Law* 397.

BUCKLAND, P. 1979. *The Factory of Grievances. Devolved Government in Northern Ireland, 1921–39* (Dublin: Gill and Macmillan).

BUCKLAND, P. 1980. *James Craig, Lord Craigavon* (Dublin: Gill and Macmillan).

CAMPBELL, C. 1994. *Emergency Law in Ireland. 1918–25* (Oxford: Clarendon Press).

CAMPBELL, J.R. 1924. *My Case* (London).

CARR, E.H. 1979. 'The Zinoviev Letter' (22) *Historical Journal* 209.

CHALLINOR, R. 1977. *The Origins of British Bolshevism* (London: Croom Helm).

CHILDS, Major General Sir W. 1930. *Episodes and Reflections* (London: Cassell).

CLEGG, H.A., FOX, A., and THOMPSON, A.F. 1985. *A History of British Trade Unionism since 1889 vol 2, 1911–1933* (Oxford: Clarendon Press).

CLYNES, J.R. 1937. *Memoirs 1924–1937* (London: Hutchinson).

COLLINS, H. 1982. *Marxism and Law* (Oxford: Clarendon Press).

Commissioner of Police of the Metropolis. 1932. *Report for the Year 1931* (Cmd. 4137).

Commissioner of Police of the Metropolis. 1933. *Report for the Year 1932* (Cmd. 4294).

Commissioner of Police of the Metropolis. 1934. *Report for the Year 1933* (Cmd. 4562).

Committee on Ministers Powers. 1932. *Report* (Cmd. 4060).

Committee to Collect Information on Russia. 1921. *Report* (Cmd. 1240).

Communist Papers. 1926. Documents Selected from those obtained in the arrest of the Communist Leaders on the 14th and 21st October 1925 (Cmd. 2682).

Communist Party of Great Britain. (n d). *The Communist Party and the Labour Party. All the Facts and All the Correspondence.*

Communist Party of Great Britain. 1921. *Constitution and Rules.*

Communist Party of Great Britain. 1921. *Report of the Executive Committee.*

Communist Party of Great Britain. 1925. *Report of the Seventh National Congress.*

Communist Party of Great Britain. 1925. *The Communist Party on Trial. Harry Pollit's Defence.*

Communist Party of Great Britain. 1925. *The Communist Party on Trial. J.R. Campbell's Defence.*

Communist Party of Great Britain. 1925. *The Communist Party on Trial. William Gallacher's Defence.*

Communist Party of Great Britain. 1926. *Report of the Eighth Congress.*

Communist Party of Great Britain. 1934. *The Sedition Bill Exposed: All About the Incitement to Disaffection Bill.*

COSGROVE, R.A. 1980. *The Rule of Law: Albert Venn Dicey, Victorian Jurist* (London: Macmillan).

CRAIG, P.P. 1995. 'Formal and Substantive Conceptions of the Rule of Law' (1) *Diritto Pubblico* 35.

CULLEN, S.M. 1993. 'Political Violence: The Case of the British Union of Fascists' (28) *Journal of Contemporary History* 245.

DAINTITH, T.C. 1966. 'Disobeying a Policeman—A Fresh Look at *Duncan v Jones*' *Public Law* 248.

DEGRAS, J. (ed.). 1956. *The Communist International 1919–1943, Documents. vol 1 1919–1922* (Oxford: Oxford University Press).

Departmental Committee on the Duties of the Police with Respect to the Preservation of Order at Public Meetings. 1909. *Report* (Cd. 4673); vol 2 (Minutes of Evidence) (Cd. 4674).

DICEY, A.V. 1885. *Lectures Introductory to a Study of the Law of the Constitution*, 2nd edn. (London: Macmillan).

DICEY, A.V. 1886. *England's Case Against Home Rule* (London: John Murray).

DICEY, A.V. 1914. *Lectures on the Relation between Law and Public Opinion in England during the Nineteenth Century*, 2nd edn. (London: Macmillan).

DICEY, A.V. 1915. 'The Development of Administrative Law in England' (31) *Law Quarterly Review* 148.

DICEY, A.V. 1915. *Introduction to the Study of the Law of the Constitution*, 8th edn. (London: Macmillan).

DICEY, A.V. 1959. *Introduction to the Study of the Law of the Constitution*, 10th edn. with an introduction by E.C.S. Wade (London: Macmillan).

Documents illustrating the Hostile Activities of the Soviet Government and Third International against Great Britain. 1927. (Cmd. 2874).

Documents relative to the Sinn Féin Movement. 1921. (Cmd. 1108).

DOHERTY, G. and KEOGH, D. (eds.). 1998. *Michael Collins and the Making of the Irish State* (Cork: Mercier Press).

DONOHUE, L.K. 2000. *Counter-Terrorist Law and Emergency Powers in the United Kingdom, 1922–2000* (Dublin: Irish Academic Press). (Forthcoming.)

DRENNAN, J. 1934. *BUF: Oswald Mosley and British Fascism* (London: John Murray).

DYSON, B. 1994. *Liberty in Britain: A Diamond Jubilee History of the National Council for Civil Liberties 1934–94* (London: Civil Liberties Trust).

EDWARDS, J.Ll.J. 1964. *The Law Officers of the Crown: A Study of the Offices of Attorney General and Solicitor General of England with an account of the Office of the Director of Public Prosecutions of England* (London: Sweet and Maxwell).

EDWARDS, J.Ll.J. 1984. *The Attorney General, Politics and the Public Interest* (London: Sweet and Maxwell).

Enquiry into certain Transactions of the Bank of Russia Trade Ltd., and the Moscow Narodny Bank Ltd. 1928. *Report: Russian Banks and Communist Funds* (Cmd. 3125).

ENRIGHT, S. 1998. 'Of Courts Martial and Writs of Habeas Corpus' (148) *New Law Journal* 1368.

EWING, K.D. 1982. *Trade Unions, the Labour Party and the Law* (Edinburgh: Edinburgh University Press).

EWING, K.D. and GEARTY, C.A. 1990. *Freedom under Thatcher: Civil Liberties in Modern Britain* (Oxford: Clarendon Press).

FARRELL, M. 1983. *Arming the Protestants. The Formation of the Ulster Special Constabulary and the Royal Ulster Constabulary, 1920–7* (London: Pluto Press).

FELDMAN, D. 1993. *Civil Liberties and Human Rights in England and Wales* (Oxford: Clarendon Press).

FINE, B. 1984. *Democracy and the Rule of Law: Liberal Ideals and Marxist Critiques* (London: Pluto Press).

FOSTER, R.F. 1988. *Modern Ireland 1600–1972* (London: Allen Lane).

FOX, L.W. 1934. *The Modern English Prison* (London: George Routledge and Sons).

FRENCH, D. 1978. 'Spy Fever in Britain, 1900–1915' (21) *Historical Journal* 355.

FRÖLICH, P. 1940. *Rosa Luxemburg* (London: Gollancz).

FULFORD, R. 1957. *Votes for Women: The Story of a Struggle* (London: Faber).

GALLAGHER, W. 1936. *Revolt on the Clyde* (London: Lawrence and Wishart).

GALLAGHER, W. 1947. *The Rolling of the Thunder* (London: Lawrence and Wishart).

GEARTY, C. 1993. 'Citizenship and Freedom of Expression' in Blackburn R. (ed.), *Rights of Citizenship* (London: Mansell).

GLYNN, S. 1991. *No Alternative? Unemployment in Britain* (London: Faber).

GOODHART, A.L. 1927. 'The Legality of the General Strike' (36) *Yale Law Journal* 464.

GOODHART, A.L. 1936–8. '*Thomas v Sawkins*: A Constitutional Innovation' (6) *Cambridge Law Journal* 22.

GRIFFITH, J.A.G. 1997. *The Politics of the Judiciary*, 5th edn. (London: Fontana).

GRIFFITHS, R. 1998. *Patriotism Perverted: Captain Ramsay, The Right Club, and British Anti-Semitism, 1939–40* (London: Constable).

HANNINGTON, W. 1967. *Never on our Knees* (London: Lawrence and Wishart).

HAWKINS, K (ed.). 1997. *The Human Face of the Law: Essays in Honour of Donald Harris* (Oxford: Clarendon Press).

HELLET, A. 1972. *The 'B' Specials. A History of the Royal Ulster Constabulary* (London: Tom Stacey Ltd).

HEUSTON, R.F.V. 1964. *Essays in Constitutional Law*, 2nd edn. (London: Stevens).

HEWART, Lord. 1929. *The New Despotism* (London: Ernest Benn).

HILL, C. 1972. *Intellectual Origins of the English Revolution* (Oxford: Clarendon Press).

HINTON, J. 1971. 'The Clyde Workers' Committee and the Dilution Struggle' in

Briggs, A. and Saville, J. (eds.), *Essays in Labour History 1886–1923. vol 2* (London: Macmillan).

HOBHOUSE, L.T. 1911. *Liberalism* (London: Thornton Butterworth).

HOLDSWORTH, W.S. 1926. 'The Legality of the General Strike' *The Architect and Building News* 445.

Home Office Circular. 1926. Intimidation and Molestation. Home Office Circular addressed to Chief Constables of England and Wales, as to the Provisions of the Law relating to Intimidation and Molestation (Cmd. 2666).

HOPKIN, D. 1970. 'Domestic Censorship in the First World War' (5(4)) *Journal of Contemporary History* 151.

HOROWITZ, M. 1977. 'The Rule of Law: An Unqualified Human Good?' (86) *Yale Law Journal* 561.

HUNNINGS, N.M. 1967. *Film Censors and the Law* (London: Allen and Unwin).

Intercourse Between Bolshevism and Sinn Féin. 1921. (Cmd. 1326).

IVAMY, E.R.H. 1949. 'The Right of Public Meeting' (2) *Current Legal Problems* 183.

JACKSON, R. 1959. *The Chief: The Biography of Gordon Hewart Lord Chief Justice of England 1922–1940* (London: Harrap).

JACKSON, S. 1936. *Rufus Isaacs: First Marquess of Reading* (London: Cassell).

JACKSON, T.A. 1940. *Trials of British Freedom* (London: Lawrence and Wishart).

JACOBS, J. 1978 *Out of the Ghetto, My Youth in the East End, Communism and Fascism, 1913–39* (London: Janet Simon).

JENKINS, E.A. 1933. *From Foundry to Foreign Office: The Romantic Life Story of the Rt Hon Arthur Henderson MP* (London: Grayson and Grayson).

JENNINGS, W.I. 1932. 'The Report on Ministers Powers' (10) *Public Administration* 333.

JENNINGS, W.I. 1937. 'Public Order' (8) *Political Quarterly* 7.

JENNINGS, W.I. 1952. *The Law and the Constitution*, 4th edn. (London: University of London Press).

JOWELL, J. 1994. 'The Rule of Law Today' in Jowell, J., and Oliver, D. (eds.), *The Changing Constitution*, 3rd edn. (Oxford: Clarendon Press, 1994).

JOWELL, J., and OLIVER, D. (eds.). 1994. *The Changing Constitution*, 3rd edn. (Oxford: Clarendon Press).

KEETON, G.W. 1942. 'Liversidge v Anderson' (5) *Modern Law Review* 162.

KENDALL, W. 1969. *The Revolutionary Movement in Britain 1900–1921: The Origins of British Communism* (London: Weidenfeld and Nicholson).

KIDD, R. 1940. *British Liberty in Danger: An Introduction to the Study of Civil Rights* (London: Lawrence and Wishart).

KINGSFORD, P.W. 1982. *The Hunger Marchers in Britain 1920–1940* (London: Lawrence and Wishart).

KIRKWOOD, D. 1935. *My Life of Revolt* (London: Harrap).

KLUGMANN, J. 1960. 'The Foundation of the Communist Party of Great Britain' (4) *Marxism Today* 1.

KLUGMANN, J. 1968. *History of the Communist Party of Great Britain. vol 1: Formation and Early Years, 1919–1924* (London: Lawrence and Wishart).

KLUGMANN, J. 1969. *History of the Communist Party of Great Britain. vol 2: 1925–27: The General Strike* (London: Lawrence and Wishart).

Labour Party. 1936. *Annual Report*.

Law Commission. 1987. *Criminal Law. Binding Over: The Issues* (Working Paper No 103).

Law Commission. 1994. *Binding Over* (Cm. 2439).

LENIN, V.I. 1971. *Selected Works 2* (Moscow: Progress Publishers).

LENIN, V.I. 1971. *Selected Works 3* (Moscow: Progress Publishers).

LOCKE, J. 1963. *Two Treatises of Government* (Cambridge: Cambridge University Press).

LOMAS, O.G. 1980. 'The Executive and the Anti-Terrorist Legislation of 1939' *Public Law* 16.

LONDON, J. 1971. *The Iron Heel* (New York: Sagamore Press).

LOUGHLIN, M. 1992. *Public Law and Political Theory* (Oxford: Clarendon Press).

LOVELAND, I (ed.). 1995. *Frontiers of Criminality* (London: Sweet and Maxwell).

LUNN, K. and THURLOW, R.C. (eds.). 1980. *British Fascism. Essays on the Radical Right in Inter-War Britain* (London: Croom Helm).

LUXEMBURG, R. 1970. 'The Russian Revolution' in Waters, M.-A. (ed.), *Rosa Luxemburg Speaks* (1977), 365.

LYMAN, R.W. 1957. *The First Labour Government 1924* (London: Chapman and Hall).

LYONS, F.S.L. 1971. *Ireland since the Famine* (London: Weidenfeld and Nicolson).

MACARTHUR, B. 1998. *The Penguin Book of Twentieth-Century Protest* (London: Viking).

McAUSLAN, P. and McELDOWNEY, J.F. (eds.). 1985. *Law, Legitimacy and the Constitution: Essays Marking the Centenary of Dicey's Law of the Constitution* (London: Sweet and Maxwell).

MacCORMICK, D.N. 1983. 'Jurisprudence and the Constitution' (36) *Current Legal Problems* 13.

MacDOUGALL, I. (ed.). 1981. *Militant Miners* (Edinburgh: Polygon Press).

McELDOWNEY, J.F. 1985, 'Dicey in Historical Perspective—A Review Essay' in McAuslan, P. and McEldowney, J.F. (eds), *Law Legitimacy and the Constitution: Essays Marking the Centenary of Dicey's Law of the Constitution* (London: Sweet and Maxwell).

MacFARLANE, L.J. 1966. *The British Communist Party: Its Origin and Development until 1929* (London: Macgibbon and Kee).

McKIBBIN, R. 1974. *The Evolution of the Labour Party 1910–1924* (Oxford: Oxford University Press).

McKIBBIN, R. 1998. *Class and Cultures. England 1918–51* (Oxford: Oxford University Press).

McLEAN, I. 1973. *The Legend of Red Clydeside* (Edinburgh: John Donald).

MACREADY, N. 1924. *Annals of an Active Life*.

MACPHERSON, C.B. 1977. *The Life and Times of Liberal Democracy* (Oxford: Oxford University Press).

McSHANE, H. 1978. *No Mean Fighter* (London: Pluto).

MARX, K. 1975. *Early Writings* (Harmondsworth: Penguin).

MARX, K. and ENGELS, F. 1968. *Selected Works* (London: Lawrence and Wishart).

MASON, A. 1969. 'The Government and the General Strike, 1926' (14) *International Review of Social History* 1.

MILIBAND, R. 1982. *Capitalist Democracy in Britain* (Oxford: Oxford University Press).

MILIBAND, R. 1994. *Socialism for a Sceptical Age* (Cambridge: Polity Press).

MILLER, F. 1979. 'The British Unemployment Assistance Crisis of 1935' (14) *Journal of Contemporary History* 329.

MILLER, F.M. 1976. 'The Unemployment Policy of the National Government, 1931–1936' (19) *Historical Journal* 453.

MILTON, N. 1979. *John MacLean* (London: Pluto Press).

MONTAGU, I. 1934. *Blackshirt Brutality. The Story of Olympia* (London: Workers' Bookshop).

MORGAN, J. 1987. *Conflict and Order. The Police and Labour Disputes in England and Wales, 1900–1939* (Oxford: Clarendon Press).

MORRIS, G.S. 1979. 'The Emergency Powers Act 1920' *Public Law* 317.

MORRIS, M. 1976. *The General Strike* (Harmondsworth: Penguin).

MOSLEY, O. 1970. *My Life* (London: Nelson).

MURRAY, J. 1951. *The General Strike of 1926. A History* (London: Lawrence and Wishart).

National Council for Civil Liberties. 1936. *Report of a Commission of Inquiry appointed to examine the purpose and effect of the Civil Authorities (Special Powers) Acts (Northern Ireland) 1922 & 1933* (London: National Council for Civil Liberties).

National Unemployed Workers' Committee Movement. 1928. *Scottish Miners' March to Edinburgh.*

NEWARK, F.H. 1969. 'The Campbell Case and the First Labour Government' (20) *Northern Ireland Legal Quarterly* 19.

'NORTH BRITON'. 1917. *British Freedom 1914–1917.*

O'BROIN, L. 1966. *Dublin Castle and the 1916 Rising* (London: Sidgwick and Jackson).

Official Report of the Communist Unity Conference. 1920.

O'HIGGINS, P. 1980. *Cases and Materials on Civil Liberties* (London: Sweet and Maxwell).

PAGE ARNOT, R. 1926. *The General Strike* (republished in 1975 by EP Publishing, Wakefield).

PAGE ARNOT, R. 1953. *The Miners: Years of Struggle. A History of the Miners' Federation of Great Britain from 1910 onwards* (London: Allen & Unwin).

PAGE ARNOT, R. 1955. *A History of the Scottish Miners* (London: Allen & Unwin).

PARMOOR, Lord. 1936. *A Retrospect* (London: Heinemann).

PAYNE, S.G. 1995. *A History of Fascism, 1914–45* (Madison: University of Wisconsin Press).

PELLING, H. 1958. *The British Communist Party: A Historical Profile* (London: Adam and Charles Black).

PELLING, H. 1993. *A Short History of the Labour Party*, 10th edn. (Basingstoke: Macmillan).

PELLING, H. 1996. *A Short History of the Labour Party*, 11th edn. by A.J. Reid. (Basingstoke: Macmillan).

PHOENIX, E. 1998. 'Michael Collins: The Northern Question 1916–22' in Doherty, G. and Keogh, D. (eds.), *Michael Collins and the Making of the Irish State* (Cork: Mercier Press).

POLLOCK, F. 1920. '*Abrams v United States*' (36) *Law Quarterly Review* 334.

PRITT, D.N. 1965. *The Autobiography of D N Pritt, vol 1: From Right to Left* (London: Lawrence and Wishart).

PRITT, D.N. 1971. *Law, Class and Society. Book 2: The Apparatus of the Law* (London: Lawrence and Wishart).

Public Record Office. 1997. *MI5: The First Ten Years, 1909–1919* (London: Public Record Office).

RAE, J.M. 1970. *Conscience and Politics: The British Government and the Conscientious Objector to Military Service 1916–1919* (Oxford: Oxford University Press).

RAZ, J. 1977. 'The Rule of Law and its Virtue' (93) *Law Quarterly Review* 195.

ROBERTSON, G. 1989. *Freedom, the Individual and the Law*, 6th edn. (earlier edns. by Street, H.) (Harmondsworth: Penguin).

ROBERTSON, G. 1993. *Freedom, the Individual and the Law*, 7th edn. (Harmondsworth: Penguin).

Royal Commission on the Arrest and Subsequent Treatment of Mr Francis Sheehy Skeffington, Mr Thomas Dickson and Mr Patrick James McIntyre. 1916. *Report* (Cd. 8376).

Royal Commission on Police Powers and Procedures. 1929. *Report* (Cmd. 3297).

Royal Commission on the Rebellion in Ireland. 1916. *Report* (Cd. 8279).

RUBIN, G.R. 1987. *War, Law and Labour: The Munitions Acts, State Regulation and the Unions, 1915–21* (Oxford: Clarendon Press).

RUBIN, G.R. 1994. *Private Property, Government Requisition and the Constitution, 1914–27* (London: Hambledon Press).

SCAFFARDI, S. 1986. *Fire Under the Carpet. Working for Civil Liberties in the 1930s* (London: Lawrence and Wishart).

SCRUTTON, T.E. 1918. 'The War and the Law' (34) *Law Quarterly Review* 116.

Select Committee on National Expenditure. 1918. *Third Report* (H.C. 59).

Select Committee on National Expenditure. 1918. *Sixth Report* (H.C. 97).

SIMPSON, A.W.B. 1992. *In the Highest Degree Odious: Detention Without Trial in Wartime Britain* (Oxford: Clarendon Press).

SKIDELSKY, R. 1975. *Oswald Mosley* (London: Macmillan).

SMITH, A.T.H. 1987. *Offences Against Public Order* (London: Sweet and Maxwell).

SMITH, F.W.F., 2nd Earl of Birkenhead. 1933. *The Life of F E Smith, First Earl of Birkenhead* (London: Thornton Butterworth).

STAMMERS, N. 1983. *Civil Liberties in Britain during the 2nd World War: A Political Study* (London: Croom Helm).

STEPHEN, J. 1877. *A Digest of the Criminal Law* (London: Macmillan).

STEVENS, R. 1979. *Law and Politics. The House of Lords as a Judicial Body, 1800–1976* (London: Weidenfeld and Nicolson).

STEVENS, R. 1997. 'Judges, Politics and the Confusing Role of the Judiciary', in Hawkins, K. (ed.), *The Human Face of the Law* (Oxford: Clarendon Press).

STEVENSON, J. 1980. 'The BUF, the Metropolitan Police and Public Order' in Lunn, K. and Thurlow, R.C. (eds.), *British Fascism. Essays on the Radical Right in Inter-War Britain* (London: Croom Helm, 1980).

STEVENSON, J. and COOK, C. 1977. *The Slump: Society and Politics During the Depression* (London: Cape).

STEWART, B. 1967. *Breaking the Fetters* (London: Lawrence and Wishart).

STREET, H. 1963. *Freedom, the Individual and the Law* (Harmondsworth: Penguin).

STREET, H. and BRAZIER, R (eds.). 1981. *de Smith's Constitutional and Administrative Law* 4th edn. (Harmondsworth: Penguin).

SWARTZ, M. 1971. *The Union of Democratic Control in British Politics During the First World War* (Oxford: Clarendon Press).

SYPNOWICH, C. 1990. *The Concept of Socialist Law* (Oxford: Clarendon Press).

TAYLOR, A.J.P. 1965. *English History 1914–1945* (Oxford: Clarendon Press).

TAYLOR, H.A. 1933. *Jix—Viscount Brentford* (London: Stanley Paul).

THOMPSON, E.P. 1975. *Whigs and Hunters: The Origins of the Black Act* (London: Allen Lane).

THOMPSON, W.H. 1938. *Civil Liberties* (London: Gollancz).

THOMSON, B. 1939. *The Scene Changes* (London: Collins).

THURLOW, R. 1987. *Fascism in Britain, A History, 1918–85* (Oxford: Basil Blackwell).

TOWNSHEND, C. 1975. *The British Campaign in Ireland 1919–1921. The Development of Political and Military Policies* (London: Oxford University Press).

TOWNSHEND, C. 1979 'The Irish Republican Army and the Development of Guerrilla Warfare, 1916–1921' (94) *English Historical Review* 318.

TOWNSHEND, C. 1982. 'Martial Law: Legal and Administrative Problems of Civil Emergency in Britain and the Empire 1800–1940' (25) *Historical Journal* 167.

TOWNSHEND, C. 1983. *Political Violence in Ireland. Government and Resistance since 1848* (Oxford: Clarendon Press).

TOWNSHEND, C. 1993. *Making the Peace: Public Order and Public Security in Modern Britain* (Oxford: Oxford University Press).

Trades Union Congress. 1926. *Annual Report 1926.*

TULLOCH, H. 1980. 'A.V. Dicey and the Irish Question: 1870–1922' (15) *Irish Jurist* (n s) 137.

'ULTACH'. 1940. *Orange Terror: The Partition of Ireland* (Capuchin Annual).

VERNON, B.D. 1982. *Ellen Wilkinson 1891–1947* (London: Croom Helm).

WADE, E.C.S. 1934. 'Police Search' (50) *Law Quarterly Review* 354.

WADE, E.C.S. 1936–1939. 'Police Powers and Public Meetings' (6) *Cambridge Law Journal* 175.

WALKER, D.M. 1980. *Oxford Companion to Law* (Oxford: Clarendon Press).

WALKER, S. 1990. *In Defence of American Liberties: A History of the ACLU* (Oxford: Oxford University Press).

WALKER-SMITH, D. 1938. *The Life of Lord Darling* (London: Cassell).

WARD, A.J. 1974. 'Lloyd George and the 1918 Irish Conscription Crisis' (17) *Historical Journal* 107.

WATERS, M.-A. (ed.). 1970. *Rosa Luxemburg Speaks* (New York: Pathfinder Press).

WEBB, S. and WEBB, B. 1920. *The History of Trade Unionism 1666–1920* (London: Longmans, Green and Co).

WEBBER, G.C. 1984. 'Patterns of Membership and Support for the British Union of Fascists' (19) *Journal of Contemporary History* 573.

WHEELER-BENNETT, J.W. 1962. *John Anderson, Viscount Waverley* (London: Macmillan).

WHITE, S. 1979. *Britain and the Bolshevik Revolution: A Study in the Politics of Diplomacy 1920–1924* (London: Macmillan).

WILKINSON, E. 1939. *The Town that was Murdered* (London: Gollancz).

WILLIAMS, D.G.T. 1965. *Not in the Public Interest* (London: Hutchinson).

WILLIAMS, D.G.T. 1967. *Keeping the Peace* (London: Hutchinson).

WILLIAMS, D.G.T. 1982. 'The Donoughmore Report in Retrospect' (60) *Public Administration* 273.

WILLIAMS, D.G.T. 1985. 'Preventive Action and Public Order: The Principle of *Thomas v Sawkins*' (16) *Cambrian Law Review* 116.

WINTER, J.M. 1986. *The Great War and the British People* (London: Macmillan).

YOUNG, G.M. 1952. *Stanley Baldwin* (London: Hart-Davis).

YOUNG, T. (with the assistance of KETTLE, M.) 1976. *Incitement to Disaffection* (London: Cobden Trust).

Index